Roger Ebert's Movie Home Companion

ROGER EBERT'S MOVIE HOME COMPANION

by Roger Ebert

Andrews, McMeel & Parker
A Universal Press Syndicate Company
Kansas City • New York

Library of Congress Cataloging in publication data.

Ebert, Roger.
    Roger Ebert's Movie home companion.

    Includes index.
    1. Moving-pictures—Reviews.   2. Video recordings—Reviews.   I. Title.   II. Title: Movie home companion
PN1995.E318   1985   791.43'75   85-17387
ISBN 0-8362-6209-3

This book is dedicated to
Robert Zonka

Acknowledgments

Donna Martin, editor and friend, was instrumental in the conception of this book. The design is by Cameron Poulter and the cover photographs by Jack Lane, fellow Chicagoans. Patty Dingus typed the reviews and she and Dorothy O'Brien prepared the manuscript. Without them, the *Movie Home Companion* would still be trapped somewhere inside the yellowing pile of tearsheets pictured on the cover of my last book.

ROGER EBERT

Contents

Key to Symbols

★ ★ ★ ★   A great film
★ ★ ★   A good film
★ ★   Fair
★   Poor

G, PG, PG-13, R   Ratings of the Motion Picture Association of America
      G   indicates that the movie is suitable for general audiences
      PG   suitable for general audiences but parental guidance is suggested
      PG-13   recommended for viewers 13 years or above; may contain material
             inappropriate for younger children
      R   recommended for viewers 17 or older

141 m.   Running time

1983   Year of theatrical release

↙   Indicates movie for which videocassette was not yet available at time of publication

Introduction

In the introduction to my last book, I wrote, "Television is just not a first-class way to watch movies." Now here I am with a companion for owners of videocassette players. Have I changed my mind? Not at all. I still believe that the best way to see a movie is in a large, darkened room, with a giant screen at one end of it, and strangers all around. The strangers are especially important, because they set up a democracy in the dark; their massed response to the movie makes it easier for us to join the communal experience, to enter into the film-going reverie and shut down our awareness of self.

And yet I own a VCR, and I use it. Last night I was watching the documentary *George Stevens: A Filmmaker's Journey*, and as I saw the famous scenes once again (Astaire courting Rogers on the dance floor, James Dean joyfully climbing to the top of a windmill), I was reminded of the first times I'd seen the original movies. I saw *Swing Time* in 1961 on a sixteen-millimeter print in an auditorium at the University of Illinois, where, watching Astaire and Rogers for literally the first time, I was so moved by the grace and beauty of their movement that I made a basic discovery: The greatness of a film often has nothing to do with the importance of its message. All that really matters is exactly what's there on the screen.

If I had seen *Swing Time* for the first time on a videocassette, would my experience have been as intense? I doubt it. The spontaneous applause in the audience that night gave me confidence in my own reaction, and, since I never took a film class, it might have been the lessons from all the audiences I was a member of that started me along the path to film criticism.

I still believe that nothing can replace the experience of seeing a movie with an audience in a theater, and although the logistics would be easier for "At the Movies" if we could occasionally review a film after seeing it only on cassette, we insist on big-screen viewings and have reviewed cassette versions of films less than half a dozen times in ten years. Frequently I hear that today's audiences "talk too much" during the movie, destroying the experience, but I have rarely heard an audience talking during a movie that really worked. Audience noise is often a response to the lack of anything interesting to see on the screen.

Now. Having got that off my chest, here we are with a guide to recent movies available on cassette. The obvious reason to own and use videocassette players is, of course, that they exist, and that unless we happen to be Hollywood moguls or American presidents with our private screening rooms, there is no other way to see the movie of our choice, at the time of our choice. In all but the largest cities, there is also the problem that many good films simply never open locally. *Porky's II* or the unrelenting *Friday the 13th* series will inevitably play every fair-sized town in America, but many of the best films in this book have played only thirty or forty American cities. Renting cassettes is the only way most people have of seeing the offbeat, innovative, noncommercial films, and I have included a lot of sleepers, documentaries, and smaller independent productions in this book with the thought that you might be intrigued by the descriptions and track them down.[1]

Seeing otherwise unseeable films is the best reason to own a VCR. The next best reason is the opportunity to see your favorite films over again, and even to own cassettes. Most cassettes are overpriced in the $70 range, however, and I agree with the market researchers who have found that $19.95 seems to be the price threshold at which many people might choose to buy instead of rent. I've personally bought very few cassettes: *Citizen Kane; The Third Man;* Keaton's *The General; Casablanca; Say Amen, Somebody.* At $19.95, or twice the price of an LP album, I might buy more freely.

As I write, there are about twenty million VCR owners in America. Cassette machines are no longer a luxury item. Good cassette *players* (not recorders) priced at less than $200 are in the pipeline from Korea, and the Japanese will no doubt match the lower prices. Cassette machines are expected to be the top-selling consumer item at Christmas, and within a year there should be forty million of them in use in this country. Eventually they will be as common as stereo sets and audiocassette decks.[2]

When there are forty, or sixty, or eighty million cassette machines in use, a revolution will take place in the way Hollywood makes movies, and the kinds of movies it makes. It will have to. The demographics of moviegoers and VCR owners split the population in two; the majority of frequent moviegoers are under twenty-five, and the majority of VCR owners are over twenty-five. The two population groups have distinctively different tastes. Theatrical movies are increasingly aimed at teen-agers, and in the first half of 1985 there were more than thirty movies with specifically teen-age themes. The older VCR owners are not as interested in teen-age movies, except for the exceptional hit like *Flashdance* or *Risky Business,* or the crossover hit that breaks through all demographic groups, like *E. T.,* or *Raiders of the Lost Ark*. Viewers over twenty-five want to see films made more or less for them, and so there's the case of a

---

[1] Many video stores, alas, seem to have shelves lined with *Porky's II*, *Friday the 13th*, nasties, pornos, and of course the usual mainstream hits. That's why a mail-order video rental organization like Home Film Festival is invaluable. After you sign up and provide credit card information, you call a toll-free number (1-800-258-3456) to order from their catalogue of art, foreign, classic, underground, documentary, sleeper, and cult films. When the cassette arrives, you have three days to watch it before returning it in a handy mailer, which is provided. This is a plug.

[2] The Koreans are on the right track by selling machines that play but do not record. Industry surveys show, incredibly, that two-thirds of VCR owners are not quite sure how to use the record function on their machines, and use them only for playing cassettes.

movie like *The Right Stuff,* which got great reviews, failed to interest teen-agers, flopped at the box office, and then went right ahead to become one of the best-selling and renting videos of 1984. There was an audience for *The Right Stuff,* all right—but it was at home, not in theater lines.

As the after-market for theatrical movies becomes more and more impor-tant, it will influence many production decisions. The day is not more than three years away when cassette rentals and sales will represent more income, for all but the biggest hits, than the traditional theatrical box office. Will this create a crisis for movie theaters? Apparently not: Industry statistics have come up with the surprising discovery that VCR owners attend theatrical movies *more* often than they did before they bought their VCRs—apparently because cassette viewing has made them more interested in new movies in general. What will happen, when the financial balance shifts to the older population group, is that Hollywood will have compelling reasons to make movies for viewers over twenty-five. More movies like *Terms of Endearment, Gandhi, On Golden Pond,* and *The Big Chill,* to go with food-fight epics.

So far, there is no evidence that people will buy or rent cassette versions of movies that have not played theatrically. Some sort of voodoo seems to be at work: Unless somebody, somewhere, sometime, has paid to walk into a theater and see a movie, VCR owners have a reluctance to buy it or rent it and bring it home.[3] If more films for adults are made, more of them will have a chance to succeed, in an industry where teen-age films have recently had a green light. (For example: Albert Brooks's *Lost in America,* about a couple in their thirties, was postponed by one studio so it could use the same money to budget *National Lampoon's Class Reunion.*) If these trends hold up, we may see a different mix at the American box office: Teen-age films, yes, but better ones (*The Breakfast Club* instead of *Fraternity Reunion*), and more films aimed at audiences over twenty-five. Some of those films may be using theaters as a way-station on the road to video stores, but at least they will be made, and they will have a chance.

* * *

In this book, I've concentrated on movies made since 1980; they represent more than 90 percent of all video rentals. I have not, however, concentrated only on box office hits. By limiting myself to the 1980s and including more than four hundred films, I've been able to include a good number of sleepers (*Repo Man, The Long Good Friday*), cult films (*This Is Spinal Tap, Choose Me*), great documentaries (*Say Amen, Somebody, Streetwise*), independent American pro-ductions (*El Norte, Testament*), and unclassifiable but indispensable films (*My Dinner with André, Secret Honor*). I have also included a few older films that became available recently in restored versions, like *A Star Is Born.* Foreign films are a problem, because subtitles are notoriously hard to read on TV screens, and dubbing usually sounds false, but I have included some of the best recent releases, like *Fanny and Alexander* and *Kagemusha.* I have also been

---

[3] The exception is pornography; 70 percent of porno film income now comes from cassettes, and adult theaters are closing all over the country.

careful to include films that I despise, like *I Spit on Your Grave* and *Caligula*. You will also find virtually every film from these years that has made a substantial impact at the box office. In an Afterword, I look back into film history with the benefit of the unique poll which *Sight & Sound*, the British film magazine, conducts every ten years among the world's film critics. Using their forty years of lists of the "greatest films of all time" as a guideline, you could, I imagine, construct a cinematic version of the Great Books program on your TV.

* * *

Someday, I know, they will perfect TV screens the size of walls. You will be able to order the film of your choice, and it will arrive in your home via cable. The sound will be in perfect stereo. Even the subtitles will be readable. When that day comes, I know I'll want the miraculous new equipment, so I can summon up *Casablanca* and hear Sam claim yet once again that he doesn't remember how to play that song. But when that day comes, I know I will still want to see new movies in real movie theaters, with real audiences, whenever I can. Who says you can't have it both ways?

ROGER EBERT

Absence of Malice ★ ★ ★
PG, 116 m., 1981

Paul Newman (Michael Gallagher), Sally Field (Megan Carter), Bob Balaban (Rosen), Melinda Dillon (Teresa), Wilford Brimley (D.A.), John Harkins (Libel Lawyer). Directed and produced by Sydney Pollack. Screenplay by Kurt Luedtke.

There are at least two ways to approach *Absence of Malice*, and I propose to take the second. The first approach, no doubt, would be to criticize this film's portrait of an investigative newspaper reporter—to say that no respectable journalist would ever do the things that Sally Field does about, to, and with Paul Newman in this movie. She is a disgrace to her profession. What journalistic sins does she commit in this film? She allows the facts of a secret investigation to be leaked to her. She prints an unattributed story about the investigation. Then she becomes "personally involved with the subject of the investigation," as they say. In other words, she falls in love with Paul Newman. Then she prints another story she should never have printed, and as a result an innocent bystander commits suicide. Then . . .

But you get the idea. Would real investigative reporters actually commit Field's mistakes, improprieties, misjudgments, indiscretions, and ethical lapses? Generally speaking, no, they wouldn't. And if they did, they shouldn't have. And furthermore, their editors would never let them get away with it. (The unbelievable laxity of the editors in *Absence of Malice* creates the movie's greatest credibility gap.) But let's face it: Sometimes reporters *do* commit acts such as Sally Field allows herself in this movie. Sometimes news of an investigation is printed without official attribution. And so on.

One of my colleagues cornered me at the water fountain to say indignantly that, whatever else you might think about this movie, you'd have to admit that no reporter would *ever* sleep with a news source.

"Oh yeah?" asked a woman who was standing by. "Who was the news source?"

"Paul Newman," I said.

"I'd sleep with that news source in a second," she said.

And that leads us out of the first, or socially responsible, approach to *Absence of Malice*, and into the second, or romantic, approach. I not only liked this movie despite its factual and ethical problems—I'm not even so sure they matter so much to most viewers. In the newspaper business we're quick to spot the errors of movies about newspaper reporters, but where were we when the archaeologists squirmed over Harrison Ford's barbaric conduct in *Raiders of the Lost Ark?* The fact is, this movie is *really* about a woman's spunk and a common man's sneaky revenge. And on that level it's absorbing and entertaining. Sally Field's newspaper reporter is created through a quietly original performance that is *not* Norma Rae with a pencil behind her ear, but is an earnest, nervous, likable young woman who makes mistakes when she listens too closely to her heart, her ambition, or her editor (which of us cannot admit the same?).

Paul Newman's character is a liquor distributor who is (presumably) totally innocent of the murder for which he is being investigated. But because his father was a Mafioso, he finds his name being dragged through the press, and he achieves a vengeance that is smart, wicked, appropriate, and completely satisfying to the audience. Besides these two performances, there are some other good ones, most notably one by Wilford Brimley, as a district attorney who takes brusque command of an informal hearing and reduces everyone but Newman to quivering surrender, and another by John Harkins, as a newspaper libel lawyer who is able to make the restraints (and freedoms) of libel law clear not only to Sally Field but even to us.

There's a story about a legendary Chicago editor who was presented with a major scoop obtained by dubious means. First he convinced himself the story was factually sound. Then he issued the classic instruction: "Print it tonight, and call the lawyers in the morning." Now there's an editor who might have enjoyed *Absence of Malice*. He would not have approved of what Sally Field does in this movie. But he would have understood it.

After the Rehearsal ★ ★ ★ ★
R, 72 m., 1984

Erland Josephson (Henrik Vogler), Ingrid Thulin (Rakel), Lena Olin (Anna Egerman), Nadja Palmstjerna-Weiss (Anna at Twelve). Directed by Ingmar Bergman and produced by Jorn Donner. Screenplay by Bergman.

Ingmar Bergman's *After the Rehearsal* seems to be as simple and direct as a tape recording of actual conversations, and yet look at the thickets of interpretation it has inspired in its critics. After seeing it, I thought I understood the film entirely. Now I am not so sure. Like so many of Bergman's films, and especially the spare "chamber films" it joins *(Winter Light, Persona)*, it consists of unadorned surfaces concealing fathomless depths.

It is safest to begin with the surfaces. All of the action takes place on a stage prepared for a production of Strindberg's *A Dream Play*. An aging director sits among the props, and every chair and table reminds him of an earlier production. The rehearsal has ended some time ago, and now the director simply sits, as if the stage were his room. A young actress returns to the stage for a missing bracelet. But of course the bracelet is an excuse, and she wants to talk to the great man, and perhaps to begin a relationship with him (as, perhaps, she has heard that many other actresses have done over the years). The old director was once the lover of the girl's mother. It is even possible that this girl is his daughter. They talk. Then an older actress enters. She has a few lines in the play, and wants to know—frankly, brutally—if her career as a leading actress is really over because she is known as a drunk. She cries, she rants, she bares her breasts to show the old man that her body is still sound, if sodden. The director is tempted: He was once this woman's lover, and perhaps her daughter is his.

The young girl stays on stage during the extraordinary display of the older actress. When the older woman leaves, the director and ingenue talk again, and this time the old man, who has been through the turmoil of love too many times, talks her through their probable future: We could make love, we could have an affair, we would call it part of our art, you would be the student, I would

be the teacher, I would grow tired, you would feel trapped, all our idealism would turn into ashes. Since the relationship is foredoomed, why bother with it?

Just in terms of these spare passages of dialogue and passion, *After the Rehearsal* is an important and painful confessional, for the old director, of course, bears many points of resemblance to Bergman, whose lovers have included his actresses Harriet Andersson, Bibi Anderson, and Liv Ullmann, among others, and whose daughter by Ullmann appeared in *Face to Face*. But the film is not a scandalous revelation: It is actually more of a sacramental confession, as if Bergman, the son of a Lutheran bishop, now sees the stage as his confessional and is asking the audience to bless and forgive him. (His gravest sin, as I read the film, is not lust or adultery, but the sin of taking advantage of others—of manipulating them with his power and intellect.)

If that were the extent of *After the Rehearsal*, it would be deep enough. But Bergman has surrounded the bare bones of his story with mystifying problems of interpretation. Just as in *Persona* he included scenes in which his characters exchanged personalities and engaged in scenes that might have or might not have been fantasies and dreams, so here, too, he gives us things to puzzle over. Reading the earlier reviews of the film, I discover that one critic realized only belatedly that the younger actress, Anna, was onstage the whole time the older actress, Rakel, poured out her heart. Strange, and yet another critic thought the whole scene with Rakel was the director's own dream. Yet another suggested that Anna represents not only herself but also Rakel's absent daughter. And another theory is that Anna is the daughter of the director and Rakel, and is brought into being by the residual love between them, as a sort of theatrical Holy Spirit. The age of Anna has been variously reported as ranging from twelve to twenty, with one critic reporting that both ages of the character are represented.

Which is the correct interpretation? They are all correct. Each and every one is equally correct; otherwise what is the use of a dream play? The point is not to find the literal meaning, anyway, but to touch the soul of the director, and find out what still hurts him after all these years. After all the sex and all the promises, all the lies and truths and messy affairs, there is still one critical area where he is filled with guilt and passion. It is revealed when Anna tells him she is pregnant. He is enraged. How could she, a young actress given the role of a lifetime, jeopardize her career and his play by getting pregnant? Then she tells him she has had an abortion, for the sake of the play. And then he really is torn in two, for he does not believe, after all, that a play—not even his play—is worth the sacrifice of a life. What we are left with at the end of *After the Rehearsal*, however, is the very strong sense of an artist who has sacrificed many lives for the sake of his art, and now wonders if perhaps one of those lives was his own.

Against All Odds ★ ★ ★
R, 128 m., 1984

Rachel Ward (Jessie Wyler), Jeff Bridges (Terry Brogan), James Woods (Jake Wise), Alex Karras (Hank Sully), Jane Greer (Mrs. Wyler), Richard Widmark (Ben Caxton). Directed by Taylor Hackford and produced by Hackford and William S. Gilmore. Screenplay by Eric Hughes.

There have been too many sweet girls in thrillers. What we need are more no-good, double-dealing broads who can cross their legs and break your heart. *Against All Odds* has a woman like that, and it makes for one of the most intriguing movie relationships in a long time; in thirty-five years, to be exact, which is when they told this story for the first time. You may remember the original movie. It was called *Out of the Past*. It starred Robert Mitchum and Kirk Douglas, and it was the greatest cigarette-smoking movie of all time. Mitchum and Douglas smoked all the way through every scene, and they were always blowing sinister, aggressive clouds of smoke at each other. The movie was shot so there was always a lot of light on the place in midair where their smoke was aimed. The only drawback to the fact that smoking is no longer fashionable in movies is that we don't get any great smoking scenes anymore. Anyway, if you remember that movie, you remember that Kirk Douglas was a hoodlum and Robert Mitchum was a guy who would

take a job for a buck, and Douglas hired Mitchum to track down his missing girlfriend, who was played by Jane Greer. After Mitchum found Greer, they had a big love affair—or so Mitchum thought. But Greer, that no-good, two-timing, double-crossing broad, liked security more than passion.

Against All Odds is not really a remake of *Out of the Past*. The only similarity between the two movies is in the cynical love triangle. And it was a real inspiration to tell that story again, since it makes for an intriguing, complicated, interesting romance. This time, the bad guy is a gambler, played by James Woods. His girlfriend (Rachel Ward) is the daughter of the owner of a pro-football team (played by Jane Greer, of all people). And the guy who tracks her down (Jeff Bridges), is a team player who's just been fired after a knee injury.

There is a lot of plot in this movie—probably too much. The best thing to do is to accept the plot, and then disregard it, and pay attention to the scenes of passion. They really work. Bridges and Ward have an interesting sexual tension in *Against All Odds*, since their relationship is not simply sweetness and light, but depends upon suspicion, dislike, and foul betrayal. That's ever so much more interesting than just falling in love. And the situation liberates Ward from the trap she'd been in; the trap of playing attractive, sexy, strong heroines. This time, as a complicated schemer, she's fascinating.

The movie has a lot of muted social criticism in it, involving professional sports and ecology. The Jane Greer character has a plan to destroy several beautiful canyons to build houses. The Bridges character is a victim of unfair labor practices. And so on. Sometimes we get the idea we're watching a clone of *Chinatown*—but not with that jealous triangle. Woods is the villain, so he does smoke, of course. But Bridges and Ward are so consumed with passion, they don't even need to.

Airplane! ★ ★ ★
PG, 88 m., 1980

Lloyd Bridges (McCroskey), Peter Graves (Captain Oveur), Kareem Abdul-Jabbar (Murdock), Julie Hagerty (Elaine), Robert

Hays (Ted Striker), Leslie Nielsen (Dr.
Rumack), Howard Jarvis (Man in Taxi), Ethel
Merman (Lieutenant Hurwitz). Directed and
written by Jim Abrahams, David Zucker, and
Jerry Zucker and produced by Howard W.
Koch.

Airplane! is a comedy in the great tradition of
high school skits, the Sid Caesar TV show,
Mad magazine, and the dog-eared screenplays people's nephews write in lieu of earn-
ing their college diplomas. It is sophomoric,
obvious, predictable, corny, and quite often
very funny. And the reason it's funny is frequently *because* it's sophomoric, predictable, corny, etc. Example:

    Doctor (Leslie Nielsen): Surely you
can't be serious!

    Airplane Captain (Peter Graves): Of
course I am! And stop calling me Shirley!

This sort of humor went out with Milton
Berle, Jerry Lewis, and knock-knock jokes.
That's why it's so funny. Movie comedies
these days are so hung up on being contemporary, radical, outspoken, and cynically
satirical that they sometimes forget to be
funny. And they've lost the nerve to be as
corny as *Airplane!*—to actually invite loud
groans from the audience. The flop *Wholly
Moses*, for example, is no doubt an infinitely
more intelligent comedy—but the problem
was, we didn't laugh.

Airplane! has a couple of sources for its
inspiration. One of them is obviously *Airport*
(1970) and all of its sequels and rip-offs. The
other might not come immediately to mind
unless you're a fan of the late show. It's *Zero
Hour!* (1957), which starred the quintessential 1950s B-movie cast of Dana Andrews,
Linda Darnell, and Sterling Hayden. *Airplane!* comes from the same studio (Para-
mount) and therefore is able to cheerfully
borrow the same plot (airliner is imperiled
after the crew and most of the passengers are
stricken with food poisoning). The *Zero
Hour!* crisis situation (how to get the airplane
down) was also borrowed for the terrible
Airport 1975, in which Karen Black played a
stewardess who tried to follow instructions
radioed from the ground.

Airplane! has two desperate people in the
cockpit: Julie Hagerty, as the stewardess,
and Robert Hays, as a former Air Force pilot
whose traumatic war experiences have made

him terrified of flying. (The cockpit also
contains a very kinky automatic pilot . . .
but never mind.)

The movie exploits the previous films for
all they're worth. The passenger list includes a little old lady (like Helen Hayes in
Airport), a guitar-playing nun (like Helen
Reddy in *Airport 1975*), and even a critically
ill little girl who's being flown to an emergency operation (Linda Blair played the role
in *Airport 1975*). Predictable results occur, as
when the nun's guitar knocks loose the little
girl's intravenous tubes, and she nearly dies
while all the passengers sing along inspira-
tionally.

The movie's funniest scene, however, occurs in a flashback explaining how the stewardess and the Air Force pilot first met and
fell in love years ago. The scene takes place
in an exotic Casablanca-style bar, which is
miraculously transformed when somebody's
hurled at the jukebox and it starts playing
"Stayin' Alive" by the Bee Gees. The scene
becomes a hilarious send-up of the disco
scenes in *Saturday Night Fever*, with the
young pilot defying gravity to impress the
girl.

Airplane! is practically a satirical anthology of classic movie clichés. Lloyd
Bridges, as the ground-control officer, seems
to be satirizing half of his straight roles. The
opening titles get an enormous laugh with an
unexpected reference to *Jaws*. The neurotic
young pilot is talked back into the cockpit in
a scene from *Knute Rockne, All American*.
And the romantic scenes are played as a soap
opera. None of this really adds up to great
comic artistry, but *Airplane!* compensates
for its lack of original comic invention by its
utter willingness to steal, beg, borrow, and
rewrite from anywhere.

All Night Long ★ ★
R, 100 m., 1981

Gene Hackman (George Dupler), Barbra
Streisand (Cheryl Gibbons), Diane Ladd
(Helen Dupler), Dennis Quaid (Freddie
Dupler), Kevin Dobson (Bobby Gibbons),
William Daniels (Richard Copleston),
Hamilton Camp (Buggoms). Directed by
Jean-Claude Tramont.

Some movies seem to bring their own moods
with them, and the mood of *All Night Long* is

dispirited mopery. Here's a movie with a high-energy cast and a promising comic plot, and the director seems to be aiming for the bittersweet. How can you possibly start out with Gene Hackman as the manager of an all-night drugstore, and Barbra Streisand as a fireman's wife who likes to swing, and wind up with a movie where everybody's sighing all the time?

Jean-Claude Tramont finds a way. He's the director of *All Night Long*, and maybe he should bear the responsibility. I've been arguing for years that Barbra Streisand would be one of the greatest comedians of all time if she'd just accept strong direction and not play it safe by controlling every detail of her films. Maybe I was wrong. Surely it wasn't Streisand's idea to play her character as a quiet, vacant-minded nonentity. Here's one of the most powerful personalities in movie history, and she doesn't have a single scene where she lets loose. She's almost intimidated by the clothes she wears.

Gene Hackman's character is also a disappointment. He plays an executive of the drug chain, and he's demoted to the all-night managerial position because he threw a chair through the boss's window. It's at this point (very early on) that the movie gets lost. It could have developed into a fascinating portrait of all-night society, but it doesn't. It assigns a few weirdos to march through the store and do their thing, but they don't feel real, they feel like actors. The story never approaches the rhythms of life. You know a movie's in trouble when it makes a running gag out of how to pronounce the hero's name.

Meanwhile, there's this would-be sex comedy trying to get started. Hackman discovers that his son is having an affair with a married cousin (Streisand). Hackman tries to break it up, but gets involved with Streisand himself. Hackman's wife (Diane Ladd) calls her lawyer. Streisand's husband (Kevin Dobson) tries to intimidate Hackman. This might have somehow been made into a farce, but the director keeps losing the pace. Scenes begin with the promise of fireworks and end with the characters at a loss for words. You *also* know a movie's in trouble when it has the heroine ride a motor scooter just to make her seem like more of a character.

Here and there, in the midst of this mess, there are some funny lines. Streisand: "So you only planned one child?" Hackman: "Nobody plans a kid like mine." But the movie never really gets going. It's got all the ingredients, but it feels a million miles from life. Was it all shot on a sound stage? In some of the shots in his office at the drugstore, Hackman stands in front of a one-way mirror looking into the store, and the store looks like a painted backdrop. Even when he's *in* the store, it's all wrong. There aren't any people there, except for the character actors who walk in and act crazy. One low point: An athletic woman tries to stick up the store, throws Hackman and the security guard around, and is dumped into the frozen pizzas. This should generate some electricity, you'd think, but no: The direction turns it into a scene that's first ugly, then pointless.

Maybe I wasn't completely wrong when I suggested that Streisand would benefit from strong direction. She didn't get any here, and the result is a complete waste of time; Hackman's time, as well. These are two of the most talented movie actors we have. They don't make that many films. Neither one really works in *All Night Long*. Life is short. They should get moving.

All of Me ★ ★ ★ ½
PG, 93 m., 1984

Steve Martin (Roger Cobb), Lily Tomlin (Edwina Cutwater), Victoria Tennant (Terry Hoskins), Madolyn Smith (Peggy), Richard Libertini (Prahka Lasa), Jason Bernard (Tyrone Wattel). Directed by Carl Reiner. Screenplay by Phil Alden Robinson.

All of Me shares with a lot of great screwball comedies a very simple approach: Use absolute logic in dealing with the absurd. Begin with a nutty situation, establish the rules, and follow them. The laughs happen when ordinary human nature comes into conflict with ridiculous developments.

We can identify with almost all of the motives of the characters in *All of Me*. There is, for example, the millionaire spinster Edwina Cutwater (Lily Tomlin), who wants to live forever and thinks she has found a way to do that. There is the unhappy lawyer Roger Cobb (Steve Martin), who is desperately unhappy with his work and will do anything to get a promotion—even cater to nut-case clients like Edwina. There is the evil Terry Hoskins (Victoria Tennant), who plans to cruelly deceive Edwina, and there is the beatific Prahka Lasa (Richard Libertini), who hopes to transfer Edwina's soul into a brass pot, and then insert it in Miss Hoskins's body. There is, however, a terrible psychic miscalculation, and when Edwina dies, she transmigrates instead into Cobb's body. When I heard *All of Me* described, I couldn't think of any way this plot could possibly work. To begin with, why put one of my favorite comedians, Tomlin, inside Martin, a man whose movies I have not admired? And yet it does work. The moment it starts to work is the first time Martin has to deal with this alien female entity inside his brain. He retains control of the left side of his body. She controls the right. They are trying to cross the sidewalk together, each in their own way, and this sets up a manic tug-of-war that is one of the funniest scenes I've seen in a long time.

There are other great scenes, some of them probably obligatory, as when Martin has to go to the bathroom. The movie doesn't just go for obvious physical jokes, however; it scores a lot of points by speculating on the ways in which a man and a woman could learn to coexist in such close quarters. Against all the odds, a certain tenderness and sweetness develops by the end of the film. Although it is Tomlin who disappears into Martin's body, she does not disappear from the movie. For one thing, her reflection can be seen in mirrors, and there is some exquisite timing involved in the way they play scenes with each other's mirror images. For another thing (and this is really curious), there is a real sense of her presence even when Martin is alone on the screen: The film's premise, which seems so unlikely, begins to work.

The movie is filled with good supporting performances. My favorites are Richard Libertini, as the guru of transmigration, who speaks incomprehensible words in a tone of complete agreement, and Jason Bernard, as a black musician who is Martin's friend and partner during several tricky scenes of body-snatching and brain-grabbing. *All of Me* is in a class with *Ghostbusters*, and for some of the same reasons.

. . . All the Marbles ★ ★
R, 113 m., 1981

Peter Falk (Harry), Vicki Frederick (Iris), Laurene Landon (Molly), Burt Young (Eddie Cisco), Tracy Reed (Diane). Directed by Robert Aldrich and produced by William Aldrich. Screenplay by Mel Frohman.

The wrestling in this movie is terrific. I want to say that right up front, because the two actresses in . . . *All the Marbles* obviously made a complete commitment to learning how to wrestle convincingly. They deliver amazingly well in the action scenes, but the rest of the movie lets them down.

The actresses are Vicki Frederick and Laurene Landon. Frederick is the brunette. She's a Broadway actress who won a Critics Circle Award for her performance in *Dancin'*. Landon is the tall blonde. She's been in such forgettable movies as *Roller Boogie*. Neither of them, needless to say, has a background in women's wrestling, and yet they play female wrestlers in this movie and do all their own stunts and you can see that they're personally flying through the air and landing on their heads during what the ringside announces breathlessly describes as "The Airplane! Look out below!"

The film's director, Robert Aldrich, must have demanded complete dedication from these two women, who go through an ordeal in the film and come out looking good. They must have been thrilled to be working with the director of *The Dirty Dozen* and *Twilight's Last Gleaming*, and co-starring with a name actor like Peter Falk. But Aldrich has marooned them in an idiotic, meandering script, and Falk's character is never fleshed out into an interesting person.

They play a wrestling tag team named the California Dolls, and Falk is their manager, a down-and-out guy with a beat-up old Cadillac convertible and a book full of phone numbers of people who don't want to receive his calls. They travel around the country wrestling for a few hundred bucks a night in sleazy places like Akron Arena ("the House Rubber Built"). Their goal is to make it into the big time and a championship match at the MGM Grand Hotel. (The fact that the movie was produced by Metro-Goldwyn-Mayer Inc., may help explain this particular plot point.) Lots of good things could have been done with this material. Characters could have been lovingly rounded out into Damon Runyonesque originals. The relationships of the two women and their manager could have been explored. Something could have been said about success and failure in America. Who knows? Maybe the movie could have even taken us inside the world of professional wrestling, and explained whether the women *really* take those brutal-looking falls.

But this movie can't be bothered with details like that. It introduces us to sleazy characters like a fight promoter named Cisco (Burt Young), and then leaves him hanging without a final payoff scene. The movie ends in a climactic championship fight, of course, but it doesn't level with us about that fight. Without giving away the plot, let me just say that the movie wants us to believe that the fight is fixed, but that neither one of the two tag teams is in on the fix. Sure. And when our heroines start throwing the referee around the ring and banging his head onto the canvas—I dunno a whole lot about pro wrestling, but wouldn't that be a foul?

The good qualities of this movie are mostly contained in the performances of Frederick and Landon, and in their skill in the wrestling scenes. Falk is okay, but we've seen this particular raspy-voiced Falk performance many times before, and the screenplay gives him nobody new to be. . . . *All the Marbles* is filled with great raw material, but I guess they thought the raw material would be enough. Too bad. I hope Landon and Frederick didn't break any bones, and I guess they know by now that the movie business can break your heart.

All the Right Moves ★ ★ ★
R, 91 m., 1983

Tom Cruise (Stef), Craig T. Nelson (Nickerson), Lea Thompson (Lisa). Directed by Michael Chapman and produced by Stephen Deutsch. Screenplay by Michael Kane.

I started on newspapers as a sportswriter, covering local high school teams. That was a long time ago, and I had almost forgotten, until I saw *All the Right Moves*, how desperately important every game seemed at the time. When the team members and the fans are all teen-agers, and when a school victory reflects in a significant way upon your own feelings of worth, when "We won!" means that we won, a football game can take on aspects of Greek tragedy.

All the Right Moves remembers the strength of those feelings, but does not sentimentalize them. The movie stars Tom Cruise (from *Risky Business*) as a high school football player in a small Pennsylvania mill town where unemployment is a way of life. His ticket out of town is a football scholarship to a good engineering school. The high school football coach (Craig T. Nelson) also is looking for a ticket, to an assistant coaching job in a college. On the night of the big game, these two people get into a position where each one seems to have destroyed the hopes of the other.

The movie plays this conflict against an interesting background. This isn't another high school movie with pompom girls and funny principals and weirdo chem teachers. The movie gets into the dynamics of the high school student body and into the tender, complicated relationship between the Cruise character and his girlfriend (Lea Thompson).

After all the junk high school movies in which kids chop each other up, seduce the French teacher, and visit whorehouses in Mexico, it is so wonderful to see a movie that remembers that most teen-agers are vulnerable, unsure, sincere, and fundamentally decent. The kid, his girlfriend, and all of their friends have feelings we can recognize as real. The plot feels real, too, because it centers around those kinds of horrible misunderstandings and mistakes that we all remember from high school. A lot of teen-agers walk around all day feeling guilty, even if they're totally innocent. Get them into a situation that gives them the appearance of guilt and they're in trouble. And it is so easy to get into trouble when you are old enough to do wrong but too young to move independently to avoid it. A lot of kids who say they were only along for the ride are telling the simple truth.

The movie frames the Cruise character in a situation like that, one we can identify with. And then it does an interesting thing. Instead of solving the problem with a plot twist, it solves it through the exercise of genuine human honesty: Two people finally tell each other the truth. This is, of course, an astonishing breakthrough in movies about teen-agers, and *All the Right Moves* deserves credit for that achievement.

Altered States ★ ★ ★ ½
R, 103 m., 1980

William Hurt (Eddie Jessup), Blair Brown (Emily Jessup), Bob Balaban (Arthur Rosenberg), Charles Haid (Mason Parrish), Thaao Penghlis (Eccheverria), Miguel Godreau (Primal Man). Directed by Ken Russell and produced by Howard Gottfried. Screenplay by Sidney Aaron.

Altered States is one hell of a movie—literally. It hurls its characters headlong back through billions of years to the moment of creation and finds nothing there except an anguished scream of "No!" as the life force protests its moment of birth. And then, through the power of the human ego to insist on its own will even in the face of the implacable indifference of the universe, it turns "No!" into "Yes!" and ends with the basic scene in all drama, the man and the woman falling into each other's arms.

But hold on just a second here: I'm beginning to sound like the movie's characters, a band of overwrought pseudo-intellectuals who talk like a cross between Werner Erhard, Freud, and Tarzan. Some of the movie's best dialogue passages are deliberately staged with everybody talking at once: It doesn't matter what they're saying, only that they're incredibly serious about it. I can tell myself intellectually that this movie is a fiendishly constructed visual and verbal roller coaster, a movie deliberately intended to overwhelm its audiences with sensual excess. I know all that, and yet I *was* overwhelmed, I *was* caught up in its headlong energy.

Is that a worthy accomplishment for a movie? Yes, I suppose it is, if the movie earns it by working as hard as *Altered States* does. This is, at last, the movie that Ken Russell was born to direct—the same Ken Russell whose wretched excesses in the past include *The Music Lovers, The Devils,* and *Liszto-*

mania. The formula is now clear. Take Russell's flair for visual pyrotechnics and apocalyptic sexuality, and channel it through just enough scientific mumbo jumbo to give it form. The result may be totally meaningless, but while you're watching it you are not concerned.

The movie is based on a Paddy Chayevsky novel, which was, in turn, inspired by the experiments of Dr. John Lilly, the man who placed his human subjects in total immersion tanks—floating them in total darkness so that their minds, cut off from all external reality, could play along the frontiers of sanity. In *Altered States,* William Hurt plays a Harvard scientist named Jessup who takes such an experiment one step further, by ingesting a drug made from the sacred hallucinatory mushrooms of a primitive tribe. The strange thing about these mushrooms, Hurt observes in an easily missed line of dialogue in the movie, is that they give everyone who takes them the same hallucinatory vision. Perhaps it is our cellular memory of creation: There is chaos, and then a ball of light, and then the light turns into a crack, and the crack opens onto Nothing, and that is all there was and all there will be, except for life, which has its only existence in the mind.

Got that? It hardly matters. It is a breathtaking concept, but *Altered States* hardly slows down for it. This is the damnedest movie to categorize. Just when it begins to sound like a 1960s psychedelic fantasy, a head trip—it turns into a farce. The scientist immerses himself in his tank for too long, he regresses to a simian state, physically turns into some kind of ape, attacks the campus security guards, is chased by a pack of wild dogs into the local zoo, and kills and eats a sheep for his supper before turning *back* into the kindly Professor Jessup, the Intellectual Hulk.

The movie splits up into three basic ingredients: The science, the special effects, and the love relationship between the professor and his wife. The science is handled deliciously well. We learn as much as we need to (that is, next to nothing) about total immersion, genetics, and the racial memory. Then come the special effects, in four long passages and a few short bursts. They're good. They may remind you at times of the sound-and-light extravaganza toward the end of

2001, but they are also supposed to evoke the birth of the universe in a pulsating celestial ovum. In the center of this vision is Dr. Jessup, his body pulsing in and out of an ape-shape, his mouth pulled into an anguished "O" as he protests the hell of being born. These scenes are reinforced by the music and are obviously intended to fuel the chemically altered consciousness of the next generation of movie cultists.

But then there is the matter of the love relationship between the professor and his wife (Blair Brown), and it is here that we discover how powerful the attraction of love really is. During the professor's last experiment, when he is disappearing into a violent whirlpool of light and screams on the laboratory floor, it is his wife who wades into the celestial mists, gets up to her knees in eternity, reaches in, and pulls him out. And this is despite the fact that he has filed for divorce. The last scene is a killer, with the professor turning into the protoplasm of life itself, and his wife turning into a glowing shell of rock-like flesh, with her inner fires glowing through the crevices (the effect is something like an overheated Spiderman). They're going through the unspeakable hell of reliving the First Moment, and yet as the professor, as Man, bangs on the walls and crawls toward her, and she reaches out, and the universe rocks, the Man within him bursts out of the ape-protoplasm, and the Woman within her explodes back into flesh, and they collapse into each other's arms, and all the scene really needs at that point is for him to ask, "Was it as good for you as it was for me?"

Altered States is a superbly silly movie, a magnificent entertainment, and a clever and brilliant machine for making us feel awe, fear, and humor. That is enough. It's pure movie and very little meaning. Did I like it? Yeah, I guess I did, but I wouldn't advise trying to think about it very deeply.

Amadeus ★ ★ ★ ★
PG, 158 m., 1984

F. Murray Abraham (Salieri), Tom Hulce (Mozart), Elizabeth Berridge (Constanze), Simon Callow (Emanuel Schikaneder), Roy Dotrice (Leopold Mozart), Christine Ebersole (Katerina Cavalieri), Jeffrey Jones (Joseph II). Directed by Milos Forman and produced by Saul Zaentz. Screenplay by Peter Shaffer.

Milos Forman's *Amadeus* is one of the riskiest gambles a filmmaker has taken in a long time—a lavish movie about Mozart that dares to be anarchic and saucy, and yet still earns the importance of tragedy. This movie is nothing like the dreary educational portraits we're used to seeing about the Great Composers, who come across as cobwebbed profundities weighed down with the burden of genius. This is Mozart as an eighteenth-century Bruce Springsteen, and yet (here is the genius of the movie) there is nothing cheap or unworthy about the approach. *Amadeus* is not only about as much fun as you're likely to have with a movie, it also is disturbingly true. The truth enters in the character of Salieri, who tells the story. He is not a great composer, but he is a good enough composer to know greatness when he hears it, and that is why the music of Mozart breaks his heart. He knows how good it is, he sees how easily Mozart seems to compose it, and he knows that his own work looks pale and silly beside it.

The movie begins with the suggestion that Salieri might have murdered Mozart. The movie examines the ways in which this possibility might be true, and by the end of the film we feel a certain kinship with the weak and jealous Salieri—for few of us can identify with divine genius, but many of us probably have had dark moments of urgent self-contempt in the fact of those whose effortless existence illustrates our own inadequacies. Salieri, played with burning intensity by F. Murray Abraham, sits hunched in a madhouse confessing to a priest. The movie flashes back to his memories of Wolfgang Amadeus Mozart, the child genius who composed melodies of startling originality and who grew up to become a prolific, driven artist.

One of the movie's wisest decisions is to cast Mozart not as a charismatic demigod, not as a tortured superman, but as a goofy, immature, likable kid with a ridiculous laugh. The character is played by Tom Hulce, and if you saw *Animal House*, you may remember him as the fraternity brother who tried to seduce the mayor's daughter, while an angel and a devil whispered in his ears. Hulce would seem all wrong for Mozart, but he is absolutely right, as an unaffected young man filled with delight at his own gifts, unaware of how easily he wounds Salieri and others, tortured only by the guilt of having offended his religious and domineering father.

The film is constructed in wonderfully well-written and acted scenes—scenes so carefully constructed, unfolding with such delight, that they play as perfect compositions of words. Most of them will be unfamiliar to those who have seen Peter Shaffer's brooding play, on which this film is based; Shaffer and Forman have brought light, life, and laughter to the material, and it plays with grace and ease. It's more human than the play; the characters are people, not throbbing packages of meaning. It centers on the relationships in Mozart's life: with his father, his wife, and Salieri. The father never can be pleased, and that creates an undercurrent affecting all of Mozart's success. The wife, played by delightful, buxom Elizabeth Berridge, contains in one person the qualities of a jolly wench and a loving partner: She likes to loll in bed all day, but also gives Mozart good, sound advice and is a forceful person in her own right. The patrons, especially Joseph II, the Austro-Hungarian emperor, are connoisseurs and dilettantes, slow to take to Mozart's new music but enchanted by the audacity with which he defends it. And then there is Salieri (F. Murray Abraham), the gaunt court composer whose special torture is to understand better than anybody else how inadequate he is, and how great Mozart is.

The movie was shot on location in Forman's native Czechoslovakia, and it looks exactly right; it fits its period comfortably, perhaps because Prague still contains so many streets and squares and buildings that could be directly from the Vienna of Mozart's day. Perhaps his confidence in his locations gave Forman the freedom to make Mozart slightly *out* of period. Forman directed the film version of *Hair*, and Mozart in this movie seems to share a spirit with some of the characters from *Hair*. Mozart's wigs do not look like everybody else's. They have just the slightest suggestion of punk, just the smallest shading of pink. Mozart seems more a child of the 1960's than of any other age, and this interpretation of his personality—he was an irreverent proto-hippie who trusted, if you will, his own vibes—sounds risky, but works.

I have not mentioned the music. There's probably no need to. The music provides the understructure of the film, strong, confident, above all, *clear* in a way that Salieri's simple muddles only serve to illustrate. There are times when Mozart speaks the words of a child, but then the music says the same things in the language of the gods, and all is clear.

Amadeus is a magnificent film, full and tender and funny and charming—and, at the end, sad and angry, too, because in the character of Salieri it has given us a way to understand not only greatness, but our own lack of it. This movie's fundamental question, I think, is whether we can learn to be grateful for the happiness of others, and that, of course, is a test for sainthood. How many movies ask such questions and succeed in being fun, as well?

American Gigolo ★ ★ ★ ½
R, 117 m., 1980

Richard Gere (Julian), Lauren Hutton (Michelle), Hector Elizondo (Sunday), Nina Van Pallandt (Anne), Bill Duke (Leon Jaimes), Brian Davies (Stratton). Directed by Paul Schrader and produced by Jerry Bruckheimer. Screenplay by Schrader.

The bare outline of its plot makes *American Gigolo* sound like a fairly sleazy package: A Hollywood male prostitute is framed in a kinky murder case, tracks down the pimp who's responsible for the framing, watches in horror as the pimp himself is killed, and then finds himself faced with prison unless the wife of a senator provides him with an alibi. This is strong stuff—almost sensational enough for daytime soap opera.

But the film *American Gigolo* is a stylish and surprisingly poignant handling of this material. The experiences in the film may be alien to us, but the emotions of the characters are not: Julian Kay, the gigolo of the title, is played by Richard Gere as tender, vulnerable, and a little dumb. We care about him. His business—making love to rich women of a certain age—allows him to buy the baubles by which Beverly Hills measures success, and he has his Mercedes, his expensive wardrobe, his antique vases, his entrée to country clubs.

But he says he's in business for reasons other than money, and we believe him, if only because he hardly seems to value his possessions as anything other than props. He feels a sense of satisfaction when he makes a middle-aged woman happy, he says. He seems to see himself as a cross between a sexual surrogate and a therapist, and the movie does, too: Why, he's hardly a whore at all, not even counting his heart of gold.

The movie sentimentalizes on this point, setting up the character of Julian Kay as so sympathetic that we forgive him his profession. That's a tactic that *American Gigolo*'s writer and director, Paul Schrader, is borrowing from one of his own heroes, the French director Robert Bresson, whose *Pickpocket* make a criminal into an antihero. Schrader is setting the stage for the key relationship in the film, between Julian and the senator's wife (Lauren Hutton).

He tries to pick her up in an exclusive restaurant, but breaks off their conversation when he decides she's not a likely client. But she is all *too* likely, and tracks him down to his apartment. They fall in love, at about the time he's being framed for the murder of a Palm Springs socialite, and the movie wants us to believe in the power of love to redeem both characters: Julian learns to love unselfishly, without money, and the woman learns to love honestly, without regard for her husband's position.

This business of redemption would work better if *American Gigolo* had at least a few more scenes developing the relationship between Gere and Hutton: Her character, so central to the movie's upbeat conclusion, isn't seen clearly enough. We aren't shown the steps by which she moves from sex to love with him (unless she's simply been won over by the old earth-shaking orgasm ploy). We aren't given enough detail about their feelings.

That's a weakness, but not a fatal one, because when Schrader cuts away from their relationship, it's to develop a very involving story about the murder, the framing, and the police investigation. The movie has an especially effective performance by Hector Elizondo as a cigar-chomping vice detective

who cheerfully admits he thinks Gere is guilty as sin.

Gere tries to find out who's framing him by descending into the Los Angeles sexual underground. Schrader explored this same universe in his previous film, *Hardcore*, but this time he seems more restrained: The sexual netherlands seem less lurid, more commonplace and sad.

The whole movie has a winning sadness about it; take away the story's sensational aspects and what you have is a study in loneliness. Richard Gere's performance is central to that effect, and some of his scenes—reading the morning paper, rearranging some paintings, selecting a wardrobe—underline the emptiness of his life. We leave *American Gigolo* with the curious feeling that if women weren't paying this man to sleep with them, he'd be paying them: He needs the human connection and he has a certain shyness, a loner quality, that makes it easier for him when love seems to be just another deal.

An American Werewolf in London ★ ★

R, 95 m., 1981

David Naughton (David), Griffin Dunne (Jack), Jenny Agutter (Alex), John Woodvine (Dr. Hirsch). Directed by John Landis and produced by George Folsey, Jr. Screenplay by Landis.

An American Werewolf in London seems curiously unfinished, as if director John Landis spent all his energy on spectacular set-pieces and then didn't want to bother with things like transitions, character development, or an ending. The movie has sequences that are spellbinding, and then long stretches when nobody seem sure what's going on. There are times when the special effects almost wipe the characters off the screen. It's weird. It's not a very good film, and it falls well below Landis's work in the anarchic *National Lampoon's Animal House* and the rambunctious *Blues Brothers*. Landis never seems very sure whether he's making a comedy or a horror film, so he winds up with genuinely funny moments acting as counterpoint to the gruesome undead. Combining horror and comedy is an old tradition (my favorite example is *The Bride of Franken-stein*), but the laughs and the blood co-exist very uneasily in this film.

One of the offscreen stars of the film is Rick Baker, the young makeup genius who created the movie's wounds, gore, and werewolves. His work is impressive, yes, but unless you're single-mindedly interested in special effects, *American Werewolf* is a disappointment. And even the special effects, good as they are, come as an anticlimax if you're a *really* dedicated horror fan, because if you are, you've already seen this movie's high point before: the onscreen transformation of a man into a werewolf was anticipated in *The Howling*, in which the special effects were done by a Baker protegé named Rob Bottin.

The movie's plot involves two young American students (David Naughton and Griffin Dunne), who are backpacking across the English moors. They stumble into a country pub where everyone is ominously silent, and then one guy warns them to beware the full moon and stick to the road. They don't, and are attacked by werewolves. Dunne is killed, Naughton is severely wounded, and a few days later in the hospital Naughton is visited by the decaying cadaver of Dunne—who warns him that he'll turn into a werewolf at the full moon. Naughton ignores the warning, falls in love with his nurse (Jenny Agutter), and moves in with her when he's discharged from the hospital. Then follows a series of increasingly gruesome walk-ons by Dunne, who begs Naughton to kill himself before the full moon. Naughton doesn't, turns into a werewolf, and runs amok through London. That gives director Landis his chance to stage a spectacular multi-car traffic accident in Piccadilly Circus; crashes have been his specialty since the homecoming parade in *Animal House* and the nonstop carnage in *Blues Brothers*.

The best moments in *American Werewolf* probably belong to Dunne, who may be a decaying cadaver but keeps right on talking like a college student: "Believe me," he says at Naughton's bedside, "this isn't a whole lot of fun." The scene in which Naughton turns into a werewolf is well done, with his hands elongating and growing claws, and his face twisting into a snout and fangs. But it's as if John Landis thought the technology would be enough. We never get a real feeling for the characters, we never really believe the places (especially that awkwardly phony pub and its stagy customers), and we are particularly disappointed by the ending. I won't reveal the ending, such as it is, except to say it's so sudden, arbitrary, and anticlimactic that, although we are willing for the movie to be over, we still can't quite believe it.

Amityville II: The Possession ★ ★
R, 110 m., 1982

Burt Young (Father), James Olson (Priest), Jack Magner (Son), Diane Franklin (Daughter). Directed by Damiano Damiani and produced by Dino De Laurentiis. Screenplay by Tommy Lee Wallace.

This movie is actually slightly better than *The Amityville Horror* (1979), maybe because it rips off superior source material. It starts with the most notorious piece of real estate in North America. Then it lifts ingredients from *The Exorcist*, *Poltergeist*, and *Murder in Amityville*, which was the book about the *original* Amityville horror. Perhaps a bit of history is called for. Although there is great doubt about whether the best-selling *The Amityville Horror* was fact or fiction, there seems to be no doubt that a terrible mass murder did occur in the infamous Amityville house, some years prior to the events in *Horror*. A young man living in the house went berserk and killed his parents, two sisters, and a brother. After he was institutionalized, the house stood empty for a while before being sold to the Bill Lutz family. As all Amityville fans already know, the Lutzes soon began to wonder if they'd made a good buy after the house filled up with green slime, swarms of flies, and pigs with glowing red eyes. They eventually fled the house. (These days, of course, a lot of people would be happy to live with the slime and the flies if they could assume the Lutzes' 8½ percent mortgage.)

Amityville II is actually a prequel, then, instead of a sequel, since it tells what happened in the house before the Lutzes entered the picture. The movie itself is vague about exactly when it's set, however, and although *Amityville Horror* came out in 1979, this prequel contains 1982 automobiles.

The movie opens with a foggy shot of the house, with those eerie attic windows gleaming like diabolical eyes. There is a "For Sale" sign in the front yard—which inspired me, I fear, to laugh out loud. Before long, though, a family moves in. The father is Burt Young (Rocky's brother-in-law). He beats his wife and kids. The wife weeps and refuses to sleep with him. Meanwhile, the older brother (Jack Magner) successfully seduces his sister (Diane Franklin), who confesses to the local priest (James Olson). The house is already acting up. It was, we learn, built over an ancient Indian burial ground (cf. *Poltergeist*) and contains a secret room leading to a crypt (this room is different in *Amityville Horror,* but never mind). After the incestuous son begins hearing voices, he shoots everyone in his family, and is jailed. Then the priest realizes the lad has been possessed by an evil spirit, and the last act of the movie turns into a rehash of *The Exorcist.*

For a movie that's filled with crucifixes, monsignors, confessionals, and Bibles, *Amityville II* is curiously inattentive to such theological questions as (a) Why would the desecration of a pagan burial ground be offensive to evil spirits, as opposed to benevolent ones? and (b) Why does this case call for a Catholic priest instead of a Mohawk medicine man? But never mind. There are some good performances here, by Jack Magner and Olson in particular, and some good technical credits, especially Sam O'Steen's editing. It's just that this whole Amityville saga is such absolute horse manure.

Angelo My Love ★ ★ ★ ½
R, 91 m., 1983

Angelo Evans, Michael Evans, Steve Tsigonoff, Millie Tsigonoff. Written and directed by Robert Duvall. Associate producer, Gail Youngs.

The late Italian director Vittoria De Sica once said that anyone can play at least one role—himself—better than anybody else possibly could. De Sica illustrated that belief in his late-1940s neo-realist films like *Bicycle Thief,* and now the American actor Robert Duvall proves it again, in a wonderful and unique movie he has written and directed, named *Angelo My Love.* Here is a movie that could not exist without the people who are in it—and of how many movies is that true? The film is about the lives, feuds, rivalries, and dreams of a group of New York Gypsies, and Duvall has recruited real Gypsies to play themselves. His inspiration for the movie came when he saw a young Gypsy boy named Angelo Evans conning a much older woman during an argument on a Manhattan sidewalk.

Duvall thought Angelo belonged in the movies. Having seen the movie, I agree. Here is a street-smart, inventive kid of about eleven or twelve who has some of the moves and some of the cynicism of an experienced con man. ("He's got his tiny macho moves down so pat," David Anson wrote in *Newsweek,* "he's like a child impersonator.") Angelo is the product of a culture that has taught him that the world owes him a living, and he cheerfully agrees. What we sometimes almost forget is that Angelo is also a child, vulnerable and easily wounded, and that a lot of his act is a veneer.

Duvall weaves his story around Angelo. We meet his mother, father, sister, and girlfriend, and a couple of villainous Gypsies who steal a ring that Angelo had intended to present to his future bride. All of these people play themselves, more or less. Angelo's family really is his family; the villains are played by a brother and sister, Steve and Millie Tsigonoff, whom Duvall met in Los Angeles. Although the movie's plot is basically a device for letting us watch the lives of the characters, it's the kind of plot, I suspect, that Gypsies might be able to identify with—involving theft, pride, thwarted justice, and revenge. After the Tsigonoffs steal the ring, there's an ill-advised chase to Canada to get it back (and a wonderful set-piece in a Gypsy camp supposedly under attack by ghosts). Then there's a trial scene in the backroom of an Irish-American bar in Brooklyn. It's all done with great energy and seriousness, even though by the movie's end the ring hardly seems to matter.

Angelo also stars in several fairly self-contained scenes that abundantly illustrate why Duvall found him so fascinating. He makes a defiant mess of his one day in school. He attempts to pick up a pretty country singer who is at least ten years older than he is. He and his sister engage in a long, ingratiating conversation with an old lady in a cafeteria; they want to inveigle her into their mother's fortune-telling parlor, but the lady is a New Yorker and wasn't born yesterday.

All of these scenes have a special magic because we sense that they're real, that they come out of people's lives. *Angelo My Love* is technically a fictional film, but Duvall has worked so close to his sources that it has the conviction of a documentary. Maybe because he's such a good actor, Duvall has been able to listen to his characters, to really see *them* rather than his own notion of how they should move and behave. There are moments in this movie when the camera lingers for an extra moment, and scenes that do not quite dovetail into everything else, and we sense that Duvall left them in because they revealed something about his Gypsies that he had observed and wanted to share.

At the end of the movie we ask ourselves a question the movie does not attempt to answer: What will become of Angelo in the years to come? It's one thing to be a cute, street-wise kid. It's another thing to try to carry that role on through life with you. Angelo might be able to pull it off, but the movie doesn't try to sell us that romanticized hope. Instead, Duvall seems to be suggesting that Angelo is more than a colorful Gypsy kid; that he has real potential as a person, if he can grow out of the trap of his glib mannerisms and is not too badly scarred by his upside-down childhood. Who knows? One day ten years from now, there might be a movie named *Angelo My Friend*.

Annie ★ ★ ★
PG, 128 m., 1982

Aileen Quinn (Annie), Albert Finney (Daddy Warbucks), Carol Burnett (Miss Hannigan), Bernadette Peters (Lily), Ann Reinking (Grace Farrell), Tim Curry (Rooster), Geoffrey Holder (Punjab), Edward Herrmann (F.D.R.). Directed by John Huston and produced by Ray Stark. Screenplay by Carol Sobieski.

In the abstract, *Annie* is fun. It has lots of movement and color, dance and music, sound and fury. In the particular, it has all sorts of problems, and I guess the only way to really enjoy the movie is to just ignore the particulars. I will nevertheless mention a few

particulars. One is the story itself, about how Little Orphan Annie is rescued from a cruel orphanage by a billionaire who wants a Rent-An-Orphan for Christmas. This is said to be a universal story. Critics have written that you just can't help cheering for Annie as she faces the cold world with pluck and courage. I didn't find myself cheering much, though, since Annie didn't seem to need the encouragement; as played by the feisty young Aileen Quinn, she is the sort of child who makes adults run for the hills.

The adventures she gets herself into are likewise questionable. I've never thought of *Oliver!* as a particularly realistic musical, but at least when its little hero said "Please, sir, more food?" there was a hint of truth. *Annie* has been plunged into pure fantasy, into the mindless sort of musical boosterism that plays big for Broadway theater parties but almost always translates to the movie screen as sheer contrivance. *Annie* is not *about* anything. It *contains* lots of subjects (such as cruel orphanages, the Great Depression, scheming conmen, heartless billionaires, and President Franklin Delano Roosevelt) but it isn't *about* them. It's not even really about whether Annie will survive her encounters with them, since the book of this musical is so rigorously machine-made, so relentlessly formula, it's one of those movies where you can amaze your friends by leaving the auditorium, standing blindfolded in the lobby and correctly predicting the outcome.

And yet I sort of enjoyed the movie. I enjoyed the energy that was visible on the screen, and the sumptuousness of the production numbers, and the good humor of several of the performances—especially those by Albert Finney, as Daddy Warbucks, and Carol Burnett, as the wicked orphanage supervisor, Miss Hannigan. Aileen Quinn sort of grew on me, too. She cannot be said to really play a child—at least not the sort of plausible flesh-and-blood child that Henry Thomas creates in *E. T.* But Quinn is talented, can dance well and sing passably, and does not seem to be an overtrained puppet like, say, Ricky Schroeder. She seems more like the kind of kid who will get this acting out of her system and go on to be student body president.

If there is a center to the film, it belongs to Albert Finney. He has a thankless task: He must portray Daddy Warbucks as a self-centered, smug rich man who has everything in the world, except love, and who learns to love through the example of a little girl. This is the sort of role actors kill over—to avoid playing. Albert Finney has the true grit. He's gone through this personality transformation twice; he starred in *Scrooge* in 1970. This time, he even pulls it off, by underplaying. He isn't too aloof at the beginning, and he's not too softhearted at the end. He has a certain detachment. Annie may win his heart, but she'll still have to phone for an appointment.

Will kids like the movie? I honestly don't know. When I was a kid, I didn't much like movies about other kids, maybe because I was jealous (why does *that* kid get to ride a horse in the Derby?). The movie was promoted as a family entertainment, but was it really a family musical, even on the stage? I dunno. I think it was more of a product, a clever concoction of nostalgia, hard-sell sentiment, small children, and cute dogs. The movie is the same mixture as before. It's like some kind of dumb toy that doesn't do anything or go anywhere, but it is fun to watch as it spins mindlessly around and around.

Any Which Way You Can ★ ★
PG, 116 m., 1980

Clint Eastwood (Philo Beddoe), Sondra Locke (Lynne), Geoffrey Lewis (Orville), William Smith (Jack Wilson), Harry Guardino (James Beekman), Ruth Gordon (Ma). Directed by Buddy Van Horn and produced by Fritz Manes. Screenplay by Stanford Sherman.

Clint Eastwood's *Any Which Way You Can* is not a very good movie, but it's hard not to feel a grudging affection for it. Where else, in the space of 116 minutes, can you find a country and western road picture with two fights, a bald motorcycle gang, the Mafia, a love story, a pickup truck, a tow truck, Fats Domino, a foul-mouthed octogenarian, an oversexed orangutan, and a contest for the bare-knuckle championship of the world?

The movie seems designed as a free-association exercise involving all of the above elements, in no particular order. That gives it a certain clarity of form. It opens, for example, with a bare-knuckle fight between Eastwood and someone else. (Who else? Doesn't matter). While Eastwood is slugging it out, his highly intelligent orangutan, Clyde, is relieving himself in the front seat of a state police car. And somehow we know—never mind how, we just *know*—that one of the recurring subjects of this movie is going to be orangutan crap in squad cars. We are correct. It's that kind of movie.

After seeing the big fight, Eastwood returns to his home, which seems to be an Okie hovel somewhere in a large Western state. He still lives with Ma, played by Ruth Gordon as a cross between Ma Kettle and Ma Barker. Clint and his partner, Orville Boggs, spend all day hard at work banging on things with wrenches. Occasionally Clyde amuses himself by ripping apart old Mercurys with his bare hands. Then the Mafia decides to set up a bare-knuckle fight between Eastwood and the defending Eastern champion, a guy named Jack Wilson.

It was to my immense delight that I immediately recognized the actor playing Jack Wilson. He is William (Big Bill) Smith, who played a lot of motorcycle gang leaders in films of the late 1960s, and still looks as fearsome as ever. He and Eastwood meet while out jogging one morning, and then he falls off a cliff and is rescued by Eastwood, after which he beats up a lot of guys who insult Eastwood's girlfriend in a bar. All in a day's work.

The girlfriend is played by Sondra Locke, who was also in *Every Which Way But Loose*, the prequel to the present film. You gotta give Eastwood and Locke credit. Unlike Burt Reynolds and Sally Field, who spent the first half of *Smokey and the Bandit II* holding a deep, interpersonal philosophical argument about the issues raised by their relationship in *Smokey and the Bandit*, Eastwood and Locke don't agonize over their reunion. Two minutes after their meeting in a country and western bar, Locke is being consoled by Eastwood's orangutan. Ten minutes later, they're starting a riot at the YWCA. It's that kind of movie.

Anyway, the Mafia kidnaps Sondra Locke in order to force Eastwood to fight. Then Big Bill Smith and Eastwood wipe out the Mafia, but decide to fight anyway. It is some fight. It's one of those brawls where everytime somebody gets hit on the chin, it sounds like they're beating the hell out of a Naugahyde sofa with a Ping-Pong paddle. If we had any slight lingering doubts that this was a Clint Eastwood movie, they are dispelled when Eastwood breaks his right arm during the fight, gets up off the floor and growls, "It's not over yet."

Arthur ★ ★ ★ ½
PG, 97 m., 1981

Dudley Moore (Arthur Bach), Liza Minelli (Linda Marolla), John Gielgud (Hobson), Geraldine Fitzgerald (Martha Bach), Jill Eikenberry (Susan), Stephen Elliott (Burt), Tod Ross (Bitterman), Barney Martin (Linda's Father). Directed and written by Steve Gordon. Produced by Robert Greenhut.

Only someone with a heart of stone could fail to love a drunk like Arthur Bach, who spends his wasted days in a poignant search for someone who will love him, will care for him, will inflame his passions, and soothe his pain, and who, most of all, will laugh at his one-liners. Arthur is such a servant of humanity that he even dedicates himself to thinking up new one-liners and holding them in reserve, lest he be unprepared if someone walks into his life and needs a laugh, quick.

Arthur, played by Dudley Moore, is the alcoholic hero of *Arthur*, a comedy about a man who is worth $750 million and who would never think of trying to buy anyone's love with his money. Arthur is like the woman in the poem by Yeats, who spent her days in innocent good will, and her nights in argument, till her voice grew shrill. Arthur, God love him, is a drunk. He slips into his bath of a morning, and his butler brings him a martini. After he completes his bath, Arthur sets about the day's business, which consists of staying drunk, and being driven about Manhattan in a limousine in his endless quest for love.

Now the problems with searching for love while you are drunk are many. They include (a) no one will want to love you while you are drunk, (b) you are not at your best while you are drunk, so they won't know what they're missing, (c) you may be too drunk to notice it if someone does finally fall in love with you, and (d) if you survive all of these pitfalls, you will nevertheless wake up hung

over, and scientific studies prove that hangovers dissolve love. All of these things having been said, Arthur, against all odds, does find love. He finds it in the person of Linda (Liza Minelli), a smart cookie who doesn't care about his money but is overwhelmed by the dimensions of his needs. Arthur would like to marry Linda. But his billionaire father insists that he marry a perfectly boring WASP (Jill Eikenberry) whose idea of a good holiday is probably the January white sales.

Arthur turns for help to his loyal butler, Hobson, who is played by John Gielgud with an understated elegance and a naughty tongue. Hobson is dying. But Hobson wishes to see Arthur prevail, for once, against Arthur's father, a sadistic puppet-master. So Hobson subtly manipulates the situation so that the lovers are thrown together at the party announcing Arthur's engagement to the WASP. That inspires a rupture within the family, and a very drunken odyssey by Arthur, who wants to press $100,000 upon Linda, and visits her at home. When Linda turns him down, her father (Barney Martin) becomes a grown man who sheds tears, creating perhaps the funniest moment in the movie.

Dudley Moore became a star, of course, with *10*, playing a man who became obsessed with Bo Derek, and who could blame him? In *Arthur*, he makes his bid for world-class status as a comic character actor. He brings a wonderful intensity to scenes like the one near the beginning of the film where he has invited a hooker to dinner at the Plaza and then forgotten who she is, and what she is, or why he is with her. It is marvelous to see him try to focus his attention, which he seems to believe is all concentrated in his eyebrow muscles.

Apart from Moore, the treasure of *Arthur* is in its many supporting performances, especially Gielgud's, although everyone in this movie has great moments. You might be tempted to think that *Arthur* would be a bore, because it is about a drunk who is always trying to tell you stories. You would be right if *Arthur* were a party and you were attending it. But *Arthur* is a movie. And so its drunk, unlike real drunks, is more entertaining, more witty, more human, and more poignant than you are. He embodies, in fact, all the wonderful human qualities that drunks fondly, mistakenly believe the booze brings out in them.

The Awakening ★
R, 102 m., 1980

Charlton Heston (Matthew Corbeck), Susannah York (Jane Turner), Jill Townsend (Anne Corbeck), Stephanie Zimbalist (Margaret Corbeck), Patrick Drury (Whittier), Bruce Myers (Dr. Khalid). Directed by Mike Newell and produced by Robert Solo. Screenplay by Allan Scott, Chris Bryant, and Clive Exton.

I would like to begin with a simple argument. If you are going to make a horror film about the mummy of a four-thousand-year-old Egyptian princess, anything you can do to make the story more realistic will also make it more frightening. A lot of us probably harbor sneaky suspicions that the ancient Egyptians were up to *something*, and if you can surround a mummy with pseudo-science you can trigger that primordial instinct, deep within the thriller fan, that your story is not only scary, but just maybe possible.

The Exorcist was able to trigger that nerve; it surrounded its demon-possession with a convincing apparatus of theological and psychic research. The original *Omen* began with all that malarky in the Middle East, just to establish a plausible framework for its story of a reawakened demon. But there's none of that groundwork in *The Awakening*, which is such an old-fashioned movie we're almost surprised, halfway through, that it's not in black and white and it doesn't feature actors who've been dead for thirty years.

The Awakening is bad in so many ways that I'll just name a few. It is, for example, completely implausible in its approach to the science of archaeology—so hilariously inaccurate, indeed, that I can recommend this movie to archaeologists without any reservations whatsoever. They'll bust a gut. Example. Charlton Heston, a British archaeologist, is searching for the long-lost tomb of the Egyptian queen Kara. He finds it. Well, no wonder: It's "hidden" behind a gigantic stone door in a mountainside, with big, bold hieroglyphics written all over it. It's about as hard to find as Men's Clothing at Marshall Field's. Anyway, having found this priceless and undisturbed tomb, Heston immediately begins pounding away at the door with a sledgehammer.

Now, even if your knowledge of archaeology is limited to leafing through back issues of *National Geographic* at the dentist's, you know that when they make a major find, they're supposed to spend years dusting off everything with little brushes and making a fetish of not disturbing anything. Not Heston. He even has a team of laborers with pickaxes standing by as back-up.

Well, wouldn't you know, every time Heston hammers at the tomb, his pregnant wife, back at the camp, doubles up in pain. That's because, as the movie makes abundantly clear, the spirit of Kara is being reborn in Heston's baby daughter. There's also some nonsense about how Heston ignores his wife to be with his comely young assistant (Susannah York), and then the movie flashes forward eighteen years, and we veteran *Omen*-watchers prepare for the scenes in which the child becomes aware that she is possessed by a spirit, and that Her Time Has Come.

Great! And none too soon, we're all thinking. But the movie's climax is so filled with impossibilities that we're too busy with the mental rewrite to get scared. For example: Do you believe a priceless tomb would be left open, eighteen years later, so that people could walk right into it? That the operation of a secret door could elude generations of grave-robbers, but be discovered twice in a matter of minutes? That Heston could walk into a modern museum, move a sarcophagus around on a freight elevator, light candles, lift a two-ton lid with his bare hands and conduct arcane rituals without attracting the inquiry of a security guard? If you can believe all those things, then, at the end, when the reborn priestess Kara turns and snarls at the audience, you'll believe that *The Awakening* is setting itself up for a sequel. Call me an optimist, but I believe this movie is so bad it'll never be reborn.*

*As of 1985, I am still correct.

Baby, It's You ★ ★ ★
R, 105 m., 1983 ✓

Rosanna Arquette (Jill), Vincent Spano
(Sheik), Joanna Merlin (Mrs. Rosen), Jack
Davidson (Dr. Rosen). Directed by John
Sayles and produced by Griffin Dunne and
Amy Robinson. Screenplay by Sayles.

Rosanna Arquette has a way about her. She's
a natural actress, and by that I don't mean
she was born talented (although perhaps she
was), but that she is able to appear onscreen
with such an unaffected natural quality that
I feel as if I'm looking past the script and
direction and actually experiencing the life
of her character. That's the feeling I got
during *Baby, It's You*, a sometimes very
good, sometimes disappointingly uneven
movie that she carries from beginning to
end. Even when her scenes aren't working,
her character is, and we're getting to know
this young woman she plays, this Jill Rosen,
who turns from an uncommonly engaging
high school student to a scared-stiff college
freshman.

The movie is by John Sayles, who has built
a career for himself out of the carefully observed events that make up ordinary lives.
His first film was *Return of the Secaucus
Seven*, about some thirty-fiveish survivors of
the 1960s. Then he made *Lianna*, about a
thirty-fiveish faculty wife who discovers,
with fear and some anticipation, that she is a
lesbian. Now here is Jill Rosen, a high school
student from the 1960s who could, we suspect, easily grow up to be any of the women
in Sayles's first two films.

Jill is smart and pretty, especially when
she smiles. Her brains and her smile are only
the half of it. She's also got a personal style.
She has this way of letting you know she's
listening, even when she seems to be ignoring you. A way of caring for you, even when
she's mad at you. You get the feeling this is a
woman whose love would be a very important thing for you to count on. And that's
certainly the opinion of the Sheik (Vincent
Spano), a semi-greaser who is consumed by
his desire to be exactly like Frank Sinatra.
The Sheik and (actually) a lot of this movie
seem to belong more to the fifties than the
sixties—but never mind. Here is a kid who's
a sharp dresser, has a lot of apparent self-
confidence, and doesn't mind that he stands

out like a sore thumb with his brazen ways
and his Sinatra wardrobe. He's a rebel with
ambitions. Jill loves him, but when she
leaves Trenton, New Jersey, and enters the
uncertain world of Sarah Lawrence College,
the Sheik doesn't fit in.

Baby, It's You does two things with this
material. First, it remembers it accurately,
right down to the irritating mannerisms of
preppy college boys with too much un-
earned self-confidence. Then, it uses it as a
meditation on growing up—which means
learning to listen to your heart as well as to
your ambitions. The movie works best in its
high school segments, and the opening hour
is wonderful. Then the infuriating stuff begins, when this movie that has been so sure-
footed loses its way in the college scenes, and
allows us to wonder at times what we're
supposed to be thinking. Rosanna Arquette
is equally good, however, in the good parts
and the disappointing ones.

Baby . . . The Secret of
the Lost Legend ★
PG, 95 m., 1985

William Katt (George), Sean Young (Susan),
Patrick McGoohan (Dr. Kiviat), Julian
Fellowes (Nigel), Kyalo Mativo (Caphu), Olu
Jacobs (The Colonel). Directed by B.W.L.
Norton and produced by Jonathan T. Taplin.
Screenplay by Clifford and Ellen Green.

The death of Sinbad, the elderly gorilla at
the Lincoln Park Zoo, was a reminder of
how we like to sentimentalize animals, turning them into images of cute, incomplete
human beings, instead of loving them for
their differences from us. *Baby*, a comedy
about an infant brontosaurus, is another example, a dreary one, of the glory of nature
being turned into a cliché of man. Imagine
that somewhere in the heart of Africa, a
colony of dinosaurs still survives. Wouldn't
it be a great wonder to actually see one of
them, living evidence of the world of one
hundred million years ago? I'd think I'd
rather see a brontosaurus than see a man
walk on the moon, because I am less amazed
by technology than by the wonders that life
has provided on its own.

If *Baby* has shared that sense of wonder, it
might have been a really special movie. The
raw materials were in place: the special ef-

fects in this movie provide surprisingly believable dinosaurs, and if the screenplay had been equally believable, they might have had something here. Instead, *Baby* turns out to be a real no-brainer. The movie even blows the one moment you'd assume couldn't fail—the first sighting of a brontosaurus. Instead of a moment of quiet awe, the movie gives us the gee-whiz approach of a *Godzilla* remake. But then maybe that's not surprising: This movie has no serious ambition at all, and is content to surround its wonderful creatures with a plot that even the kids have seen too many times before.

Here you have a family of dinosaurs, and the filmmakers use it as a prop in a movie about good guys and bad guys. The good guys are a couple of Peace Corps volunteers (William Katt and Sean Young), who trek off into the wilderness to find and protect the creatures. The bad guys include a greedy scientist (Patrick McGoohan), his bitchy sidekick (Julian Fellowes), and a trigger-happy African mercenary (Olu Jacobs). The bad guys actually drug the female brontosaurus, and fly around in a helicopter firing machine guns at the male. Why? To rid the jungle of all those bothersome brontosauri?

Meanwhile, the husband-and-wife team finds a baby brontosaurus and tries to drag the cute little thing back to civilization and safety. Their mission is accompanied by a great many manufactured discussions; the wife is a feminist, and we learn in the movie that feminists feel strongly on the issue of Brontosaurus Rights. The whole story is trivial. The scenes that work best are the ones where the little dinosaur acts like a baby, and playfully nuzzles the people or carelessly uproots their tent. But is this why we need a brontosaurus? So it can do its clever puppy imitation? Wasn't there anybody who saw this story idea as more than a cheap gimmick? The movie is subtitled *The Secret of the Lost Legend*, and that sounds like an exciting movie they might want to make sometime.

Bachelor Party ★ ★ ★
R, 100 m., 1984

Tom Hanks (Rick), Tawny Kitaen (Debbie), Adrian Zmed (Jay), George Grizzard (Mr. Thompson), Robert Prescott (Cole). Directed by Neal Israel and produced by Ron Moler and Bob Israel. Screenplay by Neal Israel and Pat Proft.

Bachelor Party is 1984's version of the Annual Summer Food Fight Movie. With a movie like this, it doesn't really matter whether anyone actually throws mashed potatoes across the room; what matters is whether the movie is faithful to the spirit of Blotto Bluto in *Animal House* when he yelled "Food fight!" and the madness began. The story this time is about this guy who decides to get married, and his friends decide to throw him a bachelor party. That's about it. The first half of the movie sets up the party and the second half of the movie is the party. Both halves of the movie are raunchy, chaotic, and quite shameless in aiming at the lowest possible level of taste, of course.

The bachelor in the movie is played by Tom Hanks. He was the guy from *Splash* who the mermaid fell in love with. I didn't think he was all that terrific in *Splash*—I thought he was miscast, and they should have gone for somebody who was less of a conventional leading man—but in *Bachelor Party* he's a lot more funny and I enjoyed the performance. He plays the kind of guy who goes over to his fiancée's house for dinner and drops table scraps onto the floor in *case* they have a dog. He has a great one-liner when he has to introduce himself to his fiancée's nerdy ex-boyfriend: "The name is Bond. James Bond." During the chaos of the party itself, one of his primary roles is simply to direct traffic.

The idea during the party, I think, is to approximate the spirit of one of those Jack Davis drawings in *Mad* magazine, where dozens of people are running around like crazy, and down in the corners you can see strange little figures doing inexplicable things. Most of the gags depend on varieties of public embarrassment and some of them are pretty funny, especially when the women decide to have their revenge by visiting a male go-go bar.

Is *Bachelor Party* a great movie? No. Why do I give it three stars? Because it honors the tradition of a reliable movie genre, because it tries hard, and because when it is funny, it is very funny. It is relatively easy to make a comedy that is totally devoid of humor (cf.

my review of *Cannonball Run II*), but not all that easy to make a movie containing some genuine laughs. *Bachelor Party* has some great moments and qualifies as a raunchy, scummy, grungy Blotto Bluto memorial.

Back Roads ★ ★
R, 94 m., 1981

Sally Field (Amy Post), Tommy Lee Jones (Elmore Pratt), David Keith (Mason), Miriam Colon (Angel). Directed by Martin Ritt and produced by Ronald Shedio. Screenplay by Gary Devore.

What we have here is a movie about a Good Ol' Girl, made with the Good Ol' Boy formula. The Good Ol' Person gets in trouble with the law, hitches up with another drifter of the opposite sex, and hits the road for California. After a series of adventures involving weird people and tight scrapes, the two persons learn to trust each other and have more confidence in themselves. The movie ends on a note of moral triumph: In this case, for example, the heroes find the courage to keep *on* heading for California.

If I'm somewhat muted in my enthusiasm for *Back Roads*, it's because the movie is so relentlessly willing to follow the Road Movie formula. One of the most predictable things about movies such as this is that the filmmakers remain under the delusion that *this* time, they can find an original approach by populating their formula screenplay with bizarre, eccentric, colorful characters. This approach might work, if they didn't always discover the same colorful characters that a dozen other movies have already discovered. In *Back Roads*, for example, we are expected to be newly astonished by a tough-talking Latino madam, a hard-drinking fight promoter, a bullet-headed evil bruiser, and a homesick sailor. The movie's two leads also are less than amazingly original: Sally Field plays a hooker with a heart of gold, and Tommy Lee Jones is a corrupt ex-prizefighter with one good fight left in him.

How could they take this material and make it *really* original? Maybe by refusing to be seduced by the screenwriter's stock Hollywood "originality" and probing more deeply into the real human lives of the characters. The people in *Back Roads* are so heavily laden with schtick that they never

have a chance to develop personalities. Take, for example, the hooker. Field plays the part with enormous appeal and gives a performance that cannot be faulted. But the character she's been given to play is a complete fiction. We are expected to believe the usual clichés about how she got to be a hooker: She was taken advantage of by a sailor; she had to give her little boy up for adoption; she weeps every time she sees the little tyke walking into school; she has to prostitute herself in order to eat. She meets another street person (Jones); he sleeps with her and doesn't pay her; they team up together and hitch to the coast.

This is all out of the Damon Runyon school of romantic realism. Think how much more interesting this movie would have been if the screenplay had played tough and uncompromising with the characters. Let's face it: The Field character is a low-life street hooker who's over the hill. In real life, she would undoubtedly be a drug addict or alcoholic. She'd hustle because she couldn't get her act together for two consecutive hours of straight work. She would not trust anybody and possibly would be so emotionally and physically crippled by her habit that a trip to California would kill her.

Instead, the movie's lovebirds hitchhike for days on end. They sleep in the open, they get soaked in ditches, they rob cops and customers, and all the time we're expected to believe that it is an act of growth and courage for them to keep heading west. Actually, it's just another self-deceiving escape, and if the movie had been willing to deal honestly with the plight of its characters, it wouldn't need to be cluttered up with eccentrics and hearts of gold.

Bad Boys ★ ★ ★ ½
R, 123 m., 1983

Sean Penn (Mick O'Brien), Reni Santoni (Ramon Herrera), Esai Morales (Paco Moreno), Jim Moody (Gene Daniels), Eric Gurry (Horowitz), Clancy Brown (Viking Lofgren). Directed by Richard Rosenthal and produced by Robert Solo. Screenplay by Richard Di Lello.

Bad Boys tells the story of some tough Chicago street-gang kids who get in a lot of trouble, get sent to a juvenile correctional institution, and get in a lot more trouble once they're inside. Following the tradition governing such movies, the story eventually comes to a moral crossroad at which a bad boy has to decide whether to become a good man—and that's too bad, because until the movie turns predictable it is very, very good. The acting, the direction, and the sense of place in *Bad Boys* is so strong that the movie deserves more than an obligatory fight scene for its conclusion.

The movie stars Sean Penn as Mick O'Brien, a teen-age Irish-American hood and Esai Morales as Paco, a Latino hood. They are both tough, mean, anti-social kids; this movie doesn't sentimentalize street gangs. Their paths cross in connection with a drug deal that Paco is doing with a black gang. There's a misunderstanding, a sudden, shocking exchange of gunfire, and Paco's kid brother is dead. Mick killed him. Mick is sent to prison, and then Paco has his revenge by raping Mick's girlfriend (Ally Sheedy). Paco is caught and sent to the same prison where Mick is being held. Mick already has learned the ropes, and Paco learns them quickly: The prison guards preside sincerely but ineffectually over a reign of terror enforced by the toughest kids in the prison. Violence and sexual crimes are commonplace. The strongest survive. This situation is complicated, of course, by the fact that everyone in the prison immediately knows that Mick and Paco will have to fight to the death over the feud of honor.

And it's at precisely that moment, when the two kids are being set up for an eventual showdown, that *Bad Boys* begins to unwind. The first hour of this movie is so good it's scary; Penn and Morales and the supporting actors are completely convincing, and *Bad Boys* is the first movie I've seen in which the street gangs are not glamorized *(West Side Story)*, stylized *(The Warriors)*, or romanticized *(The Wanderers)*. We believe, watching *Bad Boys*, that we are observing an approximation of the real thing. The direction, by Richard Rosenthal, is sure-footed, confident, and fluid; we are in the hands of a fine director, even if he *did* make *Halloween II*. Sean Penn is mean and defiant in a real star performance, and the other kids in the prison include such inimitable characters as Horowitz (Eric Gurry), a bright kid who

invents things and talks casually of his arson conviction; Viking (Clancy Brown), the hard but vulnerable boss of the prisoners; and Tweety (Robert Lee Rush), who rules at Viking's side.

These performances are good. That's why it's such a disappointment when the movie allows itself to become just another prison picture. Although the second half of the movie continues its close, convincing observations of everyday life in the youth prison, the story structure begins to feel programmed: We know we're heading for a big fight, we think we know who'll win—and what is this, anyway? They've *already* made *Rocky* three times. *Bad Boys* misses its chance at greatness, but it's saying something that this movie *had* a chance. It stands as one of those benchmark movies that we'll look back at for the talent it introduced. On the basis of their work here, Penn, Morales, and Rosenthal prove they have important careers ahead of them, and some of the supporting actors do, too. This movie's not a complete success, but it's a damned good try.

Being There ★ ★ ★ ★
PG, 130 m., 1980

Peter Sellers (Chance), Shirley MacLaine (Eve Rand), Melvyn Douglas (Ben Rand), Jack Warden (President), Richard Dysart (Dr. Allenby), Richard Basehart (Skrapinov). Directed by Hal Ashby and produced by Andrew Braunsberg. Screenplay by Jerzy Kosinski.

There's an exhilaration in seeing artists at the very top of their form: It almost doesn't matter what the form is, if they're pushing their limits and going for broke and it's working. We can sense their joy of achievement—and even more so if the project in question is a risky, off-the-wall idea that could just as easily have ended disastrously.

Hal Ashby's *Being There* is a movie that inspires those feelings. It begins with a cockamamie notion, it's basically one joke told for two hours, and it requires Peter Sellers to maintain an excruciatingly narrow tone of behavior in a role that has him onscreen almost constantly. It's a movie based on an idea, and all the conventional wisdom agrees that emotions, not ideas, are the best to make movies from. But *Being There* pulls off its long shot and is a confoundingly provocative movie.

Sellers plays a mentally retarded gardener who has lived and worked all of his life inside the walls of an elegant Washington town house. The house and its garden are in a decaying inner-city neighborhood, but what goes on outside is of no concern to Sellers: He tends his garden, he watches television, he is fed on schedule by the domestic staff, he is content.

Then one day the master of the house dies. The household is disbanded. Sellers, impeccably dressed in his employer's privately tailored wardrobe, wanders out into the city. He takes along the one possession he'll probably need: His remote-control TV channel switcher. He uses it almost immediately; surrounded by hostile street kids, he imperturbably tries to switch channels to make them go away. He hasn't figured out that, outside his garden, life isn't television.

And that is the movie's basic premise, lifted intact from a Jerzy Kosinski novel. The Sellers character knows almost nothing about real life, but he has watched countless hours of television and he can be pleasant, smile, shake hands, and comport himself; he learned from watching all those guests on talk shows. He knows nothing about *anything*, indeed, except gardening. But when he stumbles into Washington's political and social upper crust, his simple truisms from the garden ("Spring is a time for planting") are taken as audaciously simple metaphors. This guy's a Thoreau! In no time at all, he's the closest confidant of a dying billionaire industrialist (Melvyn Douglas)—and the industrialist is the closest confidant of the president.

This is, you can see, a one-joke premise. It has to be if the Sellers performance is to work. The whole movie has to be tailored to the narrow range within which Sellers's gardener can think, behave, speak, and make choices. The ways in which this movie could have gone out of control, could have been relentlessly boring on the one hand, or manic with its own audacity on the other, are endless. But the tone holds. That's one of the most exhilarating aspects of the joy you can sense, as Ashby pulls this off: Every

scene needs the confidence to play the idea completely straight.

There are wonderful comic moments, but they're never pushed so far that they strain the story's premise. Some of them involve: a battle between the CIA and the FBI as to which agency destroyed the gardener's files; Shirley MacLaine unsuccessfully attempts to introduce Sellers to the concept of romance; Sellers as a talk-show guest himself (at last!), and Sellers as the hit of a Washington cocktail party. The movie also has an audacious closing shot that moves the film's whole metaphor into a brand-new philosophical arena.

What is *Being There* about? I've read reviews calling it an indictment of television. But that doesn't fit; Sellers wasn't warped by television, he was retarded to begin with, and has TV to thank for what abilities he *has* to move in society. Is it an indictment of society, for being so dumb as to accept the Sellers character as a great philosophical sage? Maybe, but that's not so fascinating either. I'm not really inclined to plumb this movie for its message, although I'm sure that'll be a favorite audience sport. I just admire it for having the guts to take this weird conceit and push it to its ultimate comic conclusion.

Best Boy ★ ★ ★ ★
NO MPAA RATING, 111 m., 1980

A documentary produced, directed, and edited by Ira Wohl.

Sometimes there are movies that absorb you so completely that you forget you're watching them: They're simply happening to you. Ira Wohl's *Best Boy* is a movie like that. To see it is to participate in the lives of other people and to learn just a little more about being human. *Best Boy*, which won the 1980 Academy Award as best documentary, is the story of an only son named Philly, whose parents have always been too protective of him. But as the movie opens, it is time for Philly to go out a little more on his own—to go down to the corner for an ice cream cone, for example, or to look forward to his first day of school. Philly is fifty-two years old. He is mentally retarded, but otherwise, as a psychiatrist explains in the film, "quite normal." He is also warm and lovable, and when Wordsworth wrote that heaven was all about us when we were children, did he guess that would also be true for someone like Philly, who will never really leave childhood?

Best Boy deals intelligently with real people and their problems. It is not simply a documentary; it contains the surprises of true drama, and it is put together so thoughtfully that it takes what could have been a case study and turns it into a cliffhanger. That is largely due to the complete access that the filmmaker, Ira Wohl, had to his subject. Philly is Wohl's cousin, and Philly's parents are Wohl's aunt and uncle. All the time he was growing up, Ira knew Philly—he played with him, presumably, when he was four or five and Philly seemed to be about the same age. Philly stayed four or five. As Wohl grew older, he realized that sooner or later Philly's parents would die, and that Philly's total dependence on them would leave him defenseless.

Philly had been at home almost all his life. The movie begins as his parents make the first reluctant, tentative steps to allow him a little more independence—to set him free. *Best Boy* moves very delicately around this subject, and with good reason: As we watch it, we realize that the parents have come to depend on Philly, too. He provided them with a rationale for their own lives and choices. He is their crutch as well as their burden. And there is yet another drama that unfolds within the film—unfolds so subtly we barely realize it is there, and yet concludes so inevitably that it casts a light back on all the scenes that went before. Philly's father is dying. There is a time in the film when the father clearly knows that and no one else in the film does, but we, strangers, share his secret with him.

You see what I mean when I say *Best Boy* isn't a case study. It's not about what should be done with Philly, and it has little to do with the "problem" of mental retardation. It is so specifically about Philly and his family and their daily choices in life that we almost feel adopted into the family. And we get to like Philly so much! He is sweet and cheerful, patient and good-humored, with a child's logic that cuts right through so much of the confusion adults surround him with.

There is a wonderful scene with a psychiatrist, who is trying to administer a series of questions Philly obviously feels are silly. There is a visit to the theater, where Philly is allowed backstage to meet Zero Mostel, and they sing "If I Were a Rich Man" together. Why is it, the movie asks but never answers, that Philly can remember songs better than speech?

Best Boy suffers, I suppose, from being labeled a documentary: Some small-minded people make it a policy never to watch one. But at the Toronto Festival of Festivals, where the patrons are asked to vote for their favorite film, it astonished everyone by defeating all the features in the festival and placing first. It's a wonderfully positive experience.

The Best Little Whorehouse in Texas ★ ★
R, 114 m., 1982

Burt Reynolds (Ed Earl), Dolly Parton (Miss Mona), Charles Durning (Governor), Dom DeLuise (Melvin Thorpe), Jim Nabors (Deputy), Lois Nettleton (Dulcie Mae), Theresa Merritt (Jewel). Directed by Colin Higgins and produced by Thomas L. Miller, Edward K. Milkis, and Robert L. Boyett. Screenplay by Larry L. King, Peter Masterson, and Higgins.

If I were asked what image dominates *The Best Little Whorehouse in Texas*, the honest answer would have to be: Dolly Parton's plunging neckline. I am not trying to be cute. The awesome swell of her wondrous bosom dominates every scene Dolly appears in, and that includes just about every scene in the movie. W.C. Fields, the old scene-stealer, rebelled against appearing on screen with an animal, a child, or a plunging neckline, on the not unreasonable grounds that audiences would not be looking at him. Fields could have appeared incognito in *Whorehouse*, as, indeed, Burt Reynolds occasionally does.

The puzzling thing about the Parton décolletage is that so little is made of so much. You'd think there would be sizzling chemistry between Parton and Reynolds, who are two of my favorite movie sex symbols simply because they always seem so full of good cheer. But that isn't the case here. They're great looking, they smile a lot, they've been provided with good dialogue, but somehow they seem a little bored with each other, as if their affair has been going on a little too long; they're a happy old cheatin' couple. There is some passion in the movie, but it's concentrated in two scenes where Dolly is absent. In both of them, Reynolds lets loose with a non-stop cussing barrage, chewing out a foppish TV interviewer (Dom DeLuise) and a slippery governor (Charles Durning). Dolly never *really* gets to let go, and the limitless exuberance she displayed in *9 to 5* seems as tightly corseted here as her costumes are.

What's the problem? I think maybe the movie's story got misplaced somewhere in the middle of the movie's legend. The best little whorehouse of the movie's title was a legendary Texas brothel named the Chicken Ranch, which was immortalized first by generations of young Texans and later in a Broadway play by Larry King and Peter Masterson. Whorehouses, Texas ones included, are not exactly very nice places, but the whorehouse in this movie almost seems like a refuge for wayward girls. The story has been cleaned up so carefully to showcase Parton and Reynolds that the scandal has been lost; the movie has been turned into a defense of free enterprise and a hymn to romance.

That's too bad. I kept waiting for Dolly Parton to be sexy in this movie, and she never was. She was cheerful, spunky, energetic, angry, sad, and loyal, but she was never sexy—not even in bed. Her feelings for Reynolds seemed to be largely therapeutic, and I believe there were even times when they discussed the nature of their relationship. Since just the mere word "relationship" is profoundly subversive to eroticism and sexuality, we're a little baffled to see the madam and the sheriff turned into the sort of couple that discusses itself in first-person articles for *Cosmo*. This is carried so far that Parton's only reference to her bosom (indeed, the only moment in the movie when anyone deigns to even *notice* it) is about her problems "luggin' these around." It's all so matter-of-fact, it's asexual.

Parton and Reynolds are pleasant enough in *Whorehouse*, and we expect that from two

such likable actors. Dom DeLuise is wildly improbable and distractingly bizarre as the TV investigative reporter who wants to shut down the Chicken Ranch. Charles Durning has a lot of fun with a sly song-and-dance routine. Lois Nettleton has a thankless role as Reynold's "other" mistress (we never do know what to make of *their* relationship, which must have been mangled in the editing). There are a few funny jokes, some raunchy one-liners, some mostly forgettable songs set to completely forgettable choreography, and then there is Dolly Parton. If they ever give Dolly her freedom and stop packaging her so antiseptically, she could be terrific. But Dolly and Burt and *Whorehouse* never get beyond the concept stage in this movie.

Betrayal ★ ★ ★ ★
R, 95 m., 1983

Jeremy Irons (Jerry), Ben Kingsley (Robert), Patricia Hodge (Emma). Directed by David Jones and produced by Sam Spiegel. Screenplay by Harold Pinter.

Love stories have beginnings, but affairs . . . affairs have endings, too. Even sad love stories begin in gladness, when the world is young and the future reaches out cheerfully forever. Then, of course, eventually you get Romeo and Juliet dead in the tomb, but that's the price you have to pay. Life isn't a free ride. Think how much *more* tragic a sad love story would be, however, if you could see into the future, so that even *this* moment, *this* kiss, is in the shadow of eventual despair.

The absolutely brilliant thing about *Betrayal* is that it is a love story told backward. There is a lot in this movie that is wonderful—the performances, the screenplay by Harold Pinter—but what makes it all work is the structure. When Pinter's stage version of *Betrayal* first appeared, back in the late 1970s, there was a tendency to dismiss his reverse chronology as a gimmick. Not so. It is the very heart and soul of this story. It means that we in the audience know more about the unhappy romantic fortunes of Jerry and Robert and Emma at *every moment* than they know about themselves. Even their joy is painful to see.

Jerry is a youngish London literary agent, clever, good-looking, confused about his feelings. Robert, his best friend, is a publisher. Robert is older, stronger, smarter, and more bitter. Emma is Robert's wife and becomes Jerry's lover. But that is telling the story chronologically. And the story begins at the end, with Robert and Emma fighting, and with Robert slapping her, and with Emma and Jerry meeting in a pub for a painful reunion two years after their affair is over. Each additional scene takes place further back in time, and the sections have uncanny titles: Two years earlier. Three years earlier. We aren't used to this. At a public preview of the film, some people in the audience actually *resisted* the backward timeframe, as if the purpose of the playwright was just to get on with the story, damn it all, and stop this confounded fooling around.

The *Betrayal* structure strips away all artifice. It shows, heartlessly, that the very capacity for love itself is sometimes based on betraying not only other loved ones, but even ourselves. The movie is told mostly in encounters between two of the characters; all three are not often on screen together, and we never meet Jerry's wife. These people are smart and they talk a lot—too much, maybe, because there is a peculiarly British reserve about them that sometimes prevents them from quite saying what they mean. They lie and they half-lie. There are universes left unspoken in their unfinished sentences. They are all a little embarrassed that the messy urges of sex are pumping away down there beneath their civilized deceptions.

The performances are perfectly matched. Ben Kingsley (of *Gandhi*) plays Robert, the publisher, with such painfully controlled fury that there are times when he actually is frightening. Jeremy Irons, as Jerry, creates a man whose desires are stronger than his convictions, even though he spends a lot of time talking about his convictions, and almost none acknowledging his desires. Patricia Hodge, as Emma, loves them both and hates them both and would have led a much happier life if they had not been her two choices. But how could she know that when, in life, you're required by the rules to start at the beginning?

Beverly Hills Cop ★ ★ ½
R, 105 m., 1984

Eddie Murphy (Axel Foley), Judge Reinhold (Detective Billy Rosewood), John Ashton (Sergeant Taggart), Lisa Eilbacher (Jenny), Ronny Cox (Lieutenant Bogomil). Directed by Martin Brest and produced by Don Simpson and Jerry Bruckheimer. Screenplay by Daniel Petrie.

Eddie Murphy looks like the latest victim of the Star Magic Syndrome, in which it is assumed that a movie will be a hit simply because it stars an enormously talented person. Thus it is not necessary to give much thought to what he does or says, or to the story he finds himself occupying. *Beverly Hills Cop* is a movie with an enormously appealing idea—a tough black detective from Detroit goes to Beverly Hills to avenge the murder of a friend—but the filmmakers apparently expected Murphy to carry this idea entirely by himself.

Murphy plays a street-wise rebel who is always getting in trouble with his commanding officer because he does things his own way. The movie opens with an example of that: Murphy is single-handedly running a sting operation when the cops arrive unexpectedly, setting off a wild car-truck chase through the city streets. Even while we're watching the thrilling chase, however, stirrings of unease are beginning to be felt: Any movie that *begins* with a chase is not going to be heavy on originality and inspiration. Then Murphy's old friend comes to town, fresh from a prison term and six months of soaking up the rays in California. The friend has some negotiable bonds with him, and then some friends of the guy who owns the bonds turn up and murder Murphy's friend. That makes Eddie mad, and he drives his ancient beater out to Beverly Hills, where it sort of stands out among the Porsches and Mercedes. He also meets a childhood friend (Lisa Eilbacher) who now works for an art dealer.

At this point, the movie can go in one of two directions. It can become a perceptive and pointed satire about American attitudes, showing how the ultrachic denizens of Beverly Hills react to this black cop from Detroit. Or it can go for broad, cheap laughs, and plug into a standard plot borrowed from countless TV crime shows. *Beverly Hills Cop* doesn't pause a moment before taking the low road. We figure that out right away, when Murphy tries to register in a hotel and is told there isn't any room. He loudly pulls both ranks and race, claiming to be a correspondent from *Rolling Stone* and accusing the desk clerk of racism. This is (a) not funny, and (b) not convincing, because Beverly Hills desk clerks were not born yesterday. If the people who made this movie had been willing to listen to the ways that real people really talk, they could have made the scene into a jewel instead of an embarrassment.

Meanwhile, the plot thickens. It turns out that the killers of Eddie's friend were employees of the evil Victor Maitland (Steven Berkoff), a Beverly Hills criminal whose art gallery—where Eilbacher works—is a front for cocaine smuggling. When Murphy tries to move against Maitland, he comes up against the Beverly Hills Cops, including an Abbott and Costello team that supplies unnecessary pratfalls, successfully undermining the credibility of any police scene that threatens to work. But wait a minute. What's this movie about, anyway? Is it a comedy or an action picture? Audiences may expect a comedy, but the closing shootout seems inspired by the machine gun massacre at the end of Brian De Palma's *Scarface*, and the whole business with the cocaine is so very, very tired that when we see the boss and his henchmen in the warehouse, we feel like we've switched to another movie—maybe a dozen other movies. Murphy is one of the smartest and quickest young comic actors in the movies. But he is not an action hero, despite his success in *48 Hours*, and by plugging him into an action movie, the producers of *Beverly Hills Cop* reveal a lack of confidence in their original story inspiration. It's like they had a story conference that boiled down to: "Hey gang! Here's a great idea! Let's turn it into a standard idea and fill it with clichés, and take out the satire and put in a lot of machine guns!"

Beyond the Limit ★ ★ ½
R, 103 m., 1983

Michael Caine (Charlie Fortnum), Richard Gere (Eduardo Plan), Bob Hoskins (Colonel Perez), Joaquim De Alameia (Leon), Elpidia Carrilo (Clara). Directed by John Mackenzie and produced by Norma Heyman. Screenplay by Christopher Hampton.

There are times when this movie is a mess. There are other times when it becomes quietly moving. *Beyond the Limit* has one of the best endings I can remember in a mediocre film, an ending that goes a long way toward redeeming some of the sloppiness that went before. And all through the film, there is a remarkable performance by Michael Caine, who has been around for so long, in so many movies, that it's easy to forget what a fine actor he is.

The film is based on *The Honorary Consul*, Graham Greene's novel about a bungled South American terrorist kidnapping. The movie tells most of the same story, involving the alcoholic British honorary consul (Caine), the young half-British doctor (Richard Gere), the priest turned revolutionary (Joaquim De Alameia), and the beautiful Indian prostitute (Elpidia Carrilo) who becomes Caine's wife and Gere's lover. The film is also fairly faithful to Greene's ending, a study in conflicting morality, where the priest kidnaps the worthless British consul under the impression he is the American ambassador—and then the doctor's loyalties are torn between his friend the consul, his lover the consul's wife, and his old friend the priest.

What is not faithful to the novel is the casting of Gere as the doctor. Gere is so wrong for the role that he undermines every scene he's in, distracting attention from Caine's understated, quietly poignant performance. Halfway through the movie, as I was witnessing the obligatory Gere sex scene, I began to grow angry. Not at Gere, who can be effective in the right role, but at the producers, who chose his popular appeal over the obvious demands of the material. The doctor in the Greene novel is not a swaggering bodybuilder with a smoldering sexuality, but a troubled, worried, overworked young man with a conscience. The amoral way in which Gere possesses his friend's wife is totally false to the spirit of the book.

What is true, though, is the Michael Caine performance. The character he plays is Charlie Fortnum, a pathetic drunk holding onto the honorary consulship as a last vestige of dignity, investing all of his higher feelings into love for his wife. Caine gives a great performance, sweaty, exhausted, red-eyed, filled with false bonhomie, always with his eye on the level in the whiskey bottle. There is a kind of nobility in the way he accepts his fate, after the terrorists kidnap him and nobody, frankly, cares enough to ransom him. There is also a real person here, in a performance that suggests Fortnum's life up until this point, his history of failure, his essential good nature. The movie's final scene, between Caine and Carrillo, is one of the best scenes Caine has ever played.

Unhappily, it comes in a movie that never comes together, and that lingers too long on a Richard Gere who seems to have wandered in from another movie, would-be British accent and all. The casting is one of the movie's mysteries; another one is the change to a meaningless and forgettable title; a third is how Michael Caine succeeded in delivering an intact performance right there in the middle of all the lost dreams.

The Big Brawl ★ ½
R, 95 m., 1980

Jackie Chan (Jerry), Jose Ferrer (Dominici), Kristine De Bell (Nancy), Mako (Herbert), Ron Max (Leggetti), David Sheiner (Morgan), Rosalind Chao (Mae), Lenny Montana (John). Directed and written by Robert Clouse and produced by Fred Weintraub and Terry Morse, Jr.

This movie is idiotic—but it's *nice* idiotic, you know? It's the first kung fu movie I can remember where the hero is a whimsical show-off instead of a human machine bent on vengeance. The hero is Jackie Chan, the most successful of the countless spin-offs of Bruce Lee, and *The Big Brawl* portrays him as a kid from Chicago whose father runs a Chinese restaurant.

The movie opens in 1938, on the eve of a gigantic free-for-all that's going to be held in the town of Battle Creek, Texas. I thought Battle Creek was in Michigan, but maybe kung fu fans don't read cereal boxes. Anyway, the most powerful dons of the Mafia are each sponsoring fighters in the brawl, and the Chicago don (Jose Ferrer, of all people)

hears about this Chinese kid who "fights funny."

The kid also acts funny. The movie opens with him out on a date with his American girlfriend, Kristine De Bell. You may not have heard of De Bell, but I've been following her career since she made the most charming of all the big-budget soft-porno films, *Alice in Wonderland.* She's been in several mainstream movies since then, never with very big roles, but she has charm and an absolutely stunning smile. Not that Jackie Chan notices. He parks their roadster under a bridge, climbs up into the ironwork, and does gymnastics.

At home, his father wants him to take over the family restaurant. But instead, he studies the martial arts with his uncle. The plot includes several big and well-choreographed kung fu production numbers, including one at a roller derby race, another one in an alley, and the final big brawl in Texas. It's here that Jackie Chan demonstrates why he's the biggest star in Asia. Instead of acting ferocious and snarling all the time, he wipes out his opposition while smiling, talking with a lisp, doing slapstick falls, and acting goofy. And he's really very good: The fights are choreographed around props such as tables, broomsticks, and swords, and the timing is impeccable. There's a real physical grace on the screen.

Unfortunately, not much can be said about the screenplay. For example, one crucial plot development involves Jackie Chan's future sister-in-law. The poor girl gets off the boat from China, is immediately kidnapped by the Mafia, and is used as a hostage to force Jackie to fight in Texas. Meanwhile, since the brother has never met his bride-to-be, a San Francisco hooker is brought in as a substitute. The movie ends without the brother ever finding out about the substitution. Who knows? Maybe he wasn't complaining.

The Big Chill ★ ★ ½
R, 108 m., 1983

Tom Berenger (Sam), Glenn Close (Sarah), William Hurt (Nick), Jeff Goldblum (Michael), Meg Tilly (Chloe), Kevin Kline (Harold), Mary Kay Place (Meg), JoBeth Williams (Karen).

Directed by Lawrence Kasdan. Screenplay by Kasdan and Barbara Benedek.

I was going through some old papers the other night, from cardboard boxes that were packed at the end of college and have followed me around ever since. To open them up was like walking into a time capsule. There they were, the little campus literary magazines and the yellowing issues of the University of Illinois' *Daily Illini*, and a photo of a political demonstration on the steps of the student union.

On the other hand, I was going through my mail today and I got a letter from a teenager who wanted to know why they were making so many movies about the 1960s. "These are the 1980s," he informed me. "Who cares what happened in the olden days?" I think "olden days" was an attempt at humor.

In any event, I wrote back that the 1960s were big in the movies right now because the people who make the movies were students in the 1960s, and that the teen-agers of 2001 would no doubt be sick and tired of the olden days of the 1980s. And then I thought about *The Big Chill*, a movie in which survivors of the 1960s ask themselves how they could possibly be in their thirties. This is the second movie on almost exactly the same theme—a weekend reunion among college friends from the sixties, during which they relive the past, fear the present, and regret the interim. They could have called it *Son of the Return of the Secaucus Seven*.

It's a good movie. It's well acted, the dialogue is accurately heard, and the camera is extremely attentive to details of body language. It observes wonderfully well how its veterans of the 1960s have grown up into adulthood, consumerhood, parenthood, drunkenhood, adulteryhood, and regrethood. These people could all be wearing warm-up jackets with *poignancy* stenciled on the backs.

The movie begins at a funeral. One of the old college friends has killed himself, for reasons that never become clear. The others gather for his funeral and stay for a weekend in a big old summer house. We get to meet them: the intellectual, the failed writer, the confused TV star, the woman who wants to have a baby and can't tear her eyes away

from the biological clock. They eat, they drink, they pair up in various combinations, and they ask themselves questions like, Who were we? Who are we now? What happened to us? What will happen to us?

Because they are all graduates of the University of Michigan at Ann Arbor, they phrase these questions with style, of course. The dialogue sounds like a series of bittersweet captions from *New Yorker* cartoons. And at the end, of course, nothing is really discovered, nothing is really settled, and they go back into holding patterns until the next funeral.

The Big Chill is a splendid technical exercise. It has all the right moves. It knows all the right words. Its characters have all the right clothes, expressions, fears, lusts, and ambitions. But there's no payoff and it doesn't lead anywhere. I thought at first that was a weakness of the movie. There also is the possibility that it's the movie's message.

The Big Red One ★ ★ ★
PG, 113 m., 1980

Lee Marvin (Sergeant), Mark Hamill (Griff), Robert Carradine (Zab), Bobby Di Cicco (Vinci), Kelly Ward (Johnson), Siegfried Rauch (Schroeder), Stephanie Audran (Walloon). Directed and written by Samuel Fuller and produced by Gene Corman.

Sam Fuller's *The Big Red One* is a lot of war stories strung together in a row, almost as if the director filmed it for the thirty-fifth reunion of his old Army outfit, and didn't want to leave anybody out. That's one of the most interesting things about it—the feeling that the movie's events are included, not because they help the plot or make a point, but just because they happened.

Some of them happened to Fuller himself, he tells us, and there's a kid in the movie who's obviously supposed to be young Sam. Other scenes are based on things Fuller heard about. Some of them are brutal and painful, some of them are romantic, a lot of them are corny. The movie takes no position on any of them: This movie is resolutely nonpolitical, is neither pro- nor anti-war, is deliberately just a record of five dogfaces who found themselves in the middle of the action.

The movie's title refers to the U.S. Army's First Infantry Division, and the action follows one rifle squad through the entire war. The squad leader is a hard-bitten sergeant, played by Lee Marvin with the kind of gravel-voiced, squint-eyed authority he had more than a decade before in *The Dirty Dozen*. His four squad members are kids in their teens, and his job is to whip them into shape. He does. The squad is so efficient, or competent, or just plain lucky, that it survives to see action in half the major theaters of the war in Europe. At a rough count, they fight in North Africa, Tunis, Sicily, Normandy, Omaha Beach, rural France, Belgium, Czechoslovakia, and Germany. Halfway through this litany, we begin to suspect that *The Big Red One* is supposed to be something more than plausible.

The squad fights in so many places, stays together in one piece for so long, experiences so many of the key events of World War II (from the invasion of Europe to the liberation of the Nazi death camps) that of course these characters are meant to be symbols of all the infantrymen in all the battles. But Fuller, who fought in the First Division, seems determined to keep his symbols from illustrating a message. They fight. They are frightened. Men kill, other men are killed. What matters is if you're still alive. "I don't cry because that guy over there got hit," Fuller said in an interview, "I cry because I'm gonna get hit next."

This leads to a deliberately anecdotal structure for the film. One battle ends, another begins. A little orphan kid appears out of the smoke, is befriended, braids flowers into the netting of a helmet, is forgotten for the rest of the film. What we have is a series of experiences so overwhelming that the characters can't find sense or pattern in them, and so simply try to survive them through craft and experience.

Is this all Fuller got out of the war? He seems to believe it's all anybody really gets, that the vast patterns of war's meaning are really just the creations of novelists, filmmakers, generals, and politicians, and that for the guy under fire there is no pattern, just the desperately sincere desire to get out in one piece.

The Big Red One is Sam Fuller's first film in more than a decade, and by far the most expensive and ambitious film he's ever made. It's like a dream come true, the capstone of a long career. Fuller began as a newspaperman in New York, he fought in the war, he went to Hollywood and he directed a lot of B-action pictures that are considered by connoisseurs to be pulp landmarks: *I Shot Jesse James, Pickup on South Street, Hell and High Water, Shock Corridor.* His previous film, hardly seen in this country, was a 1972 West German production with the marvelous title *Dead Pigeon on Beethoven Street.*

While this is an expensive epic, he hasn't fallen to the temptations of the epic form. He doesn't give us a lot of phony meaning, as if to justify the scope of the production. There aren't a lot of deep, significant speeches. In the ways that count, *The Big Red One* is still a B-movie—hard-boiled, filled with action, held together by male camaraderie, directed with a lean economy of action. It's one of the most expensive B-pictures ever made, and I think that helps it fit the subject. "A" war movies are about War, but "B" war movies are about soldiers.

Birdy ★ ★ ★ ★
R, 120 m., 1985

Nicolas Cage (Al), Matthew Modine (Birdy). Directed by Alan Parker and produced by Alan Marshall. Screenplay by Sandy Kroopf and Jack Behr.

The strangest thing about *Birdy*, which is a very strange and beautiful movie indeed, is that it seems to work best at its looniest level, and is least at ease with the things it takes most seriously. You will not discover anything new about war in this movie, but you will find out a whole lot about how it feels to be in love with a canary.

The movie is about two friends from South Philadelphia. One of them, Al, played by Nicolas Cage, is a slick romeo with a lot of self-confidence and a way with the women. The other, nicknamed Birdy (Matthew Modine), is goofy, withdrawn, and absolutely fascinated with birds. As kids, they are inseparable friends. In high school, they begin to grow apart, separated by their individual quests for two different kinds of birds. But they still share adventures, as Birdy hangs upside-down from elevated tracks to capture pigeons, or constructs homemade wings that he hopes will let him fly. Then the war comes. Both boys serve in Vietnam and both are wounded. Cage's face is disfigured, and he wears a bandage to cover the scars. Modine's wounds are internal: He withdraws entirely into himself and stops talking. He spends long, uneventful days perched in his room at a mental hospital, head cocked to one side, looking up longingly at a window, like nothing so much as a caged bird.

Because *Birdy* is not told in chronological order, the story takes a time to sort itself out. We begin with an agonizing visit by Cage to his friend Birdy. He hopes to draw him out of his shell. But Birdy makes no sign of recognition. Then, in flashbacks, we see the two lives that led up to this moment. We see the adventures they shared, the secrets, the dreams. Most importantly, we go inside Birdy's life and begin to glimpse the depth of his obsession with birds. His room turns into a birdcage. His special pets—including a cocky little yellow canary—take on individual characteristics for us. We can begin to understand that his love for birds is sensual, romantic, passionate. There is a wonderful scene where he brushes his fingers against a feather, showing how marvelously it is constructed, and how beautifully.

Most descriptions of *Birdy* tend to dwell on what seems to be the central plot, the story of the two buddies who go to Vietnam and are wounded, and about how one tries to help the other return to the real world. I felt that the war footage in the movie was fairly routine, and that the challenge of dragging Birdy back to reality was a good deal less interesting than the story of how he arrived at the strange, secret place in his mind. I have seen other, better, movies about war, but I have never before seen a character quite like Birdy.

As you may have already guessed, *Birdy* doesn't sound like a commercial blockbuster. More important are the love and care for detail that have gone into it from all hands, especially from Cage and Modine. They have two immensely difficult roles, and both are handicapped in the later scenes by being denied access to some of an actor's usual tools; for Cage, his face; for Modine, his whole human persona. They overcome those limitations to give us characters even more touching than the ones they started with.

The movie was directed by Alan Parker. Consider this list of his earlier films: *Bugsy Malone, Fame, Midnight Express, Shoot the Moon, Pink Floyd: The Wall.* Each one coming out of an unexpected place, and avoiding conventional movie genres. He was the man to direct *Birdy*, which tells a story so unlikely that perhaps even my description of it has discouraged you—and yet a story so interesting it is impossible to put this movie out of my mind.

The Black Marble ★ ★ ★ ½
PG, 110 m., 1980

Robert Foxworth (Sergeant Valnikov), Paula Prentiss (Sergeant Zimmerman), Harry Dean Stanton (Philo Skinner), Barbara Babcock (Madeline Whitfield), John Hancock (Clarence Cromwell), Raleigh Bond (Captain Hooker), Judy Landers (Pattie Mae), Pat Corley (Itchy Mitch). Directed by Harold Becker and produced by Frank Capra, Jr. Screenplay by Joseph Wambaugh.

The Black Marble is a delightfully twisted comedy, backing into itself, starting out in one direction, ending up somewhere else, constantly surprising us with its offbeat characters. It's so many things at once it's a juggling act: It's a police movie with lots of authentic details; it's a bizarre comedy about a kidnapped prize dog; it's a shaggy romance; it's got the most excruciating chase sequence I can remember; it's goofy, but it moves us.

The movie centers around several days in the life of a Los Angeles police sergeant named Valnikov (Robert Foxworth), an incurably romantic Russian who has been drinking too much since his partner's suicide. He gets a new partner, Sgt. Natalie Zimmerman, played by Paula Prentiss as a combination of Sally Kellerman and Lucille Ball. His new partner thinks Valnikov is insane. Maybe she's right.

The case they begin working on together involves a prize bitch that has been kidnapped and is being held for $85,000 ransom. Valnikov goes to interview the kidnapped dog's grieving owner, an attractive woman of a certain age. And, in a delightful scene that illustrates the movie's gift of being able to slide ever so lightly from drama into cheerful comedy, he winds up on the sofa with the woman, drying her tears and vowing, "Don't worry; I promise I'll get your doggie back."

The dry tone Foxworth brings to the pronunciation of such lines is one of the movie's charms. He is mustachioed, mournful-eyed, usually hung over, and filled with ancient Russian dreams and curses. It is inevitable, of course, that he and the sexy Zimmerman fall in love, and they have a wonderful seduction scene in his apartment. He puts sweepingly romantic Russian folk music on his stereo. They dance. "Translate the lyrics for me!" she whispers into his ear. He does. It does not bother either of them that there *are* no lyrics since the song is instrumental.

Meanwhile, a parallel plot involves the evil dog kidnapper, played by that uniquely malevolent character actor Harry Dean Stanton, who looks and talks like Robert Mitchum's mean kid brother. Stanton is a veterinarian who has never hurt a dog in his life. But he needs the ransom to pay a gambling debt before he is killed. Coughing, wheezing, and spitting through an endless chain of cigarettes, he makes telephone threats to the dog's owner, who counters with descriptions of her own financial plight, unpaid bills, and tax problems.

When Valnikov and the kidnapper finally meet face to face, they get into what is undoubtedly the most painful chase sequence I can remember, a chase that requires them to climb mesh fences separating a series of savage and terrified dogs that snap maniacally at their legs. The chase is another scene illustrating the curious way in which *The Black Marble* succeeds in being funny, painful, and romantic, sometimes simultaneously. The movie's not altogether a comedy, although we laugh; it's a love story that kids itself and ends up seriously; it contains violence but is not really violent. What it always does is keep us off balance. Because we can't anticipate what's going to happen next, the movie has a persistent interior life; there's never the sense that a scene is included because it's expected.

The performances go to show you that a good actor in a bad film can have a very hard time appearing to be any good. Foxworth's previous screen credits include *The Omen, Part II* and *Prophecy.* Neither film gave me the slightest reason to look forward to him in *The Black Marble*, but he's wonderful here. He gives his character weariness and craziness and then covers them both with warmth. He and Prentiss have so much fun with the long seduction scene that we can sense the joy of acting craftsmanship going into it.

The movie's the second production by Joseph Wambaugh, the L.A. cop who became a best-selling novelist only to see Hollywood doing terrible things to his novels. Wambaugh vowed to produce his own books. The industry had its doubts, especially when Wambaugh hired a little-known British director, Harold Becker, to direct his first project, *The Onion Field.* But that was a strong, edgy, effective movie, and now Wambaugh and Becker are back with this unusual and distinctive comedy. Because it is uneven and moves so easily among its various tones and moods, it's possible, I suppose, to fault it on form: This isn't a seamless piece of work, but it's infectious and charming.

The Black Stallion ★ ★ ★ ★
G, 120 m., 1980

Kelly Reno (Alec Ramsey), Mickey Rooney (Henry Dailey), Teri Garr (Alec's Mother), Clarence Muse (Snoe), Hoyt Axton (Alec's Father), Michael Higgins (Neville). The black stallion is portrayed by Cass-ole, owned by San Antonio Arabians. Directed by Carroll Ballard and produced by Francis Ford Coppola, Fred Roos, and Tom Sternberg. Screenplay by Melissa Mathison, Jeanne Rosenberg and William D. Wittliff.

The first half of *The Black Stallion* is so gloriously breathtaking that the second half, the half with all the conventional excitement, seems merely routine. We've seen the second half before—the story of the kid, the horse, the veteran trainer, and the big race. But the first hour of this movie belongs among the great filmgoing experiences. It is described as an epic, and earns the description.

The film opens at sea, somewhere in the Mediterranean, forty or so years ago, on board a ship inhabited by passengers who seem foreign and fearsome to a small boy. They drink, they gamble, they speak in foreign tongues, they wear caftans and beards and glare ferociously at anyone who comes close to their prize possession, a magnificent black stallion.

The boy and his father are on board this ship for reasons never explained. The father gambles with the foreigners and the boy roams the ship and establishes a shy rapport with the black stallion, and then a great storm sweeps over the ocean and the ship catches fire and is lost. The boy and the stallion are thrown free, into the boiling sea. The horse somehow saves the boy, and in the calm of the next morning they both find themselves thrown onto a deserted island.

This sequence—the storm, the ship's sinking, the ordeal at sea—is a triumphant use of special effects, miniature models, back projection, editing, and all the tricks of craft that go into the filming of a fantasy. The director, Carroll Ballard, used the big water tank at Cinecitta Studios in Rome for the storm sequences; a model ship, looking totally real, burns and sinks headfirst, its propellers churning slowly in the air, while the horse and boy struggle in the foreground.

The horse in this film (its name is Cassole) is required to perform as few movie horses ever have. But its finest scene is the quietest one, and takes place on the island a few days after the shipwreck. Ballard and his cinematographer, Caleb Deschanel, have already established the mood of the place, with gigantic, quiet, natural panoramas. The boy spears a fish. The horse roams restlessly from the beaches to the cliffs. And then, in a single shot that is held for a long time, Ballard shows us the boy inviting the horse to eat out of his hand.

It is crucial here that this action be seen in a *single* shot; lots of short cuts, edited together, would simply be the filmmakers at work. But the one uninterrupted shot, with the horse at one edge of the screen and the boy at the other, and the boy's slow approach, and the horse's skittish advances and retreats, shows us a rapport between the human and the animal that's strangely moving.

All these scenes of the boy and horse on the island are to be treasured, especially a montage photographed underwater and showing the legs of the two as they splash in the surf. There are also wonderfully scary sequences, such as one in which the boy awakens to find a poisonous snake a few feet away from him on the sand. This scene exploits the hatred and fear horses have for snakes, and is cut together into a terrifically exciting climax.

But then, as all good things must, the idyll on the island comes to an end. The boy and the horse are rescued. And it's here that the film, while still keeping our interest, becomes more routine. The earlier passages of the film were amazing to look at (they were shot, with great difficulty and beauty, on Sardinia). Now we're back to earth again, with scenes shot around an old racetrack in Toronto.

And we've seen the melodramatic materials of the movie's second half many times before. The boy is reunited with his mother, the horse returns home with him, and the boy meets a wise old horse trainer who admits that, yes, that Arabian *can* run like the wind—but the fool thing doesn't have any papers. The presence of Mickey Rooney, who plays the trainer, is welcome but perhaps too familiar. Rooney has played this sort of role so often before (most unforgettably in *National Velvet*) that he almost seems to be visiting from another movie. His Academy Award nomination for the performance is probably a recognition of that.

Still, the melodrama is effective. Everything depends on the outcome of the big race at the film's end. The young boy, of course, is the jockey (the Elizabeth Taylor role, so to speak). Ballard and Deschanel are still gifted at finding a special, epic look for the movie; one especially good scene has the stallion racing against time, in the dark before dawn, in the rain.

The Black Stallion is a wonderful experience at the movies. The possibility remains, though, that in these cynical times it may be avoided by some viewers because it has a G rating—and G movies are sometimes dismissed as being too innocuous. That's sure not the case with this film, which is rated G simply because it has no nudity, profanity, or violence—but it does have terrific energy, beauty, and excitement. It's not a children's movie; it's for adults *and* for kids.

The Black Stallion Returns ★ ★ ½
PG, 93 m., 1983

Kelly Reno (Alec Ramsey), Vincent Spano (Raj), Allen Goorwitz (Kurr), Woody Strode (Meslar), Jodi Thelin (Tabari), Teri Garr (Alec's Mother). Directed by Robert Dakva and produced by Francis Ford Coppola. Screenplay by Richard Kletter and Jerome Kass.

I chose *The Black Stallion* as the best movie of 1980. I was not, however, really looking forward to this sequel, because the original *Black Stallion* arrived at a completely satisfactory conclusion and was happily complete. What's more, the best parts of *The Black Stallion* were in the first half, when the boy and the horse were alone on the island. The second half, ending with the big horse race, was well done, but, let's face it, pretty predictable. Now we have *The Black Stallion Returns*, which also is well done, and which *also* ends in a big horse race, and which is *very* predictable. What odds would you give that the black stallion doesn't win? I can imagine one set of circumstances under which you might want to see this picture: If you're a kid, and you loved *The Black Stallion*, and want to see more of the same stuff, with the same kid (Kelly Reno) and the same horse (Cass-ole), then this might be the movie for you. But anyone expecting serious filmmaking or fresh imagination is going to be disappointed.

The movie begins where the first one left off. The stallion is living happily on a farm with Reno and his mother (Teri Garr). Then one night two bands of evil Arabs arrive to steal the horse, which is needed for a crucial race in the Sahara. Every five years the tribes of the desert race their steeds to determine who will rule the desert. The Arabs steal the horse, Kelly follows them, and everybody ends up back in the desert.

The Arabs are portrayed in this movie as the usual greasy, obnoxious buffoons that have been so popular in the movies ever since the oil crisis; I guess the message is that it's okay to be racist, as long as your targets live far away. The Arab villain is played by Allen Goorwitz, a good character actor who is so far off-base here it's pathetic.

Anyway, most of the movie takes place in the desert, where the young hero meets bands of vagabond Arabs, makes friends with a mysterious young nomad, meets up with a young girl about his age, marches for endless miles through the hot burning sands, nearly dies, steals the stallion back from the Arabs, loses it again, and winds up being asked by the Arabs to ride the stallion in the big race. You bet.

What's good in this film? The performances are often good, including Reno's; he has an interesting, poker-faced way of underplaying scenes that keeps him from being a stereotyped kid. The photography is good, and the desert is often breathtakingly beautiful. The final race is botched by so many parallel story lines that we lose track of where the stallion stands in the race. And the movie is sometimes so overcome by its own beauty that it forgets to be about anything.

Blade Runner ★ ★ ★
R, 114 m., 1982

Harrison Ford (Deckard), Rutger Hauer (Batty), Sean Young (Rachel), Edward James Olmos (Gaff), M. Emmet Walsh (Bryant), Daryl Hannah (Pris). Directed by Ridley Scott and produced by Michael Deeley. Screenplay by Hampton Fancher and David Peoples.

The strangest thing about the future is that *this* is now the future that was once foretold. Twenty years ago, we thought of "now" as "the year 1985," and we wondered what life would be like. Little could we have guessed that there would be no world government, that the cars would look like boxes instead of rocket ships, and that there would still be rock 'n' roll on the radio. *Blade Runner* asks us to imagine its own future, in "the year 2020." The movie takes place in a Los Angeles that looks like a futuristic Tokyo, with gigantic billboards showing smiling Japanese girls drinking Coca-Cola. I would have predicted L.A. would be Hispanic, but never mind, it looks sensational. The city is dominated by almost inconceivably huge skyscrapers. People get around in compact vehicles that fly, hover, climb, and swoop. (In a lot of fictional futures, people seem to zip around the city in private aircraft; can you imagine the traffic problems?) At ground level, however, the L.A. of the future is an urban jungle.

The movie stars Harrison Ford as a cop

who moves confidently through the city's mean streets. He is laconic, cynical, competent. He has a difficult assignment. A group of "replicants," artificial people who seem amazingly human, have escaped from "off-world," and are trying to inflict themselves on Earth. Ford's job is to track them down and eliminate them. Anyone who has read this far can predict what happens next: He falls in love with one of the replicants. She may not be quite human, but, oh, you kid.

This basic story comes from a Philip K. Dick novel with the intriguing title, *Do Androids Dream of Electric Sheep?* The book examined the differences between humans and thinking machines, and circled warily around the question of memory: Does it make an android's personal memories less valid if they are inspired by someone else's experiences—especially if the android does not know that? Ford says he originally signed on for *Blade Runner* because he found such questions intriguing. For director Ridley Scott, however, the greater challenge seemed to be creating that future world. Scott is a master of production design, of imagining other worlds of the future *(Alien)* and the past *(The Duellists)*. He seems more concerned with creating his film worlds than populating them with plausible characters, and that's the trouble this time. *Blade Runner* is a stunningly interesting visual achievement, but a failure as a story.

The special effects were supervised by Douglas Trumbull, whose credits include *2001* and *Silent Running*, and who is about as good as anyone in the world at using miniatures, animation, drawings, optical effects, and other ways of tricking the eye. The visual environments he creates for this film are wonderful to behold, and there's a sense of detail, too; we don't just get the skyways and the monolithic skyscrapers and the sky-taxis, we also get notions about how restaurants, clothes, and home furnishings will look in 2020 (not too different). *Blade Runner* is worth seeing just to witness this artistry. The movie's weakness, however, is that it allows the special effects technology to overwhelm its story. Ford is tough and low-key in the central role, and Rutger Hauer and Sean Young are effective as two of the replicants, but the movie isn't really interested in these people—or creatures. The obligatory love

affair is pro forma, the villains are standard issue, and the climax is yet one more of those cliffhangers, with Ford dangling over an abyss by his fingertips. The movie has the opposite trouble as the replicants: Instead of flesh and blood, its dreams are of mechanical men.

Blame It on Rio ★
R, 101 m., 1984

Michael Caine (Matthew), Michelle Johnson (Jennifer), Joseph Bologna (Victor). Directed and produced by Stanley Donen. Screenplay by Charlie Peters and Larry Gelbart.

As a general rule, I think it's wrong for a married man of forty-seven years to have an affair with his best friend's seventeen-year-old daughter. Don't you? And especially if the girl has emotional problems. I can imagine a movie being made about the situation, and indeed the right movie might even be sensitive and poignant. But to make a cynical sitcom out of it is questionable. That's what they've done with *Blame It on Rio*. This movie is clearly intended to appeal to the prurient interests of dirty old men of all ages. It starts with the basic idea of *10* (an unhappy man flees to a beach and discovers an agreeable nymphet of startling sexuality). But in *10* Bo Derek was old enough to take care of herself, God knows, and her affair with Dudley Moore was handled with at least some wit and sophistication.

Blame It on Rio, however, has the mind of a 1940s bongo comedy and the heart of a porno film. It's really unsettling to see how casually this movie takes a serious situation. A disturbed girl is using sex to play mind games with a middle-aged man, and the movie get its yuks with slapstick scenes where one guy goes out the window when the other guy comes in the door. What's shocking is how many first-rate talents are associated with this sleaze. The director is Stanley Donen, of *Singin' in the Rain*. The man having the affair is Michael Caine, one of my favorite actors. His friend (the father of the girl) is Joseph Bologna. The girl is played by a *zaftig* model named Michelle Johnson, who is set up as the new Bo Derek.

The plot is the usual silliness: Two families are planning a vacation in Rio, but then Caine has a disagreement with his wife, who decides to go to Club Med instead. What finally happens is that the two fathers and their teen-age daughters go to Rio, where Johnson shamelessly seduces Caine with techniques that seem more appropriate to a brazen hussy than to a seventeen-year-old kid. The rest of the movie alternates uneasily between the girl's neurotic attempts to manipulate Caine with sex, Caine's real qualms, and wildly inappropriate screwball scenes. Sample: Caine thinks Bologna has found out the secret. He has to listen as Bologna reads from his daughter's diary. The daughter mentions her new lover's great teeth. Caine tries to hide his teeth with his lips while he talks. Funny, sure, but not in a movie where the underlying subject is so potentially serious.

Does the movie have redeeming qualities? Quite frankly, yes, it does, but not the kind it makes you proud to enjoy. Johnson *could* indeed be the next Bo Derek: She has a winning way, a cheerful personality, and a body that the camera never tires of exploring. Caine does as well with the material as we could possibly hope; in the hands of a lesser actor, we wouldn't be uneasy over the material, we'd be appalled. A lot of skill has gone into the awkward subject matter of this movie, and it's thought-provoking that *Blame It on Rio* sometimes almost works.

Blood Simple ★ ★ ★ ★
R, 96 m., 1985

John Getz (Ray), Frances McDormand (Abby), Dan Hedaya (Julian Marty), M. Emmet Walsh (Detective), Samm-Art Williams (Meurice). Directed by Joel Coen and produced by Ethan Coen. Screenplay by Coen and Coen.

A lot has been written about the visual style of *Blood Simple*, but I think the appeal of the movie is more elementary. It keys into three common nightmares: (1) You clean and clean, but there's still blood all over the place; (2) You know you have committed a murder, but you are not sure quite how or why; (3) You know you have forgotten a small detail that will eventually get you into a lot of trouble. *Blood Simple* mixes those fears and guilts into an incredibly complicated plot, with amazingly gory consequences. It tells a story in which every individual detail

seems to make sense, and every individual choice seems logical, but the choices and details form a bewildering labyrinth in which there are times when even the murderers themselves don't know who they are.

Because following the plot is one of this movie's most basic pleasures, I will not reveal too much. The movie begins with a sleazy backwoods bar owner's attempt to hire a scummy private detective to murder his wife. The private eye takes the money and then pulls a neat double-cross, hoping to keep the money and eliminate the only witness who could implicate him. Neat. And then it *really* gets complicated.

The movie has been shot with a lot of style, some of it self-conscious, but deliberately so. One of the pleasures in a movie like this is enjoying the low-angle and tilt shots that draw attention to themselves, that declare themselves as being part of a movie. The movie does something interesting with its timing, too. It begins to feel inexorable. Characters think they know what has happened; they turn out to be wrong; they pay the consequences, and it all happens while the movie is marching from scene to scene like an implacable professor of logic, demonstrating one fatal error after another.

Blood Simple was directed by Joel Coen, produced by his brother, Ethan, and written by the two of them. It's their first film, and has the high energy and intensity we associate with young filmmakers who are determined to make an impression. Some of the scenes are virtuoso, including a sequence in which a dead body becomes extraordinarily hard to dispose of, and another one in which two people in adjacent rooms are trapped in the same violent showdown. The central performance in the movie is by the veteran character actor M. Emmet Walsh, who plays the private eye like a man for whom idealism is a dirty word. The other actors in the movie are all effective, but they are obscured, in a way, by what happens to them: This movie weaves such a bloody web that the characters are upstaged by their dilemmas.

Is the movie fun? Well, that depends on you. It is violent, unrelenting, absurd, and fiendishly clever. There is a cliché I never use: "Not for the squeamish." But let me put it this way. *Blood Simple* may make you squeam.

Blow Out ★ ★ ★ ★
R, 107 m., 1981

John Travolta (Jack), Nancy Allen (Sally), John Lithgow (Burke), Dennis Franz (Manny Karp), Peter Boydon (Sam), Curt May (Donohue). Directed by Brian De Palma and produced by George Litto. Screenplay by De Palma.

There are times when *Blow Out* resembles recent American history trapped in the "Twilight Zone." Episodes are hauntingly familiar, and yet seem slightly askew. What if the "grassy knoll" recordings from the police radio in Dallas had been crossed with Chappaquiddick and linked to Watergate? What if Jack Ruby had been a private eye specializing in divorce cases? What if Abraham Zapruder—the man who took the home movies of President John F. Kennedy's death—had been a sound effects man? And what if Judith Exner—remember her?—had been working with Ruby? These are some of the inspirations out of which Brian De Palma constructs *Blow Out,* a movie which continues his practice of making cross-references to other movies, other directors, and actual historical events, and which nevertheless is his best and most original work.

The title itself, of course, reminds us of *Blow Up,* the 1966 film by Michelangelo Antonioni in which a photographer saw, or thought he saw, a murder—and went mad while obsessively analyzing his photographs of the "crime." *Was* there a dead body to be found on that fuzzy negative? Was there even such a thing as reality? In *Blow Out,* John Travolta plays the character who confronts these questions. He's a sound man for a sleazy Philadelphia B-movie factory. He works on cheap, cynical exploitation films. Late one night, while he's standing on a bridge recording owls and other night sounds, he becomes a witness to an accident. A car has a blow out, swerves off a bridge, and plunges into a river. Travolta plunges in after it, rescues a girl inside (Nancy Allen), and later discovers that the car's drowned driver was a potential presidential candidate. Still later, reviewing his sound recording of the event, Travolta becomes convinced that he can hear a gunshot just before the blow out. Was the accident actually murder? He traces down Nancy Allen,

discovers that she was part of a blackmail plot against the candidate, and then comes across the trail of a slimy private eye (Dennis Franz) who wanted to cause a blow out, all right, but didn't figure on anybody getting killed.

The plot thickens beautifully. De Palma doesn't have just a handful of ideas to spin out to feature length. He has an abundance. We meet a gallery of violent characters, including Burke (John Lithgow), a dirty-tricks specialist who seems inspired by G. Gordon Liddy. The original crime is complicated by a series of other murders, designed to lay a false trail and throw the police off the scent of political conspiracy.

Meanwhile, the Travolta character digs deeper. For him, it's a matter of competence, of personal pride. Arguing with a cop about his tapes, Travolta denies that he's just imagining things: "I'm a *sound* man!" He stumbles across a series of photos of the fatal accident. In a brilliantly crafted sequence, we follow every step as he assembles the film and his recording into a movie of the event, doggedly extracting what seem to be facts from what looks like chaos.

De Palma's visual images in *Blow Out* invite comparison to many Alfred Hitchcock films, and indeed De Palma invited such comparisons when the posters for *Dressed to Kill,* described him as "Master of the Macabre." In *Blow Out* there are such Hitchcock hallmarks as a shower scene (played this time for laughs rather than for the chills of *Dressed to Kill*), several grisly murders in unexpected surroundings, violence in public places, and a chase through Philadelphia on the anniversary of the ringing of the Liberty Bell. This last extended chase sequence reminds us of two Hitchcock strategies: His juxtaposition of patriotic images and espionage, as in *North by Northwest* and *Saboteur,* and his desperate chases through uncaring crowds, reminders of *Foreign Correspondent* and *Strangers on a Train.*

But *Blow Out* stands by itself. It reminds us of the violence of *Dressed to Kill,* the startling images of *The Fury,* the clouded identities of *Sisters,* the uncertainty of historical "facts" from *Obsession,* and it ends with the bleak nihilism of *Carrie.* But it moves beyond those films, because this time De Palma is more successful than ever before at populating his plot with three-dimensional characters. We believe in the reality of the people played by John Travolta, Nancy Allen, John Lithgow, and Dennis Franz. They have all the little tics and eccentricities of life. And although they're caught in the mesh of a labyrinthine conspiracy, they behave as people probably would behave in such circumstances—they're not pawns of the plot.

Best of all, this movie is inhabited by a real cinematic intelligence. The audience isn't condescended to. In sequences like the one in which Travolta reconstructs a film and sound record of the accident, we're challenged and stimulated: We share the excitement of figuring out how things develop and unfold, when so often the movies only need us as passive witnesses.

The Blue Lagoon ½★
R, 102 m., 1980

Brooke Shields (Emmeline), Christopher Atkins (Richard), Leo McKern (Paddy Button), William Daniels (Arthur Lestrange). Directed and produced by Randal Kleiser. Screenplay by Douglas Day Stewart.

This movie made me itch. It's about a young girl and a young boy who are shipwrecked on a beautiful Pacific island. It shows how they grow up, mostly at sunset. It follows their progress as they discover sex and smile sweetly at each other, in that order. It concludes with a series of scenes designed to inspire the question: If these two young people had grown up in civilized surroundings, wouldn't they have had to repeat the fourth grade?

The Blue Lagoon was the dumbest movie of the year. It could conceivably have been made interesting, if any serious attempt had been made to explore what might really happen if two seven-year-old kids were shipwrecked on an island. But this movie isn't a realistic movie. It's a wildly idealized romance, in which the kids live in a hut that looks like a Club Med honeymoon cottage, while restless natives commit human sacrifice on the other side of the island. (It is a measure of the filmmakers' desperation that the kids and natives never meet one another and the kids leave the island without even one obligatory scene of being tied to a stake.)

Why was this movie made? Presumably because Randal Kleiser, the director and producer, read the 1903 novel it's based on and vowed that this story had to be brought to the screen. It had been filmed previously, as Jean Simmons's 1949 movie debut, but no matter. Kleiser had another go.

It's intriguing to try to guess, on the basis of the film he made, what he thought the original story had to tell us. This movie could have been made as a tale of wilderness survival: *The Swiss Family Robinson Meets Lord of the Flies*. But Kleiser's details about daily life are wildly unconvincing. This movie could have been made as an adventure epic, but, as I've already mentioned, the threat of the natives on the other side of the island is introduced only to be dropped. This movie could have been made as a softcore sex film, but it's too restrained: There are so many palms carefully arranged in front of genital areas, and Brooke Shields's long hair is so carefully draped to conceal her breasts, that there must have been a whole squad of costumers and set decorations on permanent Erogenous Zone Alert.

Let's face it. Going to this film knowing what we've heard about it, we're anticipating the scenes in which the two kids discover the joys of sex. This is a prurient motive on our part, and we're maybe a little ashamed of it, but our shame turns to impatience as Kleiser intercuts countless shots of the birds and the bees (every third shot in this movie seems to be showing a parrot's reaction to something). And there is no way to quite describe my feelings about the scene that takes place the morning after the young couple have finally made love. They go swimming, see two gigantic *turtles* copulating, and smile sweetly at each other. Based on the available evidence in the movie, they know more at this point about the sex lives of turtles than about their own.

But wait, these kids aren't finished. They have a baby, after long, puzzled months of trying to figure out those stirring feelings in the girl's stomach. "Why did you have a baby?" the boy asks. "I don't know," the girl says. They try to feed the kid fresh fruit, and then they look on in wonder as the baby demonstrates the theory and practice of breastfeeding (so *that's* what they're for!).

The movie's ending is enraging. It turns

out the boy's father has been sailing the South Seas for years, looking for the castaways, who meanwhile manage to set themselves adrift at open sea again (they lose their oars . . . but never mind). Despairing of being rescued, the kids have just eaten berries that are supposed to put them permanently asleep. Then their unconscious bodies are rescued. Will they live? Die? What were those berries, anyway? The movie cops out: The burden of contriving an ending was apparently too much for such a feeble movie to support.

The Blues Brothers ★ ★ ★
R, 133 m., 1980

John Belushi (Jake Blues), Dan Aykroyd (Elwood Blues), Ray Charles (Ray), Aretha Franklin (Waitress), James Brown (Rev. James), Cab Calloway (Curtis), Charles Napier (Good Ol' Boy), Henry Gibson (Nazi), John Candy (Burton Mercer), Murphy Dunne (Piano Player), Carrie Fisher (Mystery Lady). Directed by John Landis and produced by Robert K. Weiss. Screenplay by Dan Aykroyd and Landis.

The Blues Brothers is the Sherman tank of musicals. When it was being filmed in Chicago in 1979—with dozens of cars piling up in intersections, caroming down Lake Shore Drive and crashing through the Daley Center—it seemed less like a film than a war. The movie feels the same way. It's a big, raucous powerhouse that proves against all the odds that if you're loud enough, vulgar enough, and have enough raw energy, you can make a steamroller into a musical, and vise versa.

This is some weird movie. There's never been anything that looked quite like it; was it dreamed up in a junkyard? It stars John Belushi and Dan Aykroyd as the Blues Brothers, Jake and Elwood, characters who were created on "Saturday Night Live" and took on a fearsome life of their own. The movie tells us something of their backgrounds: They were reared in a sadistic West Side orphanage, learned the blues by osmosis, and, as the movie opens, have teamed up again after Jake's release from the Joliet pen.

The movie's plot is a simple one, to put it mildly. The brothers visit their old orphanage, learn that its future is in jeopardy because of five thousand dollars due in back taxes, and determine to raise the money by getting their old band together and putting on a show. Their odyssey takes them to several sleazy Chicago locations, including a Van Buren flophouse, Maxwell Street, and lower Wacker Drive. They find their old friends in unlikely places, like a restaurant run by Aretha Franklin, a music shop run by Ray Charles, and a gospel church run by James Brown.

Their adventures include run-ins with suburban cops, good ol' boys, and Nazis who are trying to stage a demonstration. One of the intriguing things about this movie is the way it borrows so freely and literally from news events. The plot develops into a sort of musical *Mad Mad Mad Mad World*, with the Blues Brothers being pursued at the same time by avenging cops, Nazis, and an enraged country and western band led by Charles Napier, that character actor with the smile like Jaws. The chase is interrupted from time to time for musical numbers, which are mostly very good and filled with high-powered energy.

Aretha Franklin occupies one of the movie's best scenes, in her South Side soul food restaurant. Cab Calloway, as a sort of road manager for the Blues Brothers, struts through a wonderful old-style production of *Minnie the Moocher*. The Brothers themselves star in several improbable numbers; the funniest has the band playing in a country and western bar where wire mesh has been installed to protect the band from beer bottles thrown by the customers.

I was saying the musical numbers interrupt the chases. The fact is, the whole movie is a chase, with Jake and Elwood piloting a used police car that seems, as it hurdles across suspension bridges from one side to the other, to have a life of its own. There can rarely have been a movie that made so free with its locations as this one. There are incredible, sensational chase sequences under the elevated train tracks, on overpasses, in subway tunnels under the Loop, and literally through Daley Center. One crash in particular, a pileup involving maybe a dozen police cars, has to be seen to be believed: I've never seen stunt coordination like this before.

What's a little startling about this movie is

that all of this works. *The Blues Brothers* cost untold millions of dollars and kept threatening to grow completely out of control. But director John Landis (of *Animal House*) has somehow pulled it together, with a good deal of help from the strongly defined personalities of the title characters. Belushi and Aykroyd come over as hard-boiled city guys, total cynics with a world-view of sublime simplicity, and that all fits perfectly with the movie's other parts. There's even room, in the midst of the carnage and mayhem, for a surprising amount of grace, humor, and whimsy.

Body Double ★ ★ ★ ½
R, 110 m., 1984

Craig Wasson (Jake), Melanie Griffith (Holly), Gregg Henry (Sam), Deborah Shelton (Gloria). Directed and produced by Brian De Palma. Screenplay by Robert H. Averch and De Palma.

Body Double is an exhilarating exercise in pure filmmaking, a thriller in the Hitchcock tradition in which there's no particular point except that the hero is flawed, weak, and in terrible danger—and we identify with him completely. The movie is so cleverly constructed, with the emphasis on visual storytelling rather than dialogue, that we are neither faster nor slower than the hero as he gradually figures out the scheme that has entrapped him. And the casting of a Hitchcockian average guy also helps.

The movie stars Craig Wasson, an openfaced actor with an engaging smile, as its hero, an unemployed actor named Jake. He isn't smart, he isn't dumb, he isn't perfect, he isn't bad. He is an ideal choice to set up as a witness to a murder. Jake needs a place to stay, and another actor (Gregg Henry) offers him a job house-sitting in a weird, modernistic home on stilts up in the hills above Los Angeles. The other actor also points out all the sights—including a shapely neighbor who does a nightly striptease dance in front of her open window. Jake is only human. For two nights, he uses a telescope to watch the striptease. He also begins to suspect that the woman may be in danger. In sequences inspired by *Rear Window*, he begins to follow the woman (Deborah Shelton), but he keeps his distance because he's caught in the same

dilemma as Jimmy Stewart was in the Hitchcock picture: He is, after all, technically a Peeping Tom, and he wouldn't know the woman was in danger if he hadn't been breaking the law.

Since the plot is so important in *Body Double*, and because the movie contains so many nice surprises, I won't reveal very much more of the story. Let me describe in a carefully vague way, however, some of the pleasures of the movie. After a murder does indeed seem to have been committed, Jake's path leads him into the world of pornographic filmmaking. He wants to meet and hire a porno superstar (Melanie Griffith) who he thinks can help him figure out the mystery. His attempts lead to a series of very funny conversations, as the blonde porno actress talks to him with a Runyonesque mixture of jaded sophistication and startling ignorance. The speech in which she explains exactly what she will, and will not, do in a movie is shocking, sad, and curiously moving. *Body Double*'s excursion into the world of pornography (we see some fairly mild porno scenes, shot by De Palma himself) is part of a veritable anthology of styles in this movie. The film opens with a satire on vampire movies, includes a Hitchcockian cat-and-mouse sequence, and even borrows some of the clichés of 1940s thrillers, including a detailed recapitulation at the end, complete with flashbacks. There is also a sharp 1940s look to the cinematography, which uses dramatic lighting, tilted cameras, and carefully constructed shots to make the style part of the story.

But the movie is not just an exercise in style. It is also a genuinely terrifying thriller, in which an almost clockwork plot brings the hero and the killer together without a single logical glitch. De Palma is at home in this genre. Although his *Scarface* was more of a serious social commentary, thrilling suspense movies are his specialty, and his credits include *Carrie, Obsession,* and *Dressed to Kill.* With *Body Double*, he has his most airtight plot. He also has, once again, his almost unique courage to go over the top—to push scenes beyond the edge of common sense and into cheerfully heightened and impassioned overkill. The graveyard sequence next to the Hollywood reservoir, for example, or the photography in the tunnel during one of the Jake's attacks of claustrophobia, are so uninhibited that they skirt the dangerous edge of being ridiculous. But because the story's so strong, they're not. They work.

Bolero ½★
NO MPAA RATING, 105 m., 1984

Bo Derek, George Kennedy, Andrea Occhipinti. Directed by John Derek.

Bolero is a film starring Bo Derek as a woman who believes that the cure for a man's impotence is for his woman to train as a bullfighter. "Bolero" is also the name of the composition by Ravel which Dudley Moore played in *10* while making love with Derek. So much we already know. Also, let's see here, paging through the old dictionary . . . a bolero is a Spanish dance, characterized by sharp turns and revolutions of the body and stamping of the feet, and it also is a jacket of waist-length or shorter, usually worn open. So *that* explains the jacket of waist-length or shorter, usually worn open, which is Bo Derek's only item of clothing during one scene in the movie! It also explains the sharp turns and revolutions of her body during the same scene, although there is no stamping of the feet, except in the audience.

But I am still a little confused by the relationship between Derek and the bullfighter who is her lover. If you have not seen the movie, let me explain. Derek has graduated from a fancy women's boarding school, and after mooning her professors she departs in search of a tall, dark, and handsome lover. First she meets a sheik, but he turns out to be a dud, maybe because he spends too much time inhaling the magic fumes of his hookah.

So Bo goes to Spain, where she meets this all-around guy who herds cattle on a mountaintop, owns a winery, and is a bullfighter. If he also was an investment banker whose last book read was *The Prophet*, he could be a Dewar's Profile. Bo and the guy make love at sunrise. Unfortunately, the sun rises directly into the camera at crucial moments. Then her lover goes into the ring to fight with the bull, and is gored in that portion of his anatomy he could least afford to spare in any continuing relationship with Derek. He is brave. While doctors fight to save his life, his only thought is for his dog. He asks Bo to be sure that the dog gets home safely.

Before long, Bo is observing that her lover is acting depressed and distant. Could this possibly be because of his horrible injuries? You would think so, and I would think so, but Bo tells him it doesn't matter, and then she vows that he will live to fight again another day, so to speak. Then she starts taking bullfighting lessons. Oh, but I almost forgot. The Arab sheik tears himself away from his hookah long enough to fly to Spain and kidnap her. She is tied up in his open biplane, but manages to untie herself and jump over the edge. Then Bo is immediately back in her lover's hacienda again. How did she get to the ground? For anyone with Bo's faith, all is possible, and I think this is a real good omen for the lover. If she can get down in one piece, think what he might be able to do.

Let's face it. Nobody is going to *Bolero* for the plot anyway. They're going for the Good Parts. There are two Good Parts, not counting her naked ride on horseback, which was the only scene in the movie that had me wondering how she did it. The real future of Bolero is in home cassette rentals, where your fast forward and instant replay controls will supply the editing job the movie so desperately needs.

The Bostonians ★ ★ ★
PG, 120 m., 1984

Basil Ransom (Christopher Reeve), Olive Chancellor (Vanessa Redgrave), Verena Tarrant (Madeleine Potter), Miss Birdseye (Jessica Tandy), Mrs. Burrage (Nancy Marchand). Directed and produced by Ismail Merchant, James Ivory, and Ruth Prawer Jhabvala. Screenplay by Merchant, Ivory, and Jhabvala.

One of the qualities I like best in the novels of Henry James is the way his characters talk and talk about matters of passion and the heart, and never quite seem to act. One of his favorite words, in many of his books, is "intercourse," by which, significantly, he seems to mean conversation, although you can never quite be sure. James's novels run long and deep, and because he was writing for a 19th century that was not always open to the kinds of passions felt by his characters, he beat a lot, if you will, around the bush, so to speak, with lots of commas and asides and subtle hints of unspeakable practices.

The Bostonians is a novel with a lot of asides, and hundreds of pages of hints. We can summarize it boldly: It is about a sweet and somewhat inconsequential young woman who has inspired crushes in two of her admirers. One of her would-be lovers is a straight-spoken lawyer from the South, who wants to sweep her off her feet and make her his wife. The other is a woman, who does not seem quite in touch with the true nature of her feelings; today she would know she was a lesbian, but in the world of James it is necessary for her to displace her feelings—to convince herself that she is in love with the young woman's politics. Those politics are mostly secondhand, made up of things the young woman has been told by others. The story is set at the birth of the suffragette movement, and women meet in each others homes to talk about the right to vote and, by extension, the right to lead full lives. *The Bostonians* shows us several of those woman, including the veteran leader Mrs. Birdseye (wonderfully played by Jessica Tandy) and the younger firebrand Olive Chancellor (Vanessa Redgrave).

Chancellor is in love with Verena Tarrant (Madeleine Potter). That is clear to us, but not as clear to Chancellor. She promotes the young woman as a lecturer and campaigner, filled with visions of her role in social reform—a role that will necessarily require her to become Chancellor's associate, and have little to do with men. Then the tall Southern lawyer (Christopher Reeve) arrives on the scene, and the movie turns into a tug-of-war in which nobody is quite frank about the real nature of the battle.

The Bostonians is by the veteran producer-director-writer team of Ismail Merchant, James Ivory and Ruth Prawer Jhabvala, who collaborated on a 1979 film version of Henry James's *The Europeans*. This is a much better film, intelligent and subtle and open to the underlying tragedy of a woman who does not know what she wants, a man who does not care what he wants, and a girl who does not need what she wants.

The Bounty ★ ★ ★ ★
PG, 130 m., 1984

Anthony Hopkins (Lieutenant William Bligh), Mel Gibson (Fletcher Christian), Tevaite Vernette (Mauatua), Laurence Olivier (Admiral Hood), Edward Fox (Captain Greetham), Daniel Day-Lewis (Fryer). Directed by Roger Donaldson and produced by Bernard Williams. Screenplay by Robert Bolt.

The relationship between Fletcher Christian and Captain William Bligh is one of the most familiar in the movies: We've seen it acted between Clark Gable and Charles Laughton, and between Marlon Brando and Trevor Howard, but it's never before been quite as intriguing as in *The Bounty,* the third movie based on the most famous mutiny in the history of the sea. The movie suggests that Bligh and Christian were friends, of all things, and that Bligh—far from being the histrionic martinet of earlier movies—was an intelligent, contemplative man of great complications. The story is well-known, and simple: *HMS Bounty* sets sail for the South seas, has a difficult voyage that frays everyone's tempers, and then anchors at a Polynesian island. During the trip, the original first mate has been replaced by the young Fletcher Christian, whom Bligh decides to trust. But Christian tires of the voyage and of the dangers and probable death that lie ahead. He falls in love with a native girl and leads a mutiny of sailors who choose to stay on their island paradise. Bligh is played by Anthony Hopkins in one of the most interesting performances of 1984: He is unyielding, but not mindlessly rigid; certain he is right, but not egotistical; able to be realistic about his fate and his chances, and yet completely loyal to his ideas of a British naval officer's proper duties. When Fletcher Christian leads a mutiny against his command, it is not seen simply as a revolt against cruel authority (as in the earlier movies) but as a choice between a freer life-style, and Bligh's placing of duty above ordinary human nature.

Every *Bounty* movie seems to shape its Fletcher Christian somewhat to reflect the actor who plays him. Gable's Christian was a man of action, filled with physical strength and high spirits. Brando's was introverted and tortured. Mel Gibson's is maybe the hardest to figure of the three. He is a man of very few words (the screenplay gives him little to say, and almost no philosophizing), quiet, observant, an enigma. Only in the arms of the woman he comes to love, the Tahitian girl Mauatua, does he find the utter simplicity that perhaps he was looking for when he went to sea. It is a decision of some daring to give Gibson so noticeably little dialogue in this movie, but it works.

This *Bounty* is not only a wonderful movie, high-spirited and intelligent, but something of a production triumph as well. Although this third *Bounty* film was originally conceived as a big-budget, two-part epic to be directed by David *(Dr. Zhivago)* Lean, the current version was prepared and directed after only a few months' notice by a talented young New Zealander named Roger Donaldson, whose previous credits included the brilliant *Smash Palace*, a critical hit and commercial failure. What's interesting is that Donaldson's film doesn't feel like a secondhand treatment; he directs with flair and wit, and the spectacular scenes (like a stormy crossing of the Cape) never allow the special effects to steal the film away from the actors.

The sea voyage is done with the sort of macho confidence that a good sea movie needs, and the land portions to do an interesting job of contrasting the proper, civilized British (represented by Laurence Olivier, as an admiral) with the cheerful absolute freedom of Polynesia. The romance between Gibson and the beautiful Tevaite Vernette, as his island lover, is given time to develop instead of just being thrown in as a plot point. And the Polynesians, for once, are all allowed to go topless all the time (the movie nevertheless gets the PG rating, qualifying under the *National Geographic* loophole in which nudity doesn't count south of the equator). *The Bounty* is a great adventure, a lush romance, and a good movie.

Brainstorm ★ ★
PG, 106 m., 1983

Christopher Walken (Michael Brace), Natalie Wood (Karen Brace), Louise Fletcher (Lillian Reynolds), Cliff Robertson (Alex Terson). Directed and produced by Douglas Trumbull. Screenplay by Robert Stitzel and Philip Frank Messina.

One of the most sensible suggestions I've heard about telepathy is that the human race probably evolved out of it. It was necessary for us to lose the power of telepathy in order to become individuals. If we could tap into other minds all the time, think of the trouble if the guy next door had a headache. *Brainstorm* considers problems like that. It begins with the invention of an amazing machine that gives you the impression you are actually having somebody else's experience. Plug into it, and you hear, see, feel, touch, and smell whatever's been programmed. What's more, it's telepathic; it can take those sensations out of one mind and channel them into another.

The applications are endless. In one demonstration, the wearer believes he is being chased down a mountain road by a runaway truck, and then his car misses a curve and goes sailing through the air. There also are the usual stunts like putting you in the front seat of a roller coaster. But then there's a complication. One of the scientists who developed the gadget inadvertently records her own death. And when her colleagues play back her recording, *they* have the death experience, too.

This is a good idea for a movie. Unfortunately, in *Brainstorm* it remains basically an idea. The characters take such a secondary importance to the gadget that we never feel much for them. Ironic, that the movie doesn't give us *their* sights, smells, tastes, etc. The cast is populated with actors whose full abilities aren't used. We particularly notice that in the case of Natalie Wood, who died while making this movie, and who is good to see once again, but who isn't given even one big, challenging, deep scene; she's just part of the plot machinery. Louise Fletcher is also misued. She plays a chainsmoking scientist. Period. She smokes all the time. She lights a cigarette every time the camera looks at her. Half of this mannerism would have been sufficient; it becomes a joke instead of a trait. Cliff Robertson and Christopher Walken, as the head of the computer company and his brilliant scientist, also are trapped in roles rather than characters.

But the technical effects are intriguing. Douglas Trumbull, the director, is Hollywood's legendary special effects act *(2001, Silent Running, Close Encounters)*, and he does a wonderful job of making the telepathic experiences visually exciting. He cuts back and forth between wide screen and regular format, between standard lenses and astonishing visual effects. Great, except the people get overlooked.

The Breakfast Club ★ ★ ★
R, 95 m., 1985

Emilio Estevez (Andrew Clark), Anthony Michael Hall (Brian Johnson), Judd Nelson (Carl), Molly Ringwald (Claire Standish), Ally Sheedy (Allison Reynolds), Paul Gleason (Teacher), John Kapelos (Janitor). Directed by John Hughes and produced by Ned Tanen and Hughes. Screenplay by Hughes.

The Breakfast Club begins with an old dramatic standby. You isolate a group of people in a room, you have them talk, and eventually they exchange truths about themselves and come to new understandings. William Saroyan and Eugene O'Neill have been here before, but they used saloons and drunks. *The Breakfast Club* uses a high school library and five teen-age kids.

The movie takes place on a Saturday. The five kids have all violated high school rules in one way or another, and they've qualified for a special version of detention, all day long, from eight to four, in the school library. They arrive at the school one at a time. There's the arrogant, swaggering tough guy (Judd Nelson). The insecure neurotic (Ally Sheedy) who hides behind her hair and her clothes. The jock from the wrestling team (Emilio Estevez). The prom queen (Molly Ringwald). And the class brain (Anthony Michael Hall). These kids have nothing in common, and they have an aggressive desire *not* to have anything in common. In ways peculiar to teen-agers, who sometimes have a studious disinterest in anything that contradicts their self-image, these kids aren't even curious about each other. Not at first, anyway. But then the day grows longer and the library grows more oppressive, and finally the tough kid can't resist picking on the prom queen, and then there is a series of exchanges.

Nothing that happens in *The Breakfast Club* is all that surprising. The truths that are exchanged are more or less predictable, and the kids have fairly standard hang-ups. It comes as no surprise, for example, to learn that the jock's father is a perfectionist, or

that the prom queen's parents give her material rewards but withhold their love. But *The Breakfast Club* doesn't need earthshaking revelations; it's about kids who grow willing to talk to one another, and it has a surprisingly good ear for the way they speak. (Ever notice the way lots of teen-age girls, repeating a conversation, say "she goes . . ." rather than "she says . . ."?)

The movie was written and directed by John Hughes, who also made 1984's *Sixteen Candles*. Two of the stars of that movie (Ringwald and Hall) are back again, and there's another similarity: Both movies make an honest attempt to create teen-agers who might seem plausible to other teen-agers. Most Hollywood teen-age movies give us underage nymphos or nostalgia-drenched memories of the 1950s. The performances are wonderful, but then this is an all-star cast, as younger actors go; in addition to Hall and Ringwald from *Sixteen Candles*, there's Sheedy from *WarGames* and Estevez from *Repo Man*. Judd Nelson is not yet as well known, but his character creates the strong center of the film; his aggression is what breaks the silence and knocks over the walls. The only weaknesses in Hughes's writing are in the adult characters: The teacher is one-dimensional and one-note, and the janitor is brought onstage with a potted philosophical talk that isn't really necessary. Typically, the kids don't pay much attention.

Note: The "R" rating on this film refers to language; I think a PG-13 rating would have been more reasonable. The film is certainly appropriate for thoughtful teen-agers.

Breakin' 2—Electric Boogaloo ★ ★ ★
PG, 94 m., 1984

Adolfo "Shabba-Doo" Quinones (Ozone), Michael "Boogaloo Shrimp" Chambers (Turbo), Lucinda Dickey (Kelly). Directed by Sam Firstenberg and produced by Menachem Golan and Yoram Globus. Written by Jan Ventura and Julie Reichert.

Movie musicals used to be allowed to be goofy and lightweight, but in recent years they've turned into ponderous, over-budgeted artifacts that take themselves so seriously you feel guilty if you're having a good time. Remember all the self-importance of *Annie?* That's why a modest, cheerful little movie like *Breakin' 2—Electric Boogaloo* is so refreshing. Here is a movie that wants nothing more than to allow some high-spirited kids to sing and dance their way through a silly plot just long enough to make us grin.

The movie is a sequel to 1983's very successful *Breakin'.* I guess that explains the ungainly title. It involves the same actors, including a team of street-dance artists named Shabba-Doo Quinones and Boogaloo Shrimp Chambers, who more or less seem to be playing themselves. The plot is so familiar that if you're a fan of Mickey Rooney musicals or even the Beach Party movies, you may start rubbing your eyes. But the movie is a lot of fun.

Familiar? Try this plot out on your nearest trivia expert. A bunch of kids get together to turn a run-down old theater into a community center. The center is run by a nice old guy (who is not, for some reason, called "Pops"), and the ringleaders are Shabba-Doo and Boogaloo. In the last movie, they formed a dance team with a rich girl (Lucinda Dickey), and as this movie opens she visits their center and decides to stay and pitch in, despite the opposition of her WASP parents, who want her to enroll in an Ivy League university. Then the plot thickens, when an evil real estate developer wants to tear down the center and put up a big retail development. With just a few minor modifications, this story could be about Mickey and Judy, or Frankie and Annette. But what does it matter, when the whole point of the enterprise is to provide an excuse for song and dance? Quinones, Chambers, and Dickey can indeed dance, very well, and there are a lot of other street dancers in the movie, but what's interesting is the way the traditions of street dancing are combined in this movie with the older traditions of stage dancing and chorus lines. The big extravaganza at the end (a benefit to save the center, needless to say) is a unique hybrid of old and new dance styles.

Electric Boogaloo is not a great movie, but it's inexhaustible, entertaining, and may turn out to be influential. It could inspire a boomlet of low-priced movie musicals—movies not saddled with multimillion dollar budgets, Broadway connections, and stars who are not necessarily able to sing and dance. And at a time when movie musicals (as opposed to movie sound tracks) are seriously out of touch with the music that is really being played and listened to by teenagers, that could be a revolutionary development.

Breathless ★ ★ ½
R, 100 m., 1983

Richard Gere (Jesse Lujack), Valerie Kaprisky (Monica Poiccard). Directed by Jim McBride and produced by Martin Erlichman. Screenplay by McBride and L.M. (Kit) Carson.

There are several levels of cinematic incest at work in *Breathless*, an American film inspired by a 1959 French film that was itself inspired by countless even earlier Hollywood crime films, including *Gun Crazy*—a movie that turns up in this movie. This is the kind of movie for which you need your *Filmgoer's Companion.* Or maybe not; for its announced purpose, as a lurid melodrama about sex and death, it works well enough even without the cross-references. The movie stars Richard Gere, Hollywood's ranking male sex symbol, and Valerie Kaprisky, an unknown French actress, in a story of doom and obsession adapted from Jean-Luc Godard's *Breathless.*

The 1959 *Breathless* starred Jean-Paul Belmondo as a loutish young Frenchman who modeled his behavior on Bogart and Cagney, and bluffed his way into a fatal confrontation with the cops. Jean Seberg played a young American girl who came to Paris to study, met Belmondo, and found herself sharing his bed and his fate. Godard's *Breathless* superimposed Hollywood images on French life-styles. Jim McBride's 1983 *Breathless*, from a script by L.M. (Kit) Carson, does a reverse on the same theme. This time the student (Kaprisky) is French; she's studying in Los Angeles. The lout (Gere) is an American hustler who has to get out of Las Vegas in a hurry, is chased by a highway patrolman, and kills him in a confrontation that is deliberately ambiguous: Did he mean to shoot him or not?

On the run, Gere moves in with Kaprisky, whom he knows only from a weekend fling in Vegas. They make passionate love. The girl gradually becomes aware that her lover is the subject of a statewide manhunt, and the chase leads from punk discos to the Hollywood hills. McBride and Carson position their film somewhere between plausibility (in scenes on a campus, in a grocery store, and in a Mexican restaurant) and stylized fantasy (in the garish red tones of the opening scenes and in Gere's deliberate overacting).

Although movie buffs will probably enjoy this movie's cross-references, this *Breathless* is going to depend on its appeal to ordinary audiences. I imagine they'll be attracted by the notion of Gere as an erotic outlaw on the run, but how will they like him in this role? I thought Gere was deliberately repugnant, but in an interesting way. He plays a character so conceited, so self-absorbed and, I'm afraid, so dim-witted, that there's no opportunity to ever really care for or about him. Kaprisky, as the young French student, is an unknown in a role too large and complex for her, and there are times when she seems lost in a scene, looking to Gere for guidance. The result is a stylistic exercise without any genuine human concerns we can identify with— and yet, an exercise that does have a command of its style, is good looking, fun to watch, and develops a certain morbid humor.

Broadway Danny Rose ★ ★ ★ ½
PG, 86 m., 1984

Woody Allen (Danny Rose), Mia Farrow (Tina Vitale), Nick Apollo Forte (Lou Canova). Directed by Woody Allen and produced by Robert Greenhut and Charles H. Joffe. Screenplay by Allen.

The first time we see him, he's talking fast, and his arms are working like a guy doing an imitation of an air traffic controller. His hands keep coming in for landings. This is Broadway Danny Rose, the most legendary talent agent in New York, the guy who will represent you after you've been laughed off every stage in the Catskills. He represents blind xylophonists, piano-playing birds, and has-been crooners with drinking problems. He's the kind of guy that comics sitting around on their day off tell stories about. He also is Woody Allen, but he is less like Woody Allen than some of the other

characters Allen has played. After the autobiography of *Stardust Memories,* after the whimsy of *A Midsummer Night's Sex Comedy,* and the antiseptic experimentation of *Zelig,* this movie has Allen creating a character and following him all the way through a crazy story. After a period when Allen seemed stuck in self-doubt and introspection, he loosens up and has a good time.

Broadway Danny Rose, like all of Allen's best movies, is a New York movie. It starts at the Carnegie Deli, with comedians sitting around a table trading Danny Rose stories, and then it flashes back to the best Danny Rose story of them all, about how Danny signed up this has-been alcoholic tenor and carefully nurtured his career back to the brink of stardom. Riding the nostalgia boom, Danny takes the guy and books him into Top Forty concerts, until finally he gets him a date at the Waldorf—and Milton Berle is in the audience, looking for guests for his TV special. Except the crooner has a complicated love life. He has a wife, and he also has a girlfriend. He wants Danny Rose to be the "beard" and take the girlfriend to the concert. Otherwise he won't feel right. But then the crooner and the girl have a fight, and the girl goes back to her Mafioso boyfriend, and Danny Rose winds up at a mob wedding with a gun in his face.

All of this is accomplished with wonderfully off-the-wall characterizations. Allen makes Danny Rose into a caricature, and then, working from that base, turns him back into a human being: By the end of the film, we see the person beneath the mannerisms. Nick Apollo Forte, an actor I've never seen before, plays the has-been crooner with a soft touch: he's childish, he's a bear, he's loyal, he has a monstrous ego. The real treasure among the performances, however, is Mia Farrow's work as Tina Vitale, the crooner's girlfriend. You would think that Mia Farrow would be one of the most instantly recognizable actresses in the movies with those finely chiseled features and that little-girl voice. But here she is a chain-smoking, brassy blonde with her hair piled up on top of her head, and a pair of fashionable sunglasses, and dresses that look like they came from the boutique in a Mafia resort hotel.

Broadway Danny Rose uses all of the basic

ingredients of Damon Runyon's Broadway: the pathetic acts looking for a job, the guys who get a break and forget their old friends, the agents with hearts of gold, the beautiful showgirls who fall for Woody Allen types, the dumb gangsters, big shots at the ringside tables (Howard Cosell plays himself). It all works.

The Brother from Another Planet
★ ★ ★ ½
PG, 110 m., 1984

Joe Morton (The Brother), Maggie Renzi (Noreen), Fisher Stevens (Card Trickster), John Sayles (Man in Black). Directed by John Sayles and produced by Sayles and Maggie Renzi. Screenplay by Sayles.

When the movies started to talk, they began to lose the open-eyed simplicity with which they saw the world. *The Brother from Another Planet* tells the story of a man who cannot talk, but who can read minds, listen carefully, look deep into eyes, and provide a sort of mirror for our society. That makes it sound serious, but like all the most serious movies, it's a comedy.

The film stars Joe Morton as a visitor from outer space, who looks like a black human being, unless you look carefully at the three funny toes on his feet. He arrives on Earth in a spaceship that looks borrowed from the cheapest B space operas from the 1950s, swims ashore, and finds himself on Manhattan Island. At first he is completely baffled. Before long, everyone he meets is just as baffled. It is strange to deal with people who confound all your expectations: It might even force you to reevaluate yourself.

The brother is not looking for trouble, is not controversial, wants only to make sense of this weird new world. Because his instinctive response to most situations is a sort of blank reserve, people project their own feelings and expectations upon him. They tell him what he must be thinking, and behave as if they are right. He goes along.

The movie finds countless opportunities for humorous scenes, most of them with a quiet little bite, a way of causing us to look at our society. The brother runs into hookers and connivers, tourists from Indiana, immigrant shopkeepers,and a New York weirdo who, in one of the movie's best scenes,

shows him a baffling card trick, and then demonstrates another trick that contains a cynical grain of big-city truth. The brother walks through this menagerie with a sometimes bemused, sometimes puzzled look on his face. People seem to have a lot of problems on this planet. He is glad to help out when he can; for example, curing video games by a laying on of hands. His right hand contains the power to heal machines, and it is amazing how quickly people accept that, if it is useful to them.

The Brother from Another Planet was written and directed by John Sayles, who is a one-man industry in the world of the American independent film. His credits include *Return of the Secaucus Seven, Lianna,* and *Baby, It's You,* and in this film—by using a central character who cannot talk—he is sometimes able to explore the kinds of scenes that haven't been possible since the death of silent film. There are individual moments here worthy of a Keaton, and there are times when Joe Morton's unblinking passivity in the midst of chaos really does remind us of Buster.

There is also a curious way in which the film functions as more subtle social satire than might seem possible in a low-budget, good-natured comedy. Because the hero, the brother, has literally dropped out of the skies, he doesn't have an opinion on anything. He only gradually begins to realize that on this world he is "black," and that his color makes a difference in some situations. He tries to accept that. When he is hurt or wronged, his reaction is not so much anger as surprise: It seems to him so unnecessary that people behave unkindly toward one another. He is a little surprised they would go to such an effort. His surprise, in its own sweet and uncomplicated way, is one of the most effective elements in the whole movie.

Brubaker ★ ★ ½
R, 131 m., 1980

Robert Redford (Brubaker), Yaphet Kotto (Dickie Coombes), Jane Alexander (Lillian), Murray Hamilton (Deach), David Keith (Larry Lee Bullen), Morgan Freeman (Walter), M. Emmet Walsh (C.P. Woodward), Matt Clark (Purcell), Richard Ward (Abraham). Directed by Stuart Rosenberg and produced

by Ron Silverman. Screenplay by
W.D. Richter.

Brubaker is a grim and depressing drama about prison outrages—a movie that should, given its absolutely realistic vision, have kept us involved from beginning to end. That it doesn't is the result, I think, of a deliberate but unwise decision to focus on the issues involved in the story, instead of on the characters.

All the people in this movie have roles that represent something; there's the Idealistic Reformer, the Pragmatic Politician, the Corrupt Administrator, the Noble Prisoner, the Tough Guard. The problem is that once they're assigned an ideological niche at the beginning of the movie, they behave with absolute consistency. There's no room for the spontaneity of real human personalities caught in real situations.

That's especially annoying with the character of Brubaker himself, played well but within a frustratingly narrow range by Robert Redford. Brubaker is the reform warden assigned to clean up the violence and corruption of Wakefield Prison Farm, a hellhole of sadism where no guards are needed because the prisoner trusties are armed and get time off their sentences for shooting escapees. The movie's first twenty or thirty minutes, which are sickeningly effective, document conditions in the prison, where the commonplaces include beatings, bribery, rape, and slum living conditions.

Brubaker finds out about these outrages firsthand. He has himself been brought into the prison anonymously, as a prisoner. This is supposed to provide the movie's biggest surprise, when he finally steps forward and identifies himself, but the ads for the movie spoiled the surprise by identifying Redford as the warden. What seems a little unlikely in these opening scenes is that Redford, as a new prisoner, would emerge unscathed: He observes, he listens, and he's mostly left alone by the other prisoners, even though his fellow new recruits are being raped, beaten, and forced into the prison's system of corruption.

After Redford takes charge, the movie disintegrates into predictability. He takes a position in favor of progressive reforms, and the state board of corrections takes a position in favor of corrupt business as usual. Some interesting characters are introduced, especially Yaphet Kotto as a hard-boiled trusty who can't make up his mind about the warden, and Jane Alexander, as a pragmatic aide to the state governor. Murray Hamilton, as a corrupt member of the state prison board, does his usual venal capitalist and does it well, but he has played this role so frequently (in the first two *Jaws* movies, for example), that he must know it by heart.

In the meantime, we're growing a little restless because of the movie's refusal to permit its characters more human dimensions. We want to know these people better, but the screenplay throws up a wall; they act according to the ideological positions assigned to them in the screenplay, and that's that. Half of Redford's speeches could have come out of newspaper editorials, but we never find out much about him. What's his background? Was he ever married? Is this his first prison job? What's his relationship with the Jane Alexander character, who seems to have gotten him this job? (Alexander has one almost subliminal moment when she fans her neck and looks at Redford and seems to be thinking unpolitical thoughts, but the movie hurries on.) *Brubaker* is a well-crafted film that does a harrowingly effective job of portraying the details of its prison, but it populates it with positions rather than people.

Burden of Dreams ★ ★ ★ ★
NO MPAA RATING, 94 m., 1982

Featuring Werner Herzog, Klaus Kinski, Claudia Cardinale, Jason Robards, Jr., and Mick Jagger. Directed and produced by Les Blank, with Maureen Gosling.

Les Blank's *Burden of Dreams* is one of the most remarkable documentaries ever made about the making of a movie. There are at least two reasons for that. One is that the movie being made, Werner Herzog's *Fitzcarraldo*, involved some of the most torturous and dangerous on-location shooting experiences in film history. The other is that the documentary is by Les Blank, himself a brilliant filmmaker, who is unafraid to ask difficult questions and portray Herzog, warts and all.

The story of Herzog's *Fitzcarraldo* is already the stuff of movie legend. The movie was shot on location deep within the rain forests of South America, one thousand miles from civilization. When the first version of the film was half-finished, its star, Jason Robards, was rushed back to New York with amoebic dysentery and forbidden by his doctors to return to the location. Herzog replaced Robards with Klaus Kinski (star of his *Aguirre, the Wrath of God*), but meanwhile, co-star Mick Jagger left the production because of a commitment to a concert tour. Then the Kinski version of *Fitzcarraldo* was caught in the middle of a border war between tribes of Indians. The whole production was moved twelve hundred miles, to a new location where the mishaps included plane crashes, disease, and attacks by unfriendly Indians. And all of those hardships were on top of the incredible task Herzog set himself to film: He wanted to show his obsessed hero using teams of Indians to pull an entire steamship up a hillside using only block and tackle!

Blank and his associate, Maureen Gosling, visited both locations of Herzog's film. Their documentary includes the only available record of some of the earlier scenes with Robards and Jagger. It also includes scenes in which Herzog seems to be going slowly mad, blaming the evil of the jungle and the depth of his own compulsions. In *Fitzcarraldo*, you can see the incredible strain as men try to pull a steamship up a sharp incline, using only muscle power and a few elementary principles of mechanics. In *Burden of Dreams*, Blank's camera moves back one more step, to show the actual mechanisms by which Herzog hoped to move his ship. A giant bulldozer is used to augment the block-and-pulley, but it proves barely equal to the task, and at one point the Brazilian engineer in charge of the project walks off, warning that lives will be lost.

What drives Herzog to make films that test his sanity and risk his life and those of his associates? Stanley Kauffmann, in the *New Republic*, argued that, for Herzog, the purpose of film is to risk death, and each of his films is in some way a challenge hurled at the odds. Herzog has made films on the slopes of active volcanoes, has filmed in the jungle and in the middle of the Sahara, and has made films about characters who live at the edges of human achievement. *Burden of*

Dreams gives us an extraordinary portrait of Herzog trapped in the middle of one of his wildest dreams.

Caddyshack ★ ★ ½
R, 99 m., 1980

Chevy Chase (Ty Webb), Rodney Dangerfield (Al Czervik), Ted Knight (Judge Smails), Michael O'Keefe (Danny), Bill Murray (Carl), Sarah Holcomb (Maggie). Directed by Harold Ramis and produced by Douglas Kenney. Screenplay by Brian Doyle-Murray, Ramis, and Kenney.

Caddyshack never finds a consistent comic note of its own, but it plays host to all sorts of approaches from its stars, who sometimes hardly seem to be occupying the same movie. There's Bill Murray's self-absorbed craziness, Chevy Chase's laid-back bemusement, and Ted Knight's apoplectic overplaying. And then there is Rodney Dangerfield, who wades into the movie and cleans up.

To the degree that this is anybody's movie, it's Dangerfield's—and he mostly seems to be using his own material. He plays a loud, vulgar, twitching condo developer who is thinking of buying a country club and using the land for housing. The country club is one of those exclusive WASP enclaves, a haven for such types as the judge who founded it (Knight), the ne'er-do-well club champion (Chase), and the manic assistant grounds keeper (Murray).

The movie never really develops a plot, but maybe it doesn't want to. Director Harold Ramis brings on his cast of characters and lets them loose at one another. There's a vague subplot about a college scholarship for the caddies, and another one about the judge's nubile niece, and continuing warfare waged by Murray against the gophers who are devastating the club. But Ramis is cheerfully prepared to interrupt everything for moments of comic inspiration, and there are three especially good ones: The caddies in the swimming pool doing a Busby Berkeley number, another pool scene that's a scatalogical satire of *Jaws*, and a sequence in which Dangerfield's gigantic speedboat devastates a yacht club.

Dangerfield is funniest, though, when the movie just lets him talk. He's a Henny Youngman clone, filled with one-liners and insults, and he's great at the country club's dinner dance, abusing everyone and making rude noises. Surveying the crowd from the bar, he uses lines that he has, in fact, stolen directly from his nightclub routine ("This steak still has the mark of the jockey's whip on it"). With his bizarre wardrobe and trick golf bag, he's a throwback to the Groucho Marx and W.C. Fields school of insult comedy; he has a vitality that the movie's younger comedians can't match, and they suffer in comparison.

Chevy Chase, for example, has some wonderful moments in this movie, as a studiously absent-minded hedonist who doesn't even bother to keep score when he plays golf. He's good, but somehow he's in the wrong movie: His whimsy doesn't fit with Dangerfield's blatant scenery-chewing or with the Bill Murray character. Murray, as a slob who goes after gophers with explosives and entertains sexual fantasies about the women golfers, could be a refugee from *Animal House.*

Maybe one of the movie's problems is that the central characters are never really involved in the same action. Murray's off on his own, fighting gophers. Dangerfield arrives, devastates, exits. Knight is busy impressing the caddies, making vague promises about scholarships, and launching boats. If they were somehow all drawn together into the same story, maybe we'd be carried along more confidently. But *Caddyshack* feels more like a movie that was written rather loosely, so that when shooting began there was freedom—too much freedom—for it to wander off in all directions in search of comic inspiration.

Caligula no stars
NO MPAA RATING, 143 m., 1980

Malcolm McDowell (Caligula), Teresa Ann Savoy (Drusilla), John Gielgud (Nerva), Peter O'Toole (Tiberius). Produced by Bob Guccione and Franco Rossellini.

Caligula is sickening, utterly worthless, shameful trash. If it is not the worst film I have ever seen, that makes it all the more shameful: People with talent allowed themselves to participate in this travesty. Disgusted and unspeakably depressed, I walked out of the film after two hours. This film is not only garbage on an artistic level, but it is also garbage on the crude and base level where it no doubt hopes to find its audience. *Caligula* is not good art, it is not good cinema, and it is not good porn.

I've never had anything against eroticism in movies. There are X-rated films I've enjoyed, from the sensuous fantasies of *Emmanuelle* to the pop-comic absurdities of Russ Meyer. All I can say is that the makers of *Caligula* have long since lost touch with any possible common erotic denominator, and that they suggest by the contents of this film that they are jaded, perverse, and cruel human beings. There are no scenes of joy, natural pleasure, or good sensual cheer. There is, instead, a nauseating excursion into base and sad fantasies.

This is a violent film. There are scenes depicting a man whose urinary tract is closed, and who has gallons of wine poured down his throat. His bursting stomach is punctured with a sword. There is a scene in which a man is emasculated, and his genitals thrown to dogs, who eagerly eat them on the screen. There are scenes of decapitation, evisceration, rape, bestiality, sadomasochism, necrophilia.

These scenes—indeed, the movie itself—reflect a curiously distanced sensibility. Nobody in this film really seems to be there. Not the famous actors like Malcolm McDowell and (very briefly) Peter O'Toole and John Gielgud, whose scenes have been augmented by additional porn shot later with other people inserted to spice things up. Not the director (who removed his credit from the film). Not the writer (what can it mean that this movie is "*Adapted* from an Original Screenplay by Gore Vidal"?). Not even the sound track. The actors never quite seem to be speaking their own words, which are so badly dubbed that the dialogue never seems to be emerging from the drama itself.

The film even fails to involve itself in the action. *Caligula* has been photographed and directed with such clumsiness and inelegance that pieces of action do not seem to flow together, the plot is incomprehensible, the events are frequently framed as if the camera was not sure where it was, and everything is shot in muddy, ugly, underlit dungeon tones. The music is also execrable.

So what are we left with? A movie, I am

afraid, that may be invulnerable to a review like this one. There are no doubt people who believe that if this movie is as bad as I say it is, it must be worth seeing. People who simply cannot believe any film could be this vile. But people learn fast. "This movie," said the lady in front of me at the drinking fountain, "is the worst piece of shit I have ever seen."

Cannery Row ★ ★ ½
PG, 120 m., 1982

Nick Nolte (Doc), Debra Winger (Suzy), Audra Lindley (Fauna), Frank McRae (Hazel), M. Emmet Walsh (Mack), Sunshine Parker (The Seer). Directed by David S. Ward and produced by Michael Phillips. Screenplay by Ward.

Old skid-row drunks are a lot of things. They are sick, they are lice-ridden, they are often prematurely senile and sometimes they are so far gone they're not even tragic anymore, just wasted. Two things they are not is colorful and romantic, and when the Greek chorus of winos and bums marches onscreen in *Cannery Row*, we know the movie is in trouble. Dressed in colorful rags, each one an unforgettable character, they think they're Mr. Doolittle and his pals in *My Fair Lady*. They sleep in drain pipes at night because it's colorful. I mention the bums first, not because I think *Cannery Row* has any obligation to provide us with an accurate portrait of skid row, but because they are symptomatic of what is wrong with this movie.

It was made, I suppose, out of a desire to find some larger truth by taking reality and stylizing it into colorful romanticism: To take a bunch of down-and-outers and find the essential humanity in them. Writers were always dredging the essential humanity out of the proletariat in the thirties and forties, and John Steinbeck, who wrote *Cannery Row* and *Sweet Thursday*, the novels that inspired this movie, was no exception. I doubt, though, that even Steinbeck would be able to believe the extremes to which this movie goes. It populates its gigantic and impressive set (an indoor and outdoor replica of the Monterey docks) not only with lovable bums, but also with the requisite hookers with hearts of gold and with a guy named Doc, who dreams of making a break-through in marine biology. If life were like this, Norman Rockwell would have eclipsed Edward Hopper.

Doc is played by Nick Nolte, and he is the best thing in the movie. He provides a sound, solid, dignified performance, and there are times when we even believe he's a real human being who just accidentally wandered into this fantasy. Doc was once a big-league pitcher, and he had twenty-one wins and ten losses when he suddenly quit pitching and moved to Cannery Row. There is a guilty secret in his past, and it has something to do with The Seer, a loony, saintly bum who wanders the beach and serenades the dawn. Doc stares at octopuses all day, as if he could make a great discovery about them just by *looking* hard enough. One day he meets Suzy (Debra Winger), a young girl with ambitions of becoming a floozy. Doc loves her, I guess. She loves him, I suppose. She goes to work in the local cathouse, where the madam is named Fauna, maybe because Flora was already taken. But the hookers and the bums all catch on about Doc and Suzy, and the middle of the movie is devoted to their ill-conceived schemes to get the two lovers together. All of this is photographed and written in such a mixture of the wistful, the whimsical, the eccentric, and the romantic that the characters don't even seem to be living; they seem to be auditioning. Occasionally scenes come to life; there's a real sweetness in a passage where Nolte and Winger boogie with one another.

The movie is almost always good to look at, thanks to Richard MacDonald's sets (he linked together two giant sound stages) and Sven Nykvist's photography. And Nolte and Winger are almost able to make their relationship work, if only it didn't seem scripted out of old country songs and lonely hearts columns. It's tough to pull off a movie like this, in the semi-cynical 1980s (it would have been impossible in the truly cynical seventies). I guess we no longer believe in the essential heroism of the little guy, and in the proposition that anyone can succeed with a little luck. In the movie, Doc dreams of making a big discovery and impressing those eggheads at the annual biology convention. Does he succeed? Well, I understand that the original Doc, a man named Ed Ricketts who was a drinking buddy of Steinbeck's, never did make that breakthrough and died in 1953 when his car stalled on the skid-row railroad tracks and he didn't think to get out in time. Now that would have made an ending for the eighties.

The Cannonball Run ½ ★
PG, 95 m., 1981

Burt Reynolds (J.J. McClure), Roger Moore (Seymour), Farrah Fawcett (Pamela), Dom DeLuise (Victor), Dean Martin (Jamie Blake), Sammy Davis, Jr. (Fenderbaum). Directed by Hal Needham and produced by Albert S. Ruddy. Screenplay by Brock Yates.

The Cannonball Run is an abdication of artistic responsibility at the lowest possible level of ambition. In other words, they didn't even care enough to make a good lousy movie. *Cannonball* was probably always intended as junk, as an easy exploitation picture. But it's possible to bring some sense of style and humor even to grade-zilch material. This movie doesn't even seem to be trying.

Burt Reynolds sleepwalks through a role he's played several times before, but never so indifferently. He's a hotshot driver in a big, illegal cross-country road race; first one to California wins. That means Reynolds gets to drink a lot of beer, talk like a good ol' boy, and get in the middle of a lot of crashes and other stunts. The movie was directed by Hal Needham, a onetime stuntman who graduated to directing with *Smokey and the Bandit* (1977), the first and still the best of the Burt Reynolds car-chase movies. After that, each Needham movie has been worse than the one preceding it. His downward spiral has included *Hooper, The Villain,* and *Smokey and the Bandit II.* Movie buffs will note that three of Needham's four movies have starred Burt Reynolds, one of the most important properties in Hollywood. Reynolds is so popular he can make money in almost anything—a maxim that *Cannonball Run* puts to the extreme test. Reynolds and Needham are friends, and indeed the whole cast of *Cannonball* seems to consider the movie a reunion. The film ends with outtakes—spoiled shots during which somebody breaks up or says the wrong line or otherwise goofs. It's supposed to show us how much fun everybody had. Alas, the outtakes don't

look much more goofy than the takes they intended to put in the movie; *Cannonball* assembles a giant cast around an absolutely minimal amount of screenplay, and allows them to kill time expensively. There's not much plot and no suspense. The filmmakers' excuse, no doubt, is that they were really making a comedy, not a road-race picture. That would work if there were any laughs in the movie.

But just look at the cast. It's like a cattle call. It's like an Actor's Guild picket line. It's like Hollywood Squares on Wheels. Some of the actors are talented, some are not, but they look equally awful in this movie. At one time or another during this unspeakable experience, you can share it with not only Burt Reynolds but also Roger Moore, Farrah Fawcett, Dom DeLuise, Dean Martin (looking as if a big-a pizza pie hit him straight in the eye), Sammy Davis, Jr. (looking like a severe case of vitamin deficiency), Jack Elam, Adrienne Barbeau (whose role consists of unzipping her jump suit), Terry Bradshaw, Jackie Chan, Bert Convy, Jamie Farr, Peter Fonda (as an aging Hells Angel), Michael Hui, Bianca Jagger, Molly Picon, Jimmy "the Greek" Snyder, and Mel Tillis. This isn't a cast, it's the answer to a double acrostic.

Cannonball Run II ½ ★
PG, 108 m., 1984

Burt Reynolds (J.J.), Dom DeLuise (Victor), Dean Martin (Blake), Sammy Davis, Jr. (Fenderbaum), Marilu Henner (Betty), Shirley MacLaine (Veronica). Directed by Hal Needham and produced by Albert S. Ruddy. Screenplay by Needham, Ruddy, and Harvey Miller.

The clue to *Cannonball Run II* is in Frank Sinatra's first scene, but you have to look carefully. The scene starts in Sinatra's office, and we're looking over Sinatra's head at Burt Reynolds and some other people. At least, it *looks* like Sinatra's head, except there's something a little funny about the ears. Then we see Sinatra. He talks. We see Reynolds. He talks. And so on, until, if we know something about movie editing techniques, we realize *there isn't a single shot showing Sinatra and Reynolds at the same time.* Also, there's something funny about Sinatra's voice: He doesn't seem to be quite matching the tone of the things said to him. That's the final tip-off: Sinatra did his entire scene by sitting down at a desk and reading his lines into the camera, and then, on another day, Reynolds and the others looked into the camera and pretended to be looking at him. The over-the-shoulder shots are of a double.

This is the movie equivalent to phoning it in. You can't blame Sinatra. Everybody else is walking through this movie, so why shouldn't he? Refusing to appear in a scene with your fellow actors is no worse than agreeing to appear in a scene that nobody has bothered to write. *Cannonball Run II* is one of the laziest insults to the intelligence of moviegoers that I can remember. Sheer arrogance made this picture.

The movie stars Burt Reynolds as J. J. McClure, cross-country racer. Dom DeLuise is back as his sidekick. Some of the other familiar faces from the first awful *Cannonball* movie include Dean Martin and Sammy Davis, Jr., and they are joined here by Shirley MacLaine, Jamie Farr, Susan Anton, Marilu Henner, Telly Savalas, Catherine Bach, Foster Brooks, Sid Caesar, Jackie Chan, Tim Conway, Richard ("Jaws") Kiel, Don Knotts, Ricardo Montalban, Jim Nabors, Louis Nye, Molly Picon, and the pathetic Charles Nelson Reilly. It's a roll call of shame. Some of these actors are, of course, talented. Shirley MacLaine won an Academy Award the same year she made this. Burt Reynolds can be good, but you can't tell that from this movie. *Cannonball Run II* is a day off for most of these performers, who are not given characters to play, readable dialogue to recite, or anything to do other than to make fools of themselves.

The name of the director is Hal Needham. He is a crony of Reynolds's, a former stunt driver who has brilliantly demonstrated the Peter Principle by becoming a director, thus rising far above his level of competence. This is the sixth time Needham has directed Reynolds. Greater love hath no actor, than that he sacrifice his career on the altar of friendship. When Reynolds appeared in Needham's awful *Stroker Ace* in 1983, he excused himself by saying the role had been intended for Steve McQueen; he stepped in after McQueen's death as a favor to his friend Needham. What's his excuse this time?

Cannonball Run II was made for one reason: The original picture made money. There may be a sucker born every minute, but so many of them fell for *Cannonball Run* that there may not be many left who are willing to fall twice for the same scam.

Carmen ★ ★ ★ ★
R, 95 m., 1983

Antonio Gades (Antonio), Laura Del Sol (Carmen), Paco De Lucia (Paco), Cristina Hoyos (Cristina). Sung by Regina Resnik and Maria Del Monaco. Directed by Carlos Saura and produced by Emiliano Piedra. Screenplay by Saura and Antonio Gades.

Carlos Saura's *Carmen* is an erotic roller coaster of a movie, incorporating dance into its story more effectively than any other movie I can remember. It isn't a "ballet movie," and it's not like one of those musicals where everybody is occasionally taken with the need to dance. It's a story of passion and jealousy—the story of Bizet's *Carmen*—with dance as part and parcel of its flesh and blood. The movie is based on the opera by Bizet, keeping the music and the broad outlines of the story of a poor girl whose fierce romantic independence maddens the men who become obsessed with her. Everything else is new. Saura, the greatest living Spanish film director, has collaborated with Antonio Gades, the Spanish dancer and choreographer, to make this *Carmen* into a muscular, contemporary story. Their strategy is to make a story within a story. The film begins with Gades as a dance teacher who is looking for the "perfect" Carmen. He finds one in a flamenco dancing school, and as he attempts to mold her into Carmen, their relationship begins to resemble the story of the opera.

Given this approach, *Carmen* could easily have turned into an academic exercise, one of those clever movies in which all the pieces fit but none of them matter. That doesn't happen, and one of the reasons it doesn't is the casting of a young woman named Laura Del Sol as Carmen. She is a twenty-one-year-old dancer who combines convincing technique with a healthy, athletic sexiness, and her dance duets (and duels) with Gades are bold, erotic, and uninhibited. What's fascinating is the way Saura is able to blend the dance, the opera, and the "modern" story. For example, Del Sol and Gades use dance to create a scene that begins as an argument, develops into fierce declarations of independence, and then climaxes in passionate romance. In another scene, a routine day in a dance studio becomes charged by the unexpected appearance of Carmen's other lover, an ex-convict.

I have an ambivalence about dance on film. I begin with the assumption that the ideal way to see dance is live, on a stage. Everything in dance begins with the fact that the dancers are physically present and are using their bodies to turn movement into art. Movies, with their complete freedom over time and space, break that contract between real time and the dancer. Dances can be constructed out of many different shots and even out of the work of more than one dancer (see *Flashdance*). If I can't see dancing on a stage, then, my preference is for classical movie dancing, by which I mean frankly artificial constructions of the Astaire and Rogers variety. Serious dance on film usually feels like a documentary. The great achievement of *Carmen* is that it takes serious dance and music, combines them with a plausible story, suspends our disbelief, and gives us a mesmerizing, electric experience.

Carmen ★ ★ ★ ★
PG, 152 m., 1984

Julia Migenes-Johnson (Carmen), Placido Domingo (Don Jose), Ruggero Raimondi (Escamillo), Faith Esham (Micaela), Jean-Philippe Lafont (Dancairo). Directed by Francesco Rosi and produced by Patrice Ledoux.

Bizet's *Carmen* is what movies are all about. It's one of the few modern movies that requires one of those legendary Hollywood advertising men who'd cook up copy like, for example . . .

Cheer! As Bizet's towering masterpiece blazes across the screen! Cry bravo! To passion, romance, adventure! From the bullrings of Spain to the innermost recesses of her gypsy heart, Carmen drives men mad and immortalizes herself as a romantic legend! Thrill! To the golden voice of Placido Domingo, and the *tempestuous screen debut of the smouldering Julia Migenes-Johnson!*

The temptation, of course, is to approach, a film like this with hushed voice and bended knee, uttering reverent phrases about art and music. But to hell with it: This movie is the *Indiana Jones* of opera films, and we might as well not beat around the bush. *Carmen* is a Latin soap opera if ever there was one, and the sheer passionate joy of Bizet's music is as vulgar as it is sublime, as popular as it is classical. *Carmen* is one of those operas ideally suited to the movies, and this version by Francesco Rosi is exciting, involving, and entertaining.

You are doubtless already familiar with the music. The sound track was recorded in Paris with Lorin Maazel conducting the National Orchestra of France. Placido Domingo is in great voice, and a relatively unknown American soprano named Julia Migenes-Johnson not only can sing the title role but, perhaps just as importantly, can look it and act it. There is chemistry here, and without the chemistry—without the audience's belief that the scornful gypsy Carmen could enslave the soldier Don Jose—there would only be an illustrated sound track. After the recording was completed, the movie was shot on locations in Spain by Francesco Rosi, the Italian director of *Three Brothers* and *Christ Stopped at Eboli*. He has discovered lush, sun-drenched villages on hillsides, and a bullring of such stark Spanish simplicity that the ballet within the ring for once seems as elegant as the emotions it is reflecting. He also has found moonlight, rich firelight, deep reds and yellows—colors so glowing that the characters seem to warm themselves at his palette.

Opera films are traditionally not successful. They play in festivals, they find a small audience of music lovers, maybe they make some money in Italy. Domingo broke that pattern with his *La Traviata* (1983), directed by Franco Zeffirelli. It had good long runs around the United States, and even broke through to audiences beyond the core of opera lovers. But we Americans are so wary of "culture." Opera for many of us still consists of the fat lady on "The Ed Sullivan Show." And for many of the rest, it is something that inhabits a cultural shrine and must be approached with reverence. Maybe it takes the movies, that most popular of art forms, to break that pattern. Rosi, Domingo, and Migenes-Johnson have filmed a labor of love.

Cat People ★ ★ ★ ½
R, 118 m., 1982

Nastassja Kinski (Irena Gallier), Malcolm McDowell (Paul Gallier), John Heard (Oliver Yates), Annette O'Toole (Alice Perrin), Ruby Dee (Female), Ed Begley, Jr. (Joe Creigh). Directed by Paul Schrader and produced by Charles Fries. Screenplay by Alan Ormsby.

It is a preposterous idea. Untold centuries ago, when all the world was a desert of wind-whipped, blood-orange sand, and leopards lounged lazily in barren trees and arrogantly ruled all they could see, a few members of the puny race of human beings made their own accommodation with the fearsome beasts. They sacrificed their women to them. And the leopards did not kill the women, but mated with them. From those mists of prehistory, the race they created lives even today: The Cat People.

These people have had a hard time of it. They have the physical appearance of ordinary humans, except for something feline around the eyes and a certain spring in their step. They have all the mortal appetites, too, but there are complications when they make love, because in the heat of orgasm they are transformed into savage black leopards and kill their human lovers. They should mate only with their own kind. But as our story opens, there are only two Cat People—and, like their parents before them, are brother and sister.

This is the stuff of audacious myth, combining the perverse, the glorious, and the ridiculous. The movies were invented to tell such stories. Paul Schrader's Cat People moves boldly between a slice-of-life in present-day New Orleans and the wind-swept deserts where the Cat People were engendered, and his movie creates a mood of doom, predestination, forbidden passion, and, to be sure, a certain silliness. It's fun in the way horror movies should be fun; it's totally unbelievable in between the times it's scaring the popcorn out of you.

Nastassja Kinski stars as the young sister, Irena. She is an orphan, reunited in New Orleans with her long-lost brother, Paul (Malcolm McDowell). She also is a virgin, afraid of sex and liquor because they might unleash the animal inside of her. (Little does she suspect that is literally what would happen.) She is tall, with a sensual mouth, wide-set green eyes, and a catlike walk. She catches the attention of the curator at the New Orleans zoo (John Heard). He senses danger in her. He also senses that this is the creature he has been waiting for all his life—waiting for her as the leopards in their cells wait, expecting nothing, ready for anything.

We have here, then, a most complex love triangle. Kinski fears her brother because she fears incest. She fears the curator but loves him. To love him is, eventually, to kill him. The curator is in love with the idea of her threat, but does not realize she *really* will turn into a leopard and rend his flesh. There are some supporting characters: Annette O'Toole is the sensible friend who senses danger, and Ed Begley, Jr. is the lackadaisical custodian whose arm is ripped from its socket. You shouldn't mess with leopards.

Schrader tells his story in two parallel narratives. One involves the deepening relationships among the sister, the brother, and the curator. The other, stunningly photographed, takes place in an unearthly terrain straight from Frank Herbert's Dune books. The designer, Ferdinando Scarfiotti, and the veteran special effects artist, Albert Whitlock, have created a world that looks completely artificial, with its drifting red sands and its ritualistic tableau of humans and leopards—and yet looks realistic in its fantasy. In other words, you know this world is made up, but you can't see the seams; it's like the snow planet in *The Empire Strikes Back*.

Cat People moves back and forth between its mythic and realistic levels, held together primarily by the strength of Kinski's performance and John Heard's obsession. Kinski is something. She never overacts in this movie, never steps wrong, never seems ridiculous; she just steps onscreen and convincingly underplays a leopard. Heard also is good. He never seems in the grip of an ordinary sexual passion, but possesses one of those obsessions men are willing (and often are called upon) to die for. *Cat People* is a good movie in an old tradition, a fantasy-horror film that takes itself just seriously enough to work, has just enough fun to be entertaining, contains elements of intrinsic fascination in its magnificent black leopards, and ends in one way just when we were afraid it was going to end in another.

Cat's Eye ★ ★ ★
PG-13, 94 m., 1985

Drew Barrymore (Our Girl), James Woods (Morrison), Alan King (Dr. Donatti), Kenneth McMillan (Cressner), Robert Hays (Norris), Candy Clark (Sally Ann). Directed by Lewis Teague and produced by Martha J. Schumacher. Written by Stephen King.

In the first of the three stories in *Cat's Eye*, James Woods wants to stop smoking. So he goes to a Smokequitters clinic run by Alan King, who locks the door behind him and demonstrates a sadistic torture chamber: A cat is placed on a steel mesh floor, and electric shocks make it leap crazily around the room.

"I don't think I understand," Woods says. "If I don't stop smoking, you'll shock a cat?"

"Not a cat," says King. "Your wife. If you have a second slip, we put your daughter in there. The third time . . . well, only about 5 percent of our clients ever have a third slip."

The crazy unreality of the situation has a *Twilight Zone* appeal, and indeed *Cat's Eye* is a superior Twilight-style anthology of three stories that are held together by the adventures of the cat. It's a small, scrappy tabby that survives not only electric shock (actually only special effects, so don't call the ASPCA), but also city traffic, falls from high buildings, one-way tickets to the pound, and a duel to the death with a gremlin who lives behind a little girl's bedroom wall.

The first story is about the smoker, who doesn't really believe that Alan King's spies are everywhere, until he finds a man in his downstairs closet. The second story, starring Robert Hays and Kenneth McMillan, keys off of our fear of heights, as McMillan forces Hays to walk along a narrow ledge all the way around a skyscraper. In one hair-raising moment borrowed from Harold Lloyd, Hays grabs an electric sign that rips loose from the building and dangles him above the

street far below. The special effects in this scene are effective tools; it really does look as if Hays is hanging above a sickening drop.

The third story is the best, however. It's told from the point of view of a little girl (Drew Barrymore), who *just knows* that there is a creature living behind her bedroom wall. Her parents think she's making it up. Meanwhile, the long-suffering tabby arrives at Barrymore's suburban home, and invites itself inside. The parents say she can't keep the cat; they feed her all those tall tales about how cats steal the breath of sleeping children. But in a thrilling climax, the cat battles the nasty little creature as the girl looks on.

All three of the stories in *Cat's Eye* depend on special effects: The electric room, the high-rise terror, the little gremlin (made by Carlo Rambaldi, who also constructed E.T. and King Kong). The special effects are effective and understated, allowing the foreground to be occupied by some of our basic human fears, of pain for loved ones, of falling from a great height, of suffocation. Stephen King seems to be working his way through the reference books of human phobias, and *Cat's Eye* is one of his most effective films.

Caveman ★ ½
PG, 92 m., 1981

Ringo Starr (Atouk), John Matuszak (Tonda), Barbara Bach (Lana), Dennis Quaid (Lar), Shelley Long (Tala), Avery Schreiber (Ock), Jack Gilford (Gog). Directed by Carl Gottlieb and produced by Lawrence Turman and David Foster. Screenplay by Rudy de Luca and Gottlieb.

Selections from "Caveman Basic," a word guide that was handed to patrons as they entered the theater to see *Caveman:*

AIEE: *Help! Save me!* ALOONDA: *Affection, desire.* BO-BO: *Man, friend, human.* CA-CA: *Excrement.* FECH: *Bad, no good, ugly.* GWEE: *To go.* HARAKA: *Fire, burning thing.* KUDA: *Come here, where are we now, this way, right here.* MA: *Me, myself.* MACHA: *Wild animal, beast, non-human.* NYA: *No, none, not happening, negative.* OOL: *Food.* POOKA: *Hurt, injured, messed up, no good.* WHOP: *Stop, whoa, hold it!* ZUG-ZUG: *Sexual intercourse.*

Selections from my thoughts after having seen the film:

Aieee! This movie is fech! We can hardly wait for the end so we can gwee. We kill time in between by eating popcorn and other ool. The movie is ca-ca. There are a few good moments, mostly involving the giant prehistoric dinosaurs and other machas, especially during zug-zug. But the movie is mostly fech, nya, and pooka, if you ask ma.

And yet *Caveman* is fairly successful, maybe because there's a real hunger for an *Airplane!*-type satirical spoof. It gets good laughs with scenes like the one where John Matuszak throws himself over a cliff along with a rock. But it has a basic problem, which is that there is no popular original material for it to satirize. There has never been a really successful movie set in prehistoric times, although God knows they've tried, with movies like *When Dinosaurs Ruled the Earth* and *Two Million Years B.C.* Those movies were self-satirizing; by the end, they were making fun of the way they started out.

Caveman seems more in the tradition of *Alley Oop*, crossed with Mel Brooks's Two Thousand Year Old Man. But the only artistic cross-reference it can manage is from the opening scene of Stanley Kubrick's *2001: A Space Odyssey*. In *Caveman*, the cavemen are shown in the process of discovering modern fire, cooking, and music. During their epochal discoveries, the sound track teases us by quoting from Strauss's "Thus Spake Zarathustra," but never quite getting it right. Why bother to rewrite Strauss? He's out of copyright.

The movie has an interesting cast—or *would* have an interesting cast, if the actors were given interesting things to do. Ringo Starr plays the leader of a wandering tribe, and onetime Oakland Raider Matuszak is the leader of the stronger tribe and the boyfriend of Barbara Bach, who wears push-up skunk skins. Ringo feels great aloonda for Bach, and whenever he sees her, zug-zug is not far from his mind. But Matuszak is the kind of guy who can break a dinosaur's drumstick in two, and so Ringo has to outsmart the big guy. Thus, intelligence is born.

It's a little depressing to realize how much time and money went into *Caveman*, an expensive production shot on location in Mexico. This very same material could have been filmed quickly and cheaply on a sound stage, since the production values are obviously not going to make us laugh any louder. And with the added flexibility and the lower stakes, maybe a little spontaneity could have crept into the film. As it stands, the filmmakers seem to learn comedy as slowly as the cavemen learn to whop before they step in the haraka.

The Changeling ★ ★ ½
R, 114 m., 1980

George C. Scott (John Russell), Trish Van Devere (Claire Norman), Melvyn Douglas (Sen. Carmichael), John Colicos (Capt. DeWitt), Jean Marsh (Mrs. Russell). Directed by Peter Medak and produced by Joel B. Michaels and Garth Drabinsky. Screenplay by William Gray and Diana Maddox.

If it only took craftsmanship to make a haunted house movie, *The Changeling* would be a great one. It has all the technical requirements, beginning with the haunted house itself. It's a vast Gothic pile somewhere near Seattle, with staircases winding up into the gloom and a hidden door to an attic room where a child's tiny wheelchair moves by itself.

George C. Scott plays the man who moves into the house. He's a composer who recently lost his wife and child in an auto accident, and he's come to Seattle to forget the past. He rents the big old house because it has a large music room. But the house turns out to be a little too well-furnished: it has a piano that plays itself, doors that open when nobody's there, and a habit of waking him up with loud thuds.

Scott begins to suspect something is wrong (you do not have to be a quick study when you live in this house). He consults the local historical society, and is informed by the society's staff crone that people were not meant to live in that house. More stuff happens. An old music box in the attic room plays a song Scott composed only that morning. There's a nightmare vision of a child being drowned. The house ghost identifies itself at a séance.

All of these developments are handled with a great deal of skill by director Peter Medak, whose credits include the insanely eccentric *The Ruling Class*. Medak is a little too fond of wide-angle shots (his choice of lenses makes all the rooms look wraparound), but he takes a good, basic approach to the haunting phenomena. This is a scare movie with taste. And yet, halfway through the movie, admiring the craft of the séance scene, I found myself wondering why I didn't really care what happened. And, as an admirer of George C. Scott's acting, I found myself thinking the unthinkable: that Scott wasn't creating a character I was really worried about.

That's because the Scott character is almost always self-possessed. He's the kind of man who can return alone to *another* haunted house after dark, climb down into a forgotten well where the bones of the original ghost have been found, and rummage around for more clues. He's too impassive. Maybe that was a deliberate acting choice, with Scott declining to indulge the tradition of overacting in ghost movies. And maybe, then, it reveals a need on our part for at least a little overacting, a few sweaty histrionics to cater to our childish scare instincts.

The Changeling does have some interesting ideas, especially one involving the present-day identity of the man who benefited from the long-ago death in the house. And it has two absolutely sensational shots, one looking down into the abandoned well from a teen-ager's cozy bedroom, and the other looking back up from the well. But it doesn't have that sneaky sense of awful things about to happen. Scott makes the hero so rational, normal, and self-possessed that we never feel he's in danger; we go through this movie with too much confidence.

Chapter Two ★ ★
PG, 124 m., 1980

James Caan (George), Marsha Mason (Jennie), Joseph Bologna (Leo), Valerie Harper (Faye), Alan Fudge (Lee), Judy Farrell (Gwen). Directed by Robert Moore and produced by Ray Stark. Screenplay by Neil Simon.

After the early loss of his first wife, playwright Neil Simon married again soon afterwards. Six months after the death, he fell in love at first sight with actress Marsha Mason, and they were married after a romance of only twenty-two days. Simon transformed those events of 1973 into an autobiographical play that opened in 1977, and now this film stars Mason in a role that is based, we guess, more or less upon herself.

Simon says the story isn't an actual record of what happened, but was just loosely inspired by his remarriage. There is no way for us to know. What we can say, on the basis of *Chapter Two*, is that if the key dialogue between husband and new wife wasn't taken from life, it is possibly taken from that wonderful category of what they *should* have said. And there is a great deal that they should have said. Simon is usually the most quick-footed and -witted of dialogue writers, but this time he gives us more than two hours of discussions, arguments, debates, reconciliations, and accusations that quickly become tedious.

The conversations in his screenplay are too long and too literal to begin with, but they suffer from two additional handicaps: (a) They do not take place between two characters whose motives have been well established, and (b) they have the misfortune to involve James Caan, who is so tense, uptight, and verbally constipated that it's a trial to wait out his speeches.

Caan plays the Simon-like character, a writer and new widower who is inconsolable in his grief until Mason happens along. Caan has previously survived a series of blind dates with the usual assortment of hopeless choices, and so Mason enchants him: She's outspoken, direct, spunky. Their first "trial date" lasts five minutes (one of those standard Hollywood "meet cutes"), and in no time at all they're in Bermuda on their honeymoon.

So far, not so bad. This is all the stuff of dependable romantic comedy, and we know where we stand. But we are about to find ourselves at sea for the rest of the movie, because the Caan character suddenly has agonizing second thoughts . . . his new bride gets on his nerves . . . he doesn't know what's bugging him . . . he's hurtful . . . he splits. The movie never really bothers itself with *why* he behaves this way, unless we're supposed to supply our own instant Freudian analysis. Caan is awkward all through this movie (he never seems happy playing this part), but he's never more lost than when he undergoes this dramatic character transformation. And you can't really blame him: Simon just hasn't given him the words or actions to make himself clear.

After the split, the rest of the movie is devoted to attempts by first one and then the other of the newlyweds to figure out what went wrong. Their scenes are so tediously top-heavy with dialogue that we can barely stand to listen. And then there's the added distraction of a parallel plot involving an affair between their best friends (Valerie Harper and Joe Bologna).

There is absolutely no rational reason why this subplot is in the movie. Maybe it made sense in the mechanics of the stage play, but it doesn't belong here. And it's all the more distracting because, whatdaya know, Bologna and Harper are much better than Caan and Mason at conjuring up the romantic and comic juices of a love affair. Their scenes are meaningless and unnecessary, but at least they're alive, and just when they get their emotional rhythm flowing, the movie cuts back to the nonstop marriage counseling session that occupies the main plot.

Chapter Two is called a comedy, maybe because that's what we expect from Neil Simon. It's not, although it has that comic subplot. It's a middlebrow, painfully earnest, overwritten exercise in pop sociology. I'm not exactly happy describing Neil Simon's semi-real-life in those terms, but then those are the terms in which he's chosen to present it. My notion is that Simon would have been wiser to imagine himself writing about another couple, and writing for another actress than his own wife; that way maybe he wouldn't have felt it so necessary to let both sides have the last word.

Chariots of Fire ★ ★ ★ ★
PG, 123 m., 1981

Ben Cross (Harold Abrahams), Ian Charleson (Eric Liddell), Nigel Havers (Lord Andrew Lindsay), Ian Holm (Coach Mussabini), Sir John Gielgud (Master of Trinity), Lindsay Anderson (Master of Caius), David Yelland (Prince of Wales), Nicholas Farrell (Aubrey Montague). Directed by Hugh Hudson and produced by David Puttnam. Screenplay by Colin Welland.

This is strange. I have no interest in running and am not a partisan in the British class system. Then why should I have been so deeply moved by *Chariots of Fire*, a British film that has running and class as its subjects? I've toyed with that question since I first saw this remarkable film in May 1981 at the Cannes Film Festival, and I believe the answer is rather simple: Like many great films, *Chariots of Fire* takes its nominal subjects as occasions for much larger statements about human nature.

This is a movie that has a great many running scenes. It is also a movie about British class distinctions in the years after World War I, years in which the establishment was trying to piece itself back together after the carnage in France. It is about two outsiders—a Scot who is the son of missionaries in China, and a Jew whose father is an immigrant from Lithuania. And it is about how both of them use running as a means of asserting their dignity. But it is about more than them, and a lot of this film's greatness is hard to put into words. *Chariots of Fire* creates deep feelings among many members of its audiences, and it does that not so much with its story or even its characters as with particular moments that are very sharply seen and heard.

Seen, in photography that pays grave attention to the precise look of a human face during stress, pain, defeat, victory, and joy. Heard, in one of the most remarkable sound tracks of any film in a long time, with music by the Greek composer Vangelis Papathanassiou. His compositions for *Chariots of Fire* are as evocative, and as suited to the material, as the different but also perfectly matched scores of such films as *The Third Man* and *Zorba the Greek*. The music establishes the tone for the movie, which is one of nostalgia for a time when two young and naturally gifted British athletes ran fast enough to bring home medals from the 1924 Paris Olympics.

The nostalgia is an important aspect of the film, which opens with a 1979 memorial service for one of the men, Harold Abrahams, and then flashes back sixty years to his first day at Cambridge University. We are soon introduced to the film's other central character, the Scotsman Eric Liddell. The film's underlying point of view is a poignant one: These men were once young and fast and strong, and they won glory on the sports field, but now they are dead and we see them as figures from long ago.

The film is unabashedly and patriotically British in its regard for these two characters, but it also contains sharp jabs at the British class system, which made the Jewish Abrahams feel like an outsider who could sometimes feel the lack of sincerity in a handshake, and placed the Protestant Liddell in the position of having to explain to the peeved Prince of Wales why he could not, in conscience, run on the Sabbath. Both men are essentially proving themselves, their worth, their beliefs, on the track. But *Chariots of Fire* takes an unexpected approach to many of its running scenes. It does not, until near the film's end, stage them as contests to wring cheers from the audience. Instead, it sees them as *efforts*, as endeavors by individual runners—it tries to capture the exhilaration of running as a celebration of the spirit.

Two of the best moments in the movie: A moment in which Liddell defeats Abrahams, who agonizingly replays the defeat over and over in his memory. And a moment in which Abrahams' old Italian-Arabic track coach, banned from the Olympic stadium, learns who won his man's race. First he bangs his fist through his straw boater, then he sits on his bed and whispers, "My son!"

All of the contributions to the film are distinguished. Neither Ben Cross, as Abrahams, nor Ian Charleson, as Liddell, are accomplished runners but they are accomplished actors, and they *act* the running scenes convincingly. Ian Holm, as Abrahams' coach, quietly dominates every scene he is in. There are perfectly observed cameos by John Gielgud and Lindsay Anderson, as masters of Cambridge colleges, and by David Yelland, as a foppish, foolish young Prince of Wales. These parts and others make up a greater whole.

Chariots of Fire is one of the best films of recent years, a memory of a time when men still believed you could win a race if only you wanted to badly enough.

Cheech and Chong's Next Movie ★
R, 99 m., 1980

Richard Marin (Cheech), Thomas Chong (Chong), Evelyn Guerrero (Donna), Betty Kennedy (Candy), Sy Kramer (Mr. Neatnik), Rikki (Gloria). Directed by Thomas Chong and produced by Howard Brown. Screenplay by Chong and Marin.

The problem with your average dope movie is that you have to be stoned to get the jokes. That's because there aren't any jokes. The movie has the giggles, and if the audience is in the same chemical euphoria it gets the giggles, too. Sitting there straight and just watching the movie is kind of a sad experience, because the movie's not intrinsically funny. It's one of those things where you hadda be there.

Cheech and Chong's Next Movie is an experience like that, a movie that's not particularly funny unless you happen to be laughing anyway—in which case, you don't need the movie. It's a formless, shapeless, thoughtless mess of a comedy that tries to sneak through by flattering its audience that everybody's in on the same joke.

There's a subtle blackmail at work here: If you're not laughing, does that mean you missed the point? The movie's invitation is clear. It stars Cheech and Chong, two cult comedians, one Mexican-American, one Chinese-Canadian, whose anti-establishment, pothead credentials are impeccable. Since what they're doing is funny (by their own definition), if we don't laugh that makes us part of the problem instead of part of their solution. Half the people in the basic Cheech and Chong audience are stoned (kids stoke up for this one), and they laugh, so the movie's funny, right?

Well, no. You might get a contact high from the Cheech and Chong fans, but you won't get one from the screen. This movie is embarrassing. There's no invention in it, no imagination, no new comic vision, no ideas about what might be *really* funny—instead of just dope-funny, something to laugh at if you're in the bag anyway. I didn't see *Up in Smoke*, Cheech and Chong's first movie, which grossed something like $60 million. But could it have been this bad?

Cheech and Chong's Next Movie is directed by Chong himself; he no doubt got the job, without any previous directing experience, because of the Hollywood wisdom that says if you gross $60 million you're obviously a genius in all fields. Chong isn't a genius as a director. The movie's jokes aren't funny anyway, but he sabotages them with inept camera placement: There's a gag involving a magic trick with a handkerchief, and Chong mangles the punch line by cutting to a long shot so far away from the action we almost miss it. There's no rhythm in the movie, no sense of an overall idea about the material, and when the movie ends abruptly and unexpectedly, the audience is a little surprised: Is that all?

Now, I have to report that the audience did laugh a lot at the performance I attended. Why? Maybe because Cheech and Chong portray complete, stoned irresponsibility as a life-style, and borderline idiocy as a behavioral style. I was reminded of my own childhood slapstick comedy heroes, Huntz Hall and the Bowery Boys, who also spent whole movies acting dumb and getting into trouble.

But there's a difference between Cheech and Chong and the Bowery Boys. The Boys acted silly and goofy because they were supposed to *be* silly and goofy—it was an end in itself. The gag with Cheech and Chong is that they're drug addicts. As a guy I know once said, it's not nice to laugh at dopeheads if you're not one, and not funny to laugh at them if you are one.

Choose Me ★ ★ ★ ½
R, 106 m., 1984

Genevieve Bujold (Dr. Love), Keith Carradine (Mickey), Lesley Ann Warren (Eve), Patrick Bauchau (Zack), Rae Dawn Chong (Pearl). Directed by Alan Rudolph and produced by Carolyn Pfeiffer and David Blocker. Screenplay by Rudolph.

Apart from its other qualities, which are many, Alan Rudolph's *Choose Me* is an audaciously intriguing movie. Its main purpose, indeed, may be to intrigue us—as other films aim to thrill or arouse or mystify. There is hardly a moment in the whole film when I knew for sure what was going to happen next, yet I didn't feel manipulated; I felt as if the movie were giving itself the freedom to be completely spontaneous.

The movie begins with strangers talking to each other. One of the strangers is a radio talk show host. Her name is Dr. Love, and she gives advice to the lovelorn over the radio (most of her advice seems to be variations on "That's not my problem"). One of her regular callers, we learn, is a woman named Eve who owns a bar. One day a mental patient named Mickey, a guy whose past seems filled with mysterious connections to the CIA, the space program, and the Russians, walks out of a closed ward and into the bar and meets Eve. A few days later, Dr. Love, hoping to do some research into the ways that we ordinary folk live, adopts an assumed name and goes looking for a roommate. She finds Eve and moves in with her, and neither woman knows who the other woman really is. They also don't make the connection that Eve is a regular caller to the radio program (highly unlikely, since she speaks with an accent). None of this is really as hard to follow as it sounds. And since one of the pleasures of this movie is the leisurely and logical way it explores the implications of mistaken identity, I'm not going to write another word about the confusions the characters get involved in.

Choose Me is a deliberate throwback to the *film noir* of the 1940s—to those movies made up of dark streets and wet pavements, hookers under streetlamps, pimps in shiny postwar Studebakers, and people who smoke a lot. It's also about lonely people, but it's not one of those half-witted TV movies about singles bars and single women. It's about smart, complicated people who are trying to clear a space for themselves and using romance as an excavating tool. The performances are key to this strategy. The best thing in the movie is Genevieve Bujold's performance as Dr. Love. She is interesting, if detached, as the radio personality, but when love finally does touch her life, she is so unabashedly open and confessional and red-faced and sincere that we want to hug her. Bujold just gets better and better; coming so soon after her good work in *Tightrope*, this is a reminder of how many different kinds of roles she can play so well.

Keith Carradine is the drifter with the dangerous past. We are never quite sure how seriously to take him, and that's the idea behind his performance, I think: He is able to quite sincerely tell two different women he loves them and wants to marry them, and the funny thing is, we believe him, both times. Eve, the former hooker who owns a bar, is played by Lesley Ann Warren. It's another good performance, nervous and on-edge; she's the kind of woman who seeks a different man every night as a protection against winding up with the same guy for a whole lifetime in a row. There are other intriguing characters in this story, most notably Rae Dawn Chong as a cute young alcoholic with a weird marriage, a naive way of trusting strangers, and dreamy plans of becoming a poet someday. Her husband (Patrick Bauchau) begins to get real tired of seeing the Carradine character, who through a series of misunderstandings seems to specialize in robbing him of poker pots, dates, and the attentions of his wife.

All of these people interact throughout the whole movie without *Choose Me* ever settling into familiar patterns. It's as if Rudolph wanted to tell a story as it might actually have happened, with coincidental meetings, dumb misunderstandings, random chance, and the endless surprises of human nature. At the end of the movie we haven't learned anything in particular, but we have met these people and their loneliness and punch-drunk optimism, and we have followed them a little time through the night.

Christiane F. ★ ★ ★ ½
R, 124 m., 1982

Natja Brunkhorst (Christiane), Thomas Haustein (Detlev), Jens Kuphal (Axel), Reiner Wolk (Leiche). Directed by Ulrich Edel and produced by Bernd Eichinger and Hans Weth.

This is one of the most horrifying movies I have ever seen. The fact that it's based on actual events makes it heartbreaking. *Christiane F.* is the portrait of a young girl who between her thirteenth and fifteenth years went from a fairly average childhood into the horrors of drug addiction, prostitution, and life on the brink of death.

The movie has become notorious in Europe, where both the film and book versions of Christiane's adventures have been bestsellers. The real Christiane first came to light as a witness in the trial of a man accused of having sex with minors. A reporter at the trial was intrigued by her appearance on the witness stand and tracked her down. His tape-recorded interviews with her became

the basis for a twelve-part series in *Stern*, the German news magazine, which inspired the movie.

It is one of the most unremittingly grim portraits of drug addiction ever filmed. The only American equivalent that comes to mind is Shirley Clarke's *The Connection* (1961), but in that film the hell of heroin addiction was tempered by the story construction of the film, which evolved as a well-told play. *Christiane F.* simply evolves as one lower plateau of suffering after another, until Christiane hits a low bottom.

The movie opens with Christiane as an unexceptional young teen-ager, given to such minor vices as playing rock records too loud and staying out too late. She lives in an apartment with her mother and resents the regular presence of her mother's boyfriend. With friends, she experiments with alcohol and pot, and them, after a rock concert (David Bowie, playing himself), she sniffs some heroin, "just out of curiosity." She likes the feeling it gives her. She tries to get it again. She has young friends who are already junkies, but she disregards their warnings that she'll get hooked. She mindlessly repeats the addict's ageless claim: "I can't get hooked if I just use a little, only once in a while. I can control my using." She cannot. Before long, she's shooting heroin, and not much longer after that she is selling her body to buy it.

This is a common story in the big cities of the world. It is relatively unusual among girls as young as Christiane (I hope), but even more unusual is the fact that she finds her own way into the heroin-and-hooker underground, without being enslaved by a pimp. The movie is relentless in depicting the drug culture of West Berlin. We see unspeakable sights: a junkie leaping over a toilet stall to yank the needle from Christiane's arm and plunge it into his own, stealing her fix; Christiane and her boyfriend trying to withdraw cold turkey and vomiting all over one another; the discovery of dead overdose victims, and, unforgettably, the pale, sad faces of the junkies lined up in a subway station, all hope gone from their once-young eyes.

Christiane F. made lots of the "best ten" lists of European critics in 1982, but I found it hard to judge its artistic quality because of the shockingly bad dubbing job. The film has been dubbed into mid-Atlantic British, by voices that are often clearly too old and in slang that is ten to fifteen years out of date. New World should ask for its money back from the dubbers. And yet—the movie still works. After a time we forget the bad dubbing, because the images are so powerful, the horrors so strong and the performances (by a cast of young unknowns) so utterly, bleakly, realistic. This is a movie of hell.

Christine ★ ★ ★
R, 110 m., 1983

Keith Gordon (Arnie), John Stockwell (Dennis), Alexandra Paul (Leigh), Robert Prosky (Garage owner), Harry Dean Stanton (Junkins). Directed by John Carpenter and produced by Richard Kobritz. Screenplay by Bill Phillips.

I've seen a lot of movies where the teen-age guy parks in a car with the girl he loves. This is the first one where he parks with a girl in the car he loves. I knew guys like this in high school. They spent their lives customizing their cars. Their girlfriends were accessories who ranked higher, say, than foam-rubber dice, but lower than dual carbs.

The car is named *Christine*. It's a bright red 1958 Plymouth Fury, one of those cars that used to sponsor the "Lawrence Welk Show," with tail fins that were ripped off for the *Jaws* ad campaign. This car should have been recalled, all right—to hell. It kills one guy and maims another before it's off the assembly line. Its original owner comes to a sad end in the front seat. And later, when Christine is twenty-one years old and rusting away, Arnie buys her. Arnie is a wimp. He's the kind of guy you'd play jokes on during lunch period, telling him the class slut wanted to talk to him, and then hiding his lunch tray while she was telling him to get lost. The kind of guy who was always whining, "Come on, guys—the joke's over!" But after Arnie buys Christine, he undergoes a strange metamorphosis. He becomes cool. He starts looking better. He stops with the greasy kid stuff. He starts going out with the prettiest girl in the school. That's where he makes his mistake. Christine gets jealous.

The entire movie depends on our willingness to believe that a car can have a mind of its own. I have believed in stranger things in the movies. Christine can drive around without a driver, play appropriate 1950s rock songs, lock people inside, and repair its own crushed fenders. The car is another inspiration from Stephen King, the horror novelist who specializes in thrillers about everyday objects. We saw his *Cujo*, about a rabid St. Bernard, and any day now I expect him to announce *Amityville IV: The Garage Door-Opener.*

Christine is, of course, utterly ridiculous. But I enjoyed it anyway. The movies have a love affair with cars, and at some dumb elemental level we enjoy seeing chases and crashes. In fact, under the right circumstances there is nothing quite so exhilarating as seeing a car crushed, and one of the best scenes in *Christine* is the one where the car forces itself into an alley that's too narrow for it.

Christine was directed by John Carpenter, who made *Halloween*, and his method is to take the story more or less seriously. One grin and the mood would be broken. But by the end of the movie, Christine has developed such a formidable personality that we are actually taking sides during its duel with a bulldozer. This is the kind of movie where you walk out with a silly grin, get in your car, and lay rubber halfway down the freeway.

A Christmas Story ★ ★ ★
PG, 94 m., 1983

Melinda Dillon (Mrs. Parker), Darren McGavin (The Old Man), Peter Billingsley (Ralphie). Directed by Bob Clark and produced by Rene Dupont and Clark. Screenplay by Jean Shepherd, Leigh Brown, and Clark.

Of course. That's what I kept saying during *A Christmas Story*, every time the movie came up with another one of its memories about growing up in the 1940s. Of course, any nine-year-old kid in the '40s would passionately want, for Christmas, a Daisy Brand Red Ryder repeating BB carbine with a compass mounted in the stock. Of course. And of course, his mother would say, "You'll shoot your eye out." That's what mothers always said about BB-guns. I grew up in downstate Illinois. The hero of this film, Ralphie, grew up in Gary, Ind. Looking back over a distance of more than thirty years, the two places seem almost identical—Middle American outposts where you weren't trying to keep up with the neighbors, you were trying to keep up with Norman Rockwell.

The movie is based on a nostalgic comic novel named *In God We Trust, All Others Pay Cash*, by Jean Shepherd, the radio humorist, who also narrates it. He remembers the obvious things, like fights with the bullies at school, and getting into impenetrable discussions with younger kids who do not quite know what all the words mean. He remembers legendary schoolteachers and hiding in the cupboard under the sink and having fantasies of defending the family home with a BB-gun.

But he also remembers, warmly and with love, the foibles of parents. The Old Man in *A Christmas Story* is played by Darren McGavin as an enthusiast. Not an enthusiast of anything, just simply an enthusiast. When he wins a prize in a contest, and it turns out to be a table lamp in the shape of a female leg in a garter, he puts it in the window, because it is the most amazing lamp he has ever seen. Of course. I can understand that feeling. I can also understand the feeling of the mother (Melinda Dillon), who is mortified beyond words.

The movie's high point comes at Christmastime, when Ralphie (Peter Billingsley) goes to visit Santa Claus. Visits to Santa Claus are more or less standard in works of this genre, but this movie has the best visit to Santa I've ever seen. Santa is a workaholic, processing kids relentlessly. He has one helper to spin the kid and deposit him on Santa's lap, and another one to grab the kid when the visit is over, and hurl him down a chute to his parents below. If the kid doesn't want to go, he gets Santa's boot in his face. Of course.

City Heat ½★
PG, 94 m., 1984

Clint Eastwood (Lieutenant Speer), Burt Reynolds (Mike Murphy), Jane Alexander (Addy), Madeline Kahn (Caroline Howley), Rip Torn (Prime Pitt), Irene Cara (Ginny Lee). Directed by Richard Benjamin and produced by Fritz Maners. Screenplay by Sam O. Brown and Joseph C. Stinson.

Sometimes you get the idea that the deal behind a movie was so complicated and exhausting that they just didn't have the strength left to make the movie itself. *City Heat*, for example, stars two of the top box-office attractions in the recent history of Hollywood: Clint Eastwood and Burt Reynolds. It was originally going to be directed by Blake Edwards, but he was fired after "creative differences" with the two stars, and then several other directors were approached before Richard Benjamin agreed to pick up the reins. The depth of Edwards's feelings about the whole episode can be guessed from the *nom de plume* he used for his original screenplay credit, "Sam O. Brown." Check the initials.

We will never know what Edwards might have made of *City Heat*. That's bad enough. What's worse is that we can barely tell what Benjamin made of it. This movie is a confusing mess with a plot so pointless that there's a fight scene every ten minutes, just to distract us. The movie's so bewildered it doesn't even seem sure about the relationship between Eastwood and Reynolds: Are they really enemies, or just friends who talk tough to one another, or are they former friends who became enemies and are now becoming friends again? And does it matter?

The movie's a period gangster picture, with lots of antique cars and mustaches and snap-brim fedora hats. Eastwood plays a police detective who is mild-mannered, and somebody crosses him, and then he turns into a ferocious fighting machine. Reynolds is a former cop who is now a private eye. Early in the film, he goes to his office for consultations with Richard Roundtree and Jane Alexander, and it is a measure of the film's confusion that when he mentions his partner, we are not quite sure which one he means. There are other loose ends. For example, Reynolds kisses Alexander tenderly, but then she goes on a date with Eastwood. The guys go to a boxing match that has no logical purpose other than to serve as a setup for a meeting *after* the match. A criminal gang, headed by Rip Torn, will kill to get its hands on a box that contains . . . what? Ledger records, I think. Of illegal gambling debts, I think. You know a movie is desperately in trouble when the audience isn't even sure what the bad guys are after.

There are a lot of talented people in this movie, including Irene Cara in a throwaway role as a nightclub singer, and Madeline Kahn in her basic performance as a Dietrich-esque vamp. There are also incessant fight scenes and shoot-outs, in which the bad guys are consistently unable to hit the side of a barn, and Eastwood is incapable of missing. All of this is maybe supposed to be an ironic commentary on Eastwood's Dirty Harry character, but so what? Almost every scene in the movie seems to have been a separate inspiration, thrown in with no thought for the movie as a whole.

How do travesties like this get made? I have a feeling the problem starts at the level of negotiations, in which everybody protects his own turf, and the movie suffers. There are moments here when you want to squirm, especially when Clint Eastwood allows his incomparable screen persona to be parodied. The Dirty Harry movies themselves border on parody—that's part of their charm—but they know what they're doing. *City Heat* is a movie in which people almost obviously don't have a clue.

City of Women ★ ★ ½
R, 140 m., 1981

Marcello Mastroianni (Snaporaz), Ettor Manni (Dr. Zberkock), Anna Prucnal (Elena), Bernice Stegers (Woman on Train), Donatella Damiani (Feminist on Skates). Directed by Federico Fellini. Screenplay by Fellini and Bernardino Zapponi.

If there is one central image in the work of Federico Fellini, it's of Fellini's autobiographical hero being smothered by women. They come in all shapes and ages, from old crones to young innocents, from heavybreasted mother figures to seductive nymphs. One of Fellini's favorite strategies is to gather all the women into one fantasy and place his hero at the center of it. That's what he did in the celebrated harem sequence in 8½, and that's what he does throughout *City of Women*.

There is, however, an additional twist this time. Since the basic Fellini universe was created in *La Strada*, *La Dolce Vita*, 8½, and *Juliet of the Spirits*, beliefs about the role of women have undergone a revolution, even in Italy. It is no longer enough that Fellini deal with the ways women tantalize, dominate, and possess his male heroes. Now he must also deal with the women themselves. For Fellini, this is probably not nearly so much fun. His idea of a liberated woman is fairly clear from the wife-character in 8½ (1963). She is severe, wears tailored suits and horn-rim glasses, and wants to spoil all the fun. Fellini's hero, in that film and in *City of Women*, is named Guido, is played by Marcello Mastroianni, and wants to escape from the horn-rim types and lose himself in the capacious bosom of a thoroughly undemanding sex object.

At the beginning of *City of Women*, however, Guido finds himself riding on a train across from a severe-looking woman in a tailored suit. He tries to seduce her. She sentences him to an imaginary odyssey through a series of sexual fantasies, most of them devoted to the unpleasant fates of men who do not have the correct attitude about women. Most of these fantasies, and indeed many of the specific images, are familiar to anyone who has seen several Fellini films. There is a long circus chute for Mastroianni to tumble down (*Juliet*), and a group of circus scenes (from half his other films), and a wall covered with portraits (remember *Fellini Roma*?), and an insatiable satyr, and, of course, the full-lipped, full-bosomed, smiling and inexhaustible temptress who turns up, in one manifestation or another, throughout Fellini.

City of Women does nothing original or very challenging with this material. Although it pretends to be Fellini's film about feminism, it reveals no great understanding of the subject; Fellini basically sees feminists as shrill harems of whip-wielding harridans, forever dangling the carrot of sex just out of reach of his suffering hero. Fellini has rarely been able to discover human beings hidden inside his female characters, and it's a little late for him to start blaming that on the women's liberation movement.

Is *City of Women* worth seeing? Yes, probably, even though it is not a successful movie and certainly not up to Fellini's best work. It's worth seeing because it's a bedazzling collection of images, because at times it's a graceful and fluid celebration of pure filmmaking skill, and because Fellini can certainly make a bad film but cannot quite make a boring one.

Clash of the Titans ★ ★ ★ ½
PG, 118 m., 1981

Harry Hamlin (Perseus), Judi Bowker (Andromeda), Burgess Meredith (Ammen), Laurence Olivier (Zeus), Maggie Smith (Thetis), Neil McCarthy (Calibos). Directed by Desmond Davis and produced by Charles H. Schneer and Ray Harryhausen, with special effects created by Harryhausen.

Clash of the Titans is a grand and glorious romantic adventure, filled with grave heroes, beautiful heroines, fearsome monsters, and awe-inspiring duels to the death. It is a lot of fun. It was quite possibly intended as a sort of Greek mythological retread of *Star Wars* (it has a wise little mechanical owl in it who's a third cousin of R2-D2), but it's also part of an older Hollywood tradition of special-effects fantasies, and its visual wonderments are astonishing.

The story, on the other hand, is robust and straightforward. Perseus (Harry Hamlin) is locked into a coffin with his mother and cast into the sea, after she has angered the gods. But Zeus (Laurence Olivier) takes pity and sees that the coffin washes ashore on a deserted island, where Perseus grows to manhood and learns of his mission in life. The mission, in a nutshell, is to return to Joppa and rescue Andromeda (Judi Bowker) from a fate worse than death: marriage to the hideously ugly Calibos, who was promised her hand in marriage before he was turned into a monster by the wrath of the gods. Calibos lives in a swamp and dispatches a gigantic, scrawny bird every night to fetch him the spirit of the sleeping Andromeda in a gilded cage. If Perseus is to marry Andromeda, he must defeat Calibos in combat and also answer a riddle posed by Cassiopeia, Andromeda's mother. Those who answer the riddle incorrectly are condemned to die. Love was more complicated in the old days.

There are, of course, other tests. To follow the bird back to the lair of Calibos, the resourceful Perseus must capture and tame Pegasus, the last of the great winged horses. He must also enter the lair of Medusa, who turns men to stone with one glance, and

behead her so that he can use her dead eyes to petrify the gargantuan monster Kraken, who is unchained from his cage on the ocean floor so that he can ravish Joppa in general and Andromeda in particular.

All of this is gloriously silly. But because the movie respects its material, it even succeeds in halfway selling us this story; movies that look like *Clash of the Titans* have a tendency to seem ridiculous, but this film has the courage of its convictions. It is also blessed with a cast that somehow finds its way past all the monsters and through all the heroic dialogue and gets us involved in the characters. Harry Hamlin is a completely satisfactory Perseus, handsome and solemn and charged with his own mission. Judi Bowker is a beautiful princess and a great screamer, especially in the scene where she's chained to the rock and Kraken is slobbering all over her. Burgess Meredith has a nice little supporting role as Ammon, an old playwright who thinks he may be able to turn all of this into a quick epic. And Laurence Olivier is just as I have always imagined Zeus: petulant, but a pushover for a pretty face.

The real star of the movie, however, is Ray Harryhausen, who has worked more than forty years as a creator of special effects. He uses combinations of animation, miniatures, optical tricks, and multiple images to put humans into the same movie frames as the most fantastical creatures of legend, and more often than not, they look pretty convincing: when Perseus tames Pegasus, it sure looks like he's dealing with a real horse (except for the wings, of course).

Harryhausen's credits include *Mighty Joe Young*, *Jason and the Argonauts*, and *The Golden Voyage of Sinbad*, but *Clash of the Titans* is his masterwork. Among his inspired set-pieces: the battle in the Medusa's lair, with her hair writhing with snakes; the flying horse scenes; the gigantic prehistoric bird; the two-headed wolf-dog, Dioskilos; the Stygian witches; and, of course, Kraken, who rears up from the sea and causes tidal waves that do a lot of very convincing damage to a Greek city that exists only in Harryhausen's art. The most lovable special-effects creation in the movie is little Bubo, a golden owl sent by the gods to help Perseus in his trials. Bubo whistles and rotates his head something like R2-D2 in *Star Wars,* and he has a similar personality, too, especially at the hilarious moment when he enters the film for the first time.

Clash of the Titans is a family film (there's nothing in it that would disturb any but the most impressionable children), and yet it's not by any means innocuous: It's got blood and thunder and lots of gory details, all presented with enormous gusto and style. It has faith in a story-telling tradition that sometimes seems almost forgotten, a tradition depending upon legends and myths, magical swords, enchanted shields, invisibility helmets, and the overwhelming power of a kiss.

Class ★ ★
R, 98 m., 1983

Jacqueline Bisset (Ellen), Rob Lowe (Skip), Andrew McCarthy (Jonathan), Cliff Robertson (Mr. Burroughs), Stuart Margolin (Balaban), Gary Houston (Salesman), Remak Ramsey (Headmaster). Directed by Lewis John Carlino and produced by Martin Ransohoff. Screenplay by Jim Kouf and David Greenwalt.

Class is a prep-school retread of *The Graduate* that knows some of its scenes are funny and some are serious, but never figures out quite how they should go together. The result is an uncomfortable, inconsistent movie that doesn't really pay off—a movie in which everything points to two absolutely key scenes that are, inexplicably, the two most awkward scenes in the film.

You'll understand the movie's problems when I tell you that the plot involves a love affair starring a preppy who finds out, too late, that his lover also is the mother of his roommate. How, you are asking, *how* can I give away such a crucial point? The answer is, because the movie's ads were devoted to revealing that very point.

We know going into the movie that young Jonathan (Andrew McCarthy) and Mrs. Burroughs (Jacqueline Bisset) are doomed to meet, make love, and make some embarrassing discoveries about each other. That knowledge is nearly fatal to the film. It tells us things we don't want to know, affecting our view of important early scenes in the film. It also places a lot of importance on the

two key scenes: (1) The scene when Jonathan discovers that Mrs. Burroughs is his roommate Skip's mother, and (2) the scene where Skip discovers that his roommate and his mother are lovers.

Now how should those two scenes play? As comedy? As detached social observation? As farce? *Class* doesn't seem to know. The first discovery is made when Skip invites his roommate home for the holidays, and there's a pained dinner party scene that doesn't have a satisfactory ending. The second discovery is made when Skip bursts into his pal's hotel room, finds his mother in the sack, and then is left by the screenplay with nothing appropriate to say or do. I guess it doesn't matter, since the movie resolves this embarrassment between friends by having them fight and make up.

Class seems contrived out of two different approaches to the material. It contains a lot of funny scenes, including some early prep-school practical jokes and some good characterizations of headmasters, teachers, and school clowns. But it never seems really confident around its love scenes; Bisset and McCarthy are in bed at the same time, all right, but they don't seem together. And it doesn't help to make Bisset an alcoholic with emotional problems; if she's ill, how can we laugh at her behavior, even when the movie cues us?

Then there's a disturbing subplot involving cheating on exams: The point here seems to be that friendship involves not ratting on your friend, even when he's sleeping with your mother. The ethical questions got so muddled, I gave up. In fact, the whole movie got so muddled that I lost interest. There were merry pranksters in one scene, and neurotic drunks in the next, and characters who were struck speechless by situations that absolutely demanded a verbal response. The movie is entertaining when it's not dealing with its real subject matter, painful when it is, and agonizing when it confuses rigid mortification with humor. *Class* makes you appreciate how difficult it must have been to make *The Graduate.*

The Class of 1984 ★ ★ ★ ½
R, 93 m., 1982

Perry King (Andy Norris), Timothy Van Patten (Stegman), Roddy McDowell (Terry

Corrigan). Directed by Mark Lester and produced by Lester and Merrie Lynn Ross. Screenplay by Lester, John Saxton, and Tom Holland.

Movies like this either grab you, or they don't. *The Class of 1984* grabbed me. I saw it for the first time at the 1982 Cannes Film Festival, where I wandered into the theater expecting to find the dog of the week and wandered out two hours later, a little dazed and sort of overwhelmed. *The Class of 1984* is not a great movie but it works with quiet, strong efficiency to achieve more or less what we expect from a movie with such a title. It is violent, funny, scary, contains boldly outlined characters, and gets us involved. It also has a lot of style. One of the reasons for the film's style may be that it was made by people who knew what they were doing. The whole Dead Teen-ager genre has been seriously weakened in the last several years by wave upon wave of cheap, idiotic tax shelter films from Canada and elsewhere: films in which a Mad Slasher and a lot of screaming adolescents have been substituted for talent, skill, and craft—movies such as *Prom Night* and *Terror Train* and *The Burning*.

Mark Lester's *The Class of 1984* stands head and shoulders above movies like that. It tells a strong, simple story. It is acted well. It is not afraid to be comic at times and, even better, it's not afraid at the end to pull out all the stops and give us the sort of Grand Guignol conclusion that the slasher movies always botch. You may or may not think it's any good, but you'll have to admit that it works.

The movie stars Perry King, a skilled actor who has survived a lot of junk, as a music teacher who takes a job at a big city high school. The first day he walks into class, he faces trouble, and trouble is personified by Stegman (Timothy Van Patten), the brilliant but crazed leader of the high school gang. Stegman dresses as a cross between a punk rocker and a Hell's Angel. He terrorizes half the school with his violence and mesmerizes the other half with his charisma. He also happens to be a brilliant musician. King tries to deal with him, reason with him, outthink him, and even outmuscle him, but the kid is strong, smart, and mean. The

other teachers and the school officials have mostly surrendered to the reign of terror. A few put up a fight, most memorably the biology teacher, played by Roddy McDowell. He has one of the great scenes in the movie as he pulls a gun on his class and invites them to share with him the joys of education, or else.

The movie builds toward one of those nightmarish conclusions where everything's happening at once. While the teacher prepares to lead his school orchestra in a concert, the thugs terrorize his helpless wife at home. The teacher turns the baton over to his best student, a shy young girl, and goes off to do battle with the punks. After a great deal of blood has been shed, the teacher and the gang leader are finally face to face, high in the wings over the high school auditorium stage, and the climax is a cross between *The Hunchback of Notre Dame* and *Beyond the Valley of the Dolls*.

The Class of 1984 has received some really savage criticism. Newsweek called it "*The Class of 1982* with herpes." What does that mean? I dunno. I guess it means the critic found the movie so hateful that it wasn't worth anything more than cheap wisecracks. But unless we can accept talent wherever we find it in the movies, and especially in smaller genre movies without big stars, we're going to be left with nothing but overpriced lead balloons and delicate little exercises in sensibility. *The Class of 1984* is raw, offensive, vulgar, and violent, but it contains the sparks of talent and wit, and it is acted and directed by people who cared to make it special.

Close Encounters of the Third Kind: The Special Edition ★ ★ ★ ★
PG, 152 m., 1980

Richard Dreyfuss (Roy Neary), Francois Truffaut (Claude Lacombe), Teri Garr (Ronnie Neary), Melinda Dillon (Jillian Guiler).
Directed and written by Steven Spielberg and produced by Julia Phillips and Michael Phillips.

Close Encounters of the Third Kind: The Special Edition is the movie Steven Spielberg wanted to make in the first place. The changes Spielberg has made in his original 1978 film are basic and extensive, adding up to essentially a new moviegoing experience. Spielberg's changes fall into four categories:

• He's provided an entirely new conclusion, taking us inside the alien spaceship that visits at the end of the film.

• He's provided more motivation for the strange behavior of the Richard Dreyfuss character—who is compelled by "psychic implanting" to visit the Nevada mountain where the spaceship plans to land.

• He's added additional manifestations of UFO intervention in earthly affairs—including an ocean-going freighter deposited in the middle of the Gobi Desert.

• In addition to the sensational ending, he's added more special effects throughout the film. One shot seems like a light-hearted quote from Spielberg's own *Jaws*. In that film, a high-angle shot showed the shadow of the giant shark passing under a boat. In this one, a high-angle shot shows the shadow of a giant UFO passing over a pickup truck.

Spielberg's decision to revise the original version of *Close Encounters* is all but unprecedented. Some directors have remade their earlier films (Hitchcock did British and American versions of *The Man Who Knew Too Much*), and others have thought out loud about changes they'd like to make (Robert Altman wanted to edit a nine-hour version of *Nashville* for TV). And countless directors, of course, have given us sequels—"part two" of their original hits.

Spielberg's *Special Edition* is sort of a *Close Encounters: Part 1½*. It is also a very good film. I thought the original film was an astonishing achievement, capturing the feeling of awe and wonder we have when considering the likelihood of life beyond the Earth. I gave that first version a four-star rating. This new version gets another four stars: It is, quite simply, a better film—so much better that it might inspire the uncharitable question, "Why didn't Spielberg make it this good the *first* time?"

His changes fall into three categories. He has (1) thrown away scenes that didn't work, like the silly sequence in which Dreyfuss dug up half of his yard in an attempt to build a model of the mountain in his vision; (2) put in scenes he shot three years ago but did not use, such as the Gobi sequence and Dreyfuss flipping out over the strange compulsion that has overtaken him, and (3) shot some entirely new scenes.

The most spectacular of these is the new ending, which shows us what Dreyfuss sees when he enters the spacecraft. He sees a sort of extraterrestrial cathedral, a limitless interior space filled with columns of light, countless sources of brilliance, and the machinery of an unimaginable alien technology. (The new special effects were designed by the underground artist R. Cobb, I understand; no credit is given.) This new conclusion gives the movie the kind of overwhelming final emotional impact it needed; it adds another dimension to the already impressive ending of the first version.

The movie gains impact in another way. Spielberg has tightened up the whole film. Dead ends and pointless scenes have been dropped. New scenes do a better job of establishing the characters—not only of Dreyfuss, but also of Francois Truffaut, as the French scientist. The new editing moves the film along at a faster, more absorbing pace to the mind-stretching conclusion. *Close Encounters*, which was already a wonderful film, now transcends itself; it's one of the great moviegoing experiences. If you've seen it before, I'm afraid that now you'll have to see it again.

Coal Miner's Daughter ★ ★ ★
PG, 125 m., 1980

Sissy Spacek (Loretta Lynn), Tommy Lee Jones (Mooney Lynn), Beverly D'Angelo (Patsy Cline), Levon Helm (Ted Webb), Phyllis Boyens (Clara Webb). Directed by Michael Arted and produced by Bernard Schwarts. Screenplay by Tom Rickman.

What improbable lives so many Americans lead, compared to the more orderly and predictable careers of the Swedes, say, or the French. It's not just that we're the most upwardly mobile society in history, we're the most mobile, period: We go to ruin as swiftly and and dramatically as we hit the jackpot. No wonder one of our favorite myths involves a rags to riches story in which success then destroys the hero.

Look at country music star Loretta Lynn. If we can believe *Coal Miner's Daughter* (and

I gather that, by and large, we can), here's a life which began in the poverty of the coalfields of Kentucky and led almost overnight to show-business stardom. And what's astonishing is that it wasn't even really planned that way: Loretta learned to play on a pawnshop guitar, her husband thought she could sing, and one day she just sorta found herself on stage. The movie's about Loretta Lynn's childhood, her very early marriage, her quick four kids, her husband's move to Washington State looking for a job, her humble start in show business, her apparently quick rise to stardom, and then the usual Catch-22 of self-destructivenss.

We're not surprised, somehow, that right after the scenes where she becomes a superstar, there are scenes where she starts using pills, getting headaches, and complaining that everybody's on her case all the time. We fiercely want to believe in success in this country, but for some reason we also want to believe that it takes a terrible human toll. Sometimes it does—and that always makes for a better story. Straightforward success sagas, in which the heroes just keep on getting richer, are boring. We want our heroes to suffer. We like to identify—it makes stars more human, somehow, if they get screwed by Valium, too.

What's refreshing about *Coal Miner's Daughter* is that it takes the basic material (rags to riches, overnight success, the onstage breakdown, and, of course, the big comeback) and relates them in wonderfully human terms. It's fresh and immediate. That is due most of all to the performance by Sissy Spacek as Loretta Lynn. With the same sort of magical chemistry she's shown before, when she played the high school kid in *Carrie*, Spacek at twenty-nine has the ability to appear to be almost any age onscreen. Here she ages from about fourteen to somewhere in her thirties, always looks the age, and never seems to be wearing makeup. I wonder if she does it with her posture; early in the film, as a poor coal miner's kid, she slouches and slinks around, and then later she puts on dignity with the flashy dresses she wears onstage.

The movie is mostly about Lynn's relationships with her husband, Mooney (played by Tommy Lee Jones), and her first close show-business friend and mentor, Patsy Cline (Beverly D'Angelo). Both of these relationships are developed in direct, understated, intelligent ways; we are spared, for example, a routine portrait of Mooney Lynn as Official Show Biz Husband, and given instead a portrait of a recognizable human being who is aggressive, confident, loving, and fallable. The fact that this movie felt free to portray Mooney as hard-nosed is one of the most interesting things about it: Loretta Lynn, who had a certain amount of control over the project, obviously still has her feet on the ground and didn't insist that this movie be some kind of idealized fantasy.

We are left to speculate, of course, on whether Lynn's rise to stardom was really as picaresque as *Coal Miner's Daughter* suggests. She seems to get on the Grand Ole Opry mighty fast, and Patsy Cline seems to adopt her almost before she knows her. But then the amazing thing about Loretta Lynn's life seems to be how fast everything happened, and how wide open the avenues to success are in this country—if you're talented and, of course, lucky.

The most entertaining scenes in the movie are in the middle, after the coal mines and before the Top 40, when Loretta and Mooney are tooling around the back roads trying to convince country disc jockeys to play her records. The scene with Mooney taking a publicity photo of Loretta is a little gem illustrating the press agent that resides within us all.

So, anyway . . . how good *is* this movie? I think it's one of those films people like so much while they're watching it that they're inclined to think it's better than it is. It's warm, entertaining, funny, and centered around that great Sissy Spacek performance, but it's essentially pretty familiar material (not that Loretta Lynn can be blamed that Horatio Alger wrote her life before she lived it). The movie isn't great art, but it has been made with great taste and style; it's more intelligent and observant than movie biographies of singing stars used to be. That makes it a treasure to watch, even if we sometimes have the feeling we've seen it before.

Code of Silence ★ ★ ★ ½
R, 102 m., 1985

Chuck Norris (Eddie Cusack), Henry Silva (Luis Comacho), Bert Remsen (Commander

Kates), Mike Genovese (Tony Luna), Molly Hagan (Diana Luna), Nathan Davis (Felix Scalese), Ralph Roody (Cragie). Directed by Andy Davis and produced by Raymond Wagner. Screenplay by Michael Butler, Dennis Shryack, and Mike Gray.

Chuck Norris is still identified with a series of grade-zilch karate epics, but *Code of Silence* is a heavy-duty thriller—a slick, energetic movie with good performances and a lot of genuine human interest. It grabs you right at the start with a complicated triple-cross, and then it develops into a stylish urban action picture with sensational stunts. How sensational? How about an unfaked fight on top of a speeding elevated train, ending when both fighters dive off the train into the Chicago River? The stunts are great, but not surprising; Chuck Norris is famous for the stunts he features in all of his movies. What is surprising is the number of interesting characters in *Code of Silence*. The screenplay doesn't give us the usual cardboard clichés; there's a lot of human life here, in a series of carefully crafted performances. For once, here's a thriller that realizes we have to care about the characters before we care about their adventures.

Norris stars as a veteran Chicago vice cop named Cusack. He's a straight arrow, an honest cop that his partners call a "one-man army." As the film opens, he's setting up a drug bust, but a Latino gang beats him to it, stealing the money and the drugs and leaving a roomful of dead gangsters. That sets off a Chicago mob war between the Italian and Latino factions, and as bodies pile up in the streets, Cusack begins to worry about the daughter of a Mafia chieftain—a young artist named Diana (Molly Hagan) who wants nothing to do with her father's business, but finds she can't be a bystander. After an elaborate cat-and-mouse chase through the Loop, she's kidnapped and Cusack wants to save her.

Meanwhile, the movie has an interesting subplot about a tired veteran cop (Ralph Roody) who has mistakenly shot and killed a Latino kid while chasing some mobsters through a tenement. The veteran's young partner (Joseph Guzaldo) watches him plant a gun on the dead kid and claim that the shooting was in self-defense. It's up to the

rookie, backed up by Cusack, to decide what he'll say at the departmental hearing.

The movie has a knack for taking obligatory scenes and making them more than routine. Among the small acting gems in the movie is the performance of Chicago actor Nathan Davis as Felix Scalese, a wrinkled, wise old Mafia godfather who sits on his yacht and counsels against a mob war—to no avail. Mike Genovese plays the mob chief whose daughter is kidnapped, and his first scene, as he wishes his wife a happy birthday while hurrying out the door to do battle, is wonderfully timed. Roody has some nice scenes as the tired old cop, hanging around a bar talking big and looking scared.

Holding all of the performances together is Norris's work as Cusack. Bearded, dressed in jeans for undercover street duty, and driving a battered old beater, Norris seems convincing as a cop—with, of course, the degree of heroic exaggeration you need in a role like this. By the end of the film, when he is reduced to functioning as a one-man army, we can't really believe the armored robot tank that he brings into action, but, what the hell, we accept it. Norris resembles Clint Eastwood in his insistence on the barest minimum of dialogue; there's a scene where he quietly, awkwardly tries to comfort the mobster's daughter, and it rings completely true. He also seems to be doing a lot of his own stunts, and although the credits list a lot of stuntmen and they were all obviously kept busy, it looks to me like that's really Norris on top of that elevated train.

The movie was directed by Andy Davis, who was a cinematographer on Haskell Wexler's 1968 Chicago film *Medium Cool*, and returned to some of the same locations to film this picture. Davis's directorial debut was the low-budget *Stony Island* (1977), which had moments of truth and insight but nothing like the assurance he shows this time; *Code of Silence* is a thriller so professional that it has the confidence to go for drama and humor as well as thrills. It may be the movie that moves Norris out of the ranks of dependable action heroes and makes him a major star.

Come Back to the 5 & Dime, Jimmy Dean, Jimmy Dean ★ ★ ★
PG, 109 m., 1982

Sandy Dennis (Mona), Cher (Sissy), Karen Black (Joanne), Sudie Bond (Juanita), Kathy Bates (Stella Mae), Marta Heflin (Edna). Directed by Robert Altman and produced by Scott Bushnell. Screenplay by Ed Graczyk.

If Robert Altman hadn't directed this movie, the reviews would have described it as Altmanesque. It's a mixture of the bizarre and the banal, a slice of lives that could never have been led, a richly textured mixture of confessions, obsessions, and surprises.

The movie takes place in a worn-out Woolworth's in a small Texas town not far from the locations where James Dean shot *Giant* in 1955. The story begins twenty years later, at a reunion of the local James Dean fan club; the members swore a solemn vow to get together after two decades, and they drift in one by one, greeted by the tired waitress who's still on duty. There's Sandy Dennis, the flaky, visionary local woman who's convinced that she bore a son by James Dean. Then Cher walks in—looking not like the glamorous Cher of television, but like a small-town sexpot unsure of her appeal. The last arrival is Karen Black, who drove in all the way from California, and is not surprised when nobody recognizes her at first.

The fan club members and a few local good ol' girls join in a long afternoon of memories, nostalgia, self-analysis, accusation, shocking revelations, and anger, while heat-lightning flickers offscreen. And their memories trigger flashbacks to the time twenty years earlier when the proximity of James Dean served as a catalyst in all of their lives, giving some the courage to realize their dreams and others, the timid ones, the courage at least to dream them.

Jimmy Dean was a Broadway play before it was a movie, and Altman, who directed it first on stage, stays pretty close here to Ed Graczyk's script. He works just as closely with David Gropman's extraordinary stage set, on which the movie was shot. Gropman has actually created two dime stores, one a mirror-image of the other. They're separated by a two-way mirror, so that at times we're looking at the reflection of the "front" store, and at other times, the glass is transparent and we see the second store. Altman uses the front as the present and the back as the past, and there are times when a foreground image will dissolve into a background flashback. In an age of sophisticated optical effects, this sort of dissolve looks routine—until you learn that Altman isn't using opticals, he's actually shooting through the two-way mirror. His visual effects sometimes require fancy offscreen footwork for his actors to be in two places during the same shot.

Jimmy Dean's script also requires some fancy footwork, as we reel beneath a series of predictable revelations in the last twenty minutes. This is not a great drama, but two things make the movie worth seeing: Altman's visual inventiveness and the interesting performances given by everyone in the cast. Although Sandy Dennis and Karen Black in many ways have more difficult roles, Cher is the one I watched the most because her performance here is a revelation. After years and years of giving us "Cher," she gives us a new character here, in a fine performance that creates sympathy for a sexpot who doubts her own sensuality.

The Company of Wolves ★ ★ ★
R, 95 m., 1985

Angela Lansbury (Granny), David Warner (Father), Graham Crowden (Old Priest), Brian Glover (Amorous Boy's Father), Catherine Pogson (Young Bride), Stephen Rea (Young Groom). Directed by Neil Jordan and produced by Chris Brown and Stephan Woolley. Screenplay by Angela Carter and Jordan.

A wolf is sometimes much more than he seems.—Granny

The key word there is "he." There are no female wolves in this film, or at least not in the leading roles. The wolves are all male, and the males are almost all wolves. Granny warns her young granddaughter to beware of men whose eyebrows meet, for in the full of the moon their hidden natures are likely to emerge, and they will have fangs, and sharp claws, and eyes that glow in the dark. The girl believes her, but she still puts on her red hood and walks through the woods to grandmother's house, and is surprised by what big teeth Granny has.

The Company of Wolves is a dream about werewolves and little girls and deep, dark forests. It is not a children's film and it is not an exploitation film; it is a disturbing and stylish attempt to collect some of the nightmares that lie beneath the surface of "Little Red Riding Hood." The movie begins in the present, but quickly enters the dreams of an adolescent girl. She dreams many variations on the same theme: That men may turn out to be wolves, and that little girls should never, ever, stray from the path through the woods. The movie creates its dream world on British sound stages, which have been used to make a gloomy, fantastical universe filled with gnarled trees, wicked thorn bushes, clammy mists, tortuous paths, and birds' nests filled with mirrors and lipsticks, and eggs that don't have chicks inside of them. In this world, the characters tell each other stories. All of the stories begin with those delicious words, "Once upon a time." Granny (Angela Lansbury) tells most of the stories to her granddaughter, but the girl tells stories too, and after one of them her mother says, "Granny knows a great deal, but she doesn't know everything. And if there is a beast inside every man, he meets his match in the beast inside of every woman."

Most of the stories seem to take place in the nineteenth century, in a dark forest that encircles frightened and ignorant peasants. In the night, they light great torches and go out into the woods to trap the wolves, but when they cut off a giant paw as a trophy and bring it home and look at it, they are holding a severed human hand. Wolves are men, and men are wolves, and the message that repeats itself over and over in *The Company of Wolves* is that the bridegroom may be loving and handsome on his wedding night, but should he step into the light of the moon, he may turn into a hairy demon with glowing eyes.

The movie is based on a novel and a screenplay by Angela Carter, who has taken Red Riding Hood as a starting-place for the stories, which are secretly about the fearsomeness of sexuality. She has shown us what those scary fairy tales are really telling us; she has filled in the lines and visualized the parts that the Brothers Grimm left out (and they did not leave out all that many parts). The movie has an uncanny, hypnotic force; we always know what is happening, but we rarely know why, or how it connects with anything else, or how we can escape from it, or why it seems to correspond so deeply with our guilts and fears. That is, of course, almost a definition of a nightmare.

The Competition ★ ★ ★
PG, 125 m., 1981

Richard Dreyfuss (Paul Dietrich), Amy Irving (Heidi Schoonover), Lee Remick (Greta Vandemann), Sam Wanamaker (Erskine). Directed and written by Joel Oliansky and produced by William Sackheim.

The Competition is a cornball, romantic, old-fashioned, utterly predictable movie—and enormously entertaining. It's the kind of movie where you speculate on what's going to happen next, and usually you're right. When you're wrong, somehow *that's* predictable, too, as in the big international piano competition that ends the movie. We think we know who's going to win, but the surprise ending is a built-in convention of this kind of movie.

The movie's about a big international competition in San Francisco among six world-class pianists who are fighting for a $20,000 first prize and a two-year concert contract. The movie has two counterpoints to its main theme. One involves a love affair between two of the finalists, Richard Dreyfuss and Amy Irving. The other one, ridiculous but forgivable, involves a Russian piano teacher who defects to the United States, creating an international incident that causes the competition to be postponed a week.

Both of these story lines are somehow time-honored, once we realize that *The Competition* is not intended as a deadly serious treatise on big-league pianists, but as an offbeat love story. Dreyfuss and Amy Irving have a real charm and rapport as the two lovers, especially in the scenes where they argue that love has absolutely no place in a piano competition—not if it's being used as a psychological weapon to undermine one of the competitors. That's exactly what Amy Irving's piano coach (Lee Remick) thinks the dastardly Dreyfuss is trying to do.

There are three areas that the movie gets into, superficially but earnestly. One has to do with the competition itself—with the idea of artists competing with one another. Another has to do with relationships between men and women: Will the love affair between Amy and Richard be destroyed if she should win? How will his fragile male ego be able to take that? The third has to do with the idea of the artist's career, and here Remick has several good scenes and intelligently written speeches, as she tries to explain the realities of a concert career to Irving.

There is, of course, a lot of music in this movie, in addition to all the scenes of romance, backstage butterflies, international intrigue, and self-examination. And *The Competition* does an extraordinary job of persuading us that the actors are really playing their own pianos. They're not. Stay for the credits if you want the names of the real pianists on the sound track. But Dreyfuss, Irving, and the rest really *look* as if they're playing, and it took them four months of daily rehearsal to learn to fake it so well.

The Competition isn't a great movie, but it's a warm, entertaining one. It has the nerve to tell a story about serious, interesting, complicated people, who are full of surprises, because Joel Oliansky, the writer-director, has thought about them and cared enough about them to let their personalities lead him down unexpected avenues. There's only one major lapse: the inclusion, after two hours of great piano compositions, of Lalo Schifrin's dreadful song, "People Alone," sung by Randy Crawford over the end titles as if none of those great composers should be allowed to rest in peace.

Conan the Barbarian ★ ★ ★
R, 129 m., 1982

Arnold Schwarzenegger (Conan), James Earl Jones (Thulsa Doom), Max von Sydow (King Osric), Sandahl Bergman (Valeria), Ben Davidson (Rexor). Directed by John Milius and produced by Buzz Feitshans and Rafaella de Laurentiis. Screenplay by Milius and Oliver Stone.

Not since Dumbo's mother was killed has there been a cannier movie for kids than *Conan the Barbarian*. It's not supposed to be just a kids' movie, of course, and I imagine a lot of other moviegoers will like it—I liked a lot of it myself, and with me, a few broadswords and leather jerkins go a long way. But *Conan* is a perfect fantasy for the alienated preadolescent. Consider: Conan's parents are brutally murdered by the evil Thulsa Doom, which gets *them* neatly out of the way. The child is chained to the Wheel of Pain, where he goes around in circles for years, a metaphor for grade school. The kid builds muscles so terrific he could be a pro football player. One day he is set free. He teams up with Subotai the Mongol, who is an example of the classic literary type—the Best Pal—and with Valeria, Queen of Thieves, who is a *real* best pal.

Valeria is everything you could ever hope for in a woman, if you are a muscle-bound preadolescent, of course. She is lanky and muscular and a great sport, and she can ride, throw, stab, fence, and climb ropes as good as a boy. Sometimes she engages in sloppy talk about love, but you can tell she's only kidding, and she quickly recovers herself with coverup talk about loyalty and betrayal—emotions more central to Conan's experience and maturity.

With the Mongol and the Queen at his side, Conan ventures forth to seek the evil Thulsa Doom and gain revenge for the death of his parents. This requires him to journey to the mysterious East, where he learn a little quick kung-fu, and then to the mountainside where Doom rules his slave-priests from the top of his Mountain of Power. There are a lot of battles and a few interesting nights at crude wayside inns and, in general, nothing to tax the unsophisticated. *Conan the Barbarian* is, in fact, a very nearly perfect visualization of the Conan legend, of Robert E. Howard's tale of a superman who lived beyond the mists of time, when people were so pure, straightforward, and simple that a 1930s pulp magazine writer could write about them at one cent a word and not have to pause to puzzle out their motivations.

The movie's casting is ideal. Arnold Schwarzenegger is inevitably cast as Conan, and Sandahl Bergman as Valeria. Physically, they look like artist's conceptions of themselves. What's nice is that they also create entertaining versions of their characters; they, and the movie, are not without humor and a certain quiet slyness that is never allowed to get out of hand. Schwarzenegger's slight Teutonic accent is actually even an advantage, since Conan lived, of course, in the eons before American accents.

The movie is a triumph of production design, set decoration, special effects and makeup. At a time when most of the big box-office winners display state-of-the-art technology, *Conan* ranks right up there with the best. Ron Cobb, the sometime underground cartoonist who did the production design on this film (and on *Alien*) supervises an effort in which the individual frames actually do look like blowups of panels from the Marvel Comics "Conan" books. Since this Conan could have so easily looked ridiculous, that's an accomplishment.

But there is one aspect of the film I'm disturbed by. It involves the handling of Thulsa Doom, the villain. He is played here by the fine black actor James Earl Jones, who brings power and conviction to a role that seems inspired in equal parts by Hitler, Jim Jones, and Goldfinger. But when Conan and Doom meet at the top of the Mountain of Power, it was, for me, a rather unsettling image to see this Nordic superman confronting a black, and when Doom's head was sliced off and contemptuously thrown down the flight of stairs by the muscular blonde Conan, I found myself thinking that Leni Reifenstahl could have directed the scene, and that Goebbels might have applauded it.

Am I being too sensitive? Perhaps. But when Conan appeared in the pulps of the 1930s, the character suggested in certain unstated ways the same sort of Nordic superrace myths that were being peddled in Germany. These days we are more innocent again, and Conan is seen as a pure fantasy, like his British cousin, Tarzan, or his contemporary, Flash Gordon. My only reflection is that, at a time when there are *no* roles for blacks in Hollywood if they are not named Richard Pryor, it is a little unsettling to see a great black actor assigned to a role in which he is beheaded by a proto-Nordic avenger.

That complaint aside, I enjoyed *Conan*. Faithful readers will know I'm not a fan of Sword & Sorcery movies, despite such adornments as Sandahl Bergman—having discovered some time ago that heaving bosoms may be great, but a woman with a lively intelligence and a sly wit is even greater.

The problem with *Conan* is the problem with all S & S movies. After the initial premise (which usually involves revenge) is established, we suspect there's little to look forward to *except* the sets, special effects, costumes, makeup, locations, action, and surprise entrances. Almost by definition, these movies exclude the possibility of interesting, complex characters. I'd love to see them set loose an intelligent, questing, humorous hero in one of these prehistoric sword-swingers. Someone at least as smart as, say, Alley Oop.

Conan the Destroyer ★ ★ ★
PG, 103 m., 1984

Arnold Schwarzenegger (Conan), Grace Jones (Zula), Wilt Chamberlain (Bombaata), Mako (The Wizard), Tracey Walter (Malak), Sarah Douglas (Queen). Directed by Richard Fleischer and produced by Raffaella de Laurentiis. Screenplay by Stanley Mann.

What you can see in *Conan the Destroyer*, if you look closely, is the beginning of a movie dynasty. This is the film that points the way to an indefinite series of Conan adventures—one that could even replace Tarzan in supplying our need for a noble savage in the movies. Tarzan was more or less stuck in Africa; Conan can venture wherever his sword and sorcery can take him. The first Conan movie, *Conan the Barbarian*, was a dark and gloomy fantasy about the shadows of prehistory. This second film is sillier, funnier, and more entertaining. It doesn't take place before the dawn of time, but instead in that shadowy period of movie history occupied by queens and monsters, swords and castles, warriors and fools. There's more Prince Valiant and King Arthur than *Quest for Fire*.

And Conan is defined a little differently, too. He doesn't take himself as seriously. He's not just a muscle-bound superman, but a superstitious half-savage who gets very nervous in the presence of magic. Arnold Schwarzenegger, who plays Conan again, does an interesting job of defining his pop hero: Like James Bond, Conan now stands a little aside from the incessant action around him, and observes it with a bit of relish. The story this time involves the usual nonsense. Conan is recruited by an imperious queen (Sarah Douglas, looking vampirish) to take a virgin princess (Olivia D'Abo) on a mission to an enchanted crystal palace guarded by a monster, etc. He will be joined on his quest by the head of the queen's palace guard (Wilt Chamberlain). And along the way he rescues a savage woman warrior (Grace Jones) and earns her undying gratitude.

Let's face it. The Conan series does not require extraordinary acting ability, although Schwarzenegger provides a sound professional center to the story, and the film would be impossible if he couldn't carry off Conan. The characters around him, however, are basically atmosphere, and that frees the filmmakers to abandon the usual overexposed Hollywood character actors and go for really interesting types like Chamberlain and Jones. And Grace Jones is really sensational. She has all the flash and fire of a great rock stage star, and it fits perfectly into her role as Zula, the fierce fighter. Sarah Douglas provides the necessary haughty iciness as the queen, Chamberlain gives a good try at the thankless role of the turncoat guard, and only D'Abo is a disappointment: Her princess seems to have drifted in from a teen-age sitcom.

Conan the Destroyer is more entertaining than the first Conan movie, more cheerful, and it probably has more sustained action, including a good sequence in the glass palace. Compared to the first Conan movie, which was rated R for some pretty gruesome violence, this one is milder. That's part of the idea, I think: They're repackaging Conan as your friendly family barbarian.

Continental Divide ★ ★ ★
PG, 103 m., 1981

John Belushi (Souchak), Blair Brown (Nell), Allen Goorwitz (Howard), Carlin Glynn (Sylvia), Tony Ganios (Possum), Val Avery (Yablonowitz). Directed by Michael Apted and produced by Bob Larson. Written by Lawrence Kasdan.

Here is a movie that is supposed to be about a newspaperman—a columnist for the *Chicago Sun-Times*, in fact—who is like no newspaperman I know, but exactly like every newspaperman would like to be. In my opinion, that makes it accurate. *Continental Divide* stars John Belushi as the journalist, obviously inspired by Mike Royko. He likes to walk along the lakeshore with the towers of the city outlined behind him against the lonely sky at dusk, a notebook stuck in his pocket and a cigarette stuck in his mug, on his way to rendezvous with stoolie aldermen and beautiful women.

The movie takes this character, played by Belushi with a surprising tenderness and charm, and engages him in an absolute minimum of newspaper work before spiriting him off to the Rocky Mountains for what the movie is *really* about, a romance with an eagle expert. The movie opens as if it's going to be a tough Chicago slice-of-life, with Belushi getting tips from an insider about city graft and payola, but then the columnist is beaten up by a couple of cops on an alderman's payroll. The managing editor suggests this might be a good time for Belushi to spend a few weeks out of town, and so the columnist heads for the Rockies to get an interview with a mysterious and beautiful woman (Blair Brown) who has generated worldwide curiosity by becoming a hermit to spy on the habits of bald eagles.

The whole center section of the movie takes place in the mountains, and if nothing very original happens there, we are at least reminded of several beloved movie clichés that seemed, until this film, to belong exclusively in the comedies that Katharine Hepburn and Spencer Tracy used to make together. After the city slicker Belushi crawls wearily up a mountainside (losing his booze and cigarette supply in the process), he meets the beautiful birdwatcher and falls instantly in love. She's having none of it. She's one of those independent women who marches from crag to aerie in her L.L. Bean boots and designer wardrobe.

Because Belushi's grizzled mountain guide already has disappeared down the mountain, the two of them are destined to spend the next two weeks together in a cabin. This sets up a classic situation in which the girl talks tough but starts to fall for the big lunkhead. And there are the obligatory switches on male-female roles as

Brown climbs mountains and Belushi stays home and makes goulash. Occasionally, a mountain lion attacks.

This all sounds predictable, of course, and yet this movie's predictability is one of its charms. It's rare these days to find a film that is basically content to be about a colorful man and an eccentric woman who are opposites and yet fall madly in love. It is even rarer to find a movie cast with performers who are offbeat and appealing and do not have obvious matinee-idol appeal. Belushi's character in this movie is quite unlike his self-destructive slob in *National Lampoon's Animal House;* it shows the gentleness and vulnerability that made him so appealing in some of Second City's quieter skits. Brown is also a revelation. She has been in several other movies without attracting a great deal of attention, but here she is unmistakably and wonderfully a star, a tousled-haired, big-eyed warm person who does not project sex appeal so much as warmth and humor. In other words, she has terrific sex appeal.

One of Belushi's special qualities was always an underlying innocence. Maybe he created his Blues Brothers persona in reaction to it. He's an innocent in this movie, an idealist who's a little kid at heart and who wins the love of Brown not by seducing her but by appealing to her protective qualities. That's the secret of the character's appeal. We're cheering for the romance because Belushi makes us protective, too, and we want him to have a woman who'd be good for him.

What about the movie's view of journalism? It's really just a romanticized backdrop, *The Front Page* crossed with "Lou Grant" and modernized with a computerized newsroom. The newspaper scenes in the movie were shot on location in the *Sun-Times* features department, and one of the quietly amusing things about *Continental Divide*'s view of newspaper life is that in the movie it's more sedate and disciplined than the real thing. In the "real" *Sun-Times* features department, there's a lot of informality and chaos and good-natured confusion and people shouting at one another and eating lunch at their desks. In the movie, the extras (recruited from the *Sun-Times* staff) forget about real life and sit dutifully at their video display terminals, grinding out the news.

The newspaper's managing editor is played by Allen Goorwitz, a gifted character actor who usually plays manic overcompensators, but who this time is reasonable, calm, civilized, compassionate, and understanding, just like my boss. The movie's city of Chicago is populated by colorful old newsstand operators, muggers who apologize before taking your watch, and city council bosses who make sure their shady deals don't get into the official transcript. The newsies and muggers are fiction. The movie itself is fun: goofy, softhearted, fussy, sometimes funny, and with the sort of happy ending that columnists like to find for their stories and hardly ever find themselves.

The Cotton Club ★ ★ ★ ★
R, 121 m., 1984

Richard Gere (Dixie Dwyer), Gregory Hines (Sandman Williams), Diane Lane (Vera Cicero), Lonette McKee (Lila Rose Oliver), Bob Hoskins (Owney Madden), James Remar (Dutch Schultz), Fred Gwynne (Frenchy). Directed by Francis Ford Coppola and produced by Robert Evans. Screenplay by William Kennedy and Coppola.

After all the rumors, all the negative publicity, all the stories of fights on the set and backstage intrigue and imminent bankruptcy, Francis Ford Coppola's *The Cotton Club* is, quite simply, a wonderful movie. It has the confidence and momentum of a movie where every shot was premeditated—and even if we know that wasn't the case, and this was one of the most troubled productions in recent movie history, what difference does that make when the result is so entertaining?

The movie takes place in New York in the 1920s and 1930s, where Irish and Jewish gangsters battled the Italians for the rackets. Most of their intrigues were played out in public, in flashy settings like the Cotton Club, a Harlem nightclub that featured the nation's most talented black entertainers on stage—playing before an all-white audience. By telling us two love stories, Coppola shows us both sides of that racial divide. He begins by introducing Dixie Dwyer (Richard Gere), a good-looking young musician who saves the life of a gangster and is immediately recruited into the hood's inner circle.

There he meets the gangster's teen-age girlfriend (Diane Lane), and they immediatley fall in love—but secretly, because they'll live longer that way. Then we meet Sandman Williams (Gregory Hines), a black tap dancer who dreams of appearing at the Cotton Club, and falls in love with a member of the chorus line (Lonette McKee), a mulatto who talks about her secret life among people who think she is white.

The two love stories are developed against a background of a lot of very good jazz, some great dancing, sharply etched character studies of the gang bosses, and a couple of unexpected bursts of violence that remind us, in their sudden explosion, of moments in Coppola's *Godfather* films. Indeed, there's a lot of *The Godfather* in *The Cotton Club*, especially in the movie's almost elegiac sadness: We get the feeling of time passing, and personal histories being written, and some people breaking free and other people dying or surrendering to hopelessness.

There's another reminder of *The Godfather* movies, and that's in the brilliant, in-depth casting. There's not an uninteresting face or a boring performance in this movie, but two supporting characters really stand out: Bob Hoskins, as a crooked club owner named Madden, and Fred Gwynne, as a towering hulk named Frenchy. They are friends. They also are criminal associates. Hoskins is a bantamweight filled with hostility; Gwynne is a giant with a deep voice and glowering eyes. After Gwynne is kidnapped and Hoskins pays the ransom, the scene between the two of them begins as a routine confrontation and unfolds into something surprisingly funny and touching.

Coppola has a way, in this film, of telling all the different stories without giving us the impression he's jumping around a lot. Maybe the music helps. It gives the movie a continuity and an underlying rhythm that makes all of the characters' lives into steps in a sad ballet. We like some of the characters, but we don't have much respect for them, and the movie doesn't bother with clear distinctions between good and evil. *The Cotton Club* is a somewhat cynical movie about a very cynical time, and along with the music and the romance there is racism, cruelty, betrayal, and stunning violence. Romance with a cutting edge.

The performances are well-suited to the material. Richard Gere is especially good as Dixie Dwyer, maybe because the camera has a way of seeing him off-balance, so that he doesn't dominate the center of each shot like a handsome icon; Coppola stirs him into the action. Diane Lane, herself still a teen-ager, is astonishing as the party girl who wants to own her own club. Gregory Hines and his brother, Maurice, create a wonderful moment of reconciliation when they begin to tap dance and end by forgiving each other for a lifetime's hurts. And Hoskins, the British actor who played the unforgettable mob chief in *The Long Good Friday*, is so wound-up and fierce and funny as the mobster that he takes a cliché and turns it into an original.

The Cotton Club took months to shoot, and they claim they have another 200,000 feet of footage as good as this movie. I doubt it. Whatever it took to do it, Coppola has extracted a very special film out of the checkered history of this project.

Country ★ ★ ★ ½
PG, 108 m., 1984

Jessica Lange (Jewell Ivy), Sam Shepard (Gil Ivy), Wilford Brimley (Otis Stewart), Matt Clark (Tom McMullen), Therese Graham (Marlene Ivy), Levi L. Knebel (Carlisle Ivy). Directed by Richard Pearce and produced by William D. Wittliff and Jessica Lange. Screenplay by Wittliff.

The opening moments of *Country* show a woman frying hamburgers and wrapping them up and sending them out to her men, working in the fields. The movie is using visuals to announce its intentions: It wants to observe the lives of its characters at the level of daily detail and routine, and to avoid pulling back into "Big Country" cliché shots. It succeeds. This movie observes ordinary American lives carefully, and passionately. The family lives on a farm in Iowa. Times are hard, and times are now. This isn't a movie about symbolic farmers living in some colorful American past. It is about the farm policies of the Carter and Reagan administrations, and how the movie believes that those policies are resulting in the destruction of family farms. It has been so long since I've seen a Hollywood film with specific political beliefs that a funny thing happened: The movie's anger moved me as much as its story.

The story is pretty moving, too. We meet the members of the Ivy family: Jewell Ivy (Jessica Lange), the farm wife; her husband, Gil (Sam Shepard); her father, Otis (Wilford Brimley), and the three children, especially Carlisle (Levi L. Knebel), the son who knows enough about farming to know when his father has given up. The movie begins at the time of last year's harvest. Some nasty weather has destroyed part of the yield. The Ivys are behind on their FHA loan. Ordinarily, that would be no tragedy; farming is cyclical and there are good years and bad years, and eventually they'll catch up with the loan. But this year is different. An FHA regional administrator, acting on orders from Washington, instructs his people to enforce all loans strictly, and to foreclose when necessary. He uses red ink to write his recommendation on the Ivy's loan file: *Move toward voluntary liquidation.* Since there is no way the loan can be paid off, the Ivys will lose the land that Jewell's family has farmed for one hundred years. The farm agent helpfully supplies the name of an auctioneer.

All of this sounds just a little like the dire opening chapters of a story by Horatio Alger, but the movie never feels dogmatic or forced because *Country* is so clearly the particular story of these people and the way they respond. Old Otis is angry at his son-in-law for losing the farm. Jewell defends her husband, but he goes into town to drink away his impotent rage. There are loud fights far into the night in a house that had been peaceful. The boy asks, "Would somebody mind telling me what's going on around here?"

The movie's strongest passages deal with Jewell's attempts to enlist her neighbors in a stand against the government. The most touching scenes, though, are the ones showing how abstract economic policies cause specific human suffering, cause lives to be interrupted, and families to be torn apart, all in the name of the balance sheet. *Country* is as political, as unforgiving, as *The Grapes of Wrath.*

The movie has, unfortunately, one important area of weakness, in the way it handles the character of Gil (Shepard). At the beginning we have no reason to doubt that he is a good farmer. Later, the movie raises ques-

tions about that assumption, and never clearly answers them. Gil starts drinking heavily, and lays a hand on his son, and leaves the farm altogether for several days. The local farm agent tells him, point blank, that he's a drunk and a bad farmer. Well, is he? In an affecting scene where Gil returns and asks for the understanding of his family, his drinking is not mentioned. It's good that the movie tries to make the character more complex and interesting—not such a noble hero—but if he really is a drunk and a bad farmer, then maybe that's why he's behind on the loan. The movie shouldn't raise the possibility without dealing with it.

In a movie with the power of *Country*, I can live with a problem like that because there are so many other good things. The performances are so true you feel this really is a family; we expect the quality of the acting by Lange, Shepard, and gruff old Brimley, but the surprise is Levi L. Knebel, as the son. He is so stubborn and so vulnerable, so filled with his sense of right when he tells his father what's being done wrong, that he brings the movie an almost documentary quality; this isn't acting, we feel, but eavesdropping.

Creepshow ★ ★ ★
R, 129 m., 1982

Hal Holbrook (Henry Northrup), Adrienne Barbeau (Wilma Northrup), Fritz Weaver (Dexter Stanley), Leslie Nielsen (Richard Vickers), Carrie Nye (Sylvia Graham), E.G. Marshall (Upson Pratt), Viveca Lindfors (Aunt Bedelia). Directed by George A. Romero and produced by Richard P. Rubinstein. Screenplay by Stephen King.

Creepshow plays like an anthology of human phobias. What could be more horrifying that sticking your hand into a long-forgotten packing crate and suddenly feeling teeth sink into you? Unless it would be finding yourself buried up to the neck on the beach, with the tide coming in? Or trapped in an old grave, with the tombstone toppling down on top of you? Or having green stuff grow all over you? Or how about being smothered by cockroaches?

The horrors in *Creepshow* are universal enough, and so is the approach. These stories have been inspired, right down to the very camera angles, by the classic EC Comics of the early 1950s—titles like "Tales from the Crypt," which curdled the blood of Eisenhower-era kids raised on such innocent stuff as Captain Marvel, and appalled their elders. (EC Comics almost single-handedly inspired the creation of the Comics Code Authority.) The filmmakers of *Creepshow* say they were raised on those old comics, and it would appear that their subsequent careers were guided by the Ol' Crypt-Keeper's bag of tales. The movie's director is George A. Romero, whose most famous credit is *Night of the Living Dead*, and the original screenplay is by Stephen King, who wrote *Carrie* and *The Shining*. What they've done here is to recapture not only the look and the storylines of old horror comics, but also the peculiar feeling of poetic justice that permeated their pages. In an EC horror story, unspeakable things happened to people—but, for the most part, they deserved them.

The five stories told in this film often center around a fatal flaw. Upson Pratt, for example, the hero of the fifth story, is a compulsively neat and tidy man who lives in a hermetically sealed command center, much like Howard Hughes. What could be more suitable than an invasion of his stronghold by cockroaches? The professors in the story about the thing in the box have spent their lives collecting old facts: how perfect that one long-collected piece of evidence should still bite back!

Romero and King have approached this movie with humor and affection, as well as with an appreciation of the macabre. They create visual links to comic books by beginning each segment with several panels of a comic artist's version of the story, and then dissolving from the final drawn panel to a reality that exactly mirrors it. The acting also finds the right note. Such veterans of horror as Hal Holbrook, E.G. Marshall, and Adrienne Barbeau know how to paint their personalities broadly, edging up to caricature. Nobody in this movie is a three-dimensional person, or is meant to be. They are all types. And their lives are all object lessons.

The original full name of EC Comics was "Educational Comics," and you got an education, all right. You learned it was unwise to stick your hand into a box labeled "Danger—Do Not Open." It was unwise to speak ill of the dead. And it was quite unwise to assume that cockroaches would never decide to gang up and fight back.

Crimes of Passion ★ ½
R, 102 m., 1984

Kathleen Turner (Joanna/China Blue), Anthony Perkins (Shayne), John Laughlin (Grady), Annie Potts (Amy). Directed by Ken Russell and produced by Barry Sandler. Screenplay by Sandler.

I like what George Burns said about his sex life: "I got more laughs in bed than I ever got in vaudeville." Sex is an activity of great and serious importance to its participants, but as a spectator sport it has a strange way of turning into comedy. Look, for example, at Ken Russell's overwrought film *Crimes of Passion*, in which good performances and an interesting idea are metamorphosed into one of the silliest movies in a long time.

Part of the fault for that lies with Russell. A great deal of the fault no doubt lies with the movie rating system, which required massive cuts in the movie before it could qualify for an R rating, and with New World Pictures, which was too chicken to release the movie with an X.* But some of the fault also lies with the subject of sex itself, because there is nothing quite so ridiculous as someone else's sexual fantasies, and nothing as fascinating as our own.

The movie stars Kathleen Turner in a performance which must have taken a great deal of nerve and curiosity. She plays a woman with a dual identity: by day, she's a sophisticated fashion designer named Joanne, and by night she's a kinky hooker named China Blue. The psychological reasons behind this double existence are dished up out of the usual Freudian stew. Turner's day work is photographed in a matter-of-fact way. The nighttime street scene is seen by Russell, however, as a lurid *film noir* world of flashing red neon signs, garter belts, squirming sadomasochists, and perverts like the one played by Anthony Perkins, who proves in this movie that there is probably no role he would turn down because it would be bad for his image. Perkins plays a demented street preacher who sniffs uppers, hangs out in peep shows, and brandishes a murder weapon that looks like *Jaws* crossed with the latest electronic sex toy.

Perkins is just one of the clients who enlivens Turner's evenings. Others are more poignant as when Turner is hired by the wife of a dying man, who wants her husband to feel like a man for one last time. She enters the man's room, and as they begin to talk, a touchingly authentic atmosphere is established.

The purpose of *Crimes of Passion* was apparently to explore the further shores of sexual behavior. Because of the double standard of the movie ratings system, which prizes violence more highly than sex, a great deal of the behavior is missing from the movie, and what is left is a steamy, bloody thriller. I'm not sure that's what Russell had in mind. Anthony Perkins distorts most of the scenes he's in, with overacting so blatant that the plausibility of the whole movie is undermined. Turner tries. So does John Laughlin, as a square young husband who learns a lot from her about sex and love. but when *Crimes of Passion* is over, what's left? Not much. You know you're in trouble in a sex movie when you spend more time thinking about the parts they left out than the parts they put in.

*The videocassette version restores some of the excised footage.

Curse of the Pink Panther ★ ½
PG, 110 m., 1983

Ted Wass (Clifton Sleigh), David Niven (Sir Charles), Robert Wagner (George Litton), Herbert Lom (Inspector Dreyfus), Joanna Lumley (Chandra), Harvey Korman (Professor Balls). Directed by Blake Edwards and produced by Edwards and Tony Adams.

The *real* curse of the Pink Panther seems to be Blake Edwards's compulsion to continue the series long after any real occasion for it. The adventures of Inspector Clouseau had more than their share of success over the years, from the two first (and best) movies, *The Pink Panther* (1963) and *A Shot in the Dark* (1964), down through all the permutations such as *Return of* (1975), *Strikes Back* (1976), and *Revenge of* (1978). When Peter

Sellers died, the obvious thing would have been to retire the series gracefully—especially since Alan Arkin had already proven in *Inspector Clouseau* (1968) that Sellers could not easily be replaced.

Instead, Edwards seems to have been seized with a need to keep the series alive. Perhaps he has a sentimental attachment. During a period of his career when his other movies were flops like *The Carey Treatment* and *The Tamarind Seed*, the Pink Panther movies kept him alive. But with big successes like *10*, *S.O.B.*, and *Victor/Victoria*, it's a little puzzling that he would commit such crimes against comedy as *Trail of the Pink Panther* (1982) and now this *Curse*.

They're both non-movies, preoccupied with the absence of Peter Sellers. *Trail* used Sellers outtakes from old Panther movies, uneasily stitched into a plot about Closeau's disappearance. *Curse* is *still* on the trail of the missing Closeau, and retraces much of the same ground—even to the extent of paying yet another visit to David Niven in the south of France.

In *Trail*, Niven played Sir Charles Litton, the jewel thief he introduced at the beginning of the Panther series. In a scene that played like a spot on a talk show, he denied any knowledge of the missing Clouseau. Niven's scenes in *Curse* were obviously filmed at the same time* and are essentially the same scenes. It is nice to see him, but a little sad to think of these as his last film performances. At least he gives a performance. The rest of *Curse of the Pink Panther* is made up of patented, polished bits the Panther supporting cast has perfected over the years. Herbert Lom is once again the twitching Inspector Dreyfus, and Bert Kwouk once again plays the faithful servant Cato (who else has made a career out of leaping from hiding and attacking people?), and Harvey Korman, is back as Professor Balls, the master of disguise.

The movie does not fashion a story out of their appearances. This is sort of a "best of" script, in which everything that worked before is tried again. A young actor named Ted Wass stands at center stage, as a Clouseau-like American detective assigned to the case. He has the movie's one supremely hilarious moment, involving an umbrella and a rainstorm. Everything else is just more of the same old stuff.

*With Rich Little dubbing his voice, since he was too ill to sound like himself.

D.C. Cab ★ ★
R, 100 m., 1983

Adam Baldwin (Albert), Charles Barnett (Tyrone), Mr. T (Samson), Anne De Salvo (Myrna), Max Gail (Harold), Whitman Mayo (Mr. Rhythm). Directed by Joel Schumacher and produced by Topper Carew. Screenplay by Schumacher.

D.C. Cab is not an entirely bad movie—it has its moments—but if it had used more actual taxi-riding incidents and more recognizable driver types, it could have been a little masterpiece. It's about a ramshackle Washington cab company with drivers who are misfits, an owner who is henpecked, and enemies who are trying to force it off the streets. This company is so broke it can't even afford the license to pick up fares at the airport.

The drivers include various ethnic and social types, from an earnest young trainee to the inimitable Mr. T. That's great, but where are some of the most universally recognizable taxi driver types? For example, these three main varieties of recently arrived foreign students: (a) those who speak no English; (b) those who want to practice their English; and (c) those who know a way to get to the airport using only alleys.

The underlying inspiration for *D.C. Cab* doesn't seem to have been real taxi driver experiences, and no wonder. Although the movie was shot in Washington, a city where taxis are important (how else would you get to the Tidal Basin at midnight?), the movie "package" was assembled in Los Angeles, a city where everybody owns a car, taxis have to be booked in advance, and a ride to the airport costs more than a day's car rental. Furthermore, the movie's producers are Peter Guber, formerly chief honcho of Casablanca Records, and Jon Peters who is Barbra Streisand's "ex." How many hours a year do you think they spend in cabs?

D.C. Cab feels like a movie with a split personality. The plot is fresh off the assembly line, with a lot of nonsense about two kidnapped rich kids and how the taxi drivers team up to rescue them. A lot of time is also wasted on the story of the D.C. Cab Company's battle with a rival company, its attempt to improve its image, and a fight over who will share a reward for a lost violin. These are all, as you can well imagine, paralyzingly boring plot ideas. There is vitality in the movie, however, and it comes directly from the cast. There are a lot of engaging actors onscreen, with lots of energy, and when they're set free to act goofy and clown around, it can be funny. The movie's star is Adam Baldwin, an actor seen in *My Bodyguard*, and he's likable. But he and everybody else in the cast are upstaged by Mr. T, who is billed as a supporting player but dominates every scene he's in. (If Nancy Reagan will sit on his lap while he wears a sleeveless Santa suit, you *know* he's hot.) The drivers create a moving mob scene; they race through the dumb plot with anarchic energy, and when it's all over, what have you got? Mindless, likable confusion. It's not the worst thing you can get from a movie.

Consumer note: Irene Cara is billed for appearing as "herself." That's right. She gets into a cab, smiles, gives an autograph, and that's it.

Daniel ★ ★ ½
R, 130 m., 1983

Timothy Hutton (Daniel Isaacson), Ed Asner (Jacob Ascher), Mandy Patinkin (Paul Isaacson), Lindsay Crouse (Rochelle Isaacson), Joseph Leon (Selig Mindish), Amanda Plummer (Susan Isaacson). Directed by Sidney Lumet and produced by Burtt Harris. Screenplay by E.L. Doctorow.

I can just vaguely remember the Rosenberg case from the early 1950s; long-ago adult voices echo in my memory, saying "they gave away the secret of the atomic bomb to the Russians." It is a large exaggeration to suggest that the Rosenbergs literally gave the Russians the bomb, but they were found guilty of giving them classified information and for that they were executed, in one of the most famous and painful cases in American legal history. Thirty years have passed, many books have been written on the Rosenbergs, and a controversy raged over a book published in 1982 that concluded that Julius

Rosenberg was probably guilty of spying—although his wife's involvement is less clear.

The controversy has spilled over into considerations of *Daniel*, a movie that would seem to be about the Rosenbergs and their children (what other historical figures could possibly have inspired it?), although the filmmakers claim it is not. Sidney Lumet, who directed the movie, and E.L. Doctorow, who based the screenplay on his own novel, *The Story of Daniel*, are at pains to separate themselves from the Rosenbergs—who are renamed the Isaacsons. Beyond the usual disclaimers, they say that their movie isn't really about the parents, but about the legacy of the children.

As a viewer, I don't really care. I don't expect *Daniel* to be historically accurate about the original court case, nor do I want the story of the children to follow the real lives of the Rosenberg children. What I do want, though, is for the movie to make it clear where it stands on the Isaacsons. I don't mean I want the movie to declare whether they were innocent or guilty—but whether they were good or bad. And there the movie holds back. The parents in this film are seen through such a series of filters—political, emotional, historical—that they are finally not seen at all.

The movie begins with a close-up of Daniel's eyes. He is dispassionately reciting a dictionary entry about electrocution. These stark words summarize what happened to his parents and they are about the only knowable facts about the case. Then we meet other characters—Daniel's sister, Susan, and the adoptive parents who took in the Isaacson children. Susan seems terribly scarred by her childhood; she is hysterical, angry, suicidal. Daniel is less visibly scarred, but he is brutally cruel to his young wife and we wonder if she represents, for him, the mother who left—who chose death over her children.

The movie then begins to move back and forth through time. There are warm sepia-toned flashbacks to left-wing days in the 1930s, when the Isaacsons are swept up in the euphoria of the American Communist Party. The present-day scenes, usually shot with lots of blues and greens, follow Daniel's quest for friends of his parents who might share their secrets. The frustrating thing about this approach is that the flashbacks—which presumably could contain the information Daniel desires—are noncommittal. They show how the Isaacsons behaved, but are never clear about exactly what it was they did, or didn't do. It's easy to assume that's because the flashbacks are limited to what the children themselves witnessed. But, no, there are scenes in which the only people present are the parents (for example, a scene on a subway train where Jacob lectures Rochelle about Marx). Once the movie uses a single scene with an omniscient point of view, it becomes guilty of withholding additional information; if the film can see into the Isaacson's private moments when no children were present, then it can show us whether they passed secrets to the Russians. But the film doesn't want to. Its real subjects are the euphoric moments of left-wing idealism in the 1930s and how the passions of those moments are being paid for to this day by the children. Because the Isaacsons were swept up in a movement which gave them identity, support, and a sense of participating in history, these poor, miserable kids have to pay the dues.

Now *that* would be a subject, if the kids were dealt with in-depth. But the movie tries to encompass too much. It devotes so much time to the past, to the children's childhoods, that the present-day scenes are slighted. Susan is clearly so disturbed that she's of little help as a witness, but Daniel, the character the movie *could* have examined in three dimensions, is so manipulated by the plot that he remains a mystery. He's always the detective, seeking out his parents' friends, asking impassioned questions, functioning as the story device instead of as the subject. At the end of *Daniel* we know that some emotionally careless parents left behind some emotionally crippled children. We suspect, oddly, that spy secrets and charges of subversion were not really relevant to the damage done to the children. I don't think that was the movie's intention.

The Dark Crystal ★ ★ ½
PG, 94 m., 1982

Performed by Jim Henson, Kathryn Mullen, Frank Oz, Dave Goelz, Brian Muehl, Jean Pierre Amiel, Kiran Shah. Directed by Jim Henson and Frank Oz and produced by

Henson and Gary Kurtz.

You've got to hand it to Jim Henson and Frank Oz. First they enchanted a generation of kids with the Muppets. Now they're ready to scare the pants off them with the Skeksis, the Mystics and, not least, the Garthim. Those are three new races of ugly beasties invented by the Muppeteers for *The Dark Crystal*, an otherworldly fantasy. There are others. Watching this movie, I wondered at times whether Henson and Oz, who are longtime partners in the Muppet saga, made it in violent reaction to the charm of Miss Piggy, Kermit, and the other Muppets. There is nothing charming about most of the characters in this movie. They are hairy, smelly, cadaverous, loathsome, evil, cannibalistic, vindictive, slimy, mean-spirited, dripping, scaling, unkempt, and hateful, but charming they're not.

The movie *does* have a couple of heroes, who belong to the race of Gelflings, and who look related to those solemn children with gigantic, tearful eyes that you find on paintings in re-sale shops. There are two Gelflings, a boy and a girl, and they follow in a time-hallowed tradition of monster fantasies, which says that the villains can be interesting, but the good guys have to be squeaky-voiced and innocuous.

The story takes place on a faraway planet that circles three suns. A thousand years ago, so the legend goes, the planet was prosperous and peaceful. But then there was a struggle over the Dark Crystal, a shard of it was lost and the ruling race on the planet split into two kinds of creatures: the Skeksis, who are reprehensible, and the Mystics, who are merely reptilian. (The Garthim are sort of a combination of crabs and armored beetles, and do the Skeksis's dirty work.) As the movie opens, the three suns are about to get back together again, and a little Gelfling gets a mission: Find the missing shard and repair the damage of the past millennium. *The Dark Crystal* is the story of his quest. And it *is* quite a quest, since the quest was designed and executed by some of the best special-effects people in the business, led by producer Gary *(Star Wars)* Kurtz, George Lucas's Industrial Light and Magic Co., and, of course, the Muppeteers themselves.

There are all sorts of amazing sights in this movie. An otherworldly rain forest is populated with weird plants that have lives of their own. A cliffside is the home of a race of beings who look like sponge-rubber sink scrubbers. The high point in animation is probably reached during a banquet scene—a slurpfest at which the slovenly Skeksis smear food all over their faces before bringing in the dessert, which is alive, and looks like what you fear may be lurking at the bottom of Love Canal.

The Dark Crystal is a labor of love, and on that basis, I salute it. A great deal of creativity and ingenious thinking went into the creation of these strange beings and their planet. But as a work of fiction, and more specifically as entertainment, I think it has two problems: (1) Many of the scenes last too long, because the special effects are lingered over, and (2) any kid younger than ten is probably going to lose some sleep after seeing the horrendous creatures in this movie. Sure, the Gelflings are cute, but the Garthim are unforgettable.

The Dead Zone ★ ★ ★ ½
R, 103 m., 1983

Christopher Walken (Johnny), Brooke Adams (Sarah), Herbert Lom (Dr. Weizak), Tom Skeritt (Sheriff), Martin Sheen (Candidate). Directed by David Cronenberg and produced by Debra Hill. Screenplay by Jeffrey Boam.

The Dead Zone does what only a good supernatural thriller can do: It makes us forget it is supernatural. Like *Rosemary's Baby* and *The Exorcist*, it tells its story so strongly through the lives of sympathetic, believable people that we not only forgive the gimmicks, we accept them. There is pathos in what happens to the Christopher Walken character in this movie and that pathos would never be felt if we didn't buy the movie's premise.

Walken plays a high school teacher whose life is happy (he's in love with Brooke Adams), until the night an accident puts him into a coma for five years. When he "returns," he has an extrasensory gift. He can touch people's hands and "know" what will happen to them. His first discovery is that he can foresee the future. His second is that he can change it. By seeing what "will" happen and trying to prevent it, he can bring about a different future. Of course, then he's left with the problem of explaining how he knew something "would have" happened, to people who can clearly see that it did not. Instead of ignoring that problem as a lesser movie might have, *The Dead Zone* builds its whole premise on it.

The movie is based on a novel by Stephen King and was directed by David Cronenberg, the Canadian who started with low-budget shockers *(The Brood, It Came From Within)* and worked up to big budgets *(Scanners)*. It's a happy collaboration. No other King novel has been better filmed (certainly not the dreadful *Cujo*), and Cronenberg, who knows how to handle terror, also knows how to create three-dimensional, fascinating characters.

In that he gets a lot of help from Walken, whose performance in this movie in a semi-reputable genre is the equal of his work in *The Deer Hunter.* Walken does such a good job of portraying Johnny Smith, the man with the strange gift, that we forget this is science fiction or fantasy or whatever, and just accept it as this guy's story.

The movie is filled with good performances: Adams, as the woman who marries someone else during Johnny's coma, but has a clear-eyed, unsentimental love for him at a crucial moment; Tom Skeritt, as the local sheriff who wants to enlist this psychic to solve a chain of murders; Herbert Lom as a sympathetic doctor; and Martin Sheen as a conniving populist politician. They all work together to make a movie that could have been just another scary thriller, and turn it into a believable thriller—which, of course, is even scarier.

Death Wish II   no stars
R, 89 m., 1982

Charles Bronson (Paul Kersey), Jill Ireland (Geri Nichols), Vincent Gardenia (Frank Ochoa), Anthony Frannciosa (Commissioner), Robert F. Lyons (Fred). Directed by Michael Winner and produced by Menachem Golan and Yoram Globus. Screenplay by David Engleback.

You will have noticed that I've given a "no stars" rating for *Death Wish II*, starring Charles Bronson as an urban vigilante. A word of explanation. In my movie rating

system, the most a movie can get is four stars *(My Dinner With André)* and the least is ordinarily half a star (even *The Beast Within* got a whole star). I award "no stars" only to movies that are artistically inept and morally repugnant. So *Death Wish II* joins such unsavory company as *Penitentiary II* and *I Spit on Your Grave*. And that, in a way, is a shame. I have a certain admiration for the screen presence of Charles Bronson. In his good roles, he can be lean, quiet, and efficient. He often co-stars with his wife, Jill Ireland, as he does in this movie, and she is a pleasant and capable actress. They were charming together in a little-seen movie named *From Noon to Three*.

This time, however, Bronson and Ireland and everyone else involved with *Death Wish II* create a great disappointment. Although the original *Death Wish* (1974) had its detractors, it was an effective movie that spoke directly to the law-and-order mentality of the Nixon-Ford era. It was directed with a nice slick polish by Michael Winner, and, on its own terms, it worked. *Death Wish II* is a disaster by comparison. It has the same director, Winner, but he directs the dialogue scenes as if the actors' shoes were nailed to the floor. It has two of the same stars—Bronson and New York cop Vincent Gardenia—but they seem shell-shocked by weariness in this film. It has the same plot (Bronson's loved ones are attacked, and he goes out into the streets to murder muggers). But while the first film convinced me of Bronson's need for vengeance, this one is just a series of dumb killings.

You will remember that *Death Wish* opened with home invaders killing Bronson's wife and raping his daughter. After Bronson used himself as bait to trap and kill nine New York City muggers, he became a folk hero. Gardenia, the cop, found out who he was, but decided not to arrest him. Bronson left town, and in this film, he's in Los Angeles. The film opens with his daughter being killed, and then Bronson hits the streets again. Ireland plays the woman he loves, and who suspects his guilty secret.

What's most shocking about *Death Wish II* is the lack of artistry and skill in the filmmaking. The movie is underwritten and desperately underplotted, so that its witless action scenes alternate with lobotomized dialogue passages. The movie doesn't contain an ounce of life. It slinks onto the screen and squirms for a while, and is over.

Deathtrap ★ ★ ★
R, 116 m., 1982

Michael Caine (Sidney Bruhl), Christopher Reeve (Clifford Anderson), Dyan Cannon (Myra Bruhl), Irene Worth (Psychic). Directed by Sidney Lumet, produced by Burtt Harrisand. Screenplay by Jay Presson Allen.

Deathtrap is a wonderful windup fiction machine with a few modest ambitions: It wants to mislead us at every turn, confound all our expectations, and provide at least one moment when we levitate from our seats and come down screaming. It succeeds, more or less. It's a thriller that depends on all sorts of surprises for its effects, and you may continue reading in the confidence that I'll reveal none of them.

That doesn't leave me much to write about, however. Let's see. I can tell you something about how the movie begins. Michael Caine plays a very successful Broadway playwright whose latest mystery is a total flop. We see him at the outset, standing at the back of the house, a gloomy witness to a disastrous opening night. (It's a Broadway in-joke that the play he's watching is being performed on the stage set of *Deathtrap*.) Caine gets drunk and goes home to his farmhouse in Connecticut and sinks into despair. There is perhaps, however, some small shred of hope. In the mail the next day Caine receives a manuscript from a former student (Christopher Reeve). It is a new thriller, and Caine sees at once that it's a masterpiece. It could run for years and earn millions of dollars. As he talks with his wife (Dyan Cannon) about it, he slowly develops the idea that he could *steal* the play, kill Reeve, and produce the hit himself.

A plausible plan? Perhaps. Caine and Cannon invite Reeve to come for a visit to the country. They grill him, subtly, and discover that absolutely no one else knows he has written the play. The stage is set for murder, betrayal, and at least an hour and a half of surprises. The tables are turned so many times in this movie that you would think they were on wheels.

Anyway, that's all I'll say about the plot. It is fair to observe, however, that *Deathtrap* is a comic study of ancient and honorable human defects, including greed, envy, lust, pride, avarice, sloth, and falsehood. Interest in the movie depends on its surprises, but its delight grows basically out of the human characteristics of its performers. They do a very good job. Thrillers like this don't always bother to pay attention to the human nature of their characters (for example, the Agatha Christie omnibus whodunits, with their cardboard suspects). *Deathtrap*, however, provides a fascinating, quirky character in Sydney Bruhl, played by Caine, and two strong supporting performances in his goofy, screaming wife (Cannon, looking great) and his talented, devious student (Reeve, who has a light, handsome comic touch not a million miles removed from Cary Grant's). The dialogue is witty without being Neil Simonized. The sets are so good they're almost distracting (a windmill appears to operate in close association with the Bruhls' bed). The only distraction is a strange character played by Irene Worth—a next-door neighbor who's a busybody, snooping psychic who sniffs down false leads. We don't know why she's even in the play, until it's much too late.

Deathtrap is not a great film and will not live forever, but if you're an aficionado of whodunits and haven't seen this one, it'll be a treat. It's more fiendishly complicated than, for example, Caine's similar outing in *Sleuth*. It plays absolutely fair, more or less, and yet fools us every time, more or less. And perhaps its greatest gift is the sight of three lighthearted comic actors having a good time chewing on the dialogue, the scenery, and each other.

Desperately Seeking Susan ★ ★ ★
PG-13, 103 m., 1985

Rosanna Arquette (Roberta), Madonna (Susan), Aidan Quinn (Dez), Mark Blum (Gary), Robert Joy (Jim), Laurie Metcalf (Leslie). Directed by Susan Seidelman and produced by Sarah Pillsbury and Midge Sanford. Screenplay by Leora Barish.

Desperately Seeking Susan is a movie that begins with those three words, in a classified ad. A time and place are suggested where

Susan can rendezvous with the person who is desperately seeking her. A bored housewife (Rosanna Arquette) sees the ad and becomes consumed with curiosity. Who is Susan and who is seeking her, and why? So Arquette turns up at the rendezvous, sees Susan (Madonna), and inadvertently becomes so involved in her world that for a while she even *becomes* Susan.

This sounds complicated, but, believe me, it's nothing compared to the complexities of this movie. *Desperately Seeking Susan* is a screwball comedy based on several cases of mistaken identity. Susan, for example, is a punk drifter who is in a hotel room with a mobster the first time we see her. Shortly after, the mobster is killed and the mob hit man comes back looking for Susan, who may have been a witness. But meanwhile, Susan has sold the jacket that is her trademark, and the housewife has bought it, and then the housewife has banged her head and become a temporary amnesia victim, and there are people who see her jacket and think she's Susan.

But enough of the plot. I wouldn't even dream of trying to explain how Arquette ends up being sawed in half by a nightclub magician. The plot isn't the point, anyway; once you realize the movie is going to be a series of double-reverses, you relax and let them happen. The plot is so unpredictable that, in a way, it's predictable; that makes it the weakest part of the movie.

What I liked in *Desperately Seeking Susan* was the cheerful way it hopped around New York, introducing us to unforgettable characters, played by good actors. For example, Aidan Quinn plays a guy who thinks Arquette is Susan, his best friend's girl. He lets her spend the night, and inadvertently feeds her amnesia by suggesting that she *is* Susan. Laurie Metcalf plays Arquette's yuppie sister-in-law. Robert Joy plays Susan's desperately seeking lover. Peter Maloney is the broken-down magician. New York underground characters such as Richard Hell, Anne Carlisle, and Rockets Red Glare also surface briefly. The director is Susan Seidelman, whose previous film, *Smithereens*, was a similar excursion through the uncharted depths of New York.

Desperately Seeking Susan does not move with the self-confidence that its complicated plot requires. But it has its moments, and many of them involve the different kinds of special appeal that Arquette and Madonna are able to generate. They are very particular individuals, and in a dizzying plot they somehow succeed in creating specific, interesting characters.

Diner ★ ★ ★ ½
R, 110 m., 1982

Steve Guttenberg (Eddie), Daniel Stern (Shrevie), Mickey Rourke (Boogie), Kevin Bacon (Fenwick), Timothy Daly (Billy), Ellen Barkin (Beth). Directed by Barry Levinson and produced by Jerry Weintraub. Screenplay by Levinson.

Women are not strange, not threatening, not mysterious, unless you happen to be a man. Young men in particular seem to regard women with a combination of admiration, desire, and dread that is quite out of their control. This was especially true in the late 1950s, a decade during which the Playmate of the Month was more alien than E.T. is today. Women were such a puzzling phenomenon to 1950s young men that, after a date, the best way for males to restore their equilibrium was to regroup with the guys for the therapeutic consumption of cheeseburgers, greasy fries, black coffee, chocolate malteds, Lucky Strikes, and loud arguments about football teams and pop singers. *Diner* is a story about several such young men, who live in Baltimore. They share one awkward problem: They are growing up, painfully and awkwardly, at an age when they are supposed to have already grown up. Adolescence lasts longer for some people than society quite imagines. These guys are best friends for this summer, although in the fall they will go separate ways, to schools and jobs and even marriage, and it's possible they will never be this close again. They cling to one another for security, because out there in the real world, responsibility lurks, and responsibility is spelled *woman*. They have plans, but their plans are not as real as their dreams.

Diner is structured a lot like *American Graffiti* and Fellini's *I Vitelloni*. It's episodic, as the young men venture out for romantic and sexual adventures, practical jokes, drunken Friday evenings, and long morn-ings of hangovers and doubt. Some of the movie's situations seem quite implausible, but they all fit within the overall theme of fear of women. One bizarre sequence, for example, involves a young man who insists that his fiancée pass a tough quiz about pro football before he'll agree to marry her. He's serious: If she flunks, the wedding is off. This situation doesn't seem possible to me, but it's right symbolically, since what the man is really looking for in a wife is one of the guys—a woman who will agree to become an imitation man.

Another character, already married, is much more realistic. He has absolutely no communication with his wife and no way to develop any, since he sees her only as a "wife" and not as a friend, a companion, or even a fellow human being. Her great failure is an inability to regard his life with the proper reverence; when she gets his record collection out of alphabetical order, it's grounds for a fight. He's flabbergasted that she hasn't memorized the flip sides of all the Top 40 hits of 1958, but he never even suspects that he doesn't know what's inside her mind.

Diner is often a very funny movie, although I laughed most freely not at the sexual pranks but at the movie's accurate ear, as it reproduced dialogue with great comic accuracy. If the movie has a weakness, however, it's that it limits itself to the faithful reproduction of the speech, clothing, cars, and mores of the late 1950s, and never quite stretches to include the humanity of the characters. For all that I recognized and sympathized with these young men and their martyred wives, girlfriends, and sex symbols, I never quite believed that they were three-dimensional. It is, of course, a disturbing possibly that, to the degree these young men denied full personhood to women, they didn't *have* three-dimensional personalities.

Diva ★ ★ ★ ★
R, 123 m., 1981

Wilhelmenia Wiggins Fernandez (Cynthia,) Frédéric Andrei (Jules), Richard Bohringer (Gordorish), Thay An Luu (Alba), Jacques Fabbri (Saporta), Chantal Deruaz (Nadia). Directed by Jean-Jacques Beineix and produced by Irene Silberman. Screenplay by Beineix and Jean Van Hamme.

The opening shots inform us with authority that *Diva* is the work of a director with an enormous gift for creating visual images. We meet a young Parisian mailman. His job is to deliver special delivery letters on his motor scooter. His passion is opera, and, as *Diva* opens, he is secretly tape-recording a live performance by an American soprano. The camera sees this action in two ways. First, with camera movements that seem as lyrical as the operatic performance. Second, with almost surreptitious observations of the electronic eavesdropper at work. His face shows the intensity of a fanatic: He does not simply admire this woman, he adores her. There is a tear in his eye. The operatic performance takes on a greatness, in this scene, that is absolutely necessary if we're to share his passion. We do. And, doing so, we start to like this kid.

His name is Frédéric Andrei, an actor I do not remember having seen before. But he could be Antoine Doinel, the subject of *The 400 Blows* and several other autobiographical films by Francois Truffaut. He has the same loony idealism, coexisting with a certain hard-headed realism about Paris. He lives and works there, he knows the streets, and yet he never quite believes he could get into trouble. *Diva* is the story of the trouble he gets into. It is one of the best thrillers of recent years but, more than that, it is a brilliant film, a visual extravaganza that announces the considerable gifts of its young director, Jean-Jacques Beineix. He has made a film that is about many things, but I think the real subject of *Diva* is the director's joy in making it. The movie is filled with so many small character touches, so many perfectly observed intimacies, so many visual inventions—from the sly to the grand—that the thriller plot is just a bonus. In a way, it doesn't really matter what this movie is about; Pauline Kael has compared Beineix to Orson Welles and, as Welles so often did, he has made a movie that is a feast to look at, regardless of its subject.

But to give the plot its due: *Diva* really gets under way when the young postman slips his tape into the saddlebag of his motor scooter. Two tape pirates from Hong Kong know that the tape is in his possession, and, since the American soprano has refused to ever allow any of her performances to be recorded, they want to steal the tape and use it to make a bootleg record. Meanwhile, in a totally unrelated development, a young prostitute tape-records accusations that the Paris chief of police is involved in an international white-slavery ring. The two cassette tapes get exchanged, and *Diva* is off to the races.

One of the movie's delights is the cast of characters it introduces. Andrei, who plays the hero, is a serious, plucky kid who's made his own accommodation with Paris. The diva herself, played by Wilhelmenia Wiggins Fernandez, comes into the postman's life after a most unexpected event (which I deliberately will not reveal, because the way in which it happens, and *what* happens, are enormously surprising). We meet others: A young Vietnamese girl who seems so blasé in the face of Paris that we wonder if anything truly excites her; a wealthy man-about-town who specializes in manipulating people for his own amusement; and a grab bag of criminals.

Most thrillers have a chase scene, and mostly they're predictable and boring. *Diva's* chase scene deserves ranking with the all-time classics, *Raiders of the Lost Ark*, *The French Connection*, and *Bullitt*. The kid rides his motorcycle down into the Paris Metro system, and the chase leads on and off trains and up and down escalators. It's pure exhilaration, and Beineix almost seems to be doing it just to show he knows how. A lot of the movie strikes that note: Here is a director taking audacious chances, doing wild and unpredictable things with his camera and actors, just to celebrate moviemaking.

There is a story behind his ecstasy. Jean-Jacques Beineix has been an assistant director for ten years. He has worked for directors ranging from Claude Berri to Jerry Lewis. But the job of an assistant director is not always romantic and challenging. Many days, he's a glorified traffic cop, shouting through a bullhorn for quiet on the set, and knocking on dressing room doors to tell the actors they're wanted. Day after day, year after year, the assistant director helps set up situations before the director takes control of them. The director gives the instructions,

the assistant passes them on. Perhaps some assistants are always thinking of how *they* would do the shot. Here's one who finally got his chance.

Divine Madness ★ ★ ★ ½
R, 94 m., 1980

Bette Midler, with the Harlettes (Jocelyn Brown, Ula Hedwig, Diva Gray) and Irving Sudrow as the Head Usher. Directed and produced by Michael Ritchie. Written by Jerry Blatt, Bette Midler, and Bruce Vilanch.

Think of a concert film and you think of a camera bolted to the floor in front of the stage and shooting straight up into the singer's nostrils, which are half-concealed by the microphone. Those films are all right as recordings of song performances, but as cinema they stink. Some directors have broken out of the mold by making documentaries about the event of a concert; the best of those films is still Michael Wadleigh's *Woodstock* (1970).

Here Michael Ritchie, whose background is almost entirely in dramatic features *(Downhill Racer, The Candidate, The Bad News Bears)*, tries a new approach. There are times in Ritchie's *Divine Madness* when he seems to be trying to turn a live Bette Midler stage concert into a Hollywood genre musical. He opens as if *Divine Madness* is going to be a traditional concert film—Bette charges on stage, the audience cheers, there's an electric performance feel. But from that beginning, Ritchie subtly moves into the material until there are times when we almost forget we're watching an actual concert performance.

Ritchie's first decision was to declare an absolute ban on visible cameras. At no moment during *Divine Madness* do we see any cameras or any members of Ritchie's crew onstage, even though twenty cameras were used to shoot the performance. Ritchie and Midler used a week of rehearsal to choreograph the camera moves and time them to Midler's own abundant energy. So instead of looking beyond the performer and being distracted by cinematographers carrying hand-held cameras and sneaking around in their Adidas, we see only the stage, Midler, and her backup singers, the Harlettes. Ritchie also uses camera techniques that are rarely seen in concert films. There are, for example, crane shots in this movie—shots where the camera swoops up to look down on Midler or to circle down and toward her. That's especially effective during the Magic Lady sequence, in which Bette portrays a sort of dreamy bag lady on a park bench. This sequence comes closest to capturing the feel of a studio musical. That's not to say that *Divine Madness* loses the impact of a live concert performance. This movie is amazingly alive and involving, and Midler, who has become one of the great live performers, has an energy that steamrollers through an incredible variety of material.

When you think about *Divine Madness* after it's over, you realize what a wide range of material Midler covers. She does rock 'n' roll, she sings blues, she does a hilarious stand-up comedy routine, she plays characters (including a tacky show-lounge performer who enters in a motorized wheelchair outfitted with a palm tree), she stars in bizarre pageantry, and she wears costumes that Busby Berkeley would have found excessive. That's one reason *Divine Madness* doesn't drag: Midler changes pace so often that there's never too much of the same thing.

Is there a weakness in the film? I think there's one—a curious one. I don't think Ritchie intercuts enough close-up shots of the audience. That may seem like a curious objection, since I've already praised *Divine Madness* for sometimes feeling more like a movie musical than a concert documentary. But you can use people in an audience as characters. Richard Lester did in the original Beatles film, *A Hard Day's Night* (and who can ever forget that blonde girl weeping and screaming?).

With a Midler concert, the audience is part of the show. Intercutting selected audience shots with the stage material could have set up a nice byplay in some of the numbers. But Ritchie keeps the audience mostly in long shot; it looks like a vast, amorphous mass out there in the dark. Since the film was actually edited together from three different concert performances, maybe he was concerned about matching audiences. But close-ups would have eliminated that problem.

No matter, though, really. Bette Midler is a wonderful performer with a high and infectious energy level and a split-second timing instinct that allows her to play with raunchy material instead of getting mired in it. She sings well, but she performs even better than she sings: She's giving a dramatic performance in music, and *Divine Madness* does a good job of communicating that performance without obscuring it in the distractions of most concert documentaries.

The Dogs of War ★ ★ ★
R, 102 m., 1981

Christopher Walken (Shannon), Tom Berenger (Drew), Colin Blakely (North), Hugh Millais (Endean), Maggie Scott (Gabrielle), Olu Jacobs (Customs Man), George W. Harris (Colonel Bobi), Winston Ntshona (Dr. Okoye). Directed by John Irvin and produced by Larry DeWaay. Screenplay by Gary DeVore and George Malko.

The Dogs of War seems to know a great deal about the lives and minds of mercenary soldiers—more than it's willing to share with us. Based on the bestseller by sometime mercenary Frederick Forsyth, it centers on the exploits of Shannon (Christopher Walken), a young American who stages military escapades in Central American and Africa. Early in the film we see him as a mercenary-on-leave, going to his doctor for a depressing checkup not much different from the ones James Bond and Modesty Blaise used to go through. He's falling apart. His body can't take much more torture. So he agrees to a mission in Africa.

Walken is an interesting actor to watch: His face, not unlike a young Robert Mitchum, keeps its own counsel and yet suggests that there is a lot going on underneath. We wait through this whole movie to find out what is going on in there, but we never find out. This movie is ambitious—but not, apparently, so ambitious that it's willing to sacrifice an action-packed payoff for scenes exploring the psyche of its hero. *The Day of the Jackal*, Fred Zinnemann's 1973 film based on an earlier novel by Forsyth, had a similar reticence. The plots move like clockwork, but the characters keep their secrets to themselves.

In compensation, however, the plot of *The Dogs of War* is fascinating. In the movie's best sustained sequence, Shannon goes alone to an African nation to scout the terrain for a large mining company that wants to move in. Is the government secure? Could it be toppled? How strong is the opposition? Shannon tries to pass himself off as a photographer for a nature magazine. He meets an assortment of locals and visitors who seem to have wandered in from the novels of Graham Greene or V.S. Naipaul. They have fascinating dimensions. There's Gabrielle (Maggie Scott), the beautiful black woman who gives him a guided tour; Dr. Okoye (Winston Ntshona), the progressive leader who was thrown in jail; Dexter (Thomas Baptiste), the hotelman and entrepreneur, and North (Colin Blakely), the alcoholic TV reporter doing a documentary on the country for the BBC. These characters all have their quirks and ambitions, and flesh out the world around the enigmatic Shannon.

This section of the film is so good that it sets us up for an extraordinary payoff. Alas, we get only an ordinary one, a routine action sequence with lots of fancy machine guns and exploding fortress walls. The last twenty-five minutes of The Dogs of War are essentially the same as the last twenty-five minutes of countless other movies—action that's so routine we're hardly even stirred by the violence.

What were we expecting? Well, maybe that the human involvements established in the film's middle would be continued and that the contradictions in the lives of Gabrielle and Dexter, in particular, would be developed. Instead, when Shannon returns with his fellow mercenaries to overthrow the country's government, he's an avenging angel who settles scores, distributes death, and presides over a very routine climax. There is, of course, a twist at the end, designed I suppose to show that Shannon was more complicated all along than we thought. Well, of course he was. That's why we wanted to know more about him.

Dragonslayer ★ ★ ★
PG, 108 m., 1981

Peter MacNicol (Galen), Caitlin Clarke (Valerian), Ralph Richardson (Ulrich), John Haliam (Tyrian), Peter Eyre (Casidorus Rex), Albert Saimi (Grell). Directed by Matthew Robbins and produced by Hal Barwood. Screenplay by Barwood and Robbins.

I'd like to think the Dark Ages looked something like Dragonslayer, all fearsome and muddy and overcast most of the time, and that their inhabitants walked around in a constant state of fear that something unspeakably evil was just about to eat off their ear. Dragonslayer's vision is more convincing than the Dark Ages created by John Boormann in Excalibur, with everybody riding around in suits of armor that wouldn't be invented for another seven hundred years.

The real Dark Ages must have been a time of ignorance, tyranny, and superstition. And its heroes must have been something like the two young heroes of Dragonslayer, Peter MacNicol and Caitlin Clarke, both looking about fifteen years old. In a time of disease, plague, and epidemic, fifteen was old.

Here is a movie with the courage to be grungy. Dragons live in smelly lairs deep beneath crumbling mountains, and to reach them you have to cross lakes of fire and somehow avoid being eaten alive by little baby dragons. The mission in this movie is a simple one, as all fairy-tale missions must be: Galen, a young sorcerer's apprentice (MacNicol) must travel to a faraway kingdom and kill a fearsome dragon who holds the countryside under its fiery scorn. The ruler of the kingdom has meanwhile instituted some stopgap measures. He holds a lottery every year involving all the virgins in his kingdom, and the unlucky virgin who loses the lottery is sacrificed to the dragon. Galen, the dragonslayer, vows to save the virgins by killing the dragon. (There are easier ways of saving a girl from being sacrificed as a virgin, but they didn't call these the Dark Ages for nothing.) Before he leaves on his mission, Galen is inspired by the grave words and magical death of his teacher, Ulrich the Sorcerer (Ralph Richardson, in an absolutely wonderful performance). On his way to the far-off kingdom, he meets a youth named Valerian (Caitlin Clarke), who turns out to be a girl disguised as a boy so that she can avoid being drafted in the lottery.

The scenes involving the dragon are first-rate. The beast is one of the meanest, ugliest, most reprehensible creatures I've ever seen in a film, and when it breathes flames it looks like it's *really* breathing flames. Its lair, its flaming lake, and its monstrous attacks on the population are also well handled. The real star of the movie, indeed, is the production designer, Elliott Scott, who created the look of this world. (The special effects were produced at Industrial Light and Magic Inc., which is George Lucas's shop in Marin County, Calif.)

If the movie has a flaw, it is in MacNicol's performance, which is so feckless, cheerfully adolescent, and untextured that he could almost be a surfer caught in a time warp. MacNicol isn't bad in the role, mind you—just awfully cheeky. But then maybe dragonslaying is a young man's trade, and when you grow old and wise and have a long beard and are the sorcerer, you've learned enough to send your apprentice to kill the dragon.

The Draughtsman's Contract
★ ★ ★ ★
R, 103 m., 1983

Anthony Higgins (Mr. Neville), Janet Suzman (Mrs. Herbert), Anne Louise Lambert (Mrs. Talmann). Directed by Peter Greenaway and produced by David Payne.

What we have here is a tantalizing puzzle, wrapped in eroticism and presented with the utmost elegance. I have never seen a film quite like it. *The Draughtsman's Contract* seems to be telling us a very simple story in a very straightforward way, but after it's over you may need hours of discussion with your friends before you can be sure (if even then) exactly what happened.

The film takes place in 1694, in the English countryside. A rich lady (Janet Suzman) hires an itinerant artist to make twelve detailed drawings of her house. The artist (Anthony Higgins) strikes a hard bargain. In addition to his modest payment, he demands "the unrestricted freedom of her most intimate hospitality." Since the gentleman of the house is away on business, the lady agrees, and thus begins a pleasant regime divided between the easel and the boudoir.

All of this is told in the most precise way. All of the characters speak in complete, elegant, literary sentences. All of the camera strategies are formal and mannered. The movie advances with the grace and precision of a well-behaved novel. There is even a moment, perhaps, when we grow restless at the film's deliberate pace. But then, if we are sharp, we begin to realize that strange things are happening under our very noses.

The draughtsman demands perfection. There must be no change, from day to day, in the view he paints. He aims for complete realism. But little changes do creep in. A window is left open. A ladder is found standing against a wall. There are things on the lawn that should not be on the lawn. The lady's daughter calls on the artist and suggests that a plot may be under way and that her father, the lord of the manor, may have been murdered. Furthermore, the artist may be about to be framed for the crime. As a payment for her friendship, the daughter demands the same payment in "intimate hospitality" as her mother. Now the artist is not only draughtsman but lover to mother and daughter *and* the possible object of a plot to frame him with murder.

There is more. There is a lot more, all allowed to unfold at the same deliberate pace. There is a mysterious statue in the garden. An eavesdropper. Misbehaved sheep. The raw materials of this story could have been fashioned into a bawdy romp like *Tom Jones*. But the director, Peter Greenaway, has made a canny choice. Instead of showing us everything, and explaining everything, he gives us the clues and allows us to draw our own conclusions. His movie is like a crossword puzzle for the senses.

Dreamscape ★ ★ ★
PG-13, 99 m., 1984

Dennis Quaid (Alex), Max von Sydow (Dr. Novotny), Kate Capshaw (Jane DeVries), Christopher Plummer (Bob Blair), Eddie Albert (President), David Patrick Kelly (Tommy Ray). Directed by Joseph Ruben and produced by Bruce Cohn Curtis. Screenplay by David Loughery, Chuck Russell, and Ruben.

Dreamscape is three different movies, all fighting to get inside one another. It's a political conspiracy thriller, a science fiction adventure, and sort of a love story. Most movies that try to crowd so much into an hour and a half end up looking like a shopping list, but *Dreamscape* works, maybe because it has a sense of humor.

The movie stars Dennis Quaid, that openfaced specialist in crafty sincerity, as the possessor of rare psychic powers. Once, years before, he had been the best ESP subject in the laboratory of a kindly old parapsychologist (Max von Sydow), but then he disappeared. Now he is wanted again. The government is sponsoring explosive secret research in a brand new field: It believes there is a way for people to enter other people's dreams. The possibilities are limitless. For example, a therapist could enter the nightmares of his clients and become an eyewitness to buried phobias. Jungians could rub shoulders with subconscious archetypes. Lovers could visit each other's erotic dreams. And, of course, evil dreamers could drive their victims mad, or kill them with fright.

Quaid reluctantly agrees to become a subject for dream research, and almost immediately falls in love with von Sydow's assistant, the healthy and cheerful Kate Capshaw, of *Indiana Jones*. Then the plot thickens. Christopher Plummer turns up as the head of U.S. "covert intelligence." He is best friends with the president (Eddie Albert), who is, needless to say, having trouble sleeping these days. Albert has nightmares about starting World War III, and Plummer has nightmares that Albert will turn into a pacifist. He wants to use the dreamscape program to control the presidency. All of this plot stuff alternates with visits to people's dreams, and it's here that the movie gets interesting; movie dreams are usually clichés, and *Dreamscape* remains within the tradition, but comes up with some nice touches, including a crazy staircase that zigzags into darkness and looks precarious and surreal. There is also a funny sequence in which Quaid discovers Capshaw taking a nap, and impudently enters her dream with lust on his mind.

The whole business about the plot against the president is recycled from countless other thrillers. Two things redeem it: The gimmick of the dream invasions and the quality of the acting. Science fiction movies routinely run the risk of seeming ridiculous,

and with bad performances they can inspire unwanted laughs. *Dreamscape* places its characters in a fantastical situation, and then lets them behave naturally, and with a certain wit. Dennis Quaid is especially good at that; his face lends itself to a grin, and he is a hero without ever being self-consciously heroic.

As for the dreams themselves, as I watched the movie I found myself trying to remember some of my own dreams. The movie's dreams include rooms with lots of windows and doors at crazy angles, railway coaches that are twice as wide as train tracks, and other visual distortions. I usually have more realistic dreams. Rooms and spaces have realistic proportions, and the distortions of reality come, not in the set decorating, but in the editing; flashbacks and intercutting points of view are not uncommon in my dreams, maybe because I see so many films. But movies can't use flashbacks and viewpoint tricks to manufacture dreams—because then the movie would look like a movie and not like a dream. So the movies have created a conventional dream language. What *Dreamscape* does is enlarge it with brief, sometimes funny little asides that do feel like dreams, as when Quaid is inside the nightmare of a little boy, and they're running from a Snake Man, and they see an adult seated at the end of a long table, and the kid says, "That's my dad. He won't be any help."

Dressed to Kill ★ ★ ★
R, 105 m., 1980

Michael Caine (Dr. Elliott), Angie Dickinson (Kate Miller), Nancy Allen (Liz Blake), Keith Gordon (Peter Miller), Dennis Franz (Detective Marino), David Margulies (Dr. Levy). Directed by Brian De Palma and produced by George Litto. Screenplay by De Palma.

When Alfred Hitchcock died, the obituaries puzzled over the fact that Hitchcock had created the most distinctive and easily recognizable visual style of his generation—but hadn't had a great influence on younger filmmakers. The obvious exception is Brian De Palma, who deliberately set out to work in the Hitchcock tradition, and directed this

Hitchcockian thriller that's stylish, intriguing, and very violent.

The ads for De Palma's *Dressed to Kill* describe him as "the master of the macabre," which is no more immodest, I suppose, than the ads that described Hitchcock as "the master of suspense." De Palma is not yet an artist of Hitchcock's stature, but he does earn the right to a comparison, especially after his deliberately Hitchcockian films *Sisters* and *Obsession*. He places his emphasis on the same things that obsessed Hitchcock: precise camera movements, meticulously selected visual details, characters seen as types rather than personalities, and violence as a sudden interruption of the most mundane situations.

He also has Hitchcock's delight in bizarre and unexpected plot twists, and the chief delight of the first and best hour of *Dressed to Kill* comes from the series of surprises he springs on us. Although other key characters are introduced, the central character in these early scenes is Kate Miller (Angie Dickinson), an attractive forty-fiveish Manhattan woman who has a severe case of unsatiated lust. De Palma opens with a deliberately shocking shower scene (homage to Hitch), and then follows the woman as her sexual fantasies become unexpectedly real during a lunchtime trip to the museum.

The museum sequence is absolutely brilliant, tracking Dickinson as she notices a tall, dark, and handsome stranger. She makes eye contact, breaks it, tries to attract the stranger's attention by dropping her glove, and then is tracked *by* the stranger. To her, and our, astonishment, this virtuoso scene (played entirely without dialogue) ends in a passionate sexual encounter in the back of a taxicab.

Later, she wakes up in the stranger's apartment, and De Palma shamelessly manipulates her, and us, by springing a series of plot surprises involving embarrassment and guilt: What would *you* do if you were a cheating wife and had just forgotten your wedding ring in a stranger's apartment? The plot now takes several totally unanticipated turns, and I, of course, would not dream of revealing them. Indeed, I'll be vague about the plot from now on, because De Palma's surprises are crucial to his effect.

The movie's other characters include Michael Caine, who's the psychiatrist of two of the characters in the film. Then there's Nancy Allen, who's wonderfully off-beat as a sweet Manhattan hooker who discovers a body and gets trapped in the investigation. And there's Keith Gordon: He's one of those teen-age scientific geniuses, and he invents brilliant gimmicks to investigate the crime.

Some people are going to object to certain plot details in *Dressed to Kill*, particularly the cavalier way it explains a homocidal maniac's behavior by lumping together transsexuality and schizophrenia. But I doubt that De Palma wants us to take his explanations very seriously; the pseudoscientific jargon used to "explain" the case reminds me of that terrible psychiatric explanation at the end of *Psycho*—a movie De Palma has been quoting from all along.

Dressed to Kill is an exercise in style, not narrative; it would rather look and feel like a thriller than make sense. Its plot has moments of ludicrous implausibility, it nearly bogs down at one point near the end and it cheats on us with the old "it was only a dream!" gimmick. But De Palma has so much fun with the conventions of the thriller that we forgive him and go along. And there are really nice touches in the performances: Dickinson's guilt-laden lust, Caine's analytical detachment, Allen's street-wise cool in life and death situations, Gordon's wise-guy kid. De Palma earns the title of master, all right . . . but Hitch remains the grand master.

The Dresser ★ ★ ★ ★
PG, 118 m., 1984

Albert Finney (Sir), Tom Courtenay (Norman), Edward Fox (Oxenby), Zena Walker (Her Ladyship). Directed and produced by Peter Yates. Screenplay by Ronald Harwood.

Much of mankind is divided into two categories, the enablers and the enabled. Both groups accept the same mythology, in which the enablers are self-sacrificing martyrs and the enabled are egomaniacs. But the roles are sometimes reversed; the stars are shaken by insecurities that are subtly encouraged by enablers who, in their heart of hearts, see themselves as the real stars. It's human nature. Ever hear the one about the guy who played the gravedigger in *Hamlet*? He was asked what the play was about, and he answered, "It's about this gravedigger. . . ."

The Dresser is about a guy like that, named Norman. He has devoted the best years of his life to the service of an egomaniacal actor, who is called Sir even though there is some doubt he has ever been knighted. Sir is an actor-manager who runs his own traveling theatrical troupe, touring the provinces to offer a season of Shakespeare. One night he plays King Lear. The next night, Othello. The next, Richard III. Most nights he has to ask his dresser what role he is playing. Dressers in the British theater do a great deal more than dress their employers. In *The Dresser*, Norman is also Sir's confidant, morale booster, masseur, alter ego, and physician, nursing him through hangovers with medicinal amounts of brandy. Norman has been doing this job for years, and Sir is at the center of his life. Sir, however, takes Norman very much for granted, and it is this difference between them that provides the emotional tension.

The Dresser is a backstage movie, based on a backstage play, but the movie leaves the theater for a few wonderful additions to the play, as when Sir commands a train to stop, and the train does. Mostly, though, the action is in a little provincial theater, where tonight's play is *King Lear*, and Sir looks as if he had spent the last week rehearsing the storm scene. It is Norman's job to whip him into shape. Sir is seriously disoriented. He is so hung over, shaky, and confused that he can't even remember how the play begins—indeed, he starts putting on the makeup for *Othello*. There are other problems for Norman to handle, such as Sir's relationships with his wife, his adoring stage manageress, and a young actress he is considering for Cordelia (she is slim, and would be easier to carry onstage). There are also an angry supporting player and a quaking old trouper who is being pressed into service as the Fool.

The minor characters are all well-drawn, but *The Dresser* is essentially the story of two people, and the movie has been well-cast to make the most of both of them; no wonder both actors won Oscar nominations. Norman is played by Tom Courtenay, who had the role on stage in London and New York and will also be remembered from all those British Angry Young Men films like *Billy Liar* and *Loneliness of the Long Distance Runner*. He is perfect for playing proud, resentful, self-doubting outsiders. Sir is played by Albert Finney, who manages to look far older than his forty-seven years and yet to create a physical bravura that's ideal for the role. When he shouts "Stop . . . that . . . train!" we are not too surprised when the train stops.

On the surface, the movie is a wonderful collection of theatrical lore, detail, and superstition (such as the belief that it is bad luck to say the name "Macbeth" aloud—safer to refer always to "the Scottish tragedy"). The physical details of makeup and costuming are dwelled on, and there is a great backstage moment when the primitive thunder machine is rattled to make a storm. Beneath those details, though, a human relationship arrives at a crisis point and is resolved, in a way. Sir and Norman come to the end of their long road together, and, as is the way with enablers and enabled, Norman finally understands the real nature of their relationship, while Sir, of course, can hardly be bothered. This is the best sort of drama, fascinating us on the surface with color and humor and esoteric detail, and then revealing the truth underneath.

Dune ★
PG-13, 145 m., 1984

Kyle MacLachlan (Paul), José Ferrer (Emperor), Brad Dourif (De Vries), Kenneth McMillan (Baron), Sting (Feyd-Rautha). Directed by David Lynch and produced by Raffaella DeLaurentiis. Screenplay by Lynch.

"It's like a dream," my friend from Hollywood was explaining. "It doesn't make any sense, and the special effects are straight from the dime store but if you give up trying to understand it, and just sit back and let it wash around in your mind, it's not bad." That was not exactly a rave review for a movie that someone paid $40 million to make, but it put me into a receptive frame of mind for *Dune*, the epic based on the novels by Frank Herbert. I was even willing to forgive the special effects for not being great; after all, in an era when George Lucas's *Star Wars* has turned movies into high tech, why not a film that looks like a throwback to *Flash Gordon*. It might be kind of fun.

It took *Dune* about nine minutes to completely strip me of my anticipation. This movie is a real mess, an incomprehensible, ugly, unstructured, pointless excursion into the murkier realms of one of the most confusing screenplays of all time. Even the color is no good; everything is seen through a sort of dusty yellow filter, as if the film was left out in the sun too long. Yes, you might say, but the action is, after all, on a desert planet where there isn't a drop of water, and there's sand everywhere. David Lean solved that problem in *Lawrence of Arabia*, where he made the desert look beautiful and mysterious, not shabby and drab.

The movie's plot will no doubt mean more to people who've read Herbert than to those who are walking in cold. It has to do with a young hero's personal quest. He leads his people against an evil baron and tries to destroy a galaxy-wide trade in "spice," a drug produced on the desert planet. Spice allows you to live indefinitely while you discover you have less and less to think about. There are various theological overtones, which are best left unexplored.

The movie has so many characters, so many unexplained or incomplete relationships, and so many parallel courses of action that it's sometimes a toss-up whether we're watching a story, or just an assembly of meditations on themes introduced by the novels (the movie is like a dream). Occasionally a striking image will swim into view: The alien brain floating in brine, for example, or our first glimpse of the giant sand worms plowing through the desert. If the first look is striking, however, the movie's special effects don't stand up to scrutiny. The heads of the sand worms begin to look more and more as if they came out of the same factory that produced Kermit the Frog (they have the same mouths). An evil baron floats through the air on trajectories all too obviously controlled by wires. The spaceships in the movie are so shabby, so lacking in detail or dimension, that they look almost like those student films where plastic models are shot against a tablecloth.

Nobody looks very happy in this movie. Actors stand around in ridiculous costumes, mouthing dialogue that has little or no con-text. They're not even given scenes that work on a self-contained basis; portentious lines of pop profundity are allowed to hang in the air unanswered, while additional characters arrive or leave on unexplained errands. *Dune* looks like a project that was seriously out of control from the start. Sets were constructed, actors were hired; no usable screenplay was ever written; everybody faked it as long as they could. Some shabby special effects were thrown into the pot, and the producers crossed their fingers and hoped that everybody who has read the books will want to see the movie. Not if the word gets out, they won't.

E.T.—The Extra-Terrestrial ★ ★ ★ ★
PG, 115 m., 1982* ✓

Henry Thomas (Elliott), Dee Wallace (Mary), Peter Coyote (Keys), Robert MacNaughton (Michael), Drew Barrymore (Gertie). Directed by Steven Spielberg and produced by Spielberg and Kathleen Kennedy. Screenplay by Melissa Mathison.

This movie made my heart glad. It is filled with innocence, hope, and good cheer. It is also wickedly funny and exciting as hell. *E.T.—The Extra-Terrestrial* is a movie like *The Wizard of Oz*, that you can grow up with and grow old with, and it won't let you down. It tells a story about friendship and love. Some people are a little baffled when they hear it described: It's about a relationship between a little boy and a creature from outer space that becomes his best friend. That makes it sound like a cross between *The Thing* and *National Velvet*. It works as science fiction, it's sometimes as scary as a monster movie, and at the end, when the lights go up, there's not a dry eye in the house.

E.T. is a movie of surprises, and I will not spoil any of them for you. But I can suggest some of the film's wonders. The movie takes place in and around a big American suburban development. The split-level houses march up and down the curved drives, carved out of hills that turn into forest a few blocks beyond the backyard. In this forest one night, a spaceship lands, and queer-looking little creatures hobble out of it and go snuffling through the night, looking for plant specimens, I guess. Humans arrive—

authorities with flashlights and big stomping boots. They close in on the spaceship, and it is forced to take off and abandon one of its crew members. This forlorn little creature, the *E.T.* of the title, is left behind on Earth—abandoned to a horrendous world of dogs, raccoons, automobile exhausts, and curious little boys.

The movie's hero is one particular little boy named Elliott. He is played by Henry Thomas in what has to be the best little boy performance I've ever seen in an American film. He doesn't come across as an over-coached professional kid; he's natural, defiant, easily touched, conniving, brave, and childlike. He just *knows* there's something living out there in the backyard, and he sits up all night with his flashlight, trying to coax the creature out of hiding with a nearly irresistible bait: Reese's Pieces. The creature, which looks a little like Snoopy but is very, very wise, approaches the boy. They become friends. The E.T. moves into the house, and the center section of the film is an endless invention on the theme of an extra-terrestrial's introduction to bedrooms, televisions, telephones, refrigerators, and six-packs of beer. The creature has the powers of telepathy and telekinesis, and one of the ways it communicates is to share its emotions with Elliott. That's how Elliott knows that the E.T. wants to go home.

And from here on out, I'd better not describe what happens. Let me just say that the movie has moments of sheer ingenuity, moments of high comedy, some scary moments, and a very sad sequence that has everybody blowing their noses.

What is especially wonderful about all of those moments is that Steven Spielberg, who made this film, creates them out of legitimate and fascinating plot developments. At every moment from its beginning to its end, *E.T.* is really *about* something. The story is quite a narrative accomplishment. It reveals facts about the E.T.'s nature; it develops the personalities of Elliott, his mother, brother, and sister; it involves the federal space agencies; it touches on extra-terrestrial medicine, biology, and communication, and *still* it inspires genuine laughter and tears.

A lot of those achievements rest on the very peculiar shoulders of the E.T. itself. With its odd little walk, its high-pitched squeals of surprise, its tentative imitations of human speech, and its catlike but definitely alien purring, E.T. becomes one of the most intriguing fictional creatures I've ever seen on a screen. The E.T. is a triumph of special effects, certainly; the craftsmen who made this little being have extended the boundaries of their art. But it's also a triumph of imagination, because the filmmakers had to imagine E.T., had to see through its eyes, hear with its ears, and experience this world of ours through its utterly alien experience in order to make a creature so absolutely convincing. The word for what they exercised is empathy. *E.T.—The Extra-Terrestrial* is a reminder of what movies are for. Most movies are not for any one thing, of course. Some are to make us think, some to make us feel, some to take us away from our problems, some to help us examine them. What is enchanting about *E.T.* is that, in some measure, it does all of those things.

*E.T. was held off the cassette market until after its 1985 re-release.

Easy Money ★ ★ ½
R, 95 m., 1983

Rodney Dangerfield (Monty Capuletti), Joe Pesci (Nicky Cerone), Geraldine Fitzgerald (Mrs. Monahan), Candy Azzara (Rose), Taylor Negron (Julio), Jennifer Jason Leigh (Allison). Directed by James Signorelli and produced by John Nicoletta. Screenplay by Dangerfield, Michael Enderl, P.J. O'Rourke, and Dennis Blair.

Easy Money is an off-balance and disjointed movie, but that's sort of okay, since it's about an off-balance and disjointed kinda guy. The credits call him Monty Capuletti, but he is clearly Rodney Dangerfield, gloriously playing himself as the nearest thing we are likely to get to W.C. Fields in this lifetime.

The movie's plot is simply a line to hang gags on. It stars Rodney as a baby photographer whose rich mother-in-law leaves him an inheritance of a $10 million department store. He can collect—but only if he stops drinking, gambling, smoking dope, running around late, and betting on the horses. This is a very tall order, but Rodney tries to fill it. The movie surrounds Dangerfield with a lot of good New York character actors, who populate the endless poker games and saloon scenes his life revolves around. There's also a very funny sequence involving his daughter's wedding to a Puerto Rican, an alliance that inspires a great backyard wedding party scene.

Because Rodney is Rodney, I laughed a lot during this movie. But I left it feeling curiously unsatisfied. I think maybe that was for two reasons: Because the movie introduces too many subplots that it never really deals with, and because Rodney isn't allowed to be hateful enough. First, the plot. I have the strangest feeling that *Easy Money* once had a much longer script than it has now. There are big scenes (like one where the Puerto Rican groom is sneaking into the bathroom) that end abruptly without a payoff or follow-through. There are whole sequences (like the department store's fashion show, based on Rodney's wardrobe) that seem to coexist uneasily with the rest of the movie. And the movie doesn't get enough comic mileage out of Rodney's attempt to quit drinking, smoking, and gambling (think of the fun you could have with Dangerfield attending an A.A. meeting).

Second, Rodney. I like him best when he's cynical and hard-edged. The Dangerfield of his concerts and records has been smoothed out for this movie, into a slightly more lovable guy. It looks like a masterstroke to make Rodney a baby photographer (think of W.C. Fields in that role), but not enough is done with it. He occasionally loses his temper at the little monsters, but he never seems to detest and despise them enough to be really funny. That's a problem. If you are a Rodney Dangerfield fan, it will not be insurmountable. If you are not a Dangerfield fan, of course, probably nothing on earth could induce you to go to this movie. The great Dangerfield movie, however, has still to be made. This one doesn't get quite enough respect.

Eating Raoul ★ ★
R, 87 m., 1983

Paul Bartel (Paul Bland), Mary Woronov (Mary Bland), Robert Beltran (Raoul). Directed by Paul Bartel. Screenplay by Bartel and Richard Blackburn.

Eating Raoul is one of the more deadpan black comedies I've seen: It tries to position itself somewhere between the bizarre and the banal, and most of the time, it succeeds. This has got to be the first low-key, laid-back comedy about murder, swingers' ads, and dominating women. Problem is, it's so laid-back it eventually gets monotonous. If the style and pacing had been as outrageous as the subject matter, we might have had something really amazing here.

The movie's about a happily married couple, Paul and Mary Bland, who are victims of bad times. Paul gets fired from his job in the liquor store, and there's just not much work around for a dilettante with no skills. He's spent his last rent money when providence suggests a way for the Blands to support themselves. A lecherous swinger from the upstairs apartment tries to assault Mary, and Paul bops him over the head with the frying pan. The swinger dies, and the Blands overcome their horror long enough to check out his wallet. He's loaded.

What the movie does next is to present the most outrageous events in the most matter-of-fact manner. The Blands hit upon a scheme to take ads in swingers' tabloids, lure victims to their apartment, tap them over the head with the trusty skillet, and rob them. The only problem is disposing of their victims' bodies. That's where Raoul comes in. He's a locksmith who discovers the Blands' dirty little secret and offers to sell the bodies to a dog-food factory. All's well until Raoul becomes smitten with Mary. Then Paul grows jealous, especially when he discovers that Raoul has been stealing from them. The next step is perhaps suggested by the title of the movie, or perhaps not—I wouldn't want to give anything away.

The plot of *Eating Raoul* reminds me a little of *Motel Hell*, that truly ghastly movie about a farmer who kidnapped his motel customers, buried them in the garden up to their necks, force-fed them until they were plump, and then turned them into sausages. (His motto: "It takes lots of critters to make Farmer Vincent's fritters.") I liked *Motel Hell* more than *Eating Raoul*, however, because it had the courage of its execrable taste. *Eating Raoul*, on the other hand, wants to be an almost whimsical black comedy. It's got its tongue so firmly in cheek there's no room for Raoul. The movie's got some really funny stuff in it, and I liked a lot of it, and I wouldn't exactly advise not seeing it, but it doesn't quite go that last mile. It doesn't reach for the truly unacceptable excesses, the transcendent breaches of taste, that might have made it inspired instead of merely clever.

Eddie and the Cruisers ★ ★
PG, 92 m., 1983

Tom Berenger (Frank), Michael Pare (Eddie Wilson), Joe Pantoliano (Doc Robbins), Matthew Laurence (Sal Amato), Helen Schneider (Joann Carlino), Michael 'Tunes' Antunes (Wendell Newton). Directed by Martin Davidson and produced by Joseph Brooks. Written by Martin and Arlene Davidson.

Eddie and the Cruisers is all buildup and no payoff. It tells us about this unsung rock 'n' roll genius named Eddie Wilson, whose Chevy crashed off a bridge back in 1963, and then it suggests that Eddie might still be alive. Now, leaving aside the possibility that Eddie might, in fact, have gone down with his Chevy, this premise has all sorts of possibilities. I will name some of them:

1. Eddie could have surfaced as another rock 'n' roller.
2. Eddie could have been a Buddy Holly who never died, and he disappeared to escape discovery.
3. Eddie could have been horribly disfigured and decided to spend the rest of his life in a recording studio, masterminding other people's music.
4. Eddie could have dropped out, in a grand existential gesture.

Now, I will *not* give away the ending to this movie. But I will make the following complaint: Even though one of the above possibilities does, indeed, turn out to be true—*it is still not the ending of the movie!* The movie makes the fatal flaw of arriving at a dramatic conclusion that does not settle the Eddie Wilson mystery. Instead, all we get is a big buildup to a dumb revelation. What a disappointment.

The movie makes another mistake. It never really explores Eddie Wilson as a human being. He's played in the movie by Michael Pare, a good-looking hunk. Pare does a good job of seeming to be a charis-matic rock star, a sort of Bruce Springsteen crossed with Richard Gere. But Pare has hardly any real dramatic scenes; instead, he postures a lot, makes speeches, takes stands, and is idolized onstage.

After he disappears with the Chevy, twenty years go by, and the members of the old Cruisers all make their separate peace with the Wilson legend. The key figure in the movie is Tom Berenger, playing one of the Cruisers. These days he's a high school teacher, but he still remembers his rock 'n' roll past; so do Eddie's old girlfriend (Helen Schneider) and the group's manager (Joe Pantoliano), who is now a broken-down DJ. Suddenly, there's renewed interest in the tapes of Eddie's last session. A TV investigative reporter wants to learn the real Eddie Wilson story. And then messages are received from . . . Eddie? We learn that the original tapes *were* saved; they were hidden years ago in Eddie's favorite place, a sculptor's combination of a junkyard and the Watts Towers. (Of course, the tapes have survived twenty years of rain, ice, snow, and sun.) And then . . .

You know, they could have had a good movie here. They had the cast for one and they even had the music (the sound track is terrific). If they'd just gone ahead and *dealt* with Eddie's disappearance, even in melodramatic terms, the movie would have paid off. But the ending is so frustrating, so dumb, so unsatisfactory, that it gives a bad reputation to the whole movie.

Educating Rita ★ ★
PG, 110 m., 1983

Michael Caine (Dr. Frank Bryant), Julie Walters (Rita). Directed and produced by Lewis Gilbert. Screenplay by Willy Russell.

If only I'd been able to believe they were actually reading the books, then everything else would have fallen into place. But I didn't believe it. And so *Educating Rita*, which might have been a charming human comedy, disintegrated into a forced march through a formula relationship. The movie stars Michael Caine as a British professor of literature and Julie Walters as the simple cockney girl who comes to him for nightschool lessons. She has problems: She is a working-class punk with an unimaginative

husband. He has problems: He is a drunk
whose only friends are cheating on him with
each other. They have problems: Walters
begins to idealize Caine, who then falls in
love with her.

Perhaps it would be more accurate to say
they both fall into love with the remake job
they'd like to do on each other. Caine sees
Walters as a fresh, honest, unspoiled intelligence. She sees him as a man who ought to
sober up and return to his first love, writing
poems. The idea of the curmudgeon and the
cockney was not new when Bernard Shaw
wrote *Pygmalion,* and it is not any newer in
Educating Rita. But it could have been entertaining, if only I'd believed they were reading those books. They pass the books back
and forth a lot. They sometimes read a line
or two. There is a lot of talk about Blake this
and Wordsworth that. But it's all magic. The
books are like incantations that, used properly, will exorcise cockney accents and alcoholism. But the movie doesn't really believe
that, so it departs from the stage play to
bring in a lot of phony distractions.

The original *Educating Rita,* a long-running London stage hit by Willy Russell, had
only the two characters. They were on the
stage together for a long time, and by the end
of the play we had shared in their developing
relationship. Russell's movie rewrite has
added mistresses, colleagues, husbands, in-
laws, students, and a faculty committee, all
unnecessary.

To the degree that *Educating Rita* does
work, the credit goes to Michael Caine, who
plays a man weary and kind, funny and self-
hating. There is a real character there, just as
there was in Caine's boozy diplomat in *Beyond the Limit.* In both movies, though, the
characters are not well-served by the story.
They're made to deliver speeches, take positions, and make decisions that are required
by the plot, not by their own inner prompt-
ings. When Caine's professor, at the end of
this movie, flies off to Australia to maybe
sober up and maybe make a fresh start, it's a
total cop-out—not by him, but by the
screenplay. Maybe that's what happens
when you start with an idealistic, challenging idea, and then cynically try to broaden
its appeal.

El Norte ★ ★ ★ ★
R, 141 m., 1983

Zaide Sylvia Gutierrez (Rosa), David
Villalpando (Enrique), Ernesto Gomez Cruz
(Father), Alicia del Lago (Mother), Trinidad
Silva (Monty). Directed by Gregory Nava and
produced by Anna Thomas. Screenplay by
Nava and Thomas.

From the very first moments of *El Norte,* we
know that we are in the hands of a great
movie. It tells a simple story in such a romantic and poetic way that we are touched,
deeply and honestly, and we know we will
remember the film for a long time. The
movie tells the story of two young
Guatemalans, a brother and sister named
Rosa and Enrique, and of their long trek up
through Mexico to *el Norte*—the United
States. Their journey begins in a small village and ends in Los Angeles, and their
dream is the American Dream.

But *El Norte* takes place in the present,
when we who are already Americans are not
so eager for others to share our dream. Enrique and Rosa are not brave immigrants who
could have been our forefathers, but two
young people alive now, who look through
the tattered pages of an old *Good Housekeeping* for their images of America. One of
the most interesting things about the film is
the way it acknowledges all of the political
realities of Latin America and yet resists
being a "political" film. It tells its story
through the eyes of its heroes, and it is one of
the rare films that grants Latin Americans
full humanity. They are not condescended
to, they are not made to symbolize something, they are not glorified, they are simply
themselves.

The movie begins in the fields where Ar-
turo, their father, is a *bracero*—a pair of arms.
He goes to a meeting to protest working
conditions and is killed. Their mother disappears. Enrique and Rosa, who are in their
late teens, decide to leave their village and go
to America. The first part of the film shows
their life in Guatemala with some of the same
beauty and magical imagery of Gabriel Garcia Marquez's *One Hundred Years of Solitude.*
The middle section shows them going by
bus and foot up through Mexico, which is as
harsh on immigrants from the South as
America is. At the border they try to hire a

"coyote" to guide them across, and they finally end up crawling to the promised land through a rat-infested drainage tunnel.

The final section of the film takes place in Los Angeles, which they first see as a glittering carpet of lights, but which quickly becomes a cheap motel for day laborers, and a series of jobs in the illegal, shadow job market. Enrique becomes a waiter. Rosa becomes a maid. Because they are attractive, intelligent, and have a certain naive nerve, they succeed for a time, before the film's sad, poetic ending.

El Norte is a great film, one of 1983's best, for two different kinds of reasons. One is its stunning visual and musical power; the approach of the film is not quasidocumentary, but poetic, with fantastical images that show us the joyous hearts of these two people.

The second reason is that this is the first film to approach the subject of "undocumented workers" solely through *their* eyes. This is not one of those docudramas where we half-expect a test at the end, but a film like *The Grapes of Wrath* that gets inside the hearts of its characters and lives with them.

The movie was directed by Gregory Nava and produced by Anna Thomas, who wrote it together. It's been described by *Variety* as the "first American independent epic," and it is indeed an epic film made entirely outside the studio system by two gifted filmmakers (their credits include *The Confessions of Amans*, which won a Gold Hugo at the Chicago Film Festival, and *The Haunting of M*, one of my favorite films from 1979). This time, with a larger budget and a first-rate cast, they have made their breakthrough into the first ranks of young directors.

Electric Dreams ★ ★ ★ ½
PG, 96 m., 1984

Lenny Von Dohlen (Miles), Virginia Madsen (Madeline), Maxwell Caulfield (Bill), Bud Cort (Computer). Directed by Steve Barron and produced by Rusty Lemorande and Larry DeWaay. Screenplay by Lemorande.

In a way, it's one of the oldest stories in the movies. You start with a sweet guy who's kind of a wimp. You have him rent an apartment downstairs from a good-looking blonde girl who's really classy—maybe she even plays cello in a symphony orchestra.

Then you supply the wimp with a know-it-all roommate who can do anything. Then the wimp has the roommate compose a love song for the girl upstairs. The girl falls for it, there's love at first sight, but then the wimp feels that he is living a lie. He must tell the girl the truth or he will not truly deserve her. (This begs the question, of course, of whether he should make an ethical investment in a girl who can be swayed by a single love song.)

In *Electric Dreams*, they've made one slight change in this age-old scenario, to bring it up to date. The roommate is a computer. In the old movies, there was usually a touchy moment or two when it looked like the roommate was going to fall for the girl upstairs. They even have a version of that here: The computer gets wildly jealous and possessive about its owner, and begins to inquire winsomely about the meanings of all those nice words in the love songs: How, exactly, *does* one touch? The guy in the movie is one of those cases of chronic disorganization: He's right on time but this is yesterday's training session. Somebody tells him he ought to get a computer to help him keep track of things. He buys a computer and, predictably, drops it while he is taking it out of the box. Apparently that was just what the computer needed to upgrade itself to a level of sophistication far above anything ever dreamed of by the folks at the computer store.

If *Electric Dreams* were only about this ancient old plot, it would have been a fairly routine movie. Several things make it more than that, and, in order of importance, they are: (1) the ingenious way the movie creates a personality for the computer, with the help of Bud Cort as the computer's voice; (2) the perfect casting of Lenny Von Dohlen as the wimp, and Virginia Madsen, an engaging newcomer, as the girl upstairs; (3) the graphics, and particularly the way the movie pictures the computer's wilder flights of fancy, and (4) the music by Giorgio Moroder, who seems to compose the scores for half the films in Hollywood these days, but who has certainly found the right tone for this one.

One of the nicest things about the movie is the way it maintains its note of slightly bewildered innocence. When Van Dohlen unpacks his computer and starts to assemble it, he reminds us a little of somebody like Harold Lloyd, determined to lick this thing. It's not often that a modern movie has the courage to give us a hero who doesn't seem to be a cross between a disco god and an aerobics instructor, but the Von Dohlen character is a nice change. He's likable, incompetent, and slightly dense. Virginia Madsen makes it clear right from the start that she loves her cello more than almost anything else in the world, and the movie's best single scene is the one where the computer, eavesdropping through a ventilation duct as she rehearses, joins in and plays a duet with her.

That scene, and a lot of other virtuoso moments in the movie, are photographed by Alex Thompson with a kind of fluid, poetic visual abandon that makes the movie a lot of fun to watch. The camera sweeps low over a keyboard, taking a flight that's almost as exhilarating as one of those swoops in *Star Wars*. During the songs, the screen fills with a kind of orgasmic computer screen display. They didn't stop after they figured out the story of this movie; it's obvious that the director, Steve Barron, spent a lot of time with his collaborators talking about how they could elevate their simple little story into something approaching a romantic flight of fancy. They were successful.

The Elephant Man ★ ★
PG, 123 m., 1980

Anthony Hopkins (Frederick Treves), John Hurt (John Merrick), Anne Bancroft (Mrs. Kendal), John Gielgud (Carr Gomm). Directed by David Lynch and produced by Jonathan Sanger. Screenplay by Christopher DeVore, Eric Bergren, and David Lynch.

The film of *The Elephant Man* is not based on the successful stage play of the same name, but they both draw their sources from the life of John Merrick, the original "elephant man," whose rare disease imprisoned him in a cruelly misformed body. Both the play and the movie adopt essentially the same point of view, that we are to honor Merrick because of the courage with which he faced his existence.

The Elephant Man forces me to question this position on two grounds: first, on the meaning of Merrick's life, and second, on the ways in which the film employs it. It is conventional to say that Merrick, so hideously misformed that he was exhibited as a sideshow attraction, was courageous. No doubt he was. But there is a distinction here that needs to be drawn, between the courage of a man who chooses to face hardship for a good purpose, and the courage of a man who is simply doing the best he can, under the circumstances.

Wilfrid Sheed, an American novelist who is crippled by polio, once discussed this distinction in a *Newsweek* essay. He is sick and tired, he wrote, of being praised for his "courage," when he did not choose to contract polio and has little choice but to deal with his handicaps as well as he can. True courage, he suggests, requires a degree of choice. Yet the whole structure of *The Elephant Man* is based on a life that is said to be courageous, not because of his hero's achievements, but simply because of the bad trick played on him by fate. In the film and the play (which are similar in many details), John Merrick learns to move in society, to have ladies in to tea, to attend the theater, and to build a scale model of a cathedral. Merrick may have had greater achievements in real life, but the film glosses them over. How, for example, did he learn to speak so well and eloquently? History tells us that the real Merrick's jaw was so misshapen that an operation was necessary just to allow him to talk. In the film, however, after a few snuffles to warm up, he quotes the Twenty-Third Psalm and *Romeo and Juliet*. This is pure sentimentalism.

The film could have chosen to develop the relationship between Merrick and his medical sponsor, Dr. Frederick Treves, along the lines of the bond between doctor and child in Truffaut's *The Wild Child*. It could have bluntly dealt with the degree of Merrick's inability to relate to ordinary society, as in Werner Herzog's *Kaspar Hauser*. Instead, it makes him noble and celebrates his nobility.

I kept asking myself what the film was *really* trying to say about the human condition as reflected by John Merrick, and I kept drawing blanks. The film's philosophy is this shallow: (1) Wow, the Elephant Man sure looked hideous, and (2) gosh, isn't it wonderful how he kept on in spite of everything? This last is in spite of a real possibility that John Merrick's death at twenty-seven might have been suicide.

The film's technical credits are adequate. John Hurt is very good as Merrick, somehow projecting a humanity past the disfiguring makeup, and Anthony Hopkins is correctly aloof and yet venal as the doctor. The direction, by David (Eraserhead) Lynch, is competent, although he gives us an inexcusable opening scene in which Merrick's mother is trampled or scared by elephants or raped—who knows?—and an equally idiotic closing scene in which Merrick becomes the Star Child from 2001, or something.

Endless Love ★ ★
R, 115 m., 1981

Brooke Shields (Jade), Martin Hewitt (David), Shirley Knight (Anne), Don Murray (Hugh), Richard Kiley (Arthur), Beatrice Straight (Rose), Penelope Milford (Ingrid). Directed by Franco Zeffirelli and produced by Dyson Lovell. Screenplay by Judith Rascoe.

The novel Endless Love is about a teen-age boy who remembers, with full ferocity and grief and yearning, the great love of his life, after it has been ended by fate and the adult world. The movie Endless Love is about a teen-age boy and girl who are in love, until fate and adults end their relationship. There is all the difference in the world between these two story sequences, and although there are a great many things wrong with the movie, this blunder on the narrative level is the worst.

Didn't the makers of this movie understand the poignancy at the very heart of the novel? The book begins with its hero, David, committing an act that will end all of his happiness for years. Forbidden to see his girl, Jade, for thirty days, he sets a fire of newspapers on the porch of her house—hoping to win a reprieve by being the hero who "discovers" the fire. The house burns down, and David is sent into a long exile in a mental institution. The novel's point of view is of a boy who has lost everything he values and remembers it with undying passion. But the movie rearranges the events of the book into chronological order. That means that the love affair between Jade and David, instead of being remembered as a painful loss, is seen in

the "now" as . . . well, as a teen-age romance. Its additional level of meaning is lost.

A story that began as a poem to the fierce pride of adolescent passion gets transmuted into a sociological case study. This movie contains some of the same characters and events as Scott Spencer's wonderful novel (indeed, at times it is unnecessarily faithful to situations and dialogue from the book), but it does not contain the book's reason for being. It is about events and it should be about passion.

There are many other problems in the film. One crucial mistake is in casting: Martin Hewitt, as David, the seventeen-year-old boy, is a capable actor but is too handsome, too heavily bearded, too old in appearance to suggest an adolescent bundle of vulnerability and sensitivity. Another mistake is in narrative: The sequence of events involving David's release from the institution, his trip to New York, and exactly what happens there, is so badly jumbled that some audience members will not know how and why he went to New York, and hardly anyone will be able to follow the circumstances that reunite him with Jade.

A third mistake is in this movie's ending, or rather, its lack of one: The final three minutes in this movie are enraging to anyone who has made an emotional investment in it, because they are a cop-out, a refusal to deal with the material and bring it to a conclusion. The fourth mistake is the one that made me most angry, because it deals with the central act of the narrative, with the disaster around which the story revolves. In the book, David sets fire to the newspaper as an act of passion, confusion, and grief—sure it's dumb, but he's confused and in turmoil. The movie, with offensive heavy-handedness, has another youth suggest the fire to David as a strategy. Apparently the filmmakers thought the fire had to be "explained." The result is to take a reckless act and turn it into a stupid one, diminishing both David's intelligence and the power of his passion.

The movie's central relationship, between Jade (Brooke Shields) and David, comes out as a disappointment, because their scenes are not allowed to develop human resonances. We never really feel and understand the bond between these two people. That's partly because of Hewitt's inability to project uncertainty and adolescent awkwardness; he comes on so strong and self-confident that David seems like a young man making a bold bid for a good-looking girl, rather than as one-half of a pair of star-crossed adolescent lovers.

Is there anything good in the movie? Yes. Brooke Shields is good. She is a great natural beauty, and she demonstrates, in a scene of tenderness and concern for Jewitt and in a scene of rage with her father, that she has a strong, unaffected screen acting manner. But the movie as a whole does not understand the particular strengths of the novel that inspired it, does not convince us it understands adolescent love, does not seem to know its characters very well, and is a narrative and logical mess.

Escape from New York ★ ★ ½
R, 99 m., 1981

Kurt Russell (Snake Plissken), Lee Van Cleef (Bob Hauk), Ernest Borgnine (Cabbie) Donald Pleasence (President), Harry Dean Stanton (Brain), Isaac Hayes (Duke), Season Hubley (Girl in Store), Adrienne Barbeau (Maggie). Directed by John Carpenter and produced by Larry France and Debra Hill. Screenplay by Carpenter and Nick Castle.

John Carpenter's *Escape from New York* is a cross between three of the most reliable ingredients in pulp fantasy: (1) the President Is Missing, (2) New York Is a Jungle, and (3) the Antihero as Time Bomb. Carpenter has gone after an original angle on each of the ingredients, with disappointing results. The president, for example, would be much more convincing if he were not played as a sniveling wimp by Donald Pleasence. The movie's New York of 1997 would have been more interesting if it were seen as a genuinely different prison society, rather than as a recycled version of *The Warriors*. And the antihero needs more human qualities and quirks; he seems lifted from old spaghetti Westerns.

These basic problems prevent the movie from becoming more than it is, a competent job of craftsmanship. And yet it's fun to see old standby science-fiction ingredients rehashed for our cynical times.

At the beginning of *Escape from New York*, we learn that the city was turned into a federal maximum security prison in 1987, and that

several years later the island is ruled by prowling gangs who have their own sources of power, food, and clout. When we see New York, however, it is essentially just a garbage-strewn junkyard roamed by wild-eyed crazies. How *do* people survive there? If the movie had provided specific details, it could have been fascinating. Instead, we get tantalizing hints of how things work; for example, a gang leader (Isaac Hayes) has a small oil well pumping inside his headquarters.

The president has been missing, endangered, kidnapped, blackmailed, or otherwise inconvenienced in countless other movies and novels. This time, after terrorists hijack Air Force One and crash it into Manhattan Island, the president escapes inside an ingenious armored crash pod that is never explained. He is then held hostage, along with a cassette tape that contains the means of preventing World War III. Carpenter's decision to cast Donald Pleasance in the role reminds us that Pleasance added great credibility and psychic weight to *Halloween*, in the role as the psychiatrist. But he never makes a convincing president.

The movie's plot revolves around the decision of the police commissioner (Lee Van Cleef) to send a convicted criminal into New York to bring the president back alive. The criminal is a Special Forces veteran (he fought, we learn, at Leningrad and in Siberia). If he gets the president out within twenty-four hours, he gets a pardon. If he doesn't, tiny time bombs rupture his major arteries. The criminal is played by Kurt Russell, a talented veteran of several Disney movies. Russell is so determined to shake his Disney image that he goes whole hog, with an eye patch, a three-day beard, and a growl so hoarse he seems to be moaning most of the time. It's an interesting idea for a performance, maybe, but nothing is done to give the character human qualities, and so we're allowed to remain detached about his plight.

A bunch of familiar faces turn up in supporting roles. Ernest Borgnine is the last of the wise-guy New York cabbies, *still* looking for fares in the jungle. Isaac Hayes is the gang leader, the inimitable Harry Dean Stanton is his personal advisor, and Adrienne Barbeau is his "squeeze." Making this list, I keep being reminded of the word I started out with: Ingredients. Everything is here, and it all works fairly well, but it never quite comes together into an involving story or an overpowering adventure.

Eureka ★ ★ ★
R, 130 m., 1984

Gene Hackman (Jack McCann), Theresa Russell (Tracy), Rutger Hauer (Claude), Jane Lapotaire (Helen McCann), Helena Kallianiotis (Frieda), Ed Lauter (Perkins), Mickey Rourke (D'Amato), Joe Pesci (Mayakofsky). Directed by Nicolas Roeg and produced by Jeremy Thomas. Screenplay by Paul Mayersberg.

Eureka is a strange, perverse film about passion and greed, and it leads us through a labyrinthine story to a simple message: Money can't buy you love. It stars Gene Hackman as an obsessed gold prospector in the Yukon, who screams into the wind that he will "never make a nickel off another man's sweat." He stalks out into a blizzard, almost freezes to death, and then is saved through the supernatural intervention of a fortune-teller (Helena Kallianiotis). She arranges for him to find the mother lode and become the richest man in the world.

We then flash foward to the 1930s, when he lives on his own Caribbean island. He should be a man without worries, but he is desperately unhappy because his beloved daughter (Theresa Russell) has married a scheming playboy (Rutger Hauer). While monsoons blow and parrots squawk, he bans Hauer from his table and vows to see him dead. "At first I thought you wanted my daughter. Then I thought you wanted my gold," Hackman screams at him. "Now I think you want my soul." He is right, but there is a battle over that soul, and the other contestant is the daughter herself. The film's director, Nicolas Roeg, says he has friends who seem to be the soul-clones of their parents, and apparently the closing passages of *Eureka* are meant to be seen with that notion in mind. Meanwhile, there are so many other notions to keep in mind that the film all but sinks under the weight of its inspiration.

Roeg is a fascinating director. Remember some of his films: *Walkabout, Don't Look Now, Performance, The Man Who Fell to Earth, Bad Timing.* They almost all seem to deal with supernatural intervention in the affairs of man, and with the way those mysteries get tangled up with the bedsheets. His films are also a visual feast; Roeg, a former editor, loves to construct complicated fantasies out of images and memories, shocks and beautiful meditations.

Straightforward storytelling is not his strong point. But so what? The basic facts of *Eureka* (man strikes gold, becomes rich, grows old and jealous, suffers for greed) are familiar from Jack London, Edgar Allan Poe, and von Stroheim's *Greed.* What Roeg brings to the party is a flair for the sensational, for characters who are larger than their weaknesses, who are connected to great archetypal forces. Hackman is wonderful here, with the intensity of his obsessions, and once again Russell (*still* only in her mid-twenties) is brilliant; in some ways this is her movie, and she steals scenes from everybody except, sometimes, Hackman. If *Eureka* is not completely successful—if, indeed, it is sometimes merely silly and often confusing—maybe that's the price we pay for Roeg's intensity. At least it is never boring.

Evil Under the Sun ★ ★ ★
PG, 102 m., 1982

Peter Ustinov (Hercule Poirot), Colin Blakely (Sir Horace Blatt), Jane Birkin (Christine Redfern), Nicholas Clay (Patrick Redfern), Maggie Smith (Daphne Castle), Roddy McDowall (Rex Brewster), Sylvia Miles (Myra Gardener), James Mason (Odell Gardener). Directed by Guy Hamilton and produced by John Brabourne and Richard Goodwin. Screenplay by Anthony Shaffer.

The delicious moments in an Agatha Christie film are supposed to come at the end, when the detective (in this case, the redoubtable Hercule Poirot) gathers everyone in the sitting room and toys with their guilt complexes before finally fingering the murderer. Well, there are delicious moments in the final fifteen minutes of *Evil Under the Sun,* but what I especially liked about this Christie were the opening scenes—the setup. They had a style and irreverence that reminded me curiously of *Beat the Devil,* with Bogart and Robert Morley chewing up the scenery. *Evil Under the Sun* is not, alas, as good as *Beat the Devil,* but it is the best of the recent group of Christie retreads (which include *Murder on the Orient Express, Death on the Nile,* and *The Mirror Crack'd*).

It begins in the usual way, with a corpse. It continues in obligatory fashion with the gathering of a large number of colorful and eccentric suspects in an out-of-the-way spot, which just happens to also be the destination of Hercule Poirot. It continues with the discovery of another corpse, with the liberal distribution of gigantic clues and with Poirot's lip-smacking summary of the evidence. It's the cast that makes *Evil* more fun than the previous manifestations of this identical plot. As Poirot, Peter Ustinov creates a wonderful mixture of the mentally polished and physically maladroit. He has a bit of business involving a dip in the sea that is so perfectly timed and acted it tells us everything we ever wanted to know about Poirot's appetite for exercise. He is so expansive, so beaming, so superior, in the opening scenes that he remains spiritually present throughout the film, even when he's not on screen.

All of the rest of the cast are suspects. They include Maggie Smith, a former actress who now runs an elegant spa in the Adriatic Sea; Diana Rigg, as her jealous contemporary; Sylvia Miles and James Mason, as a rich couple who produce shows on Broadway; Jane Birkin and Nicholas Clay as a young couple constantly arguing over his roving eye; Colin Blakely as a rich knight who's been taken by a gold digger; Emily Hone as the young new wife, and Roddy McDowell as a bitchy gossip columnist who knows the dirt about everybody. The newly discovered corpse belongs to one of the above. The murderer is one (or more) of the above. Nothing else I could say about the crime would be fair.

I can observe, however, that one of the delights of the movies made from Agatha Christie novels is their almost complete lack of passion: They substitute wit and style. Nobody really cares who gets bumped off, and nobody really misses the departed. What's important is that all the right clues be distributed, so that Poirot and the audience can pick them up, mull them over, and discover the culprit. Perhaps, then, one of the reasons I liked *Evil Under the Sun* was that this time, when Ustinov paused in his sum-

mation (after verbally convicting everyone in the room), and it was clear he was about to finger the real killer, I guessed the killer's identity, and I was right. Well, half right. That's better than I usually do.

Excalibur ★ ★ ½
R, 140 m., 1981

Nigel Terry (Arthur), Helen Mirren (Morgana), Nicholas Clay (Lancelot), Nicol Williamson (Merlin), Cherie Lunghi (Guenevere), Paul Geoffrey (Perceval). Directed by John Boorman and produced by Edgar F. Gross and Robert A. Eisenstein. Screenplay by Rospo Pallenberg and Boorman.

What a wondrous vision *Excalibur* is! And what a mess. This wildly ambitious retelling of the legend of King Arthur is a haunting and violent version of the Dark Ages and the heroic figures who (we dream) populated them. But it's rough going for anyone determined to be sure what is happening from scene to scene. Great armored figures clank through the forest and bury broadaxes in each other's bodies. Young Arthur frees the magic sword Excalibur from the granite boulder where it was embedded. Castles are stormed. Arthur marries Guenevere and the kingdom rejoices. Camelot reigns. Merlin the Magician enters into a doomed pact with Morgana, Arthur's half-sister, and Morgana assumes the appearance of Guenevere to seduce Arthur. She plans for their son born of incest, Mordred, to take his place as king . . .

And all of this is buried in such a wealth of detail, such an impenetrable atmosphere, such tumultuous alarms and excursions, that the audience is quite likely to lose its place. John Boorman, the director of *Excalibur,* is brilliant at staging the life and times of Arthur—the film is a triumph of production design, costumes, and special effects. But he hasn't hammered out a clear story line. His male characters, bearded and hiding within medieval helmets, sometimes look and sound like one another. If Robert Bresson's *Lancelot of the Lake* (1973) deliberately made all the knights into interchangeable, clanking clones, Boorman seems to have arrived at the same place inadvertently. This is a film we almost have to squint to see and to understand.

As a panorama of sword and sorcery, however, it is very beautiful to watch. And as a showcase for Nicol Williamson's Merlin, it is sometimes a lot of fun; Williamson plays the magician as a medieval Noel Coward, always armed with the wry witticism. His relationship with Morgana (the lovely Helen Mirren) is actually the most interesting thing in the film. Morgana borrows Merlin's magic to deceive Arthur and to stay young. Inhabiting a dragon's cave that is apparently somewhere beneath Camelot, she wears brass brassieres and other obligatory props, but she's intriguing.

It's curious how our tastes in myth change; heroes seem to be devalued and our fascination is with villains. Arthur almost recedes into the scenery toward the end of *Excalibur,* upstaged by the sins of Lancelot, the schemes of Morgana, the arch amusement of Merlin and, finally, by the astonishing appearance of Mordred—who wears a golden helmet that makes him into a muscular Cupid. *Excalibur* is a revisionist view of what Arthur's people and times looked like. But the film has a tendency to drift into soft focus and impenetrable fogs. Many scenes are shot through filters that soften and dissipate their effect. The movie's very last shot, of a ship plunging out to sea, should have been hard-edged and forlorn, but it's all misty and evanescent.

There is another problem, too: one common not only to many movie versions of Arthurian legends, but epidemic in the modern sword-and-sorcery genre. The people in this film seem doomed to their behavior. They have no choice. Arthur is courageous as a youth, but then presides over the disintegration of the Round Table, for no apparent reason. The brave and pure Lancelot, accused of being Guenevere's lover, engages in a deadly joust to defend her honor. Not much later, however, they make love. Merlin is a great and powerful magician, but allows Morgana to outwit him; he seems to decide from moment to moment whether to possess vast powers or none.

Since there is no consistency in the behavior of the characters, *Excalibur* is maddeningly arbitrary. Anyone is likely to do anything—and when they do, Boorman springs another battle scene on us, with horses whinnying and swords thumping into

flesh until the novelty wears thin. One of the joys of *Star Wars,* which is really a sword-and-sorcery fantasy of the future, is that everyone plays by the rules, lives by the Force, and is true to himself. Boorman's *Excalibur* is a record of the comings and goings of arbitrary, inconsistent, shadowy figures who are not heroes but simply giants run amok. Still, it's wonderful to look at.

Experience Preferred . . .
But Not Essential ★ ★ ★
PG, 77 m., 1983

Elizabeth Edmonds (Annie), Sue Wallace (Mavis), Geraldine Griffith (Doreen), Karen Meagher (Paula), Ron Bain (Mike), Alun Lewis (Hywel). Directed by Peter Duffell and produced by David Puttnam and Chris Griffin. Screenplay by June Roberts.

This movie is so slight and charming you're almost afraid to breathe during it, for fear of disturbing the spell. It's about ordinary people in an ordinary setting, but because the setting is a small resort hotel in Wales, and the time is the summer of 1962, there's also the strange feeling that we've entered another time and place, where some of the same rules apply, but by no means all of them.

The movie tells the story of a young woman named Annie (Elizabeth Edmonds) who comes to work for the summer in a hotel, and finds that she's entered a cozy little backstairs world with its own sets of loyalties and jealousies. All of the other waitresses at the hotel have their own stories, some funny, some sad, and Annie feels a little left out. "I'm the only one here without a past," she complains, but of course one of the reasons for spending your summer working in a hotel is to accumulate a past. The other women are suspicious of her because she's a student, but as the waitresses cram into the servants' quarters, three to a room and sometimes two to a bed, a sort of democracy sets in, and Annie is accepted.

The movie uses a wonderfully offhand style for filling us in on the characters. There's the gallant cook, who immediately takes a liking to Annie. And the redheaded bartender, who makes it a nightly habit to sleepwalk in the nude. And the conceited young waiter whose idea of a courtship is to belt his girl in the eye every once in a while. And the pretty hostess of the dining room, who owes her position and her private boudoir to the favors she supplies the hotel's owner. ("How did you get such a nice room?" Annie asks her, innocently.)

There's not much of a plot. Things just sort of happen. Young men and women work from dawn to dusk and then collapse into each other's arms, almost but not quite too exhausted for sex. And the sexual customs of the pre-Pill era take on a certain quaintness, and a certain desperation, as couples grimly try to walk the line between lust and prudence. *Experience Preferred* is charming precisely because of its inconsequential air. It's funny because it goes for whimsical little insights into human nature rather than for big, obvious jokes. It's charming because it doesn't force the charm.

Exposed ★ ★ ★ ½
R, 100 m., 1983

Nastassja Kinski (Elizabeth), Rudolph Nureyev (Daniel), Harvey Keitel (Rivas), Ian McShane (Miller), Bibi Andersson (Margaret), Pierre Clementi (Vic). Directed and produced by James Toback. Screenplay by Toback.

This movie contains moments so exhilarating they reawakened me to the infinite possibilities of movies. Yet this movie loses itself in its closing sequences and meanders through the details of a routine terrorist plot. Somewhere between its greatness and its wandering there must be a compromise, and I would strike it this way: *Exposed* contains the most exciting evidence I have seen so far that Nastassja Kinski is the next great female superstar. I do not say that she is a great actress; not yet, and perhaps not ever. I do not compare her with Meryl Streep or Kate Nelligan, Jill Clayburgh or Jessica Lange. I am not talking in those terms of professional accomplishment. I am talking about the mysterious, innate quality that some performers have to cast a special spell, to develop a relationship with the camera that you can call stardom or voodoo or magic, because its name doesn't really matter.

Kinski has it. There are moments in this film (two virtuoso scenes, in particular, and then many other small moments and parts of scenes) when she affects me in the same way that Marilyn Monroe must have affected her first viewers, in movies like *The Asphalt Jungle* or *All About Eve*. She was not yet a star and audiences did not even know her name, but there was a quality about her that could not be dismissed. Kinski has that quality. She has exhibited it before in better films, such as *Tess*, and in ambitious, imperfect films such as *Cat People* and *One from the Heart*. Now here is *Exposed*, written and directed by James Toback, who in screenplays such as *The Gambler* and his brilliant, little-seen directing debut *Fingers*, has specialized in characters who live on the edge.

There are two sequences in *Exposed* where he pulls out all the stops. In one of them, Kinski (who plays a college dropout, lonely and sexually frustrated) dances all by herself in a nearly empty apartment. In another one, she meets a violinist (Rudolph Nureyev), they fall instantly into a consuming passion, and after he has tantalized her with a violin bow they make sudden, passionate love. The sheer quality of Kinski's abandon in these two scenes made me realize how many barriers can sometimes exist between a performance and an audience: Here there are none.

The movie is wonderful for its first hour or more. It follows Kinski through a brief, unhappy love affair with her professor (played by Toback), shows her moving to New York, has her discovered by a photographer and becoming a world-famous model (because she is Kinski, this is believable), and brings her up through the love affair with Nureyev. At this moment, *Exposed* seems poised on the brink of declaring itself one of the most riveting character portraits ever made.

And that is the moment where it falters, and loses itself in the details of a plot involving Harvey Keitel, as the leader of an underground terrorist cell in Paris. It's as if Toback didn't trust the strength of this character he had created (or, more likely, didn't know when he wrote his thriller that Kinski would bring the character so completely to life). The rest of the movie is okay, I suppose, in a somewhat familiar way. But its special quality is lost in plot details. Too bad.

But if a movie can electrify me the way this one did, not once but twice and then some, I'm prepared to forgive it almost anything.

The Exterminator   no stars
R, 101 m., 1980

Christopher George (Detective Dalton), Samantha Eggar (Dr. Stewart), Robert Ginty (John Eastland), Steve James (Michael Jefferson). Directed and written by James Glickenhaus and produced by Mark Buntzman.

The Exterminator is a sick example of the almost unbelievable descent into gruesome savagery in American movies. It's a direct rip-off of *Death Wish*, a 1974 Charles Bronson hit about a man who kills muggers to avenge the death of his wife. *Death Wish* was violent, yes, but it remained within certain boundaries. It established a three-dimensional character, it gave him reasons for his actions, it allowed us to sympathize with those reasons and yet still disapprove of the murders he was committing. *The Exterminator* does none of those things. It is essentially just a sadistic exercise in moronic violence, supported by a laughable plot. The "exterminator" of the movie's title (Robert Ginty) has his life saved in Vietnam by a black man (Steve James), who becomes his closest friend. Back home in Brooklyn, they break up a gang in the process of stealing beer from a loading dock. The gang gets revenge by attacking and permanently paralyzing the black man. The hero vows revenge.

So far, so good. What's profoundly disturbing about the film is that it uses this "justification" in the plot as an excuse for revenge scenes of the sickest possible perversion. The motive is obviously to shock or titillate the audience, not to show plausible actions by the character. For example: Ginty gets one gang member to talk by tying him to a wall and threatening him with an acetylene torch. Then he machine-guns the men who attacked his buddy.

They get off easy. Determined to get money to support the family of his paralyzed friend, Ginty kidnaps a Mafia boss. He hangs him by chains over a huge meat grinder, goes to rob his house and then lowers the man into the grinder, converting him to ground meat. He justifies this crime in a letter to anchorman Roger Grimsby (who plays himself—to his horror, no doubt, when he saw this film). And then he goes on a one-man vigilante campaign to clean up New York.

To help him in his campaign, the movie shows the audience evil situations and then lets the "exterminator" remedy them. For example, a hooker is lured to a house of male prostitution, where a sadistic client disfigures her with a soldering iron. Some weeks later, the "exterminator" picks up the hooker, sees the burn scars when she undresses and decides to avenge her. He goes to the male brothel, sets the owner on fire and shoots a customer dead.

There's more, involving an insipid policeman (Christopher George) and his girlfriend (Samantha Eggar), who turns out to be the paralyzed man's doctor. This is the kind of movie that establishes their relationship by sending them to a concert and then focusing on the concert because they have no dialogue. The CIA also gets involved, but who cares? *The Exterminator* exists primarily to show burnings, shootings, gougings, grindings, and beheadings. It is a small, unclean exercise in shame.

Eye of the Needle ★ ★ ★
R, 118 m., 1981

Donald Sutherland (Faber), Kate Nelligan (Lucy), Christopher Cazenova (David), Ian Bannon (Canter). Directed by Richard Marquand and produced by Stephen Friedman. Screenplay by Stanley Mann.

Eye of the Needle resembles nothing so much as one of those downbeat, plodding, quietly horrifying, and sometimes grimly funny war movies that used to be made by the British film industry, back when there was a British film industry. They used to star Stanley Baker or Trevor Howard. This one stars Donald Sutherland, as the kind of introverted psychopath who should inhabit only black-and-white movies, although the color here is sometimes gloomy enough to suffice. I admired the movie. It is made with quiet competence, and will remind some viewers of the Alfred Hitchcock who made *The 39 Steps* and *Foreign Correspondent*. It is about a German spy, the "Needle," who dropped out of sight in Germany in 1938 and now inhabits a series of drab bed-sitting-rooms in England while he spies on the British war effort. He is known as the Needle because of his trademarked way of killing people by jabbing a stiletto into their rib cages. He kills with a singular lack of passion; this is Jack the Ripper crossed with J. Alfred Prufrock. As played by Sutherland, the Needle is a very lonely man. We are given hints to explain his isolation: He was raised by parents who did not love him, he was shipped off to boarding schools, he spent parts of his childhood in America, where he learned English. None of these experiences fully explains his ruthlessness, but then perhaps it is just a spy's job to be ruthless.

The plot is part espionage, part cliffhanger. The Needle discovers phony plywood "airplanes" intended to look, from the air, like Patton's invasion force—a ruse to throw off the Germans. His assignment is to personally deliver news of the actual Allied invasion plans to Hitler. This he intends to do with every fiber of his being, and yet we never get the feeling that the this man is a patriotic Nazi. He is more of a dogged functionary. In his attempts to rendezvous with a Nazi submarine, he's shipwrecked on an isolated island occupied only by a lighthouse-keeper and by a young married couple—a woman (Kate Nelligan), her legless husband (Christopher Cazenove), and their son. The last third of the movie turns into a bloody melodrama, as the Needle kills the husband and the lighthouse-keeper and threatens the woman, first in a psychological way and then with violence. But before the final standoff, he pretends to be merely a lost sailor. And the woman, frustrated by her husband's drunkenness and refusal to love, becomes attracted to the stranger. They make love. She grows fond of him. Does he grow fond of her? We can never be sure, but he tells her things he has told to no one else.

Some people will find the movie slow going. I preferred to think of it as deliberate. It is effective, I think, to develop a plot like this at a deliberate pace, instead of rushing headlong through it. That gives us time to meditate on the character of the Needle, and to ponder his very few, enigmatic references to his own behavior. We learn things about him that he may not even know about himself, and that is why the film's final scene is

so much more complex than it seems. "The war has come down to the two of us," Sutherland tells Nelligan, and in the final exchange of desperate looks between the man and the woman there is a whole universe left unspoken. The movie ends with Nelligan regarding a man who is either a treacherous spy or an unloved child, take your choice.

Eyewitness ★ ★ ★
R, 102 m., 1981

William Hurt (Daryll Deever), Sigourney Weaver (Tony Sokolow), Christopher Plummer (Joseph), James Woods (Aldo), Irene Worth (Mrs. Sokolow), Pamela Reed (Linda). Directed and produced by Peter Yates. Screenplay by Steve Tesich.

Somebody was explaining the difference between European and American movies to me the other day: European movies are about people, but American movies are about stories. It's an interesting idea, especially when it's applied to a thriller like *Eyewitness*, which is good precisely because it pays more attention to its people than its story. Does that make it European? Well, it was directed by Peter Yates, who is British but has directed some of the most "American" movies of the past decade, from *Bullitt* to *Breaking Away*. It is definitely set in America—from the bowels of a Manhattan boiler room to the newsroom of a TV station. But it's about such interesting, complicated, quirky, and sometimes funny people that it must at the least be mid-Atlantic.

The movie stars William Hurt as a janitor who stumbles across evidence that could lead to the solution of a murder investigation. But he doesn't go to the police with it because he's too complicated, too introspective, too distrustful of his own discovery . . . and, mostly, he's too much in love from afar with a TV news reporter (Sigourney Weaver). Maybe he can win her attention by giving her the scoop?

There are other complications. Sigourney Weaver is engaged to an Israeli agent (Christopher Plummer) who is involved in secret international negotiations to smuggle Jews out of the Soviet Union. His plan involves clandestine payments to a Vietnamese agent who got rich on the black market in

Saigon and has now moved to Manhattan. The other characters include James Woods, as Hurt's eccentric and unpredictable fellow janitor, and Steven Hill and Morgan Freeman as a couple of cops who wearily track down leads in the case (their best line: "When Aldo was a little boy, he must have wanted to grow up to be a suspect").

The development and solution of the murder mystery are handled with professional dispatch by Yates and his writer, Steve Tesich (who also wrote *Breaking Away*). A final shoot-out in a midtown riding stable has a touch of Hitchcock to it; the old master always loved to mix violence with absolutely inappropriate settings. But what makes this movie so entertaining is the way Yates and Tesich and their characters play against our expectations.

Examples. Weaver is not only a TV newswoman, but also a part-time serious pianist and the unhappy daughter of her domineering parents. Hurt is not only a janitor but also a sensitive soul who can talk his way into Weaver's heart. Woods is not only a creepy janitor but also the enthusiastic promoter of a marriage between his sister and Hurt. Hurt and the sister (Pamela Reed) carry on the courtship because they are both too embarrassed to tell the other one they're not in love. Plummer is the most complicated character of all, and it's a very good question whether he's a villain. It all depends on how you view his own personal morality.

I've seen so many thrillers that, frankly, I don't always care how they turn out—unless they're really well-crafted. What I like about *Eyewitness* is that, although it *does* care how it turns out, it cares even more about the texture of the scenes leading to the denouement. There's not a scene in this movie that exists only to provide us with plot information. Every scene develops characters. And they're developed in such offbeat fidelity to the way people do behave that we get all the more involved in the mystery, just because, for once, we halfway believe it could really be happening.

Fade to Black ★ ★ ½
R, 100 m., 1980

Dennis Christopher (Eric Binford), Tim Thomerson (Dr. Moriarty), Gwynne Gilford (Anne), Linda Kerridge (Marilyn), Morgan Paull (Gary Bially), Eve Brent Ashe (Aunt Stella). Directed by Vernon Zimmerman. Produced by George G. Braunstein and Ron Hamady. Screenplay by Zimmerman.

It will probably help to be a movie buff if you find yourself watching *Fade to Black*. This is a weird, uneven, generally intriguing thriller about a young man whose fantasy life is totally controlled by images from movies. He works in a Los Angeles film exchange, checking and shipping movie prints, and at night he comes home to his museumlike room in the home of his aunt—a shrill harridan who would feel less secure in her wheelchair if she had ever seen *Kiss of Death*.

The young man is played with a kind of creepy power by Dennis Christopher, in a role completely opposite from his performance as the hero of *Breaking Away*. He is lonely, socially isolated, hostile. He has memorized every movie ever made, although when he bets money on a trivia question, it's one with a ridiculously easy answer: He wants to know Humphrey Bogart's full name in *Casablanca*. Everybody knows that one.

Things start going wrong in the kid's life. His boss gets on his case at work. His aunt is impossible. He makes a date with a young girl (Linda Kerridge) who looks just like Marilyn Monroe, and then he thinks she stood him up. This is too much all at once, and the kid goes berserk.

In a scene we know is inevitable, he mimics Richard Widmark in *Kiss of Death* and pushes his aunt down the stairs. Then he begins masquerading as his other movie heroes—Hopalong Cassidy, James Cagney, the Mummy—and wiping out the rest of his opposition. These scenes are handled by director Vernon Zimmerman with a mixture of reality and stylized fantasy. For example, when Hoppy gets in a shoot-out, the scene is staged and lit like a movie, which heightens the effect. But it's not lit like a Hopalong Cassidy movie; it's lit to backlight and isolate the hero, and that, no doubt, is the kid's own fantasy.

I don't want to give away too many of the movie's surprises, although if you're a movie buff you'll anticipate a lot of them. The climax, though, is a bravura piece of stylistic overkill, with Christopher creeping around of the roof of Hollywood's Chinese Theater, looking like a cross between the Phantom of the Opera and Cary Grant in *To Catch a Thief.*

What's the point of all this? Just pure escapist silliness, I suppose. But I was rather moved by the Christopher character's loneliness in the earlier scenes (later, he's frankly just a caricature manipulated by the plot). I also liked the way that some of the minor roles, including Kerridge's were handled to develop the humanity of the characters rather than just the stereotypes.

The Falcon and the Snowman
★ ★ ★ ★
R, 131 m., 1985

Timothy Hutton (Christopher Boyce), Sean Penn (Daulton Lee), Pat Hingle (Mr. Boyce), Joyce Van Patten (Mrs. Boyce), David Suchet (Alex), Boris Leskin (Mikhail). Directed by John Schlesinger and produced by Gabriel Katska and Schlesinger. Screenplay by Steven Saillian.

A few years ago there were stories in the papers about a couple of California kids who were caught selling government secrets to the Russians. The stories had an air of unreality about them. Here were a couple of middle-class young men from suburban backgrounds, who were prosecuted as spies and traitors and who hardly seemed to have it quite clear in their own minds how they had gotten into the spy business. One of the many strengths of *The Falcon and the Snowman* is that it succeeds, in an admirably matter-of-fact way, in showing us exactly how these two young men got in way over their heads. This is a movie about spies, but it is not a thriller in any routine sense of the word; it's just the meticulously observant record of how naiveté, inexperience, misplaced idealism, and greed led to one of the most peculiar cases of treason in American history.

The movie stars Timothy Hutton as Christopher Boyce, a seminarian who has a crisis of conscience, drops out of school, and ends up working almost by accident for a message-routing center of the CIA. Sean Penn is his best friend, Daulton Lee. Years ago, they were altar boys together, but in recent times their paths have diverged; while Boyce was studying for the priesthood, Lee was setting himself up as a drug dealer. By the time we meet them, Boyce is earnest and clean-cut, just the kind of young man the CIA might be looking for (it doesn't hurt that his father is a former FBI man). And Lee, with a mustache that makes him look like a failed creep, is a jumpy, paranoid drug dealer who is one step ahead of the law.

The whole caper begins so simply. Boyce, reading the messages he is paid to receive and forward, learns that the CIA is engaged in dirty tricks designed to influence elections in Australia. He is deeply offended to learn that his government would be interfering in the affairs of another state, and the more he thinks about it, the more he wants to do something. For example, supply the messages to the Russians. He doesn't want to be a Russian *spy*, you understand, just to bring this injustice to light. Lee has some contacts in Mexico, where he buys drugs. One day, in a deceptively casual conversation by the side of a backyard swimming pool, the two friends decide to go into partnership to sell the information to the Soviet Embassy in Mexico City. Lee takes the documents south and launches them both on an adventure that is a lark at first, and then a challenge, and finally just a very, very bad dream.

These two young men have one basic problem. They are amateurs. The Russians don't necessarily like that any better than the Americans would; indeed, even though the Russians are happy to have the secrets that are for sale, there is a definite sense in some scenes that the key Russian contact agent, played by David Suchet, is almost offended by the sloppy way Penn deals in espionage. The only thing Penn seems really serious about is the money.

The Falcon and the Snowman never steps wrong, but it is best when it deals with the relationship between the two young American spies. The movie was directed by John Schlesinger, an Englishman whose understanding of American characters was most unforgettably demonstrated in *Midnight Cowboy*, and I was reminded of Joe Buck and Ratso Rizzo from that movie as I watched this one. There is even a quiet, understated quote to link Ratso with the

Penn character: a moment in a parking garage when Penn defies a car to pull in front of him, and we're reminded of Ratso crossing a Manhattan street and hurling the line "I'm *walking* here!" at a taxi that dares to cut him off. Instead of relying on traditional methods for creating the suspense in spy movies, this one uses the energy generated between the two very different characters, as the all-American Boyce gradually begins to understand that his partner is out of control. *The Falcon and the Snowman*, like most good movies, is not really about its plot but about its characters. These two young men could just as easily be selling stolen IBM programs to Apple, instead of CIA messages to the Russians; the point is that they begin with one set of motives and then the implacable real world supplies them with another, harder, more unforgiving set of realities.

Just as with *Midnight Cowboy*, it's hard to say who gives the better performance this time: Sean Penn, with his twitching intensity as he angles for respect from the Russians, or Timothy Hutton, the straight man, earnestly telling his girlfriend that she should remember he really loves her—"no matter what you may hear about me in a few days from now."

Falling in Love ★ ★
PG-13, 106 m., 1984

Robert De Niro (Frank Raftis), Meryl Streep (Molly Gilmore), Ann Kaczmarek (Ann Raftis), David Clennon (Brian Gilmore), Harvey Keitel (Ed Lasky). Directed by Ulu Grosbard and produced by Marvin Worth.

This movie is the clearest case I've seen in a long time of the war between movie stars and the scripts they are given. The movie is a love story. The stars are Robert De Niro and Meryl Streep—arguably the two most distinguished American movie actors under fifty. They have a genuine chemistry together on the screen and undeniable charisma. And that's it in this movie, which gives them not one memorable line of dialogue, not one inventive situation, not one moment when we don't groan at the startling array of clichés they have to march through.

Falling in Love is nothing if not upfront about its intentions. It wants to be a 1940s romance, and it makes that bountifully clear

by making the first encounter between the characters a Meet Cute. Meet Cutes are what Hollywood calls those clichéd scenes where Rosalind Russell and Cary Grant are both leaving Macy's at the same time; they run into each other, drop their packages, and bump heads as they awkwardly bend over to pick them up. Would you believe that is *exactly* how the Meet Cute works in this movie? De Niro and Streep are at a bookstore, not a department store, but as their packages drop, the movie almost could use a subtitle with the cross-reference to other films.

I'm sure there was some sort of story conference about how it would be fun to reprise a classic Meet Cute. I'm sure they had a lot of story conferences on this movie, giving one another pep talks about how the movie's total lack of substance was really a style decision. But it's just a cop-out. How can you put Streep and De Niro in a movie and not give them characters to play or interesting things to say? It's a waste of resources.

The movie's story involves two people who commute to New York on the same train. After their "Meet Cute," they are attracted to each other by instant chemistry. They meet again. There is a little awkward conversational jostling, and before long they're embarked on a chaste year-long affair in which they have lunch, go to Chinatown, visit tall buildings and trendy art galleries, and find mutual support while Streep's father dies. Art galleries and Chinatown are almost obligatory in movies like this. All true love affairs must begin with a mutual return to the infantile, as the lovestruck new partners buy hot dogs from vendors and watch the ice skating in Rockefeller Center and in other ways symbolically reenact the necessity of reliving their entire lives, from childhood on, in the company of this treasured new person.

Fine. Except that in all romances worthy of the name, there sooner or later comes a meeting of the minds: There are those rushed, excited conversations in which the two lovers realize that they are both brilliant, both insightful, both witty, and both sharing a viewpoint so unique that the rest of the world will never quite understand it. *Falling in Love* has no such passages. The dialogue is unremittingly, perhaps deliberately, banal.

The funniest line in the movie ("How much do you weigh?") is inspired by the characters' inability to think of anything to say. We learn nothing of substance about them. They are provided with spouses who are ciphers, with personalities that are shallow and narcissistic, with crises that depend upon a manipulative script.

And as if all of that were not bad enough, the movie also resorts to Idiot Plot techniques to squeeze out an infuriating ending. A final farewell between the lovers is prevented because of faulty communications. A later reunion takes place when there is only one fact that each lover needs to know—that the other is separated or divorced. Incredibly, neither character makes this revelation, because to supply that single essential fact would spoil *Falling in Love*'s manipulative and shameless ending.

Incredibly, there are passages when this movie works. They are entirely due to the chemistry, the genuine human qualities of Streep and De Niro. They carry the plot and the dimwit dialogue because of the goodwill they've built up with us, and because of their own magnetism, their ability to invest worthless dialogue with a certain personal charm. *Falling in Love* will serve as a definitive example of good performances in a bad movie.

Fame ★ ★ ★ ½
R, 133 m., 1980

Eddie Barth (Angelo), Irene Cara (Coco), Lee Curreri (Bruno), Laura Dean (Lisa), Antonia Franceschi (Hilary), Boyd Gaines (Michael), Albert Hague (Shorofsky), Tresa Hughes (Mrs. Finsecker). Directed and produced by David De Silva and Alan Marshall. Screenplay by Christopher Gore.

Mrs. Seward, the draconian rhetoric teacher who drilled literacy into generations of Urbana (Ill.) High School students, used to tell us we were having the best four years of our lives. We groaned. *Fame* is a movie that she might have enjoyed. It's about a dozen or so talented kids who enter New York's High School of the Performing Arts as freshmen and emerge four years later as future Freddie Prinzes and Benny Goodmans, Leonard Bernsteins and Mrs. Sewards.

Fame is a genuine treasure, moving and entertaining, a movie that understands being a teen-ager as well as *Breaking Away* did, but studies its characters in a completely different milieu. It's the other side of the coin: A big-city, aggressive, cranked-up movie to play against the quieter traditions of *Breaking Away*'s small Indiana college town. *Fame* is all New York City. It's populated by rich kids, ghetto kids, kids with real talent, and kids with mothers who think they have real talent. They all go into the hopper, into a high school of kids who are worked harder because they're "special"— even if they're secretly not so sure they're so special.

The movie has the kind of sensitivity to the real lives of real people that we don't get much in Hollywood productions anymore. Anyone who ever went to high school will recognize some of *Fame*'s characters: the quiet little girl who blossoms, the class genius who locks himself up in the basement with his electronic equipment, the kid who can't read but is a naturally gifted performer, the wiseass, the self-destructive type, the sexpot, the rich kid, and on and on. The cast has been recruited from New York's most talented young performers, some of them almost playing themselves. The teachers are familiar too: self-sacrificing, perfectionist, cranky, love-hate objects.

If the character types seem familiar, the movie's way of telling their stories is not. This isn't a movie that locks its characters into a conventional plot. Instead, it fragments the experiences of four years into dozens of vignettes, loosely organized into sections titled "The Auditions," "Freshman Year," and so on. We get to know the characters and their personalities gradually, as we see them in various situations. The effect is a little like high school itself; you come in as a total stranger and by the time you leave, the school has become your world.

If the kids in *Fame* are like high school kids anywhere, they're also different because they *are* talented, and the movie's at its best when it examines the special pressures on young people who are more talented than they are mature, experienced, or sure of themselves. The ghost that hovers over everyone in this school is a former graduate,

Freddie Prinze, who had the talent but never figured out how to handle it.

The movie's director, Alan Parker, seems to have a knack for isolating just those moments in the lives of his characters when growth, challenge, and talent are all on the line at once. Where did he find his insights into talented young people? Probably while he was directing his first film, the wonderful *Bugsy Malone* (1976), which was a gangster musical with an all-kid cast. *Fame* is a perfect title for this movie; it establishes an ironic distance between where these kids are now and where they'd like to be someday, and then there's also the haunting suggestion that some of the ones who find fame will be able to handle it, and some will not.

Fanny and Alexander ★ ★ ★ ★
R, 197 m., 1983

Pernilla Allwin (Fanny Ekdahl), Bertil Guve (Alexander Ekdahl), Jan Malmsjo (Bishop Vergerus), Erland Josephson (Isak Jacobi), Kabi Laretei (Aunt Emma), Gunn Wallgren (Helena Ekdahl), Ewa Froling (Emilie Ekdahl), Gunnar Bjornstrand (Filip Landahl). Directed by Ingmar Bergman and produced by Jorn Donner. Screenplay by Bergman.

There was a time when Ingmar Bergman wanted to make films reflecting the whole of human experience. He asked the big questions about death, sex, and God, and he wasn't afraid of the big, dramatic image, either. Who else (except Woody Allen) has had the temerity to show a man playing chess with Death? Bergman was swinging for the fences in those deliberately big, important films. But he has discovered that a better way to encompass all human experience is to be specific about a small part of it and let the audience draw its own conclusions. In *The Seventh Seal* (1956), he portrayed Death as a symbolic grim reaper. But in *Cries and Whispers* (1973), by showing one particular woman dying painfully while her sisters and her maid stood by helplessly, he said infinitely more about death.

His film *Fanny and Alexander* is one of the most detailed and specific he's ever made, and therefore one of the most universal. It comes directly out of his experiences as a Swede in his mid-sixties who was born into a world of rigid religious belief, grew up in a world of war and turmoil, and is now old enough, wise enough, and resigned enough to develop a sort of philosophical mysticism about life. In its chronology, the film covers only a handful of years. But in its buried implications about life, I believe, it traces the development of Bergman's thought from his school days until the day before yesterday.

Fanny and Alexander is a long film that contains many characters and many events. Very simply: In a Swedish provincial town in the early years of this century, two children are growing up within the bosom of a large, jolly extended family. Their father dies and their mother remarries. Their new stepfather is a stern, authoritarian clergyman who means well but is absolutely incapable of understanding the feelings of others. Escape from his household leads them, by an indirect path, into the life of an old Jewish antique dealer whose life still has room for the mysticism and magic of an earlier time. Not everything is explained by the end of the film, but everything is reconciled.

Bergman has confessed that a great deal of the movie is autobiographical—if not literally, then in terms of its feelings. He had, for example, a father who was a strict clergyman. But it's too easy to assume the bishop in the movie represents only Bergman's father: Can he not also represent Bergman himself, who is seen within the circle of his collaborators as an authoritarian figure with a tendency to know what is right for everyone else? Bergman has hinted that there's a little of himself, indeed, in *all* the male characters in his movie. Looking for Bergman's autobiography in his characters is one thing. I think we also can see *Fanny and Alexander* as the autobiography of his career. The warm humanism of the early scenes reflects his own beginnings in naturalism. The stern aestheticism of the middle scenes reflects his own middle period, with its obsession with both philosophical and stylistic black-and-white. The last third of the film, like the last third of his career, admits that there are more things in heaven and on Earth than dreamed of in his philosophy.

Fanny and Alexander is a big, exciting, ambitious film—more of a beginning than, as Bergman claims, the summary of his career. If you've followed him on his long trek of discovery, this will feel like a film of resolution. If you're coming fresh to Bergman, it may, paradoxically, seem to burst with the sort of invention we associate with young first-time directors. It's a film for all seasons.

Fast Times at Ridgemont High ★
R, 92 m., 1982

Sean Penn (Jeff Spicoli), Jennifer Jason Leigh (Stacy Hamilton), Judge Reinhold (Brad Hamilton), Robert Romanus (Mike Damone), Brian Backer (Rat Ratner), Phoebe Cates (Linda Barrett). Directed by Amy Heckerling and produced by Art Linson and Irving Azoff. Screenplay by Cameron Crowe.

How could they do this to Jennifer Jason Leigh? How could they put such a fresh and cheerful person into such a scuz-pit of a movie? Don't they know they have a star on their hands? I didn't even know who Leigh was when I walked into *Fast Times at Ridgemont High,* and yet I was completely won over by her. She contained so much life and light that she was a joy to behold. And then she and everybody else in this so-called comedy is invited to plunge into offensive vulgarity. Let me make myself clear. I am not against vulgarity as a subject for a movie comedy. Sometimes I treasure it, when it's used with inspiration, as in *The Producers* or *National Lampoon's Animal House.* But vulgarity is a very tricky thing to handle in a comedy; tone is everything, and the makers of *Fast Times at Ridgemont High* have an absolute gift for taking potentially funny situations and turning them into general embarrassment. They're tone-deaf.

The movie's another one of those adolescent sex romps, such as *Porky's* and *Animal House,* in which part of the humor comes from raunchy situations and dialogue. This movie is *so* raunchy, however, that the audience can't quite believe it. I went to a sneak preview thrown by a rock radio station, and the audience had come for a good time. But during a scene involving some extremely frank talk about certain popular methods of sexual behavior, even the rock fans were grossed out. There's a difference between raunchiness and gynecological detail.

The movie's cast struggles valiantly through all this dreck. Rarely have I seen so many attractive young performers invited to appear in so many unattractive scenes. Leigh, for example, plays a virginal young student at Ridgemont High. She's curious about sex, and so the script immediately turns her into a promiscuous sex machine who will go to bed with anybody. And then her sexual experiences all turn out to have an unnecessary element of realism, so that we have to see her humiliated, disappointed, and embarrassed. Whatever happened to upbeat sex? Whatever happened to love and lust and romance, and scenes where good-looking kids had a little joy and excitement in life, instead of all this grungy downbeat humiliation? Why does someone as pretty as Leigh have to have her nudity exploited in shots where the only point is to show her ill-at-ease?

If this movie had been directed by a man, I'd call it sexist. It was directed by a woman, Amy Heckerling—and it's sexist all the same. It clunks to a halt now and then for some heartfelt, badly handled material about pregnancy and abortion. I suppose that's Heckerling paying dues to some misconception of the women's movement. But for the most part this movie just exploits its performers by trying to walk a tightrope between comedy and sexploitation.

In addition to Leigh's work, however, there are some other good performances. Sean Penn is perfect as the pot-smoking space cadet who has been stoned since the third grade. Phoebe Cates is breathtaking as the more experienced girl who gives Leigh those distasteful lessons in love. Judge Reinhold has fun as a perennial fast-food cook who rebels against the silly uniforms he's supposed to wear. Ray Walston is suitably hateful as the dictatorial history teacher, Mr. Hand. But this movie could have been a *lot* more fun if it hadn't chosen to confuse embarrassment with humor. The unnecessary detail about sexual functions isn't funny, it's distasteful. Leigh looks so young, fresh, cheerful, and innocent that we don't laugh when she gets into unhappy scenes with men—we wince. The whole movie is a failure of taste, tone, and nerve—the waste of a good cast on erratic, offensive material that hasn't been thought through, or maybe even thought about.

The Fiendish Plot of Dr. Fu Manchu ★
PG, 108 m., 1980

Peter Sellers (Fu Manchu and Nayland Smith), Helen Mirren (Alice Rage), David Tomlinson (Sir Roger Avery), Sid Caesar (Joe Capone), Simon Williams (Townsend), Steven Franken (Williams), Burt Kwouk (Fu Manchu's Servant). Directed by Piers Haggard and produced by Zev Braun and Leland Nolan. Screenplay by Jim Moloney and Rudy Cochtermann.

I was going to write that it's a shame Peter Sellers had to end his career with a movie as disappointing as *The Fiendish Plot of Dr. Fu Manchu*. But maybe that's not the way to look at it. Here was a man who made fifty-two films, some of them great and some of them not, and he worked just as hard on the flops as on the others. *Fu Manchu* is a bad movie but not one to be ashamed of, and Sellers is in every scene, plugging away.

The project must have been just the kind Sellers loved to work on. He plays two of the major roles in the movie, the ancient Fu Manchu and the unflappable Nayland Smith of Scotland Yard. He also turns up in a variety of other disguises, as a Chinese chef, a foppish antique dealer, and the young Fu. The roles require complex makeup jobs (as old Fu, he looks like one of Madame Tussaud's bad dreams); then Sellers plays around with accents, props, all the schtick he can dream up.

Unfortunately, the movie itself gives him little support. The screenplay doesn't seem to have been thought through on the level of small details, and details are what makes movies like this funny. The hazard in these enterprises is that the story *sounds* so funny (Fu Manchu needs secret youth elixir, stages raid on British crown jewels) that the screenplay is never pushed to the next level of detail. By contrast, the Inspector Clouseau movies always felt meticulously thought-out.

The plot, in hindsight, is also just a little morbid, given Sellers's death, shortly after it was finished. As Fu Manchu, he plays a one hundred sixty-eight-year-old man who starts fading fast after a clumsy assistant spills the vial containing his youth potion. Manchu has to reassemble the secret ingredients, including a precious jewel, and so he stages an international crime wave. But his life force is ebbing low, and there are scenes where his assistants feed him jolts of electricity to keep him turning over. It is just a shade hard to laugh at some of these scenes knowing it was made so close to the end of Sellers's own life.

And, for that matter, they're not so funny anyway. The movie has some good moments (what Peter Sellers comedy could not have?), but the story never really involves us, the characters aren't all that interesting once you get beyond the makeup and the funny names and it's a bit disappointing that *The Fiendish Plot of Dr. Fu Manchu* doesn't grab the obvious opportunity to satirize all the old Boris Karloff late-show specials.

What the movie does have is a certain endearing, dogged professionalism. Nobody sets out to make a bad movie, but bad movies are made, and the people making them often suspect the worst, even at the time. But they have to forge ahead. Peter Sellers was in too many good comedies, I suspect, to be able to convince himself that this was another one. But he was too much of a trouper to let down. Maybe that could be his epitaph: When he was good, he was very good indeed, and when he was bad, he was still trying.

George Stevens: A Filmmaker's Journey ★ ★ ★ ½
PG, 113 m., 1985

A documentary written, produced, and directed by George Stevens, Jr. Edited by Catherine Shields. Music by Carl Davis.

The last shot of *Citizen Kane* showed the dead tycoon's storerooms, vast spaces filled with the jumble of a lifetime. One of the early shots in this documentary about George Stevens has something of the same quality. We see the memorabilia of his long career: cowboy hats, leather-bound scripts, cans of film, albums of photographs, Oscars, diaries, belt buckles—everything with a story, and half the stories already forgotten.

The voice on the sound track is the filmmaker's son, telling us about his famous father. One of the things the father told him, one day when they were driving past the warehouse where all of these memories were stored, was, "That'll all be yours when I'm gone." As he rummaged through the souvenirs of his father's lifetime, he made some extraordinary discoveries: Not only the prints and scripts of such classics as *Giant, A Place in the Sun,* and *Alice Adams,* but also documentary footage of Stevens on the set of his movies, and rare color footage Stevens shot for himself while he was leading a newsreel unit during World War II.

More than most men, Stevens seems to have been concerned to leave behind a record of his career. He began in movies almost at the beginning, as an assistant on the early silent films, and his first work as a director was on the Laurel and Hardy films. We see some of his earliest footage, and then we begin to hear the voices of the people who knew him then, and worked with him: Old directors like Rouben Mamoulian and John Huston, stars like Katharine Hepburn and Warren Beatty, writers like Irwin Shaw. Hepburn gave Stevens his real start, rescuing him from grade B features and second-unit work because she was impressed by his enthusiasm for *Alice Adams.* It became his first prestigious production, but then there was a flood of others: the definitive Astaire-Rogers musical *Swing Time,* the audacious *Gunga Din,* and *Woman of the Year,* and Stevens began to build a reputation as a man who saw his own way through the standard scripts he was handed, freeing his actors so that *Gunga Din,* for example, became a high-spirited comic masterpiece instead of just another swashbuckler.

The film contains a lot of home movies and private documentary footage; Stevens shot the only color footage of the landing at Normandy, and we also see moments of Stevens at work, always quietly professional, thoughtful, not the flamboyant self-promoter so many other directors of his generation became. Stevens, more than anyone else, fashioned the image of James Dean. He directed some of Elizabeth Taylor's most memorable scenes. And he pressed on in the face of daunting odds to direct such movies as *The Greatest Story Ever Told.* Shooting in Utah, he was faced with the first snowstorms in a generation, and when he asked the cast

and crew to pitch in and shovel snow, they respected him enough that they did it.

A Filmmaker's Journey is a film biography of a movie director, and it inevitably shares some of the conventions of the genre. We see the clips of great scenes, we hear the memories of old colleagues. Two things distinguish the film: The quiet professionalism with which the materials have been edited together, and the feeling that George Stevens, Jr., really is engaging in a rediscovery of his father through the making of this film. By the end of the film, we are less aware of George Stevens as a filmmaker than as a good and gifted man who happened to use movies as a means of expressing his gifts.

The Final Conflict (Omen III) ★ ★
R, 108 m., 1981

Sam Neill (Damien), Rossano Brazzi (De Carlo), Don Gordon (Dean), Lisa Harrow (Kate), Barnaby Holm (Peter), Mason Adams (President). Directed by Graham Baker and produced by Harvey Bernhard and Mace Neufeld. Screenplay by Andrew Birkin.

The first ten minutes of *The Final Conflict* are such a masterful job of storytelling that I dared to hope that the *Omen* trilogy had pulled itself out of the bag. The story is told in images without dialogue. An earth-moving machine in Chicago digs up seven ancient daggers. A workman carries the daggers home and pawns them. An antique dealer buys the daggers from the pawnshop. They go on auction and are eventually carried to an old monastery in Italy, where the abbot solemnly prays before them. These are the daggers, we learn, that are necessary to kill the antichrist.

This is a terrific opening. But, alas, the moment *The Final Conflict* turns to dialogue and a plot, it loses its inspiration. If Armageddon is as boring as this movie, we'll need a program to tell the players. Loyal students of the *Omen* trilogy will know, of course, that this final conflict has been brewing for a long time—ever since 1976, when the original and rather effective *The Omen* was released. In that one, the U.S. ambassador to Great Britain adopted a child who, we learned, was the devil reincarnate. In *Damien: Omen II* (1978), the kid grew up, went to a military school, and set the stage for his eventual confrontation with the forces of good. A subplot was introduced, involving Thorne Industries, a multinational conglomerate with plans to dominate mankind by controlling the Third World's food supply. As *The Final Conflict* opens, the adopted son (now played by Sam Neill) is in command of Thorne Industries, and is himself named ambassador to Great Britain—as well as chairman of the United Nations Youth Committee.

He does not make a very good youth chairman. Shortly after moving to England he learns that Christ has been reborn, and orders his flunkies at Thorne to kill all the male children born between midnight and 6 A.M. on the suspected day. That includes the son of his most trusted assistant, but so carelessly is this movie assembled that we're never quite sure if the associate (a) knows and believes his boss is the son of Satan, (b) is a diabolical creation himself, or (c) is just on the payroll. *Somebody* on the staff must be in full sympathy with Damien, however, because in the attic of the U.S. Embassy in London's Berkeley Square he has a room devoted to the Black Mass, including a grotesque wooden effigy of the crucifixion. I found myself thinking irreverent thoughts, like, what did they tell the movers as they were carting that crucifix upstairs?

So it goes. In addition to its opening sequence, *The Final Conflict* has one other great scene involving a fox hunt and a plot by the priests of the Italian monastery to lure Damien away from the hunt and kill him. This scene is wonderfully staged and edited. But the movie is otherwise a growing disappointment, as we realize that the apocalyptic confrontation between the forces of good and evil is being reduced to a bunch of guys with Italian accents running around trying to stab Damien in the back.

I would not, of course, dream of revealing this movie's ending. But it's not cheating to say how disappointed I was, as Damien slinks through an abandoned cathedral screaming the equivalent of "Come on out, Nazarene! Come out and fight!" And the last scenes are a disappointing anticlimax that raise once again the ancient question: Why is evil always so much more colorful than good in the movies?

The Final Countdown ★ ★
PG, 92 m., 1980

Kirk Douglas (Captain Yelland), Martin Sheen (Warren Lasky), Katharine Ross (Laurel Scott), James Farentino (Commander Owens), Ron O'Neal (Commander Thurman), Charles Curning (Senator Chapman). Directed by Don Taylor and produced by Peter Vincent Douglas. Screenplay by David Ambrose, Gerry Davis, Thomas Hunter, and Peter Powell.

Logic is a dangerous thing to apply to science fiction. It hardly matters in *The Final Countdown*, in which the aircraft carrier *Nimitz* sails through a whirlpool in time and is thrown back forty years to the day before Pearl Harbor. It's an appealing idea: A nuclear-powered carrier with a full complement of jet warplanes, right off Pearl and knowing the Japanese attack plans. Unfortunately, the movie makes such a mess of it that the biggest element of interest is the aircraft carrier itself. The movie was shot on board, with Navy cooperation, and the operations of the carrier are shown in interesting detail.

Just try to forget the plot. It has the *Nimitz* sailing through clear waters when suddenly a gigantic whirlpool appears in the sky. This is apparently a gateway into the past, although it looks more like a rejected test run for Disney's *Black Hole*. Thrown back to 1940, the ship is in a position to alter the course of history. Will it destroy the Japanese air fleet? *Ha.* We know it can't—because, in the future the *Nimitz* was thrown back from, it didn't, or hadn't. Anyway, just before the zero hour, the *Nimitz* is hurled back into 1980 by another whirlpool. But it leaves two people back there in 1940.

And that sets up this insoluble time-travel paradox: If a guy from 1980 travels forty years back in time, and then lives for another forty years, could he have a meeting with himself? It almost happens in this movie: A mysterious limousine arrives just as the *Nimitz* is sailing on its ill-fated 1980 cruise. Inside is an old man who, as a young man, sailed on the cruise, was thrown back in time, was stranded on a desert island, lived forty years . . . and arrived in the limousine to see the ship off.

But hold on a minute. Doesn't that mean that the same man, before and after, is on the

same dock at the same time? By my count, that makes two bodies for one person, which violates everything they taught us in high school physics.

So, okay, say I'll buy the paradox. That still leaves me with other problems. For example, *Nimitz* commander Kirk Douglas launches an air attack against the arriving Japanese Air Force . . . and then calls it off at the last minute, just as the *Nimitz* is sailing back into the second whirlpool. Why change his mind and call it off? Is he reluctant to play God? I dunno and he doesn't say. (I can think of one good reason for calling the planes back: When the *Nimitz* is snatched back to 1980, they'd be left flying around the Pacific with no place to land.) The movie dodges all sorts of fundamental questions like that, and it moves so slowly, alas, that we have lots of time to ponder them.

Still, the footage aboard the carrier is good. We get an interesting notion of life on ship, and we see lots of takeoffs and even an emergency landing. This is the kind of movie that some kids would probably enjoy—it's filled with technology, special effects, and action. But it just doesn't make any sense. And it lacks the wit to have fun with its time travel paradoxes, as the wonderful *Time After Time* did. It just plows ahead. Or behind. Or somewhere.

Firefox ★ ★ ★ ½
PG, 136 m., 1982

Clint Eastwood (Mitchell Gant), Freddie Jones (Kenneth Aubrey), David Huffman (Buckholz), Warren Clarke (Pavel Upenskoy), Ronald Lacey (Semelovsky), Kenneth Colley (Colonel Kontarsky), Stefan Schnabel (First Secretary). Directed and produced by Clint Eastwood. Screenplay by Alex Lasker and Wendell Wellman.

Clint Eastwood's *Firefox* is a slick, muscular thriller that combines espionage with science fiction. The movie works like a well-crafted machine, and it's *about* a well-crafted machine. The *Firefox* of the title is a top-secret Russian warplane capable of flying six times the speed of sound while remaining invisible on radar. Eastwood's mission, if he chooses to accept it: Infiltrate the Soviet Union disguised as a Las Vegas drug smug-gler, and then steal the Firefox by flying it to the West.

This is one of those basic movie plots that can generate a lot of entertainment if it's handled properly. *Firefox* knows the territory. It complicates things slightly by making Eastwood a Vietnam veteran who is sometimes overcome by the hallucination that he's still in combat. The movie calls it Post-Combat Stress Syndrome. But the CIA man who recruits him explains that the government isn't much worried, because you don't have the syndrome while you're *in* combat, you see, but only afterward. Somebody ought to compile a textbook of psychology as practiced in movies.

Anyway, Eastwood trains for the mission, is disguised with a mustache and horn-rim glasses, and survives some uncomfortable moments at Moscow customs before he makes it into Russia. Then he makes contact with a confederation of spies and double agents who lead him to a Jewish dissident who is such a brilliant scientist that he is still being allowed to work on Firefox. Why does the dissident *want* to work on it? Because he knows how Eastwood could steal the plane. All of these scenes include obligatory shots, which are kind of fun to anticipate, if you're a fan of the Alistair Maclean–James Bond–"Mission: Impossible"–*Guns of Navarone* genre. The one indispensable scene is probably the Introduction of the MacGuffin. A MacGuffin, you will remember, was what Alfred Hitchcock called that element of the plot that everybody thinks is important. In this case, it's the Firefox, a long, sleek, cruel-looking machine that looks like a cross between a guided missle and a DeLorean. Eastwood and the camera circle it lovingly; this is the sexiest shot in a movie without a romantic subplot. The movie's climax involves Eastwood's attempt to fly this plane north to the Arctic Circle, make a refueling rendezvous, and then take it on home. His flight is intercut with comic opera scenes involving members of the Russian high command, who argue and bicker while looming over an illuminated map that casts an eerie underlight on their faces, making them look like ghouls from old E.C. comics.

Does Eastwood make it out in one piece? Does he bring along the plane? I wouldn't dream of giving away the plot. But I will say

that the movie's climax is a sensational high-altitude dogfight between two different Firefoxes, and that as Eastwood occupies the Firefox cockpit, surrounded by video screens and computer displays of flight patterns and missile trajectories, it looks as if Dirty Harry has died and gone to Atari heaven. The special effects are really pretty good in this movie. The planes looked surprisingly real to me, and the choreography of the dogfight was not only realistic but understandable. There's one sensational chase sequence that's an homage to *Star Wars*. Remember the *Star Wars* scene where the two ships chased each other between the towering walls of the city in space? Eastwood and his Russian pursuer rocket through a crevice between two ice cliffs, and it looks great even while we're realizing it's logically impossible. I guess that goes for the whole movie.

Firestarter ★ ★
R, 115 m., 1984

David Keith (Andrew McGee), Drew Barrymore (Charlie McGee), Freddie Jones (Dr. Wanless), Martin Sheen (Captain Hollister), George C. Scott (John Rainbird), Art Carney (Irv Manders), Louise Fletcher (Norma Manders). Directed by Mark L. Lester and produced by Frank Capra, Jr. Screenplay by Stanley Mann.

Firestarter contains a little girl who can start fires with her mind; her father, whose own ESP causes him to have brain hemorrhages; an Indian child molester who is a CIA killer; a black scientist; a kindly farmer; a government bureaucrat; and a brilliant scientist whose experiments kill 75 percent of his subjects but leave the others with powers beyond the imagination of mortal man. The most astonishing thing in the movie, however, is how boring it is.

The little girl is played by Drew Barrymore, from *E.T.*, where she was the kid sister. Her father is played by David Keith, who was Richard Gere's buddy in *An Officer and a Gentleman*. The child molester is played by George C. Scott. The farmer is Art Carney. And so on. There isn't a role in this movie not filled by a capable actor. And there's not a character in this movie that is convincing, even for a moment, nor a line in this movie that even experienced performers can make real.

Firestarter was the fifth movie in a year that was based on a best-selling thriller by Stephen King. The others were *Christine*, *Cujo*, *The Dead Zone*, and *Children of the Corn*. The best of those—and the one most similar to *Firestarter*—is *The Dead Zone*, which starred Christopher Walken as a man cursed with the ability to foretell the future. The movie approached Walken as an ordinary man burdened with a power that should belong only to God, and allowed us to empathize with his terrible gift. But in *Firestarter*, we don't feel sorry for Barrymore because she's never developed as a believable little girl—just a plot gimmick. She gets mad, her eyes narrow, and things catch on fire. Her father is even less interesting; although he can use ESP to hypnotize people to obey his will, he gets a nosebleed every time he does it, and the way he clasps his hands to his head and strains makes ESP look like physical labor.

Of the other characters, the most totally confused is John Rainbird, the Indian played by Scott. Rainbird shows every sign of being a character who was rewritten so extensively that finally nothing was left except the notes. He's an Indian, I guess, judging by his name and ponytail. He wants the little girl because he dreams of killing her with one karate blow to the nose. He has a couple of gruesomely detailed speeches in which he outlines this ambition, but the movie spares us the sight of Scott carrying out his plan. Thanks for small favors. The film's crucial flaw is the lack of a strong point to the story. A little girl has her dangerous power, some government agents want to examine her, others want to destroy her, and things catch on fire. That's about it.

First Blood ★ ★ ★
R, 94 m., 1982

Sylvester Stallone (Rambo), Richard Crenna (Trautman), Brian Dennehy (Teasle), David Caruso (Mitch). Directed by Ted Kotcheff and produced by Buzz Feitshans. Screenplay by Michael Kozoll, William Sackheim, and Q. Moonblood.

Sylvester Stallone is one of the great physical actors in the movies, with a gift for throwing

himself so fearlessly into an action scene that we can't understand why somebody doesn't *really* get hurt. When he explodes near the beginning of *First Blood*, hurling cops aside and breaking out of a jail with his fists and speed, it's such a convincing demonstration of physical strength and agility that we never question the scene's implausibility. In fact, although almost all of *First Blood* is implausible, because it's Stallone on the screen, we'll buy it.

What we can't buy in this movie is the message. It's handled in too heavy-handed a way. Stallone plays a returned Vietnam veteran, a Green Beret skilled in the art of jungle survival and fighting, and after a small-town police force sadistically mishandles him, he declares war on the cops. All of this is set up in scenes of great physical power and strength—and the central sections of the movie, with Stallone and the cops stalking each other through the forests of the Pacific Northwest, have a lot of authority. But then the movie comes down to a face-off between Stallone and his old Green Beret commander (Richard Crenna), and the screenplay gives Stallone a long, impassioned speech to deliver, a speech in which he cries out against the injustices done to him and against the hippies who demonstrated at the airport when he returned from the war, etc. This is all old, familiar material from a dozen other films—clichés recycled as formula. Bruce Dern did it in *Coming Home* and William Devane in *Rolling Thunder*. Stallone is made to say things that would have much better been implied; Robert De Niro, in *Taxi Driver*, also plays a violent character who was obviously scarred by Vietnam, but the movie wisely never makes him talk about what happened to him. Some things are scarier and more emotionally moving when they're left unsaid.

So the ending doesn't work in *First Blood*. It doesn't necessarily work as action, either. By the end of the film, Stallone has taken on a whole town and has become a one-man army, laying siege to the police station and the hardware store and exploding the pumps at the gas station. This sort of spectacular conclusion has become so commonplace in action movies that I kind of wonder, sometimes, what it would be like to see one end with a whimper rather than a bang.

Until the last twenty or thirty minutes, however, *First Blood* is a very good movie, well-paced, and well-acted not only by Stallone (who invests an unlikely character with great authority) but also by Crenna and Brian Dennehy, as the police chief. The best scenes come as Stallone's on the run in the forest, using a hunting knife with a compass in the handle, and living off the land. At one point he's trapped on a cliffside by a police helicopter, and we really feel for this character who has been hunted down through no real fault of his own. We feel more deeply for him then, in fact, than we do later when he puts his grievances into words. Stallone creates the character and sells the situation with his presence itself. The screenplay should have stopped while it was ahead.

The First Deadly Sin ★ ★ ★
R, 112 m., 1980

Frank Sinatra (Edward Delaney), Faye Dunaway (Barbara Delaney), David Dukes (Daniel Blank), George Coe (Dr. Bernardi), Brenda Vaccaro (Monica Gilbert), Martin Gabel (Chris Langley), Joe Spinell (Doorman), Anthony Zerba (Captain Broughton). Directed by Brian Hutton and produced by George Pappas and Mark Shanker. Screenplay by Mann Rubin.

Who would have thought, in all honesty, that Frank Sinatra had this performance still left in him? Ten years after his previous film, the dismal *Dirty Dingus Magee*, and longer than that since the schlock of *Tony Rome* and *Lady in Cement*, here he is again with a quiet, poignant, and very effective performance as the centerpiece of *The First Deadly Sin*. Sinatra plays Ed Delaney, a New York police detective with only a few weeks until his retirement. He goes out to investigate a routine mugging and discovers that the victim has been killed by a strange weapon: The impact on the skull is like nothing he's seen before. He stumbles over a couple of related cases and begins to suspect that the same madman is responsible for them all. Delaney's boss would basically just like him to forget about it and retire, but some small core of stubbornness won't let Delaney let go.

At the same time, things are not going well in his private life. His wife (Faye Dunaway) has had a kidney removed and is in the hospital, critically ill. Delaney is living a bachelor's existence in their town house—which reflects her taste with the antiques and plants that stand ready as a backdrop to his retirement. He is a quiet man, firm but not demonstrative, and even his determination to follow through on the murder case isn't heroic, it's just dogged.

The movie surrounds Sinatra with a gallery of good character actors in good roles: There's the raspy coroner (James Whitmore) and the oily doorman (Joe Spinell) and the little old curator of antiquities (George Coe) who improbably figures out what was probably used as the murder weapon. There's a less satisfactory treatment of the killer (David Dukes), who is never really established as a personality and exists only as a shadowy, frightened cipher. The movie's never consistent in the way it shows him. We're apparently omniscient at times and can watch the killer alone in his coldly efficient High Tech apartment. But at other times we're deliberately kept ignorant of his plans and movements. The movie wants to have things both ways, but thrillers are more effective when they establish rules and play by them. Still, the failure to develop the killer isn't really crucial to the movie; we know enough about him and can guess enough more from other movies and pop psychology, to fill in his blanks. What definitely doesn't work in this movie is the character of Delaney's wife, as played by Dunaway. The movie opens with Delaney called off a case to go to her bedside, where the emergency operation was just performed—and then, all during the rest of the film, the police action alternates with visits to the bedside. Dunaway's role has to be the longest-running deathbed scene I can remember. All we know for sure is that she'll look worse every time Sinatra goes to the hospital. After a few brave and cheerful remarks at the outset, she has hardly any dialogue, and so we don't learn much about their relationship.

The fact that she is dying is intended, of course, as counterpoint to the professional pressures bearing down on the detective. But (and here the movie miscalculates) we don't need to see her dying to feel those pressures. It might have been more effective to let her die offscreen, and to let us imagine her suffering while identifying with his grief.

The handling of the wife's character could have been fatal to the movie, but it's not. That's due to Sinatra, who plays this role close to his chest, and who looks and acts very touchingly like a tired old cop on the threshold of retirement. We can empathize with him, and that's partly because he resists any temptation to give us a reprise of those wisecracking wise-asses he played in the 1960s. This is a new performance, built from the ground up.

Firstborn ★ ★
PG, 100 m., 1984

Teri Garr (Wendy Livingston), Peter Weller (Sam), Christopher Collet (Jake Livingston), Corey Haim (Brian Livingston). Directed by Michael Apted and produced by Paul Junger Witt and Tony Thomas. Screenplay by Ron Koslow.

Firstborn has such a sudden and unnecessary breakdown that it almost makes you wonder how the movie's ending was decided upon. Was there a final failure of will? The movie creates such an urgent situation, and fills it with such interesting characters, that when everything goes wrong at the end I felt more than disappointed, I felt cheated.

The movie is about a quiet and happy little suburban family that is violated by the appearance of the wrong man at the wrong time. The family consists of a divorced mother (Teri Garr) and her two sons. The man is Garr's new lover, and he arrives almost in response to a crisis in her life—when her ex-husband, a man she still loves, suddenly decides to remarry. On the rebound, she comes home with a young man (Peter Weller) whom she says she loves. Well, maybe she *does* love him. Love is blind. But her sons are not blind—especially not the older teen-ager (Christopher Collet), who spots this guy right away for a phony. Weller announces that he has lots of big plans for his new family. He and Garr are going to open a home security service. Or maybe a restaurant. He has lots of ideas. All he needs is capital.

Meanwhile, he spends all day sitting around the house, watching TV, and raiding the icebox. And when Collet challenges him too closely about his plans, he slaps the kid just a little too hard on the back, and tells him to get off his case. Collet tries to talk to his mom, but she won't listen. She's under this guy's spell, and it gets even worse when he turns out to be a small-time drug dealer and Garr begins to experiment with cocaine.

Up until about this point in the movie, *Firstborn* has been a very accurately observed family drama, one that even bears comparison to *Ordinary People*. The performances are strong, the plot moves with a compelling simplicity, and the dialogue shows a good ear for the way the movie's different kinds of characters might really speak. I was experiencing that special confidence you feel when a movie is making the right choices: This was going to be a good one.

It did not, alas, turn out to be so good. Having raised its issues, having trapped the children in a cruel dilemma (how can they turn in the boyfriend without implicating their mother in a drug case?), having created in a dramatic form the kind of problem that does confront real families, *Firstborn* throws away all its good work on a canned, formula ending.

Would you believe a chase and a fight? Would you believe the little brother coming to the rescue with a baseball bat? Would you believe a three-dimensional, sensitive family drama that tries to resolve itself like a TV action show? The climactic scenes in *Firstborn* are so dismally predictable that I even got a little angry. The movie had been so good that somehow it didn't have the right to evade all the issues it had raised and just turn into a suburban thriller.

What happened? Did somebody think the ending would be commercial? Did they think it would save a problematical movie from becoming too "serious"? Maybe so. But how could mistakes that basic be made by the same people with the taste to make the opening and middle segments of this movie? Love isn't all that's blind.

Fitzcarraldo ★ ★ ★ ★
PG, 157 m., 1982

Klaus Kinski (Fitzcarraldo), Claudia Cardinale (Molly), Jose Lewgoy (Don Aquilino), Miguel Angel Fuentes (Cholo). Directed by Werner Herzog. Screenplay by Herzog.

Werner Herzog's *Fitzcarraldo* is a movie in the great tradition of grandiose cinematic visions. Like Coppola's *Apocalypse Now* or Kubrick's *2001*, it is a quest film in which the hero's quest is scarcely more mad than the filmmaker's. Movies like this exist on a plane apart from ordinary films. There is a sense in which *Fitzcarraldo* is not altogether successful—it is too long, we could say, or too meandering—but it is still a film that I would not have missed for the world. The movie is the story of a dreamer named Brian Sweeney Fitzgerald, whose name has been simplified to "Fitzcarraldo" by the Indians and Spanish who inhabit his godforsaken corner of South America. He loves opera. He spends his days making a little money from an ice factory and his nights dreaming up new schemes. One of them, a plan to build a railroad across the continent, has already failed. Now he is ready with another: He seriously intends to build an opera house in the rain jungle, twelve hundred miles upstream from the civilized coast, and to bring Enrico Caruso there to sing an opera.

If his plan is mad, his method for carrying it out is madness of another dimension. Looking at the map, he becomes obsessed with the fact that a nearby river system offers access to hundreds of thousands of square miles of potential trading customers—if only a modern steamship could be introduced into that system. There is a point, he notices, where the other river is separated only by a thin finger of land from a river that already is navigated by boats. His inspiration: Drag a steamship across land to the other river, float it, set up a thriving trade, and use the profits to build the opera house—and then bring in Caruso! This scheme is so unlikely that perhaps we should not be surprised that Herzog's story is based on the case of a real Irish entrepreneur who tried to do exactly that.

The historical Irishman was at least wise enough to disassemble his boat before carting it across land. In Herzog's movie, however, Fitzcarraldo determines to drag the boat up one hill and down the other side in one piece. He enlists engineers to devise a system of blocks-and-pulleys that will do the trick, and he hires the local Indians to work the levers with their own muscle power. And it is here that we arrive at the thing about *Fitzcarraldo* that transcends all understanding: Werner Herzog determined to literally drag a real steamship up a real hill, using real tackle and hiring the local Indians! To produce the movie, he decided to do personally what even the original Fitzgerald never attempted.

Herzog finally settled on the right actor to play Fitzcarraldo, author of this plan: Klaus Kinski, the shock-haired German who starred in Herzog's *Aguirre, the Wrath of God* and *Nosferatu*, is back again to mastermind the effort. Kinski is perfectly cast. Herzog's original choice for the role was Jason Robards, who is also gifted at conveying a consuming passion, but Kinski, wild-eyed and ferocious, consumes the screen. There are other characters important to the story, especially Claudia Cardinale as the madam who loves Fitzcarraldo and helps finance his attempt, but without Kinski at the core it's doubtful this story would work.

The story of Herzog's own production is itself well-known, and has been told in Les Blank's *Burden of Dreams*, a brilliant documentary about the filming. It's possible that every moment of *Fitzcarraldo* is colored by our knowledge that Herzog was "really" doing the things we see Fitzcarraldo do. (The movie uses no special effects, no models, no opticals, no miniatures.) Perhaps we're even tempted to give the movie extra points because of Herzog's ordeal in the jungle. But *Fitzcarraldo* is not all sweat and madness. It contains great poetic images of the sort Herzog is famous for: An old phonograph playing a Caruso record on the desk of a boat spinning out of control into a rapids; Fitzcarraldo frantically oaring a little rowboat down a jungle river to be in time to hear an opera; and of course the immensely impressive sight of that actual steamship, resting halfway up a hillside.

Fitzcarraldo is not a perfect movie, and it never comes together into a unified statement. It *is* meandering, and it is slow and formless at times. Perhaps the conception was just too large for Herzog to shape. The movie does not approach perfection as *Aguirre* did. But as a document of a quest

and a dream, and as the record of man's audacity and foolish, visionary heroism, there has never been another movie like it.

The Flamingo Kid ★ ★ ★ ½
PG-13, 100 m., 1984

Matt Dillon (Jeffrey Willis), Hector Elizondo (Arthur Willis), Molly McCarthy (Ruth Willis), Martha Gehman (Nikki Willis), Richard Crenna (Phil Brody), Jessica Walter (Phyllis Brody), Carole R. Davis (Joyce Brody). Directed by Garry Marshall and produced by Michael Phillips. Screenplay by Neal and Garry Marshall.

"When I was eighteen, my father was ignorant on a great many subjects," Mark Twain once said, "but by the time I was twenty-five, it was amazing the things the old man had learned." Here is a movie that condenses that process into one summer. The summer begins with a kid from a poor Brooklyn neighborhood taking a job as a cabana boy at a posh beach club out on Long Island. That's against the advice of his father, a plumber, who wants his son to get a job where he can learn about hard work. By the middle of the summer, the kid has started to idolize a flashy car dealer who's the champion of the gin rummy tables. By Labor Day, he has found out more about the car dealer than he wanted to know. And he has come to love and understand his father in a new way.

The Flamingo Kid stars Matt Dillon as the teen-ager, Hector Elizondo as his father, and Richard Crenna as the car dealer. There are other characters—in particular, a bikinied goddess who helps sell Matt on life at the beach—but these are the three characters who stand at the heart of the story. Elizondo is a hard-working man who still remembers how to dream, but knows that life has few openings for dreamers. In some of the movie's most poetic passages, he reveals a lifelong obsession with ships, and the ways of harbor pilots. Crenna, on the other hand, is a man who firmly believes "You are what you wear," and values his status as the club's gin rummy champion as if it really meant something.

Dillon is a revelation in this movie. Perhaps because of his name, Matt Dillon has risked being confused with your average teen-age idol, the kind the pimple magazines put on their covers. Yet he has been an extraordinarily sensitive actor ever since his first appearance, in the unsung 1977 movie about alienated teen-agers, *Over the Edge*. In two movies based on novels by S.E. Hinton, *Tex* and *Rumble Fish*, he had the kind of clarity, the uncluttered relationship with the camera, that you see in only a handful of actors: He was a natural. He is here, too. His role in *The Flamingo Kid* could easily have been turned into an anthology of twitches and psychic anguish as he wrestles with the meaning of life. But Dillon has the kind of acting intelligence that allows him to play each scene for no more than that particular scene is really about; he's not trying to summarize the message in every speech. That gives him an ease, an ability to play the teen-age hero as if every day were a whole summer long.

We fall into the rhythm of the beach club. Into the sunny days where all the members have lots of time to know and envy each other, and time is so plentiful that it can take hours for a nasty rumor to sweep through the cabanas. Dillon hurries from one member to another with drinks, towels, club sandwiches, messages. He feels acutely that he does not belong at this level of society—and when Richard Crenna takes notice of him, and even more when Crenna's daughter invites him home for dinner, Dillon feels that he's cutting loose from the boring life back in Brooklyn. But this will be a summer of learning, and by autumn he will have learned how wise and loving his own father is, and how easy it is to be deceived by surfaces. Along the way to that lesson, *The Flamingo Kid* has a lot of fun (I hope I haven't made this social comedy sound dreary), and at the end it has a surprisingly emotional impact.

Flash Gordon ★ ★ ½
PG, 110 m., 1980

Sam J. Jones (Flash Gordon), Melody Anderson (Dale Arden), Topol (Dr. Zarkov), Max von Sydow (Emperor Ming), Ornella Muti (Princess Aura), Timothy Dalton (Prince Barin), Mariangela Melato (Kala). Directed by Mike Hodges and produced by Dino De Laurentiis. Screenplay by Lorenzo Semple, Jr.

Flash Gordon opens with an ominous crisis facing mankind, but Earth scientists are playing it cool: A NASA spokesman denies that there's anything unusual about an unexpected total eclipse of the sun. Unusual? That the moon is out of its orbit? Ha! It takes a mad scientist like Dr. Hans Zarkov to realize that the Earth is under attack, and speed to the rescue in his private space ship—with Flash Gordon and Dale Arden aboard as unwilling passengers. This new Dino De Laurentiis production is true to the tacky pop origins of the Flash Gordon comic strip and the serials starring Buster Crabbe. At a time when *Star Wars* and its spinoffs have inspired special-effects men to bust a gut making their interplanetary adventures look real, *Flash Gordon* is cheerfully willing to look as phony as it is.

You *can* make a city float in the clouds and look marginally realistic (as in *The Empire Strikes Back*), but there's something sort of fun about the *Flash Gordon* city that floats in the clouds and looks like a large miniature model floating in fake clouds. And as the spaceships lumbered past on the screen, I really wouldn't have minded if they'd left a tube of model airplane glue lying in the lower left-hand corner.

Flash Gordon is played for laughs, and wisely so. It is no more sophisticated than the comic strip it's based on, and that takes the curse off of material that was old before it was born. This is space opera, a genre invented by Edgar Rice Burroughs, Hugo Gernsback and other men of unlimited imagination harnessed to limited skills. It's fun to see it done with energy and love and without the pseudo-meaningful apparatus of the Force and the Trekkie Power.

The plot is simple: The Emperor Ming (Max von Sydow), bored with life in the universe, decides to pick on Earth. After warming up with a few hurricanes and earthquakes, he sends the moon spinning down toward the planet. Meanwhile, Zarkov, Flash (Sam J. Jones, Bo Derek's husband in *10*) and Dale (Melody Anderson) crash-land in Ming's imperial space city. There are intrigues afoot, but meanwhile Dale catches Ming's eye, he determines to marry her, and Flash finds himself fighting for his life with a gladiator.

Mike Hodges, the British director hired

by De Laurentiis to orchestrate this comic space opera, is true to the visual tradition of the original serials: Everyone is dressed in capes and ridiculous boots and headdresses, and stands around on the command decks of ornate spaceships. There's an imperial court to applaud and boo at the appropriate times. And there's a cliff-hanging showdown when the Hawk Men, looking amazingly like the winged angels in De Laurentiis's production of *Barbarella* (1968), engage the crew of a space ship in hand-to-hand battle (you know there's something lacking with the Ming technology when the commander of the rocket ship shouts, "Stand by to the repel invaders!"). Is all of this ridiculous? Of course. Is it fun? Yeah, sort of, it is.

Flashdance ★ ½
R, 96 m., 1983

Jennifer Beals (Alex), Michael Nouri (Nicky), Belinda Bauer (Katie Hurley), Lilia Skala (Hanna Long). Directed by Adrian Lyne and produced by Don Simpson and Jerry Bruckheimer. Screenplay by Tom Hedley and Joe Eszterhas.

I have a friend who has a simple test for a movie: Is this movie as interesting as the same things would be, happening in real life? A lot of movies aren't, and *Flashdance* sure isn't. If this movie had spent just a little more effort getting to know the heroine of its story, and a little less time trying to rip off *Saturday Night Fever*, it might have been a much better film.

My friend's simple test applies to this movie in another way: The movie is *not* as interesting as the real-life story of Jennifer Beals, the young actress who stars in it. Beals launched a career as a model (covers on *Town & Country* and *Vogue*) at the age of 15, after being discovered by Chicago photographer Victor Skrebneski. She enrolled in Yale, took some acting classes in New York, went to an audition, and won this role. The irony is that her story, simply and directly told, might have been a lot more interesting than the story of *Flashdance*, which is so loaded down with artificial screenplay contrivances and flashy production numbers that it's waterlogged. This is one of those movies that goes for a slice of life and ends up with three pies.

Jennifer Beals plays Alex, an eighteen-year-old who is a welder by day, *and* a go-go dancer by night, *and* dreams of being a ballet star, *and* falls in love with the Porsche-driving boss of the construction company. These are a lot of "character details" even if she *didn't* also have a saintly old woman as a mentor, a big slobbering dog as a friend, a bicycle she rides all over Pittsburgh, a loft the size of a sweatshop, a sister who ice skates, a grumpy old pop, *and* the ability to take off her bra without removing her sweatshirt. This poor kid is so busy performing the pieces of business supplied to her by the manic screenwriters that she never gets a chance to develop a character.

Meanwhile, the movie has a disconcerting way of getting sidetracked with big dance scenes. The heroine works in the most improbable working-class bar ever put on film, a joint named Mawby's that has a clientele out of Miller's Beer TV ads, stage lighting reminiscent of Vegas, go-go dancers who change their expensive costumes every night, *and* put on punk rock extravaganzas, *and* never take off all their clothes, *and* never get shouted at by the customers for not doing so.

Flashdance is like a movie that won a free ninety-minute shopping spree in the Hollywood supermarket. The director (Adrian Lyne, of the much better *Foxes*) and his collaborators race crazily down the aisles, grabbing a piece of *Saturday Night Fever*, a slice of *Urban Cowboy*, a quart of *Marty*, and a two-pound box of "Archie Bunker's Place." The result is great sound and flashdance, signifying nothing. But Jennifer Beals shouldn't feel bad. She is a natural talent, she is fresh and engaging here, and only needs to find an agent with a natural talent for turning down scripts.

Fletch ★ ★ ½
PG, 110 m., 1985

Chevy Chase (I.M. Fletcher), Joe Don Baker (Chief Karlin), Dana Wheeler-Nicholson (Gail Stanwyk), Richard Libertini (Walker), Tim Matheson (Alan Stanwyck), M. Emmet Walsh (Dr. Dolan). Directed by Michael Ritchie and produced by Alan Greisman and Peter Douglas. Screenplay by Andrew Bergman.

Why did Chevy Chase want to play I.M. Fletcher, the laconic hero of Gregory McDonald's best sellers? Was it because Chase saw a way to bring Fletch to life? Or was it because Chase thought Fletch was very much like himself? The problem with *Fletch* is that the central performance is an anthology of Chevy Chase mannerisms in search of a character. Other elements in the movie are pretty good: the supporting characters, the ingenious plot, the unexpected locations. But whenever the movie threatens to work, there's Chevy Chase with his monotone, deadpan cynicism, distancing himself from the material.

Fletch is not the first movie that Chase has undercut with his mannerisms, but it is the best one—since *Foul Play*, anyway. His problem as an actor is that he perfected a personal style on "Saturday Night Live" all those many years ago, and has never been able to work outside of it. The basic Chevy Chase personality functions well at the length of a TV sketch, when there's no time to create a new character, but in a movie it grows deadening. *Fletch* is filled with a series of extraordinary situations, and Chase seems to react to all of them with the same wry dubiousness. His character this time is an investigative reporter for a Los Angeles newspaper. Deep into an investigation of drug traffic on the city's beaches, Fletch is approached by a young man (Tim Matheson) with a simple proposition: He wants to be killed. The story is that Matheson is dying of cancer and wants to die violently so his family can qualify for enlarged insurance benefits, but Fletch doesn't buy it. Something's fishy, and Fletch pretends to take the job, while conducting his own investigation.

The case leads him to an extraordinary series of interesting characters; the film's director, Michael Ritchie is good at sketching human originals, and we meet an aging farm couple in Utah, a manic editor, a nononsense police chief, a mysterious drug dealer, a slimy doctor, a beautiful wife, and a lot of mean dogs. Every one of the characters is played well, with the little details that Ritchie loves: The scene on a farmhouse porch in Utah is filled with such sly, quiet social satire that it could stand by itself. The movie's physical comedy is good, too. A scene where Fletch breaks into a realtor's office—scaling a fence and outsmarting vicious attack dogs—is constructed so carefully out of comedy and violence that it's a little masterpiece of editing.

The problem is, Chase's performance tends to reduce all the scenes to the same level, at least as far as he's concerned. He projects such an inflexible mask of cool detachment, of ironic running commentary, that we're prevented from identifying with him. If he thinks this is all just a little too silly for words, what are we to think? If we're more involved in the action than he is, does that make us chumps? *Fletch* needed an actor more interested in playing the character than in playing himself.

The Fog ★ ★
R, 91 m., 1980

Adrienne Barbeau (Stevie Wayne), Hal Holbrook (Father Malone), Janet Leigh (Kathy Williams), Jamie Lee Curtis (Elizabeth Solley), John Houseman (Machen), Tommy Atkins (Nick Castle), Nancy Loomis (Sandy Fadel). Directed by John Carpenter and produced by Debra Hill. Screenplay by Carpenter and Hill.

The problem is with the fog. It must have seemed like an inspired idea to make a horror movie in which clouds of fog would be the menace, but the idea just doesn't work out in *The Fog*, John Carpenter's next thriller after *Halloween*. The movie's made with style and energy, but it needs a better villain.

And it also needs a slightly more plausible plot. We don't really care about the logic of the plot in horror movies, of course, but there has to be *some* plausibility, just so we know what the rules are. Carpenter's fog—which contains the ghosts of murdered sailors—is too unpredictable. When it rolls in, it's likely to kill anyone, no matter whether or not their ancestors were responsible for killing the sailors one hundred years ago.

It's easy to see, though, why this project must have been appealing to Carpenter, a talented young filmmaker who built a cult audience with the low-budget genre films *Dark Star* and *Assault on Precinct 13* before breaking through to enormous ratings with the made-for-TV *Elvis*. Carpenter's *Halloween* was one of the major box office successes of 1979 (*Variety* called it the most profitable independent film ever made) and it demonstrated his favorite approach: He likes films that manipulate audiences, films designed, quite simply, to cause emotions—and his favorite response is shock.

The Fog basically has the same structure as *Halloween*. It gives us a small American town. It introduces a few of its inhabitants, especially isolated women. It establishes a threat. And then the rest of the movie is devoted to scenes in which the threat either does or does not destroy its intended victims.

Very simple. The threat need not even be believable; *Halloween*'s psychotic killer, wrapped in sheets and apparently invulnerable, just kept on coming while a platoon of baby-sitters bit the dust. But *Halloween*'s killer was a person, and had at least a bit of personal background (we saw a traumatic scene from his childhood and heard a psychiatrist describe him as evil incarnate).

The narrative background in *The Fog* is presented stylishly—John Houseman tells a ghost story around a campfire on the beach, little kids listen with their mouths hanging open, we learn that shipwrecked sailors were murdered near this town a century ago, and that they vowed to return one hundred years later. And, of course, tonight's the night.

But when the sailors' ghosts return, wrapped in fog, we can't figure out what their motives are. Do they want to kill the descendants of their murderers? Are they angry at the town itself? Are they indeed *there* in the fog, or are the victims hallucinating?

We wouldn't care about the answers to these questions if *The Fog* were as scary as *Halloween*. But because *The Fog* has a historical plot, because its events are inspired by the past, it should make more sense. A sentient fog may be photogenic (and this is a good-looking movie), but can we identify with it? Is it the kind of villain we love to hate? Not really.

Footloose ★ ½
PG, 106 m., 1984

Kevin Bacon (Ren), Lori Singer (Ariel), John Lithgow (Reverend Moore). Directed by Herbert Ross and produced by Lewis J. Rachmil and Craig Zadan. Screenplay by Dean Pitchford.

Footloose is a seriously confused movie that tries to do three things, and does all of them badly. It wants to tell the story of a conflict in a town, it wants to introduce some flashy teen-age characters, and part of the time it wants to be a music video. It's possible that no movie with this many agendas *can* be good; maybe somebody should have decided, early on, exactly what the movie was supposed to be about. The film tells the story of a Chicago kid named Ren (Kevin Bacon), who has a fashionable haircut and likes to dance. He moves with his mother to a small town named Bomont, which is somewhere in the Midwest, although I seriously doubt a town like this exists anywhere outside of standard movie clichés. The old fuddies in Bomont have imposed a total ban on rock 'n' roll and dancing. The ban is led by an uptight preacher named Shaw Moore (John Lithgow), who is still grieving because he lost a child in a car wreck five years ago. To the Reverend Moore, dancing and rock lead to booze and drugs.

Ren falls in love with the preacher's daughter (Lori Singer). He also has the usual standard showdowns with the locals, including the high school bully. Ren decides what this town needs is a dance. His assignment, should he choose to accept it, is to (1) win the approval of the preacher and the town council to allow dancing, (2) beat up the bully, and (3) star in at least three segments of the movie that can be used as TV music videos. The basic conflict in this movie was not new when the *Beach Party* gang discovered it. Remember Annette and Frankie trying to persuade the old folks to let them hold a dance on the beach? If the movie had only relaxed and allowed itself to admit how silly the situation is, it could have been more fun. Instead, it gets bogged down in the peculiar personality of the preacher, who is played by Lithgow as a man of agonizing complexity.

Footloose makes one huge, inexplicable error with the Lithgow character. It sets him up as an unyielding reactionary, and then lets him change his mind 180 degrees without a word of explanation. In one scene, the preacher's daughter confronts her dad in church and announces she isn't a virgin (the movie never remembers to tell us whether she really is or not). The preacher turns livid, starts to scream, and then is interrupted by news that they're burning books down at the library. In the *very next scene*, the preacher is arguing against the book burners—and before long, without any meaningful transitional scenes, he has caved in to the idea of the dance. It's cheating to set up Lithgow as the enemy and then turn him into a friend without a word of explanation.

I mentioned the flashy teen-age characters. The one who gave me the most trouble was that preacher's daughter. She enjoys suicidal games of chicken, like balancing with her legs on the doors of a speeding car and a speeding truck while a speeding semi bears down on her. This trick is, of course, impossible to do in real life, and so it simultaneously makes her into an idiot and a stuntwoman. As for the music video scenes: On three different occasions, the movie switches gears and goes into prepackaged MTV-type production numbers, with the fancy photography and the flashy quick cuts. These scenes may play well on TV, but they break what little reality the story has, and expose *Footloose* as a collection of unrelated ingredients that someone thought would be exploitable.

For Your Eyes Only ★ ★
PG, 127 m., 1981

Roger Moore (James Bond), Carole Bouquet (Melina), Topol (Columbo), Julian Glover (Kristatos), Cassandra Harris (Lisl), Janet Brown (Prime Minister). Directed by John Glen and produced by Albert R. Broccoli. Screenplay by Richard Malbaum and Michael Wilson.

For Your Eyes Only is a competent James Bond thriller, well-crafted, a respectable product from the 007 production line. But it's no more than that. It doesn't have the special sly humor of the Sean Connery Bonds, of course, but also doesn't have the visual splendor of such Roger Moore Bonds as *The Spy Who Loved Me*, or special effects to equal *Moonraker*. And in this era of jolting, inspired visual effects from George Lucas and Steven Spielberg, it's just not quite in the same league. That will no doubt come as a shock to Producer Albert (Cubby)

Broccoli, who has made the James Bond series his life's work.

Broccoli and his late partner, Harry Saltzman, all but invented the genre that Hollywood calls "event films" or "special effects films." The ingredients, which Bond popularized and others imitated, always included supervillains, sensational stunts, sex, absurd plots to destroy or rule the world and, of course, a hero. The 007 epics held the patent on that formula in the late '60s and early '70s, but they are growing dated. *For Your Eyes Only* doesn't have any surprises. We've seen all the big scenes before, and when the villains turn out to be headquartered in an impregnable mountaintop fortress, we yawn. After *Where Eagles Dare* and *The Guns of Navarone* and the hollow Japanese volcano that Bond himself once infiltrated, let's face it: When you've seen one impregnable mountaintop fortress, you've seen 'em all.

The movie opens with James Bond trapped inside a remote-controlled helicopter being guided by a bald sadist in a wheelchair. After Bond triumphs, the incident is never referred to again. *This* movie involves the loss of the secret British code controlling submarine-based missiles. The Russians would like to have it. Bond's mission: Retrieve the control console from a ship sunk in the Aegean. The movie breaks down into a series of set-pieces. Bond and his latest Bondgirl (long-haired, undemonstrative Carole Bouquet) dive in a mini-sub, engage in a complicated chase through the back roads of Greece, crawl through the sunken wreck in wet suits, are nearly drowned and blown up, etc. For variety, Bond and Bouquet are dragged behind a powerboat as shark bait, and then Bond scales the fortress mountain. A fortress guard spots Bond dangling from a rope thousands of feet in the air. What does he do? Does he just cut the rope? No, sir, the guard descends part way to tantalize Bond by letting him drop a little at a time. The rest is predictable.

In a movie of respectable craftsmanship and moderate pleasures, there's one obvious disappointment. The relationship between Roger Moore and Carole Bouquet is never worked out in an interesting way. Since the days when he was played by Sean Connery, agent 007 has always had a dry, quiet, humorous way with women. Roger Moore has risen to the same challenge, notably opposite Barbara Bach in *The Spy Who Loved Me*. But Moore and Bouquet have no real chemistry in *For Your Eyes Only*. There's none of that kidding byplay. It's too routine. The whole movie is too routine.

The Formula ★ ★
R, 117 m., 1980

George C. Scott (Detective), Marlon Brando (Adam Steifel), Marthe Keller (Lisa), John Gielgud (Dr. Esau), G.D. Spradlin (Clements). Directed by John Avildsen and produced and written by Steve Shagan.

One of the ironies of *The Formula* is that if it had only been made from an old Hollywood formula—*any* formula—we might have been able to understand it better. As it stands, it's so thoroughly baffling that we find ourselves asking, not only who-did-it, but what they did, and who they were. The movie is no help. Since *The Formula* is intended as a thriller, its completely muddled plot is a disaster: There can be no joy in unraveling a plot that is a mystery even to itself.

The movie's based on Steve Shagan's best-selling novel, which began with the premise that the Nazis discovered a cheap formula for synthetic fuel thirty-five years ago, and that the giant oil corporations have been suppressing it ever since. In the movie, the oil companies are represented by Marlon Brando, who appears in three fascinating scenes and leaves us wishing for more. The good guys are boiled down in the person of George C. Scott, as a Los Angeles detective who starts out investigating the murder of a friend and stumbles onto a trail that leads him to Europe and possessors of that secret formula.

Of *that* much I'm sure. Various other questions remain unanswered. For example, in Europe Scott takes up with a young lady who seems to be on the same side he's on. She's played by Marthe Keller as the same sort of beautiful international enigma she has played before. But what's she *really* up to? In interviews, Steve Shagan explains that she's from the Palestine Liberation Organization. In the movie, we learn she has guilt feelings because her Nazi father murdered Jews. Then why would she be in the PLO? It

hardly matters, since her affiliation, if any, is never made clear in the movie.

There are other puzzles. As Scott tracks down the formula, everyone he talks to is killed almost immediately after he talks to them. Why? Because he's being led on a wild goose chase, and each character is eliminated after serving his function? Because the killers are trying to discourage Scott—and just can't seem to kill him, too? It's a mystery. I must also admit that at the movie's end, I still did not know for sure who was doing the shooting. I assumed it was a conspiracy by Brando's oil company, but I couldn't be sure.

The Formula apparently is a mess because of a post-production fight between Shagan, as writer-producer, and John Avildsen, as director; they exchanged acrimonious letters in the *Los Angeles Times*, and Avildsen failed in an attempt to have his name removed from the picture. They way they tell it, Avildsen wanted the movie to make more sense as a thriller, while Shagan was more concerned with his "message."

Well. One of the problems with his message is that it is not based on fact; it's a fantasy. Even though it may be true that the multinational oil companies try to manipulate the energy market, it is apparently not true that a formula exists that could turn coal into cheap synthetic fuel. Yet the movie's publicity calls the existence of a secret Nazi formula a "proven fact."

I have here an article from the November 1980 issue of *Science* magazine, noting that the "synthesis used by the Germans are more in the nature of textbook processes than Mobil secrets" and that the film, "as history, is bunkum."

If the film cannot be taken seriously as an exposé, and it is hopelessly confused as a thriller, what's left? Two marvelous performances. Scott, as the detective, is a harried, tired, deeply cynical man who fills the crevices of his role with an actor's details that make the cop a human being. Brando, who designed his makeup to resemble Occidental Oil's Armand Hammer, has a great speech at the end of the film and several other classic lines ranging from "You're missing the point—we *are* the Arabs," to the succinct offer "Milk Dud?" What happens during *The Formula* is that we eventually give up trying to make any sense out of the movie and content ourselves with regarding these performances. They are subtle and lovingly crafted, and it is just too bad there's no substance surrounding them.

Fort Apache, The Bronx ★ ★
R, 123 m., 1981

Paul Newman (Murphy), Edward Asner (Connolly), Ken Wahl (Corelli), Danny Aiello (Morgan), Rachel Ticotin (Isabella), Pam Grier (Charlotte), Kathleen Beller (Theresa). Directed by Daniel Petrie and produced by Martin Richards and Tom Fiorello. Screenplay by Heywood Gould.

It's sort of insidious, the way a formula can take over and smother a good idea for a movie. *Fort Apache, The Bronx* apparently began as such an idea. It's said to be based on the experiences of a couple of real cops in the worst area of New York's Bronx. The area looks like a bomb site, with burned-out buildings and people. The filmmakers wanted to go into this area and use a police story as a framework for showing how people live and suffer there, and how public agencies such as the police grow frustrated trying to deal with an impossible situation. That was their intention, anyway. What they came out with is the most complete collection of cop-movie clichés since John Wayne played a Chicago cop in *McQ*.

There were authentic perceptions and ideas available to this film—and you can see them on the screen. You can see them in the look of some of the shots, tracking across the urban wasteland, and in the sound and feel of a scene where a pimp beats and berates one of his girls, and the grim humor of a scene where a thief outruns a cop—who pauses, gasping for breath, and lights a cigarette.

But then there's a story line that keeps getting in the way. There are too many scenes that are necessary to the plot but not to the movie, scenes where the life of the movie stops so story details can be filled in. And we realize that somehow Hollywood hasn't wanted to get *too* close to this material. Instead, it has borrowed a look of grim authenticity and grafted it to assorted cop show situations.

The movie stars Paul Newman. He's good in his role, as a cop named Murphy who simultaneously falls in love with a nurse, witnesses his fellow officers committing a murder, and has a battle of will with his commanding officer. The chief is played by Edward Asner, who is in the movie so briefly that, effective as he is, we have trouble remembering he's a cop. He's still Lou Grant, barking orders in the sqaud room instead of the city room.

The movie has several story threads that lead nowhere. One involves Pam Grier, as a junkie prostitute who wanders the streets in a daze, kills a couple of cops—and then turns out to have been basically a walk-on, and *not* the key to the movie's mysteries. There are also several whole scenes that seem to have been put in without much purpose, including one in which Newman and his partner try to talk a transvestite out of jumping off a building, and another in which Newman delivers a baby. Then there's a big climactic scene, with drug dealers holed up with hostages and the SWAT boys (and Newman, of course) crashing through windows on the ends of ropes.

These scenes all seem to be in the movie because the filmmakers thought they belonged in any self-respecting cop movie. Too bad. The purely human story in this movie would have been much more interesting. It involves Newman's relationship with the Puerto Rican nurse (wonderfully well-played by Rachel Ticotin) and the crisis of conscience he goes through about whether to turn in his fellow officers after he saw them throw a kid off a roof.

Do the filmmakers feel we're not ready for issues like that, served straight? Do we need violence and action to keep our attention? Is our attention span so short that no strand of character development can be followed for long without throwing in some kind of sensational diversion? I hope not. To throw in all the stock characters and shopworn situations from old TV cop shows is an insult to the abilities of the actors and to the real lives this movie pretends to reflect.

48 Hours ★ ★ ★ ½
R, 100 m., 1982

Nick Nolte (Cates), Eddie Murphy (Reggie), James Remar (Ganz), Sonny Landham (Billy

Bear), Annette O'Toole (Elaine). Directed by Walter Hill and produced by Lawrence Gordon and Joel Silver. Screenplay by Roger Spottiswoode, Hill, Larry Gross, and Steven E. de Souza.

Sometimes an actor becomes a star in just one scene. Jack Nicholson did it in *Easy Rider*, wearing the football helmet on the back of the motorcycle. It happened to Faye Dunaway when she looked sleepily out of a screen window at Warren Beatty in *Bonnie and Clyde*. And in *48 Hours*, it happens to Eddie Murphy. His unforgettable scene comes about halfway through *48 Hours*. He plays a convict who has done thirty months for theft and will do six more unless he helps out Nick Nolte, a hungover hot dog of a detective who's on the trail of some cop killers. Nolte has sprung Murphy from jail for forty-eight hours, with the promise of freedom if they get the killers. Murphy thinks there's a bartender who may have some information. The thing is, the bar is a redneck country joint, the kind where urban cowboys drink out of longneck bottles and salute the Confederate flag on the wall. Murphy has been jiving Nolte about how he can handle any situation. Nolte gives him a chance. And Murphy, impersonating a police officer, walks into that bar, takes command, totally intimidates everybody, and gets his information. It's a great scene—the mirror image of that scene in *The French Connection* where Gene Hackman, as Popeye Doyle, intimidated the black regulars in a Harlem bar.

Murphy has other good moments in this movie, and so does Nolte, who gives a wonderful performance as a cynical, irresponsible, and immature cop who's always telling lies to his girlfriend and sneaking a jolt of whiskey out of his personal flask. The two men start out suspicious of each other in this movie and work up to a warm dislike. But eventually, grudgingly, a kind of respect starts to grow.

The movie's story is nothing to write home about. It's pretty routine. What makes the movie special is how it's made. Nolte and Murphy are good, and their dialogue is good, too—quirky and funny. Character actor James Remar makes a really slimy killer, genuinely evil. Annette O'Toole gets third billing as Nolte's lover, but it's another one of those thankless women's roles. Not only could O'Toole have phoned it in—she does, spending most of her scenes on the telephone calling Nolte a no-good bum. The direction is by Walter Hill, who has never been any good at scenes involving women and doesn't improve this time. What he is good at is action, male camaraderie and atmosphere. His movies almost always feature at least one beautifully choreographed, unbelievably violent fight scene (remember Charles Bronson's bare-knuckle fight in *Hard Times?*), and the fight scene this time is exhausting.

Where Hill grows in this movie is in his ability to create characters. In a lot of his earlier movies (*The Warriors, The Driver, Long Riders, Southern Comfort*) he preferred men who were symbols, who represented things and so didn't have to be human. In *48 Hours*, Nolte and Murphy are human, vulnerable, and touching. Also mean, violent, and chauvinistic. It's that kind of movie.

Four Friends ★ ★ ★ ★
R, 114 m., 1981

Craig Wasson (Danilo Prozor), Jodi Thelen (Georgia Miles), Jim Metzler (Tom Donaldson), Michael Huddleston (David Levine), Reed Birney (Louie Carnahan), Julie Murray (Adrienne Carnahan), Miklos Simon (Mr. Prozor). Directed by Arthur Penn and produced by Penn and Gene Lasko. Screenplay by Steven Tesich.

Somewhere in the middle of *My Dinner with André*, Andre Gregory wonders aloud if it's not possible that the 1960s were the last decade when we were all truly alive—that since then we've sunk into a bemused state of self-hypnosis, placated by consumer goods and given the illusion of excitement by television. Walking out of *Four Friends*, I had some of the same thoughts. This movie brings the almost unbelievable contradictions of that decade into sharp relief, not as nostalgia or as a re-creation of times past, but as a reliving of all of the agony and freedom of the weirdest ten years any of us is likely to witness.

The movie is told in the form of a loose-knit autobiography, somewhat inspired by the experiences of Steve Tesich, the son of Yugoslavian parents who moved to this country as a boy and lived in the neighborhoods of East Chicago, Indiana, that provide the film's locations. If the film is his emotional autobiography, it is also perhaps the intellectual autobiography of Arthur Penn, the film's director, whose *Bonnie and Clyde* was the best American film of the 1960s and whose *Alice's Restaurant* (1970) was an earlier examination of that wonderful and haunted time.

Their movie tells the stories of four friends. When we meet them, they're entering their senior year of high school. It is 1961. That is so long ago that nobody has yet heard of the Beatles. One of the friends is a young woman (Jodi Thelen), who imagines she is the reincarnation of Isadora Duncan, and who strikes attitudes and poses in an attempt to appear altogether too much of an artistic genius for East Chicago to contain. The other three friends are male classmates. They all love the girl in one way or another, or perhaps it's just that they've never seen anyone like her before. In the ten years to follow, these four people will have lives that were not imaginable in 1961. They will have the opportunity to break out of the sedate conservatism of the Eisenhower era and into the decade of "alternative life-styles."

The movie is ambitious. It wants to take us on a tour of some of the things that happened in the 1960s, and some of the ways four midwestern kids might have responded to them. It also wants to be a meditation on love, and on how love changes during the course of a decade. When Thelen turns up at the bedroom window of her "real" true love (Craig Wasson) early in the movie and cheerfully offers to sleep with him, Wasson refuses, not only because he's a high school kid who's a little afraid of her—but also because he's too much in love with his idea of love to want to make it real. By the time they finally do come back together, years later, they've both been through bad scenes, through madness, drug abuse, and the trauma of the war in Vietnam. They have also grown up, some. The wonder is not that *Four Friends* covers so much ground, but that it makes many of its scenes so memorable that we learn more even about the supporting characters than we expect to.

There are individual scenes in this movie that are just right. One of them involves a crowd of kids walking home in the dusk after school. Another happens between Wasson and Miklos Simon, who plays his gruff, defensive Yugoslavian father, and who finally, painfully, breaks down and smiles after a poker-faced lifetime. A relationship between Wasson and a dying college classmate (Reed Birney) is well drawn, to remind us of undergraduate friendships based on idealism and mutual discovery. And the scene where Wasson and Thelen see each other after many years is handled tenderly and with just the right notes of irony.

Four Friends is a very good movie. Like *Breaking Away,* the story of growing up in Bloomington, Indiana (for which Tesich also wrote the original screenplay), this is a movie that remembers times past with such clarity that there are times it seems to be making it all up. Did we really say those things? Make those assumptions? Live on the edge of what seemed to be a society gone both free and mad at once? Some critics have said the people and events in this movie are not plausible. I don't know if they're denying the movie's truth, or arguing that from a 1980s point of view the '60s were just a bad dream. Or a good one.

The Fox and the Hound ★ ★ ★
G, 83 m., 1981

With the voices of Pearl Bailey (Big Mama), Kurt Russell (Copper), Mickey Rooney (Tod), Sandy Duncan (Vixey), Pat Buttram (Chief), Jack Albertson (Slade). Directed by Art Stevens, Ted Berman, and Richard Rich and produced by Wolfgang Reitherman and Stevens. Screenplay by Larry Clemmons and others.

In all the old familiar ways, *The Fox and the Hound* looks like a traditional production from Walt Disney animators. In has cute little animals and wise old owls. It has a villain in the shape of a mountainous grizzly bear, and comic relief in a long-standing feud between a woodpecker and a caterpillar. And it has songs that contain such uncontroversial wishes as, "If only the world wouldn't get in the way . . . If only the world would let us play." And yet, for all of its familiar qualities, this movie marks something of a departure for the Disney studio, and its movement is in an interesting direction. *The*

Fox and the Hound is one of those relatively rare Disney animated features that contains a useful lesson for its younger audiences. It's not just cute animals and frightening adventures and a happy ending; it's also a rather thoughtful meditation on how society determines our behavior.

The movie is a fable about a small puppy named Tod and an orphaned fox named Copper. At the outset we sense something unusual—after the camera traces a gloomy path through the shadows of the forest, a mother fox and her baby come running terrified out of the woods, chased by hunters and hounds. Will the mother and child escape? They almost do. But then the mother hides her baby and sacrifices her life to draw attention away from him. This is the cruel world, without any magical cartoon escapes.

The little fox is taken under the wing, so to speak, by wise old Big Mama Owl, who arranges for the baby to be adopted by a kindly farm woman. It's at this point that the puppy comes into the plot. Puppy and fox become great friends in their childhoods and pledge to be loyal to each other forevermore. But then the quickly growing hound is taken away to be trained as a hunter, and the next time the two friends meet, the hound is savagely trying to chase down the fox. After they are almost killed by the bear, there is a reconciliation of sorts. They realize (and perhaps the kids in the audience will realize, too) how quickly our better impulses can be drowned out by the noise of society. The message is not heavy-handed, nor does it need to be, because the lessons in the movie are so firmly illustrated by the lives of the animals.

Although *The Fox and the Hound* is the first Disney animated feature to have been made mostly by a newer generation of artists at the studio, the film's look still is in the tradition of *The Rescuers* (1977) and other Disney work in the 1970s. That means we don't get the painstaking, frame-by-frame animation of individual leaves and flowers and birds that made *Snow White* magical back when animator man-hours were cheaper. But we do get a lot of life and energy on the screen.

The star of the movie's sound track is Pearl Bailey as Big Mama Owl. She sings three songs, dispenses advice with a free hand, and struts around in the forest as a sort of feathered Ann Landers. The animators have done a wonderful job of giving their cartoon owl some of Pearlie Mae's personality traits, but the two leading characters (with Mickey Rooney as the fox and Kurt Russell as the hound) are more straightforward.

The bottom line, I suppose, is: Will kids like this movie? And the answer is, sure, I think so. It's a fast-moving, colorful story, and as I watched the animated images on the screen, I was suddenly reminded of a curious belief I held when I was a kid. I believed that cartoons looked more real than "live" features, because everything on the screen had sharper edges. I outgrew my notion, but I'm not sure that represents progress.

Foxes ★ ★ ★
R, 106 m., 1980

Jodie Foster (Jeanie), Scott Baio (Brad), Sally Kellerman (Mary), Randy Quaid (Jay), Lois Smith (Mrs. Axman), Adam Faith (Bryan), Cherie Currie (Annie), Marilyn Kagan (Madge), Kandice Stroh (Dierdre). Directed by Adrian Lyne and produced by David Puttnam and Gerald Ayres. Screenplay by Ayres.

God help us if many American teen-agers are like the ones in this movie—but God love *them*, for that matter, for surviving in the teen-age subculture of Los Angeles. *Foxes* is a movie about four teen-age girls who live in the San Fernando Valley, who come from broken or unhappy homes, who are surrounded by a teen-age subculture of sex, dope, booze, and rock and roll . . . and who aren't bad kids, not really.

They run in a pack, sleeping over at each other's homes, going to school together, hanging out together, forming a substitute family because home doesn't provide a traditional one. They form the fierce loyalties that all teen-agers depend upon—loyalties of friendship that run deeper than the instant romances and sudden crushes that are a dime a dozen. They live in a world where sixteen-year-old kids are somehow expected to live in adult society, make decisions about adult vices, and yet not be adult. That's what's scariest about *Foxes:* Our knowledge that alcohol, pot, and pills *are* available to teen-agers unwise enough to go looking for them, and that they can provide emotional overloads far beyond the ability of the kids to cope.

One of the kids in this movie does cope fairly well, though. She's Jeanie, played by Jodie Foster as a sort of teen-age mother hen, a young girl who's got problems of her own but is intelligent, balanced, and enough of a survivor to clearly see the mistakes the others are making. That doesn't mean she rejects her friends. She runs with the pack and she takes her chances, but she's not clearly doomed. And some of the others are.

The movie follows its four foxes through several days and several adventures. It's a loosely structured film, deliberately episodic to suggest the shapeless form of these teen-agers' typical days and nights. Things happen on impulse. Stuff comes up. Kids stay out all night, or run away, or get drunk, or get involved in what's supposed to be a civilized dinner party until it's crashed by a mob of greasers.

The subject of the movie is the way these events are seen so very differently by the kids and their parents. And at the heart of the movie is one particular, wonderful, and complicated parent-child relationship, between Jodie Foster and Sally Kellerman. They only have a few extended scenes together, but the material is written and acted with such sensitivity that we really understand the relationship. And we understand Kellerman, as an attractive woman in her thirties, divorced from a rock promoter, who is trying to raise a sixteen-year-old, attend college, and still have a love life of her own. Kellerman has a line that evokes whole lives, when she talks about "all those desperately lonely, divorced UCLA undergraduates."

The parallels here are obvious. The Kellerman character, we suspect, got swept up in the rock and drug subculture, got married too young, got pregnant immediately, and now, the mother of a sixteen-year-old, is *still* in the process of growing up herself. She doesn't want her kid to go through what she went through. But kids grow up so fast these days that, oddly enough, these two women are almost in the same boat.

Foxes is an ambitious movie, not an exploitation picture. It's a lot more serious, for example, than the hit *Little Darlings*. It contains the sounds and rhythms of real teen-age lives; it was written and directed after a lot of research, and is acted by kids who are to one degree or another playing themselves. The movie's a rare attempt to provide a portrait of the way teen-agers really do live today in some suburban cultures.

Frances ★ ★ ★ ½
R, 139 m., 1983

Jessica Lange (Frances Farmer), Sam Shepard (Harry York), Bart Burns (Farmer). Directed by Graeme Clifford and produced by Jonathan Sanger. Screenplay by Eric Bergren, Christopher Devore, and Nicholas Kazan.

Graeme Clifford's *Frances* tells the story of a small-town girl who tasted the glory of Hollywood and the exhilaration of Broadway and then went on to lead a life during which everything went wrong. It is a tragedy without a villain, a sad story with no moral except that there, but for the grace of God, go we. The movie is about Frances Farmer, a beautiful and talented movie star from the 1930s and 1940s who had a streak of independence and a compulsion toward self-destruction, and who went about as high and about as low as it is possible to go in one lifetime. She came out of Seattle as a high school essay-contest winner and budding intellectual. She was talented and pretty enough to make her way fairly easily into show business, where she immediately gravitated to the left-wing precincts of the Group Theater and such landmark productions as Clifford Odets's *Waiting for Lefty*. She also became a movie star, and there was a time when her star shone so brightly that it seemed it would last forever.

It did not. She was a stubborn, opinionated star who fought with the studio system, defied the bosses, drank too much, took too many pills, and got into too much trouble. Her strong-willed mother stepped in to help her, and that's when Frances's troubles really began. The mother orchestrated a series of hospitalizations in bizarre mental institutions, where Frances Farmer was brutally mistreated and finally, horrifyingly, lobotomized. She ended her days as a vague, pleasant middle-age woman who did a talk show in Indianapolis and finally died of alcoholism.

Jessica Lange plays Frances Farmer in a performance that is so driven, that contains so many different facets of a complex personality, that we feel she has an intuitive understanding of this tragic woman. She is just as good when she portrays Farmer as an uncertain, appealing teen-ager from the Northwest as she is when she plays her much later, snarling at a hairdresser and screaming at her mother. All of those contradictions were inside Farmer, and if she had learned to hide or deal with some of them she might have lived a happier life.

The story of Frances Farmer makes a fascinating movie, if only because it's such a contrast to standard show-business biographies. They usually come in two speeds: rags to riches, or rags to riches to victim. *Frances* never really lays blame for the tragedy of Farmer's life. It presents a number of causes for Farmer's destruction. (A short list might include her combative personality, her shrewish mother, the studio system, betrayal by her lovers, alcoholism, drug abuse, psychiatric malpractice, and the predations of a mad lobotomist.) But the movie never comes right out and says what it believes "caused" Farmer's tragedy. That is good, I think, because no simple explanation will do for Farmer's life. The movie is told from her point of view, and from where she stood, she was surrounded. On one day she had one enemy, and on another day, another enemy. Always, of course, her worst enemy was herself. The movie doesn't let us off the hook by giving us someone to blame. Instead, it insists on being a bleak tragedy, and it argues that sometimes it is quite possible for everything to go wrong. Since most movies are at least optimistic enough to provide a *cause* for human tragedy, this one is sort of daring.

It is also well made by Clifford, whose credits as a film editor include such virtuoso work as *McCabe and Mrs. Miller* and *Don't Look Now.* In his debut as a director Clifford has made a period picture that wears its period so easily that we're not distracted by it, a movie that is bleak without being unwatchable.

There are a few problems with his structure, most of them centering around an incompletely explained friend of Farmer's, played by Sam Shepard as a guy who seems to drift into her life whenever the plot requires him. Kim Stanley plays Farmer's mother on a rather thankless note of shrillness, and the lobotomist in the picture seems to have wandered over from a nearby horror film. (He apparently gave the same impression in real life.) But Lange provides a strong emotional center for the film, and when it is over we're left with the feeling that Farmer never really got a chance to be who she should have been, or to do what she should have done. She had every gift she needed in life except for luck, useful friends, and an instinct for survival. She could have been one of the greatest movie stars of her time. As it is, when I was asked to name a few of Frances Farmer's best films, I had to admit that, offhand, I couldn't think of one.

Fraternity Vacation ★
R, 95 m., 1985

Stephen Geofferys (Wendell Tvedt), Sherre J. Wilson (Ashley Taylor), Cameron Dye (Joe Gillespie), Leigh McCloskey (Chas). Directed by James Frawley and produced by Robert C. Peters. Screenplay by Lindsay Harrison.

No women are hacked to pieces in *Fraternity Vacation,* but they are the victims of violence all the same—the kind of violence that denies them the opportunity to be as interesting, as aggressive, and as free to choose as all the guys in this brain-damaged film. Their basic role here is to be the prizes in a male sexual competition. Since the guys in this movie are shallow, narcissistic, self-obsessed dummies, to be the prize is to lose the game, but in a movie like this, those are the rules.

The film takes place in Palm Springs, during spring break, when a bunch of fraternity boys from Iowa descend on the town. Why Palm Springs and not Fort Lauderdale? Because Palm Springs is closer to Hollywood, and therefore a cheaper place to make a movie, that's why. So the movie glosses over the fact that Palm Springs is the most boring town in America for anyone who does not play golf and/or know Bob Hope or Betty Ford. In the movie, the college students cruise up and down the main drag in their convertibles, checking out the action, and we meet the main players. On one side there are three fraternity brothers—two jocks and a nerd. On the other side, two jocks from a rival fraternity. Everybody is out to get laid, of course, and that leads to the movie's painfully offensive opening sex scene.

You've got to see this episode to believe what pathological attitudes the movie has about women. Let me set the scene. The guys from the rival fraternity—let's call them the bad guys—have brought along a couple of girlfriends, and convince them to stage a practical joke to make the good guys think they're going to get lucky. So the women go up to the good guys' room, make out for a while, completely strip, and then play the "joke" by pretending they have herpes. What a ton of fun. Consider: What's essentially happening, in this jocular, happy-go-lucky scene, is that the girlfriends are asked to behave like hookers, and they agree. You think that's bad? Get this: After that scene, the two women *are never seen again in this movie!* They are simply dropped as characters—and as girlfriends, too, I guess. how would you feel if you were an actress auditioning for a part, and the good news was you were the girlfriend of the star, and the bad news was that after you stripped and made a herpes joke, you disappeared from the movie?

Meanwhile, the arena of sexual competition changes. There's a beautiful, mysterious blonde (Sherre J. Taylor) at poolside, and all the guys lust after her. So, they make a $1,000 bet about who will be the first to get her in the sack. The rest of the movie consists of the idiotic things all five guys do to impress the blonde. At the end of the film, of course, it's not the jocks but the nerd who wins out. Who said this movie doesn't have a conscience?

Don't get me wrong. I have nothing against dumb sex comedies. All I object to is the fact that *Fraternity Vacation* is playing with half a deck—the male half. The men are the characters and the women are the objects. That's probably because the movie was made by men who lacked the imagination to get outside their own fat heads and imagine what it might be like to be a woman—not a woman in real life, mind you, but even a woman in their trashy little movie. Think how much more interesting it could have been if the women, as well as the men, were allowed to lust, to scheme, to make bets, to have competitions, and to do all sorts of fun things, instead of just tanning themselves by the side of the pool. Of course, that would be another movie. Maybe even another universe.

The French Lieutenant's Woman
★ ★ ★ ½
R, 124 m., 1981

Meryl Streep (Sarah and Anna), Jeremy Irons (Charles and Mike), Hilton McRae (Sam), Emily Morgan (Mary), Charlotte Mitchell (Mrs. Tranter), Lynsey Baxter (Ernestina). Directed by Karol Reisz and produced by Leon Clore. Screenplay by Harold Pinter.

Reading the last one hundred pages of John Fowles's *The French Lieutenant's Woman* is like being caught in a fictional labyrinth. We think we know where we stand in the story, and who the characters are and what possibilities are open to them, and then Fowles begins an astonishing series of surprises. He turns his story inside out, suggesting first one ending, then another, always in a way that forces us to rethink everything that has gone before. That complex structure was long thought to make Fowles's novel unfilmable. How could his fictional surprises, depending on the relationship between reader and omniscient narrator, be translated into the more literal nature of film? One of the directors who tried to lick *The French Lieutenant's Woman* was John Frankenheimer, who complained: "There is no way you can film the book. You can tell the same story in a movie, of course, but not in the same way. And how Fowles tells his story is what makes the book so good." That seemed to be the final verdict, until the British playwright Harold Pinter tackled the project.

Pinter's previous screenplays, such as *The Accident* and *The Go-Between*, are known for a mastery of ambiguity, for a willingness to approach the audience on more than one level of reality, and what he and director Karel Reisz have done with their film, *The French Lieutenant's Woman*, is both simple and brilliant. They have frankly discarded the multi-layered fictional devices of John Fowles, and tried to create a new cinematic approach that will achieve the same ambiguity. Fowles made us stand at a distance from his two doomed lovers, Sarah and Charles. He told their story, of a passion that was forbidden by the full weight of Victorian convention, and then he invited us to stand back and view that passion in terms of facts and statistics about . . . well, Victorian passions in general. Pinter and Reisz create a similar distance in their movie by telling us two parallel stories. In one of them, Sarah Woodruff (Meryl Streep) still keeps her forlorn vigil for the French lieutenant who loved and abandoned her, and she still plays her intriguing cat-and-mouse game with the obsessed young man (Jeremy Irons) who must possess her.

In the other story, set in the present, two actors named Anna and Mike are playing Sarah and Charles. And Anna and Mike are also having a forbidden affair, albeit a more conventional one. For the length of the movie's shooting schedule, they are lovers offscreen as well as on. But eventually Mike will return to his family and Anna to her lover.

This is a device that works, I think. Frankenheimer was right in arguing that just *telling* the Victorian love story would leave you with . . . just a Victorian love story. The modern framing story places the Victorian lovers in ironic relief. Everything they say and do has another level of meaning, because we know the "real" relationship between the actors themselves. Reisz opens his film with a shot that boldly states his approach: We see Streep in costume for her role as Sarah, attended by a movie makeup woman. A clapboard marks the scene, and *then* Streep walks into the movie's re-creation of the British coastal village of Lyme Regis.

"It's only a movie," this shot informs us. But, of course, it's *all* only a movie, including the story about the modern actors. And this confusion of fact and fiction interlocks perfectly with the psychological games played in the Victorian story by Sarah Woodruff herself.

The French lieutenant's woman is one of the most intriguing characters in recent fiction. She is not only apparently the victim of Victorian sexism, but also (as Charles discovers) its manipulator and master. She cleverly uses the conventions that would limit her, as a means of obtaining personal freedom and power over men. At least that is one way to look at what she does. Readers of the novel will know there are others.

The French Lieutenant's Woman is a beautiful film to look at, and remarkably well-acted. Streep was showered with praise for her remarkable double performance, and she deserved it. She is offhandedly contemporary one moment, and then gloriously, theatrically Victorian the next. Opposite her, Jeremy Irons is authoritative and convincingly bedeviled as the man who is frustrated by both of Streep's characters. The movie's a challenge to our intelligence, takes delight in playing with our expectations, and has one other considerable achievement as well: It entertains admirers of Fowles's novel, but does not reveal the book's secrets. If you see the movie, the book will still surprise you, and that's as it should be.

Friday the 13th, Part II ½ ★
R, 87 m., 1981*

Amy Steel (Ginny), John Furey (Paul), Adrienne King (Alice), Kirsten Baker (Terry). Directed and produced by Steve Miner. Screenplay by Ron Kurz.

I saw *Friday the 13th Part II* at the Virginia Theater, a former vaudeville house in my hometown of Champaign-Urbana, Illinois. The late show was half-filled with high school and college students, and as the lights went down I experienced a brief wave of nostalgia. In this very theater, on countless Friday nights, I'd gone with a date to the movies. My nostalgia lasted for the first two minutes of the movie.

The pretitle sequence showed one of the heroines of the original *Friday the 13th*, alone at home. She has nightmares, wakes up, undresses, is stalked by the camera, hears a noise in the kitchen. She tiptoes into the kitchen. Through the open window, a cat springs into the room. The audience screamed loudly and happily: It's fun to be scared. Then an unidentified man sunk an ice pick into the girl's brain, and, for me, the fun stopped.

The audience, however, carried on. It is a tradition to be loud during these movies, I guess. After a batch of young counselors turns up for training at a summer camp, a girl goes out walking alone at night. Everybody in the audience imitated hoot-owls and hyenas. Another girl went to her room and started to undress. Five guys sitting together started a chant: "We want boobs!"

The plot: In the original movie, a summer camp staff was wiped out by a demented woman whose son had been allowed to drown by incompetent camp counselors. At the end of that film, the mother was decapitated by the young woman who is killed with an ice pick at the beginning of *Part II*. The legend grows that the son, Jason, did *not* really drown, but survived, and lurks in the woods waiting to take his vengeance against the killer of his mother . . . and against camp couselors in general, I guess.

That sets up the film. The counselors are introduced, very briefly, and then some of them go into town for a beer and the rest stay at the camp to make out with each other. A mystery assailant prowls around the main cabin. We see only his shadow and his shoes. One by one, he picks off the kids. He sinks a machete into the brain of a kid in a wheelchair. He surprises a boy and a girl making love, and nails them to a bunk with a spear through both their bodies. When the other kids return to the camp, it's their turn. After almost everyone has been killed in a disgusting and violent way, one girl chews up the assailant with a chain saw, *after* which we discover the mummies in his cabin in the woods, *after* which he jumps through a window at the girl, etc.

This movie is a cross between the Mad Slasher and Dead Teen-ager genres; about two dozen movies a year feature a mad killer going berserk, and they're all about as bad as this one. Some have a little more plot, some have a little less. It doesn't matter.

Sinking into my seat in this movie theater from my childhood, I remembered the movie fantasies when I was a kid. They involved teen-agers who fell in love, made out with each other, customized their cars, listened to rock and roll, and were rebels without causes. Neither the kids in those movies nor the kids watching them would have understood a world view in which the primary function of teen-agers is to be hacked to death.

*This review will suffice for the *Friday the 13th* film of your choice.

Gandhi ★ ★ ★ ★
PG, 188 m., 1983

Ben Kingsley (Mahatma Gandhi), Candice Bergen (Margaret Bourke-White), Edward Fox (General Dyer), John Gielgud (Lord Irwin), Trevor Howard (Judge Broomfield), John Mills (The Viceroy) Martin Sheen (Walker), Rohini Hattangady (Kasturba Ghandi), Ian Charleson (Charlie Andrews), Athol Fugard (General Smuts). Directed and produced by Richard Attenborough. Screenplay by John Briley.

In the middle of this epic film there is a quiet, small scene that helps explain why *Gandhi* is such a remarkable experience. Mahatma Gandhi, at the height of his power and his fame, stands by the side of a lake with his wife of many years. Together, for the benefit of a visitor from the West, they reenact their marriage vows. They do it with solemnity, quiet warmth, and perhaps just a touch of shyness; they are simultaneously demonstrating an aspect of Indian culture and touching on something very personal to them both. At the end of the ceremony, Gandhi says, "We were thirteen at the time." He shrugs. The marriage had been arranged. Gandhi and his wife had not been in love, had not been old enough for love, and yet love had grown between them. But that is not really the point of the scene. The point, I think, comes in the quiet smile with which Gandhi says the words. At that moment we believe that he is fully and truly human, and at that moment, a turning point in the film, *Gandhi* declares that it is not only a historical record but a breathing, living document.

This is the sort of rare epic film that spans the decades, that uses the proverbial cast of thousands, and yet follows a human thread from beginning to end: *Gandhi* is no more overwhelmed by the scope of its production than was Gandhi overwhelmed by all the glory of the British Empire. The movie earns comparison with two classic works by David Lean, *Lawrence of Arabia* and *Dr. Zhivago*, in its ability to paint a strong human story on a very large canvas.

The movie is a labor of love by Sir Richard Attenborough, who struggled for years to get financing for his huge but "non-commercial" project. Various actors were considered over the years for the all-important title role, but the actor who was finally chosen, Ben Kingsley, makes the role so completely his own that there is a genuine feeling that the spirit of Gandhi is on the screen. Kingsley's performance is powerful without being loud or histrionic; he is almost always quiet, observant, and soft-spoken on the screen, and yet his performance comes across with such might that we realize, afterward, that the sheer moral force of Gandhi must have been behind the words. Apart from all its other qualities, what makes this movie special is that it was obviously made by people who believed in it.

The movie begins in the early years of the century, in South Africa, where Gandhi was born and spent the first decades of his life. He was trained as a lawyer and received his degree, but, degree or not, he was a target of South Africa's system of racial segregation, in which Indians (even though they are Caucasian, and thus should "qualify") are denied full citizenship and manhood. Gandhi's reaction to the system is, at first, almost naive; an early scene on a train doesn't quite work only because we can't believe the adult Gandhi would still be so ill-informed about the racial code of South Africa. But Gandhi's response sets the tone of the film. He is nonviolent but firm. He is sure where the right lies in every situation, and he will uphold it in total disregard for the possible consequences to himself.

Before long Gandhi is in India, a nation of hundreds of millions, ruled by a relative handful of British. They rule almost by divine right, shouldering the "white man's burden" even though they have not quite been requested to do so by the Indians. Gandhi realizes that Indians have been made into second-class citizens in their own country, and he begins a program of civil disobedience that is at first ignored by the British, then scorned, and finally, reluctantly, dealt with, sometimes by subterfuge, sometimes by brutality. Scenes in this central passage of the movie make it clear that nonviolent protests could contain a great deal of violence. There is a shattering scene in which wave after wave of Gandhi's followers march forward to be beaten to the ground by British clubs. Through it all, Gandhi maintains a certain detachment; he is convinced he is right, convinced that violence is not an answer, convinced that

sheer moral example can free his nation—as it did. "You have been guests in our home long enough," he tells the British, "Now we would like for you to leave."

The movie is populated with many familiar faces, surrounding the newcomer Kingsley. Where would the British cinema be without its dependable, sturdy, absolutely authoritative generation of great character actors like Trevor Howard (as a British judge), John Mills (the British viceroy), John Gielgud, and Michael Hordern? There are also such younger actors as Ian Bannen, Edward Fox, Ian Charleson, and, from America, Martin Sheen as a reporter and Candice Bergen as the photographer Margaret Bourke-White.

Gandhi stands at the quiet center. And Ben Kingsley's performance finds the right note and stays with it. There are complexities here; *Gandhi* is not simply a moral story with a happy ending, and the tragedy of the bloodshed between the Hindu and Buddhist populations of liberated India is addressed, as is the partition of India and Pakistan, which we can almost literally feel breaking Gandhi's heart.

I imagine that for many Americans, Mahatma Gandhi remains a dimly understood historical figure. I suspect a lot of us know he was a great Indian leader without quite knowing why and—such is our ignorance of Eastern history and culture—we may not fully realize that his movement did indeed liberate India, in one of the greatest political and economic victories of all time, achieved through nonviolent principles. What is important about this film is not that it serves as a history lesson (although it does) but that, at a time when the threat of nuclear holocaust hangs ominously in the air, it reminds us that we are, after all, human, and thus capable of the most extraordinary and wonderful achievements, simply through the use of our imagination, our will, and our sense of right.

Gates of Heaven ★ ★ ★ ★
NO MPAA RATING, 85 m, 1978 ✓

A documentary produced, directed, and written by Errol Morris.

There are many invitations to laughter during this remarkable documentary, but what

Gates of Heaven finally made me feel was an aching poignancy about its subjects. They say you can make a great documentary about almost anything, if only you see it well enough and truly, and this film proves it. *Gates of Heaven*, which has no connection with the unfortunate *Heaven's Gate*, is a documentary about pet cemeteries and their owners. It was filmed in Southern California, so of course we immediately anticipate a sardonic look at peculiarities of the Moonbeam State. But then *Gates of Heaven* grows ever so much more complicated and frightening, until at the end it is about such large issues as love, immortality, failure, and the dogged elusiveness of the American Dream.

The film was made by a California filmmaker named Errol Morris, and it has been the subject of notoriety because Werner Herzog, the West German director, promised to eat his shoe if Morris ever finished it. Morris did finish it, and at the film's premiere in Berkeley, Herzog indeed boiled and ate his shoe.

Gates of Heaven is so rich and thought-provoking, it achieves so much while seeming to strain so little, that it stays in your mind for tantalizing days. It opens with a monologue by a kind-looking, somewhat heavyset paraplegic, with a slight lisp that makes him sound like a kid. His name is Floyd McClure. Ever since his pet dog was run over years ago by a Model A Ford, he has dreamed of establishing a pet cemetery. The movie develops and follows his dream, showing the forlorn, bare patch of land where he founded his cemetery at the intersection of two superhighways. Then, with cunning drama, it gradually reveals that the cemetery went bankrupt and the remains of 450 animals had to be dug up. Various people contribute to the story: One of McClure's investors, a partner, two of the women whose pets were buried in his cemetery, and an unforgettable old woman named Florence Rasmussen, who starts on the subject of pets, and switches, with considerable fire, to her no-account son. Then the action shifts north to the Napa Valley, where a go-getter named Cal Harberts has absorbed what remained of McClure's dream (and the 450 dead pets) into his own pet cemetery, the Bubbling Well Pet Memorial Park. It is here that the movie grows heartbreaking, painting a portrait of a life-style that looks chillingly forlorn, and of the people who live it with relentless faith in positive thinking.

Harberts, a patriarch, runs his pet cemetery with two sons, Phil and Dan. Phil, the older one, has returned home after a period spent selling insurance in Salt Lake City. He speaks of having been overworked. Morris lets the camera stay on Phil as he solemnly explains his motivational techniques, and his method of impressing a new client by filling his office with salesmanship trophies. He has read all of Clement Stone's books on "Positive Mental Attitude," and has a framed picture of Stone on his wall. Phil looks neat, presentable, capable. He talks reassuringly of his positive approach to things, "mentally wise." Then we meet the younger brother, Dan, who composes songs and plays them on his guitar. In the late afternoon, when no one is at the pet cemetery, he hooks up his 100-watt speakers and blasts his songs all over the valley. He has a wispy mustache and looks like a hippie. The family hierarchy is clear. Cal, in the words of Phil, is "El Presidento." Then Dan comes next, because he has worked at the cemetery longer. Phil, the golden boy, the positive thinker, is maintaining his P.M.A. in the face of having had to leave an insurance business in Salt Lake City to return home as third in command at a pet cemetery.

The cemetery itself is bleak and barren, its markers informing us, "God is love; dog is god backwards." An American flag flies over the little graves. Floyd McClure tells us at the beginning of the film that pets are put on Earth for two reasons: to love and to be loved. At the end of this mysterious and great movie, we observe the people who guard and maintain their graves, and who themselves seem unloved and very lonely. One of the last images is of old Cal, the patriarch, wheeling past on his forklift, a collie-sized coffin in its grasp.

Ghost Story ★ ★ ★
R, 110 m., 1981

Fred Astaire (Ricky Hawthorne), Melvyn Douglas (John Jeffrey), Douglas Fairbanks, Jr. (Edward Wanderly), John Houseman (Sears James), Craig Wasson (Don/David), Alice Krige (Alma/Eva), Patricia Neal (Stella).

Directed by John Irvin and produced by Burt Weissbourd. Screenplay by Lawrence D. Cohen.

Ghost stories should always begin as this one does, in shadows so deep that the flickering light of the dying fire barely illuminates the apprehensive faces of the listeners. They should be told in an old man's voice, dry as dust. They should be listened to by other men who are so old and so rich that we can only guess at the horrors they have seen. And, of course, ghost stories should be about things that happened long ago to young, passionate lovers who committed unspeakable crimes and have had to live forever after with the knowledge of them. If at all possible, some of the characters should be living in this life, filled with guilt, while others should be living the half-lives of the Undead, filled with hatred and revenge.

Peter Straub's best-selling novel *Ghost Story* contained all of those elements, and so I plugged away at it for what must have been hundreds of pages before his unspeakable prose finally got to me. At least, he knows how to make a good story, if not how to tell it, and that is one way in which the book and the movie of *Ghost Story* differ. The movie is told with style. It goes without saying that style is the most important single element in every ghost story, since without it even the most ominous events disintegrate into silliness. And *Ghost Story,* perhaps aware that if characters talk too much they disperse the tension, adopts a very economical story-telling approach. Dialogue comes in short, straightforward sentences. Background is provided without being allowed to distract from the main event. The characters are established with quick, subtle strokes. This is a good movie.

The story involves four very old men, who have formed a club to tell each other ghost stories. The casting is crucial here, and the movie's glory is in the performances and presences of Fred Astaire, the late Melvyn Douglas, Douglas Fairbanks, Jr., and John Houseman. What a crowd.

There is also a young protagonist (Craig Wasson), who has a dual role as Fairbanks's twin sons. When one comes to a dreadful end, the other begins to suspect that a mysterious woman may have something to do with it. And indeed she may. I would not dream of even hinting at exactly what connection this young woman (played with creepy charm by Alice Krige) might have with the four old men, but of course there is a connection. The movie flashes back fifty or sixty years to establish the connection, but its scariest scenes are in the present. They involve a wonderful haunted house, a long-drowned auto, a series of horrendous accidents, a group of ghostly manifestations, and a truly horrible vengeance wreaked upon the living by the not-exactly-dead.

If you like ghost stories, you will appreciate that they cannot be told with all sorts of ridiculous skeletons leaping out of closets, as in Abbott and Costello. They must be told largely in terms of fearful and nostalgic memory, since (by definition) a ghost is a ghost because of something that once happened that shouldn't have happened. *Ghost Story* understands that, and restrains its performers so that the horror of the ghost is hardly more transparent than they are.

Ghostbusters ★ ★ ★ ½
PG, 107 m., 1984

Bill Murray (Venkman), Dan Aykroyd (Stantz), Harold Ramis (Spengler), Sigourney Weaver (Dana), Ernie Hudson (Winston), Rick Moranis (Louis). Directed and produced by Ivan Reitman. Screenplay by Dan Aykroyd and Harold Ramis.

Ghostbusters is a head-on collision between two comic approaches that have rarely worked together very successfully. This time, they do. It's (1) a special effects blockbuster, and (2) a sly dialogue movie, in which everybody talks to each other like smart graduate students who are in on the joke. In the movie's climactic scenes, an apocalyptic psychic mindquake is rocking Manhattan, and the experts talk like Bob and Ray.

This movie is an exception to the general rule that big special effects can wreck a comedy. Special effects require painstaking detail work. Comedy requires spontaneity and improvisation—or at least that's what it should feel like, no matter how much work has gone into it. In movies like Steven Spielberg's *1941,* the awesome scale of the special effects dominated everything else;

we couldn't laugh because we were holding our breath. Not this time. *Ghostbusters* has a lot of neat effects, some of them mind-boggling, others just quick little throwaways, as when a transparent green slime monster gobbles up a mouthful of hot dogs. No matter what effects are being used, they're placed at the service of the actors; instead of feeling as if the characters have been carefully posed in front of special effects, we feel they're winging this adventure as they go along.

The movie stars Bill Murray, Dan Aykroyd, and Harold Ramis, three graduates of the Second City/*National Lampoon*/"Saturday Night Live" tradition. They're funny, but they're not afraid to reveal that they're also quick-witted and intelligent; their dialogue puts nice little spins on American clichés, and it uses understatement, irony, in-jokes, vast cynicism, and cheerful goofiness. Rarely has a movie this expensive provided so many quotable lines.

The plot, such as it is, involves an epidemic of psychic nuisance reports in Manhattan. Murray, Ramis, and Aykroyd, defrocked parapsychologists whose university experiments have been exposed as pure boondoggle, create a company named Ghostbusters and offer to speed to the rescue like a supernatural version of the Orkin man. Business is bad until Sigourney Weaver notices that the eggs in her kitchen are frying themselves. Her next-door neighbor, Rick Moranis, notices horrifying monsters in the apartment hallways. They both apparently live in a building that serves as a conduit to the next world. The ghostbusters ride to the rescue, armed with nuclear-powered backpacks. There is a lot of talk about arcane details of psychic lore (most of which the ghostbusters are inventing on the spot), and then an earthshaking showdown between good and evil, during which Manhattan is menaced by a monster that is twenty stories high, and about which I cannot say one more word without spoiling the movie's best visual moment.

Ghostbusters is one of those rare movies where the original, fragile comic vision has survived a multimillion-dollar production. It is not a complete vindication for big-budget comedies, since it's still true, as a general rule, that the more you spend, the fewer laughs you get. But it uses its money wisely,

and when that, ahem, monster marches down a Manhattan avenue and climbs the side of a skyscraper . . . we're glad they spent the money for the special effects because it gets one of the biggest laughs in a long time.

Give My Regards to Broad Street ★
PG, 108 m., 1984

With Paul and Linda McCartney, Ringo Starr, Barbara Bach, Sir Ralph Richardson, and Bryan Brown. Directed by Peter Webb and produced by Andros Epaminondas.

The usual thing is to see the movie and buy the sound track. With *Give My Regards to Broad Street*, I think you can safely skip the movie and proceed directly to the sound track. In fact, you already may have substantial portions of the sound track in your record library; among the Beatles songs featured in this film are "Yesterday" and "Eleanor Rigby." They've been rerecorded by Paul McCartney for this film, but they haven't been reinterpreted, and there are times when they sound uncannily like the original recordings. There are times, too, when the movie is uncanny. It seems to be a throwback to pre-Beatle days, back when pop musical films were simpleminded and shallow, back before *A Hard Day's Night* and *Help!* seemed to create a new tradition of fresh irreverence.

Give My Regards to Broad Street is about as close as you can get to a nonmovie, and the parts that do try something are the worst. The movie comes billed as "a day in the life of a famous rock star," but instead of actually giving us a day in McCartney's life (a promising idea, that), *Broad Street* supplies us with a fake crisis, paper-thin characters, and long musical interludes that have been photographed with a remarkable lack of style. The story: Tapes of a recording session have been entrusted to an ex-con who is now McCartney's employee. They, and the ex-con, have disappeared. Unless the tapes turn up by midnight, control of the multimillion-dollar McCartney musical empire will pass into the hands of slimy investors. So Paul looks desperately for his friend, while the movie treads water with idiotic dream sequences.

The most unnecessary passages in the film

are used to illustrate a long instrumental interlude in the middle of "Eleanor Rigby." I'm not sure I understood all the symbolism, but if I followed things all right, Paul and friends are in the midst of a Victorian nightmare that requires them to go on picnics and chat with Sir Ralph Richardson. The whole scene has heavy overtones of someone saying, "Hey, gang! Here's hundreds of thousands of dollars! Let's rent a camera and film an utterly meaningless interlude!"

The music is, of course, wonderful. The only scenes worth seeing in the film are the musical scenes, mostly filmed in a recording studio. Paul, Linda McCartney, and Ringo Starr perform (although Ringo reportedly refused to have anything to do with Paul's actual rerecording sessions of the Beatles classics, limiting his participation to an onscreen performance as himself). The music is wonderful, yes, but the performance photography is pedestrian. And the movie develops an inadvertent running gag in the person of Barbara Bach, Ringo's wife, who is given fourth-highest billing but does nothing except nod her head in time to the music, and play a nonspeaking guest at a dinner party at which McCartney never arrives. McCartney should have skipped the movie, too.

Gloria ★ ★ ★
PG, 123 m., 1980

Gena Rowlands (Gloria Swenson), John Adames (Phil), Buck Henry (Jack), Julie Carmen (Jeri Dawn). Directed by John Cassavetes and produced by Sam Shaw. Screenplay by Cassavetes.

Well, it's a cute idea for a movie, and maybe that's why they've had this particular idea so often. You start with tough-talking, streetwise gangster types, you hook them up with a little kid, you put them in fear of their lives, and then you milk the situation for poignancy, pathos, excitement, comedy, and anything else that turns up. It's the basic situation of *Little Miss Marker*, the Damon Runyon story that has been filmed three times. And now John Cassavetes tells it again in *Gloria*. The twists this time: The tough-talking gangster type is a woman, and the kid is Puerto Rican. Cassavetes has cast his wife, Gena Rowlands, in the title role, and

it's an infectious performance—if infectious is the word to describe a chain-smoking dame who charges around town in her high heels, dragging a kid behind her.

The kid is also well cast. He's a youngster named John Adames who has dark hair and big eyes and a way of delivering his dialogue as if daring you to change one single word. Precisely because the material of this movie is so familiar, almost everything depends on the performances. And that's where Cassavetes saves the material and redeems the corniness of his story. Rowlands propels the action with such appealing nervous energy that we don't have the heart to stop and think how silly everything is.

The movie begins with a two-bit hoodlum (Buck Henry, an inexplicable casting choice) barricaded in an apartment with his Puerto Rican wife (Julie Carmen) and their kids. Men are going to come through the door at any moment with guns blazing. There's a knock on the door. It's Rowlands, as the neighbor, with the somehow inevitable name of Gloria Swenson. She wants to borrow sugar. She winds up with the kid. She doesn't want the kid. She doesn't like kids, she tells Henry: "Especially your kids." But the kid tags along. There's a shoot-out, the kid's family is dead, and things get even more complicated when it turns out that Henry gave his kid a notebook that has information in it the mob will kill to retrieve. That's the premise for the rest of the movie, which is a cat-and-mouse chase through the sleazier districts of New York and New Jersey.

Cassavetes has a nice eye for locale. There's a crummy flophouse where the clerk tells Rowlands, "Just pick a room. They're all open." There's a garishly decorated love nest that Rowlands occasionally occupies with a mobster. There are bus stations, back alleys, dimly lit hallways, and the kinds of bars that open at dawn and do most of their business by 9 A.M. (That provides one of the movie's best scenes. Gloria and the kid argue, Gloria tells the kid to split if that's the way he feels, and then she marches into the bar, orders a beer, lights a cigarette and says to the bartender: "Listen. There are reasons why I can't turn around and look . . . but is there a little kid heading in here?").

Cassavetes remains one of the most consistently interesting Hollywood mavericks. He makes money by acting, and immediately spends it producing his own films. Most of them are passionately indulgent of the actors, who sometimes repay his indulgence with inspired performances. Rowlands won an Oscar nomination for Cassavetes's *A Woman Under the Influence*. His next picture starred Ben Gazzara in *The Murder of a Chinese Bookie* (1978), which has become an unseen, lost film—better, if the truth be known, than *Gloria*, which is fun and engaging but slight. What saves this movie is Cassavetes's reliance on a tried-and-true plot construction. For once, his characters aren't all over the map in nonstop dialogue, as they were in *Husbands*, the talkathon he made in 1970 with Peter Falk, Gazzara, and himself. *Gloria* is tough, sweet, and goofy.

The Gods Must Be Crazy ★ ★ ★
PG, 109 m., 1984 ✔

N!xau (Xi), Marius Weyers (Andrew Steyn), Sandra Prinsloo (Kate Thompson), Louw Verwey (Sam Boga), James Uys (The Reverend). Directed and produced by Jamie Uys. Screenplay by Uys.

Here's a movie that begins with a Coke bottle falling from the heavens, and ends with a Jeep up in a tree. *The Gods Must Be Crazy* is a South African movie that arrived in Europe with little fanfare in 1982, broke box office records in Japan and South America and all over Europe, and even became a cult hit here in North America, where there has not been much of a demand for comedies from South Africa.

The film begins in the Kalahari Desert. A pilot in a private plane throws his empty Coke bottle out of the window. It lands near a Bushman who is on a hunting expedition. He has never seen anything like it before. He takes it back to his tribe, where it is put to dozens of uses: It becomes a musical instrument, a patternmaker, a fire starter, a cooking utensil, and, most of all, an object of bitter controversy. Everybody in the tribe ends up fighting over the bottle, and so the Bushman, played by the Xhosa actor N!xau (the exclamation point represents a click), decides there is only one thing to do: He must return the bottle to the gods. This decision sends him on a long odyssey toward

more settled lands on the edges of the desert, where the movie develops into a somewhat more conventional comedy.

We meet some of the new characters: A would-be schoolteacher, a goofy biologist, and an insurgent leader. They are all intent on their own lives and plans, but in one way or another, the Xhosa and his Coke bottle bring them together into unexpected combinations. And the director, Jamie Uys, has the patience to develop some really elaborate sight gags, which require a lot of preparation but pay off with big laughs—particularly the sequence with an indecisive, back-and-forth Jeep.

The star of the movie is N!xau, who is so forthright and cheerful and sensible that his very presence makes some of the gags pay off. In any slapstick comedy, the gags must rest on a solid basis of logic: It's not funny to watch people being ridiculous, but it is funny to watch people doing the next logical thing, and turning out to be ridiculous. N!xau, because he approaches Western society without preconceptions, and bases all of his actions on logical conclusions, brings into relief a lot of the little tics and assumptions of everyday life. I think that reveals the thought that went into this movie: It might be easy to make a farce about screwball happenings in the desert, but it's a lot harder to create a funny interaction between nature and human nature. This movie's a nice little treasure.

The Goonies ★ ★ ★
PG, 114 m., 1985 ✔

Sean Astin (Mikey), Josh Brolin (Brand), Jeff Cohen (Chunk), Corey Feldman (Mouth), Kerri Green (Andy), Martha Plimpton (Stef), and Ke Huy Quan (Data). Directed by Richard Donner and produced by Donner and Harvey Bernhard. Executive producer, Steven Spielberg. Screenplay by Chris Columbus.

The Goonies is a smooth mixture of the usual ingredients from Steven Spielberg action movies, made special because of the high-energy performances of the kids who have the adventures. It's a fantastical story of buried pirate treasure, told with a slice-of-life approach that lets these kids use words Bogart didn't know in *Casablanca*. There used to be children's movies and adult movies. Now Spielberg has found an in-between niche, for young teen-agers who have fairly sophisticated tastes in horror. He supervises the formula and oversees the production, assigning the direction to stylish action veterans (this time, it's Richard Donner, of *Superman* and *Ladyhawke*).

Goonies, like *Gremlins*, walks a thin line between the cheerful and the gruesome, and the very scenes the adults might object to are the ones the kids will like the best: Spielberg is congratulating them on their ability to take the heavy-duty stuff. The movie begins with an assortment of engaging boys, including a smart kid, a kid with braces, a fat kid, an older brother, and an Asian kid whose clothing conceals numerous inventions. Along the way they pick up a couple of girls, whose function is to swap spit and get bats in their hair. The kids find an old treasure map and blunder into the hideout of a desperate gang of criminals—two brothers, led by a Ma Barker type. There is a third brother, a Quasimodish freak, who is kept chained down in the cellar, where he watches TV. The tunnels to the treasure begin under the hideout. The kids find the tunnels while fleeing from the bad guys, and then go looking for the treasure with the crooks on their tails. There are lots of special effects and among the set pieces are the same kinds of booby traps that Indiana Jones survived in *Raiders* (falling boulders, sharp spikes), and a toboggan ride on a water chute that will remind you of the runaway train in *The Temple of Doom*.

If the ingredients are familiar from Spielberg's high-powered action movies, the kids are inspired by *E. T.* The single most important line of dialogue in any Spielberg movie is probably the line in *E. T.* when one kid calls another kid "penis-breath." The dialogue hears and acknowledges the precocious way that kids incorporate vulgarity into their conversations, especially with each other; the line in *E. T.* created such a shock of recognition that the laughs swept away any objections.

This time, his kids say "shit" a lot, and it is a measure of Spielberg's insight that the word draws only a PG rating for the movie; Spielberg no doubt argues that most kids talk like that half the time, and he is right. His technique is to take his 13- and 14-year-olds and let them act a little older than their age. It's more refreshing than the old Disney technique, which was to take characters of all ages and have them behave as if they were 12.

Another Spielberg trademark, faithfully achieved by Donner, is a breakneck narrative speed. More things happen in this movie than in six ordinary action films. There's not just a thrill a minute; there's a thrill, a laugh, a shock, and a special effect. The screenplay has all the kids talking all at once, all the time, and there were times, especially in the first reel, when I couldn't understand much of what they were saying. The movie needs to be played loud, and with extra treble.

During *Goonies*, I was often exhilarated by what was happening. Afterwards, I was less enthusiastic. The movie is totally manipulative, which would be okay, except it doesn't have the lift of a film like *E. T.* It has the high energy without the sweetness. It uses what it knows about kids to churn them up, while *E. T.* gave them things to think about, the values to enjoy. *Goonies*, like *Gremlins*, shows that Spielberg and his directors are absolute masters of how to excite and involve an audience. *E. T.* was more like *Close Encounters;* it didn't simply want us to feel, but also to wonder, and to dream.

Gorky Park ★ ★ ★ ½
R, 128 m., 1983

William Hurt (Arkady Renko), Lee Marvin (Jack Osborne), Joanna Pakula (Irina), Brian Dennehy (Kirwell), Ian Bannen (Iamskoy). Directed by Michael Apted and produced by Gene Kirkwood and Howard W. Koch, Jr. Screenplay by Dennis Potter.

Mystery fans talk about the "police procedural," a crime novel that follows police work, step by meticulous step, from the opening of a case to its eventual resolution. The crimes aren't always solved, but then the solution isn't really the point. Instead, "procedurals" are a way to study human nature under stress, to see how a society works from the inside out and the bottom up. There are procedurals set all over the world, from Ed McBain's 87th Precinct on the East coast to the Martin Beck thrillers in Stockholm, but Martin Cruz Smith's *Gorky*

Park was the first good police procedural set in Russia. It used the procedural approach to show us an honest cop under pressure, a system that functioned only through corruption, and a conflict between socialism and Russia's homegrown capitalism.

This is the movie of that book, and it has all of the same strengths. It begins with a shocking murder (three corpses found frozen in the snow with their faces and fingerprints removed). There are no clues. A police inspector named Renko (William Hurt) is assigned to the case, and makes it his personal crusade. He recruits a physical anthropologist to try to re-create the missing faces on the bodies. He prowls the black market, where deals are made in Western currency. He meets a beautiful young woman and a mysterious American businessman. And he learns about the obsessive power of sable fur coats.

The investigation of the crime has a fascination of its own, but what makes *Gorky Park* really interesting is its views of Soviet cops, criminals, bureaucrats, and ordinary citizens. As Renko gets closer and closer to a solution to the case, his investigation leads him to powerful circles in the Soviet Union. And his heart, of course, leads him closer to the girl, who may have all of the necessary information but has been so warped by paranoia that she refuses to betray those she thinks are her friends.

The movie is directed with efficiency by Michael *(Coal Miner's Daughter)* Apted, who knows that pacing is indispensable to a procedural. Too long a pause for anything—romance, detail, speculation, explanation—and the spell is broken. He uses actors who are able to bring fully realized characters to the screen, so we don't have to stand around waiting for introductions. That involves a certain amount of typecasting. Lee Marvin, gravel-voiced, white-haired, expensively dressed, is perfect for the businessman. Joanna Pakula, a young Polish actress in her first Western role, is beautiful, vulnerable, wide-eyed, and fresh—and as an exile stranded in Paris when her Warsaw theater was closed by Poland's martial law, she doesn't have to fake her paranoia about the Soviet state.

William Hurt, as Renko, is probably the key to the picture. He makes this cop into a particular kind of person, cold, at times willfully blinded by duty, sublimating his feelings in his profession, until this case breaks him wide open. By the end of *Gorky Park*, we realize that it's not the solution that matters, but what the case itself forces the people to discover about themselves.

Gotcha! ★ ★
PG-13, 100 m., 1985

Anthony Edwards (Jonathan), Linda Fiorentino (Sasha), Nich Corri (Al), Marla Adams (Maria). Directed by Keff Kanew and produced by Paul S. Hensler. Screenplay by Dan Gordon.

Gotcha! begins with a fairly obvious inspiration, takes it to some interesting places, and then misplaces it toward the end of the film. It also selects the wrong character to be the center of the story. Other than that, it's a fairly good movie—good enough to make us wish it had tried a little harder.

The movie begins with a student game called Gotcha, which involves undergraduates who stalk each other across a college campus and "kill" each other with globs of paint. A player of the game (Anthony Edwards) talks his parents into letting him go to Paris on vacation, and he's hardly off the plane before he meets a beautiful, young Czech woman named Sasha, who is played by Linda Fiorentino. They have a sudden, passionate romance, and when she asks him to go along with her on a trip to East Germany, he accepts. Well, of course it turns out that she's a spy, and the two of them run into trouble from the East German police and Russian spymasters. Real life turns into a deadly game of Gotcha (which is the movie's fairly obvious inspiration), and the chase turns into a well-directed cat-and-mouse game. By now we enjoy the chemistry between the callow undergraduate and the slick European spy, and the movie has gotten to be fairly exciting.

Then it loses track of itself. The student returns to America, gets involved in further intrigues, and becomes convinced the Czech woman was only using him. For reasons only the screenplay writer knows for sure, there are no less than two excruciating scenes in which the student tries to explain the entire story, which is a waste of time, since we already know the entire story and would rather get on with it. The basic mistake in the movie, however, isn't in the pacing, but in the storytelling. They've made the movie about its less interesting major character. The woman is infinitely more intriguing; she's bright, exotic, resourceful, and mysterious, and yet we get the story told from the point of view of the campus nerd. Instead of Plot A (simple-minded undergraduate meets beautiful spy, then blunders through strange situations), why not Plot B (fascinating woman is forced to use dense undergraduate as an accomplice to pull off spy caper)?

That's an especially appealing idea with Fiorentino available as the spy. She's one of those movie talents who seem to materialize out of thin air, a genuine original. This is her second movie; her first was *Vision Quest*, where she played the drifter who wandered into Matthew Modine's life and encouraged his quest for a state wrestling champion (I don't write the plots, I only report them). Fiorentino has quick, dark eyes and a deep voice and an aura of being smart and sensible; how many actresses in their early twenties can play a spy and be convincing and never seem ridiculous?

Anthony Edwards, who plays the undergraduate, is fine for his role—likable and slightly goofy, and able to pull himself together in an emergency. But the very nature of this screenplay means that when he's onscreen, the most interesting things will be happening offscreen, including Fiorentino's adventures in the clutches of the police. I'll bet the men who made this movie just assumed it had to be told from his point of view, and never considered hers. Too bad. I think they missed their best chance.

The Great Muppet Caper ★ ★
G, 95 m., 1981

Charles Grodin (Nicky), Diana Rigg (Lady Holiday). With the Muppets and their performers: Jim Henson, Frank Oz, Dave Goetz, Jerry Holson, and Richard Hunt. Cameo appearances by Robert Morley, Peter Ustinov, and Jack Warden. Directed by Jim Henson and produced by Frank Oz. Screenplay by Tom Patchett, Jay Tarses, Jerry Juhl, and Jack Rose.

The Muppets are a wonderful creation, but they lose their special quality in *The Great Muppet Caper*. They behave like clones of other popular kiddie superstars—like the basic cartoon heroes they once seemed destined to replace. Jim Henson's original inspiration with the Muppets was to invest them with very real human qualities: Miss Piggy's vanity and insecurity, Kermit's insouciant inquisitiveness, Fozzie's fuzzy desire to be loved, and so on. Then he involved them in situations that revolved around their personalities, so that the kids who watched them could perhaps learn something about human nature. A lot of suspense during a Muppet story depended on how a particular Muppet would *feel* about something.

That was the approach of many of the Muppet TV episodes and of the original *Muppet Movie* (1979). This time, though, Henson and his associates haven't developed a screenplay that pays attention to the Muppet personalities. Instead, they ship them to England and dump them into a basic caper plot, treating them every bit as much like a formula as James Bond. This won't do. We don't care about some dumb diamond the size of a baseball, and as Muppet fans we're probably also indifferent to Henson's ambition to satirize old movie genres.

When he gives us a Busby Berkeley-like water ballet starring Miss Piggy, our reaction is complex. We think (a) that kids in the audience won't know what is being satirized and (b) that Miss Piggy's fantasies have become less fun as they reveal less vulnerability. And as for Miss Piggy herself . . . I really hate to say this, but she's not nearly as appealing in *The Great Muppet Caper* as she's always been before. She is also alarmingly thinner. Are we witnessing the Hollywoodization of Miss Piggy? Is she perhaps beginning to believe her own publicity? She's less vulnerable this time, less touching, with fewer instantly recognizable human frailties.

The movie involves a Muppet expedition to London, a near-affair between Charles Grodin and Miss Piggy, and some missing jewels. It also features some cameo appearances by familiar stars, but Henson seems content that the stars are merely in his movie; he doesn't use them with comic imagination. Example: When the Muppets crash-land in the middle of a British pond, they're greeted by British Airways' TV spokesman Robert Morley. But Morley plays the scene absolutely straight. Here was a great chance to have fun with Morley's TV ads: He could have brusquely informed the Muppets that hotels were $400 a night, there were no theater tickets available, not a single rental car was to be had for miles around, and that, frankly, the British wished their American cousins would stay at home.

The lack of a cutting edge hurts this movie. It's too nice, too routine, too predictable, and too safe.

The Great Santini ★ ★ ★ ★
PG, 118 m., 1980

Robert Duvall (Bull Meechum), Blythe Danner (Lillian Meechum), Michael O'Keefe (Ben Meechum), Lisa Jane Persky (Mary Anne Meechum), Stan Shaw (Toomer Smalls), Theresa Merritt (Arrabelle Smalls). Directed by Lewis John Carlino and produced by Charles A. Pratt. Screenplay by Carlino.

Like almost all of my favorite films, *The Great Santini* is about people more than it's about a story. It's a study of several characters, most unforgettably the Great Santini himself—played by Robert Duvall. Despite his name, he is not a magician or an acrobat but a lieutenant colonel in the Marines with the real name of Bull Meechum. He sees himself as the Great Santini, an ace pilot, great Marine, heroic husband and father and, in general, a sterling man among men. His family is expected to go along with this—and to go along with him, as he's transferred to a duty camp in South Carolina in the early 1960s.

There are five other members of the Meechum family. His wife (Blythe Danner) is a sweet Southern girl who calls her kids "sugar" and understands her maverick husband with a love that is deep but unforgiving. His oldest son (Michael O'Keefe) is just turning eighteen and learning to stand up to a father who issues "direct orders," calls everyone "sports fan," and expects to be called "sir." There are two more daughters and a son, but the movie's main relationship is between the father and the oldest boy.

Santini, you understand, is one hell of a guy. All he understands is competition. He's a royal pain in the ass to his Marine superiors, because he's always pulling damn fool stunts and making a spectacle out of himself. But he's a great pilot and he's said to be a good leader (even though his first briefing session for the men under him in South Carolina leaves them totally bewildered). Santini wants to win at everything, even backyard basketball with his son.

But the son is learning to be his own man. And there's a subplot involving a friendship between O'Keefe and the intense actor Stan Shaw, who plays the son of the family's black maid. Marine kids grow up nowhere and everywhere, we learn, and in South Carolina these two kids go shrimping together, trade lore together, become friends. It's a nice relationship, although a little tangential to the main thrust of the movie.

It's Robert Duvall who really makes the movie live—Duvall and Blythe Danner in a stunning performance that nothing she's done before (in *1776*, *Hearts of the West*, etc.) prepares us for. Although *The Great Santini* is set about ten years before *Apocalypse Now*, Duvall is playing essentially the same character in both films—we remember his great scene in *Apocalypse*, shouting that napalm smells to him like victory, as he gives his gung-ho speeches in this movie.

Duvall and O'Keefe go hard at each other, in the father-son confrontation, and there's an especially painful scene where the father bounces a basketball off his son's head, egging him on. But this movie is essentially a comedy—a serious, tender one, like *Breaking Away*, which is also about a son getting to know his father.

There are wonderful little moments in the dialogue (as when the Great Santini's daughter wonders aloud if females are allowed full Meechum family status, or are only sort of one-celled Meechums). There are moments straight out of left field, as when Duvall and the family's new maid (the formidable Theresa Merritt) get into an impromptu shoulder-punching contest. There are moments so unpredictable and yet so natural they feel just like the spontaneity of life itself. And the movie's conclusion is the same way: sentimental without being corny, a tearjerker with dignity.

The Great Santini is a movie to seek out and to treasure.

Gregory's Girl ★ ★ ★
PG, 93 m., 1982

Gordon John Sinclair (Gregory), Dee Hepburn (Dorothy), Chic Murray (Head-master), Jake D'Arcy (Phil), Alex Norton (Alec), John Bott (Alistair). Directed by Bill Forsyth and produced by Clive Parsons and Davina Boling. Screenplay by Forsyth.

There was a little item in the paper not long ago that should have been front page news. It was about a survey reporting that physically handsome men were less successful in business, made less money, married younger, and had less "desirable" spouses than men of average or below-average looks. The sociologists who announced these conclusions speculated that the handsome guys tended to get sidetracked in high school, spending more time on social life and less time on studies; they tended to depend on their golden boy charm instead of plowing ahead through college; and they tended, because they were more sexually active at younger ages, to marry sooner and therefore to marry women who were looking for marriage rather than careers. On the average, therefore, the weird kid with acne who's president of Chem Club will do better in the long run than the prom king.

Bill Forsyth's *Gregory's Girl* is a charming, innocent, very funny little movie about the weird kid. It is set in Scotland, where the teen-agers are quieter, more civilized and more naive than, let's say, those in *The Class of 1984*. And it is about Gregory (Gordon John Sinclair), a gangling adolescent who has started to shoot up all of a sudden and finds he is hopelessly uncoordinated on the soccer field. Gregory looks sort of like an immensely likable stork. He loses his place on the soccer team to another student who is a good deal faster and more coordinated. The other student happens to be a girl. Her name is Dorothy (Dee Hepburn), and Gregory instantly falls deeply in love with her. Nothing like this has ever hit him before, and romance becomes for him almost a physical illness. Dorothy is sweet to him, but distant, because she not only suspects

Gregory's feelings but is way ahead of him in her analysis of the whole situation.

The movie takes place mostly in a pleasant suburb of Glasgow, where the kids hang about and trade endless speculation on the impossibility of being sixteen and happy at the same time. Gregory turns for romantic advice to his younger sister, who is much more interested in ice cream. His sister, in fact, is oblivious to boys, although one pays her an earnest compliment: "She's only ten, but she has the body of a woman of thirteen." Meanwhile, Gregory consoles his best friend, who is fifteen and a half and has never known love.

This movie is a reminder that we tend to forget a lot of things about adolescence. For example: That it is no use telling a teen-ager what his faults are, because he is painfully aware of every possible fault in the minutest detail; that boys are absolutely helpless in the throes of teen-age romance, whereas girls tend to retain at least some perspective; that it is an unwritten law of the universe that no sixteen-year-old ever falls instantly in love with the right person at the right time.

The movie has a lot of gentle, civilized fun with insights like that. And along the way, Gregory the stork is led on a wild goose chase with a swan at the end. The movie contains so much wisdom about being alive and teen-aged and vulnerable that maybe it would even be painful for a teen-ager to see it; it's not much help, when you're suffering from those feelings of low self-esteem and an absolutely hopeless crush, to realize that not only are you in pain and suffering an emotional turmoil, but you're not even unique. Maybe only grown-ups should see this movie. You know, people who have gotten over the pains of unrequited love (hollow laugh).

Gremlins ★ ★ ★
PG, 111 m., 1984

Hoyt Axton (Rand Peltzer), Zach Galligan (Billy), Phoebe Cates (Kate), Scott Brady (Sheriff Frank), Polly Holliday (Mrs. Deagle). Directed by Joe Dante and produced by Michael Finnell. Executive producer Steven Spielberg. Screenplay by Chris Columbus.

Gremlins is a confrontation between Norman Rockwell's vision of Christmas and Hollywood's vision of the blood-sucking monkeys of voodoo island. It's fun. On the one hand, you have an idyllic American small town, with Burger Kings and Sears stores clustered merrily around the village square, and on the other hand you have a plague of reprehensible little beasties who behave like a rodent road company of Marlon Brando's motorcycle gang in *The Wild One*.

The whole movie is a sly series of send-ups, inspired by movie scenes so basic they reside permanently in our subconscious. The opening scene, for example, involves a visit to your basic Mysterious Little Shop in Chinatown, where, as we all know, the ordinary rules of the visible universe cease to operate and magic is a reality. Later on, after a kid's father buys him a cute little gremlin in Chinatown, we have a new version of your basic Puppy for Christmas Scene. Then there are such basic movie characters as the Zany Inventor, the Blustering Sheriff, the Clean-Cut Kid, the Cute Girlfriend, and, of course, the Old Bag.

The first half of the movie is the best. That's when we meet the little gremlins, which are unbearably cute and look like a cross between a Pekingese, Yoda from *Empire*, the Ewoks from *Jedi*, and kittens. They have impossibly big eyes, they're cuddly and friendly, and they would make ideal pets except for the fact that they hate bright lights, should not be allowed to get wet, and must never be fed after midnight. Well, of course, it's *always* after midnight; that's the tip-off that this isn't a retread of *E. T.* but comes from an older tradition, the fairy tale or magic story. And in the second half of the movie, after the gremlins have gotten wet, been fed after midnight, etc., they turn into truly hateful creatures that look like the monster in *Alien*.

The movie exploits every trick in the monster-movie book. We have scenes where monsters pop up in the foreground, and others where they stalk us in the background, and others when they drop into the frame and scare the Shinola out of everybody. And the movie itself turns nasty, especially in a scene involving a monster that gets slammed in a microwave oven, and another one where a wide-eyed teen-age girl (Phoebe Cates) explains why she hates Christmas. Her story is in the great tradition of 1950s sick jokes, and as for the microwave scene, I had a queasy feeling that before long we'd be reading newspaper stories about kids who went home and tried the same thing with the family cat.

Gremlins was hailed as another *E. T.* It's not. It's in a different tradition. At the level of Serious Film Criticism, it's a meditation on the myths in our movies: Christmas, families, monsters, retail stores, movies, boogeymen. At the level of Pop Moviegoing, it's a sophisticated, witty B movie, in which the monsters are devouring not only the defenseless town, but decades of defenseless clichés. But don't go if you still believe in Santa Claus.

The Grey Fox ★ ★ ★ ½
PG, 92 m., 1983

Richard Farnsworth (Bill Miner), Jackie Burroughs (Kate Flynn), Wayne Robson (Shorty), Ken Pogue (Jack Budd). Directed by Phillip Borsos and produced by Peter O'Brian. Screenplay by John Hunter.

Here's a lovely adventure: a movie about a stubborn, indomitable character who robs people because that's what he knows best. A man should work at his craft, shouldn't he? *The Grey Fox* tells the story of Bill Miner, a man who was thrown into prison in the heyday of the Old West, was kept behind bars for thirty-three years, and who finally emerged, confused but interested, into the twentieth century, where the movie begins in 1901. Bill Miner robbed stagecoaches. What's he supposed to do with a train? He's a whiskery old man, stubborn as a mule, and his pride hasn't grown any smaller during those years in jail. He heads for his sister's place to look for work and a roof over his head, but he doesn't get along with his brother-in-law and he also doesn't much like picking oysters for a living. He leaves. He hits the road, drifting aimlessly, a man without a mission—until the night in 1903 when he sees Edwin S. Porter's *The Great Train Robbery*. That famous movie is only eleven minutes long, but long enough to make everything absolutely clear to Miner, who realizes he has a new calling in life, as a train robber.

All of this could, of course, be an innocuous Disney movie, but it's well-written and directed, and what gives it zest and joy is the performance by Richard Farnsworth, who plays Miner. Maybe you'll recognize Farnsworth when you see him on the screen. Maybe not. His life has been one of those careers that makes you realize Hollywood is a company town, where you can make a living for years and never be a star. Farnsworth has been in more than 300 movies. He was a stuntman for thirty years. He's had speaking roles in movies ranging from *The Cowboys* to *Resurrection*. He was even in "Roots" on TV. And yet there is absolutely no mention of his name in Leslie Halliwell's *Filmgoer's Companion*. Farnsworth is one of those unstudied, graceful, absolutely natural actors who has spent a lifetime behaving exactly as he feels. I think he is incapable of a false or a dishonest moment. He makes Miner so proud, so vulnerable, such a noble rascal, that the whole movie becomes just a little more complex because he's in it.

There's one scene where you can really see Farnsworth's gift for conviction. It's a love scene with a feminist lady photographer named Kate Flynn (Jackie Burroughs), who is touring the West to document its changing times. Bill and Kate are instantly attracted to one another. And their love scene together is a warm, amusing masterpiece of quiet affection. Miner doesn't deny his age; he triumphs with it. He's not handsome but he's damned attractive, and knows it. Kate Flynn can see that this man has six times the worth of an ordinary man, and adores him. The scene is a treasure, even when you don't know whether to laugh or cry.

The director, Phillip Borsos, is able to make this a human story and still keep it exciting as an action picture. And he gives it a certain documentary feel; *The Grey Fox* is apparently based, to some degree, on truth. That doesn't matter half as much as that Farnsworth bases his performance on how he sees the truth of Bill Miner.

Greystoke ★ ★ ★
PG, 129 m., 1984

Christopher Lambert (Tarzan), Ralph Richardson (Earl of Greystoke), Ian Holm (Captain D'Arnot), Andie MacDowell (Jane Porter). Directed by Hugh Hudson and produced by Hudson and Stanley S. Canter.

Screenplay by P.H. Vazak and Michael Austin.

One of the most unforgettable mothers in the history of literature is named Kala, and she is an ape. Some people will immediately know that Kala is the great ape who adopted a shipwrecked orphan and raised him as her own, until he became Tarzan, Lord of the Apes. Other people will not know that, and for them, the movie *Greystoke* may be missing a certain resonance. I think it helps, in seeing this movie, to draw on a background of rainy Saturday afternoons when you were ten and had your nose buried in *Tarzan* books.

Greystoke, the Legend of Tarzan, Lord of the Apes is the most faithful film adaptation of the Tarzan legend ever made. That isn't saying much, because most of the forty or so Tarzan movies were laughable quickies with Tarzan trying not to be upstaged by cute chimps. *Greystoke* takes the legend seriously, and it's worthy of being taken seriously, I think, because the story of Tarzan has become one of the most durable of all the myths of the twentieth century. The obvious challenge for this movie is to convince an audience that it is actually looking at a little human baby being nurtured by wild animals. *Greystoke* passes that test. The movie combines footage of real animals with footage of human actors disguised by the special effects makeup of Rick Baker, and I was hard-pressed to tell the difference. The movie has an extended opening sequence that takes place entirely in the jungle, without spoken dialogue, and that captures the central mystery of the Tarzan legend as well as anything I've ever seen.

Unfortunately, there's one other aspect of Tarzan that *Greystoke* doesn't capture as well. The Tarzan adventures were all inspired by the imagination of a pulp writer named Edgar Rice Burroughs, who was not a stylist or a philosopher but was certainly a great plotter and knew how to entangle Tarzan in cliff-hanging melodrama. *Greystoke* isn't melodrama and doesn't try to be, and I missed that. After the great early jungle scenes, it has the grown-up Tarzan (Christopher Lambert) being discovered by a Belgian explorer (Ian Holm) who returns him to his ancestral Scottish home,

Greystoke Manor, where he meets his grand-father (Ralph Richardson) and also a young lady named Jane (Andie MacDowell). The movie has fun showing Tarzan's introduction to civilization; there's a spine-tingling moment when he growls into Jane's ear. The characters also are well-drawn, especially Ralph Richardson's Earl of Greystoke, who childishly slides down a staircase on a silver tray, and who has a touching death scene that was acted not long before Richardson himself died.

But where's the action? Shouldn't there be some sort of pulp subplot about the ant men, or the jewels of Opar, or a wild elephant on a rampage? *Greystoke* is the story of the legend of Tarzan, but it doesn't contain an adventure *involving* Tarzan. Who would have guessed there'd ever be a respectable Tarzan movie?

Halloween ★ ★ ★ ★
R, 93 m., 1978

With Donald Pleasence, Jamie Lee Curtis, P.J. Soles, and Nancy Loomis. Directed by John Carpenter and produced by Irving Yablans. Screenplay by Carpenter and Debra Hill.

"I enjoy playing the audience like a piano."—Alfred Hitchcock

So does John Carpenter. *Halloween* is an absolutely merciless thriller, a movie so violent and scary that, yes, I *would* compare it to *Psycho*. It's a terrifying and creepy film about what one of the characters calls Evil Personified. Right. And that leads us to the one small piece of plot I'm going to describe. There's this six-year-old kid who commits a murder right at the beginning of the movie, and is sent away, and is described by his psychiatrist as someone he spent eight years trying to help, and then the next seven years trying to keep locked up. But the guy escapes. And he returns on Halloween to the same town and the same street where he committed his first murder. And while the local babysitters telephone their boyfriends and watch *The Thing* on television, he goes back into action.

Period: That's all I'm going to describe, because *Halloween* is a visceral experience—we aren't seeing the movie, we're having it happen to us. It's frightening. Maybe you

don't like movies that are *really* scary: Then don't see this one. Seeing it, I was reminded of the favorable review I gave a few years ago to *The Last House on the Left*, another really terrifying thriller. Readers wrote to ask how I could possibly support such a movie. But it wasn't that I was supporting it so much as that I was describing it: You don't want to be scared? Don't see it. Credit must be paid to filmmakers who make the effort to really frighten us, to make a good thriller when quite possibly a bad one might have made as much money. Hitchcock is acknowledged as a master of suspense; it's hypocrisy to disapprove of other directors in the same genre who want to scare us too.

It's easy to create violence on the screen, but it's hard to do it well. Carpenter is uncannily skilled, for example, at the use of foregrounds in his compositions, and everyone who likes thrillers knows that foregrounds are crucial: The camera establishes the situation, and then it pans to one side, and something unexpectedly looms up in the foreground. Usually it's a tree or a door or a bush. Not always. And it's interesting how he paints his victims. They're all ordinary, everyday people—nobody's supposed to be the star and have a big scene and win an Academy Award. The performances are all the more absorbing because of that; the movie's a slice of life that is carefully painted (in drab daylights and impenetrable night-times) before its human monster enters the scene.

We see movies for a lot of reasons. Sometimes we want to be amused. Sometimes we want to escape. Sometimes we want to laugh, or cry, or see sunsets. And sometimes we want to be scared. I'd like to be clear about this. If you don't want to have a really terrifying experience, don't see *Halloween*.

Halloween II ★ ★
R, 92 m., 1981

Jamie Lee Curtis (Laurie), Donald Pleasence (Sam Loomis), Charles Cyphers (Leigh Brackett), Dick Warlock (The Shape). Directed by Rich Rosenthal and produced by Debra Hill and John Carpenter. Written by Hill and Carpenter.

It's a little sad to witness a fall from greatness, and that's what we get in *Halloween II*.

John Carpenter's original 1978 *Halloween* was one of the most effective horror films ever made, a scarifying fable of a mad-dog killer's progress through a small Illinois town on Halloween. That movie inspired countless imitations, each one worse than the last, until the sight of a woman's throat being slashed became ten times more common in the movies than the sight of a kiss.

Mad Slasher Movies, they were called, and they became a genre of their own, even inspiring a book of pseudoscholarship, *Splatter Movies*, by John McCarty. His definition of a Splatter Film is concise and disheartening, and bears quoting: "[They] aim not to scare their audiences, necessarily, nor to drive them to the edge of their seats in suspense, but to *mortify* them with scenes of explicit gore. In splatter movies, mutilation is indeed the message—many times the only one."

Halloween II fits this description precisely. It is not a horror film but a geek show. It is technically a sequel, but it doesn't even attempt to do justice to the original. Instead, it tries to outdo all the other violent *Halloween* rip-offs of the last several years. The movie does not have the artistry or the imagination of the original, but it does have new technology: For those like McCarty who keep records of such things, this movie has the first close-up I can remember of a hypodermic needle being inserted into an eyeball. We see that twice. It mortifies the viewer nicely, just as scenes in Splatter Movies are supposed to do. There are a few other moments of passable originality, as when the killer disfigures the face of a beautiful woman by plunging her repeatedly into the scalding water of a whirlpool bath. But for the most part, *Halloween II* is a retread of *Halloween* without that movie's craft, exquisite timing, and thorough understanding of horror.

The movie begins just where the last one left off—with some of the same footage, indeed. The mysterious, invincible killer (who escaped from an institution earlier that Halloween day) has just tried to kill Jamie Lee Curtis. But Donald Pleasence, a psychiatrist who has decided the killer is literally inhuman, fires six bullets at close range. The killer is down, but not out. As the first movie ended, his body had disappeared. As this

one opens, he's on the prowl again, still shuffling after screaming women at the same maddening slow pace.

The plot of *Halloween II* absolutely depends, of course, on our old friend the Idiot Plot which requires that everyone in the movie behave at all times like an idiot. That's necessary because if anyone were to use common sense, the problem would be solved and the movie would be over. So Jamie Lee Curtis and other young women consistently run into traps where the killer can corner them. In the first film, Jamie Lee locked herself in an upstairs closet. This time, it's a basement boiler room. The movie's other idiotic masterstroke comes when Curtis and a young kid are hiding in a car parked outside, and the kid slumps forward and honks the horn, revealing his hiding place. Inspired. The killer keeps coming. He's relentless. So is the movie. It uses the standard horror formula: Cause a false alarm, get a laugh, and then spring violence on the audience. You know how it works. The heroine opens a creaking door into a dark room and peers inside. A hand claps her on the shoulder. The audience screams. But whaddya know, it's only the friendly teen-age intern. Laughter. *Then* the killer strikes.

This can get monotonous. But since most of this movie takes place in a hospital, the killer has lots of props to work with. I've already mentioned the whirlpool bath and the needles. Another particularly nasty gimmick is the intravenous tube. The killer uses it to drain the blood from one of his victims. That's gruesome, but give the filmmakers credit. They use that gimmick to deliver the one scene I've been impatiently expecting for years and years in gore films: Finally, one of the characters kills himself by slipping on the wet blood and hitting his head on the floor. Sooner or later, it had to happen.

Halloween III ★ ½
R, 98 m., 1982

Tom Atkins (Dr. Challis), Stacey Nelkin (Ellie Grimbridge), Dan O'Herlihy (Conal Cochran), Ralph Strait (Buddy). Directed by Tommy Lee Wallace and produced by Debra Hill and John Carpenter. Screenplay by Wallace.

There are a lot of problems with *Halloween III*, but the most basic one is that I could never figure out what the villain wanted to accomplish if he got his way. His scheme is easy enough to figure: He wants to sell millions of Halloween masks to the nation's kiddies and then brainwash them to put them on at the same time, whereupon laser beams at the base of the neck will fry the tykes. Meanwhile, he runs a factory that turns out lifelike robots. What's his plan? Kill the kids and replace them with robots? Why?

A half-baked scheme like that feels right at home in *Halloween III*, which is a low-rent thriller from the first frame. This is one of those Identikit movies, assembled out of familiar parts from other, better movies. It begins at the end of *Halloween II*, when the monster was burned up in the hospital parking lot, but it's not still another retread of the invincible monster. In fact, the monster is forgotten, except for a lab technician who spends the whole movie sifting through his ashes. Instead, the plot follows the young daughter (Stacey Nelkin) of one of the victims, who ran a toy shop. She enlists the aid of a local doctor (Tom Atkins), and they retrace her father's steps back to an ominous toy factory run by Dan O'Herlihy. The factory has the whole town bugged and under surveillance, and the factory's guards are androids who crush their victims' heads with their hands.

Like a lot of horror movies in this age of self-conscious filmmaking, *Halloween III* is filled with references to other movies. The friendly motel owner in the company town, for example, is dressed as a dead ringer for Henry Fonda in *On Golden Pond*. The scene where the bugs and snakes crawl out of the crushed skull is a cross-reference, sort of, to *The Thing*—the last movie by John Carpenter, whose original *Halloween* was incomparably better than Parts II and III. But the funniest reference comes when the hero and heroine break into O'Herlihy's factory and are captured. Then the demented toymaker takes them on a tour of his facility, while explaining his diabolical scheme. He's got an obligatory underground mad scientist laboratory, and we know the approach by heart from all the James Bond movies: White-coated technicians scurry around with clipboards, while the boss arranges a demonstration of the weird method of kill-

ing that will soon be tried on our heroes. The funny part is that the underground lab is so cheesy. It consists of a few TV monitors on high-tech bookshelves and a papier-mâché mock-up of one of the stones from Stonehenge. (If you can figure out what Stonehenge has to do with this movie, you're smarter than anyone in it.) Next, there are lots of shots of the guy and girl running from O'Herlihy's henchmen. These are all obligatory shots where the man grabs the woman's hand and yanks her along, she of course being too dumb to run from danger on her own.(Cf. "Me-Push-Pull-You," in the Glossary.)

The one saving grace in *Halloween III* is Stacey Nelkin, who plays the heroine. She has one of those rich voices that makes you wish she had more to say and in a better role. But watch her, too, in the reaction shots: When she's not talking, she's listening. She has a kind of rapt, yet humorous, attention that I thought was really fetching. Too bad she plays her last scene without a head.

Hardly Working   no stars
R, 91 m., 1981

Jerry Lewis (Bo Hooper), Susan Oliver (Claire Trent), Roger C. Carmel (Robert Trent), Deanna Lund (Millie), Harold J. Stone (Frank Loucazi). Directed by Jerry Lewis and produced by James J. McNamara and Igo Kanter. Screenplay by Michael Janover and Lewis.

Hardly Working is one of the great non-experiences of my moviegoing life. I was absolutely stunned by the vast stupidity of this film. It was a test of patience and tolerance that a saint might not have passed—but I didn't walk out. I remained for every single last dismal wretched awful moment. I was keeping a pledge to myself.

Watching the "Today" show in a hotel room in Los Angeles, I saw Jerry Lewis being interviewed by Gene Shalit. Jerry was convinced that the critics had it in for him. He hinted, none too subtly, that the chances were Shalit would dislike the film when he saw it (Shalit claimed not to have seen it already, which was an excellent ploy). In *Variety*, I'd read that the critics were barred from the Miami premiere of the film because, and I paraphrase, Jerry Lewis makes films for the masses and critics are unequipped to understand his appeal. Horse manure. *Hardly Working* is one of the worst movies ever to achieve commercial release in this country, and it is no wonder it was on the shelf for two years before it saw the light of day. It is not just a bad film, it is incompetent filmmaking.

Jerry Lewis, as director, has no sense of timing—and timing is the soul of comedy. He leaves people standing onscreen waiting for something to be said. He throws in random, odd pieces of comic business that are inexplicable and not funny. He has made his film into an educational experience: See it, and you will learn by default what competent film editing is.

The plot stars Jerry as a born loser who is fired from his job as a circus clown (and no wonder; the film's one clown sequence is not even remotely funny). He throws himself on the mercy of his sister and brother-in-law, and then tries his hand at a variety of jobs, including gas station attendant, before finally winding up with the U.S. Postal Service. The movie sets us up for several comic set pieces, none of which deliver. Example: Applying for a job at the gas station, Jerry sneaks up behind the owner, who is making a tall stack of oil cans. Jerry scares him, and the owner tips the cans over. Later, Jerry lets a customer's gas tank overflow. The owner, nearly finished rebuilding the stack, sees what Jerry is doing and so deliberately knocks over the stack again. Why? That is an excellent question to ask again and again during this movie.

Some scenes are totally inexplicable. These include a conversation Lewis has with himself in drag (it doesn't even use trick photography, just over-the-shoulder shots with stand-ins wearing wigs); a scene in which he waits for a very long time in a supervisor's office, to no avail; and several scenes in which he spills things on people. Once, a very long time ago, Jerry Lewis made me laugh. I was seven at the time. He still seems to be making movies for the same audience.

Harry & Son ★
PG, 117 m., 1984

Paul Newman (Harry), Robby Benson (Howard), Ellen Barkin (Katie), Wilford

Brimley (Tom), Ossie Davis (Raymond), Joanne Woodward (Lilly). Directed by Paul Newman and produced by Newman and Ronald L. Buck. Screenplay by Newman and Buck.

Note: Throughout this review, the "*" will indicate a "Symbol."

This movie looks like the aftermath of an explosion in the story department. It's about everything. They give us so many relationships, so many problems, so many emotional hazards, so many colorful characters, we need a battery-lighted ballpoint, so we can take notes in the dark.

Harry & Son is about Harry and his son*. Harry (Paul Newman) is a construction worker*. His job is to operate a wrecking ball*. One day, he gets dizzy and cannot see what he's doing, and he loses control of his ball**. He returns to his home, which is isolated in the middle of a giant parking lot*, and deals with his son, Howard, who works as a car hiker* because his real ambition is to be a writer***. Other people in Harry's life include his brother* (Wilford Brimley), who runs an Army surplus store*, and his daughter*, who doesn't get along with him because he hates her husband*, a wimp*. Sometimes Harry visits the local pet store*, where the owner, a friendly widow* (Joanne Woodward), who reads craniums, has been in love with him for years.

The pet store owner has a daughter* who is the former girlfriend** of Howard, and who is now pregnant***, but not by Howard****. Howard, meanwhile, has an affair with a nymphomaniac* who parks her car in his garage**. She has orgasms caused by the sound of a camera shutter*. Howard fixes Harry up with the nymphomaniac. She'd rather take pictures*. Meanwhile, Howard gets a job as an auto repossessor*, but quits after he is caught repossessing a car belonging to Ossie Davis, who is unemployed* but snatches the opportunity to take Howard's job*. Harry is also unemployed**. He tries to get work, but has a dread, unnamed disease*** that makes him dizzy at crucial times. He feels he is a failure. He is cruel to his daughter, plays a practical joke on her husband, and gets drunk and shouts at his son, who should be looking for a job.

The son, meanwhile, finally sells a short story. He apologizes to his former girlfriend, and then assists her in delivering her child***, in the back seat of a taxi stuck in traffic*. This proves to Howard that he is a man**, and to us that he is at least a fair amateur midwife. Then Howard uses the money from his sale to finance a vacation for his father, his former girlfriend, her baby, and her mother, the pet shop owner. Harry and the pet shop owner begin to fall in love*, before the tragic ending****.

Howard, the son, behaves in such a weird way most of the time that it's a toss-up whether he's actually crazy, or just going through a really difficult period. The movie has other problems. Harry, the most interesting character, is offscreen for long periods of time while minor characters march off at right angles to the plot. The movie might have worked if it had been a satire of those awful made-for-TV "Family Problem Movies." Unfortunately, it does not seem to know it is funny, not even at the end when everybody gazes longingly at the horizon* down at the beach*, where the waves** crash eternally ashore****.

The Hearse ½ ★
PG, 97 m., 1980

Trish Van Devere (Woman), Joseph Cotten (Lawyer), David Gautreaux (Tom), Donald Hotton (Local Kid). Directed by George Bowers and produced by Mark Tenser. Screenplay by Bill Bleich.

How long has it been since we saluted our least-favorite movie ingredient, the Idiot Plot? Too long, I think we all agree. The Idiot Plot, you'll recall, is a movie plot that depends on everyone in the movie being an idiot. If they were not, the movie would be over within fifteen minutes and we could all go home. But that never happens in an Idiot Plot: The characters make such incredibly stupid blunders that we're stuck for a whole movie, watching them wander fecklessly through their own lives.

The Hearse is a classic example of an Idiot Plot. The idiot in the movie is a young woman, played by Trish Van Devere in the style of a detergent commercial, who decides to move to a small town and live in the house of her dead aunt. She makes this decision (we learn in a pointless scene with the psychiatrist) because she wants to put the events of the past year behind her. If she'd also put the events of the next year behind her, we'd all be a lot better off.

Anyway, she drives to the town late at night, and is almost run off the road by a gigantic black hearse. An ominous sign. Once in town, she's shown around the house by a crusty old attorney (Joseph Cotten) who thinks it should have been his. She also has a run-in with the local sheriff, who is crude and rude, and with the local adolescent boys, who drive past while she's jogging and scream at her brainlessly, never having seen such a sight before, I guess.

Anyway, Van Devere moves into the house, and immediately there are the usual ominous signs. Let's see how many I can remember. A music box plays by itself. A door slams by itself. The long-dead aunt appears in a mirror. She appears behind a window. There are footsteps on the stairs. Windows are broken. Doors are broken, The hardware store owner won't deliver to her house. The local minister hints at evil goings-on. While Trish is taking a shower, the camera gives us a point-of-view shot going up the stairs, approaching the shower curtain . . . and then going away (the cameraman was chicken?). On two more occasions, the hearse tries to run her off the road. Every night, another ominous manifestation terrifies her. Every morning, she's jolly again, and goes in to shop at the hardware store and be insulted by the local teen-age louts.

Meanwhile, young Tom turns up. He's polite, handsome, old-fashioned. Trish kinda likes him. This proves she's an idiot, since everybody in the audience figures out immediately that Tom is a ghost, and was the boyfriend of the dead aunt. But Trish doesn't know this. She continues to live in this house long after every single member of the audience would have moved out. This place makes the *Amityville Horror* look like open house at a condominium.

One of the real cheats of the movie is that it never provides a consistent framework for all the terrible things that take place. Things happen without any context: The minister, for example, believes the house is haunted by the devil, and arrives one night with a

Bible, rather theatrically screaming, "Get thee behind me, Satan," while obligatory gusts of wind tear at his gray locks. But is Satan involved? Is the house merely haunted? What does the hearse have to do with anything?

The Hearse qualifies as the garage sale of horror movies. It contains all the best clichés from more successful horror movies (especially *Amityville* and even *The Changeling*, which came out in April, 1980, and starred Van Devere, her husband George C. Scott, and, of course, the obligatory self-banging doors and self-playing musical instruments). But the clichés exist in a vacuum: The events in this movie happen because they have happened in other horror movies and seemed like a good idea at the time. We know better.

Heart Beat ★ ★ ½
R, 109 m., 1980

Nick Nolte (Neal Cassady), Sissy Spacek (Carolyn Cassady), John Heard (Jack Kerouac). Directed by John Byrum and produced by Alen Greisman and Michael Shamberg. Screenplay by Byrum.

Jack Kerouac's novel *On the Road* announced an end to the Eisenhower years and the beginning of the narcissistic, rebellious sixties. It told the story of the first beatniks, those dropouts from the middle class who rode the highways from Maine to Mexico and raised hell, wrote poetry, loved unwisely, drank too well, and did the basic engineering on the life-style that would eventually be run to exhaustion by the hippies. Kerouac's novel starred a heroic proto-beat named Dean Moriarty, based on the legendary underground figure Neal Cassady. In *Heart Beat* we get the story of Neal and Jack and Neal's wife. Sort of.

The movie's based on a memoir written a few years ago by Carolyn Cassady, who was not one of the heroes of *On the Road*, and who, it now appears, had good reason to be less than enchanted with the beatnik life-style. The wives of famous men often have unique outlooks on their wonderful opportunities to live so close to greatness; when Bennett Cerf, visiting the James Joyces in Paris, described Joyce as a genius, Mrs. Joyce dryly replied, "That's all very well for *you* to say—*you* don't have to live with the

bloody man." Carolyn Cassady's *Heart Beat* comes from the same fervent neighborhood of the soul.

But this movie is another matter altogether. How closely it resembles the facts I cannot say, but it paints a portrait of Jack and Neal as good buddies who drank, sang, hitchhiked, lied, and fought their way around the America of the late 1940s (Kerouac described himself and Cassady as "furtives"), and then both fell in love with Carolyn. She married Neal, who stayed at home, sometimes, between time on the road with Jack and a great deal of additional time spent on applied research into alcoholism. Jack was a drunk, too, and a lot of the movie deals with their attempts to patch things together in the little postwar suburban house in San Francisco where Carolyn tried to maintain a home.

This is not exactly the story we have in memory from the Kerouac legend, and there were long stretches of *Heart Beat* during which I found myself wishing instead for a film version of *On the Road*. That's unfair, I guess—but what is director John Byrum trying to do in *this* movie? I'm not sure. The movie's a triumph of art direction, all right; the locations, clothes, lighting, moods, music, and whole tones of the performances are designed to throw a kind of nostalgic drop cloth over the story, and we're constantly invited to read greater significance into dialogue and gestures because they took place during those now-lost times.

Fine, except that the significance doesn't seem to be there. *Heart Beat* seems to exist almost entirely as a matter of style. The characters are wonderfully well played by Nick Nolte, Sissy Spacek, and John Heard—they have scenes together in which the round-robin of everyday dialogue is almost poetic—but nobody has given their characters anything to do except to be. They exist, we watch them, the decor is inspired, that's it.

The attempts to add other characters from the period are mostly misguided. A character named Ira, inspired by Allen Ginsberg (who forbade use of his name), is so awkwardly drawn he comes off as a fifties' satire of a beatnik poet. Jazz musicians are so artfully "cool" they're paralytic. Jack and Neal move through the worlds of coffee houses and jazz clubs as if they were back-drops, not habitations.

What finally happens is that the whole period—the conformist fifties as well as the rebellious beats—gets frozen into the same flashback. *Everything* becomes part of the film's nostalgic memory. The film seems to treasure the conformity of American mainstream society if only because it provides such an ideal contrast to Neal and Jack. This movie treats its events as so long ago, so finished and done with and bathed in a yellowing afterglow, that we don't sense the very passion and rebelliousness it's supposed to be about. What an irony for the first serious film about the Beats.

Heartland ★ ★ ★
PG, 95 m., 1981

Conchata Ferrell (Elinore Randall), Rip Torn (Clyde Stewart), Barry Primus (Jack), Lilia Skala (Grandma), Megan Folsom (Jerrine). Directed by Richard Pearce and produced by Annick Smith, Michael Hausman, and Beth Ferris. Screenplay by Ferris.

Richard Pearce's *Heartland* is a big, robust, joyous movie about people who make other movie heroes look tentative. It takes place in 1910, out in the unsettled frontier lands of Wyoming, and it's about a determined young widow who packs up her daughter and moves out West to take a job as the housekeeper on a ranch. At first she is completely baffled by the rancher who has hired her ("I can't talk about anything with that man"), but in the end she marries him and digs in to fight an endless battle with the seasons, the land, and the banks.

A movie newcomer named Conchata Ferrell plays the widow, Elinore Randall. She's a big-boned, clear-eyed, wide-hipped woman of about thirty who makes us realize that most of the women in Westerns look as if they're about to collapse under the strain. She is extremely clear about her motivations. She gives a full day's work for a full day's pay, but she is tired of working for others, and would like to own her own land someday. She does not, however, speak endlessly about her beliefs and ambitions, because *Heartland* is a movie of few words.

That is partly because of the character of Clyde Stewart (Rip Torn), the rancher she goes to work for. He hardly ever says anything. He is a hard man, a realist who knows that the undisciplined Western land can break his back. But he is not unkind, and in the scene where he finally proposes to marry her, his choice of words contains understated wit that makes us smile.

Everything in this movie affirms life. Perhaps that is why *Heartland* can also be so unblinking in its consideration of death. The American West was not settled by people who spent all their time baking peach cobbler and knitting samplers, and this movie contains several scenes that will shock some audiences because of their forthright realism. We see a pig slaughtered, a calf birthed, cattle skinned, and a half-dead horse left out in the blizzard because there is simply nothing to feed it.

All of *Heartland* is stunningly photographed on and around a Montana ranch. (The movie is based on the real life of a settler named Elinore Randall Stewart.) It contains countless small details of farming life, put in not for "atmosphere" but because they work better than dialogue to flesh out the characters. The desolation of the frontier is suggested in small vignettes, such as one involving a family that could get this far and no farther, and lives huddled inside a small wagon. Among the many scenes that delight us with their freshness is one moment right after the wedding, when Ferrell realizes she got married wearing her apron and work boots, and another when she is about to give birth and her husband rides off into the storm to fetch the midwife from the next farm. We settle back here in anticipation of the obligatory scene in which the midwife arrives and immediately orders everyone to boil hot water, lots of it—but this time we're surprised. The husband returns alone; the midwife was not at her farm. Quiet little developments like that help expose the weight of cliché that holds down most Westerns.

In a movie filled with wonderful things, the very best thing in *Heartland* is Conchata Ferrell's voice. It is strong, confident, clear as a bell, and naturally musical. It is a fine instrument, bringing authenticity to every word it says. It puts this movie to a test, because we could not quite accept that voice saying words that sounded phony and contrived. In *Heartland*, we never have to.

Heat and Dust ★ ★ ★
R, 130 m., 1983

Julie Christie (Anne), Zakir Hussain (Inder Lal), Greta Scacchi (Olivia), Shashi Kapoor (The Nawab). Directed by James Ivory and produced by Ismail Merchant. Screenplay by Ruth Prawer Jhabvala.

Forster suggested in *A Passage to India* that the subcontinent would forever be beyond the understanding of Western minds, and that attempts to impose European ways upon it were bound to be futile and likely to be ridiculous. *Heat and Dust* makes the same argument by telling us two love stories, one set in the 1920s, the other set in the present day.

The heroine of the earlier love story is Olivia Rivers (Greta Scacchi), a free spirit whose independent ways do not fit in with the hidebound values of the British. Her husband demands that she conform, that she stay with the other British wives, share their values and interests, and keep India itself at arm's length. Olivia does not see it that way. She explores on her own. She becomes fascinated by India. Eventually she has an affair with the local Nawab (Shashi Kapoor), who is beguiling, attractive, cheerfully sophisticated, and possibly a murderer. When she becomes pregnant with his child, the whole fabric of British-Indian relationships is torn, because—depending on the point of view—*both* of the lovers have lowered themselves.

The second love story involves Olivia's great-niece, Anne (Julie Christie). Fascinated by hints about the long-ago family scandal, she follows Olivia's footsteps out to India and does her own exploring and has her own affair. There comes a moment in the movie when we realize, with a little shock, what the movie is really about. It's an effective scene; soon after Anne arrives at a decision about her own pregnancy, she visits the isolated cottage where the disgraced Olivia went to spend her confinement.

As Anne dreamily moves among the memories of the past, we realize that India and England, the East and the West, are not quite the issues here: that both women were made social outcasts from both societies in two different periods, simply because of biological facts. East is East and West is West, and never the twain shall meet—except possibly in a shared enthusiasm for sexist double standards.

Heat and Dust contains wonderful sights and sounds and textures. It is seductive, treating both of its love stories with seriousness; these are not romances, but decisions to dissent. It is fully at home in its times and places (the director, James Ivory, and the producer, Ismail Merchant, have spent twenty years making films about the British in India). And when it is over, we're a little surprised to find that it is angry, too. Angry that women of every class and every system, women British and Indian, women of the 1920s and of the 1980s, are always just not quite the same caste as men.

Heaven Help Us ★ ★ ½
R, 103 m., 1985

Andrew McCarthy (Michael Dunn), Mary Stuart Masterson (Danni), Kevin Dillon (Rooney), Malcolm Danare (Caesar), Donald Sutherland (Brother Thadeus), John Heard (Brother Timothy). Directed by Michael Dinner and produced by Don Wigutow and Mark Carliner. Screenplay by Charles Purpura.

If you remember those little clickers that the nuns used to use, you'll know why I liked the beginning of *Heaven Help Us* so much—and why I had such mixed feelings about the rest of it. The clickers were dime-store crickets that made a nice, loud click, perfect for signaling a First Communion class so all the kids would stand up at the same time, and kneel at the same time, and start filing down the aisle together. In an opening scene of the movie, a kid has his own clicker, and uses it to sabotage the nun's signals, so that the whole class is bobbing like a yo-yo. I thought that was funny, and I thought it set the tone for an affectionate, nostalgic, funny look back at Catholic school education in Brooklyn in the 1960s—sort of a cross between *Do Black Patent Leather Shoes Really Reflect Up?* and *Sister Mary Agnes Explains It All for You*. Unfortunately, what the movie turns into is more like a cross between *Stalag 17* and *Porky's*, as sadistic teachers beat every last glimmer of spirit out of students, and kids establish new indoor records in self-abuse.

Because *Heaven Help Us* does not have the slightest ambition to be a serious movie about Catholic high schools, I can't understand why the classroom scenes are so overplayed. As the sadistic teaching brother (Jay Patterson) slams his students against the blackboard, all we're really watching is a lapse in judgment by the moviemakers. The scenes are so ugly and depressing that they throw the rest of the movie out of balance. And that's too bad, because here and there in this movie are moments of real insight and memory. There's a special charm in the sweet, shy romance between a student (Andrew McCarthy) and the daughter (Mary Stuart Masterson) of the local soda fountain owner. I also liked the character named Caesar (Malcolm Danare), who pretends to be a snotty intellectual, as a defense against the heat he gets because he's smart.

The strange thing about the movie is the way the moments of inspiration raise our hopes, and then disappoint them. Take the scene where the school plays host to the nearby Catholic girls' school at a dance. The boys and girls are lined up on opposite sides of the room, and then an earnest little priest (Wallace Shawn, from *My Dinner with André*) stands up on the stage and delivers a lecture on "The Evils of Lust," gradually warming to his subject. The idea of the scene is funny, and it has a certain amount of underlying truth (I remember a priest once warning my class, "Never touch yourselves, boys"—without telling us where). But Shawn's speech climbs to such a hysterical pitch that it goes over the top, and the humor is lost; it simply becomes weird behavior.

Heaven Help Us has assembled a lot of the right elements for a movie about a Catholic boys' high school—the locations, the actors, and a lot of the right memories. But it has not found its tone. Maybe the filmmakers just never did really decide what they thought about the subject. For their penance, they should see *Rock and Roll High School*.

Heaven's Gate ½★
R, 220 m., 1981

Kris Kristofferson (Averill), Christopher Walken (Champion), John Hurt (Irvine), Sam Waterston (Canton), Brad Dourif (Eggleston), Isabelle Huppert (Ella), Joseph Cotten (Reverend Doctor), Jeff Bridges (John), Gordana Rashovich (Widow Kovach). Directed by Michael Cimino and produced by Joann Carelli. Screenplay by Cimino.

We begin with a fundamental question: Why is *Heaven's Gate* so painful and unpleasant to look at? I'm not referring to its content, but to its actual visual texture: This is one of the ugliest films I believe I have ever seen. Its director, Michael Cimino, opens his story at Harvard, continues it in Montana, and closes it aboard a ship. And yet a grim industrial pall hangs low over everything. There are clouds and billows of dirty yellow smoke in every shot that can possibly justify it, and when he runs out of smoke he gives us fog and such incredible amounts of dust that there are whole scenes where we can barely see anything. That's not enough. Cimino also shoots his picture in a maddening soft focus that makes the people and places in this movie sometimes almost impossible to *see*. And then he goes after the colors. There's not a single primary color in this movie, only dingy washed-out sepia tones.

I know, I know: He's trying to demystify the West, and all those other things hotshot directors try to do when they don't really want to make a Western. But this movie is a study in wretched excess. It is so smoky, so dusty, so foggy, so unfocused and so brownish yellow that you want to try Windex on the screen. A director is in deep trouble when we do not even enjoy the primary act of looking at his picture.

But Cimino's in deeper trouble still. *Heaven's Gate* has, of course, become a notorious picture, a boondoggle that cost something like $36 million and was yanked out of its New York opening run after the critics ran gagging from the theater. Its running time, at that point, was more than four hours. Perhaps length was the problem? Cimino went back to the editing room, while a United Artists executive complained that the film had been "destroyed" by an unfairly negative review by *New York Times* critic Vincent Canby. Brother Canby was only doing his job. If the film was formless at four hours, it was insipid at 140 minutes. At either length it is so incompetently photographed and edited that there are times when we are not even sure which character we are looking at. Christopher Walken is in several of the initial Western scenes before he finally gets a closeup and we see who he is. John Hurt wanders through various scenes to no avail. Kris Kristofferson is the star of the movie, and is never allowed to generate enough character for us to miss him, should he disappear.

The opening scenes are set at Harvard (well, they were actually shot in England, but never mind). They show Kristofferson, Hurt, and other idealistic young men graduating in 1870 and setting off to civilize a nation. Kristofferson decides to go West, to help develop the territory. He explains this decision in a narration, and the movie might have benefited if he'd narrated the whole thing, explaining as he went along. Out West, as a lawman, he learns of a plot by the cattlebreeders' association to hire a private army and assassinate 125 newly arrived European immigrants who are, it is claimed, anarchists, killers, and thieves. Most of the movie will be about this plot, Kristofferson's attempts to stop it, Walken's involvement in it, and the involvement of both Kristofferson and Walken in the private life of a young Montana madam (Isabelle Huppert).

In a movie where nothing is handled well, the immigrants are handled very badly. Cimino sees them as a mob. They march onscreen, babble excitedly in foreign tongues, and rush off wildly in all directions. By the movie's end, we can identify only one of them for sure. She is the Widow Kovach, whose husband was shot dead near the beginning of the film. That makes her the emblem of the immigrants' suffering. Every time she steps forward out of the mob, somebody respectfully murmurs "Widow Kovach!" in the subtitles. While the foreigners are hanging onto Widow Kovach's every insight, the cattlemen are holding meetings in private clubs and offering to pay their mercenaries $5 a day plus expenses and $50 for every other foreigner shot or hung. I am sure of those terms because they are

repeated endlessly throughout a movie that cares to make almost nothing else clear.

The ridiculous scenes are endless. Samples: Walken, surrounded by gunmen and trapped in a burning cabin, scribbles a farewell note in which he observes that he is trapped in the burning cabin, and then he signs his full name so that there will be no doubt who the note was from. Kristofferson, discovering Huppert being gang-raped by several men, leaps in with six-guns in both hands and shoots all the men, including those aboard Huppert, without injuring her. In a big battle scene, men make armored wagons out of logs and push them forward into the line of fire, even though anyone could ride around behind and shoot them. There is more. There is much more. It all adds up to a great deal less. This movie is $36 million thrown to the winds. It is the most scandalous cinematic waste I have ever seen, and remember, I've seen *Paint Your Wagon*.

Hell Night ★
R, 100 m., 1981

Linda Blair (Marti), Vincent Van Patten (Seth), Peter Barton (Jeff), Kevin Brophy (Peter). Directed by Tom De Simone and produced by Irwin Yablans and Bruce Cohn Curtis. Screenplay by Randolph Feldman.

It was that legendary Chicago film exhibitor Oscar Brotman who gave me one of my most useful lessons in the art of film-watching. "In ninety-nine films out of a hundred," Brotman told me, "if nothing has happened by the end of the first reel . . . nothing is *going* to happen." This rule, he said, had saved him countless hours over the years because he had walked out of movies after the first uneventful reel.

I seem to remember arguing with him. There are some films, I said, in which nothing happens in the first reel because the director is trying to set up a universe of ennui and uneventfulness. Take a movie like Michalengelo Antonioni's *L'Avventura*, for example,

"It closed in a week," Brotman said.

"But, Oscar, it was voted one of the top ten greatest films of all time!"

"They must have all seen it in the first week."

I was running this conversation through my memory while watching *Hell Night*.

You know a movie is in trouble when what is happening on the screen inspires daydreams. I had lasted through the first reel, and nothing had happened. Now I was somewhere in the middle of the third reel, and still nothing had happened. By "nothing," by the way, I mean nothing original, unexpected, well-crafted, interestingly acted, or even excitingly violent. *Hell Night* is a relentlessly lackluster example of the Dead Teen-ager Movie. The formula is always the same. A group of kids get together for some kind of adventure or forbidden ritual in a haunted house, summer camp, old school, etc. One of the kids tells a story about the horrible and gruesome murders that happened there years ago. He always ends the same way: ". . . and they say the killer *never died* and is still lurking here somewhere." That was the formula of *The Burning* and the Friday the 13th movies, and it's the formula again in *Hell Night*.

This time, the pretext is a fraternity-sorority initiation stunt. The venue is an old mansion. We learn that the hapless Garth family once lived there and had four deformed and handicapped children. The misfortunes of the children are described in great detail, with dialogue that's in very bad taste. But then of course *Hell Night* is in bad taste. The only child that need concern us is the youngest Garth, who was named Andrew and was born, we are told, a "gork." None of the dictionaries at my command include the word "gork," but for the purposes of *Hell Night* we can define "gork" thus:

Gork (n.) Deformed, violent creature that lurks in horror movies, jumping out of basement shadows and decapitating screaming teen-agers.

I have now, of course, given away the plot of *Hell Night*. As the fraternity and sorority kids creep through passageways of the old house, their candle flames fluttering in the wind, Andrew the gork picks them off, one by one, in scenes of bloody detail. Finally only Linda Blair is left. Why does she survive? Maybe because she's a battle-hardened veteran, having previously more or less lived through *The Exorcist*, *The Heretic*, and *Born Innocent*. At least in those movies, something happened in the first reel.

High Road to China ★ ★
PG, 107 m., 1983

Tom Selleck (O'Malley), Bess Armstrong (Eve), Jack Weston (Struts), Wilford Brimley (Bradley Tozer), Robert Morely (Bentik). Directed by Brian G. Hutton and produced by Fred Weintraub. Screenplay by Sandra Weintraub Roland and S. Lee Rogostin.

Word has it that Tom Selleck was Steven Spielberg's first choice for the lead in *Raiders of the Lost Ark*, and that Harrison Ford got the job at the last minute. I wonder if that left Selleck walking around frustrated, still wanting to play someone like Indiana Jones. That would be one explanation for *High Road to China*, an unconvincing, harmless action movie that at its best is a pale echo of *Raiders*. The movie stars Selleck as a freelance pilot who gives flying lessons at a field outside Istanbul. The year is 1920. The movie never pauses to explain how he finds enough customers to support himself by giving lessons in Turkey in 1920. It's too busy introducing Selleck to Bess Armstrong, a plucky American rich kid who has to prove that her daddy is alive or lose an inheritance of millions. Armstrong hires Selleck and his sidekick, Jack Weston, to fly off in the general direction of Tibet, where she thinks her father might be running a border war.

Well, that's the premise. What we get then is a series of more-or-less predictable scenes in which our heroes fly over mountains and deserts, sit by campfires, barely escape from the clutches of hostile Arabs, Turks, Tartars, and Mongolians, and eventually find her father. He's played by the wonderful character actor Wilford Brimley. (He played the federal attorney who came in and settled everybody's hash in the climactic scenes of *Absence of Malice*.) And he's masterminding the defense of a Tibetan hill town against the onslaughts of the barbarians below.

There has to be conflict in a movie like this, and so, of course, there is. Selleck and Armstrong start out hating each other. She gets one of his planes destroyed. Jack Weston has to stay behind. Selleck and Armstrong fly off together, have some close calls, and eventually fall in love. The movie gives them a lot of time to exchange wisecracks, tender and otherwise, and then they get to play one of my all-time favorite obligatory scenes. I call it the We're Alive! Let's Kiss! Scene. You've seen it in a hundred movies. It always starts with the hero and heroine up on their elbows in a shallow ditch. People are shooting at them. A bullet throws up a cloud of dirt, inches from their faces. They tumble down for cover, wind up in each other's arms, and zowie! All those repressed passions explode, and we realize (with well-concealed surprise) that their wisecracks disguised a growing love. Every movie star should play this scene at least once, at the most.

High Road to China is not a terrible movie, but it's a lifeless one. It follows some of the forms of *Raiders of the Lost Ark* without ever finding the comic rhythms. It's directed at a nice, steady pace, but without flair and without the feeling that anything's being risked. And it tells such an absolutely standard story that we never fear for the characters and we hardly ever believe them.

History of the World—Part I ★ ★
R, 90 m., 1981

Mel Brooks (Moses, Comicus, Torquemada, Jacques, Louis XVI), Dom DeLuise (Nero), Madeline Kahn (Empress Nympho), Harvey Korman (Count De Monet), Cloris Leachman (Madame Defarge), Ron Carey (Swiftus), Mary-Margaret Humes (Miriam). Directed and produced by Mel Brooks. Screenplay by Brooks.

Mel Brooks's movie *History of the World—Part I* is a rambling, undisciplined, sometimes embarrassing failure from one of the most gifted comic filmmakers around. What went wrong? Brooks never seems to have a clear idea of the rationale of his movie—so there's no confident narrative impetus to carry it along. His "history" framework doesn't have an approach or point of view; it's basically just a laundry-line for whatever gags he can hang on it.

What *is* this bizarre grab bag? Is it a parody of old Biblical, Roman, and French historical epics? Sometimes. Is it one-shot, comedy revue blackouts? Sometimes. Is it satire aimed at pompous targets? Sometimes. But most of the time it's basically just expensive sets sitting around waiting for Brooks to do something funny in front of them.

Brooks seems to rely on his own spontaneous comic genius in this film, and genius, even when you have it, is not something to be relied upon. He provides isolated moments that are indeed hilarious, moments that find an inspired image and zing us with it (as when a slave boogies through the streets of ancient Rome with a loud transistor radio glued to his ear). But as the movie creeps on, we realize that the inspirations are going to be rare, and that Brooks has not bothered to create a framework for the movie or to people it with characters. It's all just cardboard comic cutouts.

The film has another serious problem: It is in unfunny bad taste. That sounds strange coming from me. I've always enjoyed Brooks's ventures into taboo subject matter, and I still think his "Springtime for Hitler" from *The Producers* and the celebrated campfire scene in *Blazing Saddles* were hilarious. He seemed to be demonstrating that you could get away with almost anything in a movie, if you made it funny enough. (Told that *The Producers* was vulgar, he once responded loftily, "It rises *below* vulgarity.") But this time, the things he's trying to get away with aren't funny. There is, for example, the movie's tiresome series of jokes about urination. There must be comic possibilities in the subject (and he finds one when he shows a Stone Age critic's method of reviewing a cave painting), but there is nothing inherently funny about urination, and Brooks proves it here, again and again.

There also is nothing inherently funny about Jews, Catholics, nuns, blacks, and gays. They can all conceivably provide the makings of comedy, of course, but in *History of the World* Brooks doesn't have the patience to introduce a character and then create a comic situation *about* him. He introduces the character and expects us to laugh at the character himself. Example. Instead of developing a comic situation around Orthodox Jews, he simply shows us some, complete with beards and hats, their heads stuck through a stockade, and expects us to laugh. But while we might laugh with Brooks at a comic situation, we have no reason to laugh *at* people just because of their appearance or religion.

The same thing goes wrong with Brooks's big production number in this movie, "The

Inquisition,'' featuring a song-and-dance team of medieval monks, and a chorus line of nuns who splash in a pool, Busby Berkeley-style. We're supposed to laugh at the shocking juxtaposition of religious images and Hollywood corn. But Brooks never gives us an additional comic level, one where he's making funny points about the images. When he dresses up like a monk and then dances like Donald O'Connor, that's only funny for a second. If we knew anything about the monk as a comic character, the scene could build. Instead, it just continues.

History of the World—Part I was fairly expensive to produce, but it exists on the level of quick, disposable, television. It thumbs its nose at icons that have lost their taboo value for most of us, and between the occasional good laughs, we're a little embarrassed that the movie is so dumb and predictable. God knows Mel Brooks is straining for yuks up there on the screen, but he's like the life of the party who still has the lampshade on his head when everybody else is ready to go home.

Honkytonk Man ★ ★ ★
PG, 123 m., 1982

Clint Eastwood (Red Stovall), Kyle Eastwood (Whit), John McIntire (Grandpa), Alexa Kenin (Marlene), Verna Bloom (Emmy). Directed and produced by Clint Eastwood.

Clint Eastwood produced and directed *Honkytonk Man,* and stars in it as a Depression-era loser who drifts through the South with his young nephew, aiming eventually to get to Nashville and maybe get on the Grand Ol' Opry. The movie's credits say the screenplay is by Clancy Carlile, based on his own novel, but in speculating on what drew Eastwood to this project, I came across this entry in Ephraim Katz's *Film Encyclopedia:* "Eastwood, Clint. Actor, director. Born on May 31, 1930, in San Francisco. A child of the Depression, he spent his early boyhood trailing a father who pumped gas along dusty roads all over the West Coast . . .''

The entry goes on to list the usual odd jobs (logger, steel-furnace stoker) that all actors seem to hold down on their way to stardom, but I'd read enough to support my intuition that *Honkytonk Man* means a lot to Eastwood

in ways that may not be immediately apparent. This is a sweet, whimsical, low-key movie, a movie that makes you feel good without pressing you too hard. It provides Eastwood with a screen character who is the complete opposite of the patented Eastwood tough guys and provides a role of nearly equal importance for his son, Kyle, as a serious, independent and utterly engaging young nephew named Whit. What happens to them on the road is not quite as important in this movie as what happens between them.

The movie starts with Eastwood drunk behind the wheel of a big 1930s touring car, knocking over the windmill on his latest return to the old homestead. He's sort of a Hank Williams type. His family has seen this act before. They put him to bed and hide the bottle. The next day, with an ominous cough, Eastwood talks about his dream of heading for Nashville and cashing in some old IOUs. He's a singer and a songwriter, luckless but not untalented, and he thinks he could make it onto the Opry. He wants to take the kid along. After some hesitation, the kid's mother (Verna Bloom) agrees, mostly because she hopes her son can ride herd on Eastwood and keep him reasonably sober. She makes her son promise not to drink or fool around with women (thus putting her finger unerringly on one thing he did the night before, and another that he hopes to do as soon as possible). Old grandpa (John McIntire) also decides to go along for the ride; he's got some people in Tennessee he hasn't seen in forty years.

The road part of the picture is picaresque, photographed through a haze of romance and nostalgia, and spiced up with a visit to a gambling house and an encounter with a very individualistic young woman (Alexa Kenin) who also decides to join the traveling party. She has an amazing gift for couching the most ordinary sentiments in romantic prose. The movie's best scenes are the ones Eastwood plays in Nashville, during an audition at the Opry and, later, in a recording studio. He sings his songs with the kind of bone-weariness that doesn't hurt the right kind of country song, and there's a special moment in the studio when a supporting musician lends a hand. The movie turns out to be about realizing your dreams after all, which is sort of a surprise in a story where even the high points are only bittersweet.

This is a special movie. In making it, Eastwood was obviously moving away from his Dirty Harry image, but that's nothing new; his spectacular success in violent movies tends to distract us from his intriguing and challenging career as the director and star of such offbeat projects as *Bronco Billy* and *Play Misty For Me*. He seems to have a personal stake in this story, and we begin to feel it, too. Sometimes the simplest country songs are just telling the facts.

The Hunger ★ ½
R, 100 m., 1983

Catherine Deneuve (Miriam), David Bowie (John), Susan Sarandon (Sarah), Cliff De Young (Tom). Directed by Tony Scott. Screenplay by Ivan Davis and Michael Thomas.

The Hunger is an agonizingly bad vampire movie, circling around an exquisitely effective sex scene. Sorry, but that's the way it is, and I have to be honest. The seduction scene involves Catherine Deneuve, as an age-old vampire, and Susan Sarandon, as her latest victim. There was a great deal of controversy while the movie was being made (all sorts of rumors about closed sets, etc.), but the scene as it now appears isn't raunchy or *too* explicit—just sort of dreamily erotic. I mention the scene so prominently because it's one of the few scenes that really work in *The Hunger*, a movie that has been so ruthlessly overproduced that it's all flash and style and no story. Well, there's probably a story moping about somewhere within all the set decoration. It seems to involve Deneuve as a vampire of vaguely Egyptian origins, whose latest partner (David Bowie) is giving out on her after three or four centuries.

After an initial orgy of fancy camerawork, the movie settles down into the story of Bowie's final days. He has that chronic vampire disease where you age suddenly. He needs a lot of blood to keep going. He appeals to a medical researcher (Sarandon) for help, but she brushes him off, and by the time she realizes he's serious, he looks like Methuselah. Then Sarandon visits the lavish town house where Deneuve and Bowie live, and that's where a glass of sherry leads to the seduction scene.

I've got to be honest about this scene. Part of its interest lies in the fact that Catherine Deneuve *herself* and Susan Sarandon *herself*, are acting in the scene. That gives it a level of reality that would be lacking in a porno film, even a much more explicit one. Because we know that famous actresses don't usually agree to appear in scenes such as this, we're aware of the chance they're taking—and the documentary reality of the scene gives it an effectiveness all its own. Deneuve, of course, has made a career out of the contrast between her cool, perfect beauty and the strange, erotic predicaments her characters get involved in. (Remember *Belle de Jour?*) Sarandon's scene by the window in *Atlantic City*, bathing herself with lemons, created great sultriness. But *The Hunger* approaches its big scene on an altogether different level, with understatement, awkward little pauses in conversation, and a canny awareness of our own curiosity about whether Deneuve and Sarandon really will go ahead with this scene, or whether the director will cut away to the usual curtains blowing in the wind.

Well, he doesn't, but it's about the only time in the whole movie there aren't curtains blowing in the wind. This movie has so much would-be elegance and visual class that it never quite happens as a dramatic event. There's so much cross-cutting, so many memories, so many apparent flashbacks, that the real drama is lost—the drama of a living human being seduced into vampirism. In Herzog's *Nosferatu*, we felt some of the blood-scented lure of eternal death-in-life. Here, it's just—how would an ad put it?—Catherine Deneuve for Dracula.

Iceman ★ ★ ★ ★
PG, 99 m., 1984

Timothy Hutton (Dr. Shephard), John Lone (Iceman), Lindsay Crouse (Dr. Diane Brady). Directed by Fred Schepisi and produced by Norman Jewison and Patrick Palmer. Screenplay by John Drimmer and Chip Proser.

Iceman begins in almost exactly the same way as both versions of *The Thing*, with a team of Arctic scientists chopping a frozen mammal out of the ice. But somehow we're more interested in this discovery because the frozen object isn't simply a gimmick at the beginning of a horror picture; it is presented with real curiosity and awe.

What is it? As a helicopter lifts the discovery aloft, we can glimpse its vague, shadowy outline through the block of 40,000-year-old ice. It seems almost to be a man, with its arms outstretched. If we remember Fellini's *La Dolce Vita*, we're reminded of its famous opening scene, as the helicopter flew above Rome with the statue of Christ. In both cases, a contrast is made between the technological gimmicks of man and an age-old mystery. In both cases, also, we're aware that we are in the hands of a master director. *Iceman* is by Fred Schepisi, the Australian who made *The Chant of Jimmy Blacksmith* and Willie Nelson's *Barbarosa*. Both of those movies were about men who lived entirely apart from modern society, according to rules of their own, rules that we eventually realized made perfect sense (to them, at least). Now Schepisi has taken that story idea as far as it will go.

The block of ice is thawed. As each drop of water trickles down a stainless-steel table to the floor, we feel a real excitement. We're about to discover something, just as we were when the apes found the monolith in *2001*. Inside the block of ice is a Neanderthal man, perfectly preserved, frozen in an instant with his hands pushing out and his mouth open in a prehistoric cry of protest. Such a discovery is at least theoretically possible; mastodons have been found in Russia, frozen so quickly in a sudden global catastrophe that the buttercups in their stomachs had still not been digested. Why not a man? Of course, the man's cell tissue would have been destroyed by the freezing process, right? Not according to *Iceman*, which advances an ingenious theory.

The scene in which the Neanderthal is brought back to life is one of those emergency room dramas we're familiar with from the TV medical shows, with medics pounding on the chest and administering electrical shocks. Then the movie leaves the familiar, and begins an intriguing journey into the past of the man. The Neanderthal (his name sounds like "Charlie") is placed in a controlled environment. Two scientists (Timothy Hutton and Lindsay Crouse) establish a relationship with him. Elementary communication is started—although here the movie makes a basic error in showing the scientists teaching Charlie to speak English, when of course they would want to learn his language instead.

The rest of the movie develops a theory about how Charlie was frozen and what he was looking for when that surprising event took place. There is also an argument between two branches of science: Those who are more interested in what they can learn from Charlie's body and those who want to understand his mind. This conflict seems to have been put in to generate suspense (certainly no responsible scientist, presented with a living Neanderthal man, would suggest any experiment that would endanger his life). But never mind; before it turns into conflict between good and evil, *Iceman* departs in an unexpected, mystical direction.

This movie is spellbinding storytelling. It begins with such a simple premise and creates such a genuinely intriguing situation that we're not just entertained, we're drawn into the argument. What we feel about Charlie reflects what we feel about ourselves. And what he knows—that we've forgotten—illuminates the line between man the firebuilder, and man the stargazer. Think how much more interesting *The Thing* would have been if its frozen life form had been investigated rather than destroyed, and you have an idea of *Iceman*'s appeal.

The Idolmaker ★ ★ ★
PG, 117 m., 1980

Ray Sharkey (Vince Vacarri), Tovah Feldshuh (Brenda Roberts), Peter Gallagher (Cesare), Paul Land (Tommy Dee), Joe Pantoliano (Gino Pilate). Directed by Taylor Hackford and produced by Gene Kirkwood and Howard W. Koch, Jr. Screenplay by Edward Di Lorenzo.

At the core of *The Idolmaker*, making it a better film than it might otherwise have been, is the hungry, lonely ego of the movie's hero, Vince Vacarri. He has all the skills necessary to become a rock 'n' roll idol, especially in the late-1950s world of Top Forty payola and prefabricated stars. But he doesn't have the looks. He so desperately wants stardom, though, that he tries to have it vicariously, through the "idols" he painstakingly manufactures. Maybe that makes *The Idolmaker* sound more serious than it is, but it's that core of obsession in the Ray Sharkey performance that takes a movie that might have been routine and makes it interesting. This is not a dazzlingly original idea, but the movie understands its passions well enough to entertain us with them.

The "idolmaker" of the title is based, I understand, on the real-life character of Bob Marcucci (listed as the film's "technical adviser"). He is the Philadelphia Svengali who discovered, coached, and managed Frankie Avalon and Fabian, quarterbacking them to stardom. If this movie can be believed, he was a rock 'n' roll puppetmaster, supplying the lines, the songs, the delivery and—most importantly—the stage mannerisms and "look" of his personalities.

The movie moves the story to Brooklyn, and borrows heavily from the clichés of show-biz rags to riches movies: Not only is it lonely at the top in this movie . . . it's lonely at the bottom, too, for practice. The Sharkey character manufactures his first rock star (Paul Land) out of a little raw talent, an unshaped stage presence, and sheer energy. One of the movie's most engaging scenes shows Land at a high school record hop, doggedly pantomiming his first record while Sharkey, backstage, goes through the same motions.

Land does a good job of playing the movie's first rock singer—a spoiled, egotistical creation renamed "Tommy Dee." We can predict what will happen. He'll be pushed to the top by Sharkey, develop an inflated opinion of himself, and think he did it all alone. That's exactly what happens, but Land moves through these stages with a conviction that makes them seem fairly new, even while we're recognizing them.

Meanwhile, Sharkey has another discovery waiting in the wings. He spots a busboy (Peter Gallagher) in his brother's restaurant. The guy can't keep time, can't sing, and has one enormous hairy eyebrow all the way across his face. No problem: Sharkey pounds rhythm into him, grooms him, renames him Caesare and fast-talks him onto the movie's version of "American Bandstand." It turns out that this kid *does* have a

natural rapport with the prepubescent girls in his audiences, and he's on his way.

None of this would work if *The Idolmaker* didn't have convincing actors playing the two rock singers. It does. Land and Gallagher can sing and move well enough to convince us they're plausible teen idols. They can also act well enough to modulate their stage performances—they start out terrible and work their way up to levels that Fabian himself must only have dreamed about. And the movie has fun with its production numbers. The songs are all standard late-fifties rock dreck (but newly composed for the movie), but the stage performances are a little sneaky. They're not as ridiculous as many of the late-fifties adolescent heroes actually were; they seem to owe a lot not only to Elvis (naturally) but also to such performers of a decade later as Mick Jagger.

All of this is not to say that *The Idolmaker* is a masterpiece. But it is a well-crafted movie that works, that entertains, and that pulls us through its pretty standard material with the magnetism of the Ray Sharkey performance. Because we sense his hungers, his isolations, and his compulsive needs, we buy scenes that might otherwise have been unworkable.

The Incredible Shrinking Woman
★ ★ ½
PG, 88 m., 1981

Lily Tomlin (Pat Kramer and Judith Beasley), Charles Grodin (Vance Kramer), Ned Beatty (Dan Beame), Henry Gibson (Dr. Nortz). Directed by Joel Schumacher and produced by Hank Moonjean. Screenplay by Jane Wagner.

This is a terrific movie for kids and teenagers. It's a melancholy fact of the times we live in that any movie of even moderate ambition is supposed to become a blockbuster—and that "family movies," with few exceptions, are inane, innocent, and boring. But *The Incredible Shrinking Woman* is not inane, is sometimes wickedly knowing, and is only periodically boring. It strikes a note of quiet desperation that appeals to the teenager in all of us. When Lily Tomlin's character has shrunk to twenty-four inches in height and is desperately screaming for help because she is about to be flushed down the garbage disposal unit— who among us cannot say he has felt exactly the same way?

I suppose that at some basic level *The Incredible Shrinking Woman* is a protest against the lot of the housewife in American society. As Lily Tomlin slaves away in her suburban dream home, her husband (Charles Grodin) gets big raises and promotions for advertising home-care products. And eventually one of those products (was it the dye? detergent? glue?) causes Lily Tomlin to start shrinking. One of the intriguing things about the movie is that the smaller Tomlin gets, the more people treat her like a child. She even winds up living in a doll's house. I would like to argue that this is a dilemma not limited to housewives. A lot of people know this feeling. Kids can identify with the maddening sensation that they are smaller than everyone else in the world and *no one is listening!* Teen-agers have grown accustomed to being stuck down the garbage disposal of life: Nobody wants them around, and most people would probably like to hit a switch and make them disappear.

So there's a certain poignant comedy in *The Incredible Shrinking Woman* that strikes some chords. The movie is also funny in its visual approach, showing us a suburban world in which everything is done in hideously jolly colors and everybody, even the TV anchorman, wears peach blazers. America in this movie looks like a gigantic paint-color chart.

It's too bad, I suppose, that *The Incredible Shrinking Woman* succeeds on the levels I've mentioned without ever breaking through to become a really inspired comedy. Lily Tomlin is such a funny woman that we expect her to hit home runs in every movie. She doesn't in this one, but she does something almost as hard. She creates a character that is halfway believable, in the midst of chaos. She causes us to feel a certain comic sympathy for her plight. And, for that matter, she inhabits a plight that is interesting. Most "family movies" these days are uninspired, moronic, and directed and acted without any visible style. *The Incredible Shrinking Woman* at least has an intelligence behind it. It is engaging a lot of the time and funny some of the time, especially when a

gorilla helps the two-inch-tall Tomlin escape from captivity.

Indiana Jones and the Temple of Doom ★ ★ ★ ★
PG, 118 m., 1984 ✓

Harrison Ford (Indiana Jones), Kate Capshaw (Willie Scott), Ke Huy Quan (Short Round), Amrish Puri (Mola Ram), Philip Stone (Captain Blumburtt), Roshan Seth (Chattar Lal). Directed by Steven Spielberg and produced by George Lucas. Screenplay by Willard Huyck and Gloria Katz.

Steven Spielberg's *Indiana Jones and the Temple of Doom* is one of the greatest Bruised Forearm Movies ever made. You know what a Bruised Forearm Movie is. That's the kind of movie where your date is always grabbing your forearm in a viselike grip, as unbearable excitement unfolds on the screen. After the movie is over, you've had a great time but your arm is black-and-blue for a week. This movie is one of the most relentlessly nonstop action pictures ever made, with a virtuoso series of climactic sequences that must last an hour and never stop for a second. It's a roller coaster ride, a visual extravaganza, a technical triumph, and a whole lot of fun. And it's not simply a retread of *Raiders of the Lost Ark*, the first Indiana Jones movie. It works in a different way, and borrows from different traditions.

Raiders was inspired by Saturday afternoon serials. It was a series of cliffhanging predicaments, strung out along the way as Indiana Jones traveled from San Francisco to Tibet, Egypt, and other romantic locales. It was an exotic road picture. *Indiana Jones* mostly takes place on one location, and belongs more to the great tradition of the Impregnable Fortress Impregnated. You know the kind of fortress I'm talking about. You see them all the time in James Bond pictures. They involve unbelievably bizarre hideaways, usually buried under the earth, beneath the sea, on the moon, or inside a volcano. They are ruled over by megalomaniac zealots who dream of conquest, and they're fueled by slave labor. Our first glimpse of an Impregnable Fortress is always the same: An ominous long shot, with Wagnerian music, as identically uniformed functionaries hurry about their appointed tasks.

The role of the hero in a movie like this is to enter the fortress, steal the prize, and get away in one piece. This task always involves great difficulty, horrendous surprises, unspeakable dangers, and a virtuoso chase sequence. The very last shots at the end of the sequence are obligatory: The fortress must be destroyed. Hopefully, there will be great walls of flame and water, engulfing the bad guys as the heroes race to freedom, inches ahead of certain death.

But enough of intellectual film criticism. Let's get back to Indiana Jones. As *Temple of Doom* opens, Indiana is in a nightclub somewhere in Shanghai. Killers are after him. He escapes in the nick of time, taking along a beautiful nightclub floozy (Kate Capshaw), and accompanied by his trusty young sidekick, Short Round (Ke Huy Quan). Their getaway leads them into a series of adventures: A flight over the Himalayas, a breathtaking escape from a crashing plane, and a meeting with a village leader who begs Indiana to find and return the village's precious magic jewel—a stone which disappeared along with all of the village's children. Indiana is a plucky chap and agrees. Then there's a dinner in the palace of a sinister local lord. The dinner scene, by the way, also is lifted from James Bond, where it's an obligatory part of every adventure: James is always promised a sure death, but treated first to an elegant dinner with his host, who boasts of his power and takes inordinate pride in being a sophisticated host. After Indiana and Willie retire for the night, there's the movie's only slow sequence, in which such matters as love are discussed. (Make some popcorn.) Then the movie's second half opens with a breathtaking series of adventures involving the mines beneath the palace—mines that have been turned into a vision of hell.

The set design, art direction, special effects, and sound effects inside this underground Hades are among the most impressive achievements in the whole history of Raiders and Bond-style thrillers. As dozens of little kids work on chain gangs, the evil maharajah keeps them in slavery by using the sinister powers of the missing jewel and its two mates. Indiana and his friends look on in astonishment, and then Indiana attempts to steal back the jewel. Some of the film's great setpieces now take place: Human victims are lowered into a subterranean volcano in a steel cage, weird rituals are celebrated, and there is a chase scene involving the mine's miniature railway. This chase has to be seen to be believed. Spielberg has obviously studied Buster Keaton's *The General*, that silent classic that solved the obvious logistic problem of a chase on railway tracks (i.e., what to do about the fact that one train seemingly always has to be behind the other one). As Indiana and friends hurtle in the little out-of-control mine car, the pursuers are behind, ahead, above, below, and beside them, and the scene will wring you out and leave you breathless. *Indiana Jones and the Temple of Doom* makes no apologies for being exactly what it is: Exhilarating, manic, wildly imaginative escapism.

No apologies are necessary. This is the most cheerfully exciting, bizarre, goofy, romantic adventure movie since *Raiders*, and it is high praise to say that it's not so much a sequel as an equal. It's quite an experience. You stagger out with a silly grin—and a bruised forearm, of course.

Into the Night ★
R, 117 m., 1985

Jeff Goldblum (Ed Okin), Michelle Pfeiffer (Diana), Richard Farnsworth (Jack Caper), Irene Papas (Shaheen), Kathryn Harrold (Christie), Paul Mazursky (Bud Herman), Bruce McGill (Brother [Elvis]), David Bowie (Colin Morris). Directed by John Landis and produced by George Folsey, Jr., and Ron Koslow. Screenplay by Koslow.

Into the Night is a fitfully funny, aimless, unnecessary thriller. That would not necessarily be enough to make it a bad movie; *Beverly Hills Cop* is also fitfully funny, aimless, and unnecessary, but it is also a more successful movie because it has a sense of style and because it has Eddie Murphy at its center. This movie has no center, even though the wonderful actor Jeff Goldblum was available to supply one. I have a theory about that.

The movie was directed by John Landis, who has filled it with countless cameo appearances. Everybody knows that a lot of

Hollywood directors have walk-ons in *Into the Night*, but that's just the beginning. Everybody and his cousin dirfts through this movie. And I have a notion that the set began to resemble a party, with a different guest list every day. As Landis played host and tried to make all of his nonactors feel comfortable, some degree of vital tension was lost. Creating the experience became more important than making the movie. Look at the guest list. Among the directors who appear in the film are David Cronenberg, Colin Higgins, Daniel Petrie, Paul Mazursky, Paul Bartel, Don Siegel, Jim Henson, Amy Heckerling, Roger Vadim, Lawrence Kasdan, Jonathan Demme, Carl Gottleib, and Landis himself. Not sure who all of them are? That's all right; they probably had a great time at the Director's Guild screening. Other bit players in the film include actors Dan Ackroyd, Vera Miles, Clu Gulanger, and Irene Papas, cinematographer Robert Paynter, publicist Saul Kahan, car dealer Cal Worthington, rock star David Bowie, writer Waldo Salt, computer software expert Hadi Sadjadi, body-builder Jake Steinfeld, cartoonist Bruce McGill (who is very good as an Elvis freak), special effects makeup artist Rick Baker, country singer Carl Perkins, assistant director David Sosna, second assistant cameraman Christopher George, sound mixer William B. Kaplan, and makeup man Wes Dawn. And I'll bet I missed a few.

What's the idea here? To make a home movie? If I had been the agent for one of the stars, like Goldblum, Michelle Pfeiffer, Richard Farnsworth, or Kathryn Harrold, I think I would have protested to the front office that Landis was engaging in cinematic autoeroticism and that my clients were getting lost in the middle of the family reunion.

The irony is that *Into the Night* opens so promisingly. Goldblum plays an aerospace engineer who is unhappily married, unhappily employed, depressed, and restless. When he finds out his wife is having an affair, he gets up in the middle of the night and drives his car to the airport—planning to fly off into the night. At this point, wonderful things could have happened. Instead, Michelle Pfeiffer lands on the hood of his car, pursued by four murderous Arabs. Goldblum saves her life and gets caught in an intrigue involving stolen jewels, black-mar-

ket con games, and an international network of thieves. And the movie gets reduced to a mindless, shapeless mess, with the Arabs chasing him around in a Mercedes, looking like the Four Stooges. There was never a moment when I cared about the plot. And there have been so many chase scenes in the movies that Hollywood should open a franchise: Chase 'n' Shoot, regular or crispy, with or without cheesecake.

Landis is not a bad director. Look at his credits like *Animal House*, *The Blues Brothers*, and *Trading Places*. Some of the scenes in this movie work, including a funny beachfront episode with Mazursky and Harrold, Farnsworth's touching work as a dying old man and McGill's hilarious supporting role as an angry Elvis imitator. Maybe what the movie needed was more professional discipline and less geniality. As a rule, it's probably better to throw the party after the filming is finished.

Irreconcilable Differences ★ ★ ★ ½
PG, 112 m., 1984

Ryan O'Neal (Albert Brodsky), Shelley Long (Lucy Van Patten Brodsky), Drew Barrymore (Casey Brodsky), Sam Wanamaker (David Kessler), Allen Garfield (Phil Hanner), Hortensia Colorado (Maria Hernandez). Directed by Charles Shyer and produced by Arlene Sellers and Alex Winitsky. Screenplay by Nancy Myers and Shyer.

The opening moments of *Irreconcilable Differences* are not promising. A lawyer is advising his client about divorce—and when we see the client, she turns out to be a little girl. Her plan is to divorce her parents, because they have (she stumbles over the word) ir . . . ir . . . rec . . . concilable differences. Right away, I was bracing myself for one of those smarmy movies about cute kids and mean parents. I could foresee the series this movie would inspire: "Kids' Court," with a different little plaintiff every week. It turns out that I was too cynical. *Irreconcilable Differences* is sometimes cute, and is about mean parents, but it also is one of the funnier and more intelligent movies of 1984, and if viewers can work their way past the ungainly title, they're likely to have a surprisingly good time.

The movie stars Drew Barrymore as the

little girl. You may remember her from *E. T.,* when she hid E.T. in the closet with her stuffed animals. She has grown up just a little, but she still has that slight lisp and that air of preternaturally concentrated seriousness: She is the right actress for this role precisely because she approaches it with such grave calm. A kid trying to be funny would be a mistake. Her parents are played by Shelley Long of "Cheers," who is one of my favorite actresses, and Ryan O'Neal, who is not usually one of my favorite actors but is right for this role and good in it. They have a Meet-Cute while he is hitchhiking and she is returning her car to her tall, muscular boyfriend. It's love at first sight, even after Bink, the boyfriend, bursts into their motel room and figures out that his engagement is over.

O'Neal plans to be a great movie director. (His character seems inspired by Peter Bogdanovich, right down to the style of his glasses.) Long starts out to be a helpful wife and good mother, but then, after O'Neal's career hits the skids, she has great success as a writer. The point is that one parent or the other is always so busy, so successful, so much in demand, that the little girl gets overlooked. The only place she really feels loved and comfortable is when she goes home with the family's Mexican maid. So the kid sues for divorce. She wants to give the maid custody of herself. The parents are shocked. The media have a circus. The plot drifts dangerously toward a series of stagy confrontations, but avoids the obvious: This movie has been written with so much wit and imagination that even obligatory scenes have a certain freshness and style.

It also has a real edge, even a suggestion of bitterness, in its scenes about Hollywood. Although *Irreconcilable Differences* is a movie about family life, it's also a perceptive portrait of success and failure in Hollywood, with a good ear for the way people use the language of Leo Buscaglia to describe the behavior of Machiavelli.

The Drew Barrymore character sees right through all of this. She doesn't care about careers, she wants to be given a happy home and her minimum daily requirement of love, and, in a way, the movie is about how Hollywood (and American success in general) tends to cut adults off from the natural func-

tions of parents. The theory is that kids will wait but a deal won't. Actually, it's just the opposite.

I Spit on Your Grave   no stars
R, 98 m., 1980

With Camille Keaton, Eron Tabor, Richard Pace, and Anthony Nichols. Directed by Meir Zarchi and produced by Joseph Zbeda. Screenplay by Zarchi.

I Spit on Your Grave is a vile bag of garbage that is so sick, reprehensible, and contemptible that I can hardly believe it played in respectable theaters. But it did. Attending it was one of the most depressing experiences of my life.

This is a film without a shred of artistic distinction. It lacks even simple craftsmanship. There was no possible motive for exhibiting it, other than the totally cynical hope that it might make money. And it did make money: When I saw it at 11:20 A.M. on a Monday, the theater contained a larger crowd than usual.

It was not just a large crowd, it was a profoundly disturbing one. I do not often attribute motives to audience members, nor do I try to read their minds, but the people who were sitting around me on that Monday morning made it easy for me to know what they were thinking. They talked out loud. And if they seriously believed the things they were saying, they were vicarious sex criminals.

The story of *I Spit on Your Grave* is told with moronic simplicity. A girl goes for a vacation in the woods. She sunbathes by a river. Two men speed by in a powerboat. They harass her. Later, they tow her boat to a rendezvous with two of their buddies. They strip the girl, beat her, and rape her again. She crawls home. They are already there, beat her some more, and rape her again.

Two weeks later, somewhat recovered, the girl lures one of the men out to her house, pretends to seduce him, and hangs him. She lures out another man and castrates him, leaving him to bleed to death in a bathtub. She kills the third man with an axe and disembowels the fourth with an outboard engine. End of movie.

These horrible events are shown with an absolute minimum of dialogue, which is so poorly recorded that it often cannot be heard. There is no attempt to develop the personalities of the characters—they are, simply, a girl and four men, one of them mentally retarded. The movie is nothing more or less than a series of attacks on the girl and then her attacks on the men, interrupted only by an unbelievably grotesque and inappropriate scene in which she enters a church and asks forgiveness for the murders she plans to commit.

How did the audience react to all of this? Those who were vocal seemed to be eating it up. The middle-aged, white-haired man two seats down from me, for example, talked aloud. After the first rape: "That was a good one!" After the second: "That'll show her!" After the third: "I've seen some good ones, but this is the best." When the tables turned and the woman started her killing spree, a woman in the back row shouted: "Cut him up, sister!" In several scenes, the other three men tried to force the retarded man to attack the girl. This inspired a lot of laughter and encouragement from the audience.

I wanted to turn to the man next to me and tell him his remarks were disgusting, but I did not. To hold his opinions at his age, he must already have suffered a fundamental loss of decent human feelings. I would have liked to talk with the woman in the back row, the one with the feminist solidarity for the movie's heroine. I wanted to ask if she'd been appalled by the movie's hour of rape scenes. As it was, at the film's end I walked out of the theater quickly, feeling unclean, ashamed, and depressed.

This movie is an expression of the most diseased and perverted darker human natures. Because it is made artlessly, it flaunts its motives: There is no reason to see this movie except to be entertained by the sight of sadism and suffering. As a critic, I have never condemned the use of violence in films if I felt the filmmakers had an artistic reason for employing it. *I Spit on Your Grave* does not. It is a geek show. I wonder if its exhibitors saw it before they decided to play it, and if they felt as unclean afterward as I did.

The Jazz Singer ★
PG, 115 m., 1980

Neil Diamond (Jess Robin), Laurence Olivier (Cantor Rabinovitch), Lucie Arnaz (Molly Bell), Catlin Adams (Rivka Rabinovitch). Directed by Richard Fleischer and produced by Jerry Leider. Screenplay by Herbert Baker.

The Jazz Singer has so many things wrong with it that a review threatens to become a list. Let me start with the most obvious: This movie is about a man who is at least twenty years too old for such things to be happening to him. *The Jazz Singer* looks ridiculous giving us Neil Diamond going through an adolescent crisis.

The movie is a remake, of course, of Al Jolson's 1927 *The Jazz Singer*, which was the first commercially successful talking picture. The remake has played with time in an interesting way: It sets the story in the present, but it places the characters in some kind of time warp. Their behavior seems decades out of date, and some scenes are totally inexplicable in *any* context. For example: In the film, Diamond plays a young Jewish cantor at his father's synagogue. He is married, and he appears settled down to a lifetime of religion. But he also writes songs for a black group—and when one of the quartet gets sick, Diamond takes his place, appearing in a black nightclub in blackface. Oh yeah? This scene is probably supposed to be homage to Jolson's blackface performance of "Mammy" in the original, but what it does now is get the movie off to an unintentionally hilarious start.

The bulk of the movie concerns Diamond's decision to leave New York, his father, and his wife, and go to Los Angeles, where he hopes to break into the music industry. This whole business of leaving the nest, of breaking the ties with his father, seems so strange in a middle-aged character: Diamond is just too old to play these scenes. But no matter; the movie is ridiculous for lots of other reasons.

When he arrives in L.A., for example, he's instantly "discovered" in a recording studio by Lucie Arnaz, who plays an agent and is filled with energy and spunk—she's the best thing in the movie. She thinks he has promise, so she gets him a job as the opening act for a comic. This gives Diamond a chance to sing, and his onstage appearances, I guess, are supposed to be the big deal in this movie. Because of that, the film sacrifices any attempt to present them realistically: For his West Coast debut as a warm-up for a comic, Diamond is backed up by dozens of onstage musicians, which look like the L.A. Philharmonic and, at union scale, would cost thousands of dollars. Sure.

The plot plods relentlessly onward. Laurence Olivier plays the aging father in the film, in a performance that seems based on that tortured German accent he also used in *The Boys from Brazil, Marathon Man* and *A Little Romance:* Is it too much to hope that Sir Laurence will return to the English language sometime soon? Father and son fight, split, grudgingly meet again, hold a tearful reunion—all in scenes of deadly predictability. One sequence that is not predictable has Neil Diamond abandoning (the now pregnant) Lucie Arnaz in order to hit the highway and become a road-show Kristofferson. This stretch of the film, with Diamond self-consciously lonely and hurting, is supposed to be affecting, but is misfires, it drips with so much narcissism.

But then Diamond's whole presence in this movie is offensively narcissistic. His songs are melodramatic, interchangeable, self-aggrandizing groans and anguished shouts, backed protectively by expensive and cloying instrumentation. His dramatic presence also looks overprotected, as if nobody was willing to risk offending him by asking him to seem involved, caring, and engaged.

Diamond plays the whole movie looking at people's third shirt buttons, as if he can't be bothered to meet their eyes and relate with them. It's strange about the Diamond performance: It's not just that he can't act. It's that he sends out creepy vibes. He seems self-absorbed, closed off, grandiose, out of touch with his immediate surroundings. His fans apparently think Neil Diamond songs celebrate worthy human qualities. I think they describe conditions suitable for treatment.

Johnny Dangerously ★ ★
PG-13, 90 m., 1984

Michael Keaton (Johnny), Joe Piscopo (Danny Vermin), Marilu Henner (Lil), Maureen Stapleton (Mom Kelly), Peter Boyle (Jocko), Griffin Dunne (D.A.), Glynnis O'Connor (Sally). Directed by Amy Heckerling and produced by Michael Hertzberg. Screenplay by Norman Steinberg, Bernie Kukoff, Harry Colomby, and Jeff Harris.

The opening scenes of *Johnny Dangerously* are so funny you just don't see how they can keep it up. And you're right: They can't. But they make a real try. The movie wants to do for gangster films what *Airplane!* did for *Airport*, and *Top Secret* did for spy movies. It has its work cut out; this formula consumes comic inspiration at an exhausting rate, and the gangster movie is not exactly an original target for satire. What distinguishes *Johnny Dangerously* from the other attempts in this direction is the caliber of the actors: This is a high-class cast, having fun with the material, and bringing a certain reality to some of the characters almost in spite of themselves.

Michael Keaton, from *Mr. Mom*, plays Johnny as a sweet, sort of gentle gangster who doesn't see any need to stir things up. His archenemy is Danny Vermin, played by Joe Piscopo, and there are a lot of other interesting characters around, including Marilu Henner as a sex bomb who spends some of her most intimate moments on top of a piano; Peter Boyle as an eminently reasonable mob patriarch, and Maureen Stapleton as Johnny's long-suffering mom.

The movie begins with the promise that it will grow into a great comedy. There's a title song out of left field, sung by Weird Al Yankovich, and then we see Johnny as a middle-aged pet store owner, stamping prices on his animals using one of those tape labeling machines they use in grocery stores. A kid tries to shoplift, and that inspires Johnny to remember the days when he began his own career in crime. The flashback then develops more or less along standard gangster movie lines, with of course a comic twist on every cliché. It's a little dizzying trying to spot all of the cameo roles as they go by; everybody who wandered onto the 20th Century Fox lot must have been hired to walk through this movie. but what gradually occurs to us is that we aren't laughing as often; the movie keeps trying, but it runs out of steam.

Too bad. And especially too bad for Joe Piscopo, who is such an accomplished mimic that he once literally had me thinking I was watching Jerry Lewis on "Saturday Night Live." Since masters of disguise are a fixture in gangster movies, why didn't they let Piscopo play a most-wanted criminal who was desperately trying to alter his appearance, and kept running up against incompetent gangland plastic surgeons? He plays Danny Vermin well enough, but the role seems rather limiting.

Just the Way You Are ★ ½
PG-13, 95 m., 1984

Kristy McNichol (Susan), Michael Ontkean (Peter), Kaki Hunter (Lisa), Andre Dussollier (Francois), Catherine Salviat (Nicole), Robert Carradine (Sam). Directed by Edouard Molinaro and produced by Leo L. Fuchs. Screenplay by Allan Burns.

It annoys me when trivial movies try to gain points by introducing serious themes. *Just the Way You Are*, for example, is a movie without a single brain in its head, and yet it pretends to be the story of people who learn to accept themselves, and each other, just the way they are. Despite this large message, there is still time in the movie for a ski resort, a hot-air balloon, and several one-night stands.

The movie stars Kristy McNichol as a classical flute player who wears a leg brace because of a crippling childhood disease, and who goes on a European concert tour so she can have time to decide whether she wants to marry a Dallas stockbroker. One guy (not the stockbroker, who remains a sexual enigma) has already struck out in the sack because her leg bothers him. In France, she gives a recital and then cancels two more so she can go to a ski resort. And to conceal her handicap, she has her leg put in a cast. Then she seeks to discover herself through a series of one-night stands. The critical turning point comes when her girlfriend rejects a handsome and wealthy ski manufacturer because he is missing one leg, and then Kristy falls in love with a guy and is afraid he will reject her if she tells him the truth.

By this point in the movie, any genuinely handicapped people in the audience will have already thrown their crutches at the screen. *Just the Way You Are* betrays not the slightest awareness of the self-sufficiency and pride that is so characteristic of most of the handicapped. It uses the handicap as a gimmick, and condescends to the character and the audience. But there's more, and it's worse.

If the movie had been simply a dreadful soap opera about Kristy, her leg, and her men, it would have been bad enough. But the addition of a love affair turns it into an endless Semi-Obligatory Lyrical Interlude, during which bad music plays while we watch ski scenes, fireside scenes, love scenes, the Gimp Olympics, and public displays of cuteness. The climax, I am afraid, is inevitable: The movie produces a hot-air balloon for a trip across the Alps to Switzerland.

I don't have any firm statistics on this, but I think we can say, as a general rule, that no truly great movie has ever been made in which there was a hot-air balloon. I include *Around the World in 80 Days*, despite Cantinflas. Among the casualties are *Bobby Deerfield*, with Al Pacino and Marthe Keller, floating over the Alps, that Disney picture where the family and their dog escaped from East Germany in a balloon, and the Luciano Pavarotti movie where he arrived by balloon at the food fight. Is it something about balloons?

Kagemusha ★ ★ ★ ★
PG, 160 m., 1980

Tatsuya Nakadai (Shingen and Kagemusha), Tsutomu Yamazaki (Nobukado), Kenichi Hagiwara (Katsuyori), Jinpachi Nezu (Bodyguard), Shuji Otaki (Fire General). Directed by Akira Kurosawa and produced by Kurosawa and Tomoyuki Tanaka. Screenplay by Kurosawa and Masato Ide.

Kagemusha, we learn, means "shadow warrior" in Japanese, and Akira Kurosawa's great film tells the story of a man who becomes the double, or shadow, of a great warrior. It also teaches the lesson that shadows or appearances are as important as reality, but that men cannot count on either shadows or reality.

Kagemusha is a samurai drama by the director who most successfully introduced the genre to the West (with such classics as *The*

Seven Samurai and *Yojimbo*), and who, at the age of seventy, made an epic that dares to wonder what meaning the samurai code—or any human code—really has in the life of an individual man. His film is basically the story of one such man, a common thief who, because of his astonishing resemblance to the warlord Shingen, is chosen as Shingen's double. When Shingen is mortally wounded in battle, the great Takeda clan secretly replaces him with the double—so their enemies will not learn that Shingen is dead. Thus begins a period of three years during which the kagemusha is treated by everyone, even his son and his mistresses, as if he were the real Shingen. Only his closest advisers know the truth.

But he is not Lord Shingen. And so every scene is undercut with irony. It is important that both friends and enemies believe Shengen is alive; his appearance, or shadow, creates both the respect of his clan and the caution of his enemies. If he is unmasked, he is useless; as Shingen's double, he can send hundreds of men to be killed, and his own guards will willingly sacrifice their lives for him. But as himself, he is worthless, and when he *is* unmasked, he's banished into the wilderness.

What is Kurosawa saying here? I suspect the answer can be found in a contrast between two kinds of scenes. His film contains epic battle scenes of astonishing beauty and scope. And then there are the intimate scenes in the throne room, the bedroom, the castles, and battlefield camps. The great battle scenes glorify the samurai system. Armies of thousands of men throw themselves heedlessly at death, for the sake of pride. But the intimate scenes undermine that glorious tradition; as everyone holds their breath, Shingen's double is tested in meetings with his son, his mistresses, and his horse. They know him best of all. If they are not fooled, all of the panoply and battlefield courage is meaningless, because the Tanaka clan has lost the leader who is their figurehead; the illusion that he exists creates the clan's reality.

Kurosawa made this film after a decade of personal travail. Although he is often considered the greatest living Japanese director, he was unable to find financial backing in Japan when he first tried to make *Kagemusha*.

He made a smaller film, *Dodeskaden*, which was not successful. He tried to commit suicide, but failed. He was backed by the Russians and went to Siberia to make the beautiful *Dersu Uzala* (1976), about a man of the wilderness. But *Kagemusha* remained his obsession, and he was finally able to make it only when Hollywood directors Francis Ford Coppola and George Lucas helped him find U.S. financing.

The film he finally made is simple, bold, and colorful on the surface, but very thoughtful. Kurosawa seems to be saying that great human endeavors (in this case, samurai wars) depend entirely on large numbers of men sharing the same fantasies or beliefs. It is entirely unimportant, he seems to be suggesting, whether or not the beliefs are based on reality—all that matters is that men accept them. But when a belief is shattered, the result is confusion, destruction, and death. At the end of *Kagemusha*, for example, the son of the real Lord Shingen orders his troops into a suicidal charge, and their deaths are not only unnecessary but meaningless, because they are not on behalf of the sacred person of the warlord.

There are great images in this film: Of a breathless courier clattering down countless steps, of men passing in front of a blood-red sunset, of a dying horse on a battlefield. But Kurosawa's last image—of the dying kagemusha floating in the sea, swept by tidal currents past the fallen standard of the Takeda clan—summarizes everything: ideas and men are carried along heedlessly by the currents of time, and historical meaning *seems* to emerge when both happen to be swept in the same way at the same time.

The Karate Kid ★ ★ ★ ★
PG, 126 m., 1984

Ralph Macchio (Daniel), Noriyuki "Pat" Morita (Miyagi), Elisabeth Shue (Ali), Martin Kove (Kreese), William Zabka (Johnny). Directed by John G. Avildsen and produced by Jerry Weintraub. Written by Robert Mark Kamen.

I didn't want to see this movie. I took one look at the title and figured it was either (a) a sequel to *Toenails of Vengeance*, or (b) an adventure pitting Ricky Schroeder against the Megaloth Man. I was completely wrong.

The Karate Kid was one of the nice surprises of 1984—an exciting, sweet-tempered, heart-warming story with one of the most interesting friendships in a long time. The friends come from different worlds. A kid named Daniel (Ralph Macchio) is a New Jersey teen-ager who moves with his mother to Los Angeles. An old guy named Miyagi (Pat Morita) is the Japanese janitor in their apartment building. When Daniel starts to date the former girlfriend of the toughest kid in the senior class, the kid starts pounding on Daniel's head on a regular basis. Daniel tries to fight back, but this is a Southern California kid, and so of course he has a black belt in karate. Enter Mr. Miyagi, who seems to be a harmless old eccentric with a curious hobby: He tries to catch flies with chopsticks. It turns out that Miyagi is a karate master, a student not only of karate fighting but of the total philosophy of the martial arts. He agrees to take Daniel as his student.

And then begins the wonderful center section of *The Karate Kid*, as the old man and the kid from Jersey become friends. Miyagi's system of karate instruction is off-beat, to say the least. He puts Daniel to work shining cars, painting fences, scrubbing the bottoms of pools. Daniel complains that he isn't learning karate, he's acting as free labor. But there is a system to Mr. Miyagi's training.

The Karate Kid was directed by Ralph Avildsen, who made *Rocky*. It ends with the same sort of climactic fight scene; Daniel faces his enemies in a championship karate tournament. But the heart of this movie isn't in the fight sequences, it's in the relationships. And in addition to Daniel's friendship with Miyagi, there's also a sweet romantic liaison with Ali (Elisabeth Shue), who is your standard girl from the right side of town and has the usual snobbish parents.

Macchio is an unusual, interesting choice for Daniel. He's not the basic handsome Hollywood teen-ager but a thin, tall, intense kid with a way of seeming to talk to himself. His delivery always sounds natural, even offhand; he never seems to be reading a line. He's a good, sound, interesting lead, but the movie really belongs to Pat Morita, an actor who has been around a long time (he was Arnold on "Happy Days") without ever

having a role anywhere near this good. Morita makes Miyagi into an example of applied serenity. In a couple of scenes where he has to face down a hostile karate coach, Miyagi's words are so carefully chosen they don't give the other guy any excuse to get violent; Miyagi uses the language as carefully as his hands or arms to ward off blows and gain an advantage. It's refreshing to see a completely original character like this old man. *The Karate Kid* is a sleeper with a title that gives you the wrong idea: It's one of 1984's best movies.

The Killing Fields ★ ★ ★ ★
R, 139 m., 1984

Sam Waterston (Sydney Schanberg), Dr. Haing S. Ngor (Dith Pran), John Malkovich (Al Rockoff), Craig T. Nelson (Military Attaché), Athol Fugard (Dr. Sundesval). Directed by Roland Joffe and produced by David Puttnam. Screenplay by Bruce Robinson.

There's a strange thing about stories based on what the movies insist on calling "real life." The haphazard chances of life, the unanticipated twists of fate, have a way of getting smoothed down into Hollywood formulas, so that what might once have happened to a real person begins to look more and more like what might once have happened to John Wayne. One of the risks taken by *The Killing Fields* is to cut loose from that tradition, to tell us a story that does not have a traditional Hollywood structure, and to trust that we'll find the characters so interesting that we won't miss the cliché. It is a risk that works, and that helps make this into a really affecting experience.

The "real life" story behind the movie is by now well-known. Sydney Schanberg, a correspondent for the *New York Times*, covered the invasion of Cambodia with the help of Dith Pran, a local journalist and translator. When the country fell to the communist Khmer Rouge, the lives of all foreigners were immediately at risk, and Schanberg got out along with most of his fellow Western correspondents. He offered Pran a chance to leave with him, but Pran elected to stay. And when the Khmer Rouge drew a bamboo curtain around Cambodia, Pran disappeared into a long silence. Back home in New York,

Schanberg did what he could to discover information about his friend; for example, he wrote about four hundred letters to organizations like the Red Cross. But it was a futile exercise, and Schanberg had given up his friend for dead, when one day four years later word came that Pran was still alive and had made it across the border to a refugee camp. The two friends were reunited, in one of the rare happy endings that come out of a period of great suffering.

As a human story, this is a compelling one. As a Hollywood story, it obviously will not do because the last half of the movie is essentially Dith Pran's story, told from his point of view. Hollywood convention has it that the American should fight his way back into the occupied country (accompanied by renegade Green Berets and Hell's Angels, and Rambo, if possible), blast his way into a prison camp, and save his buddy. That was the formula for *Uncommon Valor* and *Missing in Action,* two box-office hits, and in *The Deer Hunter* one friend went back to Vietnam to rescue another. Sitting in New York writing letters is not quite heroism on the same scale. And yet, what else could Schanberg do? And, more to the point, what else could Dith Pran do, in the four years of his disappearance, but try to disguise his origins and his education, and pass as an illiterate peasant—one of the countless prisoners of Khmer Rouge work camps? By telling his story, and by respecting it, *The Killing Fields* becomes a film of an altogether higher order than the Hollywood revenge thrillers.

The movie begins in the early days of the journalistic coverage of Cambodia. We meet Schanberg (Sam Waterston) and Pran (played by Dr. Haing S. Ngor, whose own story is an uncanny parallel to his character's), and we sense the strong friendship and loyalty that they share. We also absorb the conditions in the country, where warehouses full of Coca-Cola are blown up by terrorists who know a symbolic target when they see one. Life is a routine of hanging out at cafes and restaurants and official briefings, punctuated by an occasional trip to the front, where the American view of things does not seem to be reflected by the suffering that the correspondents witness.

The whole atmosphere of this period is suggested most successfully by the character of an American photographer, played by John Malkovich as a cross between a dopehead and a hard-bitten newsman. He is not stirred to action very easily, and still less easily stirred to caring, but when an occasion rises (for example, the need to forge a passport for Pran), he reveals the depth of his feeling. As the Khmer Rouge victory becomes inevitable, there are scenes of incredible tension, especially one in which Dith Pran saves the lives of his friends by some desperate fast talking with the cadres of adolescent rebels who would just as soon shoot them. Then there is the confusion of the evacuation of the U.S. Embassy and a last glimpse of Dith Pran before he disappears for four years.

In a more conventional film, he would, of course, have really disappeared, and we would have followed the point of view of the Schanberg character. But this movie takes the chance of switching points of view in midstream, and the last half of the film belongs to Dith Pran, who sees his country turned into an insane parody of a one-party state, ruled by the Khmer Rouge with instant violence and a savage intolerance for any reminders of the French and American presence of the colonial era. Many of the best scenes in the film's second half are essentially played without dialogue, as Pran works in the fields, disguises his origins, and waits for his chance.

The film is a masterful achievement on all the technical levels—it does an especially good job of convincing us with its Asian locations—but the best moments are the human ones, the conversations, the exchanges of trust, the waiting around, the sudden fear, the quick bursts of violence, the desperation. At the center of many of those scenes is Dr. Haing S. Ngor, a non-actor who was recruited for the role from the ranks of Cambodian refugees in California, and who brings to it a simple sincerity that is absolutely convincing. Sam Waterston is effective in the somewhat thankless role of Sydney Schanberg, and among the carefully drawn vignettes are Craig T. Nelson as a military attaché and Athol Fugard as Dr. Sundesval.

The American experience in Southeast Asia has given us a great film epic *(Apocalypse Now)* and a great drama *(The Deer*

Hunter). Here is the story told a little closer to the ground, of people who were not very important and not very powerful, who got caught up in events that were indifferent to them, but never stopped trying to do their best and their most courageous.

The King of Comedy ★ ★ ★
PG, 101 m., 1983

Robert De Niro (Rupert Pupkin), Jerry Lewis (Jerry Langford), Diahnne Abbott (Rita), Sandra Bernhard (Masha), Ed Herlihy (Himself). Directed by Martin Scorsese. Screenplay by Paul Zimmerman.

Martin Scorsese's *The King of Comedy* is one of the most arid, painful, wounded movies I've ever seen. It's hard to believe Scorsese made it; instead of the big-city life, the violence and sexuality of his movies like *Taxi Driver* and *Mean Streets*, what we have here is an agonizing portrait of lonely, angry people with their emotions all tightly bottled up. This is a movie that seems ready to explode—but somehow it never does. That lack of release seriously disturbed me the first time I saw *The King of Comedy*. I kept straining forward, waiting for the movie to let loose, and it kept frustrating me. Maybe that was the idea. This is a movie about rejection, with a hero who never admits that he has been rejected, and so there is neither comic nor tragic release—just the postponement of pain.

I left that first screening filled with dislike for the movie. Dislike, but not disinterest. Memories of *The King of Comedy* kept gnawing at me, and when people asked me what I thought about it, I said I wasn't sure. Then I saw the movie a second time, and it seemed to work better for me—maybe because I was able to watch without any expectations. I knew it wasn't an entertainment, I knew it didn't allow itself any emotional payoffs, I knew the ending was cynical and unsatisfactory, and so, with *those* discoveries no longer to be made, I was free to simply watch what was on the screen.

What I saw the second time, better than the first, were the performances by Robert De Niro, Jerry Lewis, Diahnne Abbott, and Sandra Bernhard, who play the movie's most important characters. They must have been difficult performances to deliver, be-cause there's almost no feedback in this movie. The actors can't bounce emotional energy off each other, because nobody *listens* in this film; everybody's just waiting for the other person to stop talking so they can start. And everybody's so emotionally isolated in this movie that they don't even seem able to guess what they're missing.

The movie stars De Niro, as Rupert Pupkin, a nerdish man in his thirties who fantasizes himself as a television star. He practices in his basement, holding conde-scending conversations with life-size cardboard cutouts of Liza Minnelli and Jerry Lewis. His dream is to get a stand-up comedy slot on the late-night talk show hosted by Lewis (whose name in the movie is Jerry Langford). The movie opens with Rupert's first meeting with Jerry; he barges into Jerry's limousine and is immediately on an obnoxious first-name basis. Jerry vaguely promises to check out Rupert's comedy routine, and the rest of the movie is devoted to Rupert's single-minded pursuit of fame. He arrives at Jerry's office, is politely brushed off, returns, is ejected, arrives at Jerry's country home with a "date" in tow, is ejected again, and finally decides to kidnap Jerry.

This *sounds* like an entertaining story, I suppose, but Scorsese doesn't direct a single scene for a payoff. The whole movie is an exercise in *cinema interruptus;* even a big scene in a bar, where Rupert triumphantly turns on the TV set to reveal himself on television, is deliberately edited to leave out the payoff shots—reaction shots of the amazed clientele. Scorsese doesn't want laughs in this movie, and he also doesn't want release. The whole movie is about the inability of the characters to get any kind of a positive response to their bids for recognition.

The King of Comedy is not, you may already have guessed, a fun movie. It is also not a bad movie. It is frustrating to watch, unpleasant to remember, and, in its own way, quite effective. It represents an enormous departure for Scorsese, whose movies teemed with life before he filmed this emotional desert, and whose camera used to prowl restlessly before he nailed it down this time. Scorsese and De Niro are the most creative, productive director/actor team in the movies right now, and the fact that they feel the freedom to make such an odd, stimulating, unsatisfying movie is good news, I guess. But *The King of Comedy* is the kind of film that makes you want to go and see a Scorsese movie.

Koyaanisqatsi ★ ★ ★
NO MPAA RATING, 87 m., 1983

Produced and directed by Godfrey Reggio.

ko·yaa·nis·qatsi, n. (Hopi). 1. crazy life. 2. life in turmoil. 3. life disintegrating. 4. life out of balance. 5. a state of life that calls for another way of living.

I give the definition because it is the key to the movie. Without it, you could make a sincere mistake. *Koyaanisqatsi* opens with magnificent images out of nature: great canyons and limitless deserts and a world without man. Through the use of speeded-up images, clouds climb the sides of mountains and speed across the sky, their shadows painting the landscape. Then the movie turns to images of smokestacks, factories, and expressways. There is an assumption on the part of the filmmaker, Godfrey Reggio, that we'll immediately get the message. And the message, I think, is that nature is wonderful, but that American civilization is a rotten despoiler that is creating a "crazy life."

But I am irreverent, and given to my own thoughts during the film. After I have admired its visionary photography (this is a beautiful movie) and fallen under the spell of its music (an original sound track by the distinguished composer Philip Glass), there is still time to think other thoughts, such as:

This film has one idea, a simplistic one. It contrasts the glory of nature with the mess made by man. But man *is* a messy beast, given to leaving reminders of his presence all over the surface of planet Earth. Although a Hopi word is used to evoke unspoiled nature, no Hopis are seen, and the contrast in the movie doesn't seem to be between American Indian society and Los Angeles expressways, but between expressways and a beautiful world *empty* of man. Thanks, but no thanks.

I had another problem. *All* of the images in this movie are beautiful, even the images of man despoiling the environment. The first shots of smokestacks are no doubt supposed to make us recoil in horror, but actually I thought they looked rather noble. The shots of the expressways are also two-edged. Given the clue in the title, we can consider them as an example of life out of control. *Or*—and here's the catch—we can marvel at the fast-action photography and reflect about all those people moving so quickly to their thousands of individual destinations. What a piece of work is a man! And what expressways he builds!

Koyaanisqatsi, then, is an invitation to knee-jerk environmentalism of the most sentimental kind. It is all images and music. There is no overt message except the obvious one (the Grand Canyon is prettier than Manhattan). It has been hailed as a vast and sorrowful vision, but to what end? If the people in all those cars on all those expressways are indeed living crazy lives, their problem is not the expressway (which is all that makes life in L.A. manageable) but perhaps social facts such as unemployment, crime, racism, drug abuse, and illiteracy—issues so complicated that a return to nature seems like an elitist joke at their expense. Having said that, let me add that *Koyaanisqatsi* is an impressive visual and listening experience, that Reggio and Glass have made wonderful pictures and sounds, and that this film is a curious throwback to the 1960s, when it would have been a short subject to be viewed through a marijuana haze. Far-out.

Lassiter ★ ★ ★
R, 100 m., 1984

Tom Selleck (Lassiter), Jane Seymour (Sara), Lauren Hutton (Kari), Bob Hoskins (Becker). Directed by Roger Young and produced by Albert S. Ruddy. Screenplay by David Taylor.

Here's a basic rule about thrillers: Style is a lot more important than plot. What happens isn't nearly as important as how it happens and who it happens to—and if you doubt me, think back over to your favorite James Bond movies. *Lassiter* is a good example. Here's a movie with a plot spun out of thin air. That doesn't matter, though, because the movie is acted and directed with such style that we have fun slogging through the silliness. And part of the fun comes from watching Tom

Selleck, the hero of "Magnum, P.I.," in a movie that does him justice. He was wasted in *High Road to China*, which looked like a *Raiders of the Lost Ark* rip-off with Selleck plugged into the Harrison Ford role. *Lassiter* is a movie that seems to have been made with Selleck in mind, and he delivers—he's clearly one of the few actors capable of making the leap from TV to the big screen.

The movie stars Selleck as Nick Lassiter, an American thief in London on the eve of World War II. A hardheaded police inspector (Bob Hoskins) gets the goods on him and makes him a flat offer: Either Lassiter breaks into the German Embassy and steals $10 million in jewels, or he goes into the slammer. Lassiter goes for the jewels. That involves seducing the kinky, sadistic German countess (Lauren Hutton) who has the diamonds in her bedroom inside the well-guarded embassy. The movie misses a bet here: It spends a lot of time establishing the Hutton character (who has an unusual taste for blood), and we see her killing one of her bed partners. Yet when Lassiter finally goes to bed with her, the movie cuts to the morning after instead of showing how he survived the night. And there's no big final confrontation with the countess; at a crucial moment, Lassiter knocks her cold, and that's that.

Other characters are handled more carefully. We meet Lassiter's sweet girlfriend (Jane Seymour, looking more than ever like a perfect porcelain portrait); Hoskins, who played the mob boss in *The Long Good Friday*, and assorted creeps. Selleck occupies this world effortlessly. He is a big man, and yet he moves gracefully, wears a tuxedo well, makes charming small talk, doesn't seem to be straining himself during the fight scenes, and, in general, stands at the center of a lot of action as if he belonged there. He would make a good James Bond. *Lassiter* knows that, and knows that style and movement are a lot more important than making sense of everything. I squirm when the action stops in a thriller while the characters explain everything to one another; I think of those speeches as memos from the screenwriter to the director. *Lassiter* stops for nothing.

The Last Dragon ★ ★ ½
PG-13, 110 m., 1985

Taimak (Leroy), Vanity (Laura), Julius J. Carry III (Sho'Nuff), Chris Murney (Eddie). Directed by Michael Schultz and produced by Rupert Hitzig. Screenplay by Louis Venosta.

The Last Dragon opens with its hero learning from his karate master that he has at last reached the final level of realization; he no longer needs a master, because what remains to be learned can only be found within himself. When he achieves the final level, he will know it because of a glow all over his body. This is not an idle promise; by the end of the film, the hero glows like somebody who has just tapped into the wrong power lines. Setups like that are obligatory in karate movies; there's an unwritten law that the movie must begin with five minutes of solemn, portentous philosophy before the action can begin. Once past its prologue, however, *The Last Dragon* turns into a funny, high-energy combination of karate, romance, rock music, and sensational special effects. It's so entertaining that I could almost recommend it—if it weren't for an idiotic subplot about a gangster and his girlfriend, a diversion that brings the movie to a dead halt every eight or nine minutes.

The Last Dragon stars two remarkably attractive and likable actors, who have one name apiece. The hero is played by Taimak, a twenty-year-old karate student who has not acted before, but who has a natural screen presence, and the heroine is Vanity, the rock singer discovered by Prince and used as a warm-up act at some of his concerts prior to the *Purple Rain* tour. Of Vanity, let it be said that she has the sort of rapport with the camera that makes us like her instantly; she has a sunny smile, and an inner happiness, and in the middle of this plot about gangsters and night clubs and bloody fights, she floats serenely, a joy to behold. In the same year, Prince introduced two electrifying actresses, Appolonia Kotero from *Purple Rain*, and now Vanity.

There's another engaging actor in the movie, a man named Julius J. Carry III, who describes himself as the Shogun of Harlem, and who presides over a hilarious early scene where he marches into a movie theater full of Bruce Lee fans and threatens to fight everyone in the house. Taimak is in the front row, so loyal to the Bruce Lee mystique that he's eating his popcorn with chopsticks, and after he has a showdown with the Shogun, it becomes inevitable that they will have to endure a fight to the finish. Meanwhile, Vanity is working as a video disc jockey at a private club, and a gangster (Chris Murney) decrees that she should play a video he has produced, starring his girlfriend (Faith Prince, no relation). Vanity refuses, and she is rescued from the gangster's thugs not once but twice by the brave Taimak, who barehandedly demolishes the hitmen.

That sets up the movie's basic situation: Taimak must defeat both the Shogun and the gangster—and fall in love with the girl, of course. There are also some nice scenes involving Taimak's father, who proudly runs New York's best black pizza parlor, and his little brother, who is a lot more street-smart than the otherworldly karate master.

The Last Dragon surrounds this simple plot with a lot of technology. The movie is backed by Berry Gordy's Motown Records, which has supplied it with a digital sound track, and the scenes in the disco make much use of back-projected music videos and scenes from old Bruce Lee movies. This is an expensive, high tech production. But then there's that whole business of the gangsters. They've been borrowed from a hundred other movies, they say things that have been said a hundred other times, and they walk around draining the movie of its vitality. They're tired old clichés getting in the way of the natural energy of Taimak, Vanity, and the Shogun character. Take out the gangsters, pump up the Shogun role, give Taimak and Vanity a little more screen time, and you'd have a great entertainment instead of simply a great near-miss.

The Last Flight of Noah's Ark ½★
G, 97 m., 1980

Elliott Gould (Noah Dugan), Genevieve Bujold (Bernadette), Ricky Schroeder (Bobby), Tammy Lauren (Julie), Vincent Gardenia (Stoney), John Fujioka (Cleveland). Directed by Charles Jarrott and produced by Ron Miller. Screenplay by Steven W. Carabatsos, Sandy Glass, and George Arthur Bloom.

Walt Disney's *The Last Flight of Noah's Ark* is a dreadful movie, bankrupt of creative imagination—an Identi-kit film, assembled from familiar pieces but with no identity of its own. It's so depressingly predictable that in the last half hour we're sitting there thinking: Let's see . . . the raft has put out to sea, so there has to be at least one shark attack and one bad storm before they're rescued. There are.

What's most discouraging about this film is that, with its G rating and Disney trademark, it will no doubt attract children. Parents know Disney movies are OK because there won't be any nudity or profanity. But isn't it also poisonous for kids to be exposed to stupid characters, lame-brained plots, and humorless "gags?" To a movie lacking the sense of excitement, invention, and fun that children's movies should have above all else? Isn't it damaging to expose a child to two hours of dreck?

The plot could possibly have led to a much better movie. It's about how pilot Elliott Gould is hired by missionary Genevieve Bujold to pilot a decrepit old B-26 to a Pacific island, where she hopes to start a missionary colony. The plane is loaded with breeding animals, and, of course, with two pint-sized stowaways (Ricky Schroeder and Tammy Lauren). The plane crash-lands on an unmapped island, the survivors run into two Japanese soldiers who think World War II is still being fought, and everybody pitches in to turn the top half of the airplane shell into a raft (thus Maurice Jarre's obnoxiously insipid song, "Half of Me," which is sung twice to no avail.)

If any effort had been made to explore the possible realities of this situation, the movie might have been more absorbing. But no. The Japanese are turned into offensive cartoon stereotypes, the kids go swimming, and between Gould and Bujold there springs up one of those Disney relationships that consist of fighting a lot and then suddenly falling into romanticized respect, interrupted by chaste kisses.

There are no high points to the movie, but there is a real low point at the end. The raft is launched, it floats for an undetermined number of days, and then our heroes are rescued by the U.S. *Coast Guard!* Therefore, they must have floated into U.S. coastal waters. Therefore, they floated *halfway across the Pacific* and the movie hasn't even gotten excited about it. This movie isn't just boring, it's bored.

The Last Metro ★ ★ ★
NO MPAA RATING, 133 m., 1980

Catherine Deneuve (Marion Steiner), Gerard Depardieu (Bernard Granger), Jean Poiret (Jean-Loup), Heinz Bennent (Lucas Steiner), Andrea Ferreol (Arlette), Paulette Dubost (Germaine), Jean-Louis Richard (Daxlat). Directed by Francois Truffaut. Screenplay by Truffaut, Suzanne Schiffman, and Jean-Claude Grumberg.

Francois Truffaut said he wanted to satisfy three old dreams by making *The Last Metro*. He wanted to take the camera backstage in a theater, to evoke the climate of the Nazi occupation of France, and to give Catherine Deneuve the role of a responsible woman. He has achieved the first and last dreams, but he doesn't evoke the occupation well enough to make *The Last Metro* more than a sentimental fantasy.

The film takes place backstage, and below-stage, at a theater in Paris. The theater's director is German Jew (Heinz Bennent) who already has fled from Nazi Germany and now, with the occupation of Paris, goes into permanent hiding in the basement of his theater. Upstairs, his wife (Deneuve) spreads the rumor that he has fled to South America. Then she relays his instructions as the theater attempts to save itself from bankruptcy by presenting a new production.

There are many other characters in the movie, which at times resembles Truffaut's history of a film production in *Day for Night*. Gerard Depardieu plays the leading man for the new production. The supporting cast includes a young woman who will do anything for a job in the theater, an older woman of ambiguous sexuality, an avuncular stage manager, a gay director, and a powerful critic who is such an evil monster that he must surely have been inspired by a close Truffaut friend. Most of the movie's events take place within the walls of the theater; this is a backstage film, not a war film. We see the rehearsals under way, with Bennent downstairs listening through an air duct. There are the romantic intrigues among the cast members. There are occasional walk-throughs by Nazis. There are moments of great danger, somewhat marred by the fact that Truffaut does not resolve them realistically. And there is an unforgivably sentimental ending that ties up everything without solving anything.

The problem, I think, is that Truffaut sees the Nazi presence in Paris simply as a plot device to create tension within his theatrical troupe. It is ever so much more dramatic if the show must go on despite raids, political directives, and an electrical blackout that requires the stagehands to power a generator by bicycle-power. It's all too cute. Nobody seems to *really* understand that there's a war on out there. And yet, within the unfortunate limitations that Truffaut sets for himself, he does deliver an entertaining movie. Catherine Deneuve is as beautiful as ever, and as enigmatic (it is typical of her performance that at the end we have to wait for the screenplay to tell us who she does, or does not, really love). Depardieu is gangly and sincere, a strong presence. Bennent, as the husband downstairs, is wan and courageous in the Paul Henreid role. And the most fascinating character in the cast is of course the villain, Daxlat, the pro-Nazi critic. He at least seems in touch with the true evil that the others, and Truffaut, see as backdrop.

The Last Starfighter ★ ★ ½
PG, 100 m., 1984

Lance Guest (Alex Rogan), Dan O'Herlihy (Grig), Catherine Mary Stewart (Maggie), Barbara Bosson (Jane Rogan), Robert Preston (Centauri). Directed by Nick Castle and produced by Gary Adelson and Edward O. Denault. Screenplay by Jonathan Betuel.

The way to get rich, they say is to invent something that's cheap and habit-forming, and get a patent on it. I guess video games would qualify. Kids pump quarters into them by the hour, turning into video junkies as they watch gorillas climbing little electronic ladders. Are the games educational? Sure, if you want to grow up to be a professional video game player.

Those arcade video games had to come from somewhere, and *The Last Starfighter* has an interesting theory to explain why they seemed to pop up all over the world, almost overnight. They came from outer space.

Just as I've always suspected. That's right, they were put on Earth by representatives of the Star League, who use them as testing devices. If you break a record on a video game, they come and get you and turn you into an intergalactic fighter pilot. Meanwhile, your place on Earth is taken by a robot.

The Last Starfighter starts in a trailer camp in California. We know it's in California because all the residents are fugitives from mainstream life-styles. A kid (Lance Guest) lives in the camp and sets a record on a Starfighter game, and a Star League recruiter (Robert Preston) whisks him into outer space to join the battle against the evil race of Ko-Dan. At first the kid is a little reluctant. He'd rather stay on Earth and neck with his girlfriend. But he's persuaded that he's all that stands between the Ko-Dan and intergalactic civilization as we know it. So he agrees to become a Starfighter, and is tutored by a wise old lizard-warrior named Grig, who is played by Dan O'Herlihy in makeup inspired by the heartbreak of psoriasis.

The Last Starfighter is not a terrifically original movie. The video game concept seems inspired by Walt Disney's *Tron,* and the battles in space are such close copies of the Star Wars movies that George Lucas might have a lawsuit. For example, when Grig gives the kids lessons in how to fire from the cockpit of his rocket, the cockpit's swivel chair looks directly inspired by the original *Star Wars.* If the movie isn't original in its special effects, it tries to make up for that in the trailer camp scenes. A large gallery of eccentric supporting actors is trotted onscreen, all with a few colorful lines to say, and there's a subplot about the love affair between the kid's girlfriend and the robot who has replaced the kid (every time the girl tries to lick his ear, he gets a short circuit).

This is all pretty lame material. *The Last Starfighter* is a well-made movie. The special effects are competent. The acting is good, and I enjoyed Robert Preston's fast-talking *Music Man* reprise (we've got trouble, right here in the galaxy) and the gentle wit of Dan O'Herlihy's extraterrestrial. But the final spark was missing, the final burst of inspiration that might have pulled all these concepts and inspirations and retreads together into a good movie.

Let's Spend the Night Together
★ ★ ½
PG, 94 m., 1983

Featuring The Rolling Stones. Directed by Hal Ashby and produced by Ronald L. Schwary.

It all comes down to the difference between a "concert film" and a documentary. *Let's Spend the Night Together* is essentially a concert film—a film recording an "ideal" Rolling Stones concert, put together out of footage shot at several outdoor and indoor Stones concerts. If that's what you want, enjoy this movie. I wanted more. I would have been interested in a film exploring the phenomenon of the Rolling Stones, who bill themselves as the greatest rock 'n' roll band in the world, and are certainly the most durable. I would have liked to know more about the staging of a modern rock concert, which is arguably the most sensually overpowering nonwartime spectacle in human history, and which may have been invented, in form and in its focus on a single charismatic individual, at Hitler's mass rallies. I would have liked to know more about Mick Jagger; how does it feel for an educated, literate, civilized man in his early forties, with a head for figures and a gift for contracts and negotiations, to strut with a codpiece before tens of thousands of screaming, drug-crazed fans?

Let's Spend the Night Together does not answer these questions—nor, to be fair, was it intended to. It is wall-to-wall music. The movie sells well in home video form; it's a cinematic Top Forty with Jagger and the Stones performing many of their best-known hits. But after a certain point it grows monotonous. At the beginning of the film I was caught up in the Stones' waves of sound energy, and fascinated by Jagger's exhilarating, limitless onstage energy. By the end of the film I was simply stunned, and not even "(Can't Get No) Satisfaction" could quite rouse me.

The movie was directed by Hal Ashby, a feature director whose credits include *Shampoo* and *The Last Detail.* It was reportedly photographed with twenty-one cameras, under the direction of cinematographers Caleb Deschanel and Gerald Feil. They've got a lot of good stuff on film, but they haven't bro-

ken any new ground. The best rock documentary is still *Woodstock* (1970), and the
best concert film is probably Bette Midler's
Divine Madness (1980). The Stones have
been filmed more powerfully before, too, in
Gimme Shelter, the stunning 1969 documentary of the Stones' Altamont concert, at
which a man was killed.

The worst passages in *Let's Spend the
Night Together* are the songs in which Ashby
and his collaborators try to get seriously
symbolic. There is, for example, a montage
of images from a suffering world: starving
children, a Buddhist monk immolating himself, the skeleton-like bodies of famine victims, decapitated heads of political
prisoners, etc. The idea, I guess, is to provide visual counterpoint to the Stones'
apocalyptic images. The effect is disgusting;
this particular movie has not earned the
right to exploit those real images.

The best passages involve Jagger, who is
just about the whole show, with the exception of a truncated Keith Richards solo and a
strange interlude during which would-be
beauty queens invade the stage and dance
along to "Honky Tonk Woman." Jagger is,
as always, the arrogant hermaphrodite,
strutting proudly before his fans and conducting the songs, the band, and the audience with his perfectly timed body
movements. There is an exciting moment
when he climbs down into the crowd and,
carrying a hand-held mike, sings as he is
lifted on a surge of security guards from one
side of the auditorium to another.

It's fun, but it's about the only time we see
the audience in this movie; Ashby apparently made a directorial decision to keep the
audience in long-shot, making them into a
collective, pulsating mass. But that limits his
possibilities for setting up visual rhythms in
his editing. In such landmarks rock films as
A Hard Day's Night (1964) and *Woodstock*,
the audience provided not only counterpoint
but also emotional feedback. *Let's Spend the
Night Together* seems to have been pretty
closely calculated as just simply the record of
a performance, and if that's what you want,
that's what you get.

Lianna ★ ★ ★ ½
R, 110 m., 1983

Linda Griffiths (Lianna), Jane Hallaren
(Ruth), Jon DeVries (Dick), Jo Henderson
(Sandy), John Sayles (Jerry). Directed by
John Sayles. Produced by Jeffrey Nelson
and Maggie Renzi. Screenplay by Sayles.

Movies are good at showing us people who
make great changes in their lives, but not so
good at showing us the consequences of
those changes. It's easier to present the sudden dramatic revelation than to follow
through into all the messy complications in
everyday life. John Sayles's *Lianna*, the story
of a woman who discovers in her early thirties that she is a lesbian, follows through.
Instead of being the simple, dramatic story
of a woman who "comes out," it is the complex, interesting story of what happens then.

The woman is named Lianna (Linda
Griffiths). When she was an undergraduate,
she fell in love with her teacher—a pattern
she is about to repeat. Her husband is a film
professor and the father of their two small
children. He tends to treat her like one of the
children, lecturing to the general audience at
the dinner table as if his wife was about as
bright as the kids. He is a boor. Lianna,
unhappy, tries to change her life. She signs
up for a night class in child psychology, and
finds herself attracted to the professor, a
woman who has a quick sense of humor and
really seems to care about her students.

The woman, Ruth (Jane Hallaren), has
been a lesbian for years, and is attracted to
Lianna. But it is Lianna who makes the first,
subtle moves, staying after class for a moment's chat, just as perhaps she did years ago
with her husband. The two women become
lovers fairly quickly, and although there are
love scenes, the movie is not really about that
side of their relationship. If *Personal Best* was
an exploration of the physical aspects of les-
bianism, *Lianna* explores the consequences.
They are many. Lianna's husband throws her
out and tries to block access to their children.
Lianna's oldest friend, Sandy, is suddenly
cold and distant. Ruth, a little surprised at the
intensity of the affair, confesses that she has a
long-standing relationship with another
woman in another city. Lianna rents a room
off-campus and begins a life-style that is free,
yes, but also lonely and filled with guilt.

As *Lianna* looks into the large and small things that have changed in the life of its heroine, we become increasingly aware of the perception of the filmmaker, John Sayles, who wrote, directed, and edited. In this movie and his previous work, *Return of the Secaucus Seven*, he seems in touch with the kinds of changes that some Americans in their thirties are going through; his movies are cinematic versions of Gail Sheehey's *Passages*. He is attentive to what is said, what is worn, what attitudes are taken, what goes unsaid—and he is particularly interested, in both movies, in the ways that a generation raised to "do your own thing" now tries to decide when personal freedom ends and responsibility begins.

It's in that particular area that *Lianna* is a little shaky. It never quite dealt, I thought, with the issue of Lianna's two children. Although Lianna's lover is a child psychologist and Lianna herself seems to be a responsible and loving mother as the film opens, the kids are sort of left hanging. There are a couple of brief scenes with the kids, but no real resolution of the questions that a newly gay mother would have to answer. (Since the husband is presented as such a twerp, this absence of follow through is doubly bothering.) Still, in many other scenes, including two in which Lianna has a subtly class-conscious affair with a woman in the armed services, *Lianna* is an intelligent, perceptive movie. And the performances, especially by Griffiths and Hallaren, are so specific that we're never looking at "lesbians"—only at people.

Little Darlings ★ ★
R, 95 m., 1980

Tatum O'Neal (Ferris), Kristy McNichol (Angel), Armand Assante (Gary), Matt Dillon (Randy), Maggie Blye (Ms. Bright), Krista Errickson (Cinder). Directed by Ronald F. Maxwell and produced by Stephen J. Friedman. Screenplay by Kimi Peck and Dalene Young.

There's one moment in *Little Darlings* that very nearly redeems a lot of the movie's weaknesses. It belongs to the young actress Kristy McNichol. She plays a fifteen-year-old who has just experienced sex for the first time. It was not, of course, quite like she expected it to be. She sits quietly in a corner of a deserted summer cottage, her thoughts a million miles away from her teen-age boyfriend. At last she says, "I feel so lonely."

The feelings implied in that single line of dialogue are completely true to the scene and to the character. She is lonely because she has suddenly and rather unhappily passed on from the ranks of pubescent girls. She is now an individual, possessed of the sometimes uncomfortable freedom to make decisions. Sexual intercourse, she tells the boy, "made me feel like you could see right through me." She slept with him for childish reasons, but now, we feel, she will never approach the decision so casually again.

Because this key scene is played so honestly (and because another key scene involving Tatum O'Neal is also written and acted with sensitivity), *Little Darlings* earns the right to its subject matter—even though some of the scenes unashamedly exploit the subject matter.

The movie is about two fifteen-year-old girls at summer camp, and how they're egged on into a bet about who will be the first to lose her virginity. The movie begins with inexperienced teen-agers who have an uninformed, frivolous attitude toward sex, and it moves rather awkwardly through would-be comic scenes in which O'Neal and McNichol attempt to seduce their target males and win the bet. But the scenes in which they actually confront the realities of sex are handled so thoughtfully and tastefully that they almost seem to belong to another movie.

That's possibly because *Little Darlings* really wanted to be two movies at once: A fairly serious film about teen-agers and sex, but also a box-office winner like *Animal House* or *Meatballs*. That's why we get awkwardly forced comedy like the food-fight scene. The movie also suffers from uncertain direction. When O'Neal and McNichol first meet on the bus to camp, for example, the way in which they get involved in a fight is very unconvincing. Their whole personal feud, in fact, feels phony, and parts of this movie are so badly handled that we can only marvel that *Little Darlings* somehow does succeed in treating the awesome and scary subject of sexual initiation with some of the dignity it deserves.

The Little Drummer Girl ★ ★
R, 155 m., 1984

Diane Keaton (Charlie), Yorgo Voyagis
(Joseph), Klaus Kinski (Kurtz), Sami Frey
(Khalil). Directed by George Roy Hill and
produced by Robert L. Crawford. Screenplay
by Loring Mandel.

The Little Drummer Girl lacks the two essential qualities it needs to work: It's not
comprehensible, and it's not involving.
They made a real effort to pull of the daunting task of filming John Le Carre's labyrinthine bestseller, but the movie doesn't
work. It is so jammed with characters and
incidents and mystifications that everything
seems to get equal, cursory attention. And
not a single one of the characters comes
alive. Not Kurtz, the brusque, scarred,
touchingly human chief of Israeli intelligence, who was my favorite character in the
book. Not Charlie, the American actress
who is recruited by the Israelis to play a
dangerous double game with a Palestinian
terrorist. And certainly not Joseph, the man
who is delegated to make Charlie fall in love
with him. Those three characters, Kurtz
and Charlie especially, are among the most
vivid creations in recent fiction. In this
movie version they are pale shadows of the
people I imagined as I was turning the pages.

At least I have the advantage of having
read the novel. If you haven't read the book,
I suspect that a lot of *The Little Drummer Girl*
will escape you, unless you focus on every
piece of information with unwavering attention. The book was long and complicated,
weaving a story of intrigue, double-cross,
and betrayal. The movie is relatively long,
but not long enough to do justice to Le
Carre's plot. What's amazing is how many
plot details are in the movie. Most of the
characters turn up (even such minor walk-
ons as Charlie's agent and the fake Red Cross
men), and most of the twists and turns of the
events are here. But the movie maintains a
breathless pace to squeeze everything in; at
the end we're stunned with information, but
not moved by emotion. There is no time to
linger on the emotional significance of the
story—and surely what distinguished the Le
Carre book was the way it combined a topical
thriller with a deeper appreciation of the
human issues involved in the Middle East.

Because the screenplay doesn't really provide the characters with time and space to
grow and breathe, it may be unfair to criticize the actors: How much can you do with
the Cliff's Notes edition of a story? Nevertheless, the movie has crucial failures in
the two key roles. Diane Keaton's Charlie is
not young enough, passionate enough or, if I
may say so, sluttish enough, to recapture the
wild, sloppy character in Le Carre's book.
And Klaus Kinski's performance as Kurtz
seems intended for a standard thriller. There
is no sense of the man's past, of his intelligence, of his torn emotions, of the doubts
he has about the job that Charlie is being
asked to do.

What would have helped? Maybe the director, George Roy Hill, could have pared
the story down to one specific element, such
as Charlie's recruitment, training, and mission. Maybe we didn't need the scenes involving the capture of the red Mercedes, or
the surveillance in the town square, or the
stuff about Charlie's theatrical career in
London. Even then, we'd be left with performances that did not resonate. It's not that
Keaton and Kinski are bad actors, just that
they were miscast. Unfortunately, there has
hardly been another novel in recent years for
which the casting of the movie version was
more crucial.

Local Hero ★ ★ ★ ★
PG, 112 m., 1983

Burt Lancaster (Happer), Peter Riegert
(Mac), Peter Capaldi (Danny), Fulton McKay
(Ben), Denis Lawson (Urquhart). Directed by
Bill Forsyth and produced by David Puttnam.
Screenplay by Forsyth.

Here is a small film to treasure; a loving,
funny, understated portrait of a small Scottish town and its encounter with a giant oil
company. The town is tucked away in a spar-
kling little bay, and is so small that everybody is well aware of everybody else's
foibles. The oil company is run by an eccentric billionaire (Burt Lancaster) who would
really rather have a comet named after him
than own all the oil in the world. And what
could have been a standard plot about con-
glomerates and ecology, etc., turns instead
into a wicked study of human nature.

The movie opens in Houston, but quickly

moves to the fishing village of Ferness. The oil company assigns an earnest young American (Peter Riegert) and a whimsical Scot (Peter Capaldi) to go to Ferness, and buy it up, lock, stock, and beachline, for a North Sea oil-refining complex. This is a simpler job than it appears, since a lot of the locals are all too willing to soak the oil company for its millions of dollars, sell the beach, and go in search of the bright lights of Edinburgh. But there are complications. One of them is old Ben, the cheerful philosopher who lives in a shack on the beach. It turns out that the beach has been the legal property of Ben's family for four centuries, ever since an ancestor did a favor for the king. And Ben doesn't want to sell: "Who'd look after the beach then? It would go to pieces in a short matter of time."

The local negotiations are handled by the innkeeper, Urquhart (Denis Lawson). He also is the accountant, and sort of the mayor, I guess, and is so much in love with his pretty wife that they're forever dashing upstairs for a quickie. Meanwhile, Riegert and Capaldi fall under the spell of the town, settle into its rhythms, become wrapped up in its intrigues, and, in general, are co-opted by a place whose charms are seductive.

What makes this material really work is the low-key approach of the writer-director, Bill Forsyth, who also made the charming *Gregory's Girl* and has the patience to let his characters gradually reveal themselves to the camera. He never hurries, and as a result, *Local Hero* never drags: Nothing is more absorbing than human personalities, developed with love and humor. Some of the payoffs in this film are sly and subtle, and others generate big laughs. Forsyth's big scenes are his little ones, including a heartfelt, whiskey-soaked talk between the American and the innkeeper, and a scene where the visitors walk on the beach and talk about the meaning of life. By the time Burt Lancaster reappears at the end of the film, to personally handle the negotiations with old Ben, *Local Hero* could hardly have anything but a happy ending. But it's a fairly close call.

Lone Wolf McQuade ★ ★ ★ ½
107 m., 1983

Chuck Norris (J.J. McQuade), David Carradine (Rawley), Barbara Carrera (Lola), Robert Beltran (Kayo Ramas), Sharon Farrell (Molly), Leon Isaac Kennedy (Jackson). Directed by Steve Carver.

To really understand *Lone Wolf McQuade*, you have to go back to those original spaghetti Westerns that made Clint Eastwood a star. They weren't great movies, and some critics attacked them for trashing the classic forms of the Western. But they had presence, style, and energy, and at the center of them they had a perfectly realized hero in Clint Eastwood. He was called The Man With No Name. He dealt violence with implacable fury. He stood at the middle of the maelstrom and remained untouched. And, in his own way, he was powerfully charismatic. Eastwood and Sergio Leone, his director, created a new kind of Western, pared down to its bare essentials of men and guns, horses and deserts, sweat and flies, and rotgut.

Now comes Chuck Norris. He's been in a series of karate and kung fu movies that were almost always better than average—but not a lot better than average. (The best of them was *Eye for an Eye*, directed by Steve Carver, who also directed *McQuade*.) The most you could say for a Chuck Norris film was that it did not have downright contempt for its action audiences; it tried to be better than the interchangeable chop-socky movies from Hong Kong, and Norris made an energetic, likable star. What Norris was really looking for in all those pictures, I guess, was the right character. Like Eastwood's Man With No Name, he needed a personality that would fit, that would contain his kung fu skills and allow him ways of expression not limited to flying fists and deadly elbows. That's what he's found in *Lone Wolf McQuade*.

This is an action movie. It makes no apology for that. But it's high-style action. Norris plays J.J. McQuade, a renegade modern-day Texas Ranger who walks alone, likes to work with machine guns, deals out justice on the spot, and hardly ever says much of anything. The movie surrounds him with a gallery of interesting characters, played by colorful stars: David Carradine is Rawley, the evil local criminal and karate master; Barbara Carrera is lovely, as usual, as Carradine's wife and Norris's mistress; Robert Beltran plays Kaya Ramas, Norris's Mexican-American sidekick; Leon Issac Kennedy is the federal officer; grizzled L.Q. Jones lopes through a few scenes; and Sharon Farrell is counterpoint as Norris's former wife. All of these people are thrown together into a plot that is, of course, essentially meaningless. But the movie respects the plot, and keeps it moving, and a lot of excitement is generated.

Series characters always have one archetypal scene. With Eastwood, it was the time he killed three men with one bullet. Lone Wolf McQuade has a classic. He's shot. They think he's dead. They bury him in his supercharged, customized pickup truck. He comes to. Pours a beer over his head. Floors the accelerator and drives that mother right out of the grave. You get the idea.

The Lonely Guy ★ ½
R, 91 m., 1984

Steve Martin (Larry), Charles Grodin (Warren), Judith Ivey (Iris), Steve Lawrence (Jack), Robyn Douglass (Danielle), Dr. Joyce Brothers (Herself). Directed and produced by Arthur Hiller. Screenplay by Ed Weinberger and Stan Daniels.

I saw *The Lonely Guy* all by myself. It was one of those Saturday afternoons where the snow is coming down gray and mean, and you can't even get a decent recorded message on the answering machines of strangers.

There was a warm glow coming out of the windows of a tanning parlor. At a table in the window of a hot dog joint, three bums were laughing warmly, sharing a joke and a cup of coffee. I stuck my hands down deep into the pockets of my jeans and hunched my shoulders against the cold. I tried to force a smile to my frozen lips: Hey, I was going to the movies!

I walked up to the ticket booth of the Esquire theater and with a flourish presented my Plitt Theaters pass.

"What's this?" asked the ticket person.

"A pass to the Plitt Theaters," I said.

"I don't know," the person said. "I'll have to phone and check it out." I turned

my back to the wind until the pass was verified, and then walked into the theater's priceless and irreplaceable Art Deco lobby, which cheered me somewhat.

"It's a shame they're tearing this theatre down," said a young woman to her date, as they swept past me on their way to the street. I ordered a box of popcorn, and went into the theater.

"Good luck," an usher told me. "You're going to need it."

He was right. *The Lonely Guy* is the kind of movie that seems to have been made to play in empty theaters on overcast January afternoons. It stars Steve Martin, an actor who inspires in me the same feelings that fingernails on blackboards inspire in other people. He plays a lonely guy. His girl leaves him, and he keeps losing the phone number of the only girl in New York who will talk to him. This could have been fun, if the movie were only a little more upbeat about his loneliness. But it isn't. *The Lonely Guy* is a dreary slog through morose situations, made all the worse by Martin's deadpan delivery, his slightly off-balance sense of timing, and his ability to make you cringe with his self-debasing smarminess. In a movie crawling with bad scenes, the worst is probably the bedroom scene with Iris (Judith Ivey), the above-mentioned only girl in New York who will talk to him. She has never had an orgasm. He convinces her that she will have an orgasm every time he sneezes. She fakes it by screaming "gesundheit!"

The Lonely Guy is the kind of movie that inspires you to distract yourself by counting the commercial products visible on the screen, and speculating about whether their manufacturers paid fees to have them worked into the movie. I counted two Diet 7-Ups, two Tabs, and Steve Martin.

The Lonely Lady ½★
R, 92 m., 1983

Pia Zadora (Jerilee Randall), Lloyd Bochner (Walter Thornton), Bibi Besch (Veronica Randall), Joseph Cali (Dacosta), Anthony Holland (Guy). Directed by Peter Sasdy and produced by Robert R. Weston. Screenplay by John Kershaw and Shawn Randall.

If *The Lonely Lady* had even a shred of style and humor, it could qualify as the worst movie of 1983. Unfortunately, it's not that good. It's a dog-eat-dog world, and it's not enough to be merely awful. You need something to set yourself apart. Pia Zadora tries, and she has pluck, but she's just not bad enough all by herself. The movie is bad in all the usual ways, and it would be easy enough to simply list them: The overacting, the use of "voice-over" narration to bridge awkward chasms between scenes, the predictable plot. But why don't we take all of those things for granted and move on to the truly unspeakable things in this movie. We could make a list:

1. I suppose it was necessary to have a scene in which the heroine is cruelly treated by men. But (a) couldn't they have thought of something other than rape by a garden hose, and (b) shouldn't such a traumatic event have had some *effect* on the character?

2. After the rape, Pia is seen being comforted in bed by her mother and a doctor. A single thread of stage makeup, representing blood, has trickled out of her mouth and dried. It is left in place for the entire scene, suggesting that at no point did the doctor, her mother, or any other medical personnel or family member care enough to disturb the makeup in order to make the scene realistic by wiping away the blood.

3. Proper nouns are missing from this movie. It seems to exist in a generic alternative universe in which nothing has its own name. The Oscars are known as "these awards" or "the awards." After Pia and her first lover leave a movie, they have this conversation: "I liked him better." "I liked her better." No him or her is identified. This is the kind of conversation that results when a screenplay says, *They leave the theater and briefly discuss the movie,* but the screenplay doesn't care what movie they saw.

4. The movie has no time for emotional transitions. When Pia marries the successful Hollywood writer, he is attentive and caring in one scene, and a sadist in the next, simply because the plot requires him to act that way. No motivation. When Pia goes crazy, it's not so much in reaction to what's been happening to her (she survived the garden hose with nary a backward glance) but because the script requires it, so that, later, she can pull herself back together again just as arbitrarily.

5. The movie's whole plot hinges on Pia's ability to rewrite a scene better than her jealous writer-husband. When the star of her husband's movie weeps that she can't play a certain graveyard scene, Pia whips out the portable typewriter and writes brilliant new dialogue for the star. What, you may ask, does Pia write? Here's what: She has the grieving widow kneel by the side of the open grave and cry out (are you ready for this?) "Why? Why!!!"

That's it. That's the brilliant dialogue. And it can be used for more than death scenes, let me tell you. In fact, I left this movie saying to myself, "Why? Why!!!"

The Long Good Friday ★ ★ ★ ★
R, 118 m., 1982

Bob Hoskins (Harold Shand), Helen Mirrin (Victoria), Eddie Constantine (Charlie), Derek Thompson (Jeff), Bryan Marshall (Harris), Paul Freeman (Collin). Directed by John Mackenzie and produced by Barry Hanson. Screenplay by Barrie Keeffe.

Harold is as hard as a rock and he will crush you. He runs the London docks and he wants to put together the biggest real estate deal in Europe. He has Mafia money from America and the tacit cooperation of the London criminal organization. He's short, barrel-chested, with his thinning hair combed forward above a round face and teeth that always seem to be grinding. He cannot believe that in one weekend his whole world can come apart. Harold Shand is a hood, but he lives in a penthouse, anchors a world-class yacht in the Thames, has the love of an intelligent and tactful mistress and talks obsessively about the ten years of peace he has helped negotiate in the London underground. Then a bomb blows up his Rolls Royce, killing his chauffeur. Another bomb demolishes the lovingly restored landmark pub he owns. A third bomb is found inside Harold's Mayfair casino, but fails to detonate. Who is after him? Who is his enemy? And why has the enemy chosen this worst of all possible times to come after him—the Easter weekend when an American Mafioso is in town to consider investing millions in his real estate project?

The Long Good Friday, which is a masterful and very tough piece of filmmaking, eventually does answer these questions. But the point of the film isn't to analyze Harold Shand's problems. It's to present a portrait of this man. And I have rarely seen a movie character so completely alive. Shand is an evil, cruel, sadistic man. But he's a mass of contradictions, and there are times when we understand him so completely we almost feel affectionate. He's such a character, such an overcompensating Cockney, sensitive to the slightest affront, able to strike fear in the hearts of killers, but a pushover when his mistress raises her voice to him. Shand is played by a compact, muscular actor named Bob Hoskins, in the most-praised film performance of the year from England. Hoskins has the energy and the freshness of a younger Michael Caine, if not the good looks, of course. There are scenes where he hangs his enemies upside down from meat hooks and questions them about the bombings, and other scenes, moments later, where he solemnly kids with the neighborhood juvenile delinquents and tries to soft-talk the American out of his millions.

He's an operator. He's a con man who has muscled his way to the top by knowing exactly how things work and what buttons to push, and now here he is, impotent before this faceless enemy. *The Long Good Friday* tells his story in a rather indirect way, opening with a montage of seemingly unrelated events, held together by a hypnotic music theme. Everything is eventually explained. It's all a big misunderstanding, based on stupid decisions taken by Shand's underlings and misinterpreted by the IRA. But although we know the real story, and Harold Shand does, the IRA never does—and the movie's final shots are, quite simply, extraordinary close-ups, held for a long time, of Shand's ratlike face in close-up, as his eyes shift from side to side, and his mouth breaks into a terrified grin, and he realizes how it feels to get a dose of his own medicine. This movie is one amazing piece of work, not only for the Hoskins performance but also for the energy of the filmmaking, the power of the music, and, oddly enough, for the engaging quality of its sometimes very violent sense of humor.

The Lords of Discipline ★ ★
R, 103 m., 1983

David Keith (Will), Robert Prosky (Bear), G.D. Spradlin (General Durrell), Barbara Babcock (Abigail), Michael Biehn (Alexander), Rick Rossovich (Pig), Mark Breland (Pearce). Directed by Frank Roddam and produced by Herb Jaffe and Gabriel Katzka. Screenplay by Thomas Pope and Lloyd Fonvielle.

I knew the military school in *Taps* (1981) was a fiction, but I didn't mind, because it was a fiction that worked to support a group of compelling characters. I also know that the military school in *The Lords of Discipline* is a fiction, and this time I *do* mind, because the whole function of the school here is to provide a framework for a nasty, cruel little thriller.

The movie takes place in the South, in the mid-1960s. A famous private military academy is struggling to haul itself into the twentieth century. A few cadets have been admitted who "don't belong," including a kid too gauche to fit in with the polished cadets, and another kid who is the school's first black. The story is told mostly through the eyes of one cadet who stands up for the underdogs. He's played by David Keith, who was the naval officer's candidate who hanged himself in *An Officer and a Gentleman.*

The school is a little odd. Although it has a magnificent, galleried library (where secret notes are hidden in the pages of Spengler's *The Decline of the West*), it apparently has no classrooms, no academic program, and no faculty members except two: the school's president, a slimy retired general (G.D. Spradlin), and a crusty old colonel named Bear (Robert Prosky), who lights a cigar every time he has anything to say. Keith is elected head of the cadet corps and determines to protect the rights of the misfit and the black. But then he begins to hear about a mysterious organization named "The Ten," a secret society within the school; its origins lost in the mists of time, its duty to "protect" the school's sacred honor against contamination by undesirable elements. Before long, it's Keith against "The Ten."

The Lords of Discipline starts out fairly well, and David Keith and the other actors in the movie are good, convincing performers. So it's only gradually that we realize the movie is essentially a ridiculous revenge melodrama. There's a scene where a cadet plunges to his death from the top of a school building, but that's nothing compared to the really creepy scenes where the black student is cut with a razor blade, attacked in a shower, and finally—in an offensively gratuitous scene—kidnapped, held in an old plantation, and tortured with electrical charges to his genitals. There's a funny thing about the way the movie handles that scene. David Keith tracks down the kidnappers, looks in a window, sees the electrical shock torture, sees the masked members of "The Ten" pour gasoline over the helpless student, sees them set a rag on fire and dangle it over him, watches all that happen, and *then* tries to stop the torture. Why didn't he act sooner? I'm afraid the answer, a sick one, is that the movie was so happy to linger over the scene that it didn't want to interrupt the sadism with a quick rescue. This is not a nice movie.

Lost in America ★ ★ ★ ★
R, 90 m., 1985

Albert Brooks (David Howard), Julie Hagerty (Linda Howard), Garry K. Marshall (Casino Boss), Art Frankel (Job Counselor). Directed by Albert Brooks and produced by Marty Katz. Screenplay by Brooks and Monica Johnson.

Every time I see a Winnebago motor home, I have the same fantasy as the hero of *Lost in America*. In my dream, I quit my job, sell everything I own, buy the Winnebago, and hit the open road. Where do I go? Look for me in the weather reports. I'll be parked by the side of a mountain stream, listening to Mozart on compact discs. All I'll need is a wok and a paperback.

In *Lost in America*, Albert Brooks plays an advertising executive in his thirties who realizes that dream. He leaves his job, talks his wife into quitting hers, and they point their Winnebago down that long, lonesome highway. This is not, however, a remake of *The Long, Long Trailer*. Brooks puts a different spin on things. For example, when movie characters leave their jobs, it's usually because they've been fired, they've decided to

take an ethical stand, or the company has gone broke. Only in a movie by Brooks would the hero quit to protest a "lateral transfer" to New York. There's something intrinsically comic about that: He's taking a stand, all right, but it's a narcissistic one. He's quitting because he wants to stay in Los Angeles, he thinks he deserves to be named vice president, and he doesn't like the traffic in New York.

Lost in America is being called a yuppie comedy, but it's really about the much more universal subjects of greed, hedonism, and panic. What makes it so funny is how much we can identify with it. Brooks plays a character who is making a lot of money, but not enough; who lives in a big house, but is outgrowing it; who drives an expensive car, but not a Mercedes-Benz; who is a top executive, but not a vice president. In short, he is a desperate man, trapped by his own expectations.

On the morning of his last day at work, he puts everything on hold while he has a long, luxurious telephone conversation with a Mercedes dealer. Brooks has great telephone scenes in all of his movies, but this one perfectly captures the nuances of consumerism. He asks how much the car will cost—including *everything*. Dealer prep, license, sticker, add-ons, extras, *everything*. The dealer names a price.

"That's *everything?*" Brooks asks.

"Except leather," the dealer says.

"For what I'm paying, I don't get leather?" Brooks asks, aghast.

"You get Mercedes leather."

"*Mercedes* leather? What's that?"

"Thick vinyl."

This is the kind of world Brooks is up against. A few minutes later, he's called into the boss's office and told that he will not get the promotion he thinks he deserves. Instead, he's going to New York to handle the Ford account. Brooks quits, and a few scenes later, he and his wife (Julie Hagerty) are tooling the big Winnebago into Las Vegas. They have enough money, he conservatively estimates, to stay on the road for the rest of their lives. That's before she loses their nest egg at the roulette tables.

Lost in America doesn't tell a story so much as assemble a series of self-contained comic scenes, and the movie's next scene is probably the best one in the movie. Brooks the adman tries to talk a casino owner (Garry K. Marshall) into giving back the money. It doesn't work, but Brooks keeps pushing, trying to sell the casino on improving its image ("I'm a high-paid advertising consultant. These are professional opinions you're getting.") There are other great scenes, as the desperate couple tries to find work to support themselves: An interview with an unemployment counselor, who listens, baffled, to Brooks explaining why he left a $100,000-a-year job because he couldn't "find himself." And Brooks's wife introducing her new boss, a teen-age boy.

Lost in America has one strange flaw. It doesn't seem to come to a conclusion. It just sort of ends in midstream, as if the final scenes were never shot. I don't know if that's the actual case, but I do wish the movie had been longer and had arrived at some sort of final destination. What we do get, however, is observant and very funny. Brooks is especially good at hearing exactly how people talk, and how that reveals things about themselves. Take that line about "Mercedes leather." A lot of people would be very happy to sit on "Mercedes leather." But not a Mercedes owner, of course. How did Joni Mitchell put it? "Don't it always seem to go, that you don't know what you've got, till it's gone."

Love Letters ★ ★ ★ ½
R, 98 m., 1984

Jamie Lee Curtis (Anna), James Keach (Oliver), Amy Madigan (Wendy), Matt Clark (Mr. Winter). Directed by Amy Jones and produced by Roger Corman. Screenplay by Jones.

Love Letters teaches this lesson: Passion can exist between two people who know their relationship is wrong, but love cannot exist, because love demands to know that it is right. The movie stars Jamie Lee Curtis, in the best performance she has ever given, as Anna, a bright young woman who has an affair with a married man. She tries to make herself see their relationship as existing above conventional morality, but she can't, not after she sees the man's wife and kids.

The affair begins at a crossroads in her life. She's an announcer for a public radio station in San Francisco, and within a period of a few weeks her mother dies, and she gets a job offer from a larger station. She doesn't take the job, though, because something else happens. She meets a photographer (James Keach), who is a sensitive, intelligent, married man, and feels powerfully drawn to him. And she finds her mother's love letters, which reveal that her mother once had an affair. The old letters are used as a counterpoint to the events in the present. They're read on the sound track in the voice of the man who wrote them—a man we don't meet until the movie is almost over. They are letters about love, separation, loneliness, and loyalty. Anna learns to her astonishment that her mother continued the affair for years and years during her marriage, finally ending it only because she had decided to stay with her husband.

We meet the husband, Anna's father. He is a self-pitying alcoholic who believes he was never good enough for Anna's mother, and who smothers Anna with neurotic demands. What happens then is fascinating, and the movie treats it with great intelligence. Anna is already attracted to the James Keach character. Now, reading the old love letters, she begins to develop a romantic idea about affairs. She hates her father, and so, perhaps, did her mother. Her mother cheated on her father—and so will she, by having an affair with Keach. She will become the same kind of noble, romantic outsider that the author of the love letters must have been.

All of this is handled with as much subtlety as Ingmar Bergman brought to similar situations in *Scenes from a Marriage*. This isn't a soap opera romance; it's an investigation into how we can intellectualize our way into situations where our passions are likely to take over. Anna and the photographer spend happy times together. They are "in love." Anna thinks she only wants an affair, but she grows possessive in spite of herself. And when she spies on Keach's family, she sees that his wife is a good woman and there is love in their home. Her life refuses to parallel the love letters.

Love Letters was written and directed by Amy Jones, whose previous credit was *The Slumber Party Massacre*. This is perhaps another case of a young filmmaker beginning with exploitation movies and finally getting the chance to do ambitious work. What she accomplishes here is wonderful. She creates a story of passion that is as absorbing as a thriller. She makes a movie of ideas that never, ever, seems to be just a message picture. And she gives Jamie Lee Curtis the best dramatic role of her career; this role, side-by-side with Curtis's inspired comic acting in *Trading Places*, shows her with a range we couldn't have guessed from all her horror pictures. *Love Letters* is one of those treasures that slips through once in a while: A movie that's as smart as we are, that never goes for cheap shots, that's about passion but never blinded by it.

Love Streams ★ ★ ★ ★
PG-13, 141 m., 1984

Gena Rowlands (Sarah Lawson), John Cassavetes (Robert Harmon), Diahnne Abbott (Susan), Seymour Cassel (Jack Lawson), Margaret Abbott (Margarita). Directed by John Cassavetes and produced by Menachem Golan and Yoram Globus. Screenplay by Ted Allan and Cassavetes.

John Cassavetes's *Love Streams* is the kind of movie where a woman brings home two horses, a goat, a duck, some chickens, a dog, and a parrot, and you don't have the feeling that the screenplay is going for cheap laughs. In fact, there's a tightening in your throat as you realize how desperate an act you're witnessing, and how unhappy a person is getting out of the taxi with all those animals. The menagerie scene occurs rather late in the film, after we've already locked into Cassavetes's method. This is a movie about mad people, and they are going to be acting in crazy ways, but the movie isn't going to let us off the hook by making them funny or picaresque or even symbolic (as in *King of Hearts*). They are, quite simply, desperate.

The brother, Robert (played by Cassavetes), is a writer who lives up in the Hollywood Hills in one of those houses that looks like *Architectural Digest* Visits a Motel. He writes trashy novels about bad women. A parade of hookers marches through his life; he gathers them by the taxi load, almost as a hobby, and dismisses them with lots of meaningless words about how he loves them, and how they're sweethearts and babies and dolls. The circular drive in front of his house is constantly filled with the cars

of the lonely and the desperate. He is an alcoholic who stays up for two or three days at a stretch, as if terrified of missing one single unhappy moment. The sister, Sarah (Gena Rowlands), is as possessive as her brother is evasive. She is in the process of a messy divorce from her husband (Seymour Gassel), and her daughter is in flight from her. Rowlands thinks that maybe she can buy love: First she buys the animals, later she talks about buying her brother a baby, because that's what he "needs."

At least Cassavetes and Rowlands can communicate. They share perfect trust, although it is the trust of two people in the same trap. There are other characters in the movie that Cassavetes talks at and around, but not with. They include a bemused young singer (Diahnne Abbott) who goes out with Cassavetes but looks at him as if he were capable of imploding, and a former wife (Michele Conway) who turns up one day on the doorstep with a small boy and tells him: "This is your son." The way Cassavetes handles this news is typical of the movie. The woman wonders if maybe he could baby sit for a weekend. He says he will. He brings the kid into the house, scares him away, chases him halfway down Laurel Canyon, brings him back, pours him a beer, has a heart-to-heart about "Women, Life and Marriage," and then asks the kid if he'd like to go to Vegas. Cut to Vegas. Cassavetes dumps the kid in a hotel room and goes out partying all night. He is incapable of any appropriate response to a situation requiring him to care about another human being. He fills his life with noise, hookers, emergencies, and booze to drown out the insistent whisper of duty.

The movie is exasperating, because we never know where we stand or what will happen next. I think that's one of its strengths: There's an exhilaration in this roller coaster ride through scenes that come out of nowhere. This is not a docudrama or a little psychological playlet with a lesson to be learned. It is a raw, spontaneous life, and when we laugh (as in the scene where Cassavetes summons a doctor to the side of the unconscious Rowlands), we wince.

Viewers raised on trained and tame movies may be uncomfortable in the world of Cassavetes; his films are built around lots of talk and the waving of arms and the invoking of the gods. Cassavetes has been making these passionate personal movies for twenty-five years, ever since his *Shadows* helped create American underground movies. His titles include *Minnie and Moskowitz* (in which Rowlands and Cassel got married), *Faces, A Woman Under the Influence, The Killing of a Chinese Bookie, Gloria, Opening Night,* and *Husbands.* Sometimes (as in *Husbands*) the wild truth-telling approach evaporates into a lot of empty talk and play-acting. In *Love Streams,* it works.

Lovesick ★ ★ ★
PG, 94 m., 1983

Dudley Moore (Saul Benjamin), Elizabeth McGovern (Chloe Allen), Alec Guinness (Sigmund Freud), Wallace Shawn (Otto Jaffe), Ron Silver (Ted Caruso), Larry Rivers (Jac Applezweig), John Huston (Dr. Geller). Directed by Marshall Brickman and produced by Charles Okun. Screenplay by Brickman.

The notion of a psychiatrist falling in love with his patient is not exactly new, but there are whole moments at a time when it *seems* new in *Lovesick,* a comedy where the psychiatrist is played by Dudley Moore and his patient is Elizabeth McGovern. They should not fall in love. It is against all the rules. It is also in violation of all the ethics of Moore's profession. But what is he to do when she turns those wide, grave eyes upon him and asks for his help? Moore actually hears about McGovern before he meets her. He gets a visit from a colleague (Wallace Shawn, who had dinner with André). Shawn needs help. He's head over heels with the woman and can't stop himself. Moore disapproves, until Shawn leaves and he himself meets McGovern. Then he is instantly smitten.

The scene in which he is smitten illustrates some of the best and worst qualities of this movie. Dudley Moore is very good at what directors call "reaction shots"—shots where we watch an actor watching someone else. In *Lovesick,* Moore's reactions as he gazes upon McGovern are comic and helpless. Her close-ups are fun, too. We find ourselves in sympathy with them. But the development of the scene is interrupted by an annoying device used throughout the film by Marshall Brickman, the director. He

stops everything for a fantasy sequence in which Moore imagines that he goes around his desk and kisses McGovern, and that she responds, and that Sigmund Freud magically appears to chastise him.

Brickman, who has written for Woody Allen, may be developing a device here that was first used in *Annie Hall.* (Remember the scene where Marshall McLuhan appeared in a theater lobby and answered a man's question?) Here, though, it doesn't work. Freud (played by Alec Guinness) appears several times during the movie, and although the gimmick no doubt seemed like a clever way to illustrate the subconscious, it brings everything grinding to a dead standstill.

It's not fatal, though, to a movie with a lot of other nice things in it. I really enjoyed the rapport between Moore and McGovern—she so limpid in her unstudied sexuality; he so dreadfully serious about the burden of his love—as if the fact that he loves her is a cross he must bear. The movie is populated with a lot of interesting supporting performances, too. In fact, you can tell it's a New York film, and you can almost guess that it comes from someone in the Woody Allen orbit because of the fun it has with celebrity cameos; the actors, professional and not, who appear in this film include not only Shawn but Alan King, artist Larry Rivers, director Gene Saks, playwright Renee Taylor, director John Huston, and several actual New York shrinks.

Lovesick isn't a great comedy but it's not a bad one. And it's a reminder that Dudley Moore is a gifted and very likable comic actor. I suppose that like all great comedians, he has urges to play serious roles, but after the dreadful *Six Weeks* (in which his principal mistake was to appear), here he is in the lovesick territory of *10* and *Arthur.* It's where he belongs.

Lust in the Dust ★ ★
R, 90 m., 1985

Tab Hunter (Abel), Divine (Rosie), Lainie Kazan (Marguerite), Geoffrey Lewis (Hard Case), Cesar Romero (Father Garcia), Gina Gallego (Ninfa). Directed by Paul Bartel and produced by Allan Glaser and Tab Hunter. Screenplay by Philip John Taylor.

Lust in the Dust would have worked better

with Divine in the Tab Hunter role. Divine was born to play Tab Hunter, a claim Hunter himself has not been able to make for several years. And Divine wouldn't have made the mistake Hunter makes, of playing his Western gunslinger as a Clint Eastwood type. Divine would have chewed the scenery before shooting at it, and *Lust in the Dust* might have been funny all the way through, instead of just for the first twenty minutes.

The movie is a comedy Western, deliberately camp, starring Tab Hunter as a silent cowboy with no name, Divine as a hapless wanderer in the desert who wants to be a saloon singer, and Lainie Kazan as the owner of the only saloon in the miserable little town of Chili Verde. Divine is, of course, the well-known transvestite who has starred in lots of John Waters's movies (including *Polyester*, where the audience was issued Scratch 'n' Sniff cards). Divine usually goes for hysterical overacting, but this time she plays a timid, wistful soul, and it doesn't work as well. We need her slinging people out the saloon doors.

The movie is apparently intended as a satire on several different classic Westerns, including *Duel in the Sun*, but a funny thing happens at about the halfway point: It settles down and starts to get involved in its story. And since we don't care about the story, that's a mistake. The movie should have continued to go for the one-liners. As it is, we get this impenetrable story about a missing treasure map, and when they find the map, believe me, it's not a pretty sight.

Good things in the movie include a rousing, high-spirited performance by Kazan, who has abandoned forever her former images and has developed into an effective comedy performer; a TV producer should take a look at this movie and develop a sitcom around her (but not a comedy Western, please!). Hunter underplays until he is almost not present in some of the scenes, Divine is misused. Cesar Romero is a distraction as the local priest, and a young saloon waitress (Gina Gallego) has what used to be called the Lainie Kazan role.

The movie was directed by Paul Bartel, whose previous credit is *Eating Raoul*. Like most of the people associated with the movie, including Tab Hunter (who shares the producer's credit), he seems convinced that simply combining Divine, Kazan, and Hunter in the same room would create a fissionable comic mass. Before he shut the door, he should have also thrown in a screenplay.

Mad Max Beyond Thunderdome
★ ★ ★ ★
R, 115 m., 1985

Mel Gibson (Mad Max), Tina Turner (Aunty Entity), Frank Thring (Collector), Angelo Rossitto (Master), Paul Larsson (Blaster), Angry Anderson (Ironbar). Directed and produced by George Miller. Co-directed by George Ogilvie. Screenplay by Miller and Terry Hayes.

It's not supposed to happen this way. Sequels are not supposed to be better than the movies that inspired them. The third movie in a series isn't supposed to create a world more complex, more visionary, and more entertaining than the first two. Sequels are supposed to be creative voids. But now here is *Mad Max Beyond Thunderdome*, not only the best of the three Mad Max movies, but one of the best films of 1985.

From its opening shot of a bizarre vehicle being pulled by camels through the desert, *Mad Max Three* places us more firmly within its apocalyptic postnuclear world than ever before. We are some years in the future; how many, it is hard to say, but so few years that the frames and sheet metal of 1985 automobiles are still being salvaged for makeshift new vehicles of bizarre design. And yet enough years that a new society is taking shape. The bombs have fallen, the world's petroleum supplies have been destroyed, and in the deserts of Australia, mankind has found a new set of rules and started on a new game.

The driver of the camels is Mad Max (Mel Gibson), former cop, now sort of a free-lance nomad. After his vehicle is stolen and he is left in the desert to die, he makes his way somehow to Bartertown, a quasi-Casablanca hammered together out of spare parts. Bartertown is where you go to buy, trade, or sell anything—or anybody. It is supervised by a Sydney Greenstreet-style fat man named the Collector (Frank Thring), and ruled by an imperious queen named Aunty Entity (Tina Turner).

And it is powered by an energy source that is, in its own way, a compelling argument against nuclear war: In chambers beneath Bartertown, countless pigs live and eat and defecate, and from their waste products, Turner's soldiers generate methane gas. This leads to some of the movie's most memorable moments, as Mad Max and others wade knee-deep in piggy-do.

Tina Turner herself lives far above the masses, in a birds'-nest throne room perched high overhead. And as Mad Max first visits Turner's sky palace, I began to realize how completely the director, George Miller, had imagined this future world. It has the crowding and the variety of a movie crossroads, but it also has a riot of hairstyles and costume design, as if these desperate creatures could pause from the daily struggle for survival only long enough to invent new punk fashions. After the clothes, the hair, the crowding, the incessant activity, the spendthrift way in which Miller fills his screen with throwaway details, Bartertown becomes much more than a movie set—it's an astounding address of the imagination, a place as real as Bogart's Casablanca or Orson Welles's Xanadu or the Vienna of *The Third Man*. That was even before the movie introduced me to Thunderdome, the arena for Bartertown's hand-to-hand battles to the death.

Thunderdome is the first really original movie idea about how to stage a fight since we got the first karate movies. The "dome" is a giant upside-down framework bowl. The spectators scurry up the sides of the bowl, and look down on the fighters. But the combatants are not limited to fighting on the floor of the arena. They are placed on harnesses with long elastic straps, so that they can leap from top to bottom and from side to side with great lethal bounds. Thunderdome is to fighting as three-dimensional chess is to a flat board. And the weapons available to the fighters are hung from the inside of the dome: Cleavers, broadaxes, sledge-hammers, the inevitable chainsaw.

It is into Thunderdome that Mad Max goes for his showdown with Aunty Entity's greatest warrior, and George Miller's most original creation, a character named Master-Blaster, who is actually two people. Blaster is a giant hulk of a man in an iron mask. Master is a dwarf who rides him like a chariot, standing in an iron harness above his shoulders. The fight between Mad Max and Master-Blaster is one of the great creative action scenes in the movies.

There is a lot more in *Mad Max Beyond Thunderdome*. The descent into the pig world, for example, and the visit to a sort of postwar hippie commune, and of course the inevitable final chase scene, involving car, train, truck, cycle, and incredible stunts. This is a movie that strains at the leash of the possible, a movie of great visionary wonders.

Making Love ★ ★
R, 111 m., 1982

Michael Ontkean (Zack), Kate Jackson (Claire), Harry Hamlin (Bart), Wendy Hiller (Winnie). Directed by Arthur Hiller and produced by Allen Adler and Daniel Melnick. Screenplay by Barry Sandler.

Arthur Hiller's *Making Love* tells the story of a couple that has been married for eight years—happily married, according to the evidence—when the husband has an affair with another man, discovers that he is gay, and decides to leave his wife. *Making Love* is limited primarily to the characters' sexual identities. There would be no movie if the husband were not homosexual; this film has nothing else to be about. Its characters, as written, aren't open to the surprises of real life, because the movie is single-mindedly about the specific nature of their sexual dilemma.

Since we already know the secrets when we start watching *Making Love* (the ads summarized the plot), we feel locked in; there's nothing to do but wait while the movie marches through its lockstep development. The stages are predictable: (a) introduction of the ideal marriage; (b) the husband's secret homosexual desires; (c) the other man; (d) passion and deception; (e) the revelation scene; (f) unhappiness and acceptance; followed by (g) a brave new tomorrow.

Every scene and almost every line seems to be programmed to make an obvious point. This movie has some of the worst dialogue one can imagine:
She: "What about passion?"
He: "What about support?"
She: "What about betrayal?"

The movie stars Kate Jackson as the wife, Michael Ontkean as her husband, and Harry Hamlin as the homosexual writer Ontkean falls in love with. Jackson's a TV executive, Ontkean's a young doctor, and their marriage (pre-Hamlin) exists in one of those Hollywood wonderlands in which young couples figure they can meet the mortgage payments if they start brown-bagging their lunch. No attempt is made to present the marriage in messy human terms; it has to be boringly happy so that Jackson can be amazed when her husband walks out.

And walk out Ontkean does, after some preliminary false starts. He visits a couple of gay bars populated exclusively by extras who look as if they should be posing for an *Ah! Men!* catalog. He drives down an alley lined with shoulder-to-shoulder hustlers. Then Hamlin comes into his office for a physical exam (the most cursory and incompetent such exam, incidentally, ever presented in a movie). Ontkean is attracted, asks him out to dinner, and the rest is predictable, right down to the obligatory scene in which Jackson tears her husband's clothes out of the closet and throws them on the floor.

Making Love is essentially a TV docudrama, in which the subject is announced loud and clear at the outset and there are no surprises. People have described the movie to me in one sentence as "Kate Jackson finds out her husband is a homosexual," and they haven't left out much.

The Man Who Loved Women ★ ★
R, 118 m., 1983

Burt Reynolds (David), Julie Andrews (Marianna), Kim Basinger (Louise), Marilu Henner (Agnes). Directed by Blake Edwards and produced by Edwards and Tony Adams. Screenplay by Edwards, Milton Wexler, and Geoffrey Edwards.

Here is a sad movie with a funny movie inside trying to get out. The sad movie tells the story of a man who is utterly obsessed with women. He thinks he loves them, but he's not a lover, he's a collector. He goes to see an analyst, but that doesn't help because he falls in love with her. Beautiful women make him restless. He letches and dreams, pursues and fantasizes, until finally his obsession kills him. Because his funeral opens

the movie, I have not given away very much. This movie is not only sad, it's also insincere and dishonest.

The funny movie inside is another matter. It's about how Burt Reynolds goes to Texas and is seduced by a sex-mad temptress whose husband is a jealous oil millionaire. She likes risk. Her encounters with Reynolds take place during cocktail parties, horse races, and on the highway. Because she is truly a sensuous woman (especially as played, with great wit, by Kim Basinger), these encounters take on a kind of surrealism. And Basinger drapes her body on Reynolds with a bold sort of leaning maneuver that would create obsession in a man of stone.

The Texas movie is funny. It reminds us of some of the best farcical work by Blake Edwards, the director, whose movies include *10* and *Victor/Victoria*. Unfortunately, the Texas sequence lasts only thirty minutes or so, and the rest of the movie is an uncomfortable mixture of psycho-babble, fake sincerity, and scenes we are supposed to take seriously even though they contain obviously impossible elements. Reynolds plays a man who, we are told, loves women too much. At his funeral, they turn out by the dozens. But nowhere in the movie do we really see him *loving* a woman. He courts them. He is nice to them. He kids with them. He goes to bed with them. He tries to be protective toward a young hooker. But he's not a lover, he's a perfect host.

This is a portrait of a lonely man. The problem with a man who loves *all* women is that he can never love *a* woman. There is always another one demanding his attention and requiring his care. When the analyst (played by Julie Andrews) makes her smarmy little speech about how he *really* and *truly* loved all of those women, each in her own way, she speaks like no woman I know. If she truly loved Reynolds and felt he truly loved her, and if she had half the brains you need to get out of Analysis 101, she would have (a) been a little hurt, (b) a little jealous, and (c) deeply suspicious of the health of his motives.

This movie is a remake, by the way, of a little-seen 1977 Francois Truffaut film. In the Truffaut, the man was seen as something of a victim, suffering from an incurable obsession that was almost a disease. The tip-off to the phoniness of the Reynolds version is that the movie seems to be recommending the disease.

The Man With Two Brains ★ ★
R, 91 m., 1983

Steve Martin (Dr. Hfuhruhurr), Kathleen Turner (Dolores), David Warner (Dr. Necessiter), Paul Benedits (Butler). Directed by Carl Reiner and produced by David V. Picker and William E. McEuen. Written by Reiner, Steve Martin, and George Gipe.

Steve Martin and Carl Reiner continue their tour of ancient movie genres with *The Man With Two Brains*, which does for Mad Scientist movies what *Dead Men Don't Wear Plaid* did for private eye pictures, which is to say, not very much. Some of the gags depend on a familiarity with classics like *Donovan's Brain, Bride of Frankenstein*—and even, in this case, Mel Brooks's *Young Frankenstein*. Other gags depend on Steve Martin's comic personality, as a guy whose elevator doesn't go all the way to the top floor. I've never found Steve Martin irresistibly funny. There's something stolid about his approach to humor, something deliberately half-paced and mannered that seems designed to be subtly irritating. I guess it's a tribute to *The Man With Two Brains* that I found myself laughing a fair amount of the time, despite my feelings about Martin. This is not a great comedy but it has scenes that don't know that.

Martin plays a brain surgeon named Dr. Michael Hfuhruhurr. The moment I heard the name I knew we were in trouble, and, sure enough, the movie never tires of making jokes based on his funny name. Since the First Law of Comedy should be *No funny names are funny unless they are used by W.C. Fields or Groucho Marx*, the name jokes are an exercise in futility. Hfuhruhurr has perfected something called the cranial screwtop method of brain surgery, and uses it to save the life of a beautiful young woman (Kathleen Turner) whom he's hit with his Mercedes. The woman, alas, turns out to be a gold digger. She seduces the gardener but refuses to have sex with Hfuhruhurr, who in his frustration falls in love with the brain of another young woman—a brain that has been pickled in a jar in the Vienna laboratory of the eccentric Dr. Necessiter (David Warner).

And so on. The movie uses the basic approach established by Brooks in *Young Frankenstein:* sight gags, cross-references, scatalogical puns, broad plotting, running gags, and so on. It filters its material through Martin's peculiar style, which is, I think, not light-footed enough. Martin is the kind of comedian who chews every line, lingering even on the throwaways.

Turner, seen in *Body Heat*, has a nice teasing quality as the hot-and-cold sexpot. David Warner (remember him from *Morgan* all those years ago?) makes a suitably cadaverous mad scientist. But the cast somehow seems underpopulated, and the characters are underdeveloped. That's one of the weaknesses of genre satires: The filmmakers depend on our knowledge of past characters as a substitute for creating new ones. And since comedy grows out of inappropriate behavior, and our notions of inappropriate behavior depend on what we know about people, the jokes all boil down to the fact that the characters in old Mad Scientist movies wouldn't behave like the characters in this one. So what?

Mask ★ ★ ★ ½
PG-13, 120 m., 1985

Cher (Rusty Dennis), Eric Stoltz (Rocky Dennis), Sam Elliott (Gar), Estelle Getty (Evelyn), Richard Dysart (Abe), Laura Dern (Diana). Directed by Peter Bogdanovich and produced by Martin Starger. Screenplay by Anna Hamilton Phelan.

When we see him for the first time, it's a glimpse through his bedroom window, half-reflected in a mirror. A second later, we see him more clearly, this teen-age boy with the strange face. We are shocked for a second, until he starts to talk, and then, without effort, we accept him as a normal kid who has had an abnormal thing happen to him. The name of his disease is craniodiaphyseal dyaplasia, and it causes calcium deposits on his skull that force his face out of shape. "What's the matter?" he likes to ask. "You never seen anyone from the planet Vulcan before?"

The kid's name is Rocky Dennis, and his mother is named Rusty. She is not your normal mom, either. She rides with a motorcycle gang, abuses drugs, shacks up with gang members, and has no visible means of employment. But within about ten minutes, we know that she is the ideal mom for Rocky. That's in the scene where the school principal suggests that Rocky would be better off in a "special" school, and she tells the principal he is a jerk, her son is a good student with good grades, and here is the name of her lawyer.

Movies don't often grab us as quickly as *Mask* does. The story of Rocky and Rusty is absorbing from the very first, maybe because the movie doesn't waste a lot of time wringing its hands over Rocky's fate. *Mask* lands on its feet, running. The director, Peter Bogdanovich, moves directly to the center of Rocky's life—his mother, his baseball cards, his cocky bravado, his growing awareness of girls. Bogdanovich handles *Mask* a lot differently than a made-for-TV movie would have, with TV's disease-of-the-week approach. This isn't the story of a disease, but the story of some people. And the most extraordinary person in the movie, surprisingly, is not Rocky, but his mother. Rusty Dennis is played by Cher as a complicated, angry, high-energy woman with a great capacity to love her son and encourage him to live as fully as he can. Rocky is a great kid, but because he succeeds so well at being a teen-ager, he is not a special case like, say, the Elephant Man. He is a kid with a handicap. It is a tribute to Eric Stoltz, who plays the role beneath the completely convincing makeup of Michael Westmore, that we accept him on his own terms.

Cher, on the other hand, makes Rusty Dennis into one of the most interesting movie characters in a long time. She is up front about her life-style, and when her son protests about her drinking and drugging, she tells him to butt out of her business. She rides with the motorcycle gang, but is growing unhappy with her promiscuity, and is relieved when the guy she really loves (Sam Elliott) comes back from a trip and moves in. She is also finally able to clean up her act, and stop drinking and using, after Rocky asks her to; she loves him that much.

Mask is based on a true story, and that doesn't come as a surprise: Hollywood wouldn't have the nerve to make a fictional tearjerker like this. The emotional peak of the movie comes during a summer that Rocky spends as an assistant at a camp for the blind. He falls in love with a blind teen-ager (Laura Dern), who feels his face and says he looks all right to her, and they have some of that special time together that only teen-agers can have: time when love doesn't mean sex so much as it means perfect agreement on the really important issues, like Truth and Beauty. Then the girl's parents come to pick her up, and their reaction to Rocky comes as a shock to us, a reminder of how completely we had accepted him.

Mask is a wonderful movie, a story of high spirits and hope and courage. It has some songs in it, by Bob Seger, and there was a lot of publicity about the fact that Peter Bogdanovich would rather the songs were by Bruce Springsteen. Let me put it this way: This is a movie that doesn't depend on its sound track. It works because of the people it's about, not because of the music they listen to.

Max Dugan Returns ★ ★ ½
PG, 98 m., 1983

Marsha Mason (Nora McPhee), Jason Robards (Max Dugan), Donald Sutherland (Brian Costello), Matthew Broderick (Michael McPhee). Directed by Herbert Ross and produced by Ross and Neil Simon. Screenplay by Simon.

Max Dugan Returns is a sweet little movie that evokes, in its shallow wholesomeness, a world that has pretty well disappeared from TV and the movies. I'm thinking of that lost American paradise inhabited by Blondie and Dagwood, Ozzie and Harriet, and the Beaver—a world where the family gets together for a cute-talk confab in the breakfast nook.

The movie takes place in the Venice Beach area south of Santa Monica. That's a world inhabited largely by movie stars, drug dealers, and transvestite roller skaters, but you wouldn't know that from *Max Dugan Returns*. The movie stars Marsha Mason as a widowed school teacher who's raising her teen-age son (Matthew Broderick) with a lot of pluck and cheerfulness. This is one of those movies that starts right out with little character touches; Mason is provided with a standard-issue Colorful Hollywood Car that bounces like a bronco and backfires on cue. Then two big things happen in her life. (1) Her car is stolen and police Lieutenant Donald Sutherland is assigned to the case. (2) After thirty years, her long-lost father (Jason Robards) returns, bearing a briefcase full of money. While Sutherland and Mason slowly fall in love, Robards moves in and explains that he swindled the money from a Las Vegas casino to even an old score, but now he has only six months to live and wants to get to know his daughter and grandson.

This is, as you will have noticed, a Plot. There is never a danger that we will confuse it with Real Life. It's unfair even to ask for realism; *Max Dugan Returns* isn't supposed to be a slice of life, it's supposed to be a series of situations leading to a semitearful happy ending. The movie was written and coproduced by Neil Simon, who is certainly facile. He can create colorful characters on a moment's notice, and spin out funny dialogue by the yard. His problem is making the characters seem somewhat three-dimensional. He defines them by their jobs, ethnic categories, costumes, and speech patterns, so we can tell them apart—but how many Simon characters can you really remember through the years? The Odd Couple, Dreyfuss and Mason in *Goodbye Girl*, Mason in *Chapter Two*, Ann-Margret in *I Ought to Be in Pictures*, Michael Caine in *California Suite*, and who else?

Simon's gift also is his downfall. He's so good at writing lightweight dialogue that it all begins to sound the same. In *Max Dugan Returns*, for example, there's a running gag about whether the dog is named Plato or Pluto, and the trouble is, the *first* time the names are confused, we know with a conviction approaching certainty that they will be confused again, and again.

Max Dugan Returns is watchable and sort of sweet. Robards gives a poignant performance as the dying father, although the movie makes him express his love through expensive gifts that are sort of off-putting. When the movie is over, however, it seems to evaporate. It doesn't have a purpose for being; it's just spun sugar and a few tears, a plot situation set into motion to create the illusion of suspense before everyone gets what he wants, or fears, or deserves. There's hardly a moment in the whole movie that would be confused with daily life as it is really lived. Maybe that's the idea.

Melvin and Howard ★ ★ ★ ½
R, 95 m., 1980

Paul Le Mat (Melvin Dummar), Jason Robards (Howard Hughes), Mary Steenburgen (Lynda Dummar), Pamela Reed (Bonnie Dummar), Michael J. Pollard (Little Red), Charles Napier (Man with Envelope), Robert Ridgely (TV Host), Melvin Dummar (Depot Counterman). Directed by Jonathan Demme and produced by Art Linson and Don Phillips. Screenplay by Bo Goldman.

Melvin Dummar is the man who claimed he gave a lift to a doddering old hitchhiker, loaned him a quarter, and was left $156 million in the hitchhiker's will. If he was telling the truth, the hitchhiker was Howard Hughes. But Jonathan Demme's wonderful comedy *Melvin and Howard* doesn't depend on whether the so-called Mormon Will was really written by Hughes. That hardly matters. This is the story of a life lived at the other end of the financial ladder from Hughes. It sees Dummar as the kind of American hero who is celebrated for being so extraordinarily ordinary.

For what, after all, constitutes heroism? And why shouldn't Dummar be considered a hero? We learn from this movie that he ventured single-handedly into the jungle of American consumerism, and lived. We see his major battles. Here's a guy who was married three times (twice to the same woman, the second time with the "Hawaiian War Chant" playing in an all-night Vegas chapel). He had three cars and a boat repossessed, he went from being Milkman of the Month to hauling his first wife off a go-go stage, he loved his children, did not drink or smoke, and stood at the brink of losing his gas station franchise on the very day when a tall, blond stranger dropped what looked a lot like Hughes's last will and testament into his life.

The genius of *Melvin and Howard* is that it is about Melvin, not Howard. The film begins and ends with scenes involving the Hughes character, who is played by Jason Robards as a desert rat with fading memories of happiness. Dummar stops in the desert to answer a call of nature, finds Hughes lying in the sagebrush, gives him a ride in his pickup truck, and gets him to sing. For reasons of his own, Hughes sings "Bye, Bye Blackbird": *Got no one to love and understand me . . . oh, what hard-luck stories they all hand me.*

Robards is a chillingly effective Hughes. But this movie belongs to Paul Le Mat, as Dummar. Le Mat played the round-faced hot-rodder in *American Graffiti*, and Dummar is the kind of guy that character might have grown up to be. He is pleasant, genial, simple of speech, crafty of mind, always looking for an angle. He angles for Milkman of the Month, he plots to get his wife on a TV game show, he writes songs like "Santa's Souped-Up Sleigh," he plays the slots at Vegas and goes through his life asking only for a few small scores.

When he gets a big score—named the beneficiary of a $156 million will that seems to have been signed by Hughes—he hardly knows what to do. Long-lost relatives and new-found friends turn up by the dozens, and press conferences are held in front of his gas station. There is a court trial, but the movie never really addresses itself to the details of the Hughes will court case. It goes instead for the drama and for the effect on Dummar and his family.

This is a slice of American life. It shows the flip side of Gary Gilmore's Utah. It is a world of mobile homes, Pop Tarts, dust, kids, and dreams of glory. It's pretty clear how this movie got made. The producers started with the notion that the story of the mysterious Hughes will might make a good courtroom thriller. Well, maybe it would have. But my hunch is that when they met Dummar, they had the good sense to realize that they could get a better—and certainly a funnier—story out of what happened to him between the day he met Hughes and the day the will was discovered. Dummar is the kind of guy who thinks they oughta make a movie out of his life. This time, he was right.

Mephisto ★ ★ ★ ★
NO MPAA RATING, 135 m., 1981

Klaus Maria Brandauer (Henrik Hofgon), Krystyna Janda (Barbara Bruckner), Ildiko Bansagi (Nicolette Von Hiebuhr), Karin Boyd (Juliette Martens). Directed and produced by Istvan Szabo. Screenplay by Szabo and Peter Dobel.

There are times in *Mephisto* when the hero tries to explain himself by saying that he's only an actor, and he has that almost right. *All* he is, is an actor. It's not his fault that the Nazis have come to power, and that as a German speaking actor he must choose between becoming a Nazi and being exiled into a foreign land without jobs for German actors. As long as he is acting, as long as he is not called upon to risk his real feelings, this man can act his way into the hearts of women, audiences, and the Nazi power structure. This is the story of a man who plays his life wearing masks, fearing that if the last mask is removed, he will have no face.

The actor is played by Klaus Maria Brandauer in one of the greatest movie performances I've ever seen. The character, Henrik, is not sympathetic, and yet we identify with him because he shares so many of our own weaknesses and fears. Henrik is not a very good actor or a very good human being, but he is good enough to get by in ordinary times. As the movie opens, he's a socialist, interested in all the most progressive new causes, and is even the proud lover of a black woman. By the end of the film, he has learned that his liberalism was a taste, not a conviction, and that he will do anything, flatter anybody, make any compromise, just to hear applause, even though he knows the applause comes from fools.

Mephisto does an uncanny job of creating its period, of showing us Hamburg and Berlin from the 1920s to the 1940s. And I've never seen a movie that does a better job of showing the seductive Nazi practice of providing party members with theatrical costumes, titles, and pageantry. In this movie, not being a Nazi is like being at a black tie ball in a brown corduroy suit. Hofgon, the actor, is drawn to this world like a magnet. From his ambitious beginnings in the provincial German theater, he works his way up into more important roles and laterally into more important society. All of his progress is based on lies. He marries a woman he does not love, because her father can do him some good. When the rise of the

Nazis destroys his father-in-law's power, he leaves his wife. He continues all this time to maintain his affair with his black mistress. He has a modest, but undeniable, talent as an actor, but prostitutes it by playing his favorite role, Mephistopheles in *Faust*, not as he could but as he calculates he should.

The obvious parallel here is between the hero of this film and the figure of tragedy who sold his soul to the devil. But *Mephisto* doesn't depend upon easy parallels to make its point. This is a human story, and as the actor in this movie makes his way to the top of the Nazi propaganda structure and the bottom of his own soul, the movie is both merciless and understanding. This is a weak and shameful man, the film seems to say, but then it cautions us against throwing the first stone.

Mephisto is not a German but a Hungarian movie, directed by the talented Istvan Szabo, who has led his country's cinema from relative obscurity to its present position as one of the best and most innovative film industries in Europe. Szabo, in his way, has made a companion film to Fassbinder's *The Marriage of Maria Braun*. The Szabo film shows a man compromising his way to the top by lying to himself and everybody else, and throwing aside all moral standards. It ends as World War II is under way. The Fassbinder film begins after the destruction of the war, showing a woman clawing her way out of the rubble and repeating the same process of compromise, lies, and unquestioning materialism.

Both the man in the Szabo film and the woman in the Fassbinder film maintain one love affair all through everything, using their love (he for a black woman, she for a convict) as a sort of token contempt for a society whose corrupt values they otherwise completely accept. The fact that they *can* still love, of course, makes it impossible for them to quite deceive themselves. That is the price they pay for their deals with the devil.

Merry Christmas, Mr. Lawrence
★ ★ ½
R, 122 m., 1983

David Bowie (Celliers) Tom Conti (Colonel Lawrence), Ryuichi Sakamoto (Captain Yonoi), Takeshi (Sergeant Hara), Jack Thompson (Hicksley-Ellis). Directed by Nagisa Oshima and produced by Jeremy Thomas. Screenplay by Oshima and Paul Mayersberg.

Here's a movie that is even stranger than it was intended to be. *Merry Christmas, Mr. Lawrence* is about a clash between two cultures (British and Japanese) and two styles of military service (patriotic and pragmatic). That would be enough for any movie, and there are scenes when it *is* enough, and the movie works pretty well. But then the movie makes another contrast that doesn't work so well, a contrast between basic views of theatrical acting styles. British tradition suggests that, everything else being equal, actors should behave as if they were real people in a real situation. The Japanese tend toward a more overwrought acting style, made of screams and grimaces, histrionics and dramatizations. Each tradition works well enough in a movie where it is the only tradition. But in a movie where British and Japanese are on the screen at the same time and are apparently sharing the same reality, the results look odd, and eventually undermine the film. We wonder, in some small irreverent corner of our minds, whether the soft-spoken British *notice* that the Japanese rant and rave over everything, including the weather, and whether the Japanese, in turn, find the British catatonic.

The movie is by Nagisa Oshima, the best-known of the younger Japanese directors, whose notorious *In the Realm of the Senses* (1976) began with a love affair between a businessman and a geisha and ended in a bloodbath of castration and suicide. He is clearly fascinated by relationships between authorities and victims, and that's the subject here. The time is 1942, in a Japanese prison camp on Java, and the story concentrates on two pairs of officers. The British are Celliers (David Bowie), very upper crust, duty-bound, guilt-ridden, and Lawrence (Tom Conti), sensitive, bilingual, trying to translate not only the words but the values of the two races. The Japanese are Yonoi (Ryuichi Sakamoto) of the warrior class, filled with pride and glory, and Hara (Takeshi), a sort of Japanese Falstaff with a streak of sadism. How these two pairs get along together will determine the fate of the British (which is complicated by their nominal leader, a blustering bully played by Jack Thompson).

The movie develops the situation in a series of scenes that owe something to *Bridge Over the River Kwai*. Rules are made, forgotten, broken, then strictly enforced. Enemies admit at weak moments that we are all human beings, after all. But then there's a breach of protocol and a crackdown from the top. The most rigid officers on each side (Celliers and Yonoi) have a sort of admiration for each other, which turns into a contest of wills. This is interesting material, especially since Oshima plunges a little more deeply into the psychology of his characters than your average prisoner-of-war movie is likely to. There are hints of a homosexual attraction between Celliers and Yonoi, eventually leading to one of the movie's most awkward moments—a parting in which the British soldier actually seems to be saying that both sides were right in the war and both sides were wrong.

It's awkward, not because of the subject matter, because of the contrasting acting styles. Here are two men trying to communicate in a touchy area and they behave as if they're from different planets. The overstatement in the Japanese acting ruins the scene. It's strange: Japanese acting styles never bother me in all-Japanese movies (especially not when they're modulated, as in the contemporary films of Kurosawa). It's only when you have actors who are clearly on different wavelengths that the Japanese histrionics become distracting. What this movie needed was a diplomatic acting coach.

Metropolis ★ ★ ★ ★
NO MPAA RATING, 120 m., 1926, 1984 (Sound version)

Alfred Abel (Leader), Gustay Frohlich (His Son), Brigitte Helm (Maria), Rudolf Klein-Rogge (Rotwang), Heinrich George (Foreman). Directed by Fritz Lang. Screenplay by Lang and Thea Von Harbou. New sound track by Giorgio Moroder.

Fritz Lang's 1926 film *Metropolis* is one of the great achievements in the silent era, a work so audacious in its vision and so angry in its message that it is, if anything, more powerful today than when it was made. But

it is rarely seen today; even in the era of insatiable home TV watching, silent films are condemned to the hinterlands of film societies and classrooms.

That is a great loss. Lang's movie is one of the great overwrought fantasies of German Expressionism, a story of a monstrous twenty-first-century city in which the workers labor like robots in their subterranean factories, while the privileged classes dance the night away, far above. The plot is broad melodrama: The son of the ruler of Metropolis visits the underground city and falls in love with a revolutionary named Maria, who makes impassioned speeches against the tyrants above. But the ruler orders a mad scientist to provide his new robot with Maria's face, creating a false Maria who will mislead the workers. Some of the individual scenes are amazing in their visual power, especially our first sight of the workers marching to their jobs, and a bizarre Art Deco factory wall where the humans are treated as parts of the machines. The movie was widely influential: The scene where the robot is turned into the false Maria was the inspiration for all the 1930s transformations of Frankenstein's monsters. Yet the original *Metropolis* is hardly known to today's filmgoers.

But now Giorgio Moroder, the composer of "Flashdance—What a Feeling" and the sound tracks for such movies as *Cat People*, has resurrected *Metropolis*, discovered or reconstructed some of its missing scenes, added some color tinting, and released it with a sound track of 1984 pop music. When this version of the movie was premiered at the 1984 Cannes Film Festival, it was sold primarily for its possibilities as a midnight cult film. In some sort of weird cultural inversion, Pat Benatar and Adam Ant would be used to sell Fritz Lang.

After you've seen the film with its new sound track, however, the notion seems almost sane. Silent films have always been accompanied by some sort of musical accompaniment—everything from orchestras to solo pianos. And in recent years such silent classes as *Napoleon* and *Peter Pan* have been resurrected with new scores. This is even the second time around for *Metropolis*, which was given a track of electronic music by the BBC in the 1970s. Moroder, however, has gone all the way and tarted up *Metropolis* with the same kinds of songs you'd expect to hear on MTV—he treats *Metropolis* like a music video. The film is too strong and original to be reduced to a formula, however; it absorbs the sound track, instead of being dominated by it, and the result is a film that works and a sound track that is an addition.

Some purists will not approve of Moroder's choice in music. Kevin Thomas of the *Los Angeles Times* was especially offended by the use of songs with words ("which sound especially silly because they're so painfully redundant"), but the words didn't bother me because, frankly, I didn't find myself listening to them. They are part of the background, and Fritz Lang's great film, so lovingly reconstructed, is the magnificent foreground.

Micki & Maude ★ ★ ★ ★
PG-13, 115 m., 1984

Dudley Moore (Rob Salinger), Amy Irving (Maude Salinger), Ann Reinking (Micki Salinger), Richard Mulligan (Leo Brody), Lu Leonard (Nurse Verbeck). Directed by Blake Edwards and produced by Tony Adams. Screenplay by Jonathan Reynolds.

The key to the whole thing is Dudley Moore's absolutely and unquestioned sincerity. He loves both women. He would do anything to avoid hurting either woman. He wants to do the right thing but, more than that, he wants to do the kind thing. And that is how he ends up in a maternity ward with two wives who are both presenting him with baby children. If it were not for those good qualities in Moore's character, qualities this movie goes to great lengths to establish, *Micki & Maude* would run the risk of turning into tasteless and even cruel slapstick. After all, these are serious matters we're talking about. But the triumph of the movie is that it identifies so closely with Moore's desperation and his essentially sincere motivation that we understand the lengths to which he is driven. That makes the movie's inevitable climax even funnier.

As the movie opens, Moore is happily married to an assistant district attorney (Ann Reinking) who has no desire to have children. Children are, however, the only thing in life that Moore himself desires; apart from that one void, his life is full and

happy. He works as a reporter for one of those TV magazine shows where weird people talk earnestly about their constitutional rights to be weird: For example, nudists defend their right to bear arms. Then he meets a special person, a cello player (Amy Irving) who has stepped in at the last moment to play a big concert. She thinks he has beautiful eyes, he smiles, it's love, and within a few weeks Moore and Irving are talking about how they'd like to have kids. Then Irving gets pregnant. Moore decides to do the only right thing, and divorce the wife he loves to marry the pregnant girlfriend that he also loves. But then his wife announces that she's pregnant, and Moore turns, in this crisis of conscience, to his best friend, a TV producer wonderfully played by Richard Mulligan. There is obviously only one thing he can do: become a bigamist.

Micki & Maude was directed by Blake Edwards, who also directed Moore in *10*, and who knows how to build a slapstick climax by one subtle development after another. There is, for example, the fact that Irving's father happens to be a professional wrestler, with a lot of friends who are even taller and meaner than he is. There is the problem that Moore's original in-laws happen to past the church where he is having his second wedding. Edwards has a way of applying absolute logic to insane situations, so we learn, for example, that after Moore tells one wife he works days and the other one he works nights, his schedule works out in such a way that he begins to get too much sleep.

Dudley Moore is developing into one of the great movie comedians of his generation. *Micki & Maude* goes on the list with *10* and *Arthur* as screwball classics. Moore has another side as an actor, a sweeter, more serious side, that shows up in good movies like *Romantic Comedy* and bad ones like *Six Weeks*, but it's when he's in a screwball comedy, doing his specialty of absolutely sincere desperation, that he reaches genius. For example: The last twenty minutes of *Micki & Maude*, as the two pregnant women move inexorably forward on their collision course, represents a kind of filmmaking that is as hard to do as anything you'll ever see on a screen. The timing has to be flawless. So does the logic: One loose end, and the inevitability of a slapstick situation is undermined. Edwards and Moore are working at the top of their forms here, and the result is a pure, classic slapstick that makes *Micki & Maude* a real treasure.

A Midsummer Night's Sex Comedy
★ ★
PG, 88 m., 1982

Woody Allen (Andrew), Mia Farrow (Ariel), Jose Ferrer (Leopold), Julie Hagerty (Dulcy), Tony Roberts (Maxwell), Mary Steenburgen (Adrian). Directed by Woody Allen and produced by Robert Greenhut. Screenplay by Allen.

The further north you go in summer, the longer the twilight lingers, until night is but a finger drawn between the dusk and the dawn. Such nights in northern climes are times of revelry, when lads and maids frolic in the underbrush to the pipes of Pan. Woody Allen's *A Midsummer Night's Sex Comedy* sneaks up rather suspiciously on this tradition; his men and women are rationalists, belong to such professions as finance, medicine, and psychiatry, and are nonchalant in the face of such modern inventions as flying bicycles. And yet here they all are, out in the country for the weekend. They gather at a little cottage somewhere in upstate New York, arriving by carriage or primitive auto, and in no time at all they are deeply unhappy about each other's sex lives. The host and hostess are Woody Allen and Mary Steenburgen. He is a stockbroker and she is his shy and sweet wife. The guests include Jose Ferrer, as an egotistical scientist, Mia Farrow, as his fiancée, Tony Roberts as a doctor, and Julie Hagerty as his abundantly sexed nurse.

During the course of their long weekend, many themes emerge, but the most common one is the enigma of male jealousy. Look at these three men, each one paired with the wonderful woman of his dreams. Allen, a part-time crackpot inventor, has a wife who loyally supports his experiments. Ferrer, an aging genius with a monstrous ego, has a beautiful young woman to hang on his arm. Roberts, an insatiable satyr, has a nubile nurse panting with desire. Are all three men happy and satiated? Not a chance. It is the most inevitable thing in the world that each man should be consumed with lust for one or more of the other women. It is not enough to have a bird in the hand; one must also have another bird in the bush. Or, as David Merrick once observed, "It is not enough for me to succeed. My enemies must fail."

From this simple and intriguing little situation, Woody Allen spins a rondelet of sexual intrigue and frustration. The basic developments: Allen pines away with the thought that he could once have made love to Farrow, but declined the chance. Ferrer conspires to meet Hagerty in the woods. Roberts attempts to seduce Farrow. And, through it all, Steenburgen steadfastly hopes for the best from everybody. To pass the time in between assignations and intrigues, the couples picnic, go for walks in the woods and express curiosity in Allen's latest inventions, which, in addition to the flying bicycle, include a metal sphere that can provide a magic lantern show that remembers the past and foresees the future.

This all sounds very charming and whimsical, and it is—almost paralyzingly so. *A Midsummer Night's Sex Comedy* is so low-key, so sweet and offhand and slight, there are times when it hardly even seems happy to be a movie. I am not quite sure what Allen had in mind when he conceived this material, but in addition to the echoes of Shakespeare and of Bergman's *Smiles of a Summer Night*, there are suggestions of John Cheever's Wapshots, Doctorow's *Ragtime* and Jean Renoir films in which nice people do nice things to little avail. This is not a "Woody Allen film," then. It is not a brash comedy, it does not really contain the Woody Allen persona, and I guess Woody wanted it that way; he says he wants to try new things instead of giving people the same old stuff all the time. It is our misfortune that he arrived at that decision just after making *Annie Hall* and *Manhattan*, two wonderful films that brought his same old stuff to an exciting new plateau.

Now, with *Stardust Memories* and this film, he seems rudderless. I don't object to *A Midsummer Night's Sex Comedy* on grounds that it's different from his earlier films, but on the more fundamental ground that it's adrift. There doesn't seem to be a driving idea behind it, a confident tone to give us the sure notion that Allen knows what he wants to do here. It's a tip-off that the story is lacking in both sex and comedy. If the film seems at a loss to know where to turn next, the ending is particularly unsatisfactory. It involves a moment of fantasy or spirituality in which one of the movie's most rational characters dies and turns into a spirit of light, and bobs away on the twilight breeze. I don't object to the development itself, but to the way Allen handles it, so briefly and incompletely that it ends the film with what can only be described as a whimsical anticlimax.

There are nice small moments here and reflective, quiet performances, and a few laughs and smiles. But when we see Woody pedaling furiously to spin the helicopter blades of his flying bicycle, we're reminded of what we're missing. Woody doesn't have to be funny in every shot and he doesn't have to become another Mel Brooks, but he should allow himself to be funny when he feels like it, without apology, instead of receding into cuteness. I had the feeling during the film that Woody Allen was softpedaling his talent, was sitting on his comic gift, was trying to be somebody that he is not—and that, even if he were, would not be half as wonderful a piece of work as the real Woody Allen.

Missing ★ ★ ★
R, 122 m., 1982

Jack Lemmon (Ed Horman), Sissy Spacek (Beth Horman), Melanie Mayron (Terry Simon), John Shea (Charles Horman), Charles Cioffi (Capt. Tower), David Clennon (Consul Putnam). Directed by Constantin Costa-Gavras and produced by Edward and Mildred Lewis. Screenplay by Costa-Gavras and Donald Stewart.

Much has already been written about the bravery of *Missing*, which dares, we are told, to make a specific attack on American policies in Chile during and after the Allende regime. I wish the movie had been even braver—brave enough to risk a clear, unequivocal, uncompromised statement of its beliefs, instead of losing itself in a cluttered mishmash of stylistic excesses. This movie might have *really* been powerful, if it could have gotten out of its own way.

The story involves the disappearance in the early 1970s of a young American journalist in a country (not named) that is obviously intended to be Chile. The young man and his wife (played by John Shea and Sissy Spacek) have gone down there to live, write, and absorb the local color. But then a civil war breaks out, martial law is declared, troops roam the streets, and one day soldiers come and take the young man away. The movie is the record of the frustrating attempts by Spacek and her father-in-law (Jack Lemmon) to discover what happened to the missing man. It suggests that the young American might have been on some sort of informal hit list of left-wing foreign journalists, that he was taken away and killed, and that (this is the controversial part) American embassy officials knew about his fate and may even have been involved in approving his death.

If that was indeed the case, then it is a cause for great anger and dismay. And the best scenes in *Missing*—the ones that make this movie worth seeing despite its shortcomings—are the ones in which Spacek and Lemmon hack their way through a bureaucratic jungle in an attempt to get someone to make a simple statement of fact. Those scenes are masterful. The U.S. embassy officials are painted as dishonest weasels, shuffling papers, promising immediate action, and lying through their teeth. Lemmon and Spacek are about as good an example of Ordinary Americans as you can find in a movie, and their flat voices and stubborn determination and even their initial dislike for one another all ring exactly true. If *Missing* had started with the disappearance of the young man, and had followed Spacek and Lemmon in a straightforward narrative as they searched for him, this movie might have generated overwhelming tension and anger. But the movie never develops the power it should have had, because the director, Constantin Costa-Gavras, either lacked confidence in the strength of his story, or had too much confidence in his own stylistic virtuosity. He has achieved the unhappy feat of upstaging his own movie, losing it in a thicket of visual and editing stunts.

Let's begin with the most annoying example of his meddling. *Missing* contains scenes that take place before the young man disappears. We see his domestic happiness with his wife and friends, we see him reading from *The Little Prince* and making plans for the future. The fact that this material is in the movie suggests, at least, that the story is being told by an omniscient author, one who can also tell us, if he wishes to, what happened to the victim. But he does not. Costa-Gavras shows us all sorts of ominous warnings of approaching trouble (including a lot of loose talk by American military men who are not supposed to be in the country, but are, and all but claim credit for a coup). He shows us a tragic aftermath of martial law, guns in the streets, vigilante justice, and the chilling sight of row after row of dead young men, summarily executed by the new junta. But he does not show us what happened to make the film's hero disappear. Or, rather, he shows us several versions—visual fantasies in which the young husband is arrested at home by a lot of soldiers, or a few, and is taken away in this way or that. These versions are pegged to the unreliable eyewitness accounts of the people who live across the street. They dramatize an uncertain human fate in a time of upheaval, but they also distract fatally from the flow of the film.

By the time *Missing* begins its crucial last half-hour, a strange thing has happened. We care about this dead American, and his wife and father, almost *despite* the movie. The performances of Spacek and Lemmon carry us along through the movie's undisciplined stylistic displays. But at the end of the film, there isn't the instant discharge of anger we felt at the end of Costa-Gavras's great *Z* (1968), because the narrative juggernaut of that film has been traded in for what is basically just a fancy meditation on the nature of reality. Something happend to the missing young man (his story is based on real events). Somebody was guilty, and somebody was lying, and he was indeed killed. But *Missing* loses its way on the road to those conclusions, and at the end Lemmon and Spacek seem almost to mourn alone, while the crew is busy looking for its next shot.

Mommie Dearest ★
PG, 129 m., 1981

Faye Dunaway (Joan Crawford), Diana Scarwid (Christina, adult), Steve Forrest (Greg Savitt), Howard Da Silva (L.B. Mayer), Mara Hobel (Christina, child), Autanya Alda (Carol Ann). Directed by Frank Perry and produced by Frank Yablans. Screenplay by Yablans, Perry, Tracy Hotchner, and Robert Getchell.

I can't imagine who would want to subject themselves to this movie. *Mommie Dearest* is a painful experience that drones on endlessly, as Joan Crawford's relationship with her daughter, Christina, disintegrates from cruelty through jealousy into pathos. It is unremittingly depressing, not to any purpose of drama or entertainment, but just to depress. It left me feeling creepy. The movie was inspired, of course, by a best-selling memoir in which adopted daughter Christina Crawford portrayed her movie-star mother as a grasping, sadistic, alcoholic wretch whose own insecurities and monstrous ego made life miserable for everyone around her. I have no idea if the book's portrait is an accurate one, but the movie is faithful to it in one key sense: It made life miserable for me.

Mommie Dearest repeats the same basic dramatic situation again and again. Baby Christina tries to do the right thing, tries to be a good girl, tries to please Mommie, but Mommie is a manic-depressive who alternates between brief triumphs and long savage tirades, infecting her daughter with resentment and guilt. In scene after scene, we are invited to watch as Joan Crawford screams at Christina, chops her hair with scissors, beats her with a wire coat hanger and, on an especially bad day, tackles her across an end table, hurls her to the carpet, bangs her head against the floor, and tries to choke her to death. Who wants to watch this?

This material is presented essentially as sensationalism. The movie makes no attempt to draw psychological insights from the life of its Joan Crawford—not even through the shorthand Freudianism much beloved by Hollywood. Mommie is a monster, that's all, and there's some mention of her unhappy childhood. Christina is a brave, smiling, pretty, long-suffering dope who might inspire more sympathy if she were not directed (in both her childhood and adult versions) to be distant and veiled.

The movie doesn't even make narrative sense. Success follows crisis without any pattern. At one moment, Joan is in triumph after winning the Oscar for *Mildred Pierce*. In the very next scene she goes so berserk we want to scrape her off the screen with a spatula. The scenes don't build, they just happen. Another example: After an especially ugly fight, Joan sends Christina to a convent school. There's a scene where the mother superior welcomes her and promises to reform her. One scene later, Christina checks out of the school, and the nun wishes her godspeed. No mention of what happened in the school, how it affected Christina, or whether the nun changed her opinion of the girl.

The movie also offers few insights into Crawford's relationships with others. There's a loyal housekeeper, but never a scene where Crawford speaks personally with her. There is a lover and a third husband, both enigmas. Crawford's acting career is treated mostly in ellipses. The sets look absolutely great, Faye Dunaway's impersonation of Crawford is stunningly suggestive and convincing, and little Mara Hobel, as Baby Christina, handles several difficult moments very well. But to what end? *Mommie Dearest* is a movie that knows exactly how it wants to look, but has no idea what it wants to make us feel.

Monsignor ★
R, 122 m., 1982

Christopher Reeve (Flaherty), Genevieve Bujold (Clara), Fernando Rey (Santoni). Directed by Frank Perry and produced by Frank Yablans. Screenplay by Abraham Polonsky and Wendell Mayes.

Monsignor is the most cynical movie ever made about organized religion. I include in that statement the anticlerical broadsides by Luis Bunuel, who attacked Catholicism with shocking imagery and gleefully flaunted his atheism but at least took the Roman Catholic Church seriously enough to treat it as a worthy adversary. *Monsignor* uses the Vatican only for a storyline—and doesn't even get a good one.

The movie takes place during World War II, when the Italian-dominated Vatican establishment, racked by in-fighting, imports a young Irish-Catholic priest (Christopher Reeve) from America. He's said to be a good accountant. He sure is. Under the sponsorship of the Vatican Secretary of State (Fernando Rey), he concocts a plan to finance the bankrupt Vatican by selling fifty thousand cartons of American cigarettes a week to the Mafia-controlled black market. This is obviously a bright young man, destined to rise in the church hierarchy. Unfortunately, despite his promising start in illegal profiteering, he turns out to have a character defect: He lusts after a young nun (Genevieve Bujold), and they have an affair.

There follows a confusing flash-forward to a point some years in the future, after Reeve has allowed $400 million of the church's money to be lost in reckless stock market speculation. *This* time, has he gone too far? Not really. At the movie's end, he's exchanging confidences with his old sponsor, who has just been elected pope. As you may already have gathered, the Catholics in this movie do everything but pray. The church is seen as a venal, corrupt, dishonest institution—I think. (The strange thing is that Reeve maintains such a veneer of saintliness through the movie that at times we really believe his sophistry as he's defending his black market sales.) I do not object to the filmmaker's desire to make a film of overwhelming cynicism about the Vatican power structure. I simply object to the film they have made.

It appears to have no purpose. It doesn't condemn dishonesty, yet neither does it applaud unscrupulous schemery. It doesn't bemoan low human weaknesses, nor does it contain heroes. In the case of the affair between the priest and the nun, it doesn't even take a stand! The flash-forward avoids the necessity of even *finishing* that aspect of the story. There are a few good things in *Monsignor*. The movie is populated with good performances in the character roles, especially by Fernando Rey (who once played one of Bunuel's anticlerical clerics), by Robert Prosky (he's an American cardinal here, and was superb as the mob fixer in *Thief*) and by Leonardo Cimino as a pope who looks uncannily like E.T. and looks forward to his own death with a grim humor. These performances, alas, do not occur in an engaging screenplay; the most cynical thing in this cynical movie is that it doesn't even bother to put its nihilistic characters in a comprehensible story.

Monty Python's Meaning of Life
★ ★ ½
R, 103 m., 1983

Written and starring: Graham Chapman, John Cleese, Terry Gilliam, Eric Idle, Terry Jones, and Michael Palin. Directed by Terry Jones and produced by John Goldstone.

Halfway through *Monty Python's Meaning of Life,* the thought struck me that One-Upmanship was a British discovery. You remember, of course, the book and movie *(School for Scoundrels)* inspired by Stephen Potter's theory of One-Upmanship, in which the goal of the practitioner was to One-Up his daily associates and, if possible, the world. A modern example:

Victim: I've just been reading Gabriel Garcia Marquez's *Chronicle of a Death Foretold* in *Vanity Fair* magazine.

One-Upman: Really? I'm afraid I missed it.

Victim: But Garcia Marquez is brilliant.

One-Upman: No doubt, dear fellow, but my subscription ran out in 1939.

I use this illustration as an approach to *Monty Python's Meaning of Life,* which is a movie that seems consumed with a desire to push us too far. This movie is so far beyond good taste, and so cheerfully beyond, that we almost feel we're being One-Upped if we allow ourselves to be offended. Take, for example, the scene featuring projectile vomiting. We don't get just a little vomit in the scene, as we saw in *The Exorcist.* No sir, we get gallons of vomit, streams of it, all a vile yellow color, sprayed all over everybody and everything in a formal dining room. The first reaction of the non-Upman is *"Yech!"* But I think the Python gang is working at another level. And, given the weakness of movie critics for discussing what "level" a movie "works" on, I find myself almost compelled to ask myself, "At what 'level' *does* the projectile vomiting 'work'?" And I think the Python One-Up reply would be, dear fellow, that it rises above vulgarity and stakes out territory in the surrealistic. Anyone who takes the vomiting literally has missed the joke; the scene isn't about vomit-

ing, but about the lengths to which Python will go for a laugh.

There are other scenes in equally poor taste in this movie, which has a little something to offend everybody. And I mean *really* offend them: This isn't a Mel Brooks movie, with friendly little ethnic in-jokes. It's a barbed, uncompromising attack on generally observed community standards. Does the attack work? Only occasionally. The opening sequence of the film is one of its best, showing the overworked old clerks in an insurance company staging a mutiny. After they've gained control of their shabby old stone building, the movie does a brilliant turn into surrealism, the building becomes a ship, and the clerks weigh anchor and set sail against the fleets of modern high-rises, firing their filing cabinets like cannons. It's a wonderful sequence.

I also liked a scene set on a military parade ground, and a joke involving a tankful of fish, and a cheerfully unfair rugby match between two teams, one made up of twelve small schoolboys, the other with eighteen schoolmasters, all huge. Balanced against these bright moments is the goriest scene in Python history, showing a liver being removed from a transplant "volunteer" by brute force. There are also a lot of religious jokes, some straightforward sexism, and the above-mentioned vomiting sequence.

By admitting to being offended by some of the stuff in this movie, I've been One-Upped. By liking the funny stuff, I've been One-Upped again. ("But you liked the jokes that were in good taste? Jolly good!") But I'm a good loser, and I don't mind being One-Upped. In fact, let's say this is a tennis match, and the Pythons are the winners. Here, I'll hold down the net while they jump over to shake hands with me. Whoops!

Moonlighting ★ ★ ★ ★
PG, 97 m., 1982

Jeremy Irons (Nowak), Eugene Lipinski (Banaszak), Jiri Stanislav (Wolski), Eugeniusz Haczkiewicz (Kudaj). Directed by Jerzy Skolimowski and produced by Mark Shivas and Skolimowski. Screenplay by Skolimowski.

Moonlighting is a wickedly pointed movie that takes a simple little story, tells it with humor and truth, and turns it into a knife in the side of the Polish government. In its own way, this response to the crushing of Solidarity is as powerful as Andrezej Wajda's *Man of Iron*. It also is more fun. The movie takes place in London, during the weeks just before and after the banning of the Solidarity movement in Poland. It begins, actually, in Warsaw, with a mystifying scene in which a group of plotters are scheming to smuggle some hardware past British customs. They're plotters, all right; their plot is to move into a small house in London and remodel it, knocking out walls, painting ceilings, making it into a showplace for the Polish government official who has purchased it. The official's plan is simplicity itself: By bringing Polish workers to London on tourist visas, he can get the remodeling done for a fraction of what British workman would cost him. At the same time, the workers can earn good wages that they can take back to Poland and buy bicycles with. The only thing nobody counts on is the upheaval after Solidarity is crushed and travel to and from Poland is strictly regulated.

Jeremy Irons, of *The French Lieutenant's Woman*, plays the lead in the film. He's the only Polish workman who can speak English. Acting as foreman, he guides his team of men through the pitfalls of London and safely into the house they're going to remodel. He advises them to keep a low profile, while he ventures out to buy the groceries and (not incidentally) to read the newspapers. When he finds out about the crisis in Poland, he keeps it a secret from his comrades. The daily life of the renovation project falls into a pattern, which the film's director, Jerzy Skolimowski, intercuts with the adventures of his hero. Jeremy Irons begins to steal things: newspapers, bicycles, frozen turkeys. He concocts an elaborate scheme to defraud the local supermarket, and some of the movie's best scenes involve the subtle timing of his shoplifting scam, which involves the misrepresentation of cash-register receipts. He needs to steal food because he's running out of money, and he knows his group can't easily go home again. There's also a quietly hilarious, and slightly sad, episode involving a salesgirl in a blue jeans store. Irons, pretending to be more

naive than he is, tries to pick the girl up. She's having none of it.

Moonlighting invites all kinds of interpretations. You can take this simple story and set it against the events of the last two years, and see it as a kind of parable. Your interpretation is as good as mine. Is the house itself Poland, and the workmen Solidarity—rebuilding it from within, before an authoritarian outside force intervenes? Or is this movie about the heresy of substituting Western values (and jeans and turkeys) for a home-grown orientation? Or is it about the manipulation of the working classes by the intelligentsia? Or is it simply a frontal attack on the Communist Party bosses who live high off the hog while the workers are supposed to follow the rules?

Like all good parables, *Moonlighting* contains not one but many possibilities. What needs to be insisted upon, however, is how much *fun* this movie is. Skolimowski, a Pole who has lived and worked in England for several years, began writing this film on the day that Solidarity was crushed, and he filmed it, on a small budget and with a small crew, in less than two months: He had it ready for the 1982 Cannes Film Festival where it was a major success. It's successful, I think, because it tells an interesting narrative in a straightforward way. Skolimowski is a natural storyteller. You can interpret and discuss *Moonlighting* all night. During the movie, you'll be more interested in whether Irons gets away with that frozen turkey.

Moscow on the Hudson ★ ★ ★ ★
R, 115 m., 1984

Robin Williams (Vladimir Ivanoff), Maria Conchita Alonso (Lucia Lombardo), Cleavant Derricks (Witherspoon), Alejandro Rey (Orlando Ramirez). Directed and produced by Paul Mazursky. Screenplay by Mazursky and Leon Capetanos.

Mike Royko likes to make fun of foreign-born taxi drivers. He uses a lot of phonetic spellings to show how funny dey speeka da Engleesh. Maybe he's missing out on some good conversations. Have you ever *talked* to a taxi driver from Iran or Pakistan or Africa? I have, and usually I hear a fascinating story about a man who has fled from poverty or persecution, who in some cases has left behind a thriving business, and who is starting out all over again in this country. I also usually get the name of a good restaurant.

I thought of some of those experiences while I was watching Paul Mazursky's *Moscow on the Hudson,* a wonderful movie about a man who defects to the United States. His name is Vladimir Ivanoff, he plays the saxophone in a Russian circus, and when the circus visits New York, he falls in love with the United States and defects by turning himself in to a security guard at Bloomingdale's. The Russian is played by Robin Williams, who disappears so completely into his quirky, lovable, complicated character that he's quite plausible as a Russian. The movie opens with his life in Moscow, a city of overcrowded apartments, bureaucratic red tape, long lines for consumer goods, secret pleasures like jazz records, and shortages so acute that toilet paper has turned into a currency of its own. The early scenes are eerily convincing, partly because Williams plays them in Russian. This isn't one of those movies where everybody somehow speaks English. The turning point of the movie occurs in Bloomingdale's, as so many turning points do, and Ivanoff makes two friends right there on the spot: Witherspoon, the black security guard (Cleavant Derricks) and Lucia, the Italian salesclerk (Maria Conchita Alonso).

They're a tip-off to an interesting casting decision by Mazursky, who populates his movie almost entirely with ethnic and racial minorities. In addition to the black and the Italian, there's a Korean taxi driver, a Cuban lawyer, a Chinese anchorwoman, all of them reminders that all of us, except for American Indians, came from somewhere else. Ivanoff moves in with the security guard's family, which greatly resembles the one he left behind in Moscow, right down to the pious grandfather. He gets a job selling hot dogs from a pushcart, he works his way up to driving a limousine, and he falls in love with the salesclerk from Italy. That doesn't go so well. She dreams of marrying a "real American," and Ivanoff, even after he trims his beard, will not quite do.

Moscow on the Hudson is the kind of movie that Paul Mazursky does especially well. It's a comedy that finds most of its laughs in the close observations of human behavior, and that finds its story in a contemporary subject Mazursky has some thoughts about. In that, it's like his earlier films *An Unmarried Woman* (women's liberation), *Harry and Tonto* (growing old), *Blume in Love* (marriage in the age of doing your own thing), and *Bob & Carol and Ted & Alice* (encounter groups). It is also a rarity, a patriotic film that has a liberal, rather than a conservative, heart. It made me feel good to be an American, and good that Vladimir Ivanoff was going to be one, too.

Motel Hell ★ ★ ★
R, 106 m., 1980

Rory Calhoun (Farmer Vincent), Paul Linke (Bruce Smith), Nancy Parsons (Ida Smith), Nina Axelrod (Terry), Wolfman Jack (Reverend Billy), Elaine Joyce (Edith Olson). Directed by Kevin Connor and produced by Steven-Charles Jaffe and Robert Jaffe. Screenplay by Jaffe and Jaffe.

Motel Hell satirizes a whole sub-basement genre of American movies that a lot of lucky people may never even have seen. I call them Sleazoid Movies; films that deliberately test our sensibilities, and our stomachs, by the subhuman and nauseating behavior of the characters on the screen. The genre includes *The Texas Chainsaw Massacre, The Hills Have Eyes, The Honeymoon Killers, Night of the Living Dead,* and *Last House on the Left.*

These films are not to be confused with those of a neighboring genre, the Women in Danger films, which spew hatred of women. Sleazoid movies seem to exist on the edge of self-parody, and their ambition is to be to the cinema what the geek show is to the circus. They're not antiwoman, they're antitaste, and their characters sink into moronic, bestial savagery. They touch on the ultimate horror of people degraded into subhuman, animalistic behavior. Some of these films, I should add, are not without merit—although this isn't the place to launch into a defense of them.

What *Motel Hell* brings to this genre is the refreshing sound of laughter. This movie *is* disgusting, of course; it's impossible to satirize this material, I imagine, without presenting the subject matter you're satirizing. But *Motel Hell* is not nearly as gruesome as the films it satirizes, and it finds the right stylistic note for its central characters, who are simple, cheerful, smiling, earnest, and resourceful cannibals.

Motel Hell (the second "e" on the neon sign has gone out) is a ramshackle place that seems to be located in the same redneck backwoods where Russ Meyer's characters all live. It is operated by friendly Farmer Vincent (Rory Calhoun) and his sister (Nancy Parsons). The district is patrolled, none too adroitly, by a relative (Paul Linke), who is the sheriff, but sees nothing wrong with burying the victims of a motorcycle crash without benefit of investigation or autopsy.

That's just as well, because Farmer Vincent's specialty is burying people. He just doesn't wait until they're dead. He waylays unsuspecting travelers, knocks them unconscious, buries them up to their necks in his secret garden, fattens them up with cattle feed, and then slaughters them, smokes them in his smokehouse, and sells them as sausage at his roadside stand. His cheerful motto: "It takes all kinds of critters . . . to make Farmer Vincent's fritters."

All right now, of *course* this is disgusting. But hold on just a dagbone minute, as Farmer Vincent might say. It isn't simply the subject matter of Sleazoid Movies that makes them reprehensible, it's their low opinion of human nature, their acquiesence in the proposition that the world is essentially an evil place. *Motel Hell*, with Rory Calhoun looking like a Norman Rockwell model in his bib overalls, pushes this material so far in such unlikely directions that, incredibly, it works as satire. A lot of horror movies used to work that way. We went to be scared, sure, but we also went to laugh, enjoying the delicious self-indulgence with which Vincent Price or Christopher Lee hammed it up. But horror movies stopped being funny. And now they're mostly just depressing, disgusting exercises in depravity.

Motel Hell is a welcome change-of-pace; it's to *Chainsaw Massacre* as *Airplane!* is to *Airport*. It has some great moments, including a duel fought with chainsaws, a hero swinging to the rescue on a meathook, and Farmer Vincent's dying confession of the shameful secret that he concealed for years. These moments illuminate the movie's basic and not very profound insight, which is that most of the sleazoids would be a lot more fun if they didn't take themselves with such gruesome solemnity.

Mother's Day   no stars
R, 98 m., 1980

With Nancy Hendrickson, Deborah Luce, Tiana Pierce, Holden McQuire, Billy Ray McQuade, and Rose Ross.

Mother's Day is a reprehensible specimen of the geek film, so-called because such films are about the activities of that subcategory of humans formerly found in the carnival sideshows, biting the heads off chickens. Like the geeks of old, a film such as this will stoop to anything in its attempt to disgust its audiences. And the audiences for geek films are not easily disgusted. After the first five minutes of *Mother's Day*—after the shot of blood spurting from the severed neck of the movie's first victim—I was ready to walk out. But no, that would have been too easy. I determined to stick this one out.

The plot: A demented old woman lives in a shack in the woods with her two cretinous sons. Their entertainment is to capture unwary campers and torture, rape, and kill them for the delight of their mother. In between, they behave like pigs. A typical dinner scene involves one of the sons shooting a can of pressurized cheese whip down his throat.

Near the beginning of the film (but after the first beheading), three young women, former college classmates, go camping in the woods. They are imprisoned inside their sleeping bags and dragged back to the shack, where they are assaulted, raped, cut up, beaten, and forced to watch unspeakable acts. The mother cackles with glee. The actresses scream relentlessly.

Later in the film, after one of the girls is dead, the two survivors come back for revenge. (This sort of "eye for an eye" conclusion is apparently a ghastly attempt at fairness on the part of the geeks who make these movies.) The girls get their revenge. In one sequence, one of the sons is stabbed with a hatchet. His brother has a can of Drano poured down his throat, and is hit over the head with a television set. Viewers can look in through the TV screen as the victim is electrocuted. The question of why anybody of any age would possibly want to see this film remains without an answer.

Mr. Mom ★ ★
PG, 92 m., 1983

Michael Keaton (Jack), Teri Garr (Caroline), Frederick Koehler (Alex), Taliesin Jaffe (Kenny), Martin Mull (Ron). Directed by Stan Dragoti and produced by Lynn Loring and Lauren Shuler. Screenplay by John Hughes.

People have been living through the basic idea of *Mr. Mom* for years. It's too bad this movie doesn't feel more like their lives and less like the pilot for a TV sitcom. The movie's about a well-paid Ford executive who gets laid off and can't find work. Then his wife finds a job at an advertising agency, and her years of experience in "the front lines of consumerism" make her a big hit with the clients. Meanwhile, her husband stays home to keep house and raise the children. There are so many genuine comedy ideas (and not a few provocative ones) rising out of this situation that it's hard to see how the filmmakers could go wrong. But go wrong they do, with gimmicky sight gags and awkward fantasy sequences, stock characters, and unbelievable situations. What a lost opportunity.

That's especially true because the cast is so promising. Michael Keaton, a kinetic young actor who gives the uncanny impression of being able to think faster than he can talk, plays the husband. Teri Garr, Dustin Hoffman's other girlfriend in *Tootsie*, is the wife. And Martin Mull is the snaky president of the advertising agency, with plans for promoting Garr into his own life. Now if they'd taken these characters and their situation and followed through on the implications, on a believable level, they might have come up with a true human comedy. Instead, everything is pushed too far, situations are overwritten and overdirected, and the movie is desperate enough to throw in vacuum cleaners with minds of their own, seductive next-door neighbors, and a team of local repairmen who show up on cue and seem straight out of TV commercials.

God knows there's enough in ordinary housework to make a comedy out of, especially if the hotshot husband is trying to learn how to run the house. Do we really need the scene in which he cheerfully puts four cups of detergent into the washer? Enough real things can go wrong around the house without the movie needing a monosyllabic female TV repairman and an exterminator who's afraid of bugs.

Meanwhile, at the ad agency, Teri Garr also is having her problems with a script that strives for the predictable. She's brought into a conference on a tuna account. The agency's failed campaign presentations line the walls. She shoots them down and comes up with a bright idea: Offer a big discount for the duration of the recession. Brilliant, eh? Except, wait a minute, the other campaigns on the bulletin board don't even look like professional presentations; they look like scrawls out of *Mad* magazine. And her bright idea is obviously only in the movie because if she *has* a bright idea, you see, she'll get the job and attract the boss. No attempt is made to be perceptive or original about the idea of a housewife returning to the job wars as an ad executive.

Mr. Mom gives itself away with its title, I think. The title was so obviously a Concept, a brief encapsulation of what the movie would be "about," that all the script needed to deliver was manufactured, artificial situations inspired, not by the experiences of joblessness or role-reversal, but by memories of old TV shows. They had a great idea here. It's too bad they didn't follow it through on a human level, instead of making it feel made-up and artificial and twice-removed from the everyday experience it pretends to be about.

The Muppets Take Manhattan ★ ★ ★
G, 94 m., 1984

With guest stars Dabney Coleman, Joan Rivers, Liza Minelli, and John Landis. Directed by Frank Oz and produced by David Lazer. Written by Oz and Jim Henson.

Dear Kermit,

I hope you will take this in the right spirit. I know you've been tortured for some years now by an identity crisis, ever since you were discovered sitting on that log down in the swamp, strumming on your ukulele. Stardom happened almost overnight, and here you are in your third starring vehicle, *The*

Muppets Take Manhattan. Yet you still don't know who you really are.

You are obviously not a frog. You have none of the attributes of a frog, except for your appearance and your name. In your first film, *The Muppet Movie*, you were sort of a greenish overgrown pop singer, an amphibian Frankie Avalon. In your second movie, *The Great Muppet Caper,* you were cast adrift in a plot that really belonged to the human guest stars. You basically had a supporting role, making the humans look good. Only in *The Muppets Take Manhattan,* your third film, do you really seem to come into your own. You take charge. You are the central figure in the plot, you do not allow yourself to get shouldered aside by Miss Piggy, and you seem thoroughly at home with the requirements of genre, stereotype, and cliché. In the 1940s, you would have been under contract to MGM.

The plot of your movie has been seen before. I doubt if that will come as news to you. *The Muppets Take Manhattan* is yet another retread of the reliable old formula in which somebody says "Hey, gang! Our senior class musical show is so good, I'll bet we could be stars on Broadway!" The fact that this plot is not original does not deter you, Kermit, nor should it. It's still a good plot.

I liked the scenes in which you persevered. I liked the way you went to New York and challenged the stubborn agents like Dabney Coleman, and upstaged Liza Minnelli in Sardi's. I especially liked the scenes where you supported yourself by waiting tables in a greasy spoon cafe with rats in the kitchen and a Greek owner who specialized in philosophical statements that didn't make any sense. I even liked Miss Piggy's scenes, especially her childhood memories. I gasped at the wedding scene, in which you finally married her. I refrained from speculating about your wedding night—and speculation is all your G-rated movie left me with.

In short, I liked just about everything about your movie. But what I liked best was your discovery of self. Kermit, you are no longer a frog with an identity crisis. You've found the right persona, old boy, and it will see you through a dozen more movies. It was clear to me from the moment you took your curtain call and basked in the spotlight. Ker-

mit, this may come as a shock, but you're Mickey Rooney in a frog suit. Think about it. You're short. You're cute. You never say die. You keep smilin'. You have a philosophy for everything. You appear only in wholesome, G-rated movies. And sex bombs like Liza Minnelli only kiss you on the cheek.

One word of advice. Dump Miss Piggy. Stage a talent search for a Liza Minnelli Muppet. Mickey Rooney made a lot of movies with Liza's mother before you were hatched, Kermit, and now it's your turn. Move fast, kid, before you croak.

My Bodyguard ★ ★ ★ ½
PG, 97 m., 1980

Chris Makepeace (Clifford), Adam Baldwin (Linderman), Matt Dillon (Moody), Ruth Gordon (Gramma), Martin Mull (Mr. Peache), John Houseman (Dobbs), Paul Quandt (Carson), Craig Richard Nelson (Griffith). Directed by Tony Bill and produced by Don Devlin. Screenplay by Alan Ormsby.

There is a terrifying moment in adolescence when suddenly some of the kids are twice as big as the rest of the kids. It is terrifying for everybody: For the kids who are suddenly tall and gangling, and for the kids who are still small and are getting beat up all the time. *My Bodyguard* places that moment in a Chicago high school and gives us a kid who tries to think his way out of it.

The kid's name is Clifford. He has everything going against him. He's smart, he's new in the school, he's slightly built. As he's played by Chris Makepeace, he is also one of the most engaging teen-age characters I've seen in the movies in a long time. Too many movie teen-agers have been sex-crazed (*Little Darlings*), animalistic food-fighters (*Meat Balls*), or hopelessly romanticized (*The Blue Lagoon*). Clifford is basically just your normal, average kid.

He has just moved to Chicago with his family. His father (Martin Mull) is the new resident manager of the Ambassador East Hotel. His grandmother (Ruth Gordon) hangs out in the lobby and picks up old men in the bar. Life is great, backstage at a hotel (he gets his meals in the kitchen or sometimes in the Pump Room). But it's not so great at school. The movie sends Clifford to

Lake View High School, where he's immediately shaken down for his lunch money.

The extortionist (Matt Dillon) is the kind of kid we all remember from high school. He's handsome in an oily way, he's going through a severe case of adolescent sadism, he's basically a coward. His threat is that unless Clifford pays protection money, he'll sic the dreaded Linderman on him.

Linderman (Adam Baldwin) is a school legend, a big, hulking kid who allegedly killed his brother, raped a teacher, hit a cop, you name it. The movie's inspiration is to have Clifford *think* his way out of his dilemma—neutralizing Linderman by hiring him as a bodyguard. This is genius, and there's a wonderful scene where Clifford springs Linderman on the rest of the kids.

Then the movie takes an interesting turn. Clifford and Linderman become friends, and we learn some of the unhappy facts of Linderman's life. It turns out Linderman isn't the Incredible Hulk after all—he's just another kid going through growing pains and some personal tragedy. This whole middle stretch is the best part of the movie, developing a friendship in a perceptive and gentle way that's almost shocking in comparison with the idiotic, violent teen-agers so many movies have given us.

The ending is predictable (it's a showdown between Linderman and another tough kid). And there are some distractions along the way from Clifford's family. Martin Mull makes an interesting hotel manager, whimsical and charming. But the movie gets off track when it follows Ruth Gordon through some of her adventures, including a romantic collision with a hotel executive played by John Houseman. These scenes just don't seem part of the same movie: The hotel stuff is sitcom, while the stuff in the high school is fresh and inventive.

That seems to apply to the performances, too. One of the strengths of *My Bodyguard* is in the casting of the younger performers—Chris Makepeace, Adam Baldwin, Matt Dillon. They look right for their parts, but, more to the point, they *feel* right. Dillon exudes creepiness, Makepeace is plausible while thinking on his feet, Linderman is convincingly vulnerable and confused, and there's another kid, the solemn-faced, wide-eyed Paul Quandt, who steals a couple of

scenes with his absolute certainty that the worst is yet to come.

My Bodyguard is a small treasure, a movie about believable characters in an unusual situation. It doesn't pretend to be absolutely realistic, and the dynamics of its big city high school are simplified for the purposes of the story. But this movie is fun to watch because it touches memories that are shared by most of us, and because its young characters are recognizable individuals, and not simplified cartoon figures like so many movie teen-agers.

My Brilliant Career ★ ★ ★ ½
NO MPAA RATING, 101 m., 1980

Judy Davis (Sybylia Melvyn), Sam Neill (Harry Beecham), Wendy Hughes (Aunt Helen), Robert Grubb (Frank Hawden), Max Cullen (Mr. McSwat), Pat Kennedy (Aunt Gussie). Directed by Gillian Armstrong and produced by Margaret Fink. Screenplay by Eleanor Witcombe.

What magic is it that sometimes allows young girls in backward districts to guess that they need not play along with the general ideas about a "woman's role"? I ask because three of my favorite writers—and now a fourth—discovered, more or less by themselves, that the possibilities in their lives were unlimited.

Two of the writers are famous: Willa Cather, who wrote of independent young women in Nebraska and points west, and Doris Lessing, whose *Children of Violence* series chronicles the liberation of a young woman from Rhodesia. The other two writers are not so well known, but the parallels in their lives are so astonishing that I'd like to sketch them, briefly, before moving on to an extraordinary film, *My Brilliant Career.* Their names are Olive Schreiner and Miles Franklin. They both led isolated childhoods in the nineteenth century, in the backwaters of the British Empire. And they both wrote novels about those lives at a very early age.

Olive Schreiner was raised on a farm in the Orange Free State, in South Africa. She learned Afrikaans along with English, read the Bible daily, and in her mid-teens wrote a classic novel, *The Story of an African Farm.* It was about the awakening of the spirit of a teen-age girl (herself, obviously) who did not see why her life had to be so limited just because she was a woman. Schreiner's later life was spent in intellectual and feminist circles in London (and for a time she filled the challenging position of being Havelock Ellis's mistress).

The other writer is someone I've just learned about recently: Miles Franklin, born in 1879 in rural Australia and raised on an isolated country station in the outback. At the age of sixteen she wrote a novel about her experiences, *My Brilliant Career*. It was published six years later in Edinburgh. Like Schreiner, Franklin became a feminist, traveled abroad in her twenties (and came to Chicago, where she and Alice Henry organized the Women's Trade Union League).

The Story of an African Farm is an established literary classic. *My Brilliant Career*, on the other hand, was relatively forgotten until a group of Australian women filmmakers made it into this remarkable film. It tells the story of a restless, high-spirited young woman whose temperament just isn't suited to the leftover Victorian standards of Australian country districts in the 1890s.

Franklin's novel is successful as a movie primarily because of a brilliant casting discovery. Judy Davis, who plays the film's heroine, is so fresh, unique, irreverent, and winning that she makes this material live. She's a young actress from Perth, a sometime pop and jazz singer, who was reportedly the second choice for the film's lead; if that's so, it was a completely fortunate second choice.

My Brilliant Career could have been just another feminist film. The director, Gillian Armstrong, could have gone to great lengths to explain the thinking and motivations of her character—and bored us in the meantime. But she doesn't. Instead, she makes her points through Judy Davis's presence and personality.

This isn't a movie that ends with any final answers or conclusions. Instead, it's about a young woman in a painful and continuing process of indecision. She's not considered by her family to be an ideal young woman at all—she's too independent, untamed, unreconciled to a woman's role. She doesn't automatically swoon at the attentions of every young man in the district. She's red-haired, freckled, feisty.

These qualities do appeal, however, to one young neighboring man, a farmer who's of two minds about her: He finds her independence appealing, and yet he tends to share the prevailing view about proper behavior for women. Can he overcome his narrow view and accept her? He does propose marriage. Can she overcome her headstrong independence and accept him? That's the film's key question, and *My Brilliant Career* is wise in never quite answering it.

The film is beautiful to look at. It was filmed on location in the outback, in warm natural colors, and the costumes and settings meticulously establish the period. But Judy Davis's performance establishes it even more, because she creates a complicated character so naturally that we feel the conflicts instead of having to understand them intellectually. This is the best kind of movie of ideas, in which the movie supplies the people and emotions and *we* come up with the conclusions.

My Dinner with André ★ ★ ★ ★
NO MPAA RATING, 110 m., 1981

Wallace Shawn (Wally), André Gregory (André), Jean Lenauer (Waiter), Roy Butler (Bartender). Directed by Louis Malle and produced by George W. George and Beverly Karp. Screenplay by Shawn and Gregory.

The idea is astonishing in its audacity: a film of two friends talking, just simply talking—but with passion, wit, scandal, whimsy, vision, hope, and despair—for 110 minutes. It sounds at first like one of those underground films of the 1960s, in which great length and minimal content somehow interacted in the dope-addled brains of the audience to provide the impression of deep if somehow elusive profundity. *My Dinner with André* is not like that. It doesn't use all of those words as a stunt. They are alive on the screen, breathing, pulsing, reminding us of endless, impassioned conversations we've had with those few friends worth talking with for hours and hours. Underneath all the other fascinating things in this film beats the tide of friendship, of two people with a genuine interest in one another.

The two people are André Gregory and Wallace Shawn. Those are their real names, and also their names in the movie. I suppose they are playing themselves. As the film opens, Shawn travels across New York City to meet Gregory for dinner, and his thoughts provide us with background: His friend Gregory is a New York theater director, well-known into the 1970s, who dropped out for five years and traveled around the world. Now Gregory has returned, with wondrous tales of strange experiences. Shawn has spent the same years in New York, finding uncertain success as an author and playwright. They sit down for dinner in an elegant restaurant. We do not see the other customers. The bartender is a wraith in the background, the waiter is the sort of presence they were waiting for in *Waiting for Godot*. The friends order dinner, and then, as it is served and they eat and drink, they talk.

What conversation! André Gregory does most of the talking, and he is a spellbinding conversationalist, able to weave mental images not only out of his experiences, but also out of his ideas. He explains that he had become dissatisfied with life, restless, filled with anomie and discontent. He accepted an invitation to join an experimental theater group in Poland. It was *very* experimental, tending toward rituals in the woods under the full moon.

From Poland, he traveled around the world, meeting a series of people who were seriously and creatively exploring the ways in which they could experience the material world. They (and Gregory) literally believed in mind over matter, and as Gregory describes a monk who was able to stand his entire body weight on his fingertips, we visualize that man and in some strange way (so hypnotic is the tale) we share the experience.

One of the gifts of *My Dinner with André* is that we share so many of the experiences. Although most of the movie literally consists of two men talking, here's a strange thing: *We* do not spend the movie just passively listening to them talk. At first, director Louis Malle's sedate series of images (close-ups, two-shots, reacton shots) calls attention to itself, but as Gregory continues to talk, the very simplicity of the visual style renders it invisible. And like the listeners at the feet of a master storyteller, we find ourselves visualizing what Gregory describes, until

this film is as filled with visual images as a radio play—*more* filled, perhaps, than a conventional feature film.

What Gregory and Shawn talk about is, quite simply, many of the things on our minds these days. We've passed through Tom Wolfe's Me Decade and find ourselves in a decade during which there will apparently be less for everybody. The two friends talk about inner journeys—not in the mystical, vague terms of magazines you don't want to be seen reading on the bus, but in terms of trying to live better lives, of learning to listen to what others are really saying, of breaking the shackles of conventional ideas about our bodies and allowing them to more fully sense the outer world.

The movie is not ponderous, annoyingly profound, or abstract. It is about living, and Gregory seems to have lived fully in his five years of dropping out. Shawn is the character who seems more like us. He listens, he nods eagerly, he is willing to learn, but—something holds him back. Pragmatic questions keep asking themselves. He can't buy Gregory's vision, not all the way. He'd like to, but this is a real world we have to live in, after all, and if we all danced with the druids in the forests of Poland, what would happen to the market for fortune cookies?

The film's end is beautiful and inexplicably moving. Shawn returns home by taxi through the midnight streets of New York. Having spent hours with Gregory on a wild conversational flight, he is now reminded of scenes from his childhood. In *that* store, his father bought him shoes. In that one, he bought ice cream with a girl friend. The utter simplicity of his memories acts to dramatize the fragility and great preciousness of life. He has learned his friend's lesson.

My Favorite Year ★ ★ ★ ½
PG, 92 m., 1982

Peter O'Toole (Alan Swann), Mark Linn-Baker (Benjy Stone), Jessica Harper (K.C. Downing), Joseph Bologna (King Kaiser), Lainie Kazan (Belle Corroca), Lou Jacobi (Uncle Morty). Directed by Richard Benjamin and produced by Michael Gruskoff. Screenplay by Norman Steinberg and Dennis Palumbo.

"Live? I can't go on *live!!* I'm a movie star—not an actor!"

Alan Swann is imploring them: Say it isn't so! He's an alcoholic British matinee idol, veteran of countless swashbuckling epics in which he faced fleets of pirates and waves of savage barbarians. Now he is being asked to accept the worst challenge of all: to appear on live television.

My Favorite Year is the story of an era when most television was live, and the great television stars were inventing the medium out of their own imaginations every Saturday night. The year is 1950. The program is "King Kaiser's Comedy Hour," obviously inspired by the old Sid Caesar and Imogene Coca programs. The British star, Alan Swann, is played by Peter O'Toole, but he could be Errol Flynn or John Barrymore or even O'Toole himself. The movie is told from the point of view of a young production assistant named Benjy (Mark Linn-Baker). His job is to shadow the great Alan Swann, get him everything he wants except booze, keep him out of trouble, and deliver him intact to the studio in time for the broadcast. Along the way, Benjy adds a priority of his own, his continuing courtship of his would-be girlfriend, K.C. (Jessica Harper).

Through Benjy's eyes, we see Swann as the great man he was, as the pathetic drunk he is, and as the hero he could become—if he survives the live telecast. We also gain some understanding of King Kaiser (Joseph Bologna), who is a big, beefy, not-too-bright guy who has an absolutely accurate understanding of his own comic talent. Translated, that means he knows what will work. What will get a laugh. He has no taste, of course; when he offends a girl, he sends her steaks instead of flowers, and he sends a business associate a gift of tires. But he's a physical comedian with a gift for pumping the laughter out of this frail new medium, and he's backed up by a whole crew of talented writers.

Swann, meanwhile, is backed up only by memories of his greatness and fears of performing in front of a live audience. But as O'Toole plays this character, he becomes one of the great comic inventions of recent movies. Swann is a drunk, but he has an uncanny ability to pass from coma through courtliness to heroics without ever quite seeming to gain consciousness. A character like Swann could probably only be played by someone who is both a great actor and a great ham, and O'Toole is both.

My Favorite Year is not a perfect movie. I could have done without the entire romantic subplot between Benjy and K.C. But I liked the movie's ability to move from one unexpected comic situation to another. That produces one of the best scenes, when Benjy takes Swann home to Brooklyn to meet his mother and weird Uncle Morty (Lainie Kazan and Lou Jacobi in hilarious performances). There is, to be sure, a force running through the movie's disorganization, and that force is O'Toole's charisma. He is so completely charming, so doomed, so funny, and so pathetically invincible as Swann that this movie succeeds despite its occasional unnecessary scenes.

My Tutor ★ ★ ★
R, 97 m., 1983

Caren Kaye (Tutor), Matt Lattanzi (Bobby), Kevin McCarthy (Father), Clark Brandon (Friend), Bruce Bauer (Friend), Kitten Natividad (Friend). Directed by George Bowers and produced by Marilyn J. Tenser. Screenplay by Joe Roberts.

Here's an amazing discovery: *My Tutor* isn't half-bad. It *looks* like sleazoid trash, and it *sounds* like a rip-off of *Private Lessons*, but it's sort of fun and sort of sweet—one of the better makeout movies of recent years. Makeout movies, of course, used to be a big deal. They promised more than they delivered, which was okay, since subtlety is a lot more sexy than explicit sex. They starred good-looking people who were struck dumb with love and spent the rest of the movie in the back seat of a 1956 Olds convertible. *My Tutor* is so complete, it even *has* the '56 Olds. It also has some good-looking people in its cast, including Matt Lattanzi, who plays Bobby, a seventeen-year-old high school graduate who has to pass a special French exam to get into Yale, and Caren Kaye, who plays his tutor, a sweet-faced twenty-nine-year-old who has just broken up with her boyfriend.

Bobby's rich father (Kevin McCarthy) hires Kaye to move into the guest cottage of his Bel Air estate and tutor Bobby all summer. McCarthy is determined that his son go to Yale. Meanwhile, Bobby and his friends unsuccessfully set about trying to lose their virginity in a brothel, where Bobby is almost smothered by the myriad charms of legendary stripper Kitten Natividad. No luck. Meanwhile, Bobby's high school girlfriend starts going out with a college jock, and Bobby sinks into despair, only to be rescued by his accommodating tutor.

All of this sounds, of course, absolutely standard. And it is. What makes *My Tutor* fun is the charm of its performances and some nice touches in the script. Lattanzi looks like an adolescent Sylvester Stallone and behaves like an altar boy. Kaye, who is required to go skinny-dipping a whole lot in this movie, is sexy and sweet in their love scenes. Bobby's best friends, who tool around in the '56 Olds, include a kid (Clark Brandon) who's sort of a reincarnated Roddy McDowell, right down to the fashions inspired by old Archie comic books.

In most movies like this, the characters speak like sitcom retreads, in simple declarative sentences. In *My Tutor*, they're sort of sly and witty. The movie has a certain satiric edge, especially in the way it handles McCarthy, as the doting, possessive father. The love scenes, which are the basic reason for the movie's existence, are more cute than steamy. And here's another thing: They're made with real affection for women. In a lot of the Horny Teen-ager Movies (*Porky's, The Last American Virgin*, etc.), women are portrayed as objects to fear, and teen-age boys play practical jokes instead of falling in love. *My Tutor* cheerfully accepts the possibility that, in the words of e.e. cummings, "girls with boys to bed will go." The move even has a happy ending: Bobby refuses to go to Yale.

The Natural ★ ★
PG, 134 m., 1984

Robert Redford (Roy Hobbs), Robert Duvall (Max Mercy), Glenn Close (Iris Gaines), Kim Basinger (Memo Paris), Wilford Brimley (Pop Fisher), Barbara Hershey (Harriet Bird), Robert Prosky (The Judge), Richard Farnsworth (Red Blow). Directed by Barry Levinson and produced by Mark Johnson.

Screenplay by Roger Towne and Phil Dusenberry.

Why didn't they make a baseball picture? Why did *The Natural* have to be turned into idolatry on behalf of Robert Redford? Why did a perfectly good story, filled with interesting people, have to be made into one man's ascension to the godlike, especially when no effort is made to give that ascension meaning? And were the most important people in the god-man's life kept mostly off-screen so they wouldn't upstage him?

Let's begin at the end of *The Natural*. Redford plays Roy Hobbs, a middle-aged ballplayer making his comeback. It's the last out of the last inning of the crucial play-off game, and everything depends on him. He's been in a slump. Can his childhood sweetheart, Iris Gaines (Glenn Close), snap him out of it? She sends him a note revealing that her child is his son. The fact that he has not already figured this out is incredible. But he is inspired by the revelation. He steps to the plate. He has been having some trouble with his stomach. Some trouble, all right. A stain of blood spreads on his baseball shirt. It's a pretty badly bleeding stomach when it bleeds right through the skin. Roy swats a homer that hits the lights, and they all explode into fireworks, showering fiery stars upon him as he makes the rounds. In the epilogue, Roy plays catch with Iris and their son—a son who has not been allowed a single onscreen word—and a woman whose role has been to sit in the stands, wreathed in ethereal light, and inspire him.

Come on, give us a break. The last shot is cheap and phony. Either he hits the homer and then dies, or his bleeding was just a false alarm. If the bleeding was a false alarm, then everything else in the movie was false, too. But I guess that doesn't matter, because *The Natural* gives every sign of a story that's been seriously meddled with. Redford has been placed so firmly in the foreground that the prime consideration is to show him in a noble light. The people in his life—baseball players, mistresses, gamblers, crooks, sportswriters—seem grateful to share the frame with him. In case we miss the point, Redford is consistently backlit to turn his golden hair into a saintly halo.

The Natural could have been a decent

movie. One reason that it is not: Of all its characters, the only one we don't want to know more about is Roy Hobbs. I'd love to get to know Pop Fisher (Wilford Brimley), the cynical, old team manager. Robert Duvall, as the evil sportswriter, Max Mercy, has had his part cut so badly that we only know he's evil because he practically tells us. Richard Farnsworth, as a kindly coach, has a smile that's more genuine than anything else in the movie. But you have to look quick. And what's with Glenn Close? She's the childhood sweetheart who doesn't hear from Roy after an accident changes the course of his life. Then she turns up years later, and when she stands up in the bleachers she is surrounded by blinding light: "Our Lady of Extra Innings." In the few moments she's allowed alone with Roy, she strikes us as complicated, tender, and forgiving. But even the crucial fact of her life—that she has borne this man's son—is used as a plot gimmick. If *The Natural* were about human beings and not a demigod, Glenn Close and Robert Redford would have spoken together, in the same room, using real words, about their child. Not in this movie.

As for the baseball, the movie isn't even subtle. When a team is losing, it makes Little League errors. When it's winning, the hits are so accurate they even smash the bad guy's windows. There's not a second of real baseball strategy in the whole film. The message is: Baseball is purely and simply a matter of divine intervention. At about the 130-minute mark, I got the idea that God's only begotten son was playing right field for the New York team.

Neighbors ★ ★ ★
R, 90 m., 1981

John Belushi (Earl Keese), Kathryn Walker (Enid Keese), Cathy Moriarty (Ramona), Dan Aykroyd (Vic). Directed by John G. Avildsen and produced by Richard D. Zanuck and David Brown. Screenplay by Larry Gelbart.

If there's one quality that middle-class Americans have in common, it's a tendency to be rigidly polite in the face of absolutely unacceptable behavior. Confronted with obnoxious rudeness, we freeze up, we get a nervous little smile, we allow our eyes to focus on the middle distance, and we cannot believe this is happening to us. It's part of our desire to avoid a scene. We'd rather choke to death in a restaurant than break a plate to attract attention. *Neighbors* is about one such man, Earl Keese (John Belushi). He is a pleasant, low-key dumpling of a fellow. He lives an uneventful life with an uneventful wife (Kathryn Walker). Then the neighbors move in, and there goes the neighborhood. They are everything we dread in neighbors. They are loud. They are blatant freeloaders. The man (Dan Aykroyd) is gung-ho macho. The woman (Cathy Moriarty, from *Raging Bull*) is oversexed and underloved. They park some kind of customized truck on their front lawn. They invite themselves to dinner.

There are compensations. For example, the woman seems to be a nymphomaniac. That would be more of a compensation for Earl if he were not terrified of aggressive woman. Earl has not the slightest notion of how to deal with these next-door maniacs, and his wife's no help: She puts on her best smile and tries to handle the situation as if everyone were playing by Emily Post's rules. The story of the Keeses and their weird neighbors was first told in Thomas Berger's novel. It was obviously a launching pad for a movie, but what sort of movie? The relationships among these neighbors depend almost entirely on the chemistry of casting: For example, obnoxious Richard Benjamin could have moved in next to meek Donald Sutherland. In *Neighbors*, however, we get Belushi and Aykroyd. I think it was brilliant casting, especially since they divided the roles somewhat against our expectations. Belushi, the most animalistic animal in *Animal House*, plays the mild-mannered Keese. And Aykroyd, who often plays straight-arrows, makes the new neighbor into a loud neo-fascist with a back slap that can kill.

The movie slides easily from its opening slices of life into a surburban nightmare. We know things are strange right at the start, when Aykroyd extorts money from Belushi to get a carry-out Italian dinner, and then secretly cooks the spaghetti right in his own kitchen. Belushi sneaks out into the night to spy on Aykroyd and catches him faking it with Ragu, but is too intimidated to say anything. The whole movie goes like that, with Belushi so intimidated that he hardly protests even when he finds himself sinking into quicksand.

Meanwhile, the women are making their own strange arrangements, especially after the Keese's college-age daughter (Lauren-Marie Taylor) comes home from school and begins attracting Moriarty's attention. The movie operates as a satire of social expectations, using polite clichés as counterpoint to deadly insults (all delivered in pleasant conversational tones).

The first hour of *Neighbors* is probably more fun than the second, if only because the plot developments come as a series of surprises. After a while, the bizarre logic of the movie becomes more predictable. But *Neighbors* is a truly interesting comedy, an offbeat experiment in hallucinatory black humor. It grows on you.

Never Say Never Again ★ ★ ★ ½
PG, 137 m., 1983

Sean Connery (James Bond), Klaus Maria Brandauer (Largo), Max von Sydow (Blofeld), Barbara Carrera (Fatima Blush), Kim Basinger (Domino), Bernie Casey (Felix Leiter). Directed by Irwin Kershner and produced by Jack Schwartzman. Screenplay by Lorenzo Semple, Jr.

Ah, yes, James, it is good to have you back again. It is good to see the way you smile from under lowered eyebrows, and the way you bark commands in a sudden emergency, and it is good to see the way you look at women. Other secret agents may undress women with their eyes. You are more gallant. You undress them, and then thoughtfully dress them again. You are a rogue with the instincts of a gentleman.

It has been several years since Sean Connery hung it up as James Bond, several years since *Diamonds Are Forever*, and Connery's announcement that he would "never again" play special agent 007. What complex instincts caused him to have one more fling at the role, I cannot guess. Perhaps it was one morning in front of the mirror, as he pulled in his gut and reflected that he was in pretty damn fine shape for a man over fifty. And then, with a bow in the direction of his friend Roger Moore, who has made his own niche as a different kind of Bond, Sean Connery went back on assignment again.

The movie is called *Never Say Never Again*. The title has nothing to do with the movie—except why Connery made it—but never mind, nothing in this movie has much to do with anything else. It's another one of those Bond plots in which the basic ingredients are thrown together more or less in fancy. We begin with a threat (SPECTRE has stolen two nuclear missiles and is holding the world at ransom). We continue with Bond, his newest gadgets, his mission briefing. We meet the beautiful women who will figure in the plot (Barbara Carrera as terrorist Fatima Blush; Kim Basinger as the innocent mistress of the evil Largo). We meet the villains (Max van Sydow as Blofeld; Klaus Maria Brandauer as Largo). We visit exotic locations, we survive near-misses, and Bond spars with the evil woman and redeems the good one. All basic.

What makes *Never Say Never Again* more fun than most of the Bonds is more complex than that. For one thing, there's more of a human element in the movie, and it comes from Klaus Maria Brandauer, as Largo. Brandauer is a wonderful actor, and he chooses not to play the villian as a cliché. Instead, he brings a certain poignancy and charm to Largo, and since Connery always has been a particularly human James Bond, the emotional stakes are more convincing this time.

Sean Connery says he'll never make another James Bond movie, and maybe I believe him. But the fact that he made this one, so many years later, is one of those small show-business miracles. There was never a Beatles reunion. Bob Dylan and Joan Baez don't appear on the same stage anymore. But here, by God, is Sean Connery as Sir James Bond. Good work, 007.

The Neverending Story ★ ★ ★
PG, 94 m., 1984

Barret Oliver (Bastian), Noah Hathaway (Atreyu), Tami Stronach (Empress), Moses Gunn (Cairon). Directed by Wolfgang Petersen and produced by Bernd Eichinger and Dieter Geissler. Screenplay by Petersen and Weigel.

How's this for a threat? The kingdom of Fantasia is about to be wiped out, and the enemy isn't an evil wizard or a thermonuclear device, it's Nothingness. That's right, an inexorable wave of Nothingness is sweeping over the kingdom, destroying everything in its path. Were children's movies this nihilistic in the old days?

The only thing standing between Fantasia and Nothingness is the faith of a small boy named Bastian (Barret Oliver). He discovers the kingdom in a magical bookstore, and as he begins to read the adventure between the covers, it becomes so real that the people in the story know about Bastian. How could that be? Well, that's the very first question Bastian asks. This is a modern kid with quite a healthy amount of skepticism, but what can he do when he turns the page and the Child Empress (Tami Stronach) is begging him to give her a name so that Fantasia can be saved?

The idea of the story within a story is one of the nice touches in *The Neverending Story*. Another one is the idea of a child's faith being able to change the course of fate. Maybe not since the kids in the audience were asked to save Tinker Bell in *Peter Pan* has the outcome of a story been left so clearly up to a child's willingness to believe. There is a lot we have to believe in *The Neverending Story*, and that's the other great strength of this movie. It contains some of the more inventive special effects work of a time when battles in outer space, etc., have grown routine. Look for example, at *The Last Starfighter*, where the special effects are competent but never original—all the visual concepts are ripped off from *Star Wars*—and then look at this movie, where an entirely new world has been created.

The world of Fantasia contains creatures inspired by Alice in Wonderland (a little man atop a racing snail), the Muppets (a cute dragon-dog that can fly), and probably B.C. (a giant made of stone, who snacks on quartz and rumbles around on his granite tricycle). Many of the special effects involve sophisticated use of Muppet-like creatures (there are scenes that reminded me of *The Dark Crystal*). They are, in a way, more convincing than animation, because they exist in three dimensions and have the same depth as their human co-stars. And that illusion, in turn, helps reinforce the more conventional effects like animation, back projection, and so on. The world of this movie looks like a

very particular place, and the art direction involved a lot of imagination. The movie's director, Wolfgang Petersen, is accustomed to creating worlds in small places; his last film, *Das Boot (The Boat)*, took place almost entirely within a submarine.

Within the world of Fantasia, a young hero (Noah Hathaway) is assigned to complete a hazardous quest, sneak past the dreaded portals of some stone amazons, and reach the Ivory Tower, where he will receive further instructions from the empress. In most movies, this quest would be told in a straightforward way, without the surrounding story about the other little boy who is reading the book. But *The Neverending Story* is *about* the unfolding of a story, and so the framing device of the kid hidden in his school attic, breathlessly turning the pages, is interesting. It lets kids know that the story isn't just somehow happening, that storytelling is a neverending act of the imagination.

1984 ★ ★ ★ ½
R, 117 m., 1984

John Hurt (Winston Smith), Richard Burton (O'Brien), Suzanna Hamilton (Julia), Cyril Cusack (Charrington), Gregor Fisher (Parsons). Directed by Michael Radford and produced by Simon Perry. Screenplay by Radford.

George Orwell made no secret of the fact that his novel *1984* was not really about the future but about the very time he wrote it in, the bleak years after World War II when England shivered in poverty and hunger. In a novel where passion is depicted as a crime, the greatest passion is expressed, not for sex, but for contraband strawberry jam, coffee, and chocolate. What Orwell feared, when he wrote his novel in 1948, was that Hitlerism, Stalinism, centralism, and conformity would catch hold and turn the world into a totalitarian prison camp. It is hard, looking around the globe, to say that he was altogether wrong.

Michael Radford's brilliant film of Orwell's vision does a good job of finding that line between the "future" world of 1984 and the grim postwar world in which Orwell wrote. The movie's 1984 is like a year arrived at through a time warp, an alternative reality that looks constructed out of old radio tubes and smashed office furniture. There is not a single prop in this movie that you couldn't buy in a junkyard, and yet the visual result is uncanny: Orwell's hero, Winston Smith, lives in a world of grim and crushing inhumanity, of bombed factories, bug-infested bedrooms, and citizens desperate for the most simple pleasures.

The film opens with Smith rewriting history: His task is to change obsolete government documents so that they reflect current reality. He methodically scratches out old headlines, obliterates the photographs of newly made "unpersons," and attends mass rallies at which the worship of Big Brother alternates with numbing reports of the endless world war that is still going on somewhere, involving somebody. Into Smith's world comes a girl, Julia, who slips him a note of stunning force. The note says, "I love you." Smith and Julia become revolutionaries by making love, walking in the countryside, and eating strawberry jam. Then Smith is summoned to the office of O'Brien, a high official of the "inner party," who seems to be a revolutionary too, and gives him the banned writings of an enemy of the state.

This story is, of course, well known. *1984* must be one of the most widely read novels of our time. What is remarkable about the movie is how completely it satisfied my feelings about the book; the movie looks, feels, and almost tastes and smells like Orwell's bleak and angry vision. John Hurt, with his scrawny body and lined and weary face, makes the perfect Winston Smith; and Richard Burton, looking so old and weary in this film that it is little wonder he died soon after finishing it, is the immensely cynical O'Brien, who feels close to people only while he is torturing them. Suzanna Hamilton is Julia, a fierce little war orphan whose rebellion is basically inspired by her hungers.

Radford's style in the movie is an interesting experiment. Like Chaplin in *Modern Times*, he uses passages of dialogue that are not meant to be understood—nonsense words and phrases, garbled as they are transmitted over Big Brother's primitive TV, and yet listened to no more or less urgently than the messages that say something. The 1954

film version of Orwell's novel turned it into a cautionary, simplistic science fiction tale. This version penetrates much more deeply into the novel's heart of darkness.

Nine to Five ★ ★ ★
PG, 111 m., 1980

Jane Fonda (Judy Bernly), Lily Tomlin (Violet Newstead), Dolly Parton (Doralee Rhodes), Dabney Coleman (Franklin Hart, Jr.), Sterling Hayden (Tinsworthy), Elizabeth Wilson (Roz). Directed by Colin Higgins and produced by Bruce Gilbert. Screenplay by Higgins and Patricia Resnick.

Nine to Five is a good-hearted, simple-minded comedy that will win a place in film history, I suspect, primarily because it contains the movie debut of Dolly Parton. She is a natural-born movie star, a performer who holds our attention so easily that it's hard to believe it's her first film. The movie has some funny moments, and then it has some major ingredients that don't work, including some of its fantasy sequences. But then it also has Dolly Parton. And she contains so much energy, so much life and unstudied natural exuberance that watching her do anything in this movie is a pleasure. Because there have been so many Dolly Parton jokes (and doubtless will be so many more), I had better say that I'm not referring to her sex appeal or chest measurements. Indeed, she hardly seems to exist as a sexual being in the movie. She exists on another plane, as Monroe did: She is a center of life on the screen.

But excuse me for a moment while I regain my composure. *Nine to Five* itself is pleasant entertainment, and I liked it, despite its uneven qualities and a plot that's almost too preposterous for the material. The movie exists in the tradition of 1940s screwball comedies. It's about improbable events happening to people who are comic caricatures of their types, and, like those Forties movies, it also has a dash of social commentary. The message has to do with women's liberation and, specifically, with the role of women in large corporate offices. Jane Fonda, Lily Tomlin, and Dolly Parton all work in the same office. Tomlin is the efficient office manager. Fonda is the newcomer, trying out her first job after a divorce.

Parton is the boss's secretary, and everybody in the office thinks she's having an affair with the boss. So the other women won't speak to her.

The villain is the boss himself. Played by Dabney Coleman, he's a self-righteous prig with a great and sincere lust for Dolly Parton. She's having none of it. After the movie introduces a few social issues (day care, staggered work hours, equal pay, merit promotion), the movie develops into a bizarre plot to kidnap Coleman in an attempt to win equal rights. He winds up swinging from the ceiling of his bedroom, attached by wires to a garage-door opener. Serves him right, the M.C.P. This whole kidnapping sequence move so far toward unrestrained farce that it damages the movie's marginally plausible opening scenes. But perhaps we don't really care. We learn right away that this is deliberately a lightweight film, despite its superstructure of social significance. And, making the necessary concessions, we simply enjoy it.

What I enjoyed most, as you have already guessed, was Dolly Parton. Is she an actress? Yes, definitely, I'd say, although I am not at all sure how wide a range of roles she might be able to play. She's perfect for this one—which was, of course, custom-made for her. But watch her in the scenes where she's not speaking, where the action is elsewhere. She's always in character, always reacting, always generating so much energy we expect her to fly apart. There's a scene on a hospital bench, for example, where Tomlin is convinced she's poisoned the boss, and Fonda is consoling her. Watch Dolly. She's bouncing in and out, irrepressibly. What is involved here is probably something other than "acting." It has to do with what Bernard Shaw called the "life force," that dynamo of energy that some people seem to possess so bountifully. Dolly Parton simply seems to be having a great time, ready to sweep everyone else up in her enthusiasm, her concern, her energy. It's some show.

An Officer and a Gentleman
★ ★ ★ ★
R, 126 m., 1982

Richard Gere (Zack Mayo), Debra Winger (Paula Pokrifki), Lou Gossett, Jr. (Sergeant Foley), David Keith (Sid Worley), Robert Loggia (Byron Mayo), Lisa Blount (Lynette), Lisa Eilbacher (Casey Seeger). Directed by Taylor Hackford and produced by Martin Elfand. Screenplay by Douglas Day Stewart.

An Officer and a Gentleman is the best movie about love that I've seen in a long time. Maybe that's because it's not about "love" as a Hollywood concept, but about love as growth, as learning to accept other people for who and what they are. There's romance in this movie, all right, and some unusually erotic sex, but what makes the film so special is that the sex and everything else is presented within the context of its characters finding out who they are, what they stand for—and what they will *not* stand for.

The movie takes place in and around a Naval Aviation Officer Candidate School in Washington state. Every thirteen weeks, a new group of young men and women come here to see if they can survive a grueling session of physical and academic training. If they pass, they graduate to flight school. About half fail. Across Puget Sound, the local young women hope for a chance to meet an eligible future officer. They dream of becoming officers' wives, and in some of their families, we learn, this dream has persisted for two generations.

After the first month of training, there is a Regimental Ball. The women turn out with hope in their hearts and are sized up by the candidates. A man and a woman (Richard Gere and Debra Winger) pair off. We know more about them than they know about one another. He is a loner and a loser, whose mother died when he was young and whose father is a drunk. She is the daughter of an officer candidate who loved and left her mother twenty years before. They dance, they talk, they begin to date, they fall in love. She would like to marry him, but she refuses to do what the other local girls are willing to do—get pregnant or fake pregnancy to trap a future officer. For his part, the man is afraid of commitment, afraid of love, incapable of admitting that he cares for someone. All he wants is a nice, simple affair, and a clean break at the end of OCS.

This love story is told in counterpoint with others. There's the parallel affair between another candidate and another local girl. She *is* willing to trap her man. His problem is, he really loves her. He's under the thumb of his family, but he's willing to do the right thing, if she'll give him the chance.

All of the off-base romances are backdrops for the main event, which is the training program. The candidates are under the supervision of a tough drill sergeant (Lou Gossett, Jr.) who has seen them come and seen them go and is absolutely uncompromising in his standards. There's a love-hate relationship between the sergeant and his trainees, especially the rebellious, resentful Gere. And Gossett does such a fine job of fine-tuning the line between his professional standards and his personal emotions that the performance deserves its Academy Award.

The movie's method is essentially to follow its characters through the thirteen weeks, watching them as they change and grow. That does wonders for the love stories, because by the end of the film we know these people well enough to care about their decisions and to have an opinion about what they should do. In the case of Gere and Winger, the romance is absolutely absorbing because it's so true to life, right down to the pride that causes these two to pretend they don't care for each other as much as they really do. When it looks as if Gere is going to throw it all away—is going to turn his back on a good woman who loves him, just because he's too insecure to deal with her love—the movie isn't just playing with emotions, it's being very perceptive about human behavior.

But maybe I'm being too analytical about why *An Officer and a Gentleman* is so good. This is a wonderful movie precisely because it's so willing to deal with matters of the heart. Love stories are among the rarest of movies these days (and when we finally get one, it's likely to involve an extra-terrestrial). Maybe they're rare because writers and filmmakers no longer believe they understand what goes on between modern men and women. *An Officer and a Gentleman* takes chances, takes the time to know and develop its characters, and by the time this movie's wonderful last scene comes along, we know exactly what's happening, and why, and it makes us very happy.

Oh, God! Book II ★ ★
PG, 94 m., 1980

George Burns (God), Louanne (Tracy), Suzanne Pleshette (Paula), David Birney (Don), John Louie (Shingo), Anthony Holland (Dr. Newell). Directed and produced by Gilbert Cates. Screenplay by John Greenfield, Hal Goldman, Fred S. Fox, Seaman Jacobs, and Melissa Miller.

Oh, God! Book II qualifies as a sequel only because of its title and the irreplaceable presence of George Burns in the title role. Otherwise, it seems to have lost faith in the film it's based on. It begins with the same great idea for a movie (what would happen if God personally came down to earth and got involved in the affairs of men?), but it winds up as a third-rate situation comedy, using its subject as a gimmick.

Neither of the *Oh, God!* movies is, of course, seriously religious; they create God as a sort of ancient Will Rogers on a Christmas card by Norman Rockwell, and then give him lots of cute lines and paradoxical comic insights. But the original film—with God appearing to a supermarket manager played by John Denver—did at least follow through on its basic premise. What if God really did turn up in the checkout line? How do you behave when God blows the whistle and challenges you to test his rules?

Oh, God! Book II doesn't seem willing to devote a whole movie to the same subject; it uses God as basically just a *deus ex machina*. He is, of course, enormously appealing, and George Burns is rich and understated in the role. But after he appears to a little girl named Tracy (played by a very little actress named Louanne), the movie uses him as a springboard for scenes involving the little girl, her parents, her school, her psychiatrist—everything except what we'd really enjoy—more scenes with God.

Tracy's basic problem, it appears, is that she can see God and talk with him, but nobody else can. Her parents and teachers think she's talking to herself. God asks her to organize an advertising campaign to promote his image on earth, and she comes up with a slogan ("Think God") which her little playmates plaster on every open space in town. But, meanwhile, a psychiatrist (Anthony Holland) determines that Tracy's got serious problems.

There are other sitcom-style distractions. Tracy's parents (Suzanne Pleshette and David Birney) are divorced. Tracy doesn't like her daddy's new girlfriend. The principal at school is a meanie. And so on. The movie's screenplay was written by no less than five collaborators, but they were so bankrupt of ideas that some scenes have a quiet desperation to them. For example: There's an awkward TV newscast staged in the movie, with Hugh Downs as the avuncular anchorman and none other than Dr. Joyce Brothers giving her opinion that little Tracy may, indeed, have seen God. It would be sad enough if the movie were using Downs and Brothers for laughs—but, God help us, they're brought in as authority figures.

There is, however, one additional small treasure in this movie, a supporting performance by Mari Gorman, who steals every scene she's in, playing Tracy's grade school teacher, Miss Hudson. She has a weird kind of off-balance walk and out-of-time speaking style that's infectious and funny. It's amazing that a movie so devoid of comic imagination would allow itself to play around with such an offbeat supporting performance. If Gorman had played, say, Tracy's mother— and if the rest of the movie had been equally willing to take chances with its approach— *Book II* could have been worth seeing.

Oh, God! You Devil ★ ★ ★ ½
PG, 96 m., 1984

George Burns (God and Harry), Ted Wass (Bobby Shelton), Roxanne Hart (Wendy), Ron Silver (Gary). Directed by Paul Bogart and produced by Robert M. Sherman. Screenplay by Andrew Bergman.

The *God* pictures are ideal for sequels; after all, the leading character has no beginning and no end. But sequels have a way of ripping off profitable ideas without anything new to say. They grow so dreary and pale that we forget why we liked the original picture in the first place. That's why *Oh, God! You Devil* is such a delight. Here is George Burns's third God movie, and not only does it have as much humor, warmth, and good cheer as the first—it actually has a better story. The story involves a young man who was placed under God's protection when he was a little baby; he had a fever, and his father's prayers were answered. The kid has grown up into an unsuccessful musician, and one day while he's performing at some dumb wedding reception, he meets an unusual guest, one Harry O. Tophet, who is, of course, the devil. Harry makes the kid an offer he should, but does not, refuse, and before long the kid is the top rock superstar in the world.

Of course, there's a catch. He has to assume the identity of another musician—an existing superstar whose deal with the devil has just run out. And worst of all, he has to remember his previous life, including the wife he loved and the child they were expecting. This whole balancing act between success and loss is unexpectedly touching, and gives the movie a genuine human heart.

Meanwhile, the devil basks in his acquisition, and then God gets into the act when the rock star prays to be released from his deal with the devil.

It's here that we get what we've been waiting for all through the picture, the scenes where God and the devil, both played by George Burns, appear on the same screen. Dual appearances through trick photography are, of course, an old Hollywood standby, but what's fun here is the way Burns plays scenes with himself: This casting was made in heaven.

Oh, God! You Devil has two different kinds of successful elements. The Burns stuff is all superb, especially when the devil reflects whimsically about the evils he's unleashed upon the earth. But the other story—the story starring Ted Wass as the condemned rock star—has an authenticity of its own. Like Warren Beatty's *Heaven Can Wait*, it starts with a fantastical idea and then develops it along plausible human lines. For the first time in the God pictures, we care so much about the human characters that it really does make a difference what God does; it's not just a celestial vaudeville act.

On Golden Pond ★ ★ ★ ★
PG, 109 m., 1981

Katharine Hepburn (Ethel Thayer), Henry Fonda (Norman Thayer, Jr.), Jane Fonda (Chelsea), Doug McKeon (Billy Ray), Dabney Coleman (Bill Ray). Directed by Mark Rydell and produced by Bruce Gilbert. Screenplay by Ernest Thompson.

Simple affection is so rare in the movies. Shyness and resentment are also seldom seen. Love is much talked-about, but how often do we really believe that the characters are in love and not simply in a pleasant state of lust and like? Fragile emotions are hard to portray in a movie, and the movies that reach for them are more daring, really, than movies that bludgeon us with things like anger and revenge, which are easy to portray.

On Golden Pond is a treasure for many reasons, but the best one, I think, is that I could believe it. I could believe in its major characters and their relationships, and in the things they felt for one another, and there were moments when the movie was witness to human growth and change. I left the theater feeling good and warm, and with a certain resolve to try to mend my own relationships and learn to start listening better. All of those achievements are small miracles for any movie, but especially for this one, which began as a formula stage play and still contains situations and characters that are constructed completely out of cardboard.

The story of On Golden Pond begins with the arrival of an old, long-married couple (Henry Fonda and Katharine Hepburn) at the lakeside cottage where they have summered for many years. They know each other very well. Hepburn, of course, knows Fonda better than he knows her—or himself, for that matter. Fonda is a crotchety, grouchy old professor whose facade conceals a great deal of shyness, we suspect. Hepburn knows that. Before long, three more people turn up at the pond: Their daughter (Jane Fonda), her fiancé (Dabney Coleman), and his son (Doug McKeon).

That's the first act. In the second act, the conflicts are established. Jane Fonda feels that her father has never really given her her due—he wanted a son, or perhaps he never

really understood how to be a father, anyway. Jane tells her parents that she's spending a month in Europe with Coleman, and, ah, would it be all right if they left the kid at the lake? Hepburn talks the old man into it. In the central passages of the movie, the old man and the kid grudgingly move toward some kind of communication and trust. There is a crisis involving a boating accident, and a resolution that brings everybody a lot closer to the realization that life is a precious and fragile thing. Through learning to relate to the young boy, old Fonda learns, belatedly, how to also trust his own daughter and communicate with her: The kid provides Henry with practice at how to be a father. There is eventually the sort of happy ending that some people cry through.

Viewed simply as a stage plot, On Golden Pond is so predictable we can almost hear the gears squeaking. Forty-five minutes into the movie, almost everyone in the audience can probably predict more or less what is going to happen to the characters, emotionally. And yet On Golden Pond transcends its predictability and the transparent role of the young boy, and becomes a film with passages of greatness.

This is because of the acting, first of all, but also because Ernest Thompson, who wrote such a formula play, has furnished it with several wonderful scenes. A conversation between old Henry Fonda and young Coleman is an early indication that this is going to be an unusual movie: A man who is forty-five asks a man who is eighty for permission to sleep in the same room with the man's daughter, and after the old man takes the question as an excuse for some cruel put-downs, the conversation takes an altogether unexpected twist into words of simple truth. That is a good scene. So are some of the conversations between Hepburn and Fonda. And so are some remarkable scenes involving the boating accident, in which there is no doubt that Hepburn, at her age, is doing some of her own stunts. It's at moments like this that stardom, acting ability, character, situation—and what the audience already knows about the actors—all come together into an irreplaceable combination.

As everybody knows, this is the first film in which Hepburn and the two Fondas have acted in any combination with one another.

Some reviews actually seem to dismiss the casting as a stunt. I believe it adds immeasurably to the film's effect. If Hepburn and Henry Fonda are legends, seen in the twilight of their lives, and if we've heard that Jane and Henry have had some of the same problems offscreen that they have in this story—does that make the movie simple gossip? No, not if the movie deals honestly with the problems, as this one does. As people, they have apparently learned something about loving and caring that, as actors, they are able to communicate, even through the medium of this imperfect script. Watching the movie, I felt I was witnessing something rare and valuable.

On the Right Track ★ ★ ½
PG, 98 m., 1981

Gary Coleman (Lester), Michael Lembeck (Juvenile Officer), Lisa Eilbacher (Cashier), Norman Fell (Mayor), Maureen Stapleton (Mary), Bill Russell (Trainer). Directed by Lee Philips and produced by Ronald Jacobs. Screenplay by Tina Pine.

If there's anything I can't stand in a movie, it's a sweet, lovable, cute little kid who is so adorable—and *knows* he's so adorable—you want to cringe. That's why seeing Gary Coleman in *On the Right Track* was so much fun for me. I don't know how other people relate to Coleman, the precocious three-foot-nine-inch star of TV's *Diff'rent Strokes*, but in my opinion he is the shortest cynical adult in the history of the movies.

It is probably true, I suppose, that Gary Coleman is cute. He is probably also capable of being sweet, and no doubt his family loves him. But Coleman doesn't bask in his own high opinion of himself. He always seems to be thinking up a scam. In a scene where a big-city mayor comes to pat Coleman on the head and tell him what a great kid he is, Coleman sizes up the mayor like he's getting ready to ask for a patronage job. Gary's tireless self-assertion in his relationships with adults is the best thing in this movie.

Unfortunately, there are also a great many other things in *On the Right Track*. What could have been a bright little comedy is so jam-packed with supporting players, sub-plots, and distractions that it seems much longer than it is, and even Coleman's fortitude doesn't get us through. Gary plays a little shoeshine boy who lives in a double locker in Chicago's Union Station. He's a little hustler who knows all the people in the station, especially the pizza man (Herb Edelman) and the cashier in the amusement arcade (Lisa Eilbacher). They look out for him, especially when the cigar-chewing boss of the shoeshine concession tries to run him out of business.

The plot involves a well-intentioned ploy by the city to move Gary from his locker in Union Station and into an orphanage (which is run by a towering matron who looks like Ilsa, She-Wolf of the S.S.). Gary doesn't like it in the orphanage. And when his police juvenile officer (Michael Lembeck) discovers that the kid has the gift of perfectly predicting the winning horses in the daily trifecta, suddenly a whole lot of adults get very protective of Coleman.

Up until this point, the movie works just fine, especially on the several occasions when Coleman steals a scene from his colleagues and just walks away with it. He has dialogue, double-takes, one-liners, and reactions that are absolutely inimitable. Unfortunately, the movie strays away from Coleman's special qualities and gets distracted with several subplots, including (a) a romance between Eilbacher and Lembeck, (b) their plan to adopt Gary, (c) the local mayor's plan to use Gary's race predictions to retire the city debt, and (d) the totally unnecessary introduction of a whole scheme involving the Mafia, and (e) Coleman's own plan to organize a bunch of other kids into a free-lance redcap operation. This abundance of plotting eventually becomes baffling, and the movie begins to resemble a headlong dash through its cast of characters. Too bad. The cast is good, even if it's too populous (Norman Fell has an especially droll scene with Gary while they're seated on top of a billboard in Union Station). And Coleman himself has special qualities worth exploring in a movie that's less manic, and more willing to give its characters time to be themselves.

On the Road Again ★ ★ ★
PG, 119 m., 1980

Willie Nelson (Buck), Dyan Cannon (Viv), Amy Irving (Lily), Slim Pickens (Garland), Joey Floyd (Jamie), Mickey Rooney, Jr. (Cotton). Directed by Jerry Schatzberg and produced by Sydney Pollack and Gene Taft. Screenplay by Carol Sobieski, William D. Wittliff, and John Binder.

The plot of Willie Nelson's *Honeysuckle Rose** is just a slight touch familiar, maybe because it's straight out of your basic country and western song. To wit: The hero, a veteran country singer still poised at the brink of stardom after twenty-five years on the road, won't listen to his wife's pleas that he leave the road and settle down with her and their son. Meanwhile, the band's guitarist, who is also the singer's best friend, retires. A replacement is needed, and the singer hires the best friend's daughter.

She is a shapely young lady who has had a crush on the singer since she was knee-high to a grasshopper. Once they go out on the road again, the singer and the best friend's daughter start sleeping with one another. This situation causes anguish for the singer, the daughter, the best friend, the wife, the son, and the band. But after going down to Mexico to slug back some tequila and think it over, the singer returns to his wife and the best friend's daughter wisely observes: "Anything that hurts this many people can't be right."

This story is totally predictable from the opening scenes of *Honeysuckle Rose*, which is a disappointment; the movie is sly and entertaining, but it could have been better. Still, it has its charms, and one is certainly the presence of Willie Nelson himself, making his starring debut at the age of forty-seven and not looking a day over sixty. He's grizzled, grinning, sweet-voiced and pleasant, and a very engaging actor. (He gave promise of that with a single one-liner in his screen debut in *Electric Horseman*, expressing his poignant desire for the kind of girl who could suck the chrome off a trailer hitch.)

The movie also surrounds Nelson with an interesting cast: Dyan Cannon is wonderful as Willie's long-suffering wife, a sexy fortyish earth-woman with streaked hair and a wardrobe from L.L. Bean. She survives the test of her big scene, an archetypical C&W confrontation in which she charges onstage to denounce her husband and his new girlfriend.

Amy Irving is not quite so well-cast as the girlfriend; she has too many scenes in which she gazes adoringly at Willie—who, on the other hand, hardly ever gazes adoringly at her. Slim Pickens, who should be registered as a national historical place, is great as the best friend. And there is a hilarious bit part, a fatuous country singer, played by Mickey Rooney, Jr.

Mercifully, the movie doesn't drag out its tale of heartbreak into a C&W soap opera. Instead, director Jerry Schatzberg *(Scarecrow)* uses an easy-going documentary style to show us life on the band bus, at a family reunion, and backstage at big concerts. All of these scenes are filled to overflowing with colors; this is one of the cheeriest, brightest looking movies I've ever seen, starting with Willie's own amazing costumes and including the spectrum at the concerts, reunions, picnics, etc. Half the movie seems to be shot during parties, and although we enjoy the texture and detail we sometimes wonder why so little seems to be happening.

The movie remains resolutely at the level of superficial cliché, resisting any temptation to make a serious statement about the character's hard-drinking, self-destructive life-style; this isn't a movie like *Payday*, in which Rip Torn re-created the last days of the dying Hank Williams. *Honeysuckle Rose* has the kind of problems that can be resolved with an onstage reconciliation in the last scene: Willie and Dyan singing a duet together and everybody knowing things will turn out all right.

If there's an edge of disappointment coming out of the movie, maybe it's inspired by that simplicity of approach to complicated problems. Willie Nelson has lived a long time, experienced a lot, and suffered a certain amount on his way to his current success, and my hunch is that he knows a lot more about his character's problems in this movie than he lets on. Maybe the idea was to film the legend and save the man for later.

*Retitled *On the Road Again* for TV and cassette.

Once Upon a Time in America
★ —short version
★ ★ ★ ★—original version
R, 137 m., 227 m., 1984

Robert De Niro (Noodles), James Woods
(Max), Elizabeth McGovern (Deborah), Treat
Williams (Jimmy), Tuesday Weld (Carol),
Burt Young (Joe). Directed by Sergio Leone
and produced by Arnon Milchan. Screenplay
by L. Benvenuti, P. De Bernardo, E. Medioli,
F. Arcalli, F. Ferrini, Leone, and S. Kaminski.

This was a murdered movie, now brought
back to life on cassette. Sergio Leone's *Once
Upon a Time in America*, which in its
intended 227-minute version is an epic poem
of violence and greed, was chopped by ninety minutes for U.S. theatrical release into an
incomprehensible mess without texture,
timing, mood, or sense. The rest of the
world saw the original film, which I saw at
the Cannes Film Festival. In America, a
tragic decision was made. When the full-
length version (now available in cassette
form) played at the 1984 Cannes Film Festival, I wrote:

"Is the film too long? Yes and no. Yes, in
the sense that it takes real concentration to
understand Leone's story construction, in
which everything may or may not be an
opium dream, a nightmare, a memory, or a
flashback, and that we have to keep track of
characters and relationships over fifty years.
No, in the sense that the movie is compulsively and continuously watchable and
that the audience did not stir or grow restless
as the epic unfolded."

The movie tells the story of five decades in
the lives of four gangsters from New York
City—childhood friends who are merciless
criminals almost from the first, but who
have a special bond of loyalty to each other.
When one of them breaks that bond, or
thinks he does, he is haunted by guilt until
late in his life, when he discovers that he was
not the betrayer but the betrayed. Leone's
original version tells this story in a complex
series of flashbacks, memories, and dreams.
The film opens with two scenes of terrifying
violence, moves to an opium den where the
Robert De Niro character is seeking to escape the consequences of his action, and
then establishes its tone with a scene of great
power: A ceaselessly ringing telephone,

ringing forever in the conscience of a man
who called the cops and betrayed his friends.
The film moves back and forth in a tapestry
of episodes, which all fit together into an
emotional whole. There are times when we
don't understand exactly what is happening,
but never a time when we don't feel confidence in the film's narrative.

That version was not seen in American
theaters, although it is now available on cassette. Instead, the whole structure of flashbacks was junked. The telephone rings
once. The poetic transitions are gone. The
movie has been wrenched into apparent
chronological order, scenes have been
thrown out by the handful, relationships are
now inexplicable, and the audience is likely
to spend much of its time in complete bewilderment. It is a great irony that this
botched editing job was intended to "clar-
ify" the film.

Here are some of the specific problems
with the shortened version. A speakeasy
scene comes before a newspaper headline
announces that Prohibition has been
ratified. Prohibition is then repealed, on
what feels like the next day but must be six
years later. Two gangsters talk about robbing
a bank in front of a woman who has never
been seen before in the film; they've removed the scene explaining who she is. A
labor leader turns up, unexplained, and involves the gangsters in an inexplicable situation. He later sells out, but to whom? Men
come to kill De Niro's girlfriend, a character
we've hardly met, and we don't know if they
come from the mob or the police. And here's
a real howler: At the end of the shortened
version, De Niro leaves a room he has never
seen before by walking through a secret
panel in the wall. How did he know it was
there? In the long version, he was told it was
there. In the short version, his startling exit
shows simple contempt for the audience.

Many of the film's most beautiful shots are
missing from the short version, among them
a bravura moment when a flash-forward is
signaled by the unexpected appearance of a
Frisbee, and another where the past becomes the present as the Beatles' "Yesterday" sneaks into the sound track. Relationships are truncated, scenes are squeezed
of life, and I defy anyone to understand the
plot of the short version. The original *Once*

Upon a Time in America gets a four-star rating. The shorter version is a travesty.

One from the Heart ★ ★
PG, 98 m., 1982

Frederic Forrest (Hank), Teri Garr (Frannie), Raul Julia (Ray), Nastassja Kinski (Leila), Lainie Kazan (Maggie), Harry Dean Stanton (Moe). Directed by Francis Ford Coppola and produced by Bernard Gersten.

Arriving after two years of sound and fury, after all the news items on the financial pages and alarms and excursions in the movie trade press, Francis Ford Coppola's *One from the Heart* is an interesting production but not a good movie. From Coppola, the brilliant orchestrator of *Apocalypse Now* and the Godfather films, it is a major disappointment. This must be the first movie in history to arrive with more publicity about its production techniques than about its stars. Everybody knows that Coppola used experimental video equipment to view and edit his movie, sealing himself into a trailer jammed with electronic gear so that he could see on TV what the camera operator was seeing through the lens. Of course the film itself was photographed on the same old celluloid that the movies have been using forever; Coppola used TV primarily as a device to speed up the process of viewing each shot and trying out various editing combinations. (Or, as an industry wisecrack had it, "He took an $8 million project and used the latest advances in video to bring it in for $23 million.")

If *One from the Heart* is the sort of film this process inspires, then Coppola should abandon it. But of course the process is neutral; films live or die according to an inner rhythm of their own. The most dismal thing about *One from the Heart* is that it lacks those rhythms. It is a ballet of graceful and complex camera movements occupying magnificent sets, and somehow the characters get lost in the process. There was never a moment in this film when I cared about what was happening to the people in it, and only one moment (a cameo by Allen Goorwitz as an irate restaurant owner) when I felt that an actor's spontaneity was able to sneak past Coppola's smothering style and into the audience.

The storyteller of *The Godfather* has become a technician here. There are chilling parallels between Coppola's obsessive control of this film and the character of Harry Caulfield, the wiretapper in Coppola's *The Conversation* (1973), who cared only about technical results and refused to let himself think about human consequences. Movies are a lot of different things, but most of the best ones are about people and for people, and *One from the Heart* pays little heed to the complexities of the human heart. Indeed, it seems almost on guard against the actors who occupy its carefully architectured scenes. They are hardly ever allowed to dominate. They are figures in a larger pattern, one that diminishes them, that sees them as part of the furniture. They aren't given many close-ups; they're often bathed in garish red glows or sickly blues and greens; they're placed in front of distractingly flamboyant sets or lost in badly choreographed crowds, and sometimes they're cut off in the middle of an emotion or a piece of business because the relentlessly programmed camera has business elsewhere.

I've neglected, in fact, to name the actors, or describe the characters they play. That's not so much of an oversight in a review of a film like this. The two main characters (Teri Garr and Frederic Forrest) inhabit a Las Vegas of disappointment, ennui, and glittering lights. For a brief time, they break out of their humdrum lives and meet new lovers (Raul Julia and Nastassja Kinski) who tease them with dreams and fantasies. The underlying story notion, I suppose, is that ordinary little people have a great night on the town, but the night and the town in Coppola's production so overwhelm them that they remain ordinary little people throughout.

There are small pleasures in this movie. One is Harry Dean Stanton's walk-through as the seedy owner of a junkyard, although Coppola resists showing us Stanton's most effective tool, his expressive eyes. Kinski, as a circus tightrope walker, has a beauty much more mature than in *Tess* and a wonderful moment when she explains "to make a circus girl disappear, all you have to do is blink your eyes." Garr is winsome, but her role makes her thanklessly passive, and Forrest (the Oscar nominee from *The Rose*) is almost transparent here, he's given such a nebbish to play.

Only When I Laugh ★
R, 120 m., 1981

Marsha Mason (Georgia), Kristy McNichol (Polly), James Coco (Jimmy), Joan Hackett (Toby), David Dukes (David). Directed by Glenn Jordan and produced by Roger M. Rothstein and Neil Simon. Screenplay by Simon.

Neil Simon's *Only When I Laugh* is basically a movie about a woman who is recovering from alcoholism, although the film also provides us with a lonely homosexual, a disturbed teen-ager, a fortyish woman losing her husband, and a *Looking for Mr. Goodbar* scene in which protagonist Marsha Mason is assaulted and raped. It comes billed as one of Neil Simon's "serious" films. That means that it is about serious subjects. It does not mean Simon examines them seriously. The film should have contained half so many problems if he hoped to provide us with insights into them. But Simon uses misfortunes as a way of creating characters. If he can create an "alcoholic," then he doesn't have to create a three-dimensional person for his film. He can just fill out the person's life with predictable crises from the disease. The same with the film's homosexual, who can complain of loneliness, rejection, feelings of inadequacy—can do everything, indeed, except be gay onscreen.

There are times, as a result, when *Only When I Laugh* seems like a series of characters reporting to headquarters. Many of the big moments take place offscreen, and then the movie stars turn up onscreen to tell us about them. Maybe that is not so bad. In the scenes where Simon does try to grapple with his film's issues, he exhibits little understanding. Take, for example, the business of his central character's alcoholism. The movie's heroine, played by Simon's wife, Marsha Mason, is an actress who is just being released from a rehabilitation program when the movie opens. The doctor congratulates her on her wonderful progress. Then she hits the streets, where her entire program for maintaining sobriety seems to consist of (a) keeping up a brave front, (b) looking noble, (c) wallowing in self-pity

with the encouragement of her neurotic friends, (d) quickly walking past bars, and (e) gulping a drink the moment things start to go wrong.

No wonder she gets drunk again. That's predictable, but couldn't Simon have spared us a lapse scene reminiscent of *The Fatal Glass of Beer?* At one point, a glass of wine looms so menacingly on a piano top in the foreground that we think this is a Hitchcock film and that the booze must be poisoned. (In other shots in the same scene, the continuity is so sloppy that the glass disappears from the piano, but never mind.) Simon and Mason must not drink, know little about drinking, and less about how to stop drinking. If Simon had cared enough to look into the subject, he might, given his undeniable comic gifts, have been inspired to write some really good stuff about the joys and pitfalls of sobriety. (Can you imagine a Neil Simon version of an AA meeting?)

But Simon's not that interested in any of the problems he hauls onscreen in *Only When I Laugh*. He'll settle for maudlin mother-daughter confrontations, cozy, clichéd scenes of "understanding" between Mason and her gay friend (James Coco), and histrionics from another friend (Joan Hackett) who comes undone upon turning forty. The only genuine moments amid the phony landscapes of this film come from Kristy McNichol, who turns in a wonderful performance as Mason's daughter. McNichol carries conviction. She suggests the real passions and hurts that her character must feel. The other people in the movie seem to be drawn from superficial medical-advice columns, advice for the lovelorn, and the character insights of popular songs. Anyone consulting this movie for insights into alcoholism would be better off asking a bartender.

Ordinary People ★ ★ ★ ★
R, 125 m., 1980

Donald Sutherland (Calvin), Mary Tyler Moore (Beth), Judd Hirsch (Berger), Timothy Hutton (Conrad), M. Emmet Walsh (Swim Coach), Elizabeth McGovern (Jeannine), Dinah Manoff (Karen). Directed by Robert Redford and produced by Ronald L. Schwary. Screenplay by Alvin Sargent.

Families can go along for years without ever facing the underlying problems in their relationships. But sometimes a tragedy can bring everything out in the open, all of a sudden and painfully, just when everyone's most vulnerable. Robert Redford's *Ordinary People* begins at a time like that for a family that loses its older son in a boating accident. That leaves three still living at home in a perfectly manicured suburban existence, and the movie is about how they finally have to deal with the ways they really feel about one another.

There's the surviving son, who always lived in his big brother's shadow, who tried to commit suicide after the accident, who has now just returned from a psychiatric hospital. There's the father, a successful Chicago attorney who has always taken the love of his family for granted. There's the wife, an expensively maintained, perfectly groomed, cheerful homemaker whom "everyone loves." The movie begins just as all of this is falling apart.

The movie's central problems circle almost fearfully around the complexities of love. The parents and their remaining child all "love" one another, of course. But the father's love for the son is sincere yet also inarticulate, almost shy. The son's love for his mother is blocked by his belief that she doesn't really love him—she only loved the dead brother. And the love between the two parents is one of those permanent facts that both take for granted and neither has ever really tested.

Ordinary People begins with this three-way emotional standoff and develops it through the autumn and winter of one year. And what I admire most about the film is that it really *does* develop its characters and the changes they go through. So many family dramas begin with a "problem" and then examine its social implications in that frustrating semifactual, docudrama format that's big on TV. *Ordinary People* isn't a docudrama; it's the story of these people and their situation, and it shows them doing what's most difficult to show in fiction—it shows them changing, learning, and growing.

At the center of the change is the surviving son, Conrad, played by a wonderfully natural young actor named Timothy Hutton. He is absolutely tortured as the film begins; his life is ruled by fear, low self-esteem, and the correct perception that he is not loved by his mother. He starts going to a psychiatrist (Judd Hirsch) after school. Things are hard for this kid. He blames himself for his brother's death. He's a semi-outcast at school because of his suicide attempt and hospitalization. He does have a few friends—a girl he met at the hospital, and another girl who stands behind him at choir practice and who would, in a normal year, naturally become his girlfriend. But there's so much turmoil at home.

The turmoil centers around the mother (Mary Tyler Moore, inspired casting for this particular role, in which the character masks her inner sterility behind a facade of cheerful suburban perfection). She does a wonderful job of running her house, which looks like it's out of the pages of *Better Homes and Gardens*. She's active in community affairs, she's an organizer, she's an ideal wife and mother—except that at some fundamental level she's selfish, she can't really give of herself, and she *has*, in fact, always loved the dead older son more. The father (Donald Sutherland) is one of those men who wants to do and feel the right things, in his own awkward way. The change he goes through during the movie is one of the saddest ones: Realizing his wife cannot truly care for others, he questions his own love for her for the first time in their marriage.

The sessions of psychiatric therapy are supposed to contain the moments of the film's most visible insights, I suppose. But even more effective, for me, were the scenes involving the kid and his two teen-age girlfriends. The girl from the hospital (Dinah Manoff) is cheerful, bright, but somehow running from something. The girl from choir practice (Elizabeth McGovern) is straightforward, sympathetic, able to be honest. In trying to figure them out, Conrad gets help in figuring himself out.

Director Redford places all these events in a suburban world that is seen with an understated matter-of-factness. There are no cheap shots against suburban life-styles or affluence or mannerisms: The problems of the people in this movie aren't caused by their milieu, but grow out of themselves. And, like it or not, the participants have to deal with them. That's what sets the film apart from the sophisticated suburban soap opera it could easily have become. Each character in this movie is given the dramatic opportunity to look inside himself, to question his *own* motives as well as the motives of others, and to try to improve his own ways of dealing with a troubled situation. Two of the characters do learn how to adjust; the third doesn't. It's not often we get characters who face those kinds of challenges on the screen, nor directors who seek them out. *Ordinary People* is an intelligent, perceptive, and deeply moving film.

Out of the Blue ★ ★ ★ ½
R, 94 m., 1982

Linda Manz (CeBe), Dennis Hopper (Don), Sharon Farrell (Kathy), Raymond Burr (Dr. Brean), Don Gordon (Charlie). Directed by Dennis Hopper and produced by Gary Jules Jouvenat. Screenplay by Leonard Yakir and Brenda Nielson.

Out of the Blue is one of the unsung treasures of independent films, a showcase for the maverick talents of two movie rebels: veteran actor Dennis Hopper, of *Easy Rider* and *Rebel Without a Cause,* and young, tough-talking Linda Manz, whose debut in *Days of Heaven* was so heartbreaking. Made in 1982, it never got a chance in commercial theaters. The movie is Hopper's comeback as a director. After the enormous international success of *Easy Rider* (1969) and the resounding thud of his next directorial effort, *Last Movie* (1971), he didn't direct again until this movie (he acted, in such films as *The American Friend* and *Apocalypse Now*). Originally hired just to act in *Out of the Blue,* he took over two weeks into production, rewrote the screenplay, found new locations and made this movie into a bitter, unforgettable poem about alienation.

Hopper is one of the movie's stars, playing an alcoholic truck driver whose semi-rig crashes into a school bus, kills children, and sends him to jail for six years. Manz plays his daughter, a leather-jacketed, punk teen-ager who combs her hair with shoe polish and does Elvis imitations. Her mother is played by Sharon Farrell as a small-town waitress who tries a reconciliation with Hopper when he gets out of prison but is undercut by her

drug addiction. Manz is the centerpiece of the film. As she demonstrated in the magnificent pastoral romance *Days of Heaven,* she has a presence all her own. She's tough and hard-edged and yet vulnerable, and in this movie we can sometimes see the scared little kid beneath the punk bravado. She lives in a world of fantasy. All but barricaded into her room, surrounded by posters of Elvis and other teen heroes, she practices her guitar (she isn't very good) and dresses up in her dad's leather jacket. He's a hero to her. She doesn't buy the story that he was responsible for the deaths of those kids. And when he finally gets out of prison, she has a father at last—but only for a few days.

Hopper's touch as a director is especially strong in a pathetic scene of reunion, including the family's day at the overcast, gloomy beach, and a "party" that turns into a violent brawl dominated by the Hopper character's drunken friend (Don Gordon). The movie escalates so relentlessly toward its violent, nihilistic conclusion that when it comes, we believe it. This is a very good movie that simply got overlooked. When it premiered at the 1980 Cannes Film Festival, it caused a considerable sensation, and Manz was mentioned as a front-runner for the best actress award. But back in North America, the film's Canadian backers had difficulties in making a distribution deal, and the film slipped through the cracks.

Paris, Texas ★ ★ ★ ★
R, 145 m., 1984

Harry Dean Stanton (Travis), Nastassja Kinski (Jane), Hunter Carson (Their Son), Dean Stockwell (Walt), Aurore Clement (Anne), Bernhard Wicki (Dr. Ulmer). Directed by Wim Wenders and produced by Don Guest. Screenplay by Sam Shepard.

A man walks alone in the desert. He has no memory, no past, no future. He finds an isolated settlement where the doctor, another exile, a German, makes some calls. Eventually the man's brother comes to take him back home again. Before we think about this as the beginning of a story, let's think about it very specifically as the first twenty minutes of a movie. When I was watching *Paris, Texas* for the first time, my immediate reaction to the film's opening scenes was one of intrigue: I had no good guesses about where this movie was headed, and that, in itself, was exciting, because in this most pragmatic of times, even the best movies seem to be intended as predictable consumer products. If you see a lot of movies, you can sit there watching the screen and guessing what will happen next, and be right most of the time.

That's not the case with *Paris, Texas*. This is a defiantly individual film, about loss and loneliness and eccentricity. We haven't met the characters before in a dozen other films. To some people, that can be disconcerting; I've actually read reviews of *Paris, Texas* complaining because the man in the desert is German, and that another character is French. Is it written that the people in movies have to be Middle Americans, like refugees from a sitcom?

The characters in this movie come out of the imagination of Sam Shepard, the playwright of rage and alienation, and Wim Wenders, a West German director who often makes "road movies," in which lost men look for answers in the vastness of great American cities. The lost man is played this time by Harry Dean Stanton, the most forlorn and angry of all great American character actors. We never do find out what personal cataclysm led to his walk in the desert, but as his memory begins to return, we learn how much he has lost. He was married, once, and had a little boy. The boy has been raised in the last several years by Stanton's brother (Dean Stockwell) and sister-in-law (Aurore Clement). Stanton's young wife (Nastassja Kinski) seems to have disappeared entirely in the years of his exile. The little boy is played by Hunter Carson, in one of the least affected, most convincing juvenile performances in a long time. He is more or less a typical American kid, despite the strange adults in his life. He meets Stanton and accepts him as a second father, but of course he thinks of Stockwell and Clement as his family. Stanton has a mad dream of finding his wife and putting the pieces of his past back together again. He goes looking, and finds Kinski behind the one-way mirror of one of those sad sex emporiums where men pay to talk to women on the telephone.

Paris, Texas is more concerned with exploring emotions than with telling a story. This isn't a movie about missing persons, but about missing feelings. The images in the film show people framed by the vast, impersonal forms of modern architecture; the cities seem as empty as the desert did in the opening sequence. And yet this film is not the standard attack on American alienation. It seems fascinated by America, by our music, by the size of our cities, and a land so big that a man like the Stanton character might easily get misplaced. Stanton's name in the movie is Travis, and that reminds us not only of Travis McGee, the private eye who specialized in helping lost souls, but also of lots of American Westerns in which things were simpler, and you knew who your enemy was. It is a name out of American pop culture, and the movie is a reminder that all three of the great German New Wave directors—Herzog, Fassbinder, and Wenders—have been fascinated by American rock music, American fashions, American mythology.

This is Wenders's fourth film shot at least partly in America (the others were *Alice in the Cities, The American Friend*, and *Hammett*). It also bears traces of *Kings of the Road*, his German road movie in which two men meet by chance and travel for a time together, united by their mutual inability to love and understand women. But it is better than those movies—it's his best work so far—because it links the unforgettable images to a spare, perfectly heard American idiom. The Sam Shepard dialogue has a way of allowing characters to tell us almost nothing about themselves, except for their most banal beliefs and their deepest fears.

Paris, Texas is a movie with the kind of passion and willingness to experiment that was more common fifteen years ago than it is now. It has more links with films like *Five Easy Pieces* and *Easy Rider* and *Midnight Cowboy*, than with the slick arcade games that are the box office winners of the 1980s. It is true, deep, and brilliant.

A Passage to India ★ ★ ★ ★
PG, 160 m., 1984

Judy Davis (Adela Quested), Victor Banerjee (Dr. Aziz), Peggy Ashcroft (Mrs. Moore), Alec Guinness (Godbole) James Fox (Fielding), Nigel Havers (Ronny Heaslop).

Directed by David Lean and produced by
John Brabourne and Richard Goodwin.
Screenplay by Lean.

"Only connect!"—E.M. Forster

That is the advice he gives us in *Howard's End,* and then, in *A Passage to India,* he creates a world in which there are no connections, where Indians and Englishmen speak the same language but do not understand each other, where it doesn't matter what you say in the famous Marabar Caves, since all that comes back is a hollow, mocking, echo. Forster's novel is one of the literary landmarks of this century, and now David Lean has made it into one of the greatest screen adaptations I have ever seen.

Great novels do not usually translate well to the screen. They are too filled with ambiguities, and movies have a way of making all their images seem like literal fact. *A Passage to India* is especially tricky, because the central event in the novel is something that happens offstage, or never happens at all—take your choice. On a hot, muggy day, the eager Dr. Aziz leads an expedition to the Marabar Caves. One by one, members of the party drop out, until finally only Miss Quested, from England, is left. And so the Indian man and the British woman climb the last path alone, at a time when England's rule of India was based on an ingrained, semiofficial racism, and some British, at least, nodded approvingly at Kipling's "East is East, and West is West, and never the twain shall meet."

In Forster's novel, it is never clear exactly what it was that happened to Miss Quested after she wandered alone into one of the caves. David Lean's film leaves that question equally open. But because he is dealing with a visual medium, he cannot make it a mystery where Dr. Aziz is at the time; if you are offstage in a novel, you can be anywhere, but if you are offstage in a movie, you are definitely not where the camera is looking. So in the film version we know, or think we know, that Dr. Aziz is innocent of the charges later brought against him—of the attempted rape of Miss Quested.

The charges and the trial fill the second half of Lean's *A Passage to India.* Lean brings us to that point by a series of perfectly modulated, quietly tension-filled scenes in which Miss Quested (Judy Davis) and the kindly Mrs. Moore (Peggy Ashcroft) sail to India, where Miss Quested is engaged to marry the priggish local British magistrate in a provincial backwater. Both women want to see the "real India"—a wish that is either completely lacking among the locals, or is manfully repressed. Mrs. Moore goes walking by a temple pool by moonlight, and meets the earnest young Dr. Aziz, who is captivated by her gentle kindness. Miss Quested wanders by accident into the ruins of another temple, populated by sensuous and erotic statuary, tumbled together, overgrown by vegetation.

Miss Quested's temple visit is not in Forster, but has been added by Lean (who wrote his own screenplay). It accomplishes just what it needed, suggesting that in Miss Quested the forces of sensuality and repression run a great deal more deeply than her sexually constipated fiancé is ever likely to suspect. Meanwhile, we meet some of the other local characters, including Dr. Godbole (Alec Guinness), who meets every crisis with perfect equanimity, and who believes that what will be, will be. This philosophy sounds like recycled fortune cookies but turns out, in the end, to have been the simple truth. We also meet Fielding (James Fox), one of those tall, lonely middle-aged Englishmen who hang about the edges of stories set in the Empire, waiting until their destiny commands them to take a firm stand.

Lean places these characters in one of the most beautiful canvases he has ever drawn (and this is the man who directed *Dr. Zhivago* and *Lawrence of Arabia*). He doesn't see the India travel posters and lurid postcards, but the India of a Victorian watercolorist like Edward Lear, who placed enigmatic little human figures here and there in spectacular landscapes that never seemed to be quite finished. Lean makes India look like an amazing, beautiful place that an Englishman can never quite put his finger on—which is, of course, the lesson Miss Quested learns in the caves.

David Lean is a meticulous craftsman, famous for going to any lengths to make every shot look just the way he thinks it should. His actors here are encouraged to give sound, thoughtful, unflashy performances (Guinness strains at the bit), and his screenplay is a model of clarity: By the end of this movie we know these people so well, and understand them so thoroughly, that only the most reckless among us would want to go back and have a closer look at those caves.

Paternity ★ ★
PG, 94 m., 1981

Burt Reynolds (Buddy Evans), Beverly D'Angelo (Maggie), Norman Fell (Larry), Paul Dooley (Kurt), Elizabeth Ashley (Sophia), Lauren Hutton (Jenny). Directed by David Steinberg and produced by Lawrence Gordon and Hank Moonjean. Screenplay by Charlie Peters.

Burt Reynolds seems to have two basic screen characters, which, for ease of classification, we can describe as Bad Burt and Good Reynolds. Bad Burt is a mean ol' boy who tools around the Southland in a souped-up sports car, infuriating sheriffs and making Sally Field cry. Good Reynolds, however, is a guy who used to be macho and heartless, but has grown into a sensitive, caring kinda guy who is trying to build bridges to women and children.

Paternity gives us the good guy. The Reynolds character is a lot like the man he played in *Starting Over* and maybe a little bit in *Hooper:* a guy torn between a self-image as a ladies' man and a desire to grow more sensitive. This time, he's the manager of Madison Square Garden, and he leads a lonely but (he thinks) idyllic existence as a New York playboy. He's got a date every night, but there's nobody to come home to. And when he shoots baskets with a friend's son, he begins to realize that he would like to have a son, too. Not a family, mind you. And certainly not a wife. But a son. He sends out feelers for a surrogate mother. All the candidates are impossible or have braces on their teeth. Then he stumbles across a pretty blonde waitress in a restaurant where he has lunch. She's a music student, wants to study in Paris, and will bear his child for a one-time payment of $50,000 (considerably higher than market price, I believe).

The waitress is played by Beverly D'Angelo. She was the rich kid in *Hair!* and Patsy Cline in *Coal Miner's Daughter.* She is wonderful in this movie: soft and warm and understanding. Of course, *we* know (although Good Reynolds is slow to catch on) that they will eventually fall in love. God knows Burt tries to hold out and play the playboy role, but eventually even his sexy dates such as Elizabeth Ashley start to like D'Angelo and to lay a guilt trip on Reynolds.

But a-ha, you are thinking, I have given the plot away. Well, yes and no. I have given the plot away in one sense, but in another sense this movie drives us to the edges of our seat with maddening frustration because it is so slow to give itself away. *Paternity* is absolutely predictable at every moment. Stop the film at any point, and nine out of ten viewers could correctly predict what was going to happen next.

The movie has another flaw. It takes its characters just a little too evenly. Although the movie was directed by David Steinberg, a comic actor with a good sense of timing, *Paternity*'s timing is so slow-paced and stately that there are times when this doesn't feel like a comedy, it feels like a historical romance. People speak at a measured pace; they move through scenes as if preprogrammed; they do not contain the passion and surprise you would expect in a story dealing with matters of sex and life and identity. Too bad. Burt Reynolds can be a most engaging actor; the movie surrounds him with other convincing actors such as Paul Dooley and Norman Fell; Elizabeth Ashley does some nice things with her small role. But *Paternity* is so preordained. It fulfills every one of our expectations with a deadening safeness. It is about a man who wants a child so that he will leave something after himself, but it never convinces us that he has a self to leave.

Pennies from Heaven ★ ★
R, 107 m., 1981

Steve Martin (Arthur), Bernadette Peters (Eileen), Christopher Walken (Tom), Jessica Harper (Joan), Vernel Barneris (Accordion Man). Directed by Herbert Ross and produced by Nora Kay and Ross. Screenplay by Dennis Potter.

Pennies from Heaven is dazzling and disappointing in equal measure. It's a musical with an idea, and ideas usually have been deadly to the musical, that most gloriously heedless of movie genres. The idea this time is that there was a great contrast between the grim reality of the Depression era, and the mindless song-and-dance of the era's favorite escapist entertainment, the musical. Well, so there was, and *viva la difference.*

Pennies from Heaven illustrates its insight by setting up a brutal constrast between its dramatic scenes and its musical numbers. The story in this film is relentlessly downbeat, cruel, and occasionally twisted: A miserable marriage leads to a cheerless love affair, both based on the sexual humiliation of women. Then, just as we are primed to hurl ourselves out of the window, the characters undergo a transmogrification into inhabitants of an upbeat 1930s musical. The voices of Bing Crosby, Connie Boswell, Fred Astaire, and other Depression recording artists issue from their mouths, and they dance their way through the most dazzling production numbers since Busby Berkeley.

The movie keeps cutting back and forth between its mean-spirited narrative and the empty-headed perfection of its musical numbers until we're as dispirited as the characters. We get it: Nothing is real except pain, and anyone who dares to sing "Let's Face the Music and Dance" is sooner or later going to have to face the music. It is the structure of *Pennies from Heaven* that works most fatally against the film. A few key scenes contrasting grim reality and movie escapism would have made the point, but two hours of contrast simply destroy our ability to get into the movie and enjoy it. The movie constantly shatters its own reality—which is, admittedly, a daring thing for a $25 million musical to do, but in this case is not a very good idea.

Original ads placed the emphasis on the movie's musical numbers and its stars, especially sheet music salesman Steve Martin and his schoolteacher mistress, Bernadette Peters (there was less emphasis on Jessica Harper, who plays Martin's desperately hapless wife). Hollywood is always pragmatic in these matters: If the filmmakers haven't made the film the studio had in mind, the studio simply advertises the film they wish had been made. That led to some thoroughly puzzled audiences, as Martin fans lined up for a wild and crazy musical and discovered they were in a musical that wanted to subvert musicals. Some of the scenes in *Pennies from Heaven* are very hard to take, especially one in which Harper pathetically tries to cater to Martin's favorite fetish, which is lipstick on the nipples; this is the most embarrassing and gratuitously cruel scene I've seen in a long time.

On the other hand, *Pennies* also contains musical scenes that are wonderfully entertaining, even if the movie has a way of ending them with emotional crash landings. The choreography has been referred to as a Busby Berkeley parody, but it's not parody, it's homage, and never have I seen such well-drilled troupes of chorus girls, song-and-dance men, and even well-scrubbed little toddlers lined up at dozens of baby grand pianos.

The production values in this movie are superb, and it's great to look at, not only during the musical interludes but even in the dramatic moments. Many of the compositions are borrowed from famous paintings or photographs of the time.

The problem is, *Pennies from Heaven* is all flash and style and no heart. That's the problem with the Steve Martin performance, too: He provides a technically excellent performance that does not seem to be inhabited by a person. Bernadette Peters has a winning way with the schoolteacher, all curls and sweetness and shattered hopes, but the emotional reality of the other characters is consistently undermined by the movie's lame-brained determination to interrupt each happy moment with a grim one, and vice versa, until we're emotionally shellshocked. Just imagine if the creativity, energy, work, talent, and money that went into *Pennies from Heaven* had been devoted instead to a cheerful film on the same topic. Boy, would we need it now.

Perfect ★ ½
R, 120 m., 1985

John Travolta (Adam), Jamie Lee Curtis (Jessie), Jann Wenner (Mark Roth), Anne De Salvo (Frankie), Marilu Henner (Sally), Laraine Newman (Linda), Matthew Reed (Roger), Kenneth Welsh (McKenzie). Produced and directed by James Bridges. Screenplay by Aaron Latham and Bridges.

They say you never enjoy a movie about a subject you know something about. You keep spotting the flaws instead of enjoying the story. Maybe that's my problem with *Perfect*, a movie that is about journalism and health clubs. I know something about journalism and nothing about health clubs, and I hated the movie's journalism scenes, but I thought Jamie Lee Curtis was really hot as the aerobics instructor.

The movie stars John Travolta as a *Rolling Stone* reporter who goes to Los Angeles to research an article about health clubs as the singles bars of the 1980s. At the same time, he's doing an exclusive interview with a white-collar criminal who bears a strong resemblance to John DeLorean. In L.A., at a health club called the Sports Connection, he meets Jamie Lee Curtis, falls in love with her, and tries to interview her. But she's been burned before by investigative reporters, and she won't talk to him. Their courtship turns into a protracted agony for them, and for the viewer. They like each other. They have a lot in common. They go out on a date, Travolta produces the tape recorder. She gets mad at him and goes home. They make up. They kiss. His tape recorder is on. She throws him out of her car. They start talking again. And so on, endlessly as Travolta plays the first reporter in history who would rather boogie with his Sony than with Jamie Lee Curtis.

The Travolta character is inspired by Aaron Latham, a *Rolling Stone* reporter who wrote the "Urban Cowboy" article for *Rolling Stone*, and recycled it into the Travolta movie of the same name. The director of both films is James Bridges. The reason the Latham-Travolta-Bridges combination doesn't work this time is that the material hasn't been transformed into fiction. With *Urban Cowboy*, the filmmakers used Latham's articles to make a movie about an urban cowboy. With *Perfect*, we get a movie about the writing of the articles. If they'd gone one step further, eliminated the scenes about the journalism, and made the movie about the Jamie Lee Curtis character, the formula might have worked again.

Instead, the movie scurries distractingly from one subplot to another. There are three: (1) the Travolta-Curtis relationship, with a backdrop of health clubs; (2) the

McKenzie case, about a businessman busted for drug sales; and (3) the *Rolling Stone* scenes, with the magazine's publisher, Jann Wenner, playing himself. The stuff about the businessman feels shoehorned into an overcrowded plot, and could have been eliminated. The *Rolling Stone* material is distracting because the Wenner character behaves in such a shockingly unethical manner that if he weren't in the movie, he'd be suing it. (At one point, he orders Travolta's article to be totally rewritten and sensationalized, without the knowledge or consent of the author.)

The movie's strategic mistake is to be about journalism instead of about health clubs. Its most interesting scenes involve people from the Sports Connection (or the "Sports Erection," as Travolta nicknames it). We meet a busty brunette (Marilu Henner) who's the star of the club's social whirl; an insecure young woman (Laraine Newman) who believes that aerobics and plastic surgery could someday make her "perfect"; and an assortment of other body worshipers who are most comfortable in front of mirrors. Curtis is a queen in this world; as the club's most popular aerobics instructor, she has a circle of groupies and commands a bigger salary.

When the movie deals with the little universe inside the health club, it's fascinating—especially when Jamie Lee is onscreen, because of her electrifying performance. Travolta can also be electrifying, but his performance is so laid-back it doesn't much matter; he seems to be doing a Carl Bernstein/Dustin Hoffman number. Cub reporters are warned not to make themselves the stars of their stories. *Perfect* needed the same advice.

Personal Best ★ ★ ★ ★
R, 124 m., 1982

Mariel Hemingway (Chris Cahill), Patrice Donnelly (Tory Skinner), Scott Glenn (Coach), Kenny Moore (Denny Stites). Directed and produced by Robert Towne. Screenplay by Towne.

Robert Towne's *Personal Best* tells the story of two women who are competitors for pentathlete berths on the 1980 U.S. Olympics team—the team that did not go to Moscow.

The women are attracted to one another almost at first sight, and what begins as a tentative exploration develops into a love relationship. Then the romance gets mixed up with the ferocity of top-level sports competition.

What distinguishes *Personal Best* is that it creates *specific* characters—flesh-and-blood people with interesting personalities, people I cared about. *Personal Best* also seems knowledgeable about its two subjects, which are the weather of these women's hearts, and the world of Olympic sports competition.

It is a movie containing the spontaneity of life. It's about living, breathing, changeable people and because their relationships seems to be so deeply felt, so important to them, we're fascinated by what may happen next. The movie stars Mariel Hemingway and Patrice Donnelly as the two women track stars, Scott Glenn as their coach, and Kenny Moore as the Olympic swimmer who falls in love with Hemingway late in the film. These four people are so right for the roles it's almost scary; it makes us sense the difference between performances that are technically excellent and other performances, like these, that may sometimes be technically rough but always find the correct emotional note.

Mariel Hemingway plays a young, naive natural athlete. We sense that she always has been under the coaching thumb of her father, a perfectionist, and that her physical excellence has been won at the cost of emotional maturity. She knows everything about working out, and next to nothing about her heart, her sexuality, her own identity. She loses an important race at a preliminary meet, is sharply handled by the father, gets sick to her stomach, is obviously emotionally distraught.

Patrice Donnelly, as a more experienced athlete, tries to comfort the younger girl. In a dormitory room that night, they talk. Donnelly shares whatever wisdom she has about training and running and winning. They smoke a joint. They kid around. They arm wrestle. At this point, watching the film, I had an interesting experience. I did not already know that the characters in the film were homosexual, but I found myself thinking that the scene was so erotically charged that, "if Hollywood could be honest," it

would develop into a love scene. Just then, it did! "This is scary," Donnelly says, and then she kisses Hemingway, who returns the kiss.

Personal Best is not simply about their romance, however, It is about any relationship in which the trust necessary for love is made to compete with the total egotism necessary for championship sports. *Can* two people love each other, and at the same time compete for the same berth on an Olympic team? Scott Glenn, the coach, doesn't think so. He accepts the fact of his two stars' homosexuality, but what bothers him is a suspicion that Donnelly may be using emotional blackmail to undercut Hemingway's performance.

This is a very physical movie, one of the healthiest and sweatiest celebrations of physical exertion I can remember. There is a lot of nudity in the film—not only erotic nudity, although there is some of that, but also locker room and steam room nudity, and messing around nudity that has an unashamed, kidding freshness to it. One scene that shocks some viewers occurs between Mariel Hemingway and Kenny Moore, when he gets up to go to the bathroom and she decides to follow along; the scene is typical of the kind of unforced, natural spontaneity in the whole film. The characters in *Personal Best* seem to be free to have real feelings. It is filled with the uncertainties, risks, cares, and rewards of real life, and it considers its characters' hearts and minds, and sees their sexuality as an expression of their true feelings for each other.

Picnic at Hanging Rock ★ ★ ★ ½
PG, 110 m., 1980

Rachel Roberts (Miss Appleyard), Dominic Guard (Fitzhubert), Helen Morse (Dianne), Jacki Weaver (Minnie). Directed by Peter Weir and produced by James and Hal McElroy. Screenplay by Cliff Green.

Peter Weir's *Picnic at Hanging Rock* has something of the same sense of mystery and buried terror as Antonioni's *L'Aventura*—another film about a sudden and disquieting disappearance. But it's more lush and seductive than Antonioni's spare black-and-white images: Weir films an Australian landscape that could be prehistoric, that suggests that men have not come this way before . . . and that, quite possibly, they should not have come this time.

"This time" is 1900, when much of Australia remained unseen by European eyes, but when a staid and proper version of European culture had been established at such places as Appleyard College, presented here as a boarding school for proper young ladies. As is almost always the case in movies about proper boarding schools, an undercurrent of repressed sexuality runs through Appleyard, and especially through the person of its headmistress (Rachel Roberts).

We get a preliminary sense of that in the film's opening scenes, which show several of the young ladies preparing to spend the day picnicking at nearby Hanging Rock, a geological outcropping from time immemorial. And then there is the picnic itself, with the girls in their bonnets and parasols and immaculate white dresses, dappled in sunlight.

The film moves here at a deliberately lazy pace. The sun beats down, insects drone— and four of the young ladies, having climbed halfway up into the rock passages, are overcome by torpor. When they awake, three of them climb farther on, never to be seen again. The fourth, badly frightened, returns to the main group. A search is set into motion, and the local constable questions witnesses who saw the young girls later on in the day, but the mystery of their disappearance remains unsolved.

It's that very inconclusiveness, linked with later scenes in which the cruel nature of the headmistress is developed, that make *Picnic at Hanging Rock* so haunting. What's going on here, we ask, knowing there is no possible answer and half-pleased by the enigma. The film opens itself to our interpretations: Is the disappearance a punishment, real or imagined, for the girls' stirring sexuality? Is it a rebuke from the ancient landscape against the brash inroads of civilization? Or is it, as it was in the famous Antonioni film, a statement of nihilism: These people have disappeared, so might we, it all matters nothing, life goes on meaninglessly.

Picnic at Hanging Rock of course subscribes to none of those readings or to any reading. I've heard its ending described as inconclusive (it is) and frustrating (ditto).

But why not? Do we want a rational explanation? Arrest and trial for vagabond kidnappers? An autopsy revealing broken necks? Poisonous snakes named as the culprits? If this film *had* a rational and tidy conclusion, it would be a good deal less interesting. But as a tantalizing puzzle, a tease, a suggestion of forbidden answer just out of earshot, it works hypnotically and very nicely indeed.

The Pirates of Penzance ★ ★
G, 112 m., 1983

Kevin Kline (Pirate King), Angela Lansbury (Ruth), Linda Ronstadt (Mabel), George Rose (Major-General), Rex Smith (Frederic), Tony Azito (Sergeant). Directed by Wilford Leach and produced by Joseph Papp. Screenplay by Leach.

Joe Papp's original Broadway production of *The Pirates of Penzance* liberated Gilbert and Sullivan from the lockstep fuddery of the traditional D'Oyly Carte productions. This movie redoes the damage. Even though the film is based on the exhilarating Broadway production, even though it has many of the same cast members and the same director and score—it feels more like an old-fashioned stage production than like Papp's uninhibited, irreverent breakthrough. The reason is so obvious it's amazing they didn't spot it. What they've done here is make an old-fashioned film of a lively stage production. No effort has been made to find ways to make a good stage event into an original movie. *The Pirates of Penzance* on film isn't even a very good musical—certainly not one to compare with the best Hollywood standards.

The director, Wilford Leach, shoots in front of cheerfully phony little sets, but he doesn't have fun with them, he just uses them as if they were on a stage (we're stuck on the same papier-mâché beach for half an hour). He uses stage choreography and expects it to photograph well (nailing down his camera and staging the dances in front of it, as if the camera were a live audience). He has wonderfully charismatic actors, including Kevin Kline and Linda Ronstadt, but they never seem quite aware of each other; his awkward use of close-ups makes them seem more aware of the camera. The result is a movie that just doesn't have the excitement of the stage presentation. The only moment in this movie that sort of creates a feeling of exuberance, irreverence, and parody is George Rose's virtuoso turn with "I Am the Very Model of a Modern Major-General"—but, of course, that's a set-piece among virtuoso tunes, and there's hardly any way to miss with it.

Are there good things in the movie? Sure. The music. Ronstadt, pretty as a picture and with that strong, clear, wonderful voice. Kline, when he's not lost in the choreographed mobs. And some cute dogs.

Places in the Heart ★ ★ ★
PG, 110 m., 1984

Sally Field (Edna Spaulding), John Malkovich (Mr. Will), Danny Glover (Mose), Lindsay Crouse (Margaret Lomax), Ed Harris (Wayne Lomax), Amy Madigan (Viola Kelsey). Directed by Robert Benton and produced by Arlene Donovan. Screenplay by Benton.

The places referred to in the title of Robert Benton's movie are, he has said, places that he holds sacred in his own heart: The small town in Texas where he grew up, various friends and relatives he remembers from those days, the little boy that he once was, and the things that happened or almost happened. His memories provide the material for a wonderful movie, and he has made it, but unfortunately he hasn't stopped at that. He tells a central story of great power, and then keeps leaving it to catch us up with minor characters we never care about.

The main story stars Sally Field as a sheriff's widow who learns from the banker that times are hard and she should sell her farm and maybe board her kids with somebody else. She refuses. She will keep the farm and keep the kids, thank you, although she's not sure just how that will work. Then a black hobo comes knocking at the back door, asking for food, and he sort of insists that he is just the man to plant her acreage in cotton and farm it. He knows all there is to know about cotton. Since Field has no choice, she takes the man at his word, and he plants the cotton. Meanwhile, the banker, trying to solve a family problem and maybe help her

at the same time, brings around a blind relative named Mr. Will, who will be a paying boarder. The three adults and the two kids form a little family that pulls together to make that farm work—and that is the central story of *Places in the Heart*.

Unfortunately, there are other stories. We meet Field's sister (Lindsay Crouse), and her brother-in-law (Ed Harris), and the local woman (Amy Madigan) he's having an affair with. Their stories function as counterpoint to the drama on the farm, but who cares? We learn just enough about the other characters to suspect that there might be a movie in their stories—but not this one, please, when their adulteries and betrayals have nothing to do with the main story.

Places in the Heart is the kind of movie where people tend to dismiss the parts they don't like. I've seen some reviews where the story of Field and the farm is the only part of the movie the critics refer to, as if Crouse, Harris, and Madigan had slipped their minds. That's wishful thinking. The subplot is there, and it's an unnecessary distraction, and it robs the movie of a lot of the sheer narrative power it would have had otherwise. It also robs us of a chance to learn more about the relationships among Field, the black farmer (Danny Glover), and the blind boarder (John Malkovich). What a group of unforgettable characters! What do they talk about in their evenings at home? Do they ever get into politics or philosophy? This is Texas in the Depression: How do they think the neighbors like the idea of a black man helping a white woman farm her land? The movie spends so much time watching the hanky-panky at the dances in town that when the Ku Klux Klan suddenly turns up in the movie, it's like it dropped out of a tree.

The movie's last scene has caused a lot of comment. It is a dreamy, idealistic fantasy in which all the characters in the film—friends and enemies, wives and mistresses, living and dead, black and white—take communion together at a church service. This is a scene of great vision and power, but it's too strong for the movie it concludes. *Places in the Heart* can't support such an ending, because it hasn't led up to it with a narrative that was straight and well-aimed as an arrow. The story was on the farm and not in the town, and although the last scene tries to draw them together, you can't summarize things that have nothing in common.

Police Academy   no stars
R, 97 m., 1984

Steve Guttenberg (Carey Mahoney), Kim Cattrall (Karen Thompson), G.W. Bailey (Lieutenant Harris), Bubba Smith (Moses Hightower), Georgina Spelvin (Hooker). Directed by Hugh Wilson and produced by Paul Maslansky. Screenplay by Neal Israel, Pat Proft, and Wilson.

Once upon a time there was a movie named *Airplane!* which had a clever notion: Wouldn't it be fun to satirize all of those *Airport* movies by combining their clichés into one gloriously confused mess, typecasting the movie with walking stereotypes, and going for every corny gag in the book? They were right. It was a great idea, and it made a very funny movie. It also inspired a dreary series of clones and rip-offs, including *Young Doctors in Love* and *Jekyll and Hyde—Together Again*. Now comes without any doubt the absolute pits of this genre, the least funny movie that could possibly have been inspired by *Airplane!* or any other movie.

It's really something. It's so bad, maybe you should pool your money and draw straws and send one of the guys off to rent it so that in the future, whenever you think you're sitting through a bad comedy, he could shake his head, and chuckle tolerantly, and explain that you don't know what bad is. This is the kind of movie where they'll bring a couple of characters onscreen and begin to set up a joke, and then, just when you realize you can predict exactly what's going to happen . . . not only doesn't it happen, but nothing happens—they just cut to some different characters! If there's anything worse than a punch line that doesn't work, it's a movie that doesn't even bother to put the punch lines in.

Among the many questions raised by *Police Academy,* the easiest is: What genre does this movie think it's satirizing? Are there any other movies about police academies? That hardly matters, since the academy in this movie resembles no police academy known to modern man, and seems, indeed, to be modeled after a cross between basic training and prep school. All of the trainee cops live on campus together, in big dorms. The head of the academy is sort of like the headmaster. The campus is green and leafy and peaceful and altogether unlike, I suspect, the training experience undergone by any real police officers.

In a movie this bad, one plot element is really idiotic. It involves the casting of Bubba Smith as a giant black recruit who only has to look at a guy, and his knees start to tremble. This is funny? Don't they know that in comedy, you need a twist—like, why not make Bubba Smith a pathological coward who's afraid of everybody? Now right there is one good idea more than you can find in this entire movie.

Poltergeist ★ ★ ★
PG, 114 m., 1982

Craig T. Nelson (Steve), Jobeth Williams (Diane), Beatrice Straight (Dr. Lesh), Dominique Dunne (Dana), Oliver Robins (Robbie), Heather O'Rourke (Carol Anne). Directed by Tobe Hooper and produced by Steven Spielberg and Frank Marshall. Screenply by Spielberg, Michael Grais, and Mark Victor.

Special effects in the movies have grown so skilled, sensational, and scary that they sometimes upstage the human actors. And they often cost a lot more. In *Poltergeist,* for example, the cast is made up of relatively unknown performers, but that's all right because the real stars are producer Steven Spielberg *(Raiders of the Lost Ark),* director Tobe Hooper *(The Texas Chainsaw Massacre),* and their reputations for special effects and realistic violence. Their names on this horror film suggest that its technology will be impeccable. And they don't disappoint us. This is the movie *The Amityville Horror* dreamed of being. It begins with the same ingredients (a happy American family, living in a big, comfortable house). It provides similar warnings of doom (household objects move by themselves, the weather seems different around the house than anywhere else). And it ends with a similar apocalypse (spirits take total possession of the house, and terrorize the family). Even some of the special effects are quite similar, as when greasy goo begins to ooze around the edges of a doorjamb.

But *Poltergeist* is an effective thriller, not so much because of the special effects, as because Hooper and Spielberg have tried to see the movie's strange events through the eyes of the family members, instead of just standing back and letting the special effects overwhelm the cast along with the audience. The movie takes place in Spielberg's favorite terrain, the American suburb (also the locale of parts of *Close Encounters, Jaws,* and *E. T.*). The haunted house doesn't have seven gables, but it does have a two-car garage. It is occupied by a fairly normal family (two parents, three kids) and the movie begins on a somewhat hopeful note with the playing of "The Star Spangled Banner" as a TV station signs off.

The opening visuals, however, are somewhat ominous. They're an extreme close-up of a TV screen, filled with the usual patriotic images (Iwo Jima, the Lincoln Memorial). Why so close? We're almost being invited to look between the dots on the screen and see something else. And indeed, the family's youngest daughter, an open-faced, long-haired, innocent little cherub, begins to talk to the screen. She's in touch with the "TV people." Before long she disappears from this plane of existence and goes to live with the TV people, wherever they are. Weird events begin to happen in the house. An old tree behaves ominously. The swimming pool seems to have a mind of its own. And the villains are the same people who were the bad guys in Spielberg's *Jaws*—the real estate developers. This time, instead of encouraging people to go back into the water, they're building a subdivision on top of an old graveyard.

This is all ridiculous, but Hooper and Spielberg hold our interest by observing the everyday rituals of this family so closely that, since the family seems real, the weird events take on a certain credibility by association. That's during the first hour of the movie. Then all hell breaks loose, and the movie begins to operate on the same plane as *Alien* or *Altered States,* as a shocking special effects sound-and-light show. A closet seems to exist in another dimension. The swimming pool is filled with grasping, despairing forms of the undead. The search for the missing little girl involves a professional psionics expert, and a lady dwarf who specializes in "cleaning" haunted homes. Nobody ever does decide whether a poltergeist really is involved in the events in the house, or who the poltergeist may be, but if that doesn't prevent them from naming the movie *Poltergeist* I guess it shouldn't keep us from enjoying it.

The Pope of Greenwich Village
★ ★ ★
R, 122 m., 1984

Eric Roberts (Paulie), Mickey Rourke (Charlie), Daryl Hannah (Diane), Geraldine Page (Mrs. Ritter), Kenneth McMillan (Barney), Tony Musante (Pete), Burt Young (Bedbug Eddie). Directed by Stuart Rosenberg and produced by Gene Kirkwood. Screenplay by Vincent Patrick.

Everybody is very ethnic in *The Pope of Greenwich Village.* They all wave their hands a lot, and hang out on street corners, and have uncles in the Mafia. They have such bonds of blood brotherhood, a cousin to them is closer than your mother is to you. And they've always got some kind of con game going on the side. Take Paulie, for example. He knows this racehorse that's selling for $15,000, only the joke is, this is a champion horse because it was sired with sperm stolen directly from the winner of the Belmont. Paulie explains about the horse while he has his mouth full of a hero sandwich that's a yard long. His cousin, Charlie, tells him he's crazy. That is a compliment in this family.

Paulie and Charlie have just been fired from their jobs at a restaurant for stealing from the management. Charlie is hard up. He can no longer support his girlfriend, a long-limbed, blonde aerobics instructor who seems attracted to his exotic ethnic charm. Paulie has the answer to their problems. He will buy the future champion racehorse with money from a juice loan and then pay off the loan by cracking a safe he has heard about. There is only one problem with this plan. The safe belongs to the Mafia godfather of Greenwich Village, and if he finds out who did it, not even Paulie's uncle in the Mafia can save them. Meanwhile, Charlie's girlfriend is pregnant, Paulie's car has been towed, a cop has killed himself falling down an elevator shaft, and on the sound track Frank Sinatra is singing "Summer Wind."

The Pope of Greenwich Village bills itself as a drama and is structured like a crime thriller, but I categorize it as basically a Behavior Movie. The real subject of the movie is the behavior of the characters, and the story is essentially an excuse for showboat performances. This movie is an actor's dream, and the actors involved are Eric Roberts, fresh from his triumph in *STAR 80*, as Paulie; Mickey Rourke, the hero of *Diner*, as Charlie; Daryl Hannah, right after her hit in *Splash*, as the aerobics instructor; and the usual supporting types like Tony Musante as the uncle, Burt Young—stuffing his face with pasta—as the godfather, and Geraldine Page as the tough-talking mother of the dead cop. Also, Kenneth McMillan has a well-acted key role as an old safecracker who gets caught in the middle of the whole deal.

There are times when *The Pope of Greenwich Village* seems to aspire to some great meaning, some insight into crime like *The Godfather* had. But the tip-off is the last shot, where the boys have a happy-go-lucky walk down the street and into a freeze-frame, while Sinatra is trotted out for his third encore. This movie is not really about anything except behavior, and the only human drama in it is the story of the safecracker and his family. That doesn't mean it's not worth seeing. The behavior is well-observed, although Eric Roberts has a tendency to go over the top in his mannered performance, and the last two scenes are highly unlikely. It's worth seeing for the acting, and it's got some good laughs in it, and New York is colorfully observed, but don't tell me this movie is about human nature, because it's not; it's about acting.

Popeye ★ ★ ★ ½
PG, 114 m., 1980

Robin Williams (Popeye), Shelly Duvall (Olive Oyl), Ray Walston (Poopdeck Pappy), Paul Dooley (Wimpy), Paul L. Smith (Bluto), Richard Libertini (Geezil). Directed by Robert Altman and produced by Robert Evans. Screenplay by Jules Feiffer.

One of Robert Altman's trademarks is the way he creates whole new worlds in his movies—worlds where we somehow don't believe that life ends at the edge of the screen, worlds in which the main characters are surrounded by other people plunging ahead at the business of living. That gift for populating new places is one of the richest treasures in *Popeye*, Altman's musical comedy. He takes one of the most artificial and limiting of art forms—the comic strip—and raises it to the level of high comedy and high spirits.

And yet *Popeye* nevertheless remains true to its origin on the comic page, and in those classic cartoons by Max Fleischer. A review of this film almost has to start with the work of Wolf Kroeger, the production designer, who created an astonishingly detailed and rich set on the movie's Malta locations. Most of the action takes place in a ramshackle fishing hamlet—"Sweethaven"—where the streets run at crazy angles up the hillsides, and the rooming houses and saloons lean together dangerously.

Sweethaven has been populated by actors who look, or are made to look, so much like their funny-page originals that it's hardly even jarring that they're *not* cartoons. Audiences immediately notice the immense forearms on Robin Williams, who plays Popeye; they're big, brawny, and completely convincing. But so is Williams's perpetual squint and his lopsided smile. Shelly Duvall, the star of so many other Altman films, is perfect here as Olive Oyl, the role she was born to play. She brings to Olive a certain . . . dignity, you might say. She's not lightly scorned, and although she may tear apart a room in an unsuccessful attempt to open the curtains, she is fearless in the face of her terrifying fiancé, Bluto. The list continues: Paul Smith (the torturer in *Midnight Express*) looks ferociously Bluto-like, and Paul Dooley (the father in *Breaking Away*) is a perfect Wimpy, forever curiously sniffing a hamburger with a connoisseur's fanatic passion. Even the little baby, Swee' Pea, played by Altman's grandson, Wesley Ivan Hurt, looks like typecasting.

But it's not enough that the characters and the locations look their parts. Altman has breathed life into this material, and he hasn't done it by pretending it's camp, either. He organizes a screenful of activity, so carefully choreographed that it's a delight, for example to watch the moves as the guests in Olive's rooming house make stabs at the plates of food on the table.

There are several set pieces. One involves Popeye's arrival at Sweethaven, another a stop on his lonely quest for his long-lost father. Another is the big wedding day for Bluto and Olive Oyl, with Olive among the missing and Bluto's temper growing until steam jets from his ears. There is the excursion to the amusement pier, and the melee at the dinner table, and the revelation of the true identity of a mysterious admiral, and the kidnapping of Swee' Pea, and then the kidnapping of Olive Oyl and her subsequent wrestling match with a savage octopus.

The movie's songs, by Harry Nilssen, fit into all of this quite effortlessly. Instead of having everything come to a halt for the musical set pieces, Altman stitches them into the fabric. Robin Williams sings Popeye's anthem, "I Yam What I Yam" with a growling old sea dog's stubborness. Bluto's "I'm Mean" has an undeniable conviction, and so does Olive Oyl's song to Bluto, "He's Large." Shelly Duvall's performance as Olive Oyl also benefits from the amazingly ungainly walking style she brings to the movie.

Popeye, then, is lots of fun. It suggests that it *is* possible to take the broad strokes of a comic strip and turn them into sophisticated entertainment. What's needed is the right attitude toward the material. If Altman and his people had been the slightest bit condescending toward Popeye, the movie might have crash-landed. But it's clear that this movie has an affection for Popeye, and so much regard for the sailor man that it even bothers to reveal the real truth about his opinion of spinach.

Porky's ★ ½
R, 94 m., 1982

Dan Monahan (Pee Wee), Mark Herrier (Billy), Wyatt Knight (Tommy), Roger Wilson (Mickey), Kim Cattrall (Honeywell), Alex Karras (Sheriff), Susan Clark (Cherry Forever), Nancy Parsons (Ms. Balbricker). Directed by Bob Clark and produced by Don Carmody and Clark.

Porky's is another raunchy teen-age sex-and-

food-fight movies. The whole genre seems fixated on the late 1950s and early 1960s, when the filmmakers, no doubt, were teenagers. Do today's teenagers really identify with jokes about locker rooms, Trojans, boobs, jockstraps, killer-dyke gym coaches, and barfing? Well, yes, probably they do. Teen-agers seem to occupy a time warp of eternally unchanging preoccupations. Hollywood originally entered that world with a certain innocence in the late 1950s with Pat Boone and beach part movies. That innocence is now long, long ago. Since *American Graffiti, National Lampoon's Animal House,* and *Meatballs,* the A.C.N.E.S. movie has turned cynical. You remember what A.C.N.E.S. stands for. It's an acronym for any movie about the dreaded Adolescent Character's Neurotic Eroticism Syndrome.

In *Porky's,* the male characters are neurotic about the usual three subjects: the size, experience, and health of their reproductive organs. The female characters, on the other hand, are seen almost entirely as an undiscovered species from a lost continent. They're whispered about, speculated about, spied upon, victimized, and, in general, feared. And it's not only Ms. Balbricker, the juggernaut gym coach, who's a heavy. All of the women in this movie are weird. One howls like a dog during sexual intercourse. Others lure unsuspecting horny teen-age boys into rooms with trapdoors, and dump them into alligator-infested waters.

In fact, the strangest thing about *Porky's* is how much it hates women. The only close friendships in the movie are between men. The movie even takes certain scenes that are usually clichés for female characters and assigns them to men. For example, you can hardly make a movie like this without a scene in which someone's caught nude in public. Remember Hot Lips in *M*A*S*H?* In *Porky's,* it's a kid named Pee Wee. He's caught with his pants down, chased into the woods, picked up by the cops, and deposited at the local drive-in hamburger stand, where he poses like September Morn.

Since the movie doesn't like women, its sex scenes all create fear and hostility, which prevents them from being funny (sex scenes *about* fear and hostility, on the other hand, can be very funny). Even in an easy scene like the one where the guys spy on the girls in the locker room, the director, Bob Clark, blows it. Peeping-tom scenes can be very funny (remember John Belushi on the ladder in *Animal House?*). Here, it's just smarmy. There's one other problem. None of the male actors in this movie look, sound, or act like teen-agers. They all look like overgrown preppies at their fraternity pledge class's fifth reunion. Jokes based on embarrassment never work unless we can identify with the embarrassed character. Here, the actors all seem to be just acting.

I see that I have neglected to summarize the plot of *Porky's*. And I don't think I will. I don't feel like writing one more sentence (which is, to be sure, all it would take).

The Postman Always Rings Twice
★ ★ ½
R, 122 m., 1981

Jack Nicholson (Frank Chambers), Jessica Lange (Cora Papadakis), John Colicos (Nick Papadakis), Michael Lerner (Katz), John P. Ryan (Kennedy), Anjelica Huston (Madge). Directed by Bob Rafelson and produced by Charles Mulvehill and Rafelson. Screenplay by David Mamet.

The Postman Always Rings Twice is an absolutely superb mounting of a hollow and disappointing production. It shows a technical mastery of filmmaking, and we are dazzled by the performances, the atmosphere, the mood of mounting violence. But by the second hour of the film we've lost our bearings: What is this movie *saying* about its characters? What does it feel and believe about them? Why was it necessary to tell their stories? The movie is based on a hard-boiled, classic novel by James M. Cain, which has already inspired three previous films, including the famous 1946 John Garfield version. It isn't difficult to guess why the director, Bob Rafelson, wanted to make it again. On the basis of his key scenes, he was attracted by the physical violence in the story and he felt that in 1981 he could deal more frankly with Cain's sexual savagery.

He was right. His film contains passages of unusual physical power, including one in which Jack Nicholson and Jessica Lange make love (if that is the word) on a kitchen table. Nicholson plays a Depression-era drifter in the film, a cheap thief, and a con man. Lange is the bored and sensuous cook in a short-order joint run by her much older Greek husband, John Colicos. Passion flares between Nicholson and Lange almost the moment they first see one another, and their lovemaking is quick, brutal, uncontrolled, and animalistic.

Eventually, they kill Colicos—although not without the greatest difficulties. This is one of those films where blood, violence, and sheer weight of human bodies are made into Hitchcockian embarrassments. And then the two lovers are put on trial, are freed through a cynical arrangement between opposing insurance companies, and then arrive at an ironic fate. Along the way, there is a brief and totally inexplicable appearance by a woman lion tamer (Anjelica Huston), who seems to be visiting from another movie.

The movie is a triumph of atmosphere. Every last weathered Coke sign, every old auto and old overcoat and old cliché have been put in with loving care. And the performances have been cranked up to levels of trembling intensity. Jessica Lange, first seen in *King Kong*, this time submits to the embrace of a wanton monster. Jack Nicholson has never been seedier, shiftier, more driven. John Colicos, as the simple, alcoholic, ambitious Greek-American, provides a wonderfully textured performance. And yet, there is no feeling of tragedy in Colicos's death. No feeling of greatness in the romantic compulsion of Lange and Nicholson. No way to tell what the movie believes about their acquittal and eventual fate. A movie such as *Bonnie and Clyde* comes to mind. It also dealt with passion, crime, and money, but so clearly that at the end of the film we felt we knew the dying characters.

We never know the people in *The Postman Always Rings Twice*. They are kept rigidly imprisoned within a tradition of absolute naturalism: They exist, they eat, they sleep, they act. That would be acceptable if the filmmakers could stand outside their characters and have feelings about them. But I never believed that was the case. Rafelson and his collaborators have gone to infinite pains, successfully, to create a film that is wonderfully achieved on the level of production. But they have not filled it with the purposes of its characters.

Prince of the City ★ ★ ★ ★
R, 167 m., 1981

Treat Williams (Daniel Ciello), Jerry Orbach (Gus Levy), Richard Foronjy (Joe Marinaro), Don Billett (Bill Mayo), Jenny Marino (Dom Bando), Bob Balaban (Sentimassino), Lindsay Crouse (Carla Ciello). Directed by Sidney Lumet and produced by Burtt Harris. Screenplay by Jay Presson Allen and Lumet.

He will not rat on his partners. This is his bottom line. He will talk to investigators about all the other guys he knows things about. He will talk about how narcotics cops get involved in the narcotics traffic, how they buy information with drugs, how they string out addicts and use them as informers, how they keep some of the money and some of the drugs after big busts. He will tell what he knows about how the other cops do these things. But he will not talk about his partners in his own unit. This is his code, and, of course, he is going to have to break it.

That is the central situation of Sidney Lumet's *Prince of the City*. While you are watching it, it's a movie about cops, drugs, and New York City, in that order. After the film starts to turn itself over in your mind, it becomes a much deeper piece, a film about how difficult it is to go straight in a crooked world without hurting people you love.

Drugs are a rotten business. They corrupt everyone they come into contact with, because they set up needs so urgent that all other considerations are forgotten. For addicts, the need is for the drug itself. For others, the needs are more complex. The members of the special police drug unit in *Prince of the City*, for example, take on an envied departmental status because of their assignment. They have no hours, no beats, no uniforms. They are elite free-lancers, modern knights riding out into the drug underworld and establishing their own rules. They do not look at it this way, but their status depends on drugs. If there were no drugs and no addicts, there would be no narcs, no princes of the city. Of course, their jobs are also cold, dirty, lonely, dangerous, thankless, and never finished. That is the other side of the deal, and that helps explain why they will sometimes keep the money they confiscate in a drug bust. It's as if they're levying their own fines. It also ex-

plains why they sometimes supply informers with drugs: They know better than anyone how horrible the addict's life can be. "A junkie can break your heart," the hero of this movie says at one point, and by the movie's end we understand what he means.

The film is based on a book by Robert Daley about Bob Leuci, a New York cop who cooperated with a 1971 investigation of police corruption. In the movie, Leuci is called Ciello, and he is played by Treat Williams in a demanding and grueling performance. Williams is almost always onscreen, and almost always in situations of extreme stress, fatigue, and emotional turmoil. We see him coming apart before our eyes. He falls to pieces not simply because of his job, or because of his decision to testify, but because he is in an inexorable trap and he *will* sooner or later have to hurt his partners.

This is a movie that literally hinges on the issue of perjury. And Sidney Lumet and his co-writer, Jay Presson Allen, have a great deal of respect for the legal questions involved. There is a sustained scene in this movie that is one of the most spellbinding I can imagine, and it consists entirely of government lawyers debating whether a given situation justifies a charge of perjury. Rarely are ethical issues discussed in such detail in a movie, and hardly ever so effectively.

Prince of the City is a very good movie and, like some of its characters, it wants to break your heart. Maybe it will. It is about the ways in which a corrupt modern city makes it almost impossible for a man to be true to the law, his ideals, and his friends, all at the same time. The movie has no answers. Only horrible alternatives.

Private Benjamin ★ ★ ★
R, 110 m., 1980

Goldie Hawn (Judy Benjamin), Eileen Brennan (Captain Lewis), Armand Assante (Henri Tremont), Robert Webber (Colonel Thornbush), Sam Wanamaker (Teddy Benjamin), Barbara Barrie (Harriet Benjamin), Harry Dean Stanton (Sergeant Ballard), Albert Brooks (Yale Goodman). Directed by Howard Zieff and written and produced by Nancy Meyers, Charles Shyer, and Harvey Miller.

Howard Zieff's *Private Benjamin* is an appealing, infectious comedy starring Goldie Hawn as Judy Benjamin, a Jewish-American princess, breathless with joy on the day of her second marriage. She has a real catch: He's named Yale, he's a professional man, he wants his study done in mushroom colors. Alas, he dies in the throes of passion on his wedding night (something his grieving mother discovers when Judy solemnly repeats his last words). And Judy goes into mourning.

What's she to do? She calls in to an all-night talk show and is promised a solution by another caller. The next day, we meet the guy with the answer. Played by Harry Dean Stanton, that wonderful character actor who could be Robert Mitchum's sneaky cousin, the guy turns out to be an Army recruiter. And he solemnly paints a picture of Army life that has Judy signing up. Her subsequent shocks of discovery provide the great laughs of the movie's best scenes. She solemnly explains to a captain (Eileen Brennan) that she *did* sign up with the Army, yes, but with another Army. Where, she asks, are the private condo living quarters the recruiter promised her? And surely the Army could have afforded some draperies? In no time at all, she's cleaning the latrines with her electric toothbrush.

This is an inspired idea for a movie comedy, and Goldie Hawn has a lot of fun with it. She finds just the right note for her performance, poised halfway between the avaricious and the slack-jawed, the calculating and the innocent. She makes some kind of impression on everyone she runs up against (or into), especially Robert Webber as the square-jawed Colonel Thornbush, commander of the Army's elite paratroop unit, the Thornbushers.

It's at about this point that the movie seems to lose its unique comic direction and turn into a more or less predictable combination of service comedy and romantic farce. After Judy's parents try to rescue her from the Army, she suddenly decides to stay and stick it out. She turns into a passable soldier. She almost inadvertently captures the entire Red team and makes them Blue prisoners of war during war games. And she is invited to join the Thornbushers by Colonel Thornbush himself (who turns out to have an alternative in mind if Judy doesn't want to jump at 13,000 feet).

Along the way, she meets a sexy and eligible French bachelor who's a gynecologist. After she blackmails Thornbush into sending her to Allied Army headquarters in Paris, she falls in love with the Frenchman (Armand Assante), and gets involved in Gallic romantic intrigues. It turns out that her would-be third husband is more interested in Sunday morning soccer games and cute little downstairs maids than in the kind of marriage Judy Benjamin was brought up to desire.

This stuff is occasionally funny, but it's kind of predictable. It turns *Private Benjamin* into areas that are too familiar: We've all seen the comic situations that grow out of the courtship with the Frenchman, and we'd really rather have seen more stuff of Private Benjamin in the Army. The movie would have been better off sticking with Goldie Hawn as a female Beetle Bailey and forgetting about the changes that allow her to find self-respect, deal with the Frenchman, etc. Still, *Private Benjamin* is refreshing and fun. Goldie Hawn, who is a true comic actress, makes an original, appealing character out of Judy Benjamin, and so the movie feels alive—not just an exercise in gags and situations.

Private School ★ ★
R, 82 m., 1983

Phoebe Cates (Christine), Betsy Russell (Jordan), Michael Zorek (Bubba), Sylvia Kristel (Teacher). Directed by Noel Black and produced by R. B. Efraim and Don Enright. Screenplay by Dan Greenburg and Suzanne O'Malley.

Is it some kind of trend in our society that the same movies that used to appeal to dirty old men are now being made for teen-agers? The original nudies of the early 1960s, movies like *The Immoral Mr. Teas* and *Not Tonight, Henry*, involved voyeuristic males who would look at, but not touch, pretty girls in various stages of undress. Those movies usually played at the kinds of theaters where you slammed down the exact admission price so you wouldn't have to linger in public view waiting for your change. *Private School* has at least as much nudity as the original skin flicks, is presented in the same spirit, and has about the same sense of humor. Only this one is different: In the old skin flicks, women were treated with a certain sense of awe; these days, female nudity is used primarily as a vehicle for inspiring cheap laughs against women.

The movie involves the libidinous young students of two private schools—the Cherryvale Academy for Women and the Freemount Academy for Men, ha ha—and it's basically just a series of gags based on the crude attempt of the men to score with the women. For variety, there are occasional episodes involving the fuddy-duddy administrators, the hypocritical parents, and the comely sex education teacher (Sylvia Kristel). The movie is well-made in a light, fluffy way, and the direction by Noel (*Pretty Poison*) Black is much better than average in the epidemic of Horny Teen-ager Movies. But why are these movies so antiwoman? Why are *all* the jokes about nudity directed at women? Why are the girls the only ones embarrassed in public? Why is it always a girl who's in a boy's room while his leering friends hide in the closet and under the bed, taking bets on how far he'll get with her? And why are we supposed to yuk when the guys dress up in drag and sneak into the girls' school—when the same scene played the other way would seem threatening to men?

I think the makers of these teen-age sex movies are uninformed about teen-age sexuality, lack the interest or the intelligence to really explore the difficult business of growing up, and are content to grind out Dirty Old Men's fantasies about pubescent sex. Hasn't anyone told them (or don't they remember?) that sex is a terrifically serious, scary, and delicate business when you're a teen-ager, and that these movies depict sexual conduct that is way out of the norm?

There are a few Teen-age Sex Movies that do deal realistically with the whole area. The list is short: *Tex; Baby, It's You;* and *Valley Girl.* The rest of these movies (*Private Lessons, Going All the Way, Losing It, The Last American Virgin, Paradise, Blue Lagoon,* etc.) depict a world in which teen-age males are initiated into sex by prostitutes or older women, while teen-age females are made the targets of jokes and public embarrassment.

This is very sick. And back to *Private School:* As I suggested, the movie's not without charm. There's a fresh, sweet relationship between one of the girls (Phoebe Cates) and her boyfriend, in which she is permitted to have the normal fears, doubts, and reservations of anyone her age. I'm not sure how that plot got into this smarmy-minded movie, but it was like a breath of fresh air.

Prizzi's Honor ★ ★ ★ ★
R, 129 m., 1985

Jack Nicholson (Charley Partanna), Kathleen Turner (Irene Walker), Anjelica Huston (Maerose), Robert Loggia (Eduardo Prizzi), John Randolph (Pop Partanna), William Hickey (Don Carrado Prizzi), Lee Richardson (Dominic). Directed by John Huston and produced by John Foreman. Screenplay by Richard Condon and Janet Roach.

John Huston's *Prizzi's Honor* marches like weird and gloomy clockwork to its relentless conclusion, and half of the time, we're laughing. This is the most bizarre comedy in many a month; a movie so dark, so cynical, and so funny that perhaps only Jack Nicholson and Kathleen Turner could have kept straight faces during the love scenes. They do. They play two professional Mafia killers who meet, fall in love, marry, and find out that the mob may not be big enough for both of them.

Nicholson plays Charley Partanna, a soldier in the proud Prizzi family, rulers of the East Coast, enforcers of criminal order. The godfather of the Prizzis, Don Corrado, is a mean little old man who looks like he has been freeze-dried by the lifelong ordeal of draining every ounce of humanity out of his wizened body. To Don Corrado (William Hickey), nothing is more important than the Prizzis' honor—not even another Prizzi. Charley Partanna is the Don's grandson. He has been raised in this ethic, and accepts it. He kills without remorse. He follows orders. Only occasionally does he disobey the family's instructions, as when he broke his engagement with Maerose Prizzi (Anjelica Huston), his cousin. She then brought disgrace upon herself and, as the movie opens, is in the fourth year of self-imposed exile.

But she is a Prizzi, and does not forget, or forgive.

The movie opens like *The Godfather*, at a wedding. Charley's eyes roam around the church. In the choir loft, he sees a beautiful blonde (Kathleen Turner). She looks like an angel. At the reception, he dances with her once, and then she disappears. Later that day, there is a mob killing. Determined to find out the name of the blonde angel, Charley discovers even more—that she was the California hitman, brought in to do the job. He turns to Maerose for advice. She counsels him to go ahead: After all, it's good to have interests in common with your wife.

Charley flies to the coast, setting up a running gag as they establish a transcontinental commute. There is instant, electrifying chemistry between the two of them, and the odd thing is, it seems halfway plausible. They're opposites, but they attract. Nicholson plays his hood as a tough Brooklynite; he uses a stiff upper lip, like Bogart, and sounds simple and implacable. Turner, who is flowering as a wonderful comic actress, plays her Mafia killer like a bright, cheery hostess. She could be selling cosmetics.

What happens between them is best not explained here, since the unfolding of the plot is one of the movie's delights. The story is by Richard Condon, a novelist who delights in devious plot construction, and here he takes two absolutes—romantic love and the Prizzis' honor—and arranges a collision between them. Because all of the motivations are so direct and logical, the movie is able to make the most shocking decisions seem inevitable.

John Huston directed this film right after *Under the Volcano*, and what other director could have put those two back-to-back? It is one of his very best films, perhaps because he made it with friends; Condon is an old pal from Ireland, Anjelica Huston is, of course, his daughter, and Nicholson has long been Anjelica's lover. Together they have taken a strange plot, peopled it with carefully overwrought characters, and made *Prizzi's Honor* into a treasure.

Protocol ★ ★ ½
PG, 96 m., 1984

Goldie Hawn (Sunny), Chris Sarandon (Michael), Richard Romanus (Emir), André Gregory (Nawaf), Gail Strickland (Mrs. St. John), Cliff De Young (Hilley). Directed by Herbert Ross and produced by Anthea Sylbert. Screenplay by Buck Henry.

The first hour of *Protocol* is so much fun, and the Goldie Hawn character is such an engaging original, that at first I couldn't believe they were going to throw away all that work by going for a standard Hollywood ending. But they did. You know a movie's in trouble when they stop dealing with the characters and start throwing things at the screen.

Maybe it's just that they started with such a good premise, such a good first and second act, that they never got around to ending the movie. *Protocol* begins with Goldie as a cocktail waitress who dresses like a big bird every night to entertain the regulars in a sleazy nightclub. She's broke and without prospects. But then one night she pushes to the front of a crowd, and when a guy pulls out a gun, she wrestles him to the ground and saves the life of the leader of an obscure Arab oil sheikdom. She is, in the process, wounded in the nether regions, and when she becomes a national heroine and the star of TV interview shows, the Arab leader falls in love with her and the White House decides to hire her as a protocol officer and more or less give her to the sheik.

The setup for the film has a lot of charm, with Goldie as a goofy heroine who rooms with a couple of gay men and asks them thoughtfully, "Do you think I might be one of those people who is referred to as cute, but none too heavy in the brains department?" Her first televised press conference after the foiled assassination is probably the movie's high point; she answers each question with such refreshing directness that she becomes an overnight star. It's right after the press conference that the movie reaches its turning point: Should it continue to develop this story along the lines of more or less realistic comedy, or should it go for the bizarre and the slapstick? It makes the second choice. We meet the sheik (Richard Romanus) and his chief aide (André Gregory), and the usual clichés about Arabs start to fly thick and fast. Goldie soon finds herself in the Middle East as a prospective harem wife. Some of this stuff is funny, but the movie really falls apart when it moves back to

Washington and Goldie invites the Arabs to a party in her old nightclub.

One of the things Hollywood has trouble learning is that wild party scenes are almost never funny (*Bachelor Party* was an exception). *Protocol*'s party scene fills the screen with the standard clichés: The Arabs, visiting Japanese businessmen, Hell's Angels, shocked diplomats, S&M couples, waitresses dressed like giraffes, and so on. It's not funny, it's desperate. We look at a lot of people going nuts and breaking glasses over each other's heads, and it's like the movie is pleading artistic bankruptcy.

There's more: A Capra-style ending, with Goldie making a patriotic, tear-jerking speech before a congressional hearing and then running for public office. None of this has much to do with the genuine comic premises that were set up at the beginning. Why couldn't they have followed Hawn's character into the labyrinth of real diplomatic protocol, and created original characters instead of off-the-shelf stereotypes? Why do so many Hollywood movies these days feel they have to go berserk in the last half hour, instead of putting in the groundwork to create a situation we care about and a conclusion that makes a difference? The character that Goldie Hawn creates in this movie is so refreshing and so interesting that they should have gone ahead and made the extra effort and written an intelligent screenplay about her.

Psycho II ★ ★ ½
R, 113 m., 1983

Anthony Perkins (Norman Bates), Vera Miles (Lila), Meg Tilly (Mary), Robert Loggia (Dr. Raymond), Dennis Franz (Toomey), Hugh Gillan (Sheriff Hunt). Directed by Richard Franklin and produced by Hilton A. Green. Screenplay by Tom Holland.

The first thing is to put Alfred Hitchcock's original 1960 *Psycho* right out of your mind. There will never be another movie like it, and no sequel could possibly capture its unique charms. If you've seen *Psycho* a dozen times and can recite the shots in the shower scene by heart, *Psycho II* is just not going to do it for you. But if you can accept this 1983 movie on its own terms, as a fresh start, and put your memories of Hitchcock on hold, then *Psycho II* begins to work. It's

too heavy on plot and too willing to cheat about its plot to be really successful, but it does have its moments, and it's better than your average, run-of-the-mill slasher movie.

Norman Bates, having been judged not guilty by reason of insanity back in 1960, has responded well to psychiatric treatment. He is released. Because of a "state budget cutback," however, there will be no halfway house to ease his transition back into society's mainstream, and no social worker to drop in from time to time. Instead, Norman's all on his own—and he moves back into that Gothic house of horrors up on the hill above the Bates Motel. The movie's homecoming scenes strike a nerve. After all, that *is* the Bates Motel, and few images of Sir Alfred's long career have remained more indelibly etched in the memories of moviegoers. Perkins plays Bates about the same as the last time we saw him, with perhaps a few additional twitches. But he's a more sympathetic character this time, more mellow, more subdued. He still is, of course, as nutty as a fruitcake. He gets a job washing dishes at the local diner, and he makes friends with a waitress named Mary (Meg Tilly), who agrees to move into the Bates home and become his roommate. And then, in Norman's words, it starts again. His "mother," long dead (as we have every reason to recall), begins telephoning him. There are some unexplained murders. The plot thickens, but I'll end my description right here, to preserve the movie's many, many, many, secrets.

Is *Psycho II* worth seeing? It is a craftsmanlike piece of filmmaking with a suitably flaky performance by Perkins, but it isn't really a sequel to *Psycho*. It continues the story, but not the spell. And it never really establishes the other characters very well. Meg Tilly, as Norman's friend, is too laid-back and dreamy to hold her own against Norman Bates *and* a fresh slasher mystery. Vera Miles, as a woman with a fierce hatred of Norman, never quite crosses the line from indignation to insanity. In a movie full of half-sketched characters and half-explained developments, Norman Bates is just too mesmerizing to fit in very easily. But then I should have guessed the sequel wouldn't make it—right from the pretitle sequence, in which Hitchcock's original shower scene is shown, but is allowed to end before the shot of the blood going down the drain! Is nothing sacred?

Pumping Iron II: The Women
★ ★ ★ ½
NO MPAA RATING, 130 m., 1985

Featuring Lori Bowen, Carla Dunlap, Bev Francis, and Rachel McLish. Directed and produced by George Butler and written by Charles Gaines.

The music is *Also Sprach Zarathustra,* the theme of *2001: A Space Odyssey.* From a concealed staircase at the back of the stage, an awesome human figure emerges. The backlighting makes it hard to discern: Is this Arnold Schwarzenegger? Sylvester Stallone? Not even close. This is Bev Francis, an Australian-born power-lifter who is the most muscular woman in the world.

The idea of women with big muscles is still a little strange. Spending some time with the stars of *Pumping Iron II: The Women* at the 1985 Cannes Film Festival, I was struck by the reactions they inspired from people on the street, who stopped, turned, and stared at these women with broad shoulders and huge biceps. Until the last few years, crowds at Cannes have traditionally been drawn by women with exaggerated feminine physiologies; now here were women from the covers of muscle magazines, and the French, usually so blasé, simply did not know how to react.

At first sight, there is something disturbing about a woman with massive muscles. She is not merely androgynous, a combination of the sexes like an Audrey Hepburn or a Mick Jagger, but more like a man with a woman's face. We are so trained to equate muscles with men, softness and slight build with women, that it seems nature has made a mistake. The impulse is to reject muscle-women as freaks, and that is probably going to be the first reaction of viewers to *Pumping Iron II,* a companion to the original *Pumping Iron,* which made Schwarzenegger a star. The intriguing thing about the movie is how it alters our original reactions, involving us in the sport of women's body-building, using the clichés of all sports to make us fans of this one, until by the end of the movie we're watching the 1983 International Women's Body-Building Competition with a connoisseur's eye. If we don't know how we feel about women with muscles, neither do the judges; the entry of Bev Francis into the competition inspires a philosophical debate about the definition of "femininity."

Because Francis is by far more muscular than any other woman in the competition—including former champions Rachel McLish and Carla Dunlap—she should be the obvious favorite, but some of the judges say she doesn't look like a woman. Should she? Is this a body-building competition, or a beauty pageant? McLish, with her Farrah Fawcett hairstyle and rhinestone bra, has an obvious cheesecake appeal. Dunlap, Lori Bowen, and others in the finals are good-looking women. Francis looks like she belongs on the wrestling team. Her entry forces the judges—a hopelessly inept group—to define their terms. Meanwhile, we go backstage. George Butler, who has directed both *Pumping Iron* films, makes no pretense that his films are *cinéma vérité.* The documentary is scripted, in the sense that scenes are set up to dramatize Butler's points—even though the subjects and their dialogue are "real." We see Francis training in Australia, Dunlap talking with her mother, Bowen confessing that she idolizes Rachel McLish, and McLish tying body-building into born-again Christianity.

There are the obligatory gymnasium scenes, as the women work out, and the movie makes no secret of the narcissism implied by the sport. The real competition is with the mirror. The stage competition, at Caesar's Palace in Las Vegas, is more of a performance. The women line up, pair off for comparisons, are judged singly and in groups, displaying their basic muscle groups. The contest is so frankly obsessed with the details of these physical bodies that it seems like a particularly honest Miss America competition: They all know what they're onstage for, and there are no essays to write or songs to sing.

If anything sets the muscle-women apart from the Miss Americas, however, it's their intelligence. Miss Americas almost always share a stunning gift for the banal, for rehearsed clichés from civics class. The body-builders are, without exception, after all, articulate about what they are doing, and why. It has taken them, after all, a great deal more effort over a much longer time to get to *their* championship competition, and they have had to spend much of that time defending the very idea of their sport.

They are also, I thought, more articulate than most other athletes of either sex. Most competitive sports come already packaged with a complete set of rationales and clichés; nobody asks a football player to defend *the idea* of football. Nobody asks Chris Evert if she thinks playing tennis means she doesn't really want to be a woman. Body-building is a sport that seems to be about defining muscles, but *Pumping Iron II* shows that it is at least as much about defining attitudes and definitions of sexuality. You walk into this movie expecting to see a lot of sweat, and you walk out with more to think about than you bargained for.

Purple Hearts ½★
R, 115 m., 1984

Ken Wahl (Don Jardian), Cheryl Ladd (Deborah Solomon), Stephen Lee (Wizard), Drew Snyder (Colonel Larrimore), David Harris (Haynes). Directed and produced by Sidney J. Furie. Screenplay by Furie and Rick Natkin.

Remember those movie ads that used to show two lovers in the foreground, and a whole war in the background? You know, where the whole world was a stage, and millions of people were fighting and dying so that these two goofballs could swap spit? I thought they'd stopped making movies like that, but nope: *Purple Hearts* dedicates itself to all the Purple Heart winners of Vietnam, and then turns that war into a lonely hearts club for a couple of lovesick medics.

The characters:

Dr. Don Jardian (Ken Wahl), Navy battlefield surgeon, attached to the Marines. A gruff cynic until he looks up during a tricky operation and sees, above her surgical mask, the eyes of . . .

Deborah Solomon (Cheryl Ladd), Navy nurse, who has already lost a husband in this war, and is not willing to risk her heart one more time on a man who could be killed, breaking it again.

Jardian is in the front lines, up to his elbows in blood, performing major surgery

on an assembly line. Then one critically wounded soldier comes in, and Jardian's superior predicts the soldier will die. Jardian doesn't think so—not if the kid can get the latest treatment at a good hospital. So he commandeers a plane, escorts the wounded soldier to a hospital in Da Nang, and meets Nurse Solomon. The soldier dies. *C'est la guerre.* The doctor and nurse fall in love. He makes a proposition. She rejects it. Disconsolate, he flies back into danger—or, as John Wayne once put it, he steers into harm's way. Later, they meet again and this time they make love. In the morning, though, she announces that they cannot have an affair because she doesn't want to "commit" herself and have another broken heart, etc. She explains that they can always treasure the memory of last night. Thanks a lot, Nurse Solomon.

Jardian volunteers for heavy-duty frontline combat assignments. There is then a great deal of rugged battle footage, in which inflamed waves of Viet Cong charge American machine gun positions. The combat looks about as authentic as in John Wayne's *The Green Berets* (which ended, you will recall, with the Duke standing on the beach, silhouetted against a sun that had to be setting in the East). Anyway, Jardian is shot down behind enemy lines and has to trek back 150 miles through the jungle with a wounded comrade on his back. Meanwhile, Nurse Solomon hears he's dead. Also meanwhile, something happens so that when Jardian returns to base, *he* thinks *she's* dead. Not since *Romeo and Juliet* has the old They-Both-Think-the-Other-One-is-Dead ploy been milked so shamelessly.

This isn't war, this is bad plotting. And this isn't romance, it's soap opera. The last half-hour of the movie is an exercise in complete frustration for the audience: We cut back and forth between the doctor and the nurse in such a way that we know everything about both of them, and they know nothing about each other. It's the kind of movie where you want to shout advice at the screen. What's disappointing is that *Purple Hearts* comes from director Sidney J. Furie, who also made *The Boys in Company C*, a Vietnam film I admired very much. It was lean and angry and filled with a bitter humor. *Purple Hearts* is just romantic goo and impossible coincidence. The boys in Company C would have thrown beer bottles at the screen.

The Purple Rose of Cairo ★ ★ ★ ★
PG, 87 m., 1985

Mia Farrow (Cecilia), Jeff Daniels (Tom Baxter/Gil Shepherd), Danny Aiello (Monk), Van Johnson (Larry), Alexander H. Cohen (Raoul Hirsh). Directed by Woody Allen and produced by Robert Greenhut. Screenplay by Allen.

About twenty minutes into Woody Allen's *The Purple Rose of Cairo,* an extraordinary event takes place. A young woman has been going to see the same movie over and over again, because of her infatuation with the movie's hero. From his vantage point up on the screen, the hero notices her out in the audience. He strikes up a conversation, she smiles and shyly responds, and he abruptly steps off the screen and into her life. No explanation is offered for this miraculous event, but then perhaps none is needed: Don't we spend our lives waiting for the same thing to happen to us in the movies?

Life, of course, is never as simple and dreamy as the movies, and so the hero's bold act has alarming consequences. The movie's other characters are still stranded up there on the screen, feeling angry and left out. The Hollywood studio is aghast that its characters would suddenly develop minds of their own. The actor who *played* the hero is particularly upset, because now there are two of him walking around, one wearing a pith helmet. Things are simple only in the lives of the hero and the woman, who convince themselves that they *can* simply walk off into the sunset, and get away with this thing.

The Purple Rose of Cairo is audacious and witty and has a lot of good laughs in it, but the best thing about the movie is the way Woody Allen uses it to toy with the very essence of reality and fantasy. The movie is so cheerful and open that it took me a day or two, after I'd seen it, to realize how deeply Allen has reached this time. If it is true, and I think it is, that most of the time we go to the movies in order to experience brief lives that are not our own, then Allen is demonstrating what a tricky self-deception we practice. Those movie lives consist of *only* what is on

the screen, and if we start thinking that real life can be the same way, we are in for a cruel awakening.

The woman in the movie is played by Mia Farrow as a sweet, rather baffled small-town waitress whose big, shiftless lug of a husband bats her around. She is a good candidate for the magic of the movies. Up on the screen, sophisticated people have cocktails and plan trips down the Nile and are recognized by the doormen in nightclubs. The hero in the movie is played by Jeff Daniels (who was Debra Winger's husband in *Terms of Endearment*). He is a genial, open-faced smoothie with all the right moves, but he has a problem: He *only* knows what his character knows in the movie, and his experience is literally limited to what happens to his character in the plot. This can cause problems. He's great at talking sweetly to a woman, and holding hands, and kissing—but just when the crucial moment arrives, the movie fades out, and therefore, alas, so does he.

Many of Allen's best moments come from exploring the paradox that the movie character knows nothing of real life. For example, he can drive a car, because he drives one in the movie, but he can't start a car, because he doesn't turn on the ignition in the movie. Mia Farrow thinks maybe they can work this out. They can learn from each other. He can learn real life, and she can learn the romance of the movies. The problem is, both of them are now living in real life, where studio moguls and angry actors and snoopy reporters are making their life miserable.

Allen's buried subject in *The Purple Rose of Cairo* is, I think, related to the subjects of his less successful movies, *Stardust Memories* (1980) and *Zelig* (1983). He is interested in the conflicts involving who you want to be, and who other people want you to be. *Stardust* was about a celebrity whose fame prevented people from relating to anything but his image. *Zelig,* the other side of the coin, was about a man whose anonymity was so profound that he could gain an identity only by absorbing one from the people around him. In *Purple Rose,* the movie hero has the first problem, and the woman in the audience has the second, and when they get together, they still don't make one whole person, just two sad halves.

Purple Rose is delightful from beginning

to end, not only because of the clarity and charm with which Daniels and Farrow explore the problems of their characters, but also because the movie is so intelligent. It's not brainy or intellectual—no one in the whole movie speaks with more complexity than your average 1930s movie hero—but the movie is filled with wit and invention, and Allen trusts us to find the ironies, relish the contradictions, and figure things out for ourselves. While we do that, he makes us laugh and he makes us think, and when you get right down to it, forget about the fantasies; those are two of the most exciting things that could happen to anybody in a movie. The more you think about *The Purple Rose of Cairo*, and about the movies, and about why you go to the movies, the deeper the damned thing gets.

Q ★ ★ ½
R, 92 m., 1982

Michael Moriarty (Quinn), Candy Clark (Girlfriend), David Carradine (Detective), Richard Roundtree (Detective), Ed Kovens (Crook). Directed by Larry Cohen and produced by Samuel Z. Arkoff. Screenplay by Cohen.

A few days after *Q* was screened at the Cannes Film Festival (under its original title, *The Winged Serpent*), the following conversation took place between Samuel Z. Arkoff, the film's producer, and Rex Reed, the critic:

Reed: Sam! I just saw *The Winged Serpent!* What a surprise! All that dreck— and right in the middle of it, a great Method performance by Michael Moriarty!
Arkoff: The dreck was my idea.

I believe him. Arkoff has been producing films for thirty years now, and even if he *was* honored with a retrospective at the Museum of Modern Art, his heart still lies with shots of a giant flying lizard attacking a woman in a bikini on top of a Manhattan skyscraper. He's just that kinda guy. There are, in fact, several shots in *Q* that owe their ancestry to Sam Arkoff. I am aware, of course, that Larry Cohen gets credit for having written and directed this movie, but where would Cohen or any other director be without the

rich heritage of a quarter-century of American-International Pictures made by Sam Arkoff? Here are examples of the shots I have in mind:

• The camera looks straight down at terrified citizens fleeing from a menace. They run crazily across the street. Some run away from the camera, some toward it, so that you can't tell for sure where the menace is, and the shot can be intercut with shots of a menace approaching from any direction.

• The hero empties his machine gun into the giant serpent and turns away from a window to issue orders: "Everybody hold your positions!" Just then the serpent reappears behind him.

• There are False Serpent Alarms in which people get hit from behind by toy birds, chairs, and their boyfriends.

• David Carradine says, "He doesn't die easy."

You get the idea. *Q* is another silly monster movie. But think how long it's *been* since we had another silly monster movie. There was a time during the golden age of Sam Arkoff's career when there were lots of monster movies. Remember, for example, *Attack of the Crab Monsters, The Viking Women and the Sea Serpent, Creature from the Haunted Sea,* and *Wasp Woman.* But in the last few years Creature Features have been replaced by Dead Teen-ager Movies, and instead of awful special effects of a monster going berserk, we get worse shots of a homicidal maniac going berserk.

Q returns to the basic formula, in which a prehistoric creature terrorizes the city. In this case, the creature is a Quetzalcoatl, a mythical Aztec monster with wings *and* four claws. It apparently has been brought back into existence in connection with some shady human sacrifices at the Museum of National History (although this particular subplot is very muddled). It lives in a nest at the top of the Chrysler Building, lays eggs, and terrorizes helpless New Yorkers, who are not sure if this is a real monster or another crazy circulation stunt by Rupert Murdoch.

Rex Reed was right, though, about the Method performance by Michael Moriarty. In the middle of this exploitation movie, there's Moriarty, rolling his eyes, improvising dialogue, and acting creepy. He's fun to watch, especially in the scene where he names his terms for leading the cops to the lizard. The cast also includes David Carradine, Richard Roundtree, and Candy Clark, good actors all, but you have to be *awfully* good not to be upstaged by the death throes of a dying Quetzalcoatl.

Still to be answered: How did *one* Quetzalcoatl get pregnant?

Quest for Fire ★ ★ ★ ½
R, 100 m., 1982

Everett McGill (Noah), Ron Perlman (Amoukar), Nameer El-Kadi (Gaw), Rae Dawn Chong (Ika). Directed by Jean-Jacques Annaud and produced by John Kemeny and Denis Heroux. Screenplay by Gerard Brach.

There are basically two ways to regard *Quest for Fire*. The movie is either (a) the moving story of how scattered tribes of very early men developed some of the traits that made them human, or (b) a laughable caveman picture in which a lot of lantern-jawed actors jump around in animal skins, snarling and swinging clubs at one another. During the movie's opening scenes, I found myself seeing it in the second way, as a borderline comedy. But then these characters and their quest began to grow on me, and by the time the movie was over I cared very much about how their lives would turn out.

Other viewers report some of the same confusion. The movie has been compared with such varied works of art as *2001: A Space Odyssey* and *Alley Oop.* The question, I suppose, is whether you can make your own leap of imagination into the world of the movie—whether you're willing to identify with these beetle-browed ancestors who made more important discoveries, in their way, than all of the Nobel laureates put together. I found I *was* willing, and I was a little surprised at how much affection the movie generated.

Quest for Fire was shot on rugged locations in Canada and Scotland and takes place at the dawn of man. It introduces us to a tribe of primitive men who guard their most precious possession, which is fire. They know how to tend it and how to use it, but not how to make it. And after a jealous tribe of less-advanced creatures attacks them and destroys their fire, three men set out on an odyssey to seek another tribe that possesses fire and to steal it from them. Along the way, there are terrifying adventures. A saber-toothed tiger chases the men up into a tree and keeps them there for days. On another occasion, the heroes are trapped between an unfriendly tribe of apes and a herd of mastodons. In each situation, the men realize that simply running away won't work; they can't run fast or far enough. And so they slowly and painfully figure out a solution to their dilemma. Climbing the tree, for example, is rather obvious, but their solution to the mastodon problem is a brave inspiration.

Eventually the men discover another tribe, a more advanced tribe that lives in primitive huts and knows how to make fire and has even developed arts (they decorate themselves with mud, and their clay pots have drawings of animals scratched on them). The leader of the wanderers lusts after one of the women of the new tribe, and after a strange initiation ceremony he has sex with her. Soon he will make one of his greatest discoveries: The difference between lust and love and how it leads to the difference between isolation—and loneliness.

Quest for Fire compresses prehistory quite radically, of course. It's a little much to expect that one man in one span of a few weeks could make the scientific, emotional, and tactical discoveries that take place in the movie. Our progress as a race must have been slower than that (although Loren Eiseley writes in his books of the amazing explosion of the size of the human brain in just a handful of generations). *Quest for Fire* isn't science, though, it's an imaginary re-creation of our past, and it uses history for inspiration, not as a data source. The only two technical advisers listed in the credits are, appropriately, a novelist and a scientific popularizer: Anthony Burgess created the special primitive languages in the film, and Desmond Morris choreographed the body language and gestures.

I suggested earlier that there's probably a temptation to laugh during *Quest for Fire,* especially during such touchy scenes as the one in which early woman teaches early man that it *wasn't* as good for her as it was for him. I smiled during those scenes. But, thinking over my response, I realize that I wasn't smiling at the movie, but at the behavior of the characters. Man is a comic beast. For all of our dignity, we are very simple in many of our wants and desires, and as we crawled out of the primeval sludge and started our long trek toward civilization, there must have been many more moments of comedy than of nobility.

Quest for Fire cheerfully acknowledges that, and indeed some of its best scenes involve man's discovery of laughter. When one of the primitive tribesmen is hit on the head by a small falling stone, the woman from the other tribe laughs and laughs. Our heroes are puzzled: They haven't heard such a noise before. But it strikes some sort of deep chord, I guess, because later, one of the tribesmen deliberately drops a small stone on his friend's head, and then everybody laughs: The three men together with the woman who taught them laughter. That's human. The guy who got hit on the head is, of course, a little slow to join in the laughter, but finally he goes along with the joke. That's civilization.

Racing with the Moon ★ ★ ★ ½
PG, 108 m., 1984

Sean Penn (Hopper), Elizabeth McGovern (Caddie), Nicholas Cage (Nicky), Suzanne Adkinson (Sally), Julie Phillips (Alice). Directed by Richard Benjamin and produced by Alain Bernheim and John Kohn. Screenplay by Steven Kloves.

I'd like to start with a hypothetical question: How long has it been since you went to a movie that ended with the words "I love you"? For me, it had been a very long time, and one of the simpler pleasures of *Racing with the Moon* was to observe the movie marching inevitably toward those three words. A deeper pleasure was that the movie arrived there with grace and charm.

The story takes place in California in 1943, with the United States at war and teen-agers volunteering for the service. We meet a couple of high school kids, Hopper and Nicky, who are pinspotters down at the bowling alley and otherwise spend their time cutting classes, shooting pool, hitching rides on trains, and talking about the meaning of life. We are reminded of Tom and Huck. One night Hopper goes to the movies. His eyes meet the girl who is selling him his ticket, and he is thunderstruck by her. Her name is Caddie. Nicky already has a girlfriend, a plump little blonde named Sally. Hopper starts a campaign to win Caddie's heart, by slipping her flowers anonymously and tracking her down in the high school library. It appears that Caddie is a rich kid who lives in the house on the hill. But she likes Hopper anyway, and he likes her, and *Racing with the Moon* turns into a love story.

So far, what we have here is a movie that could go in several different directions. It could be sappy, it could be great, it could be dripping with so much nostalgia that it would feel like a memory even while we were watching it. *Racing with the Moon* doesn't fall into the *Summer of '42* nostalgia trap, but tries to be honest with its romantic characters. The performers are probably the reason that approach works so well. The three leading actors are Sean Penn and Elizabeth McGovern, as the young lovers, and Nicholas Cage, as Penn's friend. It's a pleasure to watch them work.

Penn, in particular, shows a whole side we didn't see in movies like *Bad Boys* or, needless to say, *Fast Times at Ridgemont High*. He's somehow better-looking than before, and more relaxed and confident. He doesn't come across with a lot of distracting self-importance. He plays the kind of kid who uses a rough exterior—smoking and shooting pool—as a kind of cover-up for the intelligence and sensitivity underneath, and one of the movie's best quiet moments comes when he reveals how well he can play the piano. McGovern, who had such a sweet face and such a wicked charm as the mistress in *Ragtime*, seems younger here. She has a secret she keeps from Penn, but only because she loves him. The way she plays against him is fun to watch: She's not a flirt and she's not coy, but instead she's open with this kid and has fun teasing him; there's a scene where she sets him up for a date with her girlfriend, and it's written and choreographed so carefully that it takes you back to any soda fountain you may ever have inhabited. Cage is good, too, reckless and self-destructive and dreamy, and by the end of the movie we really have a feeling for their complex relationships with each other.

Racing with the Moon is a movie like *Valley*

Girl or *Baby, It's You,* a movie that is interested in teen-agers and willing to listen to how they talk and to observe, with great tenderness, the fragility and importance of their first big loves. It's easy to end a movie with "I love you," but it's hard to get there honestly.

Raggedy Man ★ ★ ★ ½
PG, 94 m., 1981

Sissy Spacek (Nita), Eric Roberts (Teddy), Sam Shepard (Bailey), R.G. Armstrong (Rigby). Directed by Jack Fisk and produced by Burt Weissbourd and William D. Wittliff. Screenplay by Wittliff.

Raggedy Man remembers the small-town years of World War II so exactly that, although not yet born when the war broke out, I found myself remembering things I didn't even know I knew. Things like the way kids zoomed around dusty backyards, making their arms into airplane wings and imitating the noises of dive bombers. Like the Andrews Sisters singing "Rum and Coca-Cola" on the radio. Like the absolutely correct detail of a plaster-of-paris plaque on the wall, with a child's hand print immortalized on it. Remember?

Sissy Spacek stars as the sole switchboard operator of a small-town telephone company somewhere in the wilds of Texas. She lives in a small white frame house with a slamming screen door, and tries to raise her two sons, who are almost too small to support such grown-up names as Henry and Harry. The question of her husband is a mystery. Spacek hates her job, but she can't leave it: Mr. Rigby, the president of the telephone company, barks that this is wartime and her job is "frozen." Right, and she's frozen in it, until one day a young sailor (Eric Roberts) comes looking for a pay phone so he can call home. He's got a few days' leave, and has hitchhiked for hundreds of miles on the hopes of seeing his fiancée. The phone call reveals that she has taken up with a new beau. Roberts is crestfallen. Spacek kindly offers him some coffee. More or less, a little at a time, they fall in love.

These surface events of small-town life are wonderfully observed in *Raggedy Man,* which never pushes the romance between Spacek and Roberts too far: They remain decent, sensitive, courteous people, a little shy in the presence of large emotions. The town gossips about the woman taking up with the sailor, but people will gossip. (Nobody knows that better than the telephone operator!) Unfortunately, *Raggedy Man* has a whole additional level of plotting that is not nearly as rewarding as the events I've already described. There is, for example, the mystery of the "raggedy man" himself, a strange, scarecrow character who hangs about in the background of several scenes and has a disconcerting way of disappearing just when you want to get a closer look at him. There's also the matter of the town louts, who inhabit the beer hall and lust after the slim, young telephone operator.

These two plot strands lead up to a climactic ending that, quite frankly, I thought was unnecessary. Without giving away several secrets that the movie itself takes very seriously, I can say that *Raggedy Man* would have pleased me more if it had completely avoided its violent conclusion—and if the raggedy man himself had been left totally out of the story, the movie, and especially the symbolism.

Such regrets still leave my affection for this movie pretty much untouched. The Sissy Spacek performance is a small jewel: She has the words, the movements, the very tilt of her face, down just right. There's a scene where she puts music on the radio and dances with a broom, and another scene where she has a serious talk with her two little boys, and they're nearly perfect scenes. So is another one, where Roberts takes the two boys to a carnival. Roberts himself is a revelation: He is often overwrought in his acting; here, playing more quietly, he expresses great reserve of tenderness and strength, and is very effective.

Raggedy Man was Sissy Spacek's first movie after she won the Academy Award for *Coal Miner's Daughter,* and the first movie directed by her husband, Jack Fisk. (She met him when he was the art director for her first starring movie, *Badlands,* back in 1973.) The movie was made with a lot of love and startlingly fresh memories of the early 1940s, and reminds us once again that Spacek is a treasure.

Raging Bull ★ ★ ★ ★
R, 119 m., 1980

Robert De Niro (Jake La Motta), Cathy Moriarty (Vickie La Motta), Joe Pesci (Joey), Frank Vincent (Salvy), Nicholas Colasanto (Tommy Como), Theresa Saldana (Lenore), Frank Adonis (Patsy), Mario Gallo (Mario). Directed by Martin Scorsese and produced by Irwin Winkler and Robert Chartoff. Screenplay by Paul Schrader and Mardik Martin.

Martin Scorsese's *Raging Bull* is a movie about brute force, anger, and grief. It is also, like several of Scorsese's other movies, about a man's inability to understand a woman except in terms of the only two roles he knows how to assign her: virgin or whore. There is no room inside the mind of the prizefighter in this movie for the notion that a woman might be a friend, a lover, or a partner. She is only, to begin with, an inaccessible sexual fantasy. And then, after he has possessed her, she becomes tarnished by sex. Insecure in his own manhood, the man becomes obsessed by jealousy—and releases his jealousy in violence.

It is a vicious circle. Freud called it the "madonna-whore complex." Groucho Marx put it somewhat differently: "I wouldn't belong to any club that would have me as a member." It amounts to a man having such low self-esteem that he (a) cannot respect a woman who would sleep with him, and (b) is convinced that, given the choice, she would rather be sleeping with someone else. I'm making a point of the way *Raging Bull* equates sexuality and violence because one of the criticisms of this movie is that we never really get to know the central character. I don't agree with that. I think Scorsese and Robert De Niro do a fearless job of showing us the precise feelings of their central character, the former boxing champion Jake La Motta.

It is true that the character never tells us what he's feeling, that he is not introspective, that his dialogue is mostly limited to expressions of desire, fear, hatred, and jealousy. But these very limitations—these stone walls separating the character from the world of ordinary feelings—tell us all we need to know, especially when they're reflected back at him by the other people in his life. Especially his brother and his wife, Vickie.

Raging Bull is based, we are told, on the life of La Motta, who came out of the slums of the Bronx to become middleweight champion in the 1940s, who made and squandered millions of dollars, who became a pathetic stand-up comedian, and finally spent time in a prison for corrupting the morals of an underage girl. Is this the real La Motta? We cannot know for sure, though La Motta was closely involved with the production. What's perhaps more to the point is that Scorsese and his principal collaborators, actor Robert De Niro and screenwriter Paul Schrader, were attracted to this material. All three seem fascinated by the lives of tortured, violent, guilt-ridden characters; their previous three-way collaboration was the movie *Taxi Driver.*

Scorsese's very first film, *Who's That Knocking at My Door* (1967), starred Harvey Keitel as a kid from Little Italy who fell in love with a girl but could not handle the facts of her previous sexual experience. In its sequel, *Mean Streets* (1972), the same hang-up was explored, as it was in *Taxi Driver,* where the De Niro character's madonna-whore complex tortured him in sick relationships with an inaccessible, icy blonde, and with a young prostitute. Now the filmmakers have returned to the same ground, in a film deliberately intended to strip away everything but the raw surges of guilt, jealousy, and rage coursing through La Motta's extremely limited imagination.

Raging Bull remains close to its three basic elements: a man, a woman, and prizefighting. La Motta is portrayed as a punk kid, stubborn, strong, and narrow. He gets involved in boxing, and he is good at it. He gets married, but his wife seems almost an afterthought. Then one day he sees a girl at a municipal swimming pool and is transfixed by her. The girl is named Vickie, and she is played by Cathy Moriarty as an intriguing mixture of unstudied teen-ager, self-reliant survivor, and somewhat calculated slut.

La Motta wins and marries her. Then he becomes consumed by the conviction she is cheating on him. Scorsese finds a way to visually suggest his jealousy: From La Motta's point of view, Vickie sometimes floats in slow motion toward another man. The technique fixes the moment in our minds; we share La Motta's exaggeration of an innocent event. And we share, too, the La Motta character's limited and tragic hang-ups. This man we see is not, I think, supposed to be any more subtle than he seems. He does not have additional "qualities" to share with us. He is an engine driven by his own rage. The equation between his prizefighting and his sexuality is inescapable, and we see the trap he's in: La Motta is the victim of base needs and instincts that, in his case, are not accompanied by the insights and maturity necessary for him to cope with them. The raging bull. The poor sap.

Ragtime ★ ★ ★ ½
PG, 156 m., 1981

Howard E. Rollins, Jr. (Coalhouse Walker), James Cagney (Rhinelander Waldo), Brad Dourif (Younger Brother), Mary Steenburgen (Mother), James Olson (Father), Elizabeth McGovern (Evelyn Nesbit), Kenneth McMillan (Willie Conklin), Pat O'Brien (Delmas), Mandy Patinkin (Tateh), Moses Gunn (Booker T. Washington). Directed by Milos Forman and produced by Dino De Laurentiis. Screenplay by Michael Weller.

Milos Forman apparently made a basic decision very early in his production of E.L. Doctorow's best-selling novel, *Ragtime*. He decided to set aside the book's kaleidoscopic jumble of people, places, and things, and concentrate on just one of the several narrative threads. Instead of telling dozens of stories, his film is mostly concerned with the story of Coalhouse Walker, Jr., a black piano player who insists that justice be done after he is insulted by some yahoo volunteer firemen.

Doctorow's novel was an inspired juggling act involving both actual and fictional characters, who sometimes met in imaginary scenes of good wit and imagery. The Coalhouse story was more or less equal with several others. A film faithful to the book would have had people walking in and out of each other's lives in an astonishing series of coincidences. That might have been a good film, too. It might have looked a little like Robert Altman's *Nashville* or *Buffalo Bill*, and indeed Altman was the first filmmaker signed to direct *Ragtime*. But we will never

see what Altman might have done, and Forman decided to do something different. He traces the ways in which Coalhouse Walker enters and affects the lives of an upstate New York family in the first decade of the century. The family lives in White Plains, N.Y., in a vast and airy old frame manor, and it consists of Father, Mother, and Younger Brother, with walk-ons by a grandfather and a young son.

For Younger Brother, the sirens of the big city call, in the form of an infatuation with the chorus girl Evelyn Nesbit (Elizabeth McGovern). That's before the saga of Coalhouse Walker alters his life. Coalhouse (in a superb performance by Howard E. Rollins, Jr.) meets the family by accident, or maybe by fate. A young black woman gives birth to Coalhouse's son, and then the family takes in both the woman and her son, hiring her as their maid. Coalhouse comes calling. He wants to marry the mother of his child. He has earned enough money. Everything's all set for the ceremony, when an event takes place that changes everything. The local volunteer firemen, enraged that a black man would own his own Model T, block the car's way in front of their station. They pile horse manure on the front seat. And Coalhouse, quite simply, cannot rest until he sees his car restored to him in its original condition.

The story develops quickly into a confrontation. Coalhouse barricades himself into New York's J. Pierpont Morgan Library, and issues a set of demands. The library is surrounded by police and guardsmen, led by Police Commissioner Rhinelander Waldo (the great James Cagney, out of retirement). Father (James Olson) gets drawn into negotiations, and Younger Brother (Brad Dourif) is actually one of Coalhouse's lieutenants, in blackface disguise. Meanwhile, Mother is running off with a bearded immigrant who started out making cutout silhouettes on the streets and is now one of the first film directors.

The story of *Ragtime*, then, is essentially the story of Coalhouse Walker, Jr. Forman, a Czechoslovakian with an usually keen eye for American society—his credits include *One Flew Over the Cuckoo's Nest* and *Hair!*—has made a film about black pride and rage and . . . not *only* white racism, which we sort of expect, but also white liberalism.

The great achievement of *Ragtime* is in its performances, especially Rollins and the changes he goes through in this story, from youthful romantic love to an impassioned cry "Lord, why did you fill me with such rage?" Olson, quiet and self-effacing, is subtly powerful as Father. Mary Steenburgen is clear-voiced, primly ethical Mother who springs a big surprise on everyone. Pat O'Brien has two great scenes as a corrupt, world-weary lawyer. Kenneth McMillan blusters and threatens as the racist fire chief. And when Cagney tells him "people tell me . . . you're slime," there is the resonance of movie legend in his voice.

Ragtime is a loving, beautifully mounted, graceful film that creates its characters with great clarity. We understand where everyone stands, and most of the time we even know why. Forman surrounds them with some of the other characters from the Doctorow novel (including Harry Houdini, Teddy Roosevelt, and Norman Mailer as the architect Sanford White), but in the film they're just atmosphere—window dressing. Forman's decision to stick with the story of Coalhouse is vindicated, because he tells it so well.

Raiders of the Lost Ark ★ ★ ★ ★
PG, 115 m., 1981

Harrison Ford (Indy), Ronald Lacey (Teht), John Rhys-Davies (Sallah), Karen Allen (Marion), Wolf Kahler (Dietrich). Directed by Steven Spielberg and produced by Frank Marshall. Executive producers, George Lucas and Howard Kazanjian. Screenplay by Lucas and Phillip Kaufman.

Raiders of the Lost Ark is an out-of-body experience, a movie of glorious imagination and breakneck speed that grabs you in the first shot, hurtles you through a series of incredible adventures, and deposits you back in reality two hours later—breathless, dizzy, wrung-out, and with a silly grin on your face. This movie celebrates the stories we spent our adolescence searching for in the pulp adventure magazines, in the novels of Edgar Rice Burroughs, in comics—even in the movies. There used to be a magazine named *Thrilling Wonder Stories*, and every shot in *Raiders of the Lost Ark* looks like one of its covers. It's the kind of movie where the hero gets out of bed wondering what daring exploits and astonishing, cliff-hanging, death-defying threats he will have to survive in the next ten seconds.

It's actually more than a movie; it's a catalog of adventure. For locations, it ticks off the jungles of South America, the hinterlands of Tibet, the deserts of Egypt, a hidden submarine base, an isolated island, a forgotten tomb—no, make that *two* forgotten tombs—and an American anthropology classroom. For villains, it has sadistic Nazis, slimy gravediggers, drunken Sherpas, and scheming Frenchmen. For threats, it climaxes with the wrath of God, and leads up to that spectacular development by easy stages, with tarantulas, runaway boulders, hidden spears, falling rock slabs, burning airplanes, runaway trucks, sealed tombs, and snakes. Lots of snakes. For modes of conveyance, it looks like one of those old world's fair panoramas of transportation: It has horse carts, biplanes, motorcycles, submarines, ships, horse, trains, and trucks. No bicycles.

For heroes, it has Indiana Jones (Harrison Ford) and his former and future girlfriend, Marion (Karen Allen). She's the kind of girl . . . well, to make a long story short, when they first met ten years ago, Indiana deflowered her, and that made her so mad at men that she moved to the mountains of Tibet, opened a bar, and started nightly drinking contests with the Sherpas. She'll never forgive him, almost.

The time is 1936. Indy is an American anthropologist who learns that the Nazis think they've discovered the long-lost resting place of the Ark of the Covenant, the golden casket used by the ancient Hebrews to hold the Ten Commandments. Indy's mission: Beat the Nazis to the prize. He flies to Tibet, collects Marion and a priceless medallion that holds the secret of the Ark's location, and then tries to outsmart the Nazis. What is a little amazing about *Raiders of the Lost Ark* is that this plot somehow holds together and makes some sense, even though it functions primarily as a framework for the most incredible series of action and stunt set-pieces I've ever seen in a movie. Indiana and Marion spend the entire film hanging by their fingernails—literally, at one point, over a pit of poisonous snakes.

They survive a series of gruesome and

dreadful traps, pitfalls, double-crosses, ambushes, and fates worse than death (of which this movie suggests several). And Indiana engages in the best chase scene I've seen in a film. (I include, in second place, the chase from *The French Connection*, with *Bullitt* in third.) The chase involves a truck, three jeeps, a horse, a motorcycle, and an awesomely difficult stunt in which a character is required to make a 360-degree turn of the speeding truck. All of these spectacles are achieved with flawless movie technology brought to a combination of stunts, special visual effects, and sheer sweat. The makers of this film have covered similar ground before, if perhaps never so fluently; George Lucas, the executive producer, gave birth to the *Star Wars* movies, and Steven Spielberg, the director, made *Jaws* and *Close Encounters*. The rest of the all-star crew's work includes photography by veteran British cinematographer Douglas Slocombe, appropriately stirring and haunting music by *Star Wars* composer John Williams, sets by *Star Wars* production designer Norman Reynolds and art director Les Dilley, and countless wonderments by Richard Edlund, who supervised the visual effects.

Two things, however, make *Raiders of the Lost Ark* more than just a technological triumph: its sense of humor and the droll style of its characters. This is often a funny movie, but it doesn't get many of its laughs with dialogue and only a few with obvious gags (although the biggest laugh comes from the oldest and most obvious gag, involving a swordsman and a marksman). We find ourselves laughing in surprise, in relief, in incredulity at the movie's ability to pile one incident upon another in an inexhaustible series of inventions. And the personalities of the central characters are enormously winning. Harrison Ford, as Indy Jones, does not do a reprise of his *Star Wars* work. Instead he creates a taciturn, understated, stubborn character who might be the Humphrey Bogart of *Treasure of the Sierra Madre* with his tongue in his cheek. He survives fires, crushings, shootings, burnings. He really hates snakes. Karen Allen plays the female lead with a resilient toughness that develops its own charm. She can handle herself in any situation. She *really* hates snakes.

Raiders of the Lost Ark is a swashbuckling adventure epic in the tradition of *Star Wars*, *Superman*, the James Bond pictures, and all the other multimillion-dollar special effects extravaganzas. It wants only to entertain. It succeeds. Watch it with someone you know fairly well. There will be times during the film when it will be necessary to grab somebody.

Raise the Titanic ★ ★ ½
PG, 112 m., 1980

Jason Robards (Admiral Sandecker), Richard Jordon (Dirk Pitt), David Selby (Dr. Sergram), Anne Archer (Dana Archibald), Alec Guinness (Bigalow), J.D. Cannon (Captain Burke). Directed by Jerry Jameson and produced by William Frye. Screenplay by Adam Kennedy.

Raise the Titanic is almost a good movie. It has some wonderful moments, but they're bogged down in two moronic subplots. Why is it that they always gum up great movie ideas by shoveling in those two infallible deadends, The Girl and The Russians?

The movie's basic premise—that it might be possible to raise and salvage the great ship *Titanic*—is irresistible. We get some hot scientific gobbledygook about how the *Titanic* might really be in pretty good shape, down there two miles below the frigid Atlantic, where it wouldn't rust because of the oxygen shortage in the water. Maybe so. The plan to float the *Titanic* sure is ingenious: Pump it full of plastic foam, attach giant inflatable balloons on its sides, and blast it free of the mud. Easy as pie. Reminds me of an old Uncle Scrooge comic in which Huey, Louie, and Dewey were going to raise a sunken ship by pumping it full of ping-pong balls.

Raise the Titanic is best when it sticks to the subject. The movie succeeds in re-creating some of the romance of the *Titanic* itself. It begins with old photographs of the great ship, and with a sneaky preview shot of the ship in its watery grave. The plan to raise the ship involves the use of experimental Navy submarines, and the sequences devoted to the search are tightly directed and effective. The payoff scenes work, too: The moment when the *Titanic* breaks the surface of the water is really very moving. And so is the shot of the ship being towed into New York Harbor. Some reviews of the film have criticized the special effects in those shots, but I thought they were pretty good.

I mean, of *course* they're using combinations of a smaller ship, scale models, tricks of perspective and special optical effects—but what'd you expect? The *Titanic*? If you're not prepared to go halfway with a movie named *Raise the Titanic* you are possibly in the wrong movie to begin with.

So I liked the stuff involving the ship. What I didn't like was the movie's compulsion to lay on all sorts of "human interest," as if raising the *Titanic* weren't enough. Why don't they just once make a thriller that's about its premise from beginning to end? Why didn't they have the narrative discipline to really go into the history of the *Titanic*, the odds on its still being intact, the ways of salvaging it? The newspapers have been full of stories recently about an actual expedition to find the *Titanic*, but this movie would rather blast us with a lot of hot air involving (as I was just lamenting) The Girl and The Russians.

What would hack screenwriters do without them? The Girl is the lovely Anne Archer, who plays a reporter for the *Washington Star*. She's the girlfriend of one of the guys behind the expedition. It turns out, of course, she is also the *former* girlfriend of another guy on the expedition. This other guy's name is priceless, even in the annals of pulp: "Dirk Pitt."

Anyway, after The Russians discover the secret U.S. plans to raise the *Titanic*, they leak the story to The Girl (for no apparent reason), and then she fights with her boyfriend. So what? The Girl's completely unnecessary, as were all her scenes, especially one in which she and her boyfriend go fishing all the way out in the country, just so a helicopter can immediately turn up with orders to take the guy back to town. The Russians are also unnecessary, and so is the basic premise of the plot.

The late Alfred Hitchcock had something he called "the MacGuffin," which was whatever it was in a plot that everybody was concerned about. The MacGuffin this time is a rare mineral that the U.S. needs in order to power an impregnable laser defense system. Maybe it's on the *Titanic*. The Russians want the mineral, too, and try to capture the *Titanic* after it's raised.

All of this is, of course, completely ludicrous. And the scenes of the Russians standing around saying sinister things are terminally boring. Who needs this weird mineral as an excuse to raise the *Titanic*? Wouldn't the salvage alone be worth it? Or why couldn't they raise it in the spirit of Edmund Hillary, just because it is there?

Rambo: First Blood Part II ★ ★ ★
R, 90 m., 1985

Sylvester Stallone (Rambo), Richard Crenna (Trautman), Charles Napier (Murdock), Steven Berkoff (Podovsky). Directed by George P. Cosmatos and produced by Buzz Feitshans. Screenplay by Stallone and James Cameron.

Rambo, subtitled *First Blood Part II* and continuing the adventures of Sylvester Stallone's one-man army, is two movies in one. First there's a hard-boiled, high-energy, violent action picture, which will probably find a large and enthusiastic audience. Lurking beneath the action is a political statement accusing the U.S. government of such base political motives that I was, quite simply, astonished. *Rambo* is not left wing or right wing, but belongs to the paranoid wing of American politics, in which villains left and right crawl under the covers together and conspire to annihilate John Rambo.

If you saw the original *First Blood*, which was a big hit, you remember Rambo. He is a returned Vietnam hero, a superbly trained fighting machine who is considered by his superior officers to be the finest soldier they have ever seen. But Rambo becomes unhinged by civilian life, and by the insults which he believes society is heaping on men like himself, who risked their lives to fight the war. So Rambo reverts to his military training and turns into a one-man army dedicated to destroying the establishment that does not honor him.

At the end of *First Blood*, Rambo was captured after blowing up half a town and wiping out countless civilian and military authorities. If anyone had been keeping count, he would have qualified as the nation's most prolific mass killer. In the opening scenes of *Rambo*, he is breaking rocks on a chain gang when his old superior officer (Richard Crenna) arrives with a mission:

Rambo is needed to parachute into Southeast Asia and scout out a suspected POW compound holding missing Americans. Any questions, Rambo? "Only one," he tells Crenna. "This time, do we get to win?"

His question places *Rambo* squarely within the revisionist genre of Vietnam movies, in which the war is refought with a happy ending. *Uncommon Valor,* the two *Missing in Action* movies, and this film are all about missions to free American MIAs and kill countless Asian soldiers. The basic assumption is that we lost the war because "the politicians" prevented men like Rambo from doing what they were trained to do. And indeed, again this time he has his hands tied: he's only supposed to take pictures, not engage in violence. Needless to say, if they only want pictures, they've picked the wrong mass murderer for the job.

Rambo's mission is outlined by a suspicious American intelligence officer (the square-jawed, rugged Charles Napier, a favorite of Russ Meyer *and* Jonathan Demme). Only after Rambo parachutes into the night does it become clear that Napier doesn't really want the mission to succeed. In logic so impenetrable that I would love to have somebody run it past me again, the movie argues that it would be politically embarrassing for American MIAs to be found at this late date, and that therefore it would be best if Rambo's mission fails. If he *does* come back with photos, they'll be suppressed. In that case, I was wondering, why sponsor the mission in the first place—and especially with a loose cannon like Rambo? No matter; the movie turns into an efficient action picture, with Rambo wiping out legions of North Vietnamese and Russians with a variety of weapons, including explosive-tipped arrows. Back at headquarters, Napier does all he can to sabotage the mission, but it becomes clear that Rambo could have won the Vietnam war by himself, had he been unleashed, and everything leads to a big climax, a helicopter dogfight. The strange thing about *Rambo* is that it works despite its politics. Its conspiracy theory is so angry and so unlikely that we tend to ignore it, sit back, and enjoy the action.

The Razor's Edge ★ ★ ½
PG-13, 130 m., 1984

Bill Murray (Larry Darrell), Theresa Russell (Sophie), Catherine Hicks (Isabel), Denholm Elliott (Elliot Templeton), James Keach (Gray Maturin), Brian Doyle-Murray (Piedmont). Directed by John Byrum and written by Byrum and Bill Murray. Produced by Robert P. Marcucci and Harry Benn.

Here is the story of a man who can never quite get back to a suburban frame of mind after he's seen World War I. The man is born into a world of lawn parties, polo ponies, and rich relatives who wave benignly from the shade of a cocktail shaker. He volunteers to be an ambulance driver in the war, sees death and despair, and comes back home to tell his fiancée that they'd better postpone the wedding: He wants to live in Paris for a while and find himself.

The Razor's Edge then tells a standard story of self-discovery in which the young man drops out, becomes a bohemian in the Paris of the 1920s, works as a coal miner, and takes a passage to India to discover the meaning of life. He actually gets all the way to a mountaintop, signs on with a monastery, and spends some time as a contemplative monk, before discovering within himself only a desire to return to Paris. His fiancée comes to Paris. He courts her, but is not ready to marry her. Another American woman, a wild young thing whose husband and child have been killed in a motor crash, joins them in Paris and is quickly swept into a world of drunkenness and drugs. The young man discovers that he loves this woman and tries to save her, but by the end of the film, having stared death in the face in the war and regarded infinity from a mountaintop, he realizes that nothing really makes any difference.

In other words, this is your standard 1960s hippie drama, moved back in time and adapted from the great novel by Somerset Maugham. If the movie really had a sense of its time (if it seemed to know that it took place in an era when the characters were much more unusual than they would be today), the hero's odyssey would mean more. But the flaw in this movie is that the hero is too passive, too contained, too rich in self-irony, to really sweep us along in his quest.

And that, I'm afraid, is the fault of Bill Murray, who plays the hero as if fate is a comedian and he is the straight man. Murray, who is usually such a superb actor, has taken the wrong path in this performance, giving us moments when everybody in the film and in the audience is moved, except Murray. There are times when he seems downright obstinate in his performance, giving us a ramrod posture, a poker face, and eyes that will not let us inside. Perhaps, in his desire to make a break with the comic roles we know him for, he was overreacting. That makes even more curious the moments in the film when he allows himself to be funny: The comic side of his character doesn't seem to be coming out of anything.

The movie has other flaws. It is more interested in showing him going to India than in really dealing with what he might have discovered there. It is fascinated by the character of the dissipated young woman (a wonderful performance by Theresa Russell), but never lets us really see the ex-fiancée (Catherine Hicks) as anything more than a predestined ex-fiancée. A rich uncle (Denholm Elliott) who lives in Paris is seen just enough to become intriguing, but not enough to be understood: Why did *he* become an expatriate?

The Razor's Edge is far from being a bad movie. Some of the scenes are very good, especially the uncle's deathbed farewell and Murray's first attempts to sober up Russell. But at the end I didn't feel engaged. I didn't feel that the hero's attention had been quite focused during his quest for the meaning of life. He didn't seem to be a searcher, but more of a bystander, shoulders thrown back, deadpan expression in place, waiting to see if life could make him care.

Reds ★ ★ ★ ½
PG, 200 m., 1981

Warren Beatty (John Reed), Diane Keaton (Louise Bryant), Edward Herrmann (Max Eastman), Jerzy Kosinski (Zinoviev), Jack Nicholson (Eugene O'Neill), Maureen Stapleton (Emma Goldman), Paul Sorvino (Louis Fraina), Gene Hackman (Pete Van Wherry). Directed and produced by Warren Beatty. Screenplay by Beatty and Trevor Griffiths.

The original John Reed was a dashing young man from Portland who knew a good story when he found one, and, when he found himself in the midst of the Bolshevik revolution, wrote a book called *Ten Days That Shook the World* and made himself a famous journalist. He never quite got it right again after that. He became embroiled in the American left-wing politics of the 1920s, participated in fights between factions of the Socialist Party and the new American Communist Party, and finally returned to Moscow on a series of noble fool's errands that led up, one way or another, to his death from tuberculosis and kidney failure in a Russian hospital. He is the only American buried within the Kremlin walls.

That is Reed's story in a nutshell. But if you look a little more deeply you find a man who was more than a political creature. He was also a man who wanted to be where the action was, a radical young intellectual who was in the middle of everything in the years after World War I, when Greenwich Village was in a creative ferment and American society seemed, for a brief moment, to be overturning itself. It is that personal, human John Reed that Warren Beatty's *Reds* takes as its subject, although there is a lot, and maybe too much, of the political John Reed as well. The movie never succeeds in convincing us that the feuds between the American socialist parties were much more than personality conflicts and ego-bruisings, so audiences can hardly be expected to care which faction is "the" American party of the left.

What audiences can, and possibly will, care about, however, is a traditional Hollywood romantic epic, a love story written on the canvas of history, as they used to say in the ads. And *Reds* provides that with glorious romanticism, surprising intelligence, and a consistent wit. It is the thinking man's *Dr. Zhivago*, told from the other side, of course. The love story stars Warren Beatty and Diane Keaton, who might seem just a tad unlikely as casting choices, but who are immediately engaging and then grow into solid, plausible people on the screen. Keaton is a particular surprise. I had somehow gotten into the habit of expecting her to be a touchy New Yorker, sweet, scared, and intellectual. Here, as a Portland dentist's wife who runs away with John Reed and eventually follows him halfway around the world, through blizzards and prisons and across icy steppes, she is just what she needs to be: plucky, healthy, exasperated, loyal, and funny.

Beatty, as John Reed, is also surprising. I expected him to play Reed as a serious, noble, heroic man for all seasons, and so he does, sometimes. But there is in Warren Beatty's screen persona a persistent irony, a way of kidding his own seriousness, that takes the edge off a potentially pretentious character and makes him into one of God's fools. Beatty plays Reed but does not beatify him: He permits the silliness and boyishness to coexist with the self-conscious historical mission.

The action in the movie takes Reed to Russia and back again to Portland, and off again with Louise Bryant (Keaton), and then there is a lengthy pause in Greenwich Village and time enough for Louise to have a sad little love affair with the morosely alcoholic playwright Eugene O'Neill (Jack Nicholson). Then there are other missions to Moscow, and heated political debates in New York basements, and at one point I'm afraid I entirely lost track of exactly why Reed was running behind a horsecart in the middle of some forgotten battle in an obscure backwater of the Russian empire. The fact is, Reed's motivation from moment to moment is not the point of the picture. The point is that a revolution is happening, human societies are being swept aside, a new class is in control—or so it seems—and for an insatiably curious young man, that is exhilirating, and it is enough.

The heart of the film is in the relationship between Reed and Bryant. There is an interesting attempt to consider her problems as well as his. She leaves Portland because she is sick unto death of small talk. She wants to get involved in politics, in art, in what's happening: She is so inexorably drawn to Greenwich Village that if Reed had not taken her there, she might have gone on her own. If she was a radical in Portland, however, she is an Oregonian in the Village, and she cannot compete conversationally with such experienced fast-talkers as the anarchist Emma Goldman (Maureen Stapleton). In fact, no one seems to listen to her or pay

much heed, except for sad Eugene O'Neill, who is brave enough to love her but not smart enough to keep it to himself. The ways in which she edges toward O'Neill, and then loyally returns to Reed, create an emotional density around her character that makes it really *mean* something when she and Reed embrace at last in a wonderful tear-jerking scene in the Russian train station.

The whole movie finally comes down to the fact that the characters matter to us. Beatty may be fascinated by the ins and outs of American left-wing politics sixty years ago, but he is not so idealistic as to believe an American mass audience can be inspired to care as deeply. So he gives us people. And they are seen here with such warmth and affection that we sense new dimensions not only in Beatty and Keaton, but especially in Nicholson. In *Reds*, understating his desire, apologizing for his passion, hanging around Louise, handing her a poem, throwing her out of his life, he is quieter but much more passionate than in the overwrought *The Postman Always Rings Twice*.

As as for Beatty, *Reds* is his bravura turn. He got the idea, nurtured it for a decade, found the financing, wrote most of the script, produced, and directed and starred and still found enough artistic detachment to make his Reed into a flawed, fascinating enigma instead of a boring archetypal hero. I liked this movie. I felt a real fondness for it. It was quite a subject to spring on the capitalist Hollywood movie system, and maybe only Beatty could have raised $35 million to make a movie about a man who hated millionaires. I noticed, here at the end of the credits, a wonderful line that reads:

Copyright © MCMLXXXI Barclays Mercantile Industrial Finance Limited. John Reed would have loved that.

Repo Man ★ ★ ★
R, 92 m., 1984

Harry Dean Stanton (Bud), Emilio Estevez (Otto), Tracey Walter (Miller), Olivia Barash (Leila). Directed by Alex Cox and produced by Jonathan Wacks and Peter McCarthy. Screenplay by Cox.

Repo Man is one of those movies that slips through the cracks and gives us all a little weirdo fun. It is the first movie I know about that combines (1) punk teen-agers, (2) automobile repossessors, and (3) aliens from outer space. This is the kind of movie that baffles Hollywood, because it isn't made from any known formula and doesn't follow the rules. The movie begins with a mad scientist careening down a New Mexico road in his Chevy Malibu. He is stopped by a cop, who finds some really strange things happening in the car's trunk. Then the action moves to Los Angeles, where a punk kid (Emilio Estevez) is passing the time by going to dances and banging his head against other kids' heads, to demonstrate his affection.

The kid runs into a guy named Bud (Harry Dean Stanton), who is an auto repossessor. Bud tricks the kid into driving a repo car for him, and before long the kid is a full-time auto repossessor, learning the ropes. The ropes are pretty tough. Repo men, we learn, live their lives on the edge, operating under extreme tension that is caused partly by their working conditions and partly because as Stanton explains, "I've never known a repo man who didn't use a lot of speed." Harry Dean Stanton is one of the treasures of American movies. He has appeared in a lot of films without becoming a big star, but he has that total cynicism that brings jobs like repo into focus. In the movie, he and Estevez make a nice team; the beaten veteran and the cocky kid, and they cruise the streets looking for cars.

Meanwhile (and here I will be careful to respect some surprises in the story), the government is looking for that Chevy Malibu, because it is connected to the possibility that alien beings have visited the Earth. The feds put out a $10,000 reward for the car, which makes it the jackpot every repo man in L.A. is looking for. Hot on the trail of the car, Stanton and Estevez get into a duel with the famed Rodriguez brothers, known as the bandits of repo. All of this works very nicely, but what's best about *Repo Man* is its sly sense of humor. There are a lot of running gags in the movie, and the best of them involves generic food labels, of all things. (There is a moment involving some food in a refrigerator that gave me one of the biggest laughs I'd had at the movies in a long time.) The movie also has a special way of looking at Los Angeles, seeing it through Harry Dean Stanton's eyes as a wasteland of human ambitions where a few bucks can be made by the quick, the bitter, and the sly.

I saw *Repo Man* near the end of a busy stretch on the movie beat: Three days during which I saw more relentlessly bad movies than during any comparable period in memory. Most of those bad movies were so cynically constructed out of formula ideas and "commercial" ingredients that watching them was an ordeal. *Repo Man* comes out of left field, has no big stars, didn't cost much, takes chances, dares to be unconventional, is funny, and works. There is a lesson here.

Return of the Jedi ★ ★ ★ ★
PG, 133 m., 1983 ✔

Mark Hamill (Luke Skywalker), Harrison Ford (Han Solo), Carrie Fisher (Princess Leia), Billy Dee Williams (Lando Calrissian), Anthony Daniels (C-3PO), David Prowse (Darth Vader), James Earl Jones (Vader's Voice), Alec Guinness (Obi-Wan Kenobi). Directed by Richard Marquand and produced by Howard Kazanjian. Screenplay by Lawrence Kasdan and George Lucas.

Here is just one small moment in *Return of the Jedi*, a moment you could miss if you looked away from the screen, but a moment that helps explain the special magic of the Star Wars movies. Luke Skywalker is engaged in a ferocious battle in the dungeons beneath the throne room of the loathsome Jabba the Hutt. His adversary is a slimy, gruesome, reptilian monster made of warts and teeth. Things are looking bad when suddenly the monster is crushed beneath a falling door. And then (here is the small moment) there's a shot of the monster's keeper, a muscle-bound jailer, who rushes forward in tears. He is brokenhearted at the destruction of his pet. Everybody loves somebody.

It is that extra level of detail that makes the Star Wars pictures much more than just space operas. Other movies might approach the special effects. Other action pictures might approximate the sense of swashbuckling adventure. But in *Return of the Jedi*, as in *Star Wars* and *The Empire Strikes Back*, there's such a wonderful density to the canvas. Things are happening all over. They're pouring forth from imaginations so fertile that, yes, we do halfway believe in this crazy Galactic Empire long ago and far, far away.

Return of the Jedi is both a familiar movie and a new one. It concludes the stories of the major human characters in the saga, particularly Skywalker, Han Solo, Princess Leia, and Darth Vader. It revisits other characters who seem either more or less than human, including Ben (Obi-Wan Kenobi), Yoda, Chewbacca, and the beloved robots C-3PO and R2-D2. If George Lucas persists in his plan to make nine Star Wars movies, this will nevertheless be the last we'll see of Luke, Han, and Leia, although the robots will be present in all the films.

The story in the Star Wars movies is, however, only part of the film—and a less crucial element as time goes by. What *Jedi* is really giving us is a picaresque journey through the imagination, and an introduction to forms of life less mundane than our own. In *Jedi*, we encounter several unforgettable characters, including the evil Jabba the Hutt, who is a cross between a toad and the Cheshire cat; the lovable, cuddly Ewoks, the furry inhabitants of the "forest moon of Endor"; a fearsome desert monster made of sand and teeth, and hateful little ratlike creatures that scurry about the corners of the frame. And there is an admiral for the Alliance who looks like the missing link between Tyrannosaurus Rex and Charles de Gaulle.

One thing the Star Wars movies never do is waste a lot of time on introductions. Unlike a lot of special effects and monster movies, where new creatures are introduced with laborious setups, *Jedi* immediately plunges its alien beasts into the thick of the action. Maybe that's why the film has such a sense of visual richness. Jabba's throne room, for example, is populated with several weird creatures, some of them only half-glimpsed in the corner of the frame. The camera in *Jedi* slides casually past forms of life that would provide the centerpiece for lesser movies.

The movie also has, of course, more of the amazing battles in outer space—the intergalactic video games that have been a trademark since *Star Wars*. And *Jedi* finds an interesting variation on that chase sequence in *Star Wars* where the space cruisers hurtled through the narrow canyons on the surface of the Death Star. This time, there's a break-neck chase through a forest, aboard airborne motorcycles. After several of the bad guys have run into trees and gotten creamed, you pause to ask yourself why they couldn't have simply flown *above* the treetops . . . but never mind, it wouldn't have been as much fun that way.

And *Return of the Jedi* is fun, magnificent fun. The movie is a complete entertainment, a feast for the eyes and a delight for the fancy. It's a little amazing how Lucas and his associates keep topping themselves. From the point of view of simple moviemaking logistics, there is an awesome amount of work on the screen in *Jedi* (twice as many visual effects as *Star Wars* in the space battles, Lucas claims). The fact that the makers of *Jedi* are able to emerge intact from their task, having created a very special work of the imagination, is the sort of miracle that perhaps Obi-Wan would know something about.

Return of the Secaucus Seven ★ ★ ★
NO MPAA RATING, 110 m., 1981

Mark Arnott (Jeff), Gordon Clapp (Chip), Maggie Cousineau-Arndt (Frances), Adam Le Fevre (J.T.), Bruce MacDonald (Mike), Jean Passanante (Irene), John Sayles (Howie), Maggie Renzi (Katie). Directed and written by John Sayles. Produced by William Aydelott and Jeffrey Nelson.

A friend asked me what *Return of the Secaucus Seven* was about. "It's the story of your life," I said.

"*My* life?"

Well, and my life, too. Everybody's life who was younger once and demonstrated against one thing or another, and is older now and stumped for the moment by the curiosity that the most outspoken advocate of change in our society is Ronald Reagan. The movie tells the story of a group of friends who set out during the late 1960s to join the March on the Pentagon, and were arrested in Secaucus, New Jersey, on charges they still do not fully understand. So they didn't make it to the Pentagon, where their brain power might have made the difference in Abbie Hoffman's plan to levitate that building.

Those were strange times. Even Norman Mailer, in his *Armies of the Night*, reported that when the Yippies started to chant and meditate and try to levitate the Pentagon, he looked to see if it had started to rise: An unlikely event, of course, but one that a reporter would always kick himself for if he had missed it. Years have passed since those days. The original members of the Secaucus Seven have grown older now, can taste their thirtieth birthdays, and as the movie opens have gathered for a weekend reunion in the country. The film tells the story of their weekend, as they take their measure and remember the 1960s.

The Sixties. A director once told me that he had been interviewed by a group of college editors, one of whom asked him, "Was drug usage really prevalent back in the 1960s?" He didn't know whether to laugh or cry. The Secaucus Seven has the same choice. They are never again going to be as young as they were, but they still remember their days of activism so sharply that they refuse to cut loose from them. These days, people still go through their thirtieth birthday crisis, all right, but they seem to hold it on their fortieth birthday.

The Secaucus Seven has grown slightly, with the addition of spouses, lovers, and even children. They gather to play basketball, sing songs, get drunk, fight, break up, and sleep together—or apart. In mood, the film resembles Alain Tanner's wonderful *Jonah Who Will Be 25 in the Year 2000*. Some of the Seven have become fairly successful: There are a congressional aide and a medical student. There is also a kid who is still trying to make it as a folk singer, an occupation that no longer pays very well even if he had the talent, which he does not. And another who has chosen to stay in the old hometown and pump gas.

John Sayles, who wrote and directed the movie, made it as a labor of love (and financed it by writing the screenplays for *Piranha* and *Alligator*, so he may still not quite have evened the scales). He alternates among the various couples and groupings and intrigues, and at first the movie is frankly confusing. We can't keep everybody straight, and there's too much explanation of who they all are and what they've all done. Before long, though, we have everyone sorted out. We know the relationships. And we grow quietly grateful that Sayles has chosen not to pack his weekend reunion

with a series of dramatic confrontations and crises. There are no overdoses, suicides, or murders. Only the adjustments such a weekend would be expected to bring, and the inevitable bitterness when one couple has broken up, and the old and new lovers have to confront one another.

This is not a perfect film. Odds and ends stick out, and some scenes have a certain gracelessness. But it is an absorbing film that contains shrewd observations about human nature, and more than its share of humor. We leave with mixed feelings: We feel like we've attended that reunion, and at the same time we're relieved that we did not. It is easier to be young if your friends don't age on you.

Rhinestone ★
PG, 111 m., 1984

Sylvester Stallone (Martinelli), Dolly Parton (Jake Ferris), Richard Farnsworth (Noah Ferris), Ron Liebman (Freddie). Directed by Bob Clark and produced by Howard Smith and Marvin Worth. Screenplay by Phil Alden Robinson and Sylvester Stallone.

Rhinestone takes two of the most interesting actors in the movies and puts them into a movie they're expected to carry with sheer charm. There are times when they almost pull it off. Sure, Dolly Parton has wonderful energy and a great voice, and sure, Sylvester Stallone has a gift for ham-bone physical comedy. But this movie is so thin they both seem curiously absent. The screenplay allegedly is based on the song "Rhinestone Cowboy," but that will come as a surprise to the ghost of George Bernard Shaw, who first wrote this story as *Pygmalion*, and to Lerner and Loewe, who turned it into *My Fair Lady*. This time Dolly Parton has the Henry Higgins role. She bets a New York nightclub owner that she can take any guy off the streets and turn him into a country singer in two weeks. Along comes Stallone, driving his Yellow Cab as if he were auditioning for *Cannonball Run*. Dolly talks him into the experiment and takes him down home to Tennessee, where her daddy (Richard Farnsworth) is a country musician.

The center part of the film—the country "training" sessions—could have been fun if they'd been written with a satiric edge. Unfortunately, they seem to have been written with a blunt instrument. Dolly explains that the way to "walk country" is to pretend you have jock itch. Stallone needs to have this concept explained to him. Meanwhile, of course, they fall in love, and have a sex scene so tame that Miss Piggy goes further with Kermit. There is a dumb subplot involving Dolly's old boyfriend, and a couple of idiotic fight scenes, and then of course the big lame-brained showdown in the New York country music club. What we become agonizingly aware of, after a while, is how little Dolly Parton is singing. She has a great voice, filled with character and with little quirks and riffs and inflections that find their way around the words, but in *Rhinestone* we get short-changed. And Stallone's overacting as her would-be partner is embarrassing.

One final fashion note. Dolly Parton is, of course, justly famous for her figure. It is presented in this movie with as much rigidity as the exhibit of presidential wives' inaugural gowns in the Smithsonian. The fabrics and colors change, but the basic design configuration remains identical in one dress after another, until her bosom takes on a sort of objective unreality, like Mr. Spock's ears.

Rich and Famous ★ ★ ½
R, 117 m., 1981

Jacqueline Bisset (Liz Hamilton), Candice Bergen (Merry Noel Black), David Selby (Doug Black), Hart Bochner (Chris Adams), Steven Hill (Jules Levi). Directed by George Cukor and produced by William Allyn. Screenplay by Gerald Ayres.

The lesson of *Rich and Famous* is that, although a woman cannot be too thin or too rich, she *can* be too famous. The movie stars Jacqueline Bisset and Candice Bergen as college classmates who become writers (Bisset, a serious intellectual writer and Bergen, an author of trashy bestsellers) and who maintain their friendship over the years. What threatens them most is fame, because fame seems to make the men in their lives a little goofy, and goofy men are their downfall. This film is a real curiosity. It's a good-bad movie, like *The Other Side of Midnight* or *The Greek Tycoon*. It contains scenes that make you want to squirm because of their awk-

wardness and awfulness, and yet you don't want to look away and you're not bored. The movie has the courage to go to extremes, and some of those extremes may not be art but are certainly unforgettable.

Take, for example, Candice Bergen's performance as Merry Noel Black. She's one of those tawny, plump Southern belles with a Betty Crocker hairstyle and a dirty mind. She marries well and lives on the beach and dashes off a scandalous book about her neighbors in the Malibu colony. It becomes a bestseller, and we are tantalized by hints that Bergen's character is "really" Jacqueline Susann or Judith Krantz. It doesn't matter. Bergen's performance is in the inimitable style of the late Ms. Susann, who once leaned across a luncheon table, took my hand, and informed me seriously: "You know, Roger, I've never met a dog I didn't like." Bergen plays the role broadly and with vulgar abandon, sometimes to great comic effect (although you know that with a name like "Merry Noel," she's going to have some real depressions around Christmas). Her performance is in counterpoint with the character played by Jacqueline Bisset. Bisset's character at times seems inspired by Mary McCarthy or Susan Sontag (and at other times, particularly when she is making love to strange men in airplane restrooms, seems inspired by Emmanuelle).

While Bergen grinds out the potboilers, Bisset writes one great book, and then seizes up with a severe case of writer's block. She can't write that second book, but she preaches to Bergen about honesty. Bergen somewhere dredges up the resources to write her own honest book—even, amazingly, a good book—and it's nominated for a national award. With perfect soap opera inevitability, Bisset is on the jury to award the prize. That leads into the second half of the movie, an extended sojourn in New York and thereabouts, where books are upstaged by Bisset's compulsion for strange sex. She rejects a seduction attempt from a young *Rolling Stone* reporter, but later that same day makes love with an even younger man who's a gigolo. The eroticism in that scene is particularly effective, and somewhat surprising, considering that the director is the eighty-two-year-old George Cukor. But later, when Bisset, to her amazement, falls in love with the *Rolling Stone* reporter, we're confused, because in a major casting blunder, the reporter and the gigolo look so much alike that we can't tell them apart.

No matter. The movie forges ahead through tempestuous fights and tearful reconciliations, while Bergen's alcoholic ex-husband makes a pass at Bisset, and Bergen tries to bribe all of New York to win the book prize. I was not (and am not) sure what this movie was trying to tell me about the two characters—perhaps that if you stay in touch with someone for twenty years, you can be absolutely sure that at the end of that time you still will be in touch.

Insights into human nature don't seem to be the point of the movie, anyway. It's a slick, trashy, entertaining melodrama, with too many dumb scenes to qualify as successful. A film critic for one of the national newsweeklies said, in reviewing this film, that he has a friend who has a rule: He only attends movies that are in color and are about rich people. I deplore the attitude behind that statement, but in a crazy way, I absolutely understand it.

Richard Pryor Here and Now
★ ★ ★ ★
R, 94 m., 1983

A documentary written and directed by Richard Pryor and produced by Bob Parkinson and Andy Friendly.

Is there anyone else in America who could have pulled off this film? *Richard Pryor Here and Now* is a documentary of one man talking. Pryor walks onto the stage of the Saenger Theater in New Orleans, establishes an immediate rapport with the audience, and away he goes. At the end of the movie we have been wrung out with laughter—and with a few other things, too, because Pryor is more than a comedian in this film: He's a social commentator and a man talking honestly about himself.

This is Pryor's third concert film. The first one, *Richard Pryor Live in Concert*, was made before he set himself on fire while freebasing cocaine. The second, *Richard Pryor Live on the Sunset Strip* (1982), recorded his first filmed concert after the accident, and included his description of Jim Brown's attempts to talk him out of drug use, and Pryor's own now-famous dialogue with cocaine. In *Here and Now*, filmed in August 1983 with Brown as executive producer, Pryor firmly says he hasn't used drugs or alcohol for seven months. The arithmetic would seem to suggest that he hadn't stopped using everything when he made the second film, or that he had a relapse after his initial hospitalization. I mention that only because the Richard Pryor we see on screen in *Here and Now* has obviously found some kind of peace with himself that was lacking in the *Sunset Strip* film.

He can smile more easily. He doesn't have to reach for effects. He handles audience interruptions with grace and cool. He is the master of his instrument. And he takes bigger chances. Some of his material covers familiar ground—sex, booze, race, marriages. But all along he's showing his gift for populating the stage with a lot of different characters. He goes in and out of accents, body language, and characters, giving us confused drunks, defensive husbands, shrill wives, uptight WASPs, impenetrable Africans ("Everybody speaks English," one tells him in Zimbabwe, "but what language do you speak at *home?*"). And then at the end of his act, he goes into an extended characterization of a street black shooting heroin. In this character are humor and pain, self-deception and touching honesty, and the end of the sketch comes closer to tragedy than it does to comedy.

Pryor is a spokesman for our dreams and fears, the things we find funny and the things we're frightened of. He has assumed a role that has previously been filled by such comedians as Will Rogers, Lenny Bruce, Mort Sahl, and Woody Allen—all men who, as Rogers put it, talked about what they'd just seen in the papers. Pryor works off issues and subjects that are absolutely current, and he addresses them with a humor that is aimed so well, we duck. His story could have gone either way. He could have been killed in that wasteful accident. But he was not, and now, given a second chance, he is paying his dues.

Richard Pryor Live on the Sunset Strip
★ ★ ★ ★
R, 82 m., 1982

Directed by Joe Layton and produced by
Richard Pryor.

At the beginning of this film, Richard Pryor
is clearly nervous. He is back on a stage for
the first time since he set himself on fire.
That means he is working with the stand-up
comedian's greatest handicap, the audience's awareness of his vulnerability.
Whatever else they do, comics must project
utter confidence in their material, and when
Pryor had his accident, he also had his whole
hip image blown out from under him. So it's
a shaky start. He begins by almost defiantly
using the word "fuck" as an incantation,
employing it not so much for shock value
(does it still have any?) as for punctuation.
His timing is a little off. He is not, at first,
the supremely confident, cocky Richard
Pryor of his earlier films. But as he gets
rolling, as he populates the stage with a
whole series of characters, we watch the
emergence of a Richard Pryor who is older,
wiser, and funnier than before. And the last
fifty or sixty minutes of this film are extraordinary.

Richard Pryor Live on the Sunset Strip was
filmed at the Hollywood Palladium, down at
the unfashionable east end of that legendary
street of rock clubs, restaurants, hookers
and heroes, hot-pillow motels, and some of
the most expensive real estate in the world.
The movie opens with a montage of the
strip's neon signs (including the Chateau
Marmont, where John Belushi died). Then
it cuts inside to the Palladium auditorium,
and Pryor walks onstage and lays claim to
being the most talented one-man stage show
in existence right now.

His gift is to be funny and painfully self-
analytical at the same time. Like Bill Cosby,
he gets a lot of his material out of memories
of growing up black in America. But he sees
deeper than Cosby, and his vignettes capture
small truths and build them into an attitude.
In the brilliant middle sections of this film,
he uses just his own voice and body to create
little one-act plays, such as the one where he
recalls working in a Mafia-owned nightclub
in Ohio. In that one, his Italian-American-
gangster accent is perfectly heard; in an-

other skit, about the animals in Africa, he
turns into a gifted physical comedian, getting laughs out of his impressions of the
movements of gazelles, water buffaloes, and
lions—and ending with a hilarious observation of the body language of two whites passing each other on the street in black Africa.

The whole middle passage of the film is
that good. The last twenty minutes is one of
the most remarkable marriages of comedy
and truth I have ever seen. He talks with
great honesty about his drug addiction, his
accident, and how his life has changed since
he stopped using drugs. He confesses that in
the three weeks before his accident, he holed
up alone in his room with his cocaine pipe,
which talked to him in reassuring, seductive
tones uncannily like Richard Nixon's. Then
a friend, the actor Jim Brown, came to see
him, and asked him flat-out, "Whatcha
gonna do?" There was nothing he wanted to
do but hide in drugs. What he finally did was
set himself on fire.

I saw the film the same day that actor Shay
Duffin opened his one-man evening with
Brendan Behan at the Apollo Theater Center
in Chicago. The papers that day carried the
news that Belushi had overdosed. Behan, of
course, killed himself with alcohol. Some
day, inevitably, an actor will give us an evening with John Belushi. The dramatic structure is all there, for the Behans and Belushis:
The genius, the laughter, and the doomed
drive to self-destruction. Watching *Richard
Pryor Live on the Sunset Strip*, a breathtaking
performance by a man who came within a
hair of killing himself with drugs, was like a
gift, as if Pryor had come back from the dead
to perform in his own one-man memory of
himself. It is good we still have him. He is
better than ever.

The Right Stuff ★ ★ ★ ★
PG, 193 m., 1983

Sam Shepard (Chuck Yeager), Ed Harris
(John Glenn), Fred Ward (Gus Grissom),
Dennis Quaid (Gordon Cooper), Scott Glenn
(Alan Shepard), Barbara Hershey (Glennis
Yeager), Mary Jo Deschanel (Annie Glenn),
Pamela Reed (Trudy Cooper). Directed by
Philip Kaufman and produced by Irwin
Winkler and Robert Chartoff. Screenplay by
Kaufman.

At the beginning of *The Right Stuff,* a cowboy reins in his horse and regards a strange sight in the middle of the desert: the X-1 rocket plane, built to break the sound barrier. At the end of the film, the seven Mercury astronauts are cheered in the Houston Astrodome at a Texas barbecue thrown by Lyndon B. Johnson. The contrast between those two images contains the message of *The Right Stuff,* I think, and the message is that Americans still have the right stuff, but we've changed our idea of what it is.

The original American heroes were loners. The cowboy is the perfect example. He was silhouetted against the horizon and he rode into town by himself and if he had a sidekick, the sidekick's job was to admire him. The new American heroes are team players. No wonder Westerns aren't made much anymore; cowboys don't play on teams. The cowboy at the beginning of *The Right Stuff* is Chuck Yeager, the legendary lone-wolf test pilot who survived the horrifying death rate among early test pilots (more than sixty were killed in a single month) and did fly the X-1 faster than the speed of sound. The movie begins with that victory, and then moves on another ten years to the day when the Russians sent up Sputnik, and the Eisenhower administration hustled to get back into the space race.

The astronauts who eventually rode the first Mercury capsules into space may not have been that much different from Chuck Yeager. As they're portrayed in the movie, anyway, Gus Grissom, Scott Carpenter, and Gordon Cooper seem to have some of the same stuff as Yeager. But the astronauts were more than pilots; they were a public-relations image, and the movie shows sincere, smooth-talking John Glenn becoming their unofficial spokesman. The X-1 flew in secrecy, but the Mercury flights were telecast, and we were entering a whole new era, the selling of space. There was a lot going on, and there's a lot going on in the movie, too. *The Right Stuff* is an adventure film, a special effects film, a social commentary, and a satire. That the writer-director, Philip Kaufman, is able to get so much into a little more than three hours is impressive. That he also has organized this material into one of the best recent American movies is astonishing. *The Right Stuff* gives itself the freedom to move around in moods and styles, from a broadly based lampoon of government functionaries to Yeager's spare, taciturn manner and Glenn's wonderment at the sights outside his capsule window.

The Right Stuff has been a landmark movie in a lot of careers. It announces Kaufman's arrival in the ranks of major directors. It contains uniformly interesting performances by a whole list of unknown or little-known actors, including Ed Harris (Glenn), Scott Glenn (Alan Shepard), Fred Ward (Grissom), and Dennis Quaid (Cooper). It confirms the strong and sometimes almost mystical screen presence of playwright Sam Shepard, who played Yeager. And it joins a short list of recent American movies that might be called experimental epics: movies that have an ambitious reach through time and subject matter, that spend freely for locations or special effects, but that consider each scene as intently as an art film. *The Right Stuff* goes on that list with *The Godfather, Nashville, Apocalypse Now,* and maybe *Patton* and *Close Encounters.* It's a great film.

Risky Business ★ ★ ★ ★
R, 96 m., 1983

Tom Cruise (Joel), Rebecca De Mornay (Lana), Curtis Armstrong (Miles), Bronson Pinchot (Barry), Joe Pantoliano (Guido). Directed by Paul Brickman and produced by Joe Avnet and Steve Tisch. Screenplay by Brickman.

Risky Business is a movie about male adolescent guilt. In other words, it's a comedy. It's funny because it deals with subjects that are so touchy, so fraught with emotional pain, that unless we laugh there's hardly any way we can deal with them—especially if we are now, or ever were, a teen-age boy. The teenager in the movie is named Joel. His family lives in a suburb on Chicago's North Shore. It's the sort of family that has three cars: the family station wagon, Mom's car, and Dad's Porsche. As the movie opens, Mom and Dad are going off on vacation to a sun-drenched consumer paradise and their only son, Joel, is being left alone at home. It's a busy time in Joel's life. He's got college board exams, an interview with a Princeton admissions officer, and finals at high school.

It gets to be an even busier time after his parents leave. Joel gets involved in an ascending pyramid of trouble. He calls a number in one of those sex-contact magazines and meets a young hooker who moves into the house. He runs afoul of the girl's pimp. His mother's expensive Steuben egg is stolen. His dad's Porsche ends up in Lake Michigan. The family home turns into a brothel. He blows two finals. And so on. This description may make *Risky Business* sound like a predictable sitcom. It is not. It is one of the smartest, funniest, most perceptive satires in a long time. It not only invites comparison with *The Graduate*, it earns it. Here is a great comedy about teen-age sex.

The very best thing about the movie is its dialogue. Paul Brickman, who wrote and directed, has an ear so good that he knows what to leave out. This is one of those movies where a few words or a single line says everything that needs to be said, implies everything that needs to be implied, *and* gets a laugh. When the hooker tells the kid, "Oh, Joel, go to school. Learn something," the precise inflection of those words defines their relationship for the next three scenes.

The next best thing about the movie is the casting. Rebecca De Mornay somehow manages to take that thankless role, the hooker with a heart of gold, and turn it into a very specific character. She isn't all good and she isn't all clichés: she's a very complicated young woman with quirks and insecurities and a wayward ability to love. I became quietly astounded when I realized that this movie was going to create an original, *interesting* relationship involving a teen-ager and a hooker. The teen-age kid, in what will be called the Dustin Hoffman role, is played by Tom Cruise, who also knows how to imply a whole world by what he won't say, can't feel, and doesn't understand.

This is a movie of new faces and inspired insights and genuine laughs. It's hard to make a good movie and harder to make a good comedy and almost impossible to make a satire of such popular but mysterious obsessions as guilt, greed, lust, and secrecy. This movie knows what goes on behind the closed bathroom doors of the American dream.

The River ★ ★
PG-13, 122 m., 1985

Mel Gibson (Tom Garvey), Sissy Spacek (Mae Garvey), Scott Glenn (Joe Wade), Shane Bailey (Lewis Garvey), Becky Jo Lynch (Beth Garvey), Don Hood (Senator Neiswinder). Directed by Mark Rydell and produced by Edward Lewis and Robert Cortes. Screenplay by Robert Dillon and Julian Barry.

The River has some basic problems anyway, but it might have seemed like a much fresher film if it had not been the third of Hollywood's "save the farm" movies released between September 1984 and January 1985. Like *Places in the Heart* and *Country*, it tells the story of brave, stubborn farmers who are determined not to lose their family land to the bankers. The farmers in this film have their own unique challenge—the farm is next to a river that tends to overflow—but *The River* also has a lot in common with the earlier films, including two crucial scenes that are astonishingly similar to ones in *Country*. It is some kind of cosmic bad joke on the makers of *The River*, who worked hard and earnestly on what is essentially a good film, that it came third in the parade.

The movie contains a heartfelt performance by Sissy Spacek as the Tennessee farm wife; an adequate performance by Mel Gibson as her husband; and a scene-stealing performance by Scott Glenn as the local financier who wants to buy up all the land in the valley, dam the river, and generate some jobs with cheap hydroelectric power. (The crucial flaw in the movie's plot is that Glenn's ideas, which are supposed to make him the bad guy, sound like simple common sense.) As the movie opens, Gibson is fighting the river and almost is trapped and drowned beneath a bulldozer. We remember the opening scene in *Country*, where the son of the family is almost suffocated in an overturned load of grain, and *The River* suffers in comparison: A secondary character might be killed in an opening scene, but hardly the male lead.

Then life settles down on the farm, and we get to know the Spacek and Gibson characters and their small children. These scenes of simple domestic life are good ones; a kitchen love scene between Gibson and

Spacek is warm, true, and electrifying. But then the farm gets caught in a credit crunch, and Gibson goes off to work as a scab at a struck steel mill in Birmingham, Alabama. It's here that we begin to notice a fairly heavy touch in the screenplay. After a frightened deer wanders into the mill, the strike-breakers take pity on the animal, surround it, and lead it to safety. A memorable image, which is ruined because in the very next scene, the striking workers do exactly the same favor for the scabs.

Meanwhile, back on the farm, an auction is broken up by the chants of fellow farmers, expressing solidarity: "No sale! No sale!" This scene is just like the one in *Country.* Feeling a certain amount of *déjà vu,* we listen to Scott Glenn's reasons that Gibson and Spacek should sell their farm: "Sooner or later, you'll have to. The river will flood again, or there'll be a drought, or a surplus."

I don't think the movie wants us to believe him, but he has logic on his side. You know a movie's got problems when you find yourself wishing the heroes would agree with the villain.

Of the three "save the farm" movies, which one wins the sweepstakes? My vote goes to *Country,* which is the most concerned with actual farm problems, with the credit crunch brought on by low-priced farm loans in the 1970s and falling market prices in the 1980s—and which contains the best performance, Jessica Lange's. *Places in the Heart* is more of a human fable, more concerned with its characters than with actual farm problems, but it placed second. *The River* feels too contrived in comparison with the genuine emotion of *Places* and the authentic politics of *Country.*

The Road Warrior ★ ★ ★ ½
R, 97 m., 1982

Mel Gibson (Max), Bruce Spence (Gyro Captain), Vernon Wells (Wez), Emil Minty (Feral Kid), Virginia Hey (Warrior Woman). Directed by George Miller and produced by Byron Kennedy. Screenplay by Terry Hayes, Miller, and Brian Hannant.

The Road Warrior is a film of pure action, of kinetic energy organized around the barest possible bones of a plot. It has a vision of a violent future world, but it doesn't develop that vision with characters and dialogue. It would rather plunge headlong into one of the most relentlessly aggressive movies ever made. I walked out of *The Road Warrior* a little dizzy and with my ears still ringing from the roar of the sound track; I can't say I "enjoyed" the film, but I'll hardly forget it. The movie takes place at a point in the future when civilization has collapsed, anarchy and violence reign in the world, and roaming bands of marauders kill each other for the few remaining stores of gasoline. The vehicles of these future warriors are leftovers from the world we live in now. There are motorcycles and semi-trailer trucks and oil tankers that are familiar from the highways of 1982, but there are also bizarre customized racing cars, of which the most fearsome has two steel posts on its front to which enemies can be strapped (if the car crashes, the enemies are the first to die).

The road warriors of the title take their costumes and codes of conduct from a rummage sale of legends, myths, and genres: They look and act like Hell's Angels, samurai warriors, kamikaze pilots, street-gang members, cowboys, cops, and race drivers. They speak hardly at all; the movie's hero, Max, has perhaps two hundred words. Max is played by Mel Gibson, an Australian actor who starred in *Gallipoli.* Before that, he made *Mad Max* for the makers of *The Road Warrior,* and that film was a low-budget forerunner to this extravaganza of action and violence. Max's role in *The Road Warrior* is to behave something like a heroic cowboy might have in a classic Western. He happens upon a small band of people who are trying to protect their supplies of gasoline from the attacks of warriors who have them surrounded. Max volunteers to drive a tanker full of gasoline through the surrounding warriors and take it a few hundred miles to the coast, where they all hope to find safety. After this premise is established with a great deal of symbolism, ritual, and violence (and so few words that sometimes we have to guess what's happening), the movie arrives at its true guts. The set piece in *The Road Warrior* is an unbelievably well-sustained chase sequence that lasts for the last third of the film, as Max and his semi-trailer run a gauntlet of everything the savages can throw at them.

The director of *The Road Warrior*, George Miller, compares this chase sequence to Buster Keaton's *The General*, and I can see what he means. Although *The General* is comedic, it's also very exciting, as Keaton, playing the engineer of a speeding locomotive, runs an endless series of variations on the basic possibilities of two trains and several sets of railroad tracks. In *The Road Warrior*, there is basically a truck and a road. The pursuers and defenders have various kinds of cars and trucks to chase or defend the main truck, and the whole chase proceeds at breakneck speed as quasi-gladiators leap through the air from one racing truck to another, more often than not being crushed beneath the wheels. The special effects and stunts in this movie are spectacular; *The Road Warrior* goes on a short list with *Bullitt*, *The French Connection*, and the truck chase in *Raiders of the Lost Ark* as among the great chase films of modern years.

What is the point of the movie? Everyone is free to interpret the action, I suppose, but I prefer to avoid thinking about the implications of gasoline shortages and the collapse of Western civilization, and to experience the movie instead as pure sensation. The filmmakers have imagined a fictional world. It operates according to its special rules and values, and we experience it. The experience is frightening, sometimes disgusting, and (if the truth be told) exhilarating. This is very skillful filmmaking, and *The Road Warrior* is a movie like no other.

Romancing the Stone ★ ★ ★
PG, 106 m., 1984

Michael Douglas (Jack Colton), Kathleen Turner (Joan Wilder), Danny DeVito (Thug), Alfonso Arau (Juan), Manuel Ojeda (Zolo). Directed by Robert Zemeckis and produced by Michael Douglas. Screenplay by Diane Thomas.

It may have an awkward title, but *Romancing the Stone* is a silly, high-spirited chase picture that takes us, as they say, from the canyons of Manhattan to the steaming jungles of South America. The movie's about a New York woman who writes romantic thrillers in which the hungry lips of lovers devour each other as the sun sinks over the dead bodies of their enemies. Then she gets involved in a real-life thriller, which is filled with cliff-hanging predicaments just like the ones she writes about. The writer, played by Kathleen Turner, uses her novels as a form of escape. Throbbing loins may melt together on her pages, but not in her life. Then she gets a desperate message from her sister in South America: Unless she flies to Cartagena with a treasure map showing the location of a priceless green jewel, her sister will be killed.

What follows is an adventure that will remind a lot of people of *Raiders of the Lost Ark*, but it will be a pleasant memory. After all the *Raiders* rip-offs, it's fun to find an adventure film that deserves the comparison, that has the same spirit and sense of humor. Turner lands in Colombia, and almost instantly becomes part of the plans of a whole lineup of desperadoes. There are the local police, the local thugs, the local mountain bandits, and the local hero, a guy named Jack Colton, who is played by Michael Douglas.

Movies like this work best if they have original inspirations about the ways in which the heroes can die. I rather liked the pit full of snarling alligators, for example. They also work well if the villains are colorful, desperate, and easy to tell apart. They are. Danny DeVito, from TV's "Taxi," plays a Peter Lorre type, complete with a white tropical suit and a hat that keeps getting trampled in the mud. He's a gangster from up north, determined to follow Turner to the jewel. There's also a suave local paramilitary hero named Zolo (Manuel Ojeda), who wears a French Foreign Legion cap and lusts after not only Turner's treasure map but all of her other treasures. And Alfonso Arau plays a rural bandito who turns out to have memorized all of Turner's thrillers.

Movies like this have a tendency to turn into a long series of scenes where the man grabs the woman by the hand and leads her away from danger at a desperate run. I always hate scenes like that. Why can't the woman run by herself? Don't they both have a better chance if the guy doesn't have to always be dragging her? What we're really seeing is leftover sexism from the days when women were portrayed as hapless victims. *Romancing the Stone* doesn't have too many scenes like that. It begins by being entirely about the woman, and although Douglas takes charge after they meet, that's basically because he knows the local territory. Their relationship is on an equal footing, and so is their love affair. We get the feeling they really care about each other, and so the romance isn't just a distraction from the action.

Say Amen, Somebody ★ ★ ★ ★
G, 100 m., 1983

Featuring Willie May Ford Smith, Thomas A. Dorsey, Sallie Martin, the Barrett Sisters, Edward and Edgar O'Neal, and Zella Jackson Price. Directed by George Nierenberg and produced by George and Karen Nierenberg.

Say Amen, Somebody is one of the most joyful movies I've ever seen. It is also one of the best musicals and one of the most interesting documentaries. And it's a terrific good time. The movie is about gospel music, and it's filled with gospel music. It's sung by some of the pioneers of modern gospel, who are now in their seventies and eighties, and it's sung by some of the rising younger stars, and it's sung by choirs of kids. It's sung in churches and around the dining room table; with orchestras and a capella; by an old man named Thomas A. Dorsey in front of thousands of people, and by Dorsey standing all by himself in his own backyard. The music in *Say Amen, Somebody* is as exciting and uplifting as any music I've ever heard on film.

The people in this movie are something, too. The filmmaker, a young New Yorker named George T. Nierenberg, starts by introducing us to two pioneers of modern gospel: Mother Willie May Ford Smith, who is seventy-nine, and Professor Dorsey, who is eighty-three. She was one of the first gospel soloists; he is known as the Father of Gospel Music. The film opens at tributes to the two of them—Mother Smith in a St. Louis church, Dorsey at a Houston convention— and then Nierenberg cuts back and forth between their memories, their families, their music, and the music sung in tribute to them by younger performers.

That keeps the movie from seeming too much like the wrong kind of documentary— the kind that feels like an educational film and is filled with boring lists of dates and places. *Say Amen, Somebody* never stops moving, and even the dates and places are open to controversy (there's a hilarious sequence in which Dorsey and Mother Smith disagree very pointedly over exactly which of them convened the first gospel convention).

What's amazing in all of the musical sequences is the quality of the sound. A lot of documentaries use "available sound," picked up by microphones more appropriate for the television news. This movie's concerts are miked by up to eight microphones, and the Dolby system is used to produce full stereo sound that really rocks. Run it through your stereo speakers, and play it loud.

Willie May Ford Smith comes across in this movie as an extraordinary woman, spiritual, filled with love and power. Dorsey and his longtime business manager, Sallie Martin, come across at first as a little crusty, but then there's a remarkable scene where they sing along, softly, with one of Dorsey's old records. By the end of the film, when the ailing Dorsey insists on walking under his own steam to the front of the gospel convention in Houston, and leading the delegates in a hymn, we have come to see his strength and humanity. Just in case Smith and Dorsey seem too noble, the film uses a lot of mighty soul music as a counterpoint, particularly in the scenes shot during a tribute to Mother Smith at a St. Louis Baptist church. We see Delois Barrett Campbell and the Barrett Sisters, a Chicago-based trio who have enormous musical energy; the O'Neal Twins, Edward and Edgar, whose "Jesus Dropped the Charges" is a show-stopper; Zella Jackson Price, a younger singer who turns to Mother Smith for advice; the Interfaith Choir, and lots of other singers.

Say Amen, Somebody is the kind of movie that isn't made very often, because it takes an unusual combination of skills. The filmmaker has to be able to identify and find his subjects, win their confidence, follow them around, and then also find the technical skill to really capture what makes them special. Nierenberg's achievement here is a masterpiece of research, diligence, and direction. But his work would be meaningless if the movie didn't convey the spirit of the people in it, and *Say Amen, Somebody* does that with great and mighty joy. This is a great experience.

Scarface ★ ★ ★ ★
R, 170 m., 1983

Al Pacino (Tony Montana), Steven Bauer (Manny Ray), Michelle Pfeiffer (Elvira), Mary Elizabeth Mastrantonio (Gina), Robert Loggia (Frank Lopez). Directed by Brian De Palma and produced by Martin Bregman. Screenplay by Oliver Stone.

The interesting thing is the way Tony Montana stays in the memory, taking on the dimensions of a real, tortured person. Most thrillers use interchangeable characters, and most gangster movies are more interested in action than personality, but *Scarface* is one of those special movies, like *The Godfather*, that is willing to take a flawed, evil man and allow him to be human. Maybe it's no coincidence that Montana is played by Al Pacino, the same actor who played Michael Corleone. Montana is a punk from Cuba. The opening scene of the movie informs us that when Cuban refugees were allowed to come to America in 1981, Fidel Castro had his own little private revenge and cleaned out his prison cells, sending us criminals along with his weary and huddled masses. We see Montana trying to bluff his way through an interrogation by U.S. federal agents, and that's basically what he'll do for the whole movie: bluff. He has no real character and no real courage, although for a short time cocaine gives him the illusion of both.

Scarface takes its title from the 1932 Howard Hawks movie, which was inspired by the career of Al Capone. That Hawks film was the most violent gangster film of its time, and this 1983 film by Brian De Palma also has been surrounded by a controversy over its violence, but in both movies the violence grows out of the lives of the characters; it isn't used for thrills but for a sort of harrowing lesson about self-destruction. Both movies are about the rise and fall of a gangster, and they both make much of the hero's neurotic obsession with his sister, but the 1983 *Scarface* isn't a remake, and it owes more to *The Godfather* than to Hawks. That's because it sees its criminal so clear-

ly as a person with a popular product to sell, working in a society that wants to buy. In the old days it was booze. For the Corleones, it was gambling and prostitution. Now it's cocaine. The message for the dealer remains the same: Only a fool gets hooked on his own goods. For Tony Montana, the choices seem simple at first. He can work hard, be honest, and make a humble wage as a dishwasher. Or he can work for organized crime, make himself more vicious than his competitors and get the big cars, the beautiful women, and the boot-licking attention from nightclub doormen. He doesn't wash many dishes.

As Montana works his way into the south Florida illegal drug trade, the movie observes him with almost anthropological detachment. This isn't one of those movies where the characters all come with labels attached ("boss," "lieutenant," "hit man") and behave exactly as we expect them to. De Palma and his writer, Oliver Stone, have created a gallery of specific individuals and one of the fascinations of the movie is that we aren't watching crime-movie clichés, we're watching people who are criminals.

Al Pacino does not make Montana into a sympathetic character, but he does make him into somebody we can identify with, in a horrified way, if only because of his perfectly understandable motivations. Wouldn't we all like to be rich and powerful, have desirable sex partners, live in a mansion, be catered to by faithful servants—and hardly have to work? Well, yeah, now that you mention it. Dealing drugs offers the possibility of such a life-style, but it also involves selling your soul. Montana gets it all and he loses it all. That's predictable. What is original about this movie is the attention it gives to how little Montana enjoys it while he has it. Two scenes are truly pathetic; in one of them, he sits in a nightclub with his blonde mistress and his faithful sidekick, and he's so wiped out on cocaine that the only emotions he can really feel are impatience and boredom. In the other one, trying for a desperate transfusion of energy, he plunges his face into a pile of cocaine and inhales as if he were a drowning man.

Scarface understands this criminal personality, with its links between laziness and ruthlessness, grandiosity and low self-esteem, pipe dreams and a chronic inability to be happy. It's also an exciting crime picture, in the tradition of the 1932 movie. And, like the Godfather movies, it's a gallery of wonderful supporting performances: Steven Bauer as a sidekick, Michelle Pfeiffer as a woman whose need for drugs leads her from one wrong lover to another, Robert Loggia as a mob boss who isn't quite vicious enough, and Mary Elizabeth Mastrantonio, as Pacino's kid sister who wants the right to self-destruct in the manner of her own choosing. These are the people Tony Montana deserves in his life, and *Scarface* is a wonderful portrait of a real louse.

Secret Honor ★ ★ ★ ★
NO MPAA RATING, 90 m., 1984

Philip Baker Hall (Nixon). Directed and produced by Robert Altman. Screenplay by Donald Freed and Arnold M. Stone.

The most tantalizing images in Woodward and Bernstein's *The Final Days* were those stories of a drunken Richard M. Nixon, falling to his knees in the White House, embarrassing Henry Kissinger with a display of self-pity and pathos. Was the book accurate? Even Kissinger said he had no idea who the authors' sources were (heh, heh). But as Watergate fades into history, and as revisionist historians begin to suggest that Nixon might after all have been a great president—apart from the scandals, of course—our curiosity remains. What were the real secrets of this most complex president? Robert Altman's *Secret Honor*, which is one of the most scathing, lacerating and brilliant movies of 1984, attempts to answer our questions. The film is a work of fiction. An actor is employed to impersonate Nixon. But all of the names and many of the facts are real, and the film gives us the uncanny sensation that we are watching a man in the act of exposing his soul.

The action takes place in Nixon's private office, at some point after his resignation. The shelves are lined with books, and with a four-screen video monitor for the security system. The desk top is weighted down with brass and gold. From the walls, portraits peer down. Eisenhower, Lincoln, Washington, Woodrow Wilson, Kissinger. Nixon begins by fiddling with his tape recorder; there is a little joke in the fact that he doesn't know quite how to run it. Then he begins to talk. He talks for ninety minutes. That bare description may make *Secret Honor* sound like *My Dinner with André*, but rarely have I seen ninety more compelling minutes on the screen. Nixon is portrayed by Philip Baker Hall, an actor previously unknown to me, with such savage intensity, such passion, such venom, such scandal, that we cannot turn away. Hall looks a little like the real Nixon; he could be a cousin, and he sounds a little like him. That's close enough. This is not an impersonation, it's a performance.

What Nixon the character has to say may or may not be true. He makes shocking revelations. Watergate was staged to draw attention away from more serious, even treasonous, activities. Kissinger was on the payroll of the Shah of Iran, and supplied the Shah with young boys during his visits to New York. Marilyn Monroe was indeed murdered by the CIA, and so on. These speculations are interwoven with stories we recognize as part of the official Nixon biography: the letter to his mother, signed "Your faithful dog, Richard"; the feeling about his family and his humble beginnings; his hatred for the Eastern Establishment, which he feels has scorned him.

Truth and fiction mix together into a tapestry of life. We get the sensation of a man pouring out all of his secrets after a lifetime of repression. His sentences rush out, disorganized, disconnected, under tremendous pressure, interrupted by four-letter words that serve almost as punctuation. After a while the specific details don't matter so much; what we are hearing is a scream of a brilliant, gifted man who is tortured by the notion that fate might have made him a loser.

A strange thing happened to me as I watched this film. I knew it was fiction. I didn't approach it in the spirit of learning the "truth about Nixon." But as a movie, it created a deeper truth, an artistic truth, and after *Secret Honor* was over, you know what? I had a deeper sympathy for Richard Nixon than I have ever had before.

The Secret of NIMH ★ ★ ★
G, 82 m., 1982

With the voices of Hermione Baddeley (Shrew), Elizabeth Hartman (Mrs. Brisby), Dom DeLuise (Jeremy), Derek Jacobi (Nicodemus), Arthur Malet (Mr. Ages), John Carradine (Owl), Peter Strauss (Justin). Directed by Don Bluth and produced and written by Bluth, Gary Goldman, and John Pomeroy.

The Secret of NIMH contains that absolute rarity among feature-length animated cartoons, an interesting premise. It is: What if a group of laboratory animals were injected with an experimental drug that made them as intelligent as men? There have been smart animals in the movies for years, of course, but they were always playing quasi-humans in a universe where the real humans were seen mostly from the knees down. Now here's a story that concerns itself with the problem of being a rat and having a superior intelligence.

Although the idea was what intrigued me about *The Secret of NIMH*, the movie itself represents a philosophical statement for its makers. The animators who made this film were previously employed at the Walt Disney Studios, where they were heralded as the "new breed," groomed to replace the veterans who started with Walt himself and were all past retirement age. But halfway through production of the most recent Disney animated feature, *The Fox and the Hound*, a group of new breeders walked out and, led by director Don Bluth, set up their own shop at MGM.

Their complaint was that Disney was cutting corners on painstaking traditional animating methods. Their vow was to make a non-Disney movie in the old Disney tradition. The main difference between traditional Disney animation and cheaper, newer methods is in the areas of body movements and backgrounds. Bluth and his followers wanted to make a movie in which the characters would have lots of body language (not just moving lips and rolling eyes), and in which the backgrounds would be detailed and interesting, not just repetitive roll-bys. In *The Secret of NIMH*, they have succeeded in reproducing the marvelous detail and depth of the Disney classics. This is a good-looking, interesting movie that creates a lit-tle rodent world right under the noses of the indifferent local humans. The story is perhaps a little complicated at first, especially for younger viewers, but a flashback helps make things clear, and then the adventure begins.

We learn that a group of rats and mice was injected with the secret potion in the laboratories of the National Institute of Mental Health, and that they quickly became so smart that they were able to escape from NIMH and set up a society in a barnyard. Then they were faced with an ethical dilemma: Should they continue to freeload off of the local humans, stealing grains, supplies, and even electricity—or should they set off into the wilderness to establish a new society of their own? This larger story is counterpointed with the saga of a mousy little widow named Mrs. Brisby, whose sick child is threatened by the approach of the tilling machine.

The Secret of NIMH is an artistic success. It looks good, moves well, and delights our eyes. It is not quite such a success on the emotional level, however, because it has so many characters and involves them in so many different problems that there's nobody for the kids in the audience to strongly identify with. I guess you could say that the Disney tradition lives, but that the Disney magic still remains elusive.

Seems Like Old Times ★ ★
PG, 102 m., 1980

Goldie Hawn (Glenda), Chevy Chase (Nick), Charles Grodin (Ira), Robert Guillaume (Fred), Harold Gould (Judge), George Grizzard (Governor). Directed by Jay Sandrich and produced by Ray Stark. Screenplay by Neil Simon.

Seems Like Old Times is another one of those near-misses that leaves a movie critic in a quandary. It's a funny movie, and it made me laugh out loud a lot, but in the final analysis it just didn't quite edge over the mystical line into success. And yet I found myself wanting to like the movie, and wishing it were better, because the good parts were good enough to hold out the promise for more. The movie is Neil Simon's attempt at one of those 1940s-style screwball comedies with lots of surprise entrances and hasty exits and people hiding under the bed. It would be hard to improve on the casting (Goldie Hawn, Chevy Chase, and Charles Grodin). And there are a couple of really funny sustained sequences.

The movie opens with Chevy Chase, a divorced writer, being abducted by a pair of bank robbers who want him to hold the gun and present the note to the teller. He does, and on the way out of the bank he inadvertently poses for a perfect snapshot taken by the spy camera over the door. A statewide alarm goes out; he's wanted for a bank robbery. That causes political complications, because his first wife (Goldie Hawn) is now married to the district attorney (Charles Grodin), and the state governor is considering Grodin for attorney general. It causes even more complications when Chevy Chase, on the lam, throws himself on the mercy of Goldie Hawn and she tries to hide him in the spare room over the garage.

We now have almost all the basic ingredients for bedroom farce: Chase hides under the bed while Grodin gets amorous and Hawn desperately tries to think of excuses. Meanwhile, a whole supporting cast, both animal and human, gets involved. Goldie has a houseful of stray dogs and cats, who roam through the room during every crisis. And she's a defense attorney; her clients turn up at all the wrong times, steal cars, stumble across Chevy, and otherwise complicate everything.

The movie's single best scene is probably a formal dinner party that Grodin and Hawn throw for the governor (George Grizzard). The butler gets drunk while Chevy Chase is hiding in the kitchen, so, while the statewide search for him continues, he puts on the butler's tuxedo and serves dinner. The scene develops into wonderful physical comedy. Another great scene stars only Chevy Chase's hand. He's hiding under the bed, Charles Grodin steps on his finger, and with his other hand he pantomimes his agony.

The movie's unsung hero is probably Grodin. He's made a specialty out of playing the rather dull, absolutely straight, sort of likable establishment type: He's the perfect comic foil. He played the same basic role in *The Heartbreak Kid*, *Heaven Can Wait*, *It's My Turn*, and *The Incredible Shrinking Woman*. He never pushes the character too far: He's pleasant, friendly, understanding, funny, but sometimes a bit of a bore. Unfortunately, this time, so is the movie he's in.

Sharky's Machine ★ ★ ★
R, 119 m., 1981

Burt Reynolds (Sharky), Rachel Ward (Dominoe), Vittorio Gassman (Victor), Brian Keith (Papa), Charles Durning (Frisco). Directed by Burt Reynolds and produced by Hank Moonjean. Screenplay by Gerald Di Pago.

Sharky's Machine contains all of the ingredients of a tough, violent, cynical big-city cop movie, but what makes it intriguing is the way the Burt Reynolds character plays against those conventions. His name is Sharky. As the movie opens, he's an undercover narcotics cop. He blows a big case and is demoted to the vice squad—which is a bawdy, brawling, vocal gang of misfits who act like a cross between "Hill Street Blues" and a Joseph Wambaugh nightmare.

Sharky is not happy in vice. He is, in fact, not happy anywhere, not until a young woman named Dominoe enters his life. She is a hooker. She also seems to be involved with some snaky big-money characters, and so Sharky places her under twenty-four hour surveillance. That involves moving several cops, telescopes, cameras, and bugging devices into the high-rise opposite her apartment. The cops set up housekeeping and settle down for a long wait. And it's here that the movie begins to really involve us. Reynolds, as Sharky, falls in love with the woman. It is a voyeuristic love, involving spying and eavesdropping, and Sharky is not a voyeur—so it is particularly painful for him to witness the woman's sexual involvement with others.

The central scenes of the movie, involving the call girl's private life and the probing eyes of Sharky, could easily have become tawdry—could have disintegrated into a peep show. That doesn't happen, partly because Reynolds (who also directed the film) doesn't provide cheap displays of flesh, but also because the call girl is played by British actress Rachel Ward, who brings poignancy and restraint to the role. She plays a hooker who's not a tramp. She has a husky voice and an astonishing body, but there's an innocence in her manner. Later, we discover that she has been in virtual bondage to her pimp since she was an infant. She knows no other life. This is a setup of sorts, a device in the plot to allow the female lead to be both prostitute and victim, but it clarifies the relationship between Reynolds and Ward. And when they fall in love, as they inevitably do, it provides some leftover innocence to be celebrated.

Reynolds surrounds this central relationship with a lot of cops, known as Sharky's Machine. They are played by actors who have played a lot of other cops in a lot of other movies—Brian Keith, Charles Durning—and by Bernie Casey, who is playing his first cop but does it with special grace. There's a long scene in the film, reportedly improvised, in which Casey tells Reynolds what it felt like, the first time he was shot. We are reminded that cops in the movies hardly ever talk about being shot.

Sharky's Machine has a lot of plot, most of it inspired by the original novel by William Diehl. Maybe it has too much plot for a movie that Reynolds has referred to as *Dirty Harry Goes to Atlanta*. But this is an ambitious film; it's as if something inside Reynolds was chafing at the insipid roles he was playing in one car-chase movie after another. He doesn't walk through this movie, and he doesn't allow himself the cozy little touches that break the mood while they're letting the audience know how much fun Burt is having.

The result of his ambition and restraint is a movie much more interesting than most cop thrillers. *Sharky's Machine* does have a lot of action, including an extended, exhausting, brutal shoot-out at the end. But it also has the special qualities of the relationship between Reynolds and Ward (more fully developed than the camaraderie between Reynolds and Catherine Deneuve, as another hooker in another thriller, *Hustle*, in 1974). As a director, Reynolds allows himself a few excesses (one howler is the dramatic cut from a sex scene to the phallic glory of the Peachtree Plaza Hotel). But he's put a lot of his ambition in this movie, and it reminds us that there is a fine actor within the star of *Cannonball Run*.

Sheena, Queen of the Jungle ★
PG, 117 m., 1984

Tanya Roberts (Sheena), Ted Wass (Vic Casey), Donovan Scott (Fletcher), Elizabeth of Toro (Shaman), Trevor Thomas (Prince Otwani). Directed by John Guillermin and produced by Paul Aratow. Screenplay by David Newman and Lorenzo Semple, Jr.

How can this be? I casually reached over to the old reference shelf, to find some old references to *Sheena, Queen of the Jungle*, the jungle heroine who inflamed the pubescent fantasies of lads in the early 1950s. And not only wasn't there an entry in Halliwell's *Filmgoer's Companion*, but neither the *Oxford Companion of Film* nor *The Film Encyclopedia* had ever heard of Sheena. Could this be because Sheena spent most of her time on television, where she was once played by the one, the only, Irish McCallum? I dunno, but I think they're missing a bet in Oxford if they don't have a Sheena festival right away.

I mention my old memories because the movie *Sheena* seems likely to provide me with few new memories. The movie stars Tanya Roberts as the legendary blonde jungle girl. After Sheena's parents are killed in a cave-in, she is adopted by the beautiful Shaman (played by the fashion model Elizabeth of Toro, who undoubtedly taught Sheena all about makeup, explaining Sheena's plucked eyebrows and purple eye shadow, there in the midst of the trees). Shaman's tribe considers Sheena a god, and she learns to talk to the animals, ride a zebra bareback, and fashion crude jungle bikinis out of only those simple materials one finds in a boutique. Then an American TV crew comes to the jungle to film an interview with an African prince, who is also a place kicker for a U.S. pro football team. The prince is behind a plot to assassinate his brother, the king, and the TV crew stumbles over the story and over Sheena, who the prince's jealous girlfriend has vowed to kill.

Are you following all this? Anyway, Sheena and the anchorman (Ted Wass) disappear into the jungle, where the clichés of male superiority *instantly* take hold. Get this. The clod of an anchorman, faced with a woman who can tame zebras and talk to the elephants, tells this magnificent wild creature that, and I quote, what he'd like to do is take her to Wall Street and show her the World Trade Center while they both eat peanuts.

Anyway, *Sheena* contains all too little of Sheena at some times, and all too much at others. Let me explain. The whole dumb plot about the palace coup, the evil prince, etc., is given a lot of screen time, even though it is awesomely uninteresting. Sheena, who might have been presented as sort of a female Greystoke, a real jungle creature, meanwhile takes nude baths in waterfalls and learns that American men do rude things like pressing their lips against hers. The nudity in the movie is extensive enough to raise eyebrows over its PG rating.

Is there anything good about *Sheena*? Yeah, the animals are fun to watch, especially the lions. But Tanya Roberts is about as convincing, swinging from those vines, as Carol Burnett would have been. And come to think of it, Sheena, Queen of the Jungle, is the kind of character that, in our time, perhaps only Carol Burnett could play.

Shoot the Moon ★ ★ ★ ½
R, 124 m., 1982

Albert Finney (George Dunlap), Diane Keaton (Faith Dunlap), Karen Allen (Sandy), Peter Weller (Frank), Dana Hill (Sherry). Directed by Alan Parker and produced by Alan Marshall. Screenplay by Bo Goldman.

Alan Parker's *Shoot the Moon* is a film that sometimes keeps its painful secrets even from itself. It opens with a shot of a man in agony. In another room, his wife, surrounded by four noisy daughters, dresses for a dinner that evening at which the man will be honored. The man has to pull himself together. His voice is choking with tears, he telephones the woman he loves and tells her how hard it will be to get through the evening without her. Then he puts on his rumpled tuxedo and marches out to do battle. As we watch this scene, we assume that the movie will answer several of the questions it raises, such as: What went wrong in the marriage? Why is the man in such agony? What is the nature of his love for the other woman? One of the surprises in *Shoot the Moon* is that none of these questions is

ever quite answered, and we are asked to fill in the gaps ourselves.

That is not necessarily a flaw in the film. *Shoot the Moon* is not the historical record of this marriage, but the emotional history. It starts with what should be a happy marriage. A writer of books (Albert Finney) lives with his beautiful, funky wife (Diane Keaton) and their four rambunctious daughters in a converted farmhouse somewhere in Marin County, California. Their house is one of those warm battle zones filled with books, miscellaneous furniture, and the paraphernalia for vast projects half-completed. We learn that the marriage has gone disastrously wrong. That the man is determined to stalk out and be with his new woman. That the wife, after a period of anger and mourning, is prepared to react to this decision by almost deliberately having an affair with the loutish but well-meaning young man who comes to build a tennis court. That the husband and wife still harbor fugitive feelings of love and passion for another.

We never really learn how the marriage went wrong. There is the usual talk about how one partner was not given the room to grow, or the other did not have enough "space"—concepts that love would render meaningless, but that divorce makes into savagely defended positions. We also learn just a tantalizing little about the two new lovers. Albert Finney's new woman (Karen Allen) is so cynical about their relationship in one scene that we wonder if their affair will soon end (we never learn). Diane Keaton's new man (Peter Weller) is so emotionally stiff, so closed-off, that we don't know for a long time whether Keaton really likes him, or simply desires him sexually and wants to use him to spite her husband.

Does it matter that the movie doesn't want to provide insights in these areas? I think it does. When Ingmar Bergman covered similar grounds in his *Scenes from a Marriage*, he provided us with enough concrete information about the issues in the marriage that it was possible for us to discuss the relationship afterward, taking sides, seeing both points of view. After *Shoot the Moon*, we don't discuss the relationship, we discuss our questions about it. And yet this is sometimes an extraordinary movie. Despite its flaws, despite its gaps, despite two key scenes that are dreadfully wrong, *Shoot the Moon* contains a raw emotional power of the sort we rarely see in domestic dramas.

The film's basic conflict is within Albert Finney's mind. He can no longer stay with his wife, he must leave and be with the other woman, and yet he still wants to own the family and possessions he has left behind. He doesn't want his ex-wife dating other men. He wants to observe the birthday of an eldest daughter (Dana Hill) who hates him and resents his behavior. He remodeled the house with his own hands, and cannot bear to see another man working on it. In one scene of heartbreaking power, he breaks into his own house and finds himself beating his daughter because he loves her so much and she will not love him.

In scenes like that (and in the quiet scenes where Hill asks, "Why did Daddy leave us?" and Keaton answers, "I don't think he left you; I think he left me"), *Shoot the Moon* is a great film. In scenes like the one where they fight in a restaurant, or argue in court, it ranges from the miscalculated to the disastrous. *Shoot the Moon* is a rare, good film, and yet, afterward, most of my thoughts were about how it might have been better. It is frustrating to feel that the filmmakers knew their characters intimately, but chose to reveal them only in part.

Silkwood ★ ★ ★ ★
R, 128 m., 1983

Meryl Streep (Karen Silkwood), Kurt Russell (Drew Stephens), Cher (Dolly Pelliker), Craig T. Nelson (Winston). Directed by Mike Nichols and produced by Nichols and Michael Hausman. Screenplay by Nora Ephron and Alice Arlen.

When the Karen Silkwood story was first being talked about as a movie project, I pictured it as an angry political exposé, maybe *The China Syndrome, Part 2*. There'd be the noble, young nuclear worker, the evil conglomerate, and, looming overhead, the death's-head of a mushroom cloud. That could have been a good movie, but predictable. Mike Nichols's *Silkwood* is not predictable. That's because he's not telling the story of a conspiracy, he's telling the story of a human life. There are villains in his story, but none with motives we can't understand.

After Karen is dead and the movie is over, we realize this is a lot more movie than perhaps we were expecting.

Silkwood is the story of some American workers. They happen to work in a Kerr-McGee nuclear plant in Oklahoma, making plutonium fuel rods for nuclear reactors. But they could just as easily be working in a Southern textile mill (there are echoes of *Norma Rae*), or on an assembly line, or for a metropolitan public school district. The movie isn't about plutonium, it's about the American working class. Its villains aren't monsters; they're organization men, labor union hotshots, and people afraid of losing their jobs. As the movie opens, Karen Silkwood fits naturally into this world, and the movie is the story of how she begins to stand out, how she becomes an individual, thinks for herself, and is punished for her freedom. Silkwood is played by Meryl Streep, in another of her great performances, and there's a tiny detail in the first moments of the movie that reveals how completely Streep has thought through the role. Silkwood walks into the factory, punches her time card, automatically looks at her own wristwatch, and then shakes her wrist: It's a self-winding watch, I guess. That little shake of the wrist is an actor's choice. There are a lot of them in this movie, all almost as invisible as the first one; little by little, Streep and her coactors build characters so convincing that we become witnesses instead of merely viewers.

The nuclear plant in the film is behind on an important contract. People are working overtime and corners are being cut. A series of small incidents convinces Karen Silkwood that the compromises are dangerous, that the health of the workers is being needlessly risked, and that the company is turning its back on the falsification of safety and workmanship tests. She approaches the union. The union sees some publicity in her complaints. She gets a free trip to Washington—her first airplane ride. She meets with some union officials who are much more concerned with publicity than with working conditions, and she has a little affair with one of them. She's no angel. At home in Oklahoma, domestic life resembles a revolving door, with her boyfriend (Kurt Russell) packing up and leaving, and her friend

(Cher), a lesbian, inviting a beautician to move in. It's a little amazing that established movie stars like Streep, Russell, and Cher could disappear so completely into the everyday lives of these characters.

The real Karen Silkwood died in a mysterious automobile accident. She was on her way to deliver some documents to a *New York Times* reporter when her car left the road. Was the accident caused in some way? Was she murdered? The movie doesn't say. Nor does it point suspicion only toward the company. At the end there were a lot of people mad at Karen Silkwood. *Silkwood* is the story of an ordinary woman, hard-working and passionate, funny and screwed-up, who made those people mad simply because she told the truth as she saw it and did what she thought was right.

Sixteen Candles ★ ★ ★
PG, 93 m., 1984

Molly Ringwald (Samantha Baker), Anthony Michael Hall (The Geek), Michael Schoeffling (Jake Ryan), Gedde Watanabe (Long Duk Dong), Paul Dooley (Jim Baker). Directed by John Hughes and produced by Hilton A. Green. Screenplay by Hughes.

Sixteen Candles is a sweet and funny movie about two of the worst things that can happen to a girl on her sixteenth birthday: (1) Her grandparents shrieking "Look! She's finally got her boobies!" and (2) her entire family completely and totally forgetting that it's even her birthday. The day goes downhill from there, because of (3) her sister's wedding to a stupid lunkhead, (4) her crush on the best-looking guy in the senior class, and (5) the long, involved story about how a freshman boy named the Geek managed to get possession of a pair of her panties and sell looks at them for a dollar each to all the guys in the locker room.

If *Sixteen Candles* begins to sound a little like an adolescent raunch movie, maybe it's because I haven't suggested the style in which it's acted and directed. This is a fresh and cheerful movie with a goofy sense of humor and a good ear for how teen-agers talk. It doesn't hate its characters or conde-

scend to them, the way a lot of teen-age movies do; instead, it goes for human comedy and finds it in the everyday lives of the kids in its story.

The movie stars Molly Ringwald as Samantha, a bright-eyed brunette who pulls off the difficult trick of playing a character who takes everything too seriously—without ever taking herself too seriously. The movie's told mostly from her point of view, and it's like *Valley Girl*—it's about young kids who think a lot about sex, but who are shy and inexperienced and unsure and touchingly committed to concepts like True Love. She has a crush on a senior boy named Jake (Michael Schoeffling), who looks like Matt Dillon, of course, and doesn't even know she's alive. Meanwhile, the Geek (Anthony Michael Hall) is in love with her. Also, there are complications involving Jake's stuck-up girlfriend, Samantha's impossible grandparents, various older and younger brothers and sisters, and a foreign exchange student named Long Duk Dong, who apparently has come to this country to major in partying.

Sixteen Candles contains most of the scenes that are obligatory in teen-age movies: The dance, the makeout session, the party that turns into a free-for-all. But writer and director John Hughes doesn't treat them as subjects for exploitation; he *listens* to these kids. For example, on the night of the dance, Samamtha ends up in the shop room with the Geek. They're sitting in the front seat of an old car. The Geek acts as if he's sex-mad. Samantha tells him to get lost. Then, in a real departure for this kind of movie, they really start to talk, and it turns out they're both lonely, insecure, and in need of a good friend.

There are a lot of effective performances in this movie, including Paul Dooley as Samantha's harried father, Blanche Baker as the zonked-out older sister, Hall as the Geek, and Gedde Watanabe as the exchange student (he elevates his role from a potentially offensive stereotype to high comedy). Ringwald provides a perfect center for the story, and her reaction in the first scene with her grandmother is just about worth the price of admission.

The Slugger's Wife ★ ★
PG-13, 114 m., 1985

Michael O'Keefe (Darryl Palmer), Rebecca De Mornay (Debby Palmer), Martin Ritt (Burly De Vito), Randy Quaid (Moose). Directed by Hal Ashby and produced by Ray Stark. Screenplay by Neil Simon.

The Slugger's Wife has a story that demands to be taken as lighthearted nonsense, and since the screenplay is by Neil Simon, we go in expecting to have a good time. But no, Simon's not in a lighthearted mood, and so the silliness of the story gets bogged down in all sorts of gloomy neuroses, angry denunciations, and painful self-analysis.

Now tell me if this doesn't sound like a delightful premise: An outfielder for the Atlanta Braves is in a slump when he visits a nightclub one night and sees a singer there. He falls instantly head-over-heels in love. He announces that he'll hit two homers in tomorrow's game if she'll go out with him. He does, and they do, and it's love at first sight. But then a funny thing starts to happen. His performance at the plate is tied directly to their love. As long as he knows she loves him, he slams them out of the park. When he has doubts, he goes back into his slump.

In the good old days, this would have been material for a great light comedy, maybe starring Jimmy Stewart or Dan Dailey. But Simon won't leave well enough alone. He turns the outfielder (Michael O'Keefe) into a brooding, pathologically jealous, possessive, insecure case study. And he makes the woman (Rebecca De Mornay) into a serious, independent, liberated career woman who needs time to grow and be herself. That would be a terrific combination for a made-for-TV potboiler on the hang-up of the week. It doesn't mix very well with baseball. For that matter, the baseball in this movie is pretty unconvincing, too. Every time O'Keefe slams a homer, he stands there at the plate, grinning foolishly at his girl in the stands, instead of doing what any normal young man would do, which is to run like hell in the direction of first base.

The movie has a couple of scenes that *really* don't work. One of them involves a scheme by the wise old manager (played by directer Martin Ritt) to convince O'Keefe that De Mornay still loves him. O'Keefe is in a hospital bed, half out of his mind, and Ritt and a couple of the players come in with a girl they've recruited to play the wife. She stands in the shadows and says all the right things, and O'Keefe seems temporarily taken in, which is more than we can say. This sort of scene belongs in the very worst sort of TV sitcom. It doesn't belong in a movie where we're supposed to believe it.

All of my objections aside, let me say that O'Keefe is good in this movie and De Mornay is more than good. In her first movie since *Risky Business*, she has a couple of scenes where she's so sweet, and earnest, and believable, that you wonder what would happen if she ever used that energy in a screenplay that deserved it. I guess we're going to have to wait for the answer to that question.

Smash Palace ★ ★ ★ ★
R, 100 m., 1982

Bruno Lawrence (Al Shaw), Anna Jemison (Jacqui Shaw), Greer Robson (Georgie Shaw), Keith Aberdeen (Ray Foley), Des Kelly (Tiny). Directed and produced by Roger Donaldson. Screenplay by Donaldson, Peter Hansard, and Bruno Lawrence.

Step by step, this powerful movie takes a man from perfect happiness into a personal hell. By the end of the film, the man is behaving irrationally, but here's the frightening thing: Because we've followed him every step of the way, we have to admit he's behaving as we ourselves might, in the same circumstances. The man in *Smash Palace* is Al Shaw, a Grand Prix driver who leaves the racing circuit to take over his father's auto garage in New Zealand. Played by Bruno Lawrence, Al is a straight-talking, direct man who enjoys working with his hands and takes a vast delight in the affections of his wife and the love of his small daughter. It's a long way from the Grand Prix to repairing transmissions, but he's happy with his work and content to raise a family in peace and quiet. His wife (Anna Jemison) is not so content. She wanted him to leave the racing circuit before he was killed, but now, in the quiet backwaters of New Zealand, she is going quietly stir-crazy. She begins an affair with a local cop (Keith Aberdeen) and finally tells her husband she's leaving him. She's moving into town.

Her decision starts him on a series of wrong moves that may seem logical, one by one, but which eventually add up in the minds of others to a simple conclusion: He has lost his reason. He is jealous—of course. He holds a great fury against his wife and the cop. But, much more important, he misses his daughter. He wants custody. But because he acts in ways that are violent and frightening to his wife (and because her lover is on the police force, which must respond to the domestic emergencies he creates), he works himself into a Catch-22: The more he does to take back his daughter, the closer he is to losing her. Finally, he kidnaps her. He takes her out into the woods where they live together for a time in isolation and happiness. It's an idyll that can't last. But *Smash Palace* doesn't lead up to the inevitable violent conclusion we might expect. All along the way, this film prefers the unexpected turns of actual human behavior to the predictable plot developments we might have expected, and, at the end, there's another turn, a fascinating one.

Smash Palace is one of 1982's best films, an examination of much the same ground as *Shoot the Moon*, but a better film, because it has the patience to explore the ways in which people can become consumed by anger (*Shoot the Moon* contented itself with the outward symptoms). One of the reasons the movie works so well is the performances, which are all the stronger because they come from actors we have not seen before. Bruno Lawrence, bald-headed, wiry, tough, and surprisingly tender, is just right as the man who loses his family. Anna Jemison has a difficult assignment as his wife: We're on his side, and yet we see the logic of her moves. Keith Aberdeen is properly tentative as the other man; he feels love and lust, and yet is not unaware of the unhappiness he is causing. And there's a guy named Des Kelly who plays Tiny, an employee at the Smash Palace who looks on, and sees all, and wishes he knew what to do.

The movie was directed by a young filmmaker named Roger Donaldson, who, in a sense, *is* the New Zealand film industry. He has produced six features for New Zealand television, and his first feature film, *Sleeping Dogs*, starred Warren Oates in a horrifying and plausible fantasy about the American occupation of New Zealand. Now comes this film, so emotionally wise and observant that we learn from it why people sometimes make the front pages with guns in their hands and try to explain that it's all because of love. Love, yes, but also the terrible frustration of trying to control events, to make people do what you want them to do, what you "know" would make them happy—no matter what they think. The hero of *Smash Palace* does not act wisely, but if we are honest, it's hard to see where we might have acted differently.

Smokey and the Bandit II ★
PG, 101 m., 1980

Burt Reynolds (Bandit), Jackie Gleason (Buford T. Justice), Mike Henry (Junior Justice), Jerry Reed (Snowman), Sally Field (Carrie), Dom DeLuise (The Doc). Directed by Hal Needham and produced by Hank Moonjean. Screenplay by Jerry Belson.

There is no need for this movie. That's true of most sequels, but it's especially true of *Smokey and the Bandit II*, which is basically just the original movie done again, not as well. The press releases claimed that the 1977 *Smokey* grossed $250 million, which is probably not more than a gross exaggeration. It was, you will recall, an action comedy in which Burt Reynolds and Jerry Reed were offered an enormous amount of money to smuggle a truckload of Coors beer into one of those benighted states where Coors is not sold.

Reed was the semi-truck driver. Reynolds was Bandit, the advance scout with the CB radio to alert Reed to the traps laid by Smokey, who was an apoplectic sheriff played by Jackie Gleason. They all play the same roles in the sequel, and Sally Field is also along as Burt's sometime girlfriend. New additions this time are Doc, a gynecologist played by Dom DeLuise, and Charlotte, an elephant. The plot involves a payment of four hundred thousand dollars to Reed and Reynolds if they transport Charlotte from Florida to Texas, with Gleason once again on their trail.

Given those small adjustments in the successful premise of the original movie, what's new this time? Well, the relationship between Burt Reynolds and Sally Field has changed, and the changes are almost fatal to the story. It seems that Bandit has become a folk hero of Good Ol' Boys everywhere, as a result of his original exploits. Sally doesn't like it. They argue and keep breaking up.

Why can't the movie allow Burt and Sally to have a nice, dumb, wide-eyed romantic relationship? Probably because the filmmakers suffered an attack of Creeping Realism. As everyone who has the *National Enquirer* read to them must know, in real life Sally and Burt broke up. And their spats in this movie are conducted in "meaningful" terms borrowed from freshman psychology. Bandit wants to be a kid forever. His girl wants him to grow up. They can't communicate, etc. I can almost imagine the writers having conferences with Burt and Sally while this pseudo-serious dialogue was drummed up. Why couldn't they just have had another silly flirtation?

Most of the effort in the movie has gone, once again, into the stunts. The film's director, Hal Needham, was once the most famous of Hollywood stuntmen, and he has realized his wildest dreams this time. There are cars hurtling through the air, and fifty semi-trucks roaring down on fifty squad cars, and trucks driving on top of trucks, and cars getting sandwiched between trucks, and you name it. If you like this sort of thing and do not live within commuting distance of the nearest demolition derby, I suppose this movie is just what you're looking for.

What about the elephant? Well, it provides a couple of raunchy sight gags, and an excuse for Dom DeLuise to do his schtick as a would-be veterinarian. But the movie's best moments are by Jackie Gleason as Sheriff Buford T. Justice, and Mike Henry, as his slow-witted son, Junior. Gleason has a larger role this time than in the original movie, and he glories in it. He was always the master of the slow burn, and he burns all through this movie. There's one nice scene, using trick photography, in which Gleason plays three roles (Buford and his two brothers), and the personalities are variations of characters he invented on his television show. It was nice to see them again.

But the movie as a whole is a mess. There's

not even a clear reason why the elephant has to be taken to Texas. Episodes are strung along in no particular order. Guest stars (like Mean Joe Greene and Brenda Lee) come on for a few moments, do their thing, and disappear. The original *Smokey* was a cheap little Good Ol' Boy movie that made good. This one, with an unlimited budget, is lazy. How can I say it's lazy when it has fifty trucks doing stunts in it? Because it takes a lot less thought to fill up a movie with stunts than to create a comedy that's genuinely funny.

Soldier of Orange ★ ★ ★ ½
PG, 165 m., 1980

Rutger Hauer (Erik), Jeroen Krabbe (Guus), Edward Fox (Col. Rafelli), Susan Penhaligon (Susan), Peter Faber (Will), Belinda Meuidijk (Esther), Derek De Lint (Alex). Directed by Paul Verhoeven and produced by Rob Houwer. Screenplay based on the novel by Erik Hazelhoff.

Successful war movies almost always depend on tone. We've seen so many battle films, so many soldiers and so many tanks, so many landings and invasions and spies dropped behind the lines that the actual subject matter itself is no longer enough for us. Movies like *A Bridge Too Far* may cost untold millions and be years in the making, but for the most part we're just not moved. Good war movies don't necessarily need a message, but they need a *feeling:* We want to sense what the war experience was like for a specific group of people at a particular time.

The Dutch film *Soldier of Orange** creates that feeling as effectively, probably, as it can be created. It traces the stories of six Dutch soldiers through the years before and during World War II, and at the movie's end we feel we know these people and have learned from their experiences. Although the film contains a great deal of suspense and a fair amount of violence, it's not a garish adventure movie, it's a human chronicle. And it involves us.

That's all the more remarkable because this isn't a profoundly serious little film with a somber message, but a big, colorful, expensive war movie—the most costly production in Dutch film history. Expensive war movies tend to linger forever on their great special effects; they have a tendency to pose their heroes in front of collapsing buildings and expect us to be moved. *Soldier of Orange* is big, but it's low-key. It's about how characters of ordinary human dimension might behave against the bewildering scale of a war.

The movie's based on the memoirs of Erik Hazelhoff, a Dutch war hero who escaped from Nazi-occupied Europe, landed in England, was attached to the then hopelessly disorganized and ineffectual Dutch government in exile, and spent the war on a series of espionage missions before finally joining up with the Royal Air Force and flying many missions. What's interesting is that the Hazelhoff character (played by Rutger Hauer) is shown doing all of these things, and yet he doesn't emerge as a superhero; he's just a capable, brave man doing the next right thing.

The film mostly follows Hazelhoff, but it begins in the prewar years with six friends—college students, playing tennis, hanging out together, doubting war will *really* come—and it follows all six through the war. Four of them die, one in a particularly horrible way in a concentration camp. By following all six lives over a period of years, the film suggests the historical sweep of the war for many millions of lives; *Soldier of Orange* isn't just episodes strung together (although it is episodic), but a suggestion of how long the war must have seemed, and how easily it must have seemed endless.

The narrative structure is interesting. Instead of giving us a tightly knit plot, with characters assigned to particular roles and functions, it gives us a great many specific details. There are the scenes involving Queen Wilhelmina, for example. In exile in England, the dowager queen walks stiffly in her garden, gravely absorbs the advice of her ministers, receives delegations, and conveys a dignity upon the situation through her very bearing (for, of course, she had no real authority then at all).

A subplot involving an underground Dutch radio operator is clothed in similar detail; we know enough of his character to know why he turns informer and his decision is not simply cowardly, but is almost understandable. Unforgivable, but understandable. The movie is filled with perceptions like that.

Soldier of Orange has been dubbed into English, and I'm opposed on principle to dubbing. I'd almost always rather hear the actual voices of the actors, and take my chances with subtitles. But I must report that this is an excellent job of dubbing, and that we're never distracted by it.

A Soldier's Story ★ ★ ½
PG, 99 m., 1984

Howard E. Rollins, Jr. (Captain Davenport), Adolph Caesar (Sergeant Waters), Art Evans (Private Wilkie), David Alan Grier (Corporal Cobb), David Harris (Private Smalls), Denzel Washington (Private Peterson), Patti LaBelle (Big Mary). Directed by Norman Jewison and produced by Jewison, Ronald L. Schwary, and Patrick Palmer. Screenplay by Charles Fuller.

A Soldier's Story is one of those movies that's about less than you might think. It begins with the murder of a black sergeant, who is shot near an Army base in Louisiana in 1944. Suspicion immediately points to the local whites, who are not too happy about all these blacks stationed in their branch of the deep South. An Army lawyer, a captain, is sent from Washington to handle the investigation, and he turns out to be black, too—the first black officer anyone in the movie has ever seen. As he conducts his investigation, we get to meet some of the important characters on the base, from black privates to the white officers who brag about their experiences at "commanding Negroes." Each time the captain conducts an interview, we get a flashback to another version of the events leading up to the murder. And eventually, we find out who committed the crime.

As a storytelling device, this mechanism is excruciating. The problem is in the time structure. If an investigation begins at the present moment and proceeds, suspense can build. But if the truth is going to emerge from a series of flashbacks, then obviously the movie knows who did it, and is withholding the information from us, using it as a hook to get us to sit through all of its other points. *A Soldier's Story* is not really a murder mystery, then. What is it? I guess it's supposed to be a docudrama. A great deal of the plot revolves around the character of the dead man, Sergeant Waters (Adolph Caesar), who is a scrappy little veteran of World War I, and believes that blacks should always behave so as to favorably impress whites and reflect credit upon their race. He is filled with self-hate, and takes it out on the black men under him who are not acting the way he thinks they should.

This fact is gradually revealed in a series of interviews conducted by the lawyer, Captain Davenport, who is played by Howard E. Rollins, Jr. And what a disappointing performance it is, coming from the same actor who won an Academy Award nomination for *Ragtime*. He invests his character with little humanity; he tries to seem dispassionate, curbed, correct, just a little more noble than anyone else in the picture. The result is such a laid-back performance that the lawyer seems less interested in solving the case than in keeping his cool (the murdered Sergeant Waters would have been proud of him).

The movie ends with a handshake between Davenport and one of the white officers who has made life hard for him. This is a more ironic ending than was perhaps intended, because *A Soldier's Story* was directed by Norman Jewison, the director who ended *In the Heat of the Night* with Sidney Poitier and Rod Steiger shaking hands. The ending worked in 1967, but in 1984 I think we expect a little more. Did this movie have to be so lockstep, so trapped by its mechanical plot, so limited by a murder mystery? What the movie has to say is so pale and limited that, ironically, the most interesting character in the movie is the victim—that black racist sergeant. At least he has fire and life and, misguided as he is, at least he's vital.

Somewhere in Time ★ ★
PG, 103 m., 1980

Christopher Reeve (Richard Collier), Jane Seymour (Elise McKenna), Christopher Plummer (W. F. Robinson), Teresa Wright (Laura Roberts), Bill Erwin (Arthur), Bo Clausen (Man in Elevator). Directed by Jeannot Szwarc and produced by Stephen Deutsch. Screenplay by Richard Matheson.

Somewhere in Time wants us to share its sweeping romantic idealism, about a love so great that it spanned the decades and violated the sanctity of time itself. But we keep getting distracted by nagging doubts, like, isn't it a little futile to travel sixty-eight years backward into time for a one-night stand? The movie surrounds its love story with such boring mumbo jumbo about time travel that we finally just don't care.

It didn't have to be that way. The underrated and neglected movie *Time After Time*, which had H.G. Wells and Jack the Ripper traveling forward into modern San Francisco, contained a love story that had a lot of sly fun with the notion of relationships between people of different eras. *Somewhere in Time* has a lot of qualities, but slyness and fun are not two of them. This movie drips with solemnity. It enshrines its lovers in such excessive romantic nobility that Rachmaninoff's "Rhapsody" plays almost every time they're on the screen. This is the kind of romance so sacred, so serious, so awesome, that you have to lower your voice in the presence of it. Romances like that are boring, even to the monstrous egos usually involved in them.

But back to the movie. *Somewhere in Time* stars Christopher Reeve as a playwright who visits the Grand Hotel on Mackinac Island and sees a photograph there of an actress who appeared at the hotel in 1912. He is smitten; no, he is obsessed. He researches the career of the actress, falls in love with her, learns from a pseudoscientific psychology professor that time travel is possible, and hypnotizes himself to travel back to 1912. The movie never makes it clear whether the playwright actually does travel through time, or only hypnotizes himself into thinking he does. It doesn't matter. Once he's back in 1912, or thinks he is, he meets the young actress, who is played by the preternaturally beautiful Jane Seymour. "Is it . . . *you?*" she breathes. It is! It is! A little of this goes a long way, even with Rachmaninoff. Especially with Rachmaninoff.

There is, of course, a villain. He is the young actress's manager, played by Christopher Plummer. He has guided her career since she was sixteen, and now resents the intrusion of this stranger who has come from nowhere, is dressed oddly, and threatens to steal his protégée. There are some intrigues, as the three of them steal about the rooms and grounds of the magnificent Grand Hotel. But there are never any scenes that really deal with the romance between Reeve and Seymour—and, incredibly, the movie avoids the opportunity to exploit in their relationship the fact that Reeve is from the future. All of the delightful revelations and paradoxes that could have resulted from Reeve revealing that fact are simply ignored.

This was Reeve's first movie since *Superman*, and he is not particularly convincing in it. He seems a little stolid, a little ungainly; he's so desperately earnest in his love for this actress that he always seems to be squinting a little. The whole movie is so solemn, so worshipful toward its theme, that it's finally just silly.

Songwriter ★ ★ ★ ½
R, 94 m., 1985

Willie Nelson (Doc Jenkins), Kris Kristofferson (Blackie Buck), Melinda Dillon (Honey Carder), Rip Torn (Dino McLeish), Lesley Ann Warren (Gilda), Richard Sarafian (Rocky Rodeo). Directed by Alan Rudolph and produced by Sydney Pollack. Screenplay by Matthew Leonetti.

Songwriter is one of those movies that grows on you. It doesn't have a big point to prove, and it isn't all locked into the requirements of its plot. It's about spending some time with some country musicians who are not much crazier than most country musicians, and are probably nicer than some. It also has a lot of good music.

The movie stars Willie Nelson as a country songwriter named Doc Jenkins, who has a real bad head for business. One day he gets fast-talked into selling control of his company to a slick operator named Rocky Rodeo (Richard Sarafian). Homeless and betrayed, he turns for support to his best friend, a country music star named Blackie (Kris Kristofferson). Blackie, meanwhile, is being promoted by a sleazy manager named Dino (Rip Torn), who has somewhere found a neurotic young singer named Gilda (Lesley Ann Warren). In an early scene that lets us know this movie is not going to be routine, Blackie tries to foist Gilda off on an audience that has paid to see Blackie, and when the

audience rebels, Blackie grabs the mike and starts advising them to commit anatomical impossibilities upon themselves.

During the course of some days and nights on the road and back home in Austin, Doc comes up with a clever scheme. Instead of writing any more songs for the despised Dino, he'll write his songs under a pseudonym, and give them to Gilda to record. Blackie will include Gilda on his next tour, and Dino will get screwed. This seems like a good idea to everybody, especially Gilda, who has a tricky drinking problem and thinks she might be falling in love with Doc.

The movie unwinds casually, introducing us to the other people in the lives of these characters. The most important is Doc's former wife (Melinda Dillon), and the best scene in the movie is where Doc visits her and the kids, and is shy and sweet and tremendously moving. Another good scene is one where Gilda invites Doc into her bed, and he tries to be gentle and tactful in explaining that he doesn't think that's a good idea. Willie Nelson is the key to both of those scenes, and it's interesting how subtle his acting is. Unlike a lot of concert stars whose moves tend to be too large for the intimacy of a movie, Nelson is a gifted, understated actor. Watch the expression on his face as he turns down Gilda; not many actors can say as much with their eyes.

Songwriter was directed by Alan Rudolph, who also made *Choose Me*. Rudolph's teacher was Robert Altman, and, like Altman, he specializes in offbeat rhythms of a group of characters in an unpredictable situation. We never have a clear idea of where *Songwriter* is headed; is it about Doc's love for his first wife, or Gilda's self-destruction, or Rocky Rodeo's con games? It's good that we don't know, because then we don't know what to expect next, and the movie can surprise us.

Both Rudolph and Altman also specialize in unlikely combinations of actors; Kris Kristofferson and Nelson don't, at first, seem to belong in the same movie with Warren, Torn, and Dillon, but watch them work together. One of Torn's great unsung roles was in *Payday*, the movie based on the last days of Hank Williams, Sr. This time, he's like the same character a little further down the road, a little more spaced out. Kristofferson is basically the straight man, the hero's best friend. Nelson sings less and acts more than we expected. And Lesley Ann Warren's performance is endlessly inventive: She takes the fairly standard character of a kooky would-be singer, and makes her into a touching, unforgettable creation.

Sophie's Choice ★ ★ ★ ★
R, 157 m., 1982

Meryl Streep (Sophie), Kevin Kline (Nathan), Peter MacNicol (Stingo), Greta Turken (Leslie Lapidus), Gunther Maria Halmer (Rudolf Hoess). Directed by Alan J. Pakula and produced by Pakula and Keith Barish. Screenplay by Pakula.

Sometimes when you've read the novel, it gets in the way of the images on the screen. You keep remembering how you imagined things. That didn't happen with me during *Sophie's Choice*, because the movie is so perfectly cast and well-imagined that it just takes over and happens to you. It's quite an experience.

The movie stars Meryl Streep as Sophie, a Polish-Catholic woman, who was caught by the Nazis with a contraband ham, was sentenced to a concentration camp, lost her two children there, and then was somehow spared to immigrate to Brooklyn, U.S.A., and to the arms of an eccentric charmer named Nathan. Sophie and Nathan move into an old boardinghouse, and the rooms just below them are taken by Stingo, a jug-eared kid from the South who wants to be a great novelist. As the two lovers play out their doomed, romantic destiny, Stingo falls in love with several things: with his image of himself as a writer, with his idealized vision of Sophie and Nathan's romance, and, inevitably, with Sophie herself.

The movie, like the book, is told with two narrators. One is Stingo, who remembers these people from that summer in Brooklyn, and who also remembers himself at that much earlier age. The other narrator, contained within Stingo's story, is Sophie herself, who remembers what happened to her during World War II, and shares her memories with Stingo in a long confessional. Both the book and the movie have long central flashbacks, and neither the book nor the movie is damaged by those diversions, because Sophie's story is so indispensable to

Stingo's own growth, from an adolescent dreamer to an artist who can begin to understand human suffering. The book and movie have something else in common. Despite the fact that Sophie's story, her choices, and her fate are all sad, sad stories, there is a lot of exuberance and joy in the telling of them. *Sophie's Choice* begins as a young Southerner's odyssey to the unimaginable North—to that strange land celebrated by his hero, Thomas Wolfe, who took the all-night train to New York with its riches, its women, and its romance. Stingo is absolutely entranced by this plump blonde Polish woman who moves so winningly into his life, and by her intense, brilliant, mad lover.

We almost don't notice, at first, as Stingo's odyssey into adulthood is replaced, in the film, by Sophie's journey back into the painful memories of her past. The movie becomes an act of discovery, as the naive young American, his mind filled with notions of love, death, and honor, becomes the friend of a woman who has seen so much hate, death, and dishonor that the only way she can continue is by blotting out the past, and drinking and loving her way into temporary oblivion. It's basically a three-character movie, and the casting, as I suggested, is just right. Meryl Streep is a wonder as Sophie. She does not quite look or sound or feel like the Meryl Streep we have seen before in *The Deer Hunter* or *Manhattan* or *The French Lieutenant's Woman*. There is something juicier about her this time; she is merrier and sexier, more playful and cheerful in the scenes before she begins to tell Stingo the truth about her past. Streep plays the Brooklyn scenes with an enchanting Polish-American accent (she has the first accent I've ever wanted to hug), and she plays the flashbacks in subtitled German and Polish. There is hardly an emotion that Streep doesn't touch in this movie, and yet we're never aware of her straining. This is one of the most astonishing and yet one of the most unaffected and natural performances I can imagine.

Kevin Kline plays Nathan, the crazy romantic who convinces everyone he's on the brink of finding the cure for polio and who wavers uncertainly between anger and manic exhilaration. Peter MacNicol is Stingo, the kid who is left at the end to tell the story. Kline, MacNicol, and Streep make such good friends in this movie—despite all the suffering they go through—that we really do believe the kid when he refuses to act on an unhappy revelation, insisting, "These are my *friends*. I love them!"

Sophie's Choice is a fine, absorbing, wonderfully acted, heartbreaking movie. It is about three people who are faced with a series of choices, some frivolous, some tragic. As they flounder in the bewilderment of being human in an age of madness, they become our friends, and we love them.

Southern Comfort ★ ★ ★
R, 106 m., 1981

Keith Carradine (Spencer), Powers Boothe (Hardin), Fred Ward (Reece), Franklyn Seales (Simms), T.K. Carter (Cribbs), Lewis Smith (Stuckey). Directed by Walter Hill and produced by David Filer. Screenplay by Michael Kane, Hill, and Giler.

Southern Comfort is a well-made film, but it suffers from a certain predictability. I suspect the predictability is part of the movie's point. The film is set in the Cajun country of Louisiana, in 1973, and it follows the fortunes of a National Guard unit that gets lost in the bayous and stumbles into a metaphor for America's involvement in Vietnam.

The movie's approach is direct, and its symbolism is all right there on the surface. From the moment we discover that the guardsmen are firing blanks in their rifles, we somehow know that the movie's going to be about their impotence in a land where they do not belong. And as the weekend soldiers are relentlessly hunted down and massacred by the local Cajuns (who are intimately familiar with the bayou), we think of the uselessness of American technology against the Viet Cong.

The guardsmen are clearly strangers in a strange land, and they make fatal blunders right at the outset. They cut the nets of a Cajun fisherman, they "borrow" three Cajun boats, and they mock the Cajuns by firing blank machine-gun rounds at them. The Cajuns are not amused. By the film's end, guardsmen will have been shot dead, impaled, hung, drowned in quicksand, and attacked by savage dogs. And all the time they try to protect themselves with a parody

of military discipline, while they splash in circles and rescue helicopters roar uselessly overhead. All this action is shown with great effect in *Southern Comfort*. The movie portrays the bayous as a world of dangerous beauty. Greens and yellows and browns shimmer in the sunlight, and rare birds call to one another, and the Cajuns slip noiselessly behind trees while the guardsmen wander about making fools and targets of themselves. *Southern Comfort* is a film of drum-tight professionalism.

It is also, unfortunately, so committed to its allegorical vision that it never really comes alive as a story about people. That is the major weakness of its director, the talented young Walter Hill, whose credits include *The Warriors*, *The Driver*, and *The Long Riders*. He knows how to make a movie look great, and how to fill it with energy and style. But I suspect he is uncertain about the human dimensions of his characters. And to cover that up, he makes them into larger-than-life stick figures, into symbolic units who stand for everything except themselves. That tendency was carried to its extreme in *The Driver*, a thriller in which the characters were given titles (the Driver, the Girl) rather than names. It was also Hill's approach in *The Warriors*, which translated New York gang warfare into the terms of Greek myth. His approach bothered me so much in *The Warriors* that I overlooked, I now believe, some of the real qualities of that film. It bothers me again in *Southern Comfort*.

Who *are* these men? Of the Cajuns we learn nothing: They are invisible assassins. Of the guardsmen, however, we learn little more. One is swollen with authority. One intends to look out for himself. One is weak, one is strong, and only the man played by Keith Carradine seems somewhat balanced and sane. Once we get the psychological labels straight, there are no further surprises. And once we understand the structure of the movie (guardsmen slog through bayous, get picked off one by one), the only remaining question is whether any of them will finally survive.

That's the weakness of the storytelling. The strength of the movie is in its look, in its superb use of its locations, and in Hill's mastery of action sequences that could have been repetitive. The action is also good: The actors are given little scope to play with in their characters, but they do succeed in creating plausible weekend soldiers. "We are the Guard!" they chant, and we believe them. And there is one moment of inspired irony, when they are lost, cold, wet, hungry, and in mortal fear of their lives, and one guy asks, "Why don't we call in the National Guard?"

Splash ★ ½
PG, 111 m., 1984

Tom Hanks (Allen), Daryl Hannah (Madison), Eugene Levy (Walter), John Candy (Freddie). Directed by Ron Howard and produced by Brian Grazer. Screenplay by Lowell Ganz, Babaloo Mandel, and Bruce Jay Friedman.

There is a funny movie lurking at the edges of *Splash*, and sometimes it even sneaks on screen and makes us smile. It's too bad the relentlessly conventional minds that made this movie couldn't have made the leap from sitcom to comedy. They must have thought they had such a great idea (Manhattan bachelor falls in love with mermaid) that they couldn't fail. But great ideas are a dime a dozen. *Splash* tells the story of a young man who is twice saved from drowning by a beautiful young mermaid. She falls in love with him and follows him to Manhattan, where he is a fruit and vegetable wholesaler. He falls in love with her. She can, it appears, metamorphose at will, turning her tail into legs. There are a lot of jokes about her total ignorance about all the ways of civilization. She walks naked onto Ellis Island, for example, and eats lobsters—shell and all.

All right. Now that's the situation. But the situation isn't going to be enough. We need some characters here. The mermaid is just fine. As played by the lovely Daryl Hannah, she is young and healthy and touchingly naive. But what about the guy who falls in love with her? It's here that the movie makes its catastrophic casting mistake. You see, they figured they have a comedy as long as the girl has a tail, and a romance whenever she has legs. So they gave her a romantic leading man when they should have given her a lonely guy who could swim. The leading man is Tom Hanks. He is conventionally handsome and passably appealing, and he would do in a secondary role. He'd be great,

for example, as the straight-arrow brother. Instead, they make him the mermaid's lover, and they cast John Candy as the brother.

You remember Candy from SCTV. He is the large, shambling, Charles Laughton-type who has such a natural chrisma that he's funny just standing there. They should have made Candy the lover, and Hanks the brother. Then we'd be on the side of this big lunk who suddenly has a mermaid drop into his life and has to explain her to his creepy, swinging-singles brother. Plus, there's the sweet touch that this transcendently sexy mermaid has fallen for the tubby loser with the heart of lust, and not for his slick brother. See what I mean? Instead, they go the other way. John Candy is not used much in the movie, Tom Hanks comes across as a standard young male lead, and they have to concoct a meaningless and boring subplot in order to make the movie long enough. Don't they know in Hollywood that once all the geniuses think they've finished with the screenplay, you just gotta rotate everything 180 degrees and you got a movie?

Spring Break ★
R, 101 m., 1983

David Knell (Nelson), Perry Lang (Adam), Paul Land (Stu), Steve Bassett (O.T.), Corinne Alphen (Joan). Directed and produced by Sean S. Cunningham. Screenplay by David Smilow.

Styles in exploitation films have a way of changing overnight. Just when I thought I couldn't take one single more Dead Teen-ager Movie—one more of those hundreds of movies in which screaming teen-agers were chased by maniacs and carved up with hatchets—they stopped making them. That's the good news. The bad news is, Dead Teen-ager Movies have been replaced by Horny Teen-ager Movies.

The first one was *Porky's*. It went through the roof. Then we got *The Last American Virgin*, *Private Lessons*, *Going All the Way*, and *My Tutor* (which was sort of fun). Here's *Spring Break*, a sex-and-sand epic about the annual mating rituals in Fort Lauderdale. The obvious inspiration for *Spring Break* is all the Beach Party movies from the late 1950s and early 1960s. Here's the most obvious connection between *Spring Break* and

the Beach Party flicks: They all have absolutely unnecessary subplots involving idiotic
politicians who act like complete nerds and
become apoplectic at the thought of kids
having any fun. In the late 1950s, that sort of
plot was standard. This is the 1980s, and it's
absurd. The story this time involves a clod-
dish senatorial candidate (Donald Sym-
ington) who becomes enraged when his son
sneaks off to join the gang at Fort Lauderdale. He assigns a bunch of hired goons to
patrol the beach and bring back his son.

There's another thing seriously wrong
with *Spring Break.* It doesn't know that girls
are people, too. It's only about horny teen-
age boys. Four of them—two studs, two
timid kids—become roommates in a motel
and go out looking for where the girls are.
All four have names, identities, characteristics, etc. The whole movie involves their
adventures, their quests for girls, their exploits, their big wins in the belly-flopping
contest, etc. The women in their lives are
interchangeable, and, as nearly as I can recall, *not one woman in this movie was called by
name!*

That's too bad, especially since *Spring
Break* costars a young woman named Corinne Alphen, who was *Penthouse*'s 1982 Pet
of the Year. Sad to say, most of the Pets and
Playmates who win movie roles turn out to
be sort of self-conscious and untalented as
actresses. Not Corinne Alphen. She has a
dazzling smile, a great personality, and a
relaxed naturalness on the screen that makes
the Horny Teen-ager Boys seem all the more
gauche.

A funny little movie *might* have been made
about her adventures in Fort Lauderdale,
"where the boys are." She would have had
the personality to carry it. Instead, the lockstep mentalities who made this movie tell
their story entirely from a boring male point
of view, supply us with male wimps and
studs who are equally uninteresting, and
view women only as wet T-shirt finalists.
What a letdown for horny movie critics.

STAR 80 ★ ★ ★ ★
R, 102 m., 1983

Mariel Hemingway (Dorothy Stratten), Eric
Roberts (Paul Snider), Cliff Robertson (Hugh
Hefner), Carroll Baker (Dorothy's Mother),
Roger Rees (Aram Nicholas). Directed by
Bob Fosse and produced by Wolfgang
Glattes and Kenneth Utt. Screenplay by
Fosse.

Bob Fosse dresses all in black and makes
films about the demonic undercurrents in
our lives. Look at his credits: *Cabaret, Lenny, All That Jazz,* and now *STAR 80.* Although his Broadway musicals have been
upbeat entertainment, he seems to see the
movie camera as a device for peering into our
shames and secrets. *STAR 80* is his most
despairing film. After the Nazi decadence of
Cabaret, after the drug abuse and self-destruction in *Lenny,* and the death-obsessed
hero of *All That Jazz,* here is a movie that
begins with violent death and burrows deeper. There were times when I could hardly
keep my eyes on the screen, and a moment
near the end when I seriously asked myself if
I wanted to continue watching.

And yet I think this is an important movie.
Devastating, violent, hopeless, and important, because it holds a mirror up to a part of
the world we live in, and helps us see it more
clearly. In particular, it examines the connection between fame and obscurity, between
those who have a moment of praise and notoriety, and those who see themselves as condemned to stand always at the edge of the
spotlight. Like Martin Scorsese's *Taxi Driver,* it is a movie about being an outsider and
about going crazy with the pain of rejection.

The movie tells the story of two young
people from Vancouver. One of them was
Dorothy Stratten, a shy, pretty blonde who
thought her hands and feet were too big,
who couldn't understand why anyone would
value her, and who was close enough to some
sort of idealized North American fantasy
that she became the 1979 Playmate of the
Year. The other was Paul Snider, a Vancouver small-timer who worked as a salesman, con man, and part-time pimp. When
Paul saw Dorothy behind the counter of a
hamburger stand, he knew she was his ticket
to the big time. Dorothy resisted his compli-
ments at first, but he was so relentless in his
adoration that she surrendered to his fantasies. Paul masterminded Dorothy's rise.
He arranged the photo session that attracted
the eye of *Playboy*'s talent scouts. He bought
her dresses and flowers. He pushed her into

the limelight and then edged into it next to her. But then she went to Los Angeles and found the real stardust, the flattery of the Playboy Mansion, the attentions of young men whose sports cars were bought with their own money, while Paul's was bought with hers.

Paul had a vanity license plate made: STAR 80. But Dorothy had moved out of his world, had been given a taste of a larger world that, frankly, Paul didn't have the class to appreciate. She fell in love with a movie director. She went out of town on location. She and Paul drifted apart, and he went mad with jealousy and resentment. On August 14, 1980, Dorothy went back to the shabby little North Hollywood bungalow they had rented together, and Paul murdered her.

STAR 80 begins with the murder. Everything else is in flashback, and, therefore, the film has no really happy scenes. Dorothy's triumphs are all stained with our knowledge of what will happen. Every time she smiles, it's poignant. We know Paul will go berserk and kill her, and so we can see from the beginning that he's unbalanced. Fosse knows his material is relentlessly depressing, and so he doesn't try for moments of relief. Although we enter the world of *Playboy* and see Dorothy partying in the mansion and posing in nude modeling sessions, although the whole movie is concerned with aspects of sex, there is never an erotic moment. Fosse keeps his distance, regarding Dorothy more as a case study than as a fantasy. That makes Mariel Hemingway's performance as Dorothy all the more powerful. She has been remade into the sleek, glossy Playmate image, but she still has the adolescent directness and naiveté that she used so well in *Manhattan* and *Personal Best*. She's a big kid. Her eyes open wide when she gets to Los Angeles, and she's impressed by the attention she's receiving. The character she plays is simple, uncomplicated, shallow, and so trusting that she never does realize how dangerous Paul is.

The other performances in the movie are equally strong. Eric Roberts as Paul even succeeds in persuading us to accept him as a suffering human being rather than as a hateful killer. Like Robert De Niro as Travis Bickle in *Taxi Driver*, he fills his role with so

much reality that we feel horror, but not blame. Carroll Baker, as Dorothy's mother, is heartbreakingly incapable of connecting in any meaningful way with her daughter.

What is the point of *STAR 80?* I'm not sure, just as I wasn't sure of the points of *In Cold Blood* or *Lacombe, Lucien* or "The Executioner's Song." There is no redemption in the movie, no catharsis. It unblinkingly looks at the short life of a simple, pretty girl, and the tortured man who made her into something he couldn't have, and then killed her for it. The movie seems to be saying: These things happen. After it was over, I felt bad for Dorothy Stratten. In fact, for everybody.

A Star Is Born ★ ★ ★ ★
PG, 175 m., 1954 (1983)

Judy Garland, James Mason, Jack Carson, Tommy Noonan, Charles Bickford. Directed by George Cukor.

A Star Is Born hasn't merely been restored. It has been rediscovered. George Cukor's 1954 movie, which starred James Mason and Judy Garland in the story of Hollywood lives destroyed by alcoholism, always has been considered one of the great tear-jerking Hollywood melodramas, populated with bravura performances. But has it ever been praised for its purely cinematic qualities? I don't think so, and yet it showed Cukor's mastery not only of the big effects, but also of subtle lighting and exquisite compositions. It's an irony, but if Warner Brothers hadn't chopped twenty-seven minutes out of the movie in 1954 and tried to throw them away, the whole movie never would have been rereleased in its current form. It is very good to have the missing footage back, of course, but it's even better to have the whole movie back again, a landmark of Hollywood melodrama.

Although this version is exactly as long as Cukor's final cut in 1954, it doesn't have quite all the footage. Two major production numbers and a charming little scene in a drive-in restaurant were rediscovered by film historian Ron Haver (after months of detective work). Haver also found the movie's complete stereo soundtrack, but about seven minutes of the visual footage seem to be gone forever—and so this restoration uses an effective montage of music, dialogue, and production stills to bridge the gaps. Seeing this version of the movie makes it clear what major surgery was performed by Warner Brothers. The studio chopped out an entire Judy Garland musical number, "Here's What I'm Here For," filled with fire and energy. That's wonderful to have back again, but the other major restored sequence is almost indispensable to the film.

It's a scene from fairly early in the film. The alcoholic movie star (Mason) has convinced the young band vocalist (Garland) to risk everything and try for a movie career. With his support, she's on the brink of stardom. She's recording a song with a studio orchestra, and afterward she rests on a staircase with Mason. He proposes marriage. She says he drinks too much. He promises to reform. Neither one realizes that their whole conversation is being recorded by an eavesdropping overhead mike. Then, as a joke by the director, the proposal is played back for all the musicians to hear—and Garland accepts. By taking out that proposal scene, Warner Brothers had a movie that skipped unconvincingly from Garland's movie debut to her elopement with Mason. The earlier missing footage—the scenes represented by the still photos—also represented important bridging material, covering an uncertain period during which Garland thinks Mason has forgotten about her. Without those scenes, the movie skips directly from Garland's early hopes to her first day at the studio, with no period of uncertainty.

The missing scenes are good to have back again. But the movie's central scenes are even better to see again. There is an absolutely brilliantly lit and directed scene in a darkened nightclub, with Garland singing while the camera prowls silently among the musicians' instruments; it's one of the best examples of composition I've ever seen. And near the end of the movie, there's Garland's big, bravura scene, in which she interrupts a big production number for a heart-rending dressing-room conversation with her studio chief (Charles Bickford). And then, of course, there is Mason's sad, lonely walk into the sea, and the movie's unforgettable closing line: "Good evening, everyone. This is Mrs. Norman Maine."

A Star Is Born is one of the rare films that successfully integrate music with drama; it's not exactly a musical, but it has more music than most musicals. It's also not exactly a serious drama—it's too broad and predictable for that—but it's the sort of exaggerated, wide-gauge melodrama that Rainer Werner Fassbinder would experiment with twenty years later; a movie in which larger-than-life characters are used to help us see the melodramatic clichés that we do, indeed, sometimes pattern our own lives after.

I was lucky enough to visit George Cukor at his Hollywood home in December of 1981. He said he had never seen the butchered version of A Star Is Born and never would. "If they wanted it shorter," he said, "I could have sweated out twenty-five minutes here and there, and nobody would have missed them. Instead, they took an ax to the movie." George Cukor died on the evening before he was to see a rough version of this restored print. That is sad, but then Cukor, of course, knew what his original movie looked like. Now the rest of us can know, too.

Star Trek: The Motion Picture ★ ★ ★
G, 132 m., 1979

William Shatner (Kirk), Leonard Nimoy (Spock), DeForest Kelley ("Bones" McCoy), James Doohan (Scotty), George Takei (Sulu), Walter Koenig (Chekov). Directed by Robert Wise and produced by Gene Roddenberry. Screenplay by Harold Livingston.

Two things occurred to me as I watched Star Trek:

• The producers have succeeded at great expense in creating a toy for the eyes. This movie is fun to watch.

• Epic science fiction stories, with their cosmic themes and fast truths about the nature of mankind, somehow work best when the actors are unknown to us. The presence of the Star Trek characters and actors—who have become so familiar to us on television—tends in a strange way to undermine this movie. The audience walks in with a possessive, even patronizing attitude toward Kirk and Spock and Bones, and that interferes with the creation of the "sense of wonder" that science fiction is all about.

Let's begin with the toy for the eyes. The Star Trek movie is fairly predictable in its plot. We more or less expected that two of the frequent ingredients in the television episodes would be here, and they are: a confrontation between Starship Enterprise and some sort of alien entity, and a conclusion in which basic human values are affirmed in a hostile universe. In *Star Trek: The Motion Picture*, the alien entity is an unimaginably vast alien spaceship from somewhere out at the edge of the galaxy. The movie opens as it's discovered racing directly toward Earth, and it seems to be hostile. Where has it come from, and what does it want?

The Starship Enterprise, elaborately rebuilt, is assigned to go out to intercept it, with Admiral Kirk, of course, in charge. And scenes dealing with the Enterprise and the other ship will make up most of the movie—if the special effects aren't good, the movie's not going to work. But they are good, as, indeed, they should be: The first special effects team on this movie was fired, and the film's release was delayed a year while these new effects were devised and photographed. (The effects get better, by the way, as the movie progresses. The alien ship looks great but the spaceports and futuristic cities near the film's beginning loom fairly phony.)

The Enterprise, perhaps deliberately, looks a lot like other spaceships we've seen in *2001, Silent Running, Star Wars,* and *Alien.* Kubrick's space odyssey set a visual style for the genre that still seems to be serviceable. But the look of the other spaceship in *Star Trek* is more awesome and original. It seems to reach indefinitely in all directions, the Enterprise is a mere speck inside of it, and the contents of the alien vessel include images of the stars and planets it has passed en route, as well as enormous rooms or spaces that seem to be states of a computer-mind. This is terrific stuff.

But now we get to the human level (or the half-human level, in the case of Mr. Spock). The characters in this movie are part of our cultural folklore; the *Star Trek* television episodes have been rerun time and time again. Trekkies may be unhappy with me for saying this, but there are ways in which our familiarity with the series works against the effectiveness of this movie. On the one hand we have incomprehensible alien forces and a plot that reaches out to the edge of the gal-

axy. On the other hand, confronting these vast forces, we have television pop heroes. It's great to enjoy the in-jokes involving the relationships of the Enterprise crew members and it's great that Trekkies can pick up references meant for them, but the extreme familiarity of the Star Trek characters somehow tends to break the illusion in the big scenes involving the alien ship.

Such reservations aside, *Star Trek: The Motion Picture* is probably about as good as we could have expected. It lacks the dazzling brilliance and originality of *2001* (which was an extraordinary one-of-a-kind film). But on its own terms it's a very well-made piece of work, with an interesting premise. The alien spaceship turns out to come from a mechanical or computer civilization, one produced by artificial intelligence and yet poignantly "human" in the sense that it has come all this way to seek out the secrets of its own origins, as we might.

There is, I suspect, a sense in which you can be too sophisticated for your own good when you see a movie like this. Some of the early reviews seemed pretty blasé, as if the critics didn't allow themselves to relish the film before racing out to pigeonhole it. My inclination, as I slid down in my seat and the stereo sound surrounded me, was to relax and let the movie give me a good time. I did and it did.

Star Trek II: The Wrath of Khan
★ ★ ★ ½
PG, 113 m., 1982

William Shatner (Kirk), Leonard Nimoy (Spock), Ricardo Montalban (Khan), DeForest Kelley ("Bones" McCoy), Kirstie Alley (Lieutenant Saavik). Directed by Nicholas Meyer and produced by Robert Sallin. Screenplay by Jack B. Sowards.

This is the movie they should have made the first time. The 1979 *Star Trek: The Motion Picture* cost a lot of money and made a lot of money, but is most often remembered as a dazzling bore. Its makers apparently believed that the qualities that made Star Trek a small-screen cult phenomenon wouldn't make enough of an impact on the big screen. Attempting to fashion a big-budget, special-effects extravaganza, flashy enough to impress audiences weaned on the likes of *2001* and *Star Wars*, they sacrificed the humbler, more human appeal of the original television series. While *Star Trek II* doesn't slight the special effects, the emphasis is back where it belongs: on qualities of character and the twists and turns of plot. Kirk, Spock, and the rest may inhabit the twenty-third century, but the issues they face—love and loyalty, innocence and aging, reason and emotion—are timely and timeless enough to hit home with the twentieth century viewer. This isn't a film just for Trekkies; it's for anyone who enjoys a story well told.

Taking its seed from one of the original television episodes, *Star Trek II* pits the crew of the Starship Enterprise against a marvelously malevolent Ricardo Montalban. Looking like a retiree from a heavy-metal rock 'n' roll band, the long-haired Montalban works himself into a compelling personification of absolute evil and the ravages of revenge. As for the holdovers, they've been given the opportunity by director Nicholas Meyer to broaden their characters, and have generally taken advantage. Fifteen years down the road, William Shatner's Admiral Kirk has been kicked upstairs, leaving Leonard Nimoy's Spock in charge of all the young upstarts on the Enterprise. While the veterans and their original mates struggle with the problems of growing old gracefully, the threat posed by Khan gives them the chance for a glorious last hurrah. They rise to the occasion with even more gusto than the aging jocks in the low-cal beer commercials. The plot is complicated by Kirk's former love interest, an apparently out-of-wedlock son, and the possibility of a new love interest (played attractively by Kirstie Alley, making her film debut). The only time the film drags is during the introduction of the Kirk/Khan feud, which becomes unnecessarily complicated with setting-the-scene detail before settling into a classic good/evil battle.

While much space-adventure fare appeals as pure escapism, *Star Trek II* aims a little higher, at the idealist within us. Taking its cues from *Moby Dick* and *A Tale of Two Cities* (but not heavy-handedly so), the film offers us humanity as we would like it to be, but not in such fantasized fashion that we can't accept it. This is less an escape from

life than an enrichment of it. Outer space, twenty-third century-style, seems like a pretty normal place to be—filled with the deep, rich values of humanity at its best. By comparison, it's this world that's the weird one.

Star Trek III: The Search for Spock
★ ★ ★
PG, 105 m., 1984

William Shatner (Kirk), DeForest Kelley ("Bones" McCoy), James Doohan (Scotty), Walter Koenig (Chekov), George Takei (Sulu), Nichell Nichols (Uhura), Mark Lenard (Sarek), Leonard Nimoy (Spock). Directed by Leonard Nimoy and produced by Harve Bennett. Screenplay by Bennett.

Read no further if you don't want to know whether Mr. Spock is alive at the end of *Star Trek III: The Search for Spock*. But, if you, like me, somehow had the notion that there was a 100 percent chance that they would find Spock (if only so he would be available for *Star Trek IV*), then you will be relieved to learn that his rediscovery and rebirth pay due homage to the complexities of the Vulcan civilization. By the end of this movie, all Mr. Spock has to do is raise one of those famous eyebrows, and the audience cheers.

This is a good but not great *Star Trek* movie, a sort of compromise between the first two. The first film was a disappointment, a *Star Wars* road company that depended on special effects that weren't really that good. The second movie, the best one so far, remembered what made the *Star Trek* TV series so special: not its special effects, not its space opera gimmicks, but its use of science fiction as a platform for programs about human nature and the limitations of intelligence. *Star Trek III* looks for a balance between the first two movies. It has some of the philosophizing and some of the space opera, and there is an extended special effects scene on the exploding planet Genesis that's the latest word in fistfights on the crumbling edges of fiery volcanoes.

There is also a great-looking enemy spaceship that resembles a predatory bird in flight (although why ships in the vacuum of space require wings is still, of course, a question *Star Trek* prefers not to answer).* The ship is commanded by the fairly slow-witted

Klingon warrior Kruge (played by Christopher Lloyd of "Taxi"), who falls for a neat little double cross that is audacious in its simplicity. The movie's plot involves a loyal attempt by the Enterprise crew to return to the planet Genesis in an attempt to reunite Spock's body and spirit. The alien spaceship is in the same sector, attempting to steal the secret of Genesis, a weapon from the last movie that begins by bringing life to dead planets and goes on from there. The showdown between the Klingons and the Enterprise crew resembles, at times, one of those Westerns where first Bart had the draw on Hoppy and then Hoppy had the draw on Bart, but the struggle to the death between Kirk and Kruge takes place against such a great apocalyptic background that we forgive all.

The best thing the *Star Trek* movies have going for them is our familiarity with the TV series. That makes for a sort of storytelling shorthand. At no point during this film, for example, is it ever explained that Vulcans are creatures of logic, not emotion—although we have to know that in order to understand most of the ending. It's not necessary. These characters are under our skins. They resonate, and a thin role in a given story is reinforced by stronger roles in a dozen others. That's sort of reassuring, as (a fanfare, please) the adventure continues.

*Leonard Nimoy sent me a helpful explanation: "The Klingon Bird of Prey has wings for the same reason that our own space shuttle does. It can land in an earth-like atmosphere."

Stardust Memories ★ ★
PG, 89 m., 1980

Woody Allen (Sandy), Charlotte Rampling (Dori), Jessica Harper (Violinist), Marie-Christine Barrault (Frenchwoman). Directed by Woody Allen and produced by Robert Greenhut. Screenplay by Allen.

Woody Allen's *Stardust Memories* is a deliberate homage to *8½*, the 1963 film in which Federico Fellini chronicled several days in the life of a filmmaker who had no idea where to turn next. The major difference between the two films is that Fellini's movie was *about* a director bankrupt of new ideas,

while Allen's is a movie *by* a director with no new ideas. I know that sounds harsh, especially when applied to one of the few American directors who can be counted on for freshness and intelligence, but *Stardust Memories* is an incomplete, unsatisfying film.

The movie begins by acknowledging its sources of visual inspiration. We see a claustrophobic Allen trapped in a railroad car (that's from the opening of *8½*, with Marcello Mastroianni trapped in an auto), and the harsh black and white lighting and the ticking of a clock on the soundtrack give us a cross-reference to the nightmare that opens Ingmar Bergman's *Wild Strawberries*. Are these the exact scenes Allen had in mind? Probably, but no matter; he clearly intends *Stardust Memories* to be his *8½*, and it develops as a portrait of the artist's complaints.

Most of the action of the film centers around two subjects. The first is a weekend film seminar (obviously patterned after Judith Crist's weekends at Tarrytown, N.Y.), to which the Allen character has been invited. The second subject is a very familiar one, Allen's stormy relationships with women. The subjects blend into the basic complaint of the Woody Allen persona we have to come to know and love, and can be summarized briefly: If I'm so famous and brilliant and everybody loves me, then why doesn't anybody *in particular* love me?

At the film seminar, the Allen character is constantly besieged by groupies. They come in all styles: pathetic young girls who want to sleep with him, fans who want his autograph, weekend culture vultures, and people who spend all their time at one event promoting the next one they're attending. Allen makes his point early, by shooting these unfortunate creatures in close-up with a wide-angle lens that makes them all look like Martians with big noses. They add up to a nightmare, a non-stop invasion of privacy, a shrill chorus of people whose praise for the artist is really a call for attention.

Fine, except what *else* does Allen have to say about them? Nothing. In the Fellini film, the director-hero was surrounded by sycophants, business associates, would-be collaborators, wives, mistresses, old friends, all of whom made calls on his humanity. In the Allen picture, there's no depth, no personal context: They're only making calls on his time. What's more, the Fellini character was at least trying to create something, to harass his badgered brain into some feeble act of thought. But the Allen character expresses only impotence, despair, uncertainty, discouragement. All through the film, Allen keeps talking about diseases, catastrophes, bad luck that befalls even the most successful. Yes, but that's what artists are for: to hurl their imagination, joy, and conviction into the silent maw. Sorry if I got a little carried away. *Stardust Memories* inspires that kind of frustration, though, because it's the first Woody Allen film in which impotence has become the situation rather than the problem. This is a movie about a guy who has given up. His relationships with women illustrate that; after the marvelous and complex women in *Annie Hall* and *Manhattan*, in *Stardust Memories* we get a series of enigmas and we never really feel that Allen is connecting with them. These women don't represent failed relationships, they represent walk-throughs.

Woody Allen has always loved jazz and the great mainstream American popular music. There's a lot of it in *Stardust Memories*, but it doesn't amplify or illustrate the scene this time—it steals them. There's a scene where Allen remembers a wonderful spring morning spent with a former love (Charlotte Rampling), and how he looked up in his apartment to see her there, and for a moment felt that life was perfect. As Allen shows that moment, Louis Armstrong sings "Stardust" on the soundtrack, and something happens that should not be allowed to happen. We find our attention almost entirely on Armstrong's wonderfully loose jazz phrasing.

Stardust Memories is a disappointment. It needs some larger idea, some sort of organizing force, to pull together all these scenes of bitching and moaning, and make them lead somewhere.

Starman ★ ★ ★
PG, 112 m., 1984

Jeff Bridges (Starman), Karen Allen (Jenny Hayden), Charles Martin Smith (Mark Shermin), Richard Jaeckel (George Fox). Directed by John Carpenter and produced by Larry J. Franco. Screenplay by Bruce A. Evans and Raynold Gideon.

Starman begins by reminding us of Voyager, that little spacecraft that is even now speeding beyond the solar system. Remember Carl Sagan on the "Tonight" show, explaining to Johnny about all the messages that were on board, in case someday an alien race found this postcard from Earth? Voyager carried greetings in all of the tongues of man, and there is something inevitable about the scene, early in *Starman*, when we get an extraterrestrial visitor who has studied them carefully, and is able to say "hello" a hundred different ways.

The starman of the title is a ball of glowing light. He, or it, has traveled to Earth in response to the invitation from Voyager, but of course the Air Force treats the spacecraft as a possible invader and shoots missiles at it. Knocked off course, the starman lands in rural Wisconsin, where it becomes the identical clone of a dead house painter. The painter's widow (Karen Allen) is stunned when she sees this creature from beyond the grave. It is even more difficult when she realizes this is not her husband, but something infinitely different that just happens to look exactly like her husband. The visitor is very smart, but has a lot to learn, and at first it controls its human host body with a lot of awkward lurching. Meanwhile, government officials led by Richard Jaeckel are seeking the extraterrestrial for "security" reasons, and scientist Charles Martin Smith hopes to get there first and record the historic moment of man's first meeting from a race from another world.

All of this seems like a setup for a science-fiction movie, but what's interesting is the way the director, John Carpenter, makes a U-turn and treats *Starman* as a road movie. The visitor (played by Jeff Bridges) forces Allen to start driving in the direction of the Great Meteor Crater, where he has a rendezvous with his ride home. And as the two characters spend time together as refugees from the search parties, they begin to communicate, and the woman's initial hostility turns into respect and finally into love. This is a wonderfully sweet process, especially as Allen and Bridges go about it. *Starman* contains the potential to be a very silly movie, but the two actors have so much sympathy for their characters that the movie, advertised as space fiction, turns into one of 1984's more touching love stories. Meanwhile, Carpenter provides many of the standard scenes from earlier road movies, including a stop in a roadside diner where the alien's uncertain behavior draws attention. And there's an interlude in Vegas where the extraterrestrial tries to outsmart the slots.

The most interesting thing about *Starman* is probably Bridges's approach to playing a creature from another world. The character grows gradually more human as the film moves along, but he is never completely without glitches: His head movements are birdlike, his step is a little uncertain, he speaks as if there were just a millisecond's delay between brain and tongue. Actors sometimes try to change their appearance; Bridges does something trickier, and tries to convince us that Jeff Bridges is not inhabited by himself. I think he succeeds, and that *Starman* makes Voyager seem like a good investment.

Staying Alive ★
PG, 96 m., 1983

John Travolta (Tony Manero), Cynthia Rhodes (Jackie), Finola Hughes (Laura), Julie Bovasso (Mother). Directed by Sylvester Stallone and produced by Robert Stigwood. Screenplay by Stallone and Norman Wexler.

Staying Alive is a big disappointment. This sequel to the gutsy, electric *Saturday Night Fever* is a slick, cinematic jukebox, a series of self-contained song-and-dance sequences that could be cut apart and played forever on MTV. Like *Flashdance,* it isn't really a movie at all, but an endless series of musical interludes between dramatic scenes that aren't there. It's not even as good as *Flashdance,* but it may appeal to the same audience; it's a Walkman for the eyes.

The movie has an extremely simple plot. Extremely. Six years have passed since Tony Manero (John Travolta) gazed longingly at the lights of Manhattan at the end of *Saturday Night Fever.* Now he lives in a fleabag Manhattan hotel, works as a waiter and a dance instructor, and dates a young dancer

(Cynthia Rhodes) with the patience of a saint. He's still a woman-chaser. But he meets a long-haired British dancer (Finola Hughes) who's his match. She's a queen bitch who takes him to bed and jilts him. Meanwhile, he gets a job as a dancer in her new show and when her lead dancer falters, Tony gets the job. Does this all sound familiar?

The movie was co-authored and directed by Sylvester Stallone, and is the first bad movie he's made. He remembers all the moves from his Rocky plots, but he leaves out the heart—and, even worse, he leaves out the characters. Everybody in *Staying Alive* is Identikit. The characters are clichés, their lives clichés, and God knows their dialogue is clichés. The big musical climaxes are interrupted only long enough for people to shout prepackaged emotional countercharges at each other. There is little attempt to approximate human speech. Like the Rocky movies, *Staying Alive* ends with a big, visually explosive climax. It is so ludicrous it has to be seen to be believed. It's opening night on Broadway. Tony Manero not only dances like a hero, he survives a production number of fire, ice, smoke, flashing lights, and laser beams, throws in an improvised solo—and ends triumphantly by holding Finola Hughes above his head with one arm, like a quarry he has tracked and killed. The musical he is allegedly starring in is something called *Satan's Alley,* but it's so laughably gauche it should have been called *Springtime for Tony.* Stallone makes little effort to convince us we're watching a real stage presentation; there are camera effects the audience could never see, montages that create impossible physical moves, and—most inexplicably of all—a vocal track, even though nobody on stage is singing. It's a mess. Travolta's big dance number looks like a high-tech TV auto commercial that got sick to its stomach.

What I really missed in *Staying Alive* was the sense of reality in *Saturday Night Fever*—the sense that Tony came from someplace and was somebody particular. There's no old neighborhood, no vulgar showdowns with his family (he *apologizes* to his mother for his "attitude"!), and no Brooklyn eccentricity. Tony's world has been cloned into a backstage musical. And not a good one.

Still, the movie has one great moment. A victorious Tony says "I want to strut!" and struts across Times Square while the Bee Gees sing "Stayin' Alive." That could have been the first shot of a great movie. It's the last shot of this one.

Stevie ★ ★ ★ ★
NO MPAA RATING, 102 m., 1981

Glenda Jackson (Stevie Smith), Mona Washbourne (Her Aunt), Alec McCowen (Freddie), Trevor Howard (The Man). Directed and produced by Robert Enders. Screenplay by Hugh Whitemore.

Stevie Smith came across a newspaper clipping one day that told of a man who drowned within a few hundred yards off the shore. The people on the beach saw him waving, and they waved back. The truth, as Stevie expressed it in a famous poem, was the man's problem was just like her own:

I was much too far out all my life
And not waving, but drowning.

In those lines, Stevie Smith made an image of her own life, and it is an image that Glenda Jackson's film *Stevie* expresses with clarity, wit, and love.

Stevie Smith was a British poet of considerable reputation, who died in 1971 at the age of sixty-nine. She spent almost all of her life living in a small home in the London suburb of Palmers Green, where she moved as a child. She worked every day in an office in the city, until her growing reputation as a poet allowed her to take an early retirement. She lived with an old maid aunt, and eventually she became an old maid herself. We watch this process as it is punctuated by a marriage proposal, by a visit to Buckingham Palace for tea with the queen, by a half-hearted suicide attempt. Every night, there was definitely a glass or two or more of sherry, or sometimes gin.

To the world, she must have appeared to be an exemplary example of a talented English eccentric. Her poems were irreverent, sharply satirical, and laconic. She was capable of writing one day:

The Englishwoman is so refined
She has no bosom and no behind.

And on another day, writing about death:

I have a friend
At the end
of the world.
His name is a breath
Of fresh air.

She was not waving, but drowning. The film *Stevie* captures this laconic despair, but it also does a great deal more. It gives us a very particular portrait of a woman's life. The movie is based on a play by Hugh Whitemore, and it contains one of Glenda Jackson's greatest performances. She knows this character well. She played Stevie on the London stage and on a BBC radio production before making this film. She does what great actors can do: She takes a character who might seem uninteresting, and makes us care deeply about the uneventful days of her life.

Although *Stevie* is totally dominated by Jackson's performance, it is not a one-character film by any means. The veteran British actress Mona Washbourne provides a magnificent performance as Stevie's maiden aunt, who is a little dotty and a little giggly and very loving, who likes her glass of sherry and wears flowered print dresses that Stevie says look like a seed catalog illustration titled "They All Came Up." Alec McCowen plays Freddie, the not-so-young man who comes calling, and whose proposal Stevie rejects. And the wonderful Trevor Howard has an ambiguous part as "the man." On one level, "the man" is just someone she met at a literary party and conned into giving her a rides to poetry readings. At another level, especially when he is seen by himself, telling us about Stevie and reading some of her lines, he is the understanding, forgiving father figure Stevie never had.

Movies like *Stevie* run the risk of looking like photographs of stage plays, but *Stevie* somehow never feels that way. Even though it uses the artifices of the stage (including remarks addressed by Glenda Jackson directly to the audience), and even though a lot of its dialogue is poetry, *Stevie* always feels as if it occupies this woman's life. She is the poet, we are her confidantes, and it is a privilege to get to know her. I have perhaps given the impression that *Stevie* is grim and depressing. It is not at all. It is very sad at times, of course, but there are other times of good humor and barbed wit, when she's not drowning, but waving.

The Sting II ★ ★
PG, 102 m., 1983

Jackie Gleason (Gondorff), Mac Davis (Hooker), Teri Garr (Veronica), Karl Malden (Macalinski), Oliver Reed (Lonnegan), Bert Remsen (Kid Colors), Harry James (Bandleader). Directed by Jeremy Paul Kagan and produced by Jennings Lang. Screenplay by David S. Ward.

The Sting II is a good-looking, handsomely mounted production, but it has one unavoidable problem: We've already seen *The Sting.* Now the beauty of that 1973 movie, which starred Robert Redford and Paul Newman and won the Academy Award for best picture, was that it was a constant delight. When we saw its elaborate cons unfolding, we didn't know *what* to believe. This time, though, with *The Sting II*, we know exactly what to believe: nothing. If the basic premise of a movie is that nothing is quite as it seems, then every time we're given a new piece of information, we automatically disbelieve it. That has a tendency to undermine our wonderment as *Sting II* springs its astonishments on us. And that would be the case even if the actors in this movie didn't have an unfortunate tendency to draw back and almost smirk before making their startling revelations.

The movie, I must say, looks great. It's set in New York in 1940, a world of nightclubs, fight rings, long limousines, silk scarves, silk lingerie, and champagne. Jackie Gleason inhabits this world as if he were born to it, and, indeed, in his heyday on television he created an image a lot like the life-style of his character here, a con man named Fargo Gondorff. His partners in the cons are Mac Davis and Teri Garr; his enemy when the movie opens is the slimy Oliver Reed, and his eventual target is a rich gangster played by Karl Malden.

By listing those names, though, I've edged into another problem this movie has: low energy. The original *Sting* was a light-footed, lighthearted, sly comedy that Redford, Newman and Robert Shaw danced through with meticulous timing. In *Sting II*,

Garr and Davis try to liven things up, but Malden, Reed, and even Gleason aren't much help. Malden is too serious and thoughtful for this movie; Reed is ponderous; and Gleason seems to be reading his lines and making his moves at three-quarter speed.

The Sting II is craftily calculated, however, from beginning to end. It doesn't hedge a single bet. It was produced by Jennings Lang, a likable, powerful veteran at Universal Pictures, whose career has specialized in retreads: He produced three of the *Airport* pictures and the remake of *The Front Page* and *Little Miss Marker,* as well as *Earthquake,* which was a recycled disaster picture. In *The Sting II,* he borrows from all over: His screenplay is by David Ward, who did the original picture; his music, by Lalo Schifrin, leans on the original Marvin Hamlisch score, and his ending borrows not only from *The Sting* but even from the *Rocky* movies; this film uses a big prizefight for its climax. My basic reaction was, so what? Most sequels are unnecessary, and this isn't even a sequel, really.

Stir Crazy ★ ★
R, 111 m., 1980

Gene Wilder (Skip Donahue), Richard Pryor (Harry Monroe), Georg Stanford Brown (Rory), Jobeth Williams (Meredith). Directed by Sidney Poitier and produced by Hannah Weinstein. Screenplay by Bruce Jay Friedman.

Stir Crazy seems to change its mind, halfway through, about the kind of movie it wants to be. It starts strong: It's a comedy that teams up Gene Wilder and Richard Pryor. It gives them crazy things to do, like working as performing chickens, but it also gives them interesting characters. Wilder is a playwright, Pryor is an actor, they're both out of work, and they decide to head West and seek their fortunes.

So far, great—right up to the case of mistaken identities that lands them in court. Their courtroom scene is one of the movie's high points. Their lawyer has persuaded them to plead guilty in hope of a light sentence, but they're given 125 years apiece. Wilder begins a monosyllabic scream: "Wa! Wa! Wa!" Pryor tries to explain that everything was Wilder's idea. The movie has started well and at this point it looks like it could develop into a terrific comedy.

But it doesn't. Instead, once Wilder and Pryor are thrown into prison, it seems to lose its way. There are still some funny scenes to come, especially those involving a gigantic murderer named Grossburger (who is played by Erland Van Lidth de Jeude, the motorcycle gang leader in *The Wanderers*). But, inexplicably, the movie gets bogged down in developing its own plot. That is not always the best thing for a comedy to do, because if we're not laughing it hardly matters what happens to the plot.

But to the plot: The warden of the prison has a long-standing rivalry with another warden, and they bet on the outcome of rodeos held between the inmates at their prisons. After Wilder amazingly turns out to be a "natural cowboy" who can ride any bronco, Wilder and Pryor get involved in a scheme to escape during the prison rodeo. This is a deadly mistake for the movie. We get a long, boring rodeo sequence, intercut with the repetitious process of escape. The escape route involves slipping under a loose board and climbing under the grandstand, and sneaking out of a ventilation panel and into a peanut vendor's wagon, and on and on, and about four different characters travel this route when one would have been plenty.

So that's what's wrong with the construction of this movie. The employment of Wilder and Pryor falls in another category. The movie was directed by Sidney Poitier (this is his fifth directorial job), and either Poitier or the producers made a tactical error in making Wilder the more aggressive character and Pryor the laid-back one. This is casting against type, all right: Wilder is brilliant at being meek and laid-back, and Pryor is a genius when he's allowed to be hyper. But it just doesn't feel right when Wilder goes for the high notes and Pryor hangs back.

And that's a shame, because good comedies are hard to make and this one shows a lot of promise. What went wrong? Maybe everybody got too absorbed in the details of the rodeo and the escape plan? It's possible. But long, complicated courses of action do not necessarily suit themselves to comedy, and when the characters get absorbed in them they're not free to react in comic ways.

Stop Making Sense ★ ★ ★ ½
NO MPAA RATING, 88 m., 1984

With the Talking Heads: David Byrne, Chris Frantz, Jerry Harrison, and Tina Weymouth. Guest musicians: Edna Holt, Lynn Mabry, Steve Scales, Alex Weir, and Bernie Worrell. Directed by Jonathan Demme and produced by Gary Goetzman.

The overwelming impression throughout *Stop Making Sense* is of enormous energy, of life being lived at a joyous high. And it's not the frenetic, jangled-nerves energy of a rock band that's wired; it's the high spirits and good health we associate with artists like Bruce Springsteen. There are a lot of reasons to see concert films, but the only ones that usually get mentioned are the music and the cinematography. This time the actual physical impact of the film is just as exhilarating: Watching the Talking Heads in concert is a little like rock 'n' roll crossed with "Jane Fonda's Workout." The movie was shot during two live performances of the Talking Heads, a New York rock band that centers on the remarkable talent of its lead singer, David Byrne. Like David Bowie, his stage presence shows the influence of mime, and some of his best effects in *Stop Making Sense* are achieved with outsize costumes and hand-held lights that create shadow plays on the screen behind him.

Given all the showmanship that will develop later during the film, the opening sequences are a low-key, almost anticoncert throwaway. Byrne walks on a bare stage with a ghetto-blaster in his hand, puts it down on the stage, turns it on and sings along with "Psycho Killer." Eventually he is joined onstage by Tina Weymouth on bass. Then stagehands wander out from the wings and being to assemble a platform for drummer Chris Frantz. Gear is moved into place. Electical cables are attached. The backup singers, Edna Holt and Lynn Mabry, appear. And the concert inexorably picks up tempo.

The music of the Talking Heads draws from many sources, in addition to traditional rock 'n' roll. You can hear the echoes, in Byrne's voice, of one of his heroes, country singer Hank Williams. In the music itself, there are elements of reggae and of gospel, especially in the driving repetitions of single phrases that end some of the songs. What is particularly delightful is that the Talking Heads *are* musical: For people who have passed over that invisible divide into the age group when rock sounds like noise, the Heads will sound like music.

The film is good to look at. The director is Jonathan Demme *(Melvin and Howard)*, making his first concert film, and essentially using the visuals of the Talking Heads rather than creating his own. Instead of the standard phony cutaways to the audience (phony because, nine times out of ten, the audience members are not actually reacting to the moment in the music that we're hearing), Demme keeps his cameras trained on the stage. And when Byrne and company use the stage-level lights to create a shadow play behind them, the result is surprisingly more effective than you might imagine: It's a live show with elements of *Metropolis*.

But the film's peak moments come through Byrne's simple physical presence. He jogs in place with his sidemen; he runs around the stage; he seems so happy to be alive and making music. Like Springsteen and Prince, he serves as a reminder of how sour and weary and strung-out many rock bands have become. Starting with Mick Jagger, rock concerts have become, for the performers, as much sporting events as musical and theatrical performances. *Stop Making Sense* understands that with great exuberance.

Stranger than Paradise ★ ★ ★ ★
R, 90 m., 1984

John Lurie (Willie), Eszter Balint (Eva), Richard Edson (Eddie), Cecilia Stark (Aunt Lottie), Danny Rosen (Billy), Rammellzee (Man with Money), Tom Decillo (Airline Agent). Directed by Jim Jarmusch and produced by Sara Driver. Screenplay by Jarmusch.

Stranger than Paradise is filmed in a series of uninterrupted shots; the picture fades in, we watch the scene, and when the scene is over, there's a fade to black. Then comes the next fade-in. This is not a gimmick, but a visual equivalent of the film's deadpan characters, who take a lot to get excited.

The movie's hero is Willie (John Lurie), who arrived on these shores from Hungary about ten years ago, and has spent the intervening decade perfecting his New York accent and trying to make nothing out of himself. He lives in an apartment where the linoleum is the highlight. On a good day, he'll sleep late, hang out, play a little poker. His cousin Eva arrives from Budapest. This is the last thing he needs, a 16-year-old girl who needs a place to stay. She hates him, too. But she has to kill some time before she goes to Cleveland to live with her aunt Lottie. She has good taste in American music, but not according to him. Willie's friend, Eddie, comes over occasionally and eyeballs Eva. Nothing much happens. She leaves for Cleveland.

The screen is filled with large letters: ONE YEAR LATER. This in itself is funny, that we'd get such a momentous time cue in a movie where who even knows what day it is. Eddie and Willie get in some trouble over a poker game and Eddie suddenly remembers Willie's cousin in Cleveland. They go to see her. It is cold in Cleveland. Eva has bought the American Dream and is working in a fast-food outlet. They all go to look at the lake, which is frozen. Aunt Lottie turns out to make Clara Peller look like Dame Peggy Ashcroft. The guys say to hell with it and head for Florida. Then they come back and get Eva and take her along with them. They have a postcard that makes Florida look like paradise, but they wind up living at one of those hotels where the permanent guests live in the woodwork. Everything goes sour. Eva wants to go back to Hungary. The guys lose all their money at the dog races. Creeps start hanging around. It will take a miracle to give this movie an upbeat ending. There is a miracle.

Stranger than Paradise is a treasure from one end to the other. I saw it for the first time at the 1984 Cannes Film Festival, where it was having its first public showing. Half the people in the theater probably didn't speak English, but that didn't stop them from giving the movie a standing ovation, and it eventually won the Camera d'Or prize for the best first film. It is like no other film you've seen, and yet you feel right at home in it. It seems to be going nowhere, and knows every step it wants to make. It is a constant, almost kaleidoscopic experience of discovery, and we try to figure out what the film is up to and it just keeps moving steadfastly ahead, fade in, fade out, fade in, fade out, making a mountain out of a molehill.

Streamers ★ ★ ★ ★
R, 118 m., 1984

Matthew Modine (Billy), Michael Wright (Carlyle), Mitchell Lichtenstein (Richie), David Alan Grier (Roger), Guy Boyd (Rooney), George Dzundza (Cokes). Directed by Robert Altman and produced by Altman and Nick H. Mileti. Screenplay by David Rabe.

Robert Altman's *Streamers* is one of the most intense and intimate dramas I've ever seen on film. It's based on the play by David Rabe, about young soldiers waiting around a barracks for their orders to go to Vietnam. Most directors, faced with a play that takes place on one set, find ways to "open it up" and add new locations. Altman has moved in the opposite direction, taking advantage of the one-room set to tighten the play until it squeezes like a vise. Watching this film is such a demanding experience that both times I've seen it, it has been too much for some viewers, and they've left. Those who stay, who survive the difficult passages of violence, will find at the end of the film a conclusion that is so poetic and moving it succeeds in placing the tragedy in perspective.

It is the era of Vietnam. In a barracks somewhere, three young men wait for their orders. They are Billy, who is white and middle-class; Roger, who is black and middle-class; and Richie, a dreamy young man who likes to tease the others with hints that he is a homosexual. The only other occupants of the barracks are two drunken master sergeants, Rooney and Cokes, who are best friends and who are stumbling through idiotic revelry in an attempt to drown the realization that Cokes has leukemia. Into this little world comes Carlyle, an angry young black man who is gay, and whose conversations with Richie will lead the others into anger and denial before the situation finally explodes.

There are some surprises, but the developments in *Streamers* flow so naturally out of the material that its surprises should be left intact. A lot can be said, however, about the acting, Altman's direction, and Rabe's writing. I didn't see this play on stage and don't know how it worked there, but Altman is so completely the visual master of this material that we're drawn into that barracks room and into its rhythms of boredom, drunkenness, and passion.

The actors are all unknown to me, except for George Dzundza, who plays Cokes. They are all so natural that the dialogue has an eerie double quality: We know it's written dialogue because it has a poetry and a drama unlikely in life, but Rabe's ear is so accurate it sounds real, and the performers make it so convincing there's never a false note. The two key performances are by Mitchell Lichtenstein, as Richie, and Michael Wright, as Carlyle. Richie is indeed homosexual, as we realize long before his barracks mates are willing to acknowledge it. He likes to tease the others with insinuations that they may be gay, too. Billy boasts that he is straight, but he protests too much. Roger tries to be a peacekeeper. Then Carlyle wanders in from another unit. He is drunk and angry, collapses, sleeps it off, blearily looks around, figures out Richie, and tries to make a connection.

But there is a lot more going on here than sexual competition. *Streamers* uses both sex and race as foreground subjects while the movie's real subject, war, hovers in the background and in several extraordinary monologues—one about snakes, one about a battle, and one about the realities of parachuting. As the veteran master sergeants make their drunken way through the movie, they drop these hard realities into the lives of the unseasoned kids. And when anger turns to violence and a tragedy occurs, it is up to one of the fat old guys (Dzundza) to deliver a monologue that is one of the most revealing, intimate, honest, and moving speeches I've ever heard.

Streets of Fire ★ ★ ★
PG, 93 m., 1984

Michael Pare (Tom Cody), Diane Lane (Ellen Aim), Amy Madigan (McCoy), Rich Moranis (Billy Fish), William Dafoe (Raven), Deborah Van Valkenburgh (Reva). Directed by Walter Hill and produced by Lawrence Gordon and Joel Silver. Written by Hill and Larry Gross.

Walter Hill's *Streets of Fire* begins by telling us it's a "rock 'n' roll fable . . . from another time, another place." The movie is right on the rock 'n' roll, but the alternative time and place are mysteriously convincing—especially if, like me, you believe the most beautiful postwar American cars were Studebakers. In this world, Studebakers made it. All the cops in this movie drive circa 1950 Studebakers, and all the people in the movie live in the shadow of oppressive elevated tracks, in a shabby, nighttime city inhabited mostly by cops, street gangs, rock fans, and soda jerks.

The movie begins with the kidnapping of a rock singer (Diane Lane), who is muscled off the stage by some Hell's Angels types. But first we get one of the few original approaches to rock concert photography: Full-stage photography of the singers is combined with black foreground silhouettes of the audience, waving their hands and clapping. The effect is a little like a Roger Brown painting, and it works: This looks like it's going to be a new approach to the basic street and rock images. Unfortunately, the movie doesn't live up to its opening. It turns into your basic fable about warring street gangs, with a superman (Michael Pare) and his tough female accomplice (Amy Madigan) breaking into the headquarters of the rival gang and bringing Diane Lane back alive. This ground has been covered before, most obviously in Hill's *The Warriors*, a controversial 1978 thriller that was credited with inspiring more fights in its audience than on the screen.

Hill likes characters who are broadly symbolic. He occasionally gives us people who are individuals (as in his most successful film, *48 Hours*, with Eddie Murphy and Nick Nolte). But mostly he likes characters who stand tall and represent good or evil and settle the matters of the universe with unlimited violence. That's what we get this time. What we also get is some interesting atmosphere, which owes a lot to the art direction and the background musical score by Ry Cooder. Hill came to Chicago to shoot some of his blasted landscapes of barren warehouses under ominous L tracks, and matched them with back-lot sets at Universal that suggest a city where gentrification never caught on. The cops are corrupt in this fictional city, the gangs rule the streets, and there are districts where you've got to be armed.

Side-by-side with this paramilitary society is a world of art nouveau theater marquees, corny soda fountains, and the rock singer's manager (Rick Moranis), who wears checked sport coats and bow ties and looks like the creep of the class of '57. The language is strange, too: It's tough, but not with 1984 toughness. It sounds like the way really mean guys would have talked in the late 1950s, only with a few words different—as if this world evolved a slightly different language. The performances fit this world nicely. The most engaging character is Amy Madigan's McCoy, an Army veteran who smokes cigars, blast bikers to smithereens, and tells Pare he ain't her type. Pare is your basic taciturn, implacable Hill hero, and Diane Lane has so much of the right energy in the opening concert scene that we wonder why there wasn't a lot more rock 'n' roll in the movie. Also more Studebakers, please.

Streetwise ★ ★ ★ ★
R, 92 m., 1985 ✓

Directed by Martin Bell and produced by Cheryl McCall. Reported by Mary Ellen Mark.

The mother is being frank about her daughter. She says she knows the girl is working as a prostitute, but she figures "it's just a phase she's going through." Her daughter is about fifteen years old. That is not the most harrowing moment in *Streetwise*, a heartbreaking documentary about the street children of Seattle. There are worse moments, for example the one where a street kid tries to talk to her mother about the fact that her stepfather "was fooling around . . . doing perverted things with me" when she was a baby. "Yes," says the mother philosophically, "but now he's stopped."

The subject of runaway, abducted, and abandoned children has received a lot of attention in the news, but never anything remotely like *Streetwise*, which enters into the lives of these under-age survivors as they fight for life and love on the streets of Seattle. The movie was inspired by a *Life* magazine article on a group of the kids, who, at an age when other kids are in school, are learning to be hookers, thieves, con men, pushers, and junkies. Now comes this movie, which contains extraordinary everyday footage, which the filmmakers obtained by spending months hanging out with the kids, until they gained their trust and their cameras became accepted.

The street kids lead horrifying lives, but sometimes there are moments of acceptance and happiness. They cling to each other. They relate uneasily with a social worker who seems philosophically resigned to the facts of street life. They try to dodge the cops. They live in an abandoned hotel, get money by begging and prostitution, eat by raiding the dumpsters behind restaurants. They even have a system for marking garbage so they don't eat food that's too old.

What is amazing is that some of these kids are still in touch with their parents. One girl shrugs that her mother is off to the woods for a weekend: "I've always known she don't love me or shit. So OK." She hugs herself. Another girl tries to talk to her mother, who says, "Be quiet. I'm drinking." A kid named DeWayne goes to visit his father in prison and gets a long lecture about smoking, drinking, and taking drugs, and a pie-in-the-sky speech about how they're going to open a thrift shop when the old man gets out of prison. The next time we see DeWayne, it is at his funeral; he hanged himself in a jail cell.

You walk out of *Streetwise* realizing that these aren't bad kids. They are resourceful, tough, and true to their own standards. They break the law, but then how many legal ways are there for fourteen-year-olds to support themselves? They talk about their parents in a matter-of-fact way that, we suspect, covers up great wounds, as when one girl says she's never met her natural father— "unless maybe I dated him once."

Streetwise is surprising for the frankness of the material it contains. How did the filmmakers get these people to say these things, to allow the cameras into their lives? We see moments of intimacy, of violence, of pain. The answer, I suspect, is that a lot of these kids were so starving for attention and affection that by offering both, the filmmakers were able to get whatever they wanted. Some of the scenes are possibly staged, in the sense that the characters are aware they are in a movie, but none of the scenes are false or contrived. These are children living rough in an American city, and you would blame their parents if you didn't see that the parents are just as alienated and hopeless, and that before long these kids will be damaged parents, too.

Stripes ★ ★ ★ ½
R, 105 m., 1981

Bill Murray (John), Harold Ramis (Russell), Warren Oates (Sergeant Hulka), P.J. Soles (Stella), Sean Young (Louise), John Candy (Ox). Directed by Ivan Reitman and produced by Reitman and Dan Goldberg. Screenplay by Goldberg, Len Blum, and Harold Ramis.

Stripes is an anarchic slob movie, a celebration of all that is irreverent, reckless, foolhardy, undisciplined, and occasionally scatalogical. It's a lot of fun. It comes from some of the same people involved in *National Lampoon's Animal House,* and could have been titled *National Lampoon's Animal Army* with little loss of accuracy. As a comedy about a couple of misfits who find themselves in the U.S. Army's basic training program, it obviously resembles Goldie Hawn's *Private Benjamin.* But it doesn't duplicate that wonderful movie; they could play on the same double feature. *Stripes* has the added advantage of being a whole movie about the Army, rather than half a movie (*Private Benjamin* got sidetracked with Hawn's love affair).

The movie is not only a triumph for its stars (Bill Murray and Harold Ramis) and its director (Ivan Reitman), but a sort of vindication. To explain: Reitman directed, and Murray starred in, the enormously successful *Meatballs,* which was an entertaining enough comedy but awfully ragged. No wonder. It was shot on a shoestring with Canadian tax shelter money. What Murray and Reitman prove this time is that, given a decent budget, they can do superior work— certainly superior to *Meatballs,* for starters. For Harold Ramis, who plays Murray's grave-eyed, flat-voiced, terminally detached partner in *Stripes,* this is a chance, at last, to come out from behind the camera. Ramis and Murray are both former Second City actors, but in Hollywood, Ramis has been typecast as a writer (*Animal House, Meat-*

balls, Caddyshack), maybe because he sometimes looks too goofy for Hollywood's unimaginative tastes.

In *Stripes,* Murray and Ramis make a wonderful team. Their big strength is restraint. Given the tendency of movies like this to degenerate into undisciplined slapstick, they wisely choose to play their characters as understated, laid-back anarchists. Murray enlists in the Army in a what-the-hell mood after his girlfriend throws him out, and Ramis enlists because one stupid gesture deserves another. They're older than the usual Army recruit, less easily impressed with gung-ho propaganda, and quietly amazed at their drill instructor, Sergeant Hulka, who is played by Warren Oates with tough-as-nails insanity.

The movie has especially good writing in several scenes. My favorite comes near the beginning, during a session when recruits in the new platoon get to know one another. One obviously psycho draftee, who looks like Robert De Niro, quietly announces that if his fellow soldiers touch him, touch his stuff, or interfere in any way with his person or his privacy, he will quite simply be forced to kill them. Sergeant Hulka replies: "Lighten up!"

The movie's plot follows basic training, more or less, during its first hour. Then a romance enters. Murray and Ramis meet a couple of cute young military policewomen (P.J. Soles and Sean Young), and they happily violate every rule in the book. One funny scene: Murray and Soles sneak into the kitchen of the base commander's house and do unprecedented things with kitchen utensils.

It's an unwritten law of these movies that the last half hour has to involve some kind of spectacular development. In *Animal House,* it was the homecoming parade. In *Stripes,* the climax involves the Army's latest secret weapon, which is a computerized, armored, nuclear weapons carrier disguised as a recreational vehicle. Murray's platoon is assigned to go to Europe and test it. Murray, Ramis, and their girls decide to test it during a weekend holiday swing through the Alps. After they inadvertently cross the Iron Curtain, all hell breaks loose.

Stripes is a complete success on its intended level—it's great, irreverent entertainment—but it was successful, too, as a breakthrough for Ramis, Reitman, and Murray, on their way to *Ghostbusters.* Comedy is one of the hardest film genres to work in. Nobody knows all its secrets, not even Woody Allen and Mel Brooks. Here's a comedy from people who know some of the secrets most of the time.

Stroker Ace ★ ½
PG, 96 m., 1983

Burt Reynolds (Stroker Ace), Ned Beatty (Clyde Torkle), Jim Nabors (Lugs), Parker Stevenson (Aubrey James), Loni Anderson (Pembrook Feeney), Cassandra Peterson (Girl with Lugs). Directed by Hal Needham and produced by Hank Moonjean. Screenplay by Hugh Wilson and Needham.

Burt Reynolds used to make movies about people's life-styles. Here he seems more interested in making movies that fit in with his own life-style. *Stroker Ace* is another in a series of essentially identical movies he has made with director Hal Needham, and although it's allegedly based on a novel, it's really based on their previous hits like *Smokey and the Bandit* and *The Cannonball Run.* To call the movie a lightweight, bubble-headed entertainment is not criticism but simply description. This movie is so determined to be inconsequential that it's actually capable of showing horrible, fiery racing crashes and then implying that nobody got hurt. The plot involves a feud between two NASCAR drivers (played by Reynolds and Parker Stevenson) who specialize in sideswiping each other at 140 miles per hour in the middle of a race. I don't think that's a very slick idea.

Reynolds plays the same basic Good Ol' Boy he's refined for years—the sly, woman-chasing character with a couple of good buddies and an eye on the big time. He needs somebody to sponsor his car, and he ends up with Clyde Torkle, a fried chicken king who is played by Ned Beatty with a low bow in the directions of Colonel Sanders and Jackie Gleason. Torkle makes Reynolds paint the slogan "Fastest Chicken in the West!" on the side of his car. This provides most of the dramatic conflict in the movie.

Reynolds's sidekick is an auto mechanic named Lugs (Jim Nabors), and the romantic interest is Loni Anderson. She plays a Sunday-school teacher who doesn't drink and is a virgin. So Reynolds slips her some champagne, gets her drunk and, in an unpleasant, unfunny, and creepy scene, semi-undresses her while making small talk to her unconscious body. Loni Anderson is so innocuous in this movie, they must have given her the wrong script. The movie is stolen in the sex-symbol department by a creature named Cassandra Peterson,* who has a dynamite scene with Jim Nabors. She has long black hair and a ton of eye makeup and looks like a cross between Gina Lollobrigida and Vampirella. She's the best thing in the movie.

Which brings us to the director. Hal Needham is a onetime stunt coordinator who was a legend in his field. He moved up to directing with encouragement from his old buddy Reynolds, and together they've made several *Smokey*-type movies. There is hardly a spark of inspiration in any of those films, but Reynolds can sell anything, even Needham's lead-footed direction. If Reynolds were prepared to work with a good director, he might be hailed as the superb romantic comedian he is, rather than as the assembly line product he seems determined to become.

*a.k.a. "Elvira," hostess of TV horror movies.

The Stunt Man ★ ★
R, 129 m., 1980

Peter O'Toole (Eli Cross), Steve Railsback (Cameron), Barbara Hershey (Nina Franklin), Allen Goorwitz (Sam), Alex Rocco (Jake), Sharon Farrell (Denise), Adam Roarke (Bailey), Philip Bruns (Ace). Directed and produced by Richard Rush. Screenplay by Lawrence B. Marcus and Rush.

Richard Rush's *The Stunt Man* is like one of those sets of Chinese boxes, each one with another box inside, growing smaller and smaller until finally there is nothing left at all. I don't mean that as a criticism; the film is intended to be seen in that way, as a cinematic puzzle in which there are no answers and the only question is that old standby—what is reality? The movie takes place on the set of a movie, a World War I flying daredevils-type picture of the sort that

hasn't been made since *The Blue Max*. Peter O'Toole plays the director of the film-with-in-the-film, supplying a heavily mannered performance that somehow succeeds in winning us over with its very unlikeliness. He's so very arch and fey that we realize no one like this could really exist—except, possibly, in real life.

This movie set is a chamber of horrors that already has claimed one victim, a stunt man drowned when his car crashed off a bridge. Was his death an accident? Or is O'Toole a maniac who arranged it? Who knows? The movie deliberately teases us with the possibilities. And then the hero (Steve Railsback) stumbles into the picture and, before long, onto the picture. Railsback is wanted by the cops. He has to hide out. O'Toole discovers his secret and offers him a job, replacing the missing stunt man. Railsback has little choice but to accept, and before long, blackmailed by O'Toole, he's doing the most difficult stunts himself. The only problem is that some of the stunts seem a little too real. Railsback begins to suspect that O'Toole really wants to kill him, either in the service of cinematic art or for some sadistic private purpose. And that is essentially the situation the film repeats, over and over, scene after scene, all the way to the end.

That's what bothered me. I caught on right away (it didn't take much deep thought) that the method of the movie was to deceive and mislead me. Because the ability to do that is completely within the director's ability—because I can know only what he chooses to tell me—I found the movie's approach more frustrating than challenging. *The Stunt Man* is like magic tricks done by a magician in a movie: It doesn't matter how well they're done, or even if they're really done, because cinematic special effects make it all trickery, anyway.

There's a great deal in the film that I admire: that weird O'Toole performance, Railsback's pluckiness not only as a character but also as an actor put through incredible trials, and the movie's stunts themselves. But there were times when I felt cheated. Some of the stunts are staged so that they're not only deceiving to Railsback, as intended, but plainly impossible. And I never understood why O'Toole is lifted in a director's crane even when he wasn't working—and why his offscreen activities were lit like a movie.

The stunts were also sneaky. At one moment in particular, Railsback's on a tower that's blown up in flames. We think there's no way he could have escaped alive—and the movie merely cuts to another shot of him, without explaining his escape. A film that depends on deceiving us has got to play by its own rules. If we are going to be deceived in general, fine, but then we can't be cheated on particulars.

Sudden Impact ★ ★ ★
R, 117 m., 1983

Clint Eastwood (Harry Callahan), Sondra Locke (Jennifer Spencer), Pat Hingle (Chief Jannings), Bradford Dillman (Captain Briggs). Directed and produced by Clint Eastwood. Screenplay by Joseph C. Stinson.

Most of what you hear about pop art and pop culture is pure hype. But there comes a moment about halfway through *Sudden Impact*, a Dirty Harry movie, when you realize that Harry has achieved some kind of legitimate pop status, as the purest distillation in the movies of the spirit of vengeance. To all those cowboy movies we saw in our youth, all those TV westerns and cop dramas and war movies, Dirty Harry has brought a great simplification: A big man, a big gun, a bad guy, and instant justice.

We learned early to cheer when John Wayne shot the bad guys. We cheered when the cavalry turned up, or the Yanks, or the SWAT team. What Eastwood's Dirty Harry movies do is very simple. They reduce the screen time between those cheers to the absolute minimum. *Sudden Impact* is a Dirty Harry movie with only the good parts left in. All the slow stuff, such as character, motivation, atmosphere, and plot, has been pared to exactly the minimum necessary to hold together the violence. This movie has been edited with the economy of a thirty-second commercial. As a result, it's a great audience picture. It's not plausible, it doesn't make much sense, it has a cardboard villain and, for that matter, a hero who exists more as a set of functions (grin, fight, chase, kill) than as a human being. But none of those are valid objections. *Sudden Impact* is more like a music video; it consists only of

setups and payoffs, its big scenes are self-contained, it's filled with kinetic energy, and it has a short attention span. That last is very important, because if anyone were really keeping track of what Callahan does in this movie, Harry would be removed from the streets after his third or fourth killing. Dirty Harry movies are like Roadrunner cartoons; the moment a body is dead, it is forgotten, and nobody stands around to dispose of the corpses.

The movie's basically a revenge tragedy. A young woman (Sondra Locke) and her sister are sexually attacked at a carnival by a group of quasi-human bullies. The sister goes nuts, and Locke vows vengeance. One by one, she tracks down the rapists, and murders them by shooting them in the genitals and forehead. Dirty Harry gets assigned to the case, and the rest is a series of violent confrontations. Occasionally there's comic relief, in the form of Harry's meetings with his superiors, and his grim-jawed putdowns of anyone who crosses his path. ("Suck fish heads," he helpfully advises one man.)

If the movie has a weakness, it's the plot. Because I'm not sure the plot is relevant to the success of the film, I'm not sure that's a weakness. The whole business of Locke's revenge is so mechanically established and carried out that it's automatic, and because she has a "good" motive for her murders, she doesn't make an interesting villain. If Eastwood could create a villain as single-minded, violent, economically chiseled, and unremittingly efficient as Dirty Harry Callahan, then we'd be onto something.

Supergirl ★ ★
PG, 105 m., 1984

Helen Slater (Supergirl), Faye Dunaway (Selena), Peter O'Toole (Zaltar), Mia Farrow (Alura), Brenda Vaccaro (Bianca), Peter Cook (Nigel), Simon Ward (Zor-El). Directed by Jeannot Szwarc and produced by Timothy Burrill. Screenplay by David Odell.

The best way to approach *Supergirl* is through a statement by Clint Eastwood, who once observed that his spaghetti Westerns worked only because he played them completely seriously. In the famous scene where he shoots three guys with one bullet, if the faintest wisp of a smile had creased his lips, the whole power of the scene would have been destroyed. Only by playing it straight did he make the scene work—and it worked, incidentally, as comedy.

Supergirl doesn't know that. When it goes for campy laughs, it falls flat on its face. That also was a tendency the three Superman movies had to fight. The first two Supermans were the best, because they took the essentially silly legend of Superman and played it quasi-seriously. With the second sequel, the stories got goofier, with Richard Pryor going for slapstick. But remember the opening moments of *Superman*, with Marlon Brando as Jor-El, lending an expensive but authentic solemnity to the film? And then the clean-cut Midwestern images of Superman's childhood, with Glenn Ford no less, as his father? By playing the story straight and simple, and allowing the laughs to flow naturally out of the material (as when Clark Kent did a double-take at one of those new-style phone booths), the movie became a popular triumph.

If *Supergirl* had only taken the same approach, it might have been a pretty good movie. But it trivializes itself with an almost suicidal glee. That's a shame, because there's a place, I think, for a female superhero, and Helen Slater, who plays Supergirl, has the kind of freshness, good health, high spirits, and pluck that would be just right for the character. As it is, Slater is the best thing in the film. She shares with Christopher Reeve the ability to wear a funny costume and not look ridiculous. We look at her and we see Supergirl. We look around her and we see the results of a gag-writer's convention.

The movie begins with the usual legend-building. We learn that after the planet Krypton was destroyed, little Superman was not the only survivor. While his rocket sped him toward Earth, another fragment of Krypton was hurtled into inner space, where Zaltar (Peter O'Toole), one of the survivors, created a utopian society. One day, alas, while Supergirl was out playing, she toyed with one of the new world's energy sources, and was transported to Earth, along with the source itself. That creates a giant struggle for possession of the source, which could give its owner the usual dividend, control of the Earth. And it's about here that the movie starts to break down, with the intro-

duction of Faye Dunaway as a mysterious fortune-teller, and the even less-fortunate introduction of Brenda Vaccaro as her side-kick. The relationship between the two women reminds me of *Mommie Dearest* in search of daughters.

The appearance of *Supergirl*, so soon after *Superman III*, is an indication that the producers of the Superman movies have forgotten, if they ever consciously knew it, the real secret of the movies. We do not go to Superman and Supergirl movies to laugh condescendingly at the characters (which is what the writers, directors, and even some of the actors have started to do). We go to recapture some of the lost innocence of the whole notion of superheroes. The gift of Christopher Reeve, in his best scenes and when the filmmakers allow it, is to play Superman without laughing, to take him seriously so that we can have some innocent escapist fun. Helen Slater has the same gift, but is given even less chance to exercise it in *Supergirl*, and the result is an unhappy, unfunny, unexciting movie. Why even go to the trouble of making a movie that feels like it's laughing at itself?

Superman II ★ ★ ★ ★
PG, 127 m., 1981

Christopher Reeve (Superman/Clark Kent), Gene Hackman (Lex Luthor), Ned Beatty (Otis), Margot Kidder (Lois Lane), Jackie Cooper (Perry White), Sarah Douglas (Ursa), Jack O'Halloran (Non), Valerie Perrine (Eve). Directed by Richard Lester and produced by Alexander and Ilya Salkind and Pierre Spengler. Screenplay by Mario Puzo, David Newman, and Leslie Newman.

I thought the original *Superman* was terrific entertainment—and so I was a little startled to discover that I liked *Superman II* even more. Perhaps the secret of the sequel is that it has more faith in Superman. Before the original *Superman* was released in 1978, the producers knew he could carry a speeding locomotive, all right—but could he carry a movie? They weren't sure, and since they were investing millions of dollars in the project, they didn't want to rest a whole movie on the broad shoulders of their unknown star, Christopher Reeve. So they began *Superman* ponderously, on the planet Krypton, with the presence of Marlon Brando as a sort of totem to convince audiences that this movie was big league. They told us of Superman's origins with a solemnity more befitting a god. They were very serious and very symbolic, and it wasn't until Superman came to Earth that the movie really caught fire. *Then,* half an hour or more into its length, it started giving us what we came for: Superman flying around with his red cape, saving mankind.

Superman II begins in midstream, and never looks back (aside from a brief recap of the first movie). In many ways, it's a repeat of the last ninety minutes of the first film. It has the same key characters, including archvillain Lex Luthor. It continues the love story of Lois Lane and Superman, not to mention the strange relationship of Lois and Clark Kent. It features the return of three villains from Krypton, who when last seen were trapped in a one-dimensional plane of light and cast adrift in space. And it continues those remarkable special effects.

From his earliest days in a comic book, Superman always has been an urban hero. He lived in a universe that was defined by screaming banner headlines and vast symbolic acts, and *Superman II* catches that flavor perfectly with its use of famous landmarks like the Eiffel Tower, the Empire State Building, Niagara Falls, and the Coca-Cola sign in Times Square. He was a pop hero in a pop world, and like Mickey Mouse and the original Coke trademark, he became an instantly recognizable trademark.

That's why the special effects in both *Superman* movies are so crucial. It is a great deal simpler to show a rocket ship against the backdrop of outer space than to show Kryptonian villains hurling a city bus through the air in midtown Manhattan. But the feeling of actuality makes Superman's exploits more fun. It brings the fantastic into our everyday lives; it delights in showing us the reaction of the man on the street to Superman's latest stunt. In the movie, as in the comic book, ordinary citizens seems to spend their days glued to the sidewalk, gazing skyward, and shouting things like "Superman is dead!" or "Superman has saved the world!"

In *Superman II* he saves large portions of the world, all right, but what he preserves most of all is the element of humanity within him. The Superman movies made a basic decision to give Superman and his alter ego, Clark Kent, more human feelings than the character originally possessed. So *Superman II* has a lot of fun developing his odd dual relationship with Lois Lane. At long, long last, Lois and Superman make love in this movie (after champagne, but discreetly off-screen in Superman's ice palace). But Lois and Clark Kent also spend the night together in highly compromised circumstances, in a Niagara Falls honeymoon haven. And the movie has fun with another one of those ultimate tests that Lois was always throwing at Clark to make him admit he was really Superman. Lois bets her life on it this time, hurling herself into the rapids below Niagara Falls. Either Clark can turn into Superman and save her—or she'll drown. And what then? All I can say is, Clark does *not* turn into Superman.

This scene has a lot of humor in it, and the whole film has more smiles and laughs than the first one. Maybe that's because of a change in directors. Richard Donner, who made the first *Superman* film and did a brilliant job of establishing a basic look for the series, was followed this time by Richard Lester *(A Hard Day's Night, The Three Musketeers),* and this is some of Lester's best work. He permits satire to make its way into the film more easily. He has a lot of fun with Gene Hackman, as the still-scheming, thin-skinned, egomaniacal Lex Luthor. And he draws out Christopher Reeve, whose performance in the title role is sly, knowing, and yet still appropriately square. This movie's most intriguing insight is that Superman's disguise as Clark Kent isn't a matter of looks as much as of mental attitude: Clark is disguised not by his glasses but by his ordinariness. Beneath his meek exterior, of course, is concealed a superhero. And, the movie subtly hints, isn't that the case with us all?

Superman III ★ ★ ½
PG, 125 m., 1983

Christopher Reeve (Superman/Clark Kent), Richard Pryor (Gus Gorman), Annette O'Toole (Lana Lang), Robert Vaughn (Ross Webster). Directed by Richard Lester and produced by Alexander Salkind. Screenplay by David and Leslie Newman.

Superman III is the kind of movie I feared the original *Superman* would be. It's a cinematic comic book, shallow, silly, filled with stunts and action, without much human interest. What's amazing is that the first two Superman movies avoided that description, creating a fantasy with a certain charm. They could have been manipulative special effects movies, but they were a great deal more. With this third one, maybe they've finally run out of inspiration.

The big news about *Superman III* is, of course, the presence of Richard Pryor in the cast. But Pryor isn't used very well here. He never really emerges as a person we care about. His character and the whole movie seem assembled out of prefabricated pieces. The first two films were too, in a way, but real care was taken with the dialogue, and we could occasionally halfway believe that real people had gotten themselves into this world of fantasy. Not this time. *Superman III* drops most of the threads of the first two movies—including Lois Lane's increasingly complex love affair with Clark Kent and Superman—and goes for the action. There's no real sense of what Superman, or Clark, ever really feels. The running gag about the hero's double identity isn't really exploited this time. The sheer amazingness of Superman isn't explored; the movie and the people in it take this incredible creature for granted. After the bird and the plane, it's "Superman" when it should be SUPERMAN!

The plot involves the usual scheme to control the Earth. The villain this time is Robert Vaughn, as a mad billionaire who wants to use satellites to control the Earth's crops and become even richer. He directs his satellites and weapons systems by computer, and that's how he hooks up with Pryor, as a brilliant, but befuddled, computer programmer. Superman, meanwhile, has a couple of things on his mind. After Lois Lane leaves to go on vacation at the beginning of the movie (in a particularly awkward scene), Clark goes home to his Smallville High School reunion, and has a love affair with Lana Lang (Annette O'Toole). It's sweet, but it's not half as interesting as the Ice Castle footage with Lois Lane in *Superman II*. Then Superman gets zapped with some ersatz Kryptonite and turns into a meanie, which is good for some laughs (as a practical joke, he straightens the Leaning Tower of Pisa).

All of this is sort of fun, and the special effects are sometimes very good, but there's no real sense of wonder in this film—no moments like the scene in *Superman* where California threatened to fall into the sea and Superman turned back time to save humanity. After that, who cares about Robert Vaughn's satellites? Or Richard Pryor's dilemma? Pryor can be a wicked, anarchic comic actor, and that presence would have been welcome here. Instead, like the rest of *Superman III*, he's kind of innocuous.

The Sure Thing ★ ★ ★ ½
PG-13, 94 m., 1985

John Cusack (Walter Gibson), Daphne Zuniga (Alison Bradbury), Anthony Edwards (Lance), Boyd Gaines (Jason), Tim Robbins (Gary Cooper), Lisa Jane Persky (Mary Ann Webster), Vivica Lindfors (Professor), Nicolette Sheridan (Sure Thing). Directed by Rob Reiner and produced by Roger Birnbaum. Screenplay by Steven Bloom and Jonathan Roberts.

The love story is one of Hollywood's missing genres. The movie industry seems better at teen-age movies like *Porky's*, with its sleazy shower scenes, than with screenplays that involve any sort of thought about the love lives of its characters. That's why *The Sure Thing* is a small miracle. Although the hero of this movie is promised by his buddy that he'll be fixed up with a "guaranteed sure thing," the film is not about the sure thing but about how this kid falls genuinely and touchingly into love.

The movie's love story begins in an Eastern college classroom. Walter Gibson (John Cusack) walks into his English class and falls immediately into love with Alison Bradbury (Daphne Zuniga), who is smart and good-looking and not one of your brainless movie broads. He asks her out, but succeeds, of course, in acting like a total nerd, and she invites him to get out of her life. End of act one. In act two, Walter plans to spend his Christmas vacation in Los Angeles, where his buddy says the Sure Thing is eagerly awaiting his arrival. Alison also plans to go to L.A., to visit her fiancé, who is studying to be a boring middle-class vegetable. They both sign up for rides, and, of course, they both wind up in the back seat of the same car. At first they don't talk. They they start to fight. Then they are ditched at the side of the road and have to hitchhike to L.A. together.

I know this is an obvious movie ploy. I know, in fact, that what will happen next is completely predictable: They'll fight, they'll share experiences, they'll suffer together, and eventually they'll fall in love. I know all of these things, and yet I don't care. I don't care because love is always a cliché anyway, and the only thing that makes it endlessly fascinating is that the players are always changing. These two particular characters, Walter and Alison, played by these two gifted young actors, Cusack and Zuniga, make *The Sure Thing* into a special love story.

One of the unique things about the movie is that the characters show a normal shyness about sex. Most movie teen-agers seem to be valedictorians from the Masters & Johnson Institute. They're born knowing more about sex than Rhett Butler would have been able to teach Scarlett O'Hara. They are also, of course, not shy, not insecure, not modest, and occasionally not human. Walter and Alison are closer to real teen-agers, with real doubts and hesitations and uncertainties. The other surprising thing about the film is that it successfully avoids an obligatory sex scene with the Sure Thing (Nicollette Sheridan, in a thankless role). This film is so revolutionary, it believes sex should be accompanied by respect and love! By the end of the movie, when Walter and Alison finally do kiss, it means something. It means more, in fact, than any movie kiss in a long time, because it takes place between two people we've gotten to know and who have gotten to know each other.

The Survivors ★ ½
R, 102 m., 1983

Walter Matthau (Sonny Paluso), Robin Williams (Donald Quinelle), Jerry Reed (Jack Locke), James Wainwright (Wes Huntley). Directed by Michael Ritchie and produced by William Sackheim. Screenplay by Michael Leeson.

Survivalists are very cautious people who have secret hideaways somewhere in the woods, which they've stocked with food, weapons, ammunition, and survival gear. In case of a nuclear attack, they alert each other by CB radio and light out for the trees. *The Survivors*, which attempts to have fun with their prudence, is an aimless, self-indulgent, confusing comedy that never comes to grips with its material. And it allows Robin Williams to run wild, destroying any marginal credibility the story might have had.

It's a mess. One of the reasons it's a mess is that it doesn't know whether to be a human comedy or a slapstick, satirical comedy. The first approach would have involved creating plausible characters and plugging them into a comic situation. The second approach allows anything to be funny in any way possible. *The Survivors* goes for both approaches simultaneously, which is confusing. For example, after a slapstick opening in which Williams is fired by a trained parrot, there's a scene of social satire set in an unemployment office. Even within scenes, the styles of the actors suggest they think they're in different movies. Walter Matthau manfully acts as if he's in a plausible movie, while Williams mugs, improvises, and randomly alters his accent. See the problem? If it's a "real" world, then Matthau should observe that Williams isn't playing with a full deck. If it's an anarchic satire, then the joke's on Matthau, who does not seem to realize it.

The story involves two newly unemployed men. Williams has been fired by the parrot and Matthau's gas station has been blown up. After they get discouraged by the lines at the unemployment office, they happen to go to the same diner, which is stuck up by a fierce criminal (Jerry Reed). They snatch off his ski mask and see him, and so Reed believes he has to kill these two witnesses. What happens next is very long and involved. Williams signs up for a wilderness survival training course. He hopes to become tough enough to protect himself. Reed and Matthau both find themselves at the same isolated survivalist area. The head survivalist is a reactionary paramilitary nut who believes American society is doomed to collapse. And so on.

This material is the stuff of promising satire, but the movie's director, Michael Ritchie, goes nowhere with it. His parts don't seem to fit together. One moment we'll be getting a heartfelt talk, and the next moment there's a wilderness shoot-out straight out of *The Road Runner.* The story gets so confused that the movie can't even account for why its characters happen to be in the same place at the same time; in desperation, it gives us a scene where Williams actually calls Reed and tells him where he can be found. Uh-huh.

The Survivors wouldn't be such a disappointment if it didn't employ such talented people, and if it weren't directed by Michael Ritchie, whose gift for satirizing American institutions has given us good movies like *Smile, The Bad News Bears, The Candidate,* and *Semi-Tough.* This time he seems so fast off the starting line he left his screenplay behind.

Swamp Thing ★ ★ ★
R, 102 m., 1982

Louis Jourdan (Arcane), Adrienne Barbeau (Alice), Ray Wise (Dr. Holland), Dick Durock (Swamp Thing), David Hess (Ferret), Nicholas Worth (Brung). Directed by Wes Craven and produced by Benjamin Melniker and Michael Uslan. Screenplay by Craven.

Swamp Thing had already won my heart *before* its moment of greatness, but when that moment came, I knew I'd discovered another one of those movies that fall somewhere between buried treasures and guilty pleasures. The moment comes after Dr. Alec Holland, brilliant scientist, is attacked by thugs, is splashed with his own secret formula, catches on fire, leaps into the swamp, and turns into Swamp Thing when the formula interacts with his body and the vegetation in the swamp. Crawling back onto dry land, Swamp Thing is not recognized by his former girlfriend, the beautiful Alice Cable (Adrienne Barbeau). But after the thugs fill him with machine gun bullets and hack off his left arm, Alice asks, "Does it hurt?" and Swamp Thing replies, "Only when I laugh."

That was the movie's moment of greatness. There are others that come close, as when Swamp Thing, dripping with moss and looking like a bug-eyed spinach soufflé, says "There is great beauty in the swamp . . . if you know where to look." And when the evil villain (Louis Jourdan) drinks the secret formula and confidently waits for it to transform him into a powerful genius, he discovers that the formula doesn't so much *change* you, as develop what is already latent within you. Therefore, once a horse's ass, *always* a horse's ass.

This is one of those movies like *Infra-Man* or *Invasion of the Bee Girls:* an off-the-wall, eccentric, peculiar movie fueled by the demented obsessions of its makers. *Swamp Thing* first saw the light of day, so to speak, as a hero in a celebrated series of DC Comics. The movie version was written and directed by Wes Craven, who made *Last House on the Left,* a movie I persist in admiring even in the face of universal repugnance. Craven also made *The Hills Have Eyes,* which even I found decadent, and the made-for-NBC movie *Stranger in Our House,* with Linda Blair. This time, with *Swamp Thing,* he betrays a certain gentleness and poetry along with the gore; in fact, this movie is a lot less violent than many others in the same genre. Craven's inspiration seems to come from James Whale's classic *Bride of Frankenstein* (1935), and he pays tribute in scenes where his swamp monster sniffs a flower, admires a young girl's beauty from afar, and looks sadly at a photograph in a locket. *Swamp Thing* doesn't stop there; it also contains an exact visual quote from Russ Meyer's *Lorna,* and a scene in which the jailer in a dungeon cheerfully quotes the title of a Werner Herzog film: "It's every man for himself, and God against all!"

Will you like this film? Yes, probably, if you like monster and horror movies. The movie occupies familiar ground, but it has a freshness and winsome humor to fit it, and Craven moves confidently through the three related genres he's stealing from (monster movies, mad scientist movies and transformation movies—in which people turn into strange beings). There's beauty in this movie, if you know where to look for it.

Swann in Love ★ ★ ★
R, 110 m., 1984 ⌐

Jeremy Irons (Charles Swann), Ornella Muti (Odette de Crecy), Alain Delon (Baron de Charlus), Fanny Ardant (Duchesse de Guermantes), Marie-Christine Barrault (Madame Verdurin). Directed by Volker Schlondorff and produced by Nicole Stephane. Written by Peter Brook, Jean-Claude Carriere, and Marie-Helene Estienne.

All of the reviews I've read of Volker Schlondorff's *Swann in Love* treat it like a classroom assignment. The movie is described as a version of one of the stories that make up *Remembrance of Things Past*, the epic novel by Marcel Proust, and then the exercise becomes almost academic: "Compare and contrast Proust and Schlondorff, with particular attention to the difference between fiction and the film." Imagine instead, that this is not a film based on a novel, but a new film from an original screenplay. It will immediately seem more lively and accessible. Because not one person in a hundred who sees the film will have read Proust, this is a sensible approach; it does away with the nagging feeling that one should really curl up with those twelve volumes before going to the theater.

Schlondorff's *Swann in Love*—as opposed to Proust's—is the story of a pale young man who goes one day to visit a prostitute, and is actually indifferent to her until she stands him up. Then he becomes obsessed. She is not the right woman for him, but her very wrongness becomes fascinating. Because she is vulgar, because she lies, because she toys with his affection, and most particularly because she lets him smell the orchid in her bodice, she becomes the most important person in the world to him, and he throws his life and reputation at her feet. Proper society, of course, disapproves of his affair—and talks of nothing else. In the elegant salons where ladies and gentlemen gather, Swann is not welcome if he brings along his Odette, but because he cannot be happy without her, this is no punishment. In the most humiliating scenes in the movie, he abjectly follows her through the night, knocks on a door he hopes is hers, and stands in her boudoir while she nonchalantly disrobes and dresses for an appointment with another man.

Casting is everything in a film like this. Jeremy Irons is perfect as Charles Swann, pale, deep-eyed, feverish with passion. This was his third movie (after *The French Lieutenant's Woman* and *Betrayal*) in which love seemed necessary to his nature. We can believe his passion. As Odette, Schlondorff has cast Ornella Muti, who has a sort of languorous bemusement that is maddening: We wonder if she is even capable of understanding that the man before her is mad with love and desire, and then we realize, of course, that her very *inability* to care is what creates her fatal attraction. *Swann in Love* is a stylish, period love story, surrounding its central characters with still other pathetic seekers of perfection (Alain Delon is wonderful as a gloomy homosexual who pursues an idealized form of misery). Yet at the film's end, we've probably learned nothing except that lovers were as silly in 1875 as they are now. Sillier, perhaps; they had more time.

Swing Shift ★ ★ ★
PG, 100 m., 1984

Goldie Hawn (Kay Walsh), Kurt Russell (Lucky Lockhart), Christine Lahti (Hazel Zanussi), Fred Ward (Biscuits), Ed Harris (Jack Walsh), Charles Napier (Moon). Directed by Jonathan Demme and produced by Jerry Bick. Screenplay by Rob Morton.

Girl gets husband, girl loses husband, girl gets job. That's basically what happens in *Swing Shift*, a sentimental memory of World War II, when men went to war and their wives and sweethearts manned the production lines. This is a slice-of-life movie, the kind that director Jonathan *(Melvin and Howard)* Demme is good at. It's so nostalgic that even the anger at the end—when the war ends and the women lose their jobs—seems bittersweet.

The movie stars Goldie Hawn as Kay Walsh, a sweet, cheerful, uncomplicated young woman who lives with her husband in a bungalow on a little Los Angeles courtyard. The husband is played by Ed Harris (John Glenn in *The Right Stuff*), and he's an earnest, affectionate stereotype who doesn't want his "honey" working while he's serving in the Navy. But the aircraft factories of

Southern California need workers, so she goes to work. Besides, she's lonely.

Her husband is off to sea, and the safety-control inspector is an *awfully* nice guy named Lucky (Kurt Russell). For six months, he asks Kay out for a date. She finally accepts. And then, like so many wartime spouses, she has a lot of explaining to do when her sailor returns.

What's unexpected about *Swing Shift*, and what keeps it from being predictable and makes it special, is that the relationship between Kay and Lucky isn't really at the heart of the movie. That position is reserved for the friendship between Kay and Hazel Zanussi (Christine Lahti), a leggy brunette who lives off the same courtyard and is having her own unhappy affair with a nightclub owner (Fred Ward). There's a real sense of palship and camaraderie in their friendship. The movie's last shot isn't the usual freeze-frame of the boy and the girl, but of Kay and Hazel, hugging each other because everything—even Hazel's one-night stand with Lucky—has been forgiven.

Swing Shift isn't heavily plotted. There's no melodramatic crisis. The movie covers more than four years, and is more interested in giving us a memory of how it felt on the home front than in creating some kind of false drama. Even the scene where Kay's husband finds out about Lucky is handled with such restrained emotion that it's obvious the filmmakers didn't intend this as a movie about passion. Instead, it's about women in a man's world. Kay and Hazel are riveters on a bomber assembly line. They are hazed by the plant's macho veterans, led by Charles Napier. They also learn to support themselves, to think for themselves, and to see themselves differently. There's no suspense and no big emotional payoff, but the movie is always absorbing. The best performance is Lahti as Hazel—tough, vulnerable, cynical, a real pal. This may be the first buddy movie about women.

Sylvester ★ ★ ★
PG, 103 m., 1985

Richard Farnsworth (Foster), Melissa Gilbert (Charlie), Michael Schoeffling (Matt). Directed by Tim Hunter and produced by Martin Jurow. Written by Carol Sobieski.

Hollywood has never exactly had a shortage of movies about teen-age girls and brave horses, and I was not exactly looking forward to *Sylvester*, which stars Melissa Gilbert as a teen-age girl with a horse so brave that its full name is Sylvester Stallone. I was dreading one of those movies where the horse is almost human, and after the girl starts to cry, the horse nudges her and tries to cheer her up. Maybe that's why *Sylvester* came as such a genuine surprise: There is a good movie here, obscured by a tired old formula. Gilbert plays a tough, determined teen-ager who is raising her two younger brothers herself—and trying to keep them out of the hands of court-appointed guardians. Her ambition in life is to train horses, and she starts with Sylvester, an unsophisticated Western bucking horse who does not look like the sort of animal you'd expect to see in the Olympic steeplechase trials.

The complications in the plot are set up right away: The intervention by the court officials, the challenge of training the horse, and the problem of what to do about Gilbert's old boyfriend (Michael Schoeffling), especially since they still love each other. Gilbert turns to a father figure, a grizzled, drunken old cowboy (Richard Farnsworth), who knows all about horses, all about human nature, and even a little bit about teen-age girls. She wants him to provide a home for herself and her brothers, and supervise Sylvester's training sessions. Farnsworth protests: He's already paid his dues as a father and nursemaid. But Gilbert prevails, and the scenes between the two are charged with the kinds of tension and affection that make even routine situations seem real.

Sylvester contains, of course, the usual number of obligatory scenes. We know we'll see the horse being trained. We know we'll see Gilbert almost breaking her neck. We know we'll see Farnsworth looking at his watch and allowing as how maybe that damned horse *does* have a chance. And we also rather suspect that the horse doesn't get all the way to Kentucky only to lose. The movie doesn't disappoint us at those obligatory moments, but it has a lot of surprises, as well. One of them is the low-key but mature way it treats the romance between Gilbert and Schoeffling. They have a quiet little PG-rated love scene together that is tactful, honest, and, in its own way, rather bold.

Gilbert is best known for her work on TV's "The Little House on the Prairie." This is her first movie. She has real presence, and a much more interesting and resilient acting style than you might expect from someone raised on a network assembly line. *Sylvester* itself probably started out as little more than a classy steeplechase version of *Rocky,* but Gilbert, Farnsworth, and a good script turn it into something surprisingly better.

Table for Five ★ ½
PG, 120 m., 1983

Jon Voight (J.P. Tannen), Richard Crenna (Mitchell), Marie Christine Barrault (Marie), Millie Perkins (Kathleen), Rozana Zal (Tilde), Robby Kiger (Truman-Paul), Son Hoang Bui (Trung). Directed by Robert Lieberman and produced by Robert Schaffel. Screenplay by David Seltzer.

Table for Five is a smarmy, cloying movie that insulted my intelligence while trying to bribe me emotionally with its story of forlorn little kids faced with death. It was written by David Seltzer, the same schmaltz-merchant who perpetrated *Six Weeks* and *The Other Side of the Mountain,* the story of an Olympic ski champion who was paralyzed. Looking back at his career in perspective, I now believe Seltzer's finest hour was when he wrote *The Omen,* about a little kid who was the anti-Christ and got his kick out of hurling his nanny through the attic window. Somebody should get out a cease-and-desist order on Seltzer, forbidding him to write any more movies about horrible things happening to kids.

Anyway, *Table for Five* is cornball enough as a story, but its troubles don't end there. It also has excruciating problems with casting, and with common sense. The movie stars Jon Voight as an immature, confused man who was divorced five years earlier by his sensible, kind wife (Millie Perkins). They had three children together, and she got custody. She has since remarried, and her new husband (Richard Crenna) is a brilliant lawyer who loves the kids. The kids are named Tilde, Truman-Paul, and Trung. You know

you're in trouble when Trung is not the cutesiest name in the movie.

The manic Voight comes back into their lives to whisk the kids away on a sea voyage. Perkins and Crenna have their doubts, but Voight prevails, and before long we're on board ship on a cruise to the Mediterranean. Voight has been quoted as saying he liked the idea of a sea cruise, because it gave him the opportunity to shoot scenes in front of the Pyramids, the Sphinx, the Parthenon, etc., with their reminders of eternal values. Maybe if he had shot in front of the Library of Congress the movie might have picked up some insight into human behavior. Voight, throughout this movie, acts in such a narcissistic and mannered way (putting himself down so we'll pet him) that his performance is uncomfortable to watch. There's never a moment when we believe he's a fit, responsible father for his children.

But there's more. In a jarring *deux ex machina,* a transatlantic phone call reaches the ship. There's tragic news. I cannot reveal it in this review, but expect the worst. Voight conceals the news from his kids, while we get more excruciating scenes of their "growth" together. (In the most painful, little Truman-Paul turns out to be learning disabled, and Voight blows up at him when the kid can't learn to spell *policeman* with his alphabet blocks. Yargh!) I guess the movie is supposed to be about how Voight is able to Grow as a Person during the ocean voyage, and Find Himself, and Get to Know the Kids. I didn't believe an instant of it. The Richard Crenna character in this movie has a lot of obvious advantages over Voight, including the fact that he is manifestly sane and responsible. Voight's character is narcissism run wild; he reminds me of those creepy parents whose children are souvenirs, not individuals.

On the movie's own terms, it would be a happy ending if Voight got to stay with the kids. *Table for Five* didn't work that way for me. I became convinced that if Voight took over raising those kids, he'd drive them all nuts and wind up holding them hostage in a showdown with the guys with butterfly nets. His performance is that odd. Crenna, by contrast, is so civilized and pleasant that the final scenes in the movie achieved the opposite of what Seltzer intended. So I guess

Seltzer and Voight have to share the blame: Seltzer for writing a manipulative, smarmy script, and Voight for allowing himself (as coproducer) to cast himself in a role where he sends out all the wrong signals. This movie is a mess.

Taps ★ ★ ★
PG, 126 m., 1981

George C. Scott (General Bache), Timothy Hutton (Brian Moreland), Ronny Cox (Colonel Kerby), Sean Penn (Alex), Tom Cruise (David). Directed by Harold Becker and produced by Stanley R. Jaffe and Howard B. Jaffe. Screenplay by Darryl Ponicsan and Robert Mark Kamen.

Taps is a meditation on two subjects for which some adolescents have a great capacity: idealism and authoritarianism. It takes place in a realistic setting (it was shot on location at Valley Forge Military Academy), but it is not intended as a realistic film. There are all sorts of clues, including the pointed absence of all but one of the academy's adult faculty members, to indicate that *Taps*, like the emotionally similar *Lord of the Flies*, is using its realistic texture as a setting for a fantasy about human nature.

The film begins with an emotionally stirring commencement exercise at Bunker Hill Military Academy (as the school is called in the film). Sousa marches fill the air, the cadets march around the parade ground looking gloriously proud of themselves, and the reviewing stand is dominated by the legendary old General Harlan Bache, the academy's commander. Bache is played by George C. Scott, and it is probably no accident that his performance in this movie echoes his title role in *Patton* (1970): He is an iron-willed and yet incurably romantic professional soldier.

We soon meet the leading upperclassman, Brian Moreland (Timothy Hutton). He has been selected to lead the cadet corps next year. In one of the most important evenings of his life, he is granted the great privilege of having dinner with old General Bache and sipping some of the old man's brandy. Soon after, however, this whole network of discipline, glory, and tradition is destroyed when it's revealed that the school's pigheaded trustees intend to sell the school and its land

to some condominium developers (it is almost worth the price of admission to hear Scott pronouce "condominiums"). Bache is removed from the scene, in a dramatic development I will not reveal. And then Moreland, the cadet commander, takes inventory of the school's supplies of weapons and decides to lead the student body in making a stand for it. They'll take over the school in a military occupation, bar the gates, mount machine guns, and guard posts, and issue a set of demands designed to save the school.

The central passages of *Taps* are devoted to this scheme. The students barricade themselves in the school grounds, the police and National Guard surround the school, and a standoff develops. Meanwhile, within the student body, tensions develop between those kids who are unstable and a little too violent, and those who would secretly rather be on the outside looking in. Hutton, as Moreland, does a lot of learning and soul-searching as he tries to hold his mad scheme together.

There are obviously various problems of plot (such as: Where are the other faculty members? Why are the outside authorities both so stupid and so uncompromising? Why would the trustees have no appreciation of the school's tradition? Why would the grade-school-age cadets be issued live ammunition?, etc.). These questions do not really matter. *Taps* is basically a character study, a portrait of the personalities engaged in the showdown. And, like *Lord of the Flies*, it observes that adolescent males can easily translate the idealistic lessons they have been taught into a rationale for acting in ways that are rigid, dogmatic, and self-justifying.

Taps works as an uncommonly engrossing story, primarily because the performances are so well done. All of the cadet roles are well-acted, not only by seasoned actors like Hutton (who won an Academy Award for *Ordinary People*) but even by the very young kids who struggle with guns and realities much too large for them. By the film's end, we share their love for their school, we despair at the situation they have gotten themselves into, and we are emotionally involved in the outcome. After the film, there are some ideas to think about, involving the implications when might and right are on the same side—and when they are not.

Tarzan, the Ape Man ★ ★ ½
R, 112 m., 1981

Bo Derek (Jane), Richard Harris (Parker), John Phillip Law (Holt), Miles O'Keefe (Tarzan), Akushula Seleyah (Africa), Steven Strong (Ivory King). Directed and photographed by John Derek and produced by Bo Derek. Screenplay by Tom Rowe and Gary Goddard.

Tarzan, the Ape Man is *The Blue Lagoon* with elephants. Of course it's completely ridiculous, but at the same time it has a certain disarming charm. Sure, it's easy to groan at the secondhand "plot." It's easy to laugh at the clichés and mourn the demotion of Tarzan, who started out in the movies as king of the jungle and now gets fourth billing behind a schoolgirl, an anthropologist, and a wimp. And yet when Tarzan beats his chest and screams and swings to the rescue on a vine, there is something primal happening on the screen. And when Jane and three loyal chimpanzees tenderly bathe the body of the unconscious ape-man, we're getting very close to the reasons why we watch movies, and why there will always be a few movies to reawaken the child within us.

This Bo Derek version of the "Tarzan" legend is allegedly a remake of the MGM version of 1932, starring Johnnie Weissmuller and Maureen O'Sullivan. Not in that version or in any of the others, however, did Hollywood honestly address the central mystery of the Tarzan story, which is—what, exactly, *was* the intimate relationship between Tarzan and Jane? Were they lovers? Friends? Neighbors? Business partners? They presumably made love in order to produce Boy, but the reproduction took place far, far offscreen. I always thought there was something just a little peculiar about the behavior of Weissmuller, Lex Barker, Gordon Scott, and other movie Tarzans. There they were, all alone in the jungle with the beautiful Jane, and what did they do? Swing around on vines and talk to the animals. If I'd wanted *Dr. Doolittle*, I would have seen *Dr. Doolittle*.

This 1981 version is nothing if not willing to satisfy our curiosity about sex life in the rain forest. Bo Derek (who stars and produced) and her husband John (who directed and photographed) are frankly interested only in the relationship between Tarzan and Jane. The whole movie is a setup for several steamy scenes of confrontation between the savage, muscular jungle man and the petite young girl with eyes as wide as her shoulders. When Tarzan and Jane first meet, the movie all but abandons its plot in favor of foreplay. This is not a movie to waste time on ivory-smuggling, Nazis, cities of gold, ant-men, slave girls, lost safaris, or any of the countless other plot devices Edgar Rice Burroughs used as substitutes for interpersonal relationships. It gets right down to business.

The movie opens with a vow by Bo Derek's scientist father (Richard Harris) to lead an expedition to plunder the jungle of its secrets. His real mission: To capture the legendary ape-man Tarzan and bring him back to his club—stuffed and mounted, if possible. Harris takes Bo along on his expedition, which also includes John Phillip Law in the role of the wimp assistant. Law has hardly anything to say, and is always the guy who's looking the other way when Tarzan kidnaps Jane. After a series of routine shots of the jungle march, Tarzan *does* meet Jane and finds himself powerfully attracted to her. Harris is of course insane with jealousy: "Do you know what he *really* wants?" he asks Jane. She hopes so.

Tarzan kidnaps Jane, and then the movie boringly intercuts the jealous father searching for the curious girl. Harris's role in this movie is as hapless as Jason Robards's role in *The Lone Ranger*. Nobody cares about him, his dialogue is overwrought and underwritten, and every time Tarzan and Jane are poised to jump into the bullrushes, the movie cuts back to Harris, slogging through the jungle and cursing the ape-man.

The story line was ridiculous to begin with, but it goes berserk by the time of the movie's incomprehensible climax in a village of mud worshippers. They capture Derek, smear her with paint, and prepare her for some sort of unspeakable sacrifice before Tarzan gallops to the rescue with a herd of elephants. Those friendly elephants are, of course, part of the Tarzan legend. Tarzan speaks Elephant, and there's always that great moment when he needs help, and the elephants hear his screams and perk up their ears. I've always thought it would be dangerous to ask Tarzan for help unless you really wanted it. Say you had a small problem like a missing gourd or a stolen spear, and Tarzan arrived at your village with a herd of elephants to fix things. You'd get your gourd back, maybe, but you'd be cleaning up for weeks.

But never mind. This movie's scenes between Bo Derek, as Jane, and Miles O'Keefe, as a Tarzan who never speaks a word, show them as complete sexual innocents, fascinated by the wonderment of each other's bodies. Jane's expression as she looks at the unconscious Tarzan is entrancing. Her unabashed curiosity about him is sexier than any number of steamy sex scenes would have been. Although some of Bo Derek's nude scenes have reportedly been cut from the movie at the insistence of the spoilsport Edgar Rice Burroughs estate, the remaining nude footage is remarkably free of purience. The Tarzan-Jane scenes strike a blow for noble savages, for innocent lust, for animal magnetism, and, indeed, for soft-core porn, which is ever so much sexier than the hard-core variety. If you do not agree with me, you will probably think Bo's banana scene is ridiculous. I prefer to think it was inevitable.

Teachers ★ ★
R, 106 m., 1984

Nick Nolte (Alex), JoBeth Williams (Lisa), Judd Hirsch (Roger), Ralph Macchio (Eddie), Allen Garfield (Rosenberg), Lee Grant (Dr. Burke), Richard Mulligan (Herbert), Royal Dano (Ditto). Directed by Arthur Hiller and produced by Aaron Russo. Screenplay by W.R. McKinney.

The idea here was to do for teaching what *M*A*S*H* did for the war. Unfortunately, they've done for schools what "General Hospital" did for medicine. *Teachers* has an interesting central idea, about shell-shocked teachers trying to remember their early idealism, but the movie junks it up with so many sitcom compromises that we can never quite believe the serious scenes.

The movie begins with a big-city high school where kids get stabbed, students double as drug dealers and police informers, teachers sleep through their classes, and the system is being sued for graduating students who cannot read or write. The bewildered principal is so totally out of touch with all of these developments that his only response is a pleasant nod. We meet the frontline troops. The movie stars Nick Nolte as a one-time visionary who lately has been having trouble finding his way out of hangovers. Judd Hirsch is the overwhelmed assistant principal. Royal Dano is a teacher named Ditto, who specializes in mimeographed examinations every day, so he won't have to talk to his students (he slumbers in the back of the class). There also are the usual student rebels, including Ralph Macchio *(The Karate Kid)* as a bright, alienated con man who knows everybody's weak spot.

The movie revolves around a couple of questions: Will the school lose the lawsuit? Will Nolte tell the truth in a pretrial deposition, or lie to protect the school system? Will he help a sobbing young girl get an abortion, after she has been seduced by the gym teacher? Will the hard-nosed school superintendent (Lee Grant) have Nolte fired? And, inevitably, will Nolte fall in love with the pretty young lawyer (JoBeth Williams) who used to be one of his best students?

One at a time, these questions might be worthy of answers. But *Teachers* throws them at us so relentlessly that the movie begins to feel like one of those soap operas where yesterday's old questions are answered by today's new questions. The movie has a couple of good scenes between Nolte and Macchio, and a few lines that have the zing of painful truth. But there are also scenes played entirely for cheap laughs. And a promising running gag about Ditto never pays off. I don't want to give away the punch line, but see if you're not puzzled by the way a potentially classic gag doesn't quite work. Here's the sad bottom line: *Teachers* was just interesting enough to convince me a great movie can be made about big-city high schools. This isn't it.

Tender Mercies ★ ★ ★
PG, 93 m., 1983

Robert Duvall (Mac Sledge), Tess Harper (Rosa Lee), Betty Buckley (Dixie), Wilford Brimley (Harry), Ellen Barkin (Sue Anne), Allan Hubbard (Sonny). Directed by Bruce Beresford and produced by Philip S. Hobel. Screenplay by Horton Foote.

Tender Mercies visits some fairly familiar

movie territory, and achieves some quietly touching effects. The movie's about the rhythms of a small Texas town, and about the struggle of a has-been country singer to regain his self-respect. It might remind you of parts of *The Last Picture Show* and *Honkytonk Man,* with a little bit of *Payday* thrown in (that was the movie starring Rip Torn, based on the last days of the dying Hank Williams, Sr.). This time, the broken-down country singer is named Mac Sledge. He's at the end of his personal road. He was once a big star and a hero to young musicians around the Southwest, but as his final act opens he's sitting in a fleabag motel outside a small Texas town, drinking himself to death, and fighting for the bottle with another guy he hardly even knows.

When he wakes up on the floor the next morning, the other guy is gone and Sledge is hung over, broke, and without prospects. He throws himself on the mercy of the young widow who runs the motel: He'll work for his room and board. She agrees to that, and throws in $2 an hour, but says he can't drink while he's at the motel. He agrees, and that is the day his life turns around and he begins the rebuilding process.

Tender Mercies tells the story of the relationship between the singer and the young widow in a quiet, subtle way; this isn't one of those movies that spells everything out. The key to the movie's tone is in the performance by Robert Duvall as Sledge. Duvall plays him as a bone-weary, seedy, essentially very simple man who needs some values to hold onto. The widow can provide those, and can also provide the stability of a home and family (she has a young son, whose father was killed in Vietnam). What the Duvall character wants to do, essentially, is keep a low profile, work hard, not drink, and forget about the glories of country singing. It's hard for him to remain invisible, though, after the local paper prints a story and the members of a local band start dropping around for advice. There are more complications: Sledge's ex-wife is still touring as a country singer, and would like to turn his eighteen-year-old daughter against him.

What's interesting about *Tender Mercies* is the way it refuses to approach this material as soap opera *or* as drama. The movie's told more like one of those quiet, sly *New Yorker*

stories where the big emotional moments sneak up on you, and the effects are achieved indirectly. Sometimes this movie smiles (as in a scene of a double baptism). Sometimes it simply sits there and talks straight (as in a touching speech by Sledge on the meaning of life). Sometimes its low budget allows the seams to show (as in the unconvincing concert scene involving Sledge's wife). But mostly it just lets these stories happen, lets them get to know these people, and see them dealing with life. Some of them get better, and some of them get worse. It's like a country song.

Terms of Endearment ★ ★ ★ ★
PG, 129 m., 1983

Debra Winger (Emma Horton), Shirley MacLaine (Aurora Greenway), Jack Nicholson (Breedlove), Jeff Daniels (Flap Horton), Danny DeVito (Vernon), John Lithgow (Sam Burns). Directed, produced, and written by James L. Brooks.

When families get together to remember their times together, the conversation has a way of moving easily from the tragedies to the funny things. You'll mention someone who has passed away, and there'll be a moment of silence, and then somebody will grin and be reminded of some goofy story. Life always has an unhappy ending, but you can have a lot of fun along the way, and everything doesn't have to be dripping in deep significance.

The most remarkable achievement of *Terms of Endearment,* which is filled with great achievements, is its ability to find the balance between the funny and the sad, between moments of deep truth and other moments of high ridiculousness. A lesser movie would have had trouble moving between the extremes that are visited by this film, but because *Terms of Endearment* understands its characters and loves them, we never have a moment's doubt: What happens next is supposed to happen, because life's like that. *Terms of Endearment* feels as much like life as any movie I can think of. At the same time, it's a triumph of show business, with its high comic style, its flair for bittersweet melodrama, and its star turns for the actors. Maybe the best thing about this movie is the way it combines those two different kinds of filmmaking. This is a movie with bold emotional scenes and big laughs, and at the same time it's so firmly in control of its tone that we believe we are seeing real people.

The movie's about two remarkable women, and their relationships with each other and with the men in their lives. The mother is played by Shirley MacLaine. She's a widow who lives in Houston and hasn't dated a man since her husband died. Maybe she's redirected her sexual desires into the backyard, where her garden has grown so large and elaborate that she either will have to find a man pretty quickly or move to a house with a bigger yard. Her daughter, played by Debra Winger, is one of those people who seems to have been blessed with a sense of life and joy. She marries a guy named Flap who teaches English in a series of Midwestern colleges; she rears three kids and puts up with Flap, who has an eye for coeds.

Back in Houston, her mother finally goes out on a date with the swinging bachelor (Jack Nicholson) who has lived next door for years. He's a hard-drinking, girl-chasing former astronaut with a grin that hints of unspeakable lusts. MacLaine, a lady who surrounds herself with frills and flowers, is appalled by this animalistic man and then touched by him.

There are a couple of other bittersweet relationships in the film. Both mother and daughter have timid, mild-mannered male admirers: MacLaine is followed everywhere by Vernon (Danny DeVito), who asks only to be allowed to gaze upon her, and Winger has a tender, little affair with a banker.

The years pass. Children grow up into adolescence, Flap gets a job as head of the department in Nebraska, the astronaut turns out to have genuine human possibilities of becoming quasi-civilized, and mother and daughter grow into a warmer and deeper relationship. All of this is told in a series of perfectly written, acted, and directed scenes that flow as effortlessly as a perfect day, and then something happens that is totally unexpected, and changes everything. I don't want to suggest what happens. It flows so naturally that it should be allowed to take place.

This is a wonderful film. There isn't a thing that I would change, and I was exhila-rated by the freedom it gives itself to move from the high comedy of Nicholson's best moments to the acting of Debra Winger in the closing scenes. She outdoes herself. It's a great performance. And yet it's not a "performance." There are scenes that have such a casual gaiety that acting seems to have nothing to do with it. She doesn't reach for effects, and neither does the film, because it's all right there.

Terror Train ★
R, 97 m., 1980

Ben Johnson (Carne), Jamie Lee Curtis (Alana), Hart Bochner (Doc), David Copperfield (Magician), Derek Mackinnon (Hampson), Sandee Currie (Mitchy). Directed by Roger Spottiswoode and produced by Harold Greenburg. Screenplay by T.Y. Drake.

The modern horror film market began its current reincarnation in 1978, with the release of John Carpenter's *Halloween*. There had, of course, always been horror films, but, like all movie genre films, they came and went in cycles. In the years before *Halloween*, they often shared a certain grisly sophistication, a macabre wit that was perfected in the Hammer horror films from England in the 1960s.

But *Halloween*, itself one of the year's best films, changed all that. After it racked up grosses of nearly $60 million, producers began to comb through it, looking for ways to exploit its success. They found two: It featured attacks on young girls, and it had a lot of knives and blood in it. These two exploitable elements have been in the forefront of the boom in horror movies, and they are, of course, present in *Terror Train*.

Terror Train is a curious hybrid that doesn't seem to know just what it wants to be. It has, I guess, few artistic pretensions, and yet it's not a rock-bottom budget, schlock exploitation film. It has three recognizable mid-level movie stars in it: Ben Johnson, veteran of John Ford Westerns, as a train conductor; David Copperfield, Broadway magician, as a magician; and, most notably, Jamie Lee Curtis as one of the endangered girls.

Curtis is to the current horror film glut what Christopher Lee was to the last one—or

Boris Karloff was in the 1930s. She was the star of *Halloween,* she also starred in Carpenter's disappointing *The Fog* and the utterly inept *Prom Night,* and now here she is again, in another one of those basic horror film premises, in which a horrible event from several years ago causes terrible revenge during a gala event in the present. In *Terror Train,* the party's being held on a private train, chartered by some fraternity and sorority kids. Somewhere on the train is a vicious killer with a knife. Are his murders inspired by the unspeakable experience he had as a fraternity freshman? Or is someone else the killer?

Who knows? Certainly not avuncular old Ben Johnson. As the bodies stack up and blood drips from the upper berths, he repeats things like, "Now you young ladies stay up here—it's too dangerous down in that other car." As the train hurtles crazily through the night, his calm begins to seem more and more bizarre. The use of the train itself is bizarre, for that matter; since the only places you can go on a moving train are forward and back, how can the killer pass undetected? Well, having seen the movie, I say . . . he can't. The movie cheats.

But then, why should that matter? The classic horror films of the 1930s appealed to the intelligence of its audiences, to their sense of humor and irony. Movies like *Terror Train,* and all of its sordid predecessors and its ripoffs still to come, just don't care. They're a series of sensations, strung together on a plot. Any plot will do. Just don't forget the knife, and the girl, and the blood.

Tess ★ ★ ★ ★
PG, 180 m., 1980

Nastassja Kinski (Tess), Peter Firth (Angel Clare), Leigh Lawson (Alec d'Urberville), Rosemary Martin (Mrs. Durbeyfield), Sylvia Coleridge (Mrs. d'Urberville), John Collin (John Durbeyfield), Tony Church (Parson), Brigid Erin Bates (Girl in Meadow). Directed by Roman Polanski and produced by Claude Berri. Screenplay by Gerard Brach, Polanski, and John Brownjohn.

Roman Polanski's *Tess* is a love song with a tragic ending—the best kind of love song of all, just so long as it's not about ourselves. He tells the story of a beautiful young girl,

innocent but not without intelligence, and the way she is gradually destroyed by the exercise of the male ego. The story is all the more touching because it is not an unrelenting descent into gloom, as it might have been in other hands, but a life lived in occasional sight of love and happiness. Tess is forever just on the brink of getting the peace she deserves.

The movie is based on a novel by Thomas Hardy, but Polanski never permits his film to become a Classics Illustrated; this isn't a devout rendering of a literary masterpiece, but a film that lives and breathes and has a quick sympathy for its heroine. Nastassja Kinski is just right for the title role. She has the youth, the freshness, and the naiveté of a Tess, and none of the practiced mannerisms of an actress engaged to "interpret" the role. That's good because Tess is a character who should stick out like a sore thumb in many scenes, and Kinski's occasional shy awkwardness is just right for the story of a girl who attempts to move up in social class on sheer bravado.

The story involves a young girl who will be the victim, the prey, and sometimes the lover of many men, without ever quite understanding what it is that those men want of her. The first man in her life is her father, a drunken farmer named John Durbeyfield, who discovers from the local parson that he is related to the noble local family of d'Urbervilles. The farmer and his wife immediately send their beautiful daughter, Tess, off to confront the d'Urbervilles and perhaps win a position in their household.

Tess is almost immediately seduced by a rakish cousin. She becomes pregnant, and her child dies soon after it is born. She never tells the cousin. But later, after she falls in love with the son of a local minister and marries him, she confesses her past. This is too much for her new husband to bear; he "married down" because he was attracted to Tess's humble origins. But he is not prepared to accept the reality of her past. He leaves on a bizarre mission to South America. Tess, meanwhile, descends to rough manual labor for a few pennies an hour. She is eventually reunited with her cousin (who is not a complete bastard, and complains that he should have been informed of her pregnancy). She becomes his lover. Then the wayward husband returns, and the physical and psychic contest for Tess ends in tragedy.

As a plot, these events would be right at home in any soap opera. But what happens in Polanski's *Tess* is less important than how Tess feels about it, how we feel about it, and how successfully Polanski is able to locate those events in a specific place and time. His movie is set in England, but was actually photographed in France. It is a beautifully visualized period piece that surrounds Tess with the attitudes of her time—attitudes that explain how restricted her behavior must be, and how society views her genuine human emotions as inappropriate. This is a wonderful film; the kind of exploration of doomed young sexuality that, like *Elvira Madigan*, makes us agree that the lovers should never grow old.

Testament ★ ★ ★ ★
PG, 90 m., 1983

Jane Alexander (Carol Wetherly), William Devane (Tom Wetherly), Ross Harris (Brad), Roxana Zal (Mary Liz), Lukas Haas (Scottie), Philip Anglim (Hollis), Leon Ames (Henry Abhart), Rebecca De Mornay (Mother with Baby). Directed by Lynne Littman and produced by Jonathan Bernstein and Littman. Screenplay by John Sacret Young.

Testament may be the first movie in a long time that will make you cry. It made me cry. And seeing it again for a second time, knowing everything that would happen, anticipating each scene before it came, I was affected just as deeply. But the second time I was able to see more clearly that the movie is more than just a devastating experience, that it has a message with a certain hope.

The film is about a suburban American family, and what happens to that family after a nuclear war. It is not a science fiction movie, and it doesn't have any special effects, and there are no big scenes of buildings blowing over or people disintegrating. We never see a mushroom cloud. We never even know who started the war. Instead, *Testament* is a tragedy about manners: It asks how we might act toward one another, how our values might stand up in the face of an overwhelming catastrophe.

The movie begins with one of those typical families right out of TV commercials. The father (William Devane) is a physical-fitness nut. The mother (Jane Alexander) is loving, funny, and a little harried. The kids include a daughter who practices the piano, a son who races his dad up hills on their ten-speed bikes, and a little boy who guards the "treasure" in the bottom drawer of his chest. The movie follows these people long enough for us to know them, to appreciate their personalities, their good and weak points, and then one sunny afternoon the war starts.

Most of the film is about what happens then. Anarchy does not break out. There is some looting, but it is limited. For the most part, the people in the small northern California town stick together and try to do the best that they can. There are meetings in the church. There are public-health measures. A beloved community leader (Leon Ames, of TV's "Life with Father" many years ago) is a ham-radio operator, and makes contact with a few other places. A decision is made to go ahead with the grade-school play. Life goes on . . . but death invades it, as radiation poisoning begins to take a toll, first on the babies, then on the children, until finally the cemetery is filled and the bodies have to be burned on a pyre.

The movie finds dozens of small details to suggest existence after the bomb. All the kids, for example, take the batteries out of their toys and computer games, and turn them in for emergency use. Gasoline is rationed, and then runs out. The survivors have no garbage collection, no electricity, and, worst of all, no word from elsewhere. The sky gradually grows darker, suggesting realistically that a nuclear war would finally kill us all by raising great clouds of dust that would choke the Earth's vegetation.

In the midst of this devastation, Jane Alexander, as the mother, tries to preserve love and decency. She stands by her children, watches as they grow in response to the challenges, cherishes them as she sees all her dreams for them disappear. It is a great performance, the heart of the film. In fact, Alexander's performance makes the film possible to watch without unbearable heartbreak, because she is brave and decent in the face of horror. And the last scene, in which she expresses such small optimism as is still possible, is one of the most powerful movie scenes I've ever seen.

Tex ★ ★ ★ ★
PG, 103 m., 1982

Matt Dillon (Tex), Jim Metzler (Mason), Meg Tilly (Jamie), Bill McKinney (Pop), Frances Lee McCain (Mrs. Johnson), Ben Johnson (Cole Collins). Directed by Tim Hunter and produced by Ron Miller. Screenplay by Charlie Haas and Hunter.

There is a shock of recognition almost from the beginning of *Tex*, because we're listening to the sound of American voices in an authentically American world, the world of teen-age boys trying to figure things out and make the right decisions. The voices sound right but may be a little unfamiliar, because adolescents on television are often made to talk in pseudo-hip sitcom nonspeak. Here in *Tex* are the clear voices of two young men who are worthy of attention. Their names are Tex and Mason. They're brothers, one about eighteen, the other fourteen and a half. They live by themselves in a rundown house on some land outside a rural suburb of Tulsa. Their father is a rodeo cowboy who hardly ever stops in at home and forgets to send money for weeks at a time. These two kids are raising themselves and doing a pretty good job of it.

The movie tells the story of a couple of weeks in their lives. These are the kinds of weeks when things can go either well or badly—and if they go badly, we sense, Tex could get his whole life off to the wrong start. The brothers are broke. Mason sells their horses to raise money to buy food and get the gas turned back on. That makes Tex angry and sad; he's a kid looking for trouble.

We meet the other people in their world. There's the rich family down the road, dominated by a stern father who makes his teenagers toe a strict line. His kids are just as unpredictable as anyone else's, but he doesn't believe that. He believes their two undisciplined friends, Tex and Mason, are leading them into trouble and practically dragging them to late-night beer parties. There's another complication. His daughter and Tex are beginning to fall in love.

There's another friend, a local kid who got a girl pregnant, married her, and moved to Tulsa to start a family. He's dealing drugs. Mason knows this intuitively and surely, and knows the kid is heading for trouble. Tex knows it, too, but there comes a time in this story when Tex just doesn't give a damn, and when the drug dealer happens to be there, Tex accepts a ride into Tulsa with him. Tex doesn't do drugs himself, but he gets into a very scary situation with another dealer, and there's a harrowing scene in which Tex wavers just at the brink of getting into serious trouble.

There is more to this movie's story, but the important thing about it isn't what happens, but how it happens. The movie is so accurately acted, especially by Jim Metzler as Mason and Matt Dillon as Tex, that we care more about the characters than about the plot. We can see them learning and growing, and when they have a heart-to-heart talk about "going all the way," we hear authentic teen-agers speaking, not kids who seem to have been raised at Beverly Hills cocktail parties.

Tex is based on a famous novel by S.E. Hinton, who has had two of her other novels filmed by Francis Ford Coppola. She knows a great deal about adolescents, and her work is unaffected by sentimentality and easy romance. It's authentic. But the backgrounds of the two filmmakers are also interesting. Tim Hunter and Charles Haas bought the book and wrote the screenplay, and Hunter directed. Their previous collaboration was a little movie named *Over the Edge*, about teen-agers who feel cornered and persecuted by the rigid middle-class rules of a cardboard Denver suburb. That movie, a small masterpiece containing Matt Dillon's first movie appearance, never got a fair chance in theaters. Now here are Hunter and Haas again, still remembering what it's like to be young, still getting the dialogue and the attitudes, the hang-ups and the dreams, exactly right.

That's Dancing! ★ ★ ★
PG, 105 m., 1985

With hosts Mikhail Baryshnikov, Ray Bolger, Sammy Davis, Jr., Gene Kelly, and Liza Minnelli. Directed by Jack Haley, Jr., and produced by David Niven, Jr., and Haley. Screenplay by Haley.

There is a sense in which it is impossible to dislike *That's Dancing!* and another sense in which movies like this—made by splicing together all the "good parts" —are irritating and sort of unfair to the original films. Given the choice of seeing *Singin' in the Rain* again or spending the same amount of time looking at scenes from *Singin'* and maybe sixty other films, I'd rather see the real movie all the way through. But *That's Dancing!* is not setting an either-or test for us; what it basically wants to do is entertain us with a lot of good dance scenes from a lot of good, and bad, movies, and that is such a harmless ambition that I guess we can accept it.

The movie has been put together by Jack Haley, Jr., and David Niven, Jr., and it recycles Haley's formula in *That's Entertainment!* (1973), the original slice-and-dice anthology from Hollywood's golden ages. There also has been a *That's Entertainment II* (or "too," I seem to recall), and the law of diminishing returns is beginning to apply. Sooner or later, we'll get *That's All, Folks!* In the first movie, for example, we got Gene Kelly's immortal title dance number from *Singin' in the Rain;* in the second movie, we got Donald O'Conner's equally immortal "Make 'em Laugh" sequence; and that leaves Kelly and O'Conner's only somewhat immortal "Moses Supposes" number for this film. Pretty soon we're going to be getting *That's What's Left of Entertainment!*

That's Dancing! shares with the earlier movies an irritating compulsion to masquerade as a documentary, which it isn't. The tone is set by Kelly's opening generalizations about the universality of dance, etc., while we see *National Geographic* outtakes of dancing around the world: tribes in Africa, hula skirts in Hawaii, polkas, geisha girls and so on. Kelly is later spelled by such other dance analysts as Liza Minnelli, Ray Bolger, Mikhail Baryshnikov, and Sammy Davis, Jr., all of whom can dance with a great deal more ease than they can recite pseudo-profundities.

There is, however, a lot of good dancing in this movie, including rare silent footage of Isadora Duncan. We see Busby Berkeley's meticulously choreographed dance geometries, the infinite style of Fred Astaire, the brassy joy of Ginger Rogers, the pizazz of Cyd Charisse and Eleanor Powell, a charming duet between Bill "Bojangles" Robinson and Shirley Temple, and a dazzling display by the Nicholas Brothers, who were the in-

spiration for the dance team played by the Hines brothers in *Cotton Club.* The movie is up-to-date, with John Travolta from *Saturday Night Fever* and footage from breakdance movies, *Flashdance,* and Michael Jackson's *Thriller.* But perhaps its most pleasing single moment is a little soft-shoe by Jimmy Cagney, who was perhaps not the technical equal of Astaire, but was certainly on the same sublime plane when it came to communicating sheer joy.

One of the insights offered in the narration of *That's Dancing!* is that Astaire was responsible for the theory that you should see the entire body of the dancer in most of the shots in a dance scene, and that the scene should be shown in unbroken shots, as much as possible, to preserve the continuity of the dancer's relationship with space and time. That's the kind of seemingly obvious statement that contains a lot of half-baked conclusions. True, you have to see the dancer's whole body to appreciate what he's doing (look at the disastrous choreography in Travolta's *Stayin' Alive,* which inspired Ginger Rogers to call it a dance film—"from the waist up"). But you also need the cutaways to show the faces of the dancers, and the chemistry between them, as when Astaire and Rogers have their enchanted dancing lesson in *Swing Time.* True, shooting the whole thing in one unbroken take preserves the integrity of the visual record—but what about the sensational dance sequences in *Flashdance* that were achieved by literally cutting between different dancers, all doing their own specialty? All that really matters is the end result.

What conclusions can be drawn from the movie's survey of sixty years of dancing on screen? I can think of one, sort of obvious and sort of depressing: Style has gone out of style. New dancers in recent dance movies are in superb physical shape and do amazing things on the screen, but they do not have the magical personal style of an Astaire or a Kelly. They're technicians. And there's another thing: They don't really dance together. A lot of them are soloists, or two soloists sharing the same floor. When Astaire and Rogers danced together, they danced *together.* And that is maybe what dancing is finally all about.

They Call Me Bruce ★ ★
PG, 88 m., 1983

Johnny Yune (Bruce), Margaux Hemingway (Girl), Pam Huntington (CIA Agent), Ralph Mauro (Chauffeur). Directed and produced by Elliott Hong. Screenplay by David Randolph, Johnny Yune, Hong, and Tim Clawson.

One thing you notice right away about kung fu heroes is that they don't talk much. They're men of action. They exchange a couple of curt words:

"You have offended my honor!"

"Ha! Ha! Now I will kill you!"

And then they lay into each other with fists, feet, elbows, and fingernails. Even in the early scenes, when they're setting up the plot, they keep the dialogue to an absolute minimum. The heroic kung fu expert goes to the temple to talk to a long-bearded Master, who says something like, "The students of Wong have offended the honor of the temple!" And then the hero replies, "Ha! Ha! Now I will kill them!"

The reason for the scarcity of dialogue in most kung fu movies is easy to explain. They're mass-produced in Hong Kong and shipped all over the world. The fewer words, the less the dubbing will cost. The makers of *They Call Me Bruce* aren't aiming for a global audience. They're making a spoof of kung fu movies for Americans who liked *Airplane!*, *Airplane II*, and *Dr. Jekyll and Mr. Hyde—Together Again*. That allows them to go long on dialogue and short on action, and in the process they lose their whole satirical edge.

They Call Me Bruce does have a few funny action scenes, a very few, but most of the time its humor depends on puns and other weak witticisms from Johnny Yune, who plays its hero. Yune is also credited with helping to write the screenplay—and I can believe that, since a lot of his dialogue sounds like it was made up on the spot. The plot is cheerfully idiotic. The Mafia wants to ship some cocaine from the West Coast to New York, disguised as a special brand of Oriental flour. So the top Mafioso assigns his Chinese cook, Bruce, to carry the dope East, escorted by a trusty chauffeur. Along the way, they get into the usual adventures, including run-ins with mobsters in Vegas and

Chicago. Yune's character is a blissful idiot, a Jerry Lewis retread who specializes in bad puns. Sample: "If you knew sushi, like I know sushi." He has his funny moments, though, especially in flashback memories to the wise old Master: "Always remember, son, kick them in the groin!" The real problem with *They Call Me Bruce* is that it's a satire of a nearly satire-proof genre. *Real* kung fu movies are so implausible and so inane that it's hard to make a satire that doesn't simply cover the same ground.

Thief ★ ★ ★ ½
R, 126 m., 1981

James Caan (Frank), Tuesday Weld (Jessie), Willie Nelson (Okla), James Belushi (Barry), Robert Prosky (Leo), Tom Signorelli (Attaglia), John Santucci (Urizzi), Tom Erhart (Judge). Directed by Michael Mann and produced by Jerry Bruckheimer and Ronnie Caan. Screenplay by Mann.

Michael Mann's *Thief* is a film of style, substance, and violently felt emotion, all wrapped up in one of the most intelligent thrillers I've seen. It's one of those films where you feel the authority right away: This movie knows its characters, knows its story, and knows exactly how it wants to tell us about them. At a time when thrillers have been devalued by the routine repetition of the same dumb chases, sex scenes, and gunfights, *Thief* is completely out of the ordinary.

The movie stars James Caan as a man who says he was "raised by the state" and spent eleven years in prison. As the movie opens, he's been free four years, and lives in Chicago. He is a highly skilled professional thief—a trade he learned behind bars from Okla (Willie Nelson), a master thief. The film's opening sequence establishes Caan's expertise as he cracks a safe with a portable drill. Caan sees himself as a completely independent loner. But we see him differently, as a lonely, unloved kid who is hiding out inside an adult body. He's a loner who desperately needs to belong to somebody. He trusts his partner (James Belushi), but that's not enough. He decides, on an almost abstract intellectual level, to fall in love with a cashier (Tuesday Weld), and in one of the movie's best scenes he tells this woman, who is essentially a stranger, all about his life in prison and his plans for the future. She takes his hand and accepts him.

But there is another person who comes into his life: Leo, the master criminal, the fence who sets up heists and hires people to pull them. Leo, in a wonderfully complex performance by the sad-faced Robert Prosky, knows how to enlist Caan: "Let me be your father," he says. "I'll take care of everything." He does. He even supplies Caan and Weld with an illegally obtained baby boy when they're turned down at the adoption agency. But once the thief goes with Leo, his life gets complicated. The cops seem to be on his case. His phone is bugged. Everybody knows his business. The movie leads up to one final caper, a $4 million diamond heist in Los Angeles, and then it ends in a series of double crosses and a rain of violence.

This movie works so well for several reasons. One is that *Thief* is able to convince us that it knows its subject, knows about the methods and criminal personalities of its characters. Another is that it's well cast: Every important performance in this movie successfully creates a plausible person, instead of the stock-company supporting characters we might have expected. And the film moves at a taut pace, creating tension and anxiety through very effective photography and a wound-up, pulsing score by Tangerine Dream.

If *Thief* has a weak point, it is probably in the handling of the Willie Nelson character. Nelson is set up well: He became Caan's father-figure in prison, Caan loves him more than anybody, and when he goes to visit him in prison they have a conversation that is subtly written to lead by an indirect route to Nelson's understated revelation that he is dying and does not want to die behind bars. This scene is so strong that it sets us up for big things: We expect Willie to get out, get involved in the plot, and be instrumental in the climax. That doesn't happen. There is a very nice courtroom scene, during which you'll have to pay close attention to catch on to the subverbal and illegal conversation conducted between the judge and the lawyer. But then the Nelson character quickly disappears from the movie, and we're surprised and a little disappointed. Willie has

played the character so well that we wanted more. But, then, I suppose it is a good thing when a movie creates characters we feel that strongly about, and *Thief* is populated with them. It's a thriller with plausible people in it. How rare.

The Thing ★ ★ ½
R, 108 m., 1982

Kurt Russell (MacReady), Wilford Brimley (Blair), T.K. Carter (Nauls), David Clennon (Palmer), Keith David (Childs), Richard Dysart (Dr. Copper). Directed by John Carpenter and produced by David Foster and Lawrence Turman. Screenplay by Bill Lancaster.

A spaceship crash-lands on Earth countless years ago and is buried under Antarctic ice. It has a creature on board. Modern scientists dig up the creature, thaw it out, and discover too late that it still lives—and has the power to imitate all life-forms. Its desire to live and expand is insatiable. It begins to assume the identities of the scientists at an isolated Antarctic research station. The crucial question becomes: Who is real, and who is the Thing? The original story was called *Who Goes There?* It was written by John W. Campbell, Jr., in the late 1930s, and it provided such a strong and scary story that it inspired at least four movie versions before this one: The original *The Thing* in 1952, *Invasion of the Body Snatchers* in 1956 and 1978, *Alien* in 1979, and now John Carpenter's 1982 remake, again called *The Thing*.

I mention the previous incarnations of *The Thing* not to demonstrate my mastery of *The Filmgoer's Companion*, but to suggest the many possible approaches to this material. The two 1950s versions, especially *Body Snatchers*, were seen at the time as fables based on McCarthyism; communists, like victims of the Thing, looked, sounded, and acted like your best friend, but they were infected with a deadly secret. *Alien*, set on a spaceship but using the same premise, paid less attention to the "Who Goes There?" idea and more to the special effects: Remember that wicked little creature that tore its way out of the astronaut's stomach? Now comes this elaborate version by John Carpenter, a master of suspense *(Halloween)*. His *Thing* depends on its special effects, which are among the most elaborate, nauseating, and horrifying sights yet achieved by Hollywood's new generation of visual magicians. There are times when we seem to be sticking our heads right down into the bloody, stinking maw of the unknown, as the Thing transforms itself into creatures with the body parts of dogs, men, lobsters, and spiders, all wrapped up in gooey intestines.

The Thing is a great barf-bag movie, all right, but is it any good? I found it disappointing, for two reasons: the superficial characterizations and the implausible behavior of the scientists on that icy outpost. Characters have never been Carpenter's strong point; he says he likes his movies to create emotions in his audiences, and I guess he'd rather see us jump six inches than get involved in the personalities of his characters. This time, though, despite some roughedout typecasting and a few reliable stereotypes (the drunk, the psycho, the hero), he has populated his ice station with people whose primary purpose in life is to get jumped on from behind. The few scenes that develop characterizations are overwhelmed by the scenes in which the men are just setups for an attack by the Thing.

That leads us to the second problem, plausibility. We know that the Thing likes to wait until a character is alone, and then pounce, digest, and imitate him—by the time you see Doc again, is he still Doc, or is he the Thing? Well, the obvious defense against this problem is a watertight buddy system, but, time and time again, Carpenter allows his characters to wander off alone and come back with silly grins on their faces, until we've lost count of who may have been infected, and who hasn't. That takes the fun away.

The Thing is basically, then, just a geek show, a grossout movie in which teenagers can dare one another to watch the screen. There's nothing wrong with that; I like being scared and I *was* scared by many scenes in *The Thing*. But it seems clear that Carpenter made his choice early on to concentrate on the special effects and the technology and to allow the story and people to become secondary. Because this material has been done before, and better, especially in the original *The Thing* and in *Alien*, there's no need to see this version unless you are interested in what the Thing might look like

while starting from anonymous greasy organs extruding giant crab legs and transmuting itself into a dog. Amazingly, I'll bet that thousands, if not millions, of moviegoers *are* interested in seeing just that.

This Is Elvis ★ ★ ★ ½
PG, 88 m., 1981

Voices: Elvis (Ral Donner), Joe Esposito (Joe Esposito), Linda Thompson (Linda Thompson), Priscilla Presley (Lisha Sweetnam). Directed, produced, and written by Malcolm Leo and Andrew Solt. Featuring documentary footage of Elvis Presley.

This Is Elvis is the extraordinary record of a man who simultaneously became a great star and was destroyed by alcohol and drug addiction. What is most striking about its documentary footage is that we can almost always see both things happening at once. There is hardly a time when Elvis doesn't appear to be under the influence of mind-altering chemicals, and never a time, not even when he is only weeks from death, when he doesn't possess his special charisma. The movie's lesson is brutal, sad, and inescapable: Elvis Presley was a man who gave joy to a great many people but felt very little of his own, because he became addicted and stayed addicted until the day it killed him.

This movie does not, however, intend to be a documentary about Presley's drug usage. It just turns out that way, because Presley's life turned out that way. The film is a re-creation of his life and image, and uses documentary footage from a wide variety of sources, including Presley's own professionally made home movies. Not all the footage is even really of Presley. Some early childhood scenes are fiction, with a young actor playing Elvis. They don't work, but they're soon over. A few other scenes are also faked, including one shot following Presley into his home on the night he died, and another showing him rushing to his mother's sickbed (the double is an Elvis imitator named Johnny Harra). But the faked footage adds up to only about 10 percent of the movie, and is helpful in maintaining continuity.

The rest of the film's footage is extraordinary, and about half of it has never been seen anywhere. This film isn't just a compilation of old Elvis documentaries. The filmmakers got permission from Presley's manager, Colonel Tom Parker, to use Presley's own private film archives and to shoot inside Graceland, his mansion. They include footage that was not even suspected to exist, including scenes from a birthday party Elvis had in Germany when he was still in the Army (we see a very young Priscilla at the party), scenes of Elvis's parents moving into Graceland, scenes with Elvis clowning around with buddies, and shots taken inside his limousine very near the end, when he was drunk and drugged and obviously very ill. There are also sequences during which we frankly wonder if he will be able to make it onto the stage.

The documentary also includes some of Presley's key television appearances, including his first guest appearances on the old "Dorsey Brothers Bandstand" and the "Ed Sullivan Show" (with Ed assuring America that Elvis was "a real decent, fine boy . . . Elvis, you're thoroughly all right"). There is newsreel footage of Elvis getting out of the Army (and, significantly, observing "it was so cold some nights we had to take bennies to stay awake"). There is an old kinescope, long thought to be lost, of a TV special hosted by Frank Sinatra to welcome Elvis back to civilian life (and in his duet with Sinatra, Presley is confused and apparently under the influence of tranquilizers).

The young Elvis in this movie is an entertainer of incredible energy and charisma. The charisma stays, but somewhere along the way we notice a change in his behavior, a draining away of cheerfulness, a dreadful secret scourge. And in the film's final scenes, Presley is shockingly ill: He's bloated, his skin is splotchy, he's shaking and dripping with sweat, and, in one very painful sequence shot during a concert, he cannot remember the words to his songs. But he pushes through anyway, and his final renditions of "My Way" and "Are You Lonesome Tonight?" are beautiful and absolutely heartbreaking. He may have lost his mind, but he never lost his voice or his heart.

Elvis Presley should, of course, still be alive. The film interviews his former bodyguards about his drinking and drug usage, and they argue convincingly that they could not stop him from doing what he was determined to do. But an addict, of course, has only two choices, no matter how he might deceive himself that he has many. He can either continue to use, or he can ask for help.

The irony in Presley's case is that his own doctor was apparently the source of most of his drugs. Could Elvis have stopped? Sure. Would he have been alive today? Probably. But he was never able to admit his addiction and find the will to seek help. And he was surrounded by foot-kissers and yes-men. This movie shows the disintegration and death of a talented man who backed himself into a corner. He did it his way.

This Is Spinal Tap ★ ★ ★ ★
R, 87 m., 1984

Rob Reiner (Marty DiBergi), Michael McKean (David St. Huggins), Christopher Guest (Nigel Tufnel), Harry Shearer (Derek Smalls). Directed by Rob Reiner and produced by Karen Murphy. Screenplay by Christopher Guest, Michael McKean, Harry Shearer, and Reiner.

The children born at Woodstock are preparing for the junior prom, and rock 'n' roll is still here to stay. Rock musicians never die, they just fade away, and *This Is Spinal Tap* is a movie about a British rock group that is rocketing to the bottom of the charts.

The movie looks like a documentary filmed during the death throes of a British rock band named Spinal Tap. It is, in fact, a satire. The rock group does not really exist, but the best thing about this film is that it could. The music, the staging, the special effects, the backstage feuding, and the pseudo-profound philosophizing are right out of a hundred other rock groups and a dozen other documentaries about rock.

The group is in the middle of an American tour. The tour is not going well. Spinal Tap was once able to fill giant arenas, but its audiences have grown smaller and smaller, and concert dates are evaporating as the bad news gets around. No wonder. Spinal Tap is a bad rock 'n' roll band. It is derivative, obvious, phony, and pretentious, and it surrounds itself with whatever images seem commercial at the moment (a giant death's-head on stage, for one). The movie is absolutely inspired in the subtle way it establishes Spinal Tap's badness. The satire has a deft, wicked touch. Spinal Tap is not that much worse than, not that much different from, some successful rock bands. A few breaks here or there, a successful album, and they could be back in business. (Proof of that: A sound track album, "Smell the Glove," is getting lots of air play with cuts like "Sex Farm".)

The documentary is narrated by its director, Marty DiBergi, played by Rob Reiner, the director of the real movie. He explains that he was first attracted to the band by its unusual loudness. He follows them on tour, asking profound questions that inspire deep, meaningless answers, and his cameras watch as the group comes unglued. One of the band members brings in a girlfriend from England. She feuds with the group's manager. Bookings are canceled. The record company doesn't like the cover for the group's new album. One disastrous booking takes Spinal Tap to a dance in a hangar on a military base. The movie is brilliant at telling its story through things that happen in the background and at the edges of the picture: By the end of the film, we know as much about the personalities and conflicts of the band members as if the movie had been straightforward narrative.

There are a lot of great visual jokes, which I don't want to spoil—especially the climax of the band's Stonehenge production number, or another number that involves them being reborn from womblike stage props. There also are moments of inspired satire aimed at previous styles in rock films, as when we get glimpses of Spinal Tap in its earlier incarnations (the band started as sort of a folk group, plunged into the flower-people generation, and was a little late getting into heavy metal, satanism, and punk).

This Is Spinal Tap assumes that audiences will get most of the jokes. I think that's right. "Entertainment Tonight" and music TV and Barbara Walters specials have made show-business trade talk into national gossip, and one of the greatest pleasures of the movie is that it doesn't explain everything. It simply, slyly, destroys one level of rock pomposity after another.

Ticket to Heaven ★ ★ ★ ½
R, 107 m., 1981

Nick Mancuso (David), Saul Rubinek (Larry), Meg Foster (Ingrid), Kim Cattrall (Ruthie), R.H. Thomson (Linc Strunk), Jennifer Dale (Lisa). Directed by Ralph L. Thomas and produced by Vivienne Lebosh.

Ticket to Heaven is about a young man who enters the all-encompassing world of a religious cult. What makes the movie absolutely spellbinding is that it shows us not only how he is recruited into the group, but how *anyone* could be indoctrinated into one of the many cults in America today. This is a movie that has done its research, and it is made with such artistry that we share the experience of the young man.

His name is David. He is played by Nick Mancuso, a powerful young actor, as an independent type who flies from Toronto to San Francisco to discover what has happened to a friend who joined up with the cult. He is welcomed to their communal residence, joins in a meal and some singing, and is asked if he'd like to spend the weekend at a retreat on the group's farm. He would. By the end of the weekend, he is a cult member. Can it happen that fast? I've read stories claiming that some cults need only seventy-two hours to convert almost anyone to their way. The best and the brightest make the best recruits, they say. The movie shows the three techniques used to indoctrinate new members: (1) low-calorie, low-protein diets; (2) sleep deprivation; (3) "love-bombing," which involves constant positive reinforcement, the chanting of slogans and great care *never* to allow the recruit to be alone for a moment.

Although *Ticket to Heaven* does not mention any existing cult by name, it is based on a series of newspaper articles about a former Moonie. The techniques in the film could, I suppose, be used by anybody. What makes the film so interesting is that it's not just a docudrama, not just a sensationalist exposé, but a fully realized drama that involves us on the human level as well as with its documentary material. There are scenes that are absolutely harrowing: an overhead shot of David trying to take a walk by himself and being "joined" by jolly friends; a scene where he guiltily bolts down a forbidden hamburger;

a scene where another cult member whispers one sentence that sounds to us, as much as to David, like shocking heresy. By that point in the film, we actually understand why David has become so zombie-like and unquestioning. We have shared his experience.

The final scenes in the film involve a de-programming attempt. They are not as absorbing as what went before, if only because they involve an effort of the intellect, instead of an assault on the very personality itself. I've seen *Ticket to Heaven* three times, and at first I thought the film's ending was "weaker" than the rest. Now I wonder. What cults offer is freedom from the personality. They remove from your shoulders the burden of being you. That is a very seductive offer: why else do people also seek freedom from self through drugs, alcohol, and even jogging? As David is seduced into the cult's womb, we also submit vicariously to the experience. We understand its appeal. At the end, as David's reason is appealed to, as his intellect is reawakened, as he is asked to once again take up the burden of being himself, he resists—and maybe we do, too.

Tightrope ★ ★ ★ ½
R, 114 m., 1984

Clint Eastwood (Wes Block), Genevieve Bujold (Beryl Thibodeaux), Dan Hedaya (Detective Molinari), Alison Eastwood (Amanda Block), Jennifer Beck (Penny Block). Directed by Richard Tuggle and produced by Clint Eastwood and Fritz Manes. Screenplay by Tuggle.

Most modern police thrillers are simple-minded manipulations of chases, violence, pop psychology, and characters painted in broad stereotypes. *Tightrope* contains all four of those ingredients, to be sure, but it also contains so much more that it's a throwback to the great cop movies of the 1940s—when the hero wrestled with his conscience as much as with the killer.

The movie stars Clint Eastwood as a New Orleans homicide detective who is as different as possible from Dirty Harry Callahan. The guy's name is Wes Block. His wife has recently left him, and he lives at home with his two young daughters and several dogs. He is a good but flawed cop, with a peculiar hang-up: He likes to make love to women while they are handcuffed. The movie suggests this is because he feels deeply threatened by women (a good guess, I'd say). Detective Block is well-known to most of the kinkier prostitutes in the French Quarter, but his superiors don't know that when they assign him to a big case: A mad slasher, apparently an ex-cop, is killing hookers in the Quarter. Block's problem is that he cannot easily enter this world as a policeman after having entered it often as a client. His other problem is that when he walks into that world, all of his old urges return.

The police work in *Tightrope* is more or less standard: The interviews of suspects, the paperwork, the scenes where his superiors chew him out for not making more progress on the case. What makes *Tightrope* better than just another police movie are the scenes between Eastwood and the women he encounters. Some of them are hookers. Some are victims. One of them, played by Genevieve Bujold, is a feminist who teaches women's self-defense classes. Block has always been attracted to flashy, gaudy women, like the Quarter's more bizarre prostitutes. We do not know why his wife left him, and we are given no notions of what she was like, but right away we figure that Bujold isn't his type. She's in her mid-thirties, uses no makeup, wears sweat shirts a lot, and isn't easily impressed by cops. But somehow a friendship does begin. And it becomes the counterpoint for the cop's investigation, as he goes deeper into the messy underworld of the crimes—and as more of the evidence seems to suggest that he should be one of the suspects. It's interesting that the movie gives Eastwood two challenges: To solve the murders, and to find a way out of his own hang-ups and back into an emotional state where he can trust a strong woman.

Tightrope may appeal to the Dirty Harry fans, with its sex and violence. But it's a lot more ambitious than the Harry movies, and the relationship between Eastwood and Bujold is more interesting than most recent male-female relationships in the movies, for three reasons: (1) There is something at risk in it, on both sides; (2) it's a learning process, in which Eastwood is the one who must change; (3) it pays off dramatically at the end, when their developing relationship fits into the climax of the investigation. Think how unusual it is for a major male star to appear in a commercial cop picture in which the plot hinges on his ability to accept and respect a woman. Apart from the other good things in *Tightrope*, I admire it for taking chances; Clint Eastwood can get rich making Dirty Harry movies, but he continues to change and experiment, and that makes him the most interesting of the box office megastars.

Time Bandits ★ ★ ★
PG, 98 m., 1981

Craig Warnock (Kevin), John Cleese (Robin Hood), Sean Connery (Agamemnon), Shelley Duvall (Pansy), Ian Holm (Napoleon), Ralph Richardson (Supreme Being). The Dwarfs: David Rappaport (Randall), Kenny Baker (Fidget), Jack Purvis (Wally), Mike Edmonds (Og), Malcolm Dixon (Strutter), Tiny Ross (Vermin). Directed and produced by Terry Gilliam. Screenplay by Michael Palin and Gilliam.

First reactions while viewing *Time Bandits:* It's amazingly well-produced. The historic locations are jammed with character and detail. This is the only live-action movie I've seen that literally looks like pages out of *Heavy Metal* magazine, with kings and swordsmen and wide-eyed little boys and fearsome beasts. *But* the movie's repetitive, monotonous in the midst of all this activity. Basically, it's just a kid and six dwarfs racing breathlessly through one set-piece after another, shouting at one another. I walked out of the screening in an unsettled state of mind. When the lights go up, I'm usually fairly certain whether or not I've seen a good movie. But my reaction to *Time Bandits* was ambiguous. I had great admiration for what was physically placed on the screen; this movie is worth seeing just to *watch*. But I was disappointed by the breathless way the dramatic scenes were handled and by a breakneck pace that undermined the most important element of comedy, which is timing.

Time Bandits is the expensive fantasy by Terry Gilliam, one of the resident geniuses of Monty Python's Flying Circus. It is *not* a Monty Python film. It begins with a little boy who goes up to bed one night and is astonished, as we all would be, when a horse-

man gallops through his bedroom wall and he is in the middle of a pitched battle. Before long, the little kid has joined up with a band of six intrepid dwarfs, and they've embarked on an odyssey through history. The dwarfs, it appears, have gained possession of a map that gives the location of several holes in time—holes they can pop through in order to drop in on the adventures of Robin Hood, Napoleon, and King Agamemnon, and to sail on the *Titanic*'s maiden voyage.

As a plot gimmick, this sets up *Time Bandits* for a series of comic set-pieces as in Mel Brooks's *History of the World—Part I*. But *Time Bandits* isn't revue-style comedy. It's more of a whimsical, fantastic excursion through all those times and places, and all of its events are seen through the wondering eyes of a child. That's where the superb art direction comes in—inspired work by production designer Milly Burns and costume designer Jim Acheson. I've rarely, if ever, seen a live-action movie that looks more like an artist's conception. And yet, admiring all of these good things (and I might also mention several of the performances), I nevertheless left the screening with muted enthusiasm. The movie was somehow all on the same breathless, nonstop emotional level, like an overlong Keystone Kops chase. It didn't pause to savor its delights, except right near the end, when Sir Ralph Richardson lingered lovingly over a walk-on as the Supreme Being. I had to sort things out. And I was helped enormously in that process by the review of *Time Bandits* by Stanley Kauffmann in *The New Republic*. He describes the film, unblinkingly, as a "children's movie." Of course.

There have been so many elaborate big-budget fantasies in recent years, from *Raiders* to *Superman* to *Clash of the Titans*, that we've come to assume that elaborate costume fantasies are aimed at the average eighteen-year-old filmgoer who is trying to recapture his adolescence. These movies have a level of (limited) sophistication and wickedness that is missing in *Time Bandits*. But perhaps *Time Bandits* does work best as just simply a movie for kids. I ran it through my mind that way, wondering how a kid would respond to the costumes, the panoply, the explosions, the horses and heroic figures and, of course, the breathless, nonstop pacing. And I decided that a kid would like it just fine. I'm not sure that's what Gilliam had in mind, but it allows me to recommend the movie—with reservations, but also with admiration.

The Times of Harvey Milk ★ ★ ★ ½
NO MPAA RATING, 87 m., 1985 ✔

A documentary by Robert Epstein and Richard Schmiechen, narrated by Harvey Fierstein.

Harvey Milk must have been a great guy. You get the sense watching this documentary about his brief public career that he could appreciate the absurdities of life and enjoy a good laugh at his own expense. He was also serious enough and angry enough about the political issues in his life that he eventually ran for the San Francisco Board of Supervisors and became California's first openly homosexual public official. That victory may have cost him his life.

The Times of Harvey Milk describes the lives and deaths of Milk and Mayor George Moscone, who both were shot dead in 1978 by Dan White, one of Milk's fellow supervisors. It also describes the political and social climate in San Francisco, which during the 1960s and 1970s began to attract growing numbers of gays because of its traditionally permissive attitude. Milk was one of those gays, and in old photographs we see him in his long-haired beatnik and hippie days before he eventually shaved off the beard and opened a camera store in the Castro District. It was from the Castro that Milk ran for office and was defeated three times before finally winning in the same election that placed the first Chinese-American, the first black woman, and the first avowed feminist on the board. Milk was a master at self-promotion, and the movie includes vintage TV news footage showing him campaigning on such issues as "doggy-do," and stepping, with perfect timing, into a strategically placed pile of same at the climax of the interview.

There is a lot of footage of Milk, Moscone, and White (who disapproved of homosexuals but was naive enough to once suggest that the issue be settled by a softball game between his ward and Milk's ward). It is intercut with later interviews with many of Milk's friends, including a veteran leftist who admits that he was prejudiced against gays for a long time, until he met Milk and began to understand the political issues involved. There is a Chinese-American who parallels his own radicalization with Milk's. And there is immensely moving, emotional footage of the two demonstrations inspired by the deaths of Milk and Moscone: a silent, candlelight parade of forty-five-thousand people on the night of their deaths, and an angry night of rioting when White got what was perceived as a lenient sentence.

"If Dan White had only killed George Moscone, he would have gone up for life," one person says in the film. "But he killed a gay, and so they let him off easy." This is not necessarily the case, and the weakest element in *The Times of Harvey Milk* is its willingness to let Milk's friends second-guess the jury, and impugn the jurors' motives.

Many people who observed White's trial believe that White got a light sentence, not because of antigay sentiment, but because of incompetent prosecution. Some of the jurors were presumably available to the filmmakers, and the decision not to let them speak for themselves—to depend instead on the interpretation of Milk's friends and associates—is a serious bias. That objection aside, this is an enormously absorbing film, for the light it sheds on a decade in the life of a great American city and on the lives of Milk and Moscone, who made it a better, and certainly a more interesting, place to live.

The Tin Drum ★ ★
R, 141 m., 1980

David Bennett (Oskar), Mario Adorf (Alfred), Angela Winkler (Agnes), Daniel Olbrychski (Bronski), Katherina Tahlback (Maria), Charles Aznavour (Markus). Directed by Volker Schlondorff and produced by Frank Seitz and Anatole Dauman. Screenplay by Jean-Claude Carriere, Schlondorff, Franz Seitz, and Gunter Grass.

Allegories have trouble standing for something else if they are too convincing as themselves. That is the difficulty with *The Tim Drum*, which is either (a) an allegory about one person's protest against the inhumanity of the world, or (b) the story of an obnoxious little boy. The movie invites us to see the world through the eyes of little Oskar, who on his third birthday refuses to do any more growing up because the world is such a cruel place. My problem is that I kept seeing Oskar not as a symbol of courage but as an unsavory brat; the film's foreground obscured its larger meaning.

So what does that make me? An anti-intellectual philistine? I hope not. But if it does, that's better than caving in to the tumult of praise for *The Tin Drum*, which has shared the Grand Prix at Cannes (with *Apocalypse Now*) and won the Academy Award as best foreign film, and is hailed on all fronts for its brave stand against war and nationalism and in favor of the innocence of childhood. Actually, I don't think little Oskar is at all innocent in this film; a malevolence seems to burn from his eyes, and he's compromised in his rejection of the world's evil by his own behavior as the most spiteful, egocentric, cold, and calculating character in the film (all right: except for Adolf Hitler).

The film has been adapted by the West German filmmaker Volker Schlondorff from the 1959 novel by Gunter Grass, who helped with the screenplay. It chronicles the career of little Oskar, who narrates his own life story starting with his mother's conception in a potato patch. Oskar is born into a world divided; in the years after World War I, both Germans and Poles live in the state of Danzig, where they get along about as well as Catholics and Protestants in Belfast.

Oskar has fathers of both nationalities (for reasons too complicated to explain here), and he is not amused by the nationalistic chauvinism he sees around him. So, on his third birthday, he reaches a conscious decision to stop growing. He provides a plausible explanation for his decision by falling down the basement stairs. And for the rest of the movie he remains arrested in growth: a solemn-faced, beady-eyed little tyke who never goes anywhere without a tin drum which he beats on incessantly. For his other trick, he can scream so loudly that he shatters glass. There is a scene in which Oskar's drum so confuses a Nazi marching band that it switches from a Nazi hymn to "The Blue Danube." The crashing obviousness of this

scene aside, I must confess that the symbolism of the drum failed to involve me.

And here we are at the central problem of the movie: Should I decide to take the drum as, say, a child's toy protest against the marching cadences of the German armies? Or should I allow myself to be annoyed by the child's obnoxious habit of banging on it whenever something's not to his liking? Even if I buy the wretched drum as a Moral Symbol, I'm still stuck with the kid as a pious little bastard.

But what about the other people in the movie? Oskar is right at the middle of the tug-of-war over Danzig and, by implication, over Europe. People are choosing up sides between the Poles and the Nazis. Meanwhile, all around him, adult duplicity is a way of life. Oskar's mother, for example, sneaks away on Thursday afternoons for an illicit sexual interlude. Oskar interrupts her dalliance with a scream that supplies work for half the glassmakers in Danzig. Does this make him a socialist or an Oedipus?

Soon after, he finds himself on the road with a troupe of performing midgets. He shatters glasses on cue, marches around in uniform, and listens as the troupe's leader explains that little people have to stay in the spotlight or big people will run the show. This idea is the last one Oskar needs to have implanted in his mind.

The movie juxtaposes Oskar's one-man protest with the horror of World War II. But I am not sure what the juxtaposition means. Did I miss everything? I've taken the story on a literal level, but I don't think that means I misread the film *as it stands*.

If we come in armed with the Grass novel and a sheaf of reviews, it's maybe just possible to discipline ourselves to read *The Tin Drum* as a solemn allegorical statement. But if we take the chance of just watching what's on the screen, Schlondorff never makes the connection. We're stuck with this cretinous little kid, just when Europe has enough trouble of its own.

To Be or Not To Be ★ ★ ★
R, 108 m., 1983

Mel Brooks (Bronski), Anne Bancroft (Anna Bronski), Tim Matheson (Lieutenant

Sobinski), Charles Durning (Colonel Erhardt), Jose Ferrer (Professor Siletski). Directed by Alan Johnson and produced by Mel Brooks. Screenplay by Thomas Meehan and Ronny Graham.

It's an old gag, the one about the actor who is always interrupted in the middle of Hamlet's soliloquy by a guy in the third row who has to go to the john and loudly excuses himself all the way to the end of the row. But I can't think of a better Hamlet for this particular gag than Mel Brooks. "That is the QUESTION!" he bellows, as the guy screws up his timing, his delivery, his concentration. And the punch line is that the guy is actually going backstage to have a quick assignation with the actor's wife.

Mel Brooks loves show business and has worked it into a lot of his movies, most unforgettably in *The Producers*. He also loves musicals and has worked musical numbers into the most unlikely moments in his movies. (Remember Frankenstein's monster doing the soft-shoe?) In *To Be or Not To Be*, Brooks combines a backstage musical with a wartime romance and comes up with an eclectic comedy that races off into several directions, sometimes successfully.

The movie costars Brooks and his wife, Anne Bancroft, working together for the first time on screen as Frederick and (Anna) Bronski, the impresarios of a brave little theatrical troupe in Warsaw on the brink of war. (Anna) Bronski, whose name is in parentheses because her husband has such a big ego, is a femme fatale with an eye for the handsome young servicemen that worship her nightly in the theater. Bronski is an all-over-the-map guy who does Hamlet's soliloquy and stars in a revue called *Naughty Nazis* in the same night and on the same stage. Then the Nazis march into Poland. What can a humble troupe of actors do to stop them? "Nothing!" Bronski declares—but then the troupe gets involved in an elaborate masquerade, pretending to be real Nazis in order to throw Hitler's men off-course and prevent the success of the German plans.

When *To Be or Not To Be* was originally made, by Ernst Lubitsch in 1942, the Nazis *were* in Poland, which gave a certain poignancy to every funny line. Lubitsch's stars were Jack Benny and Carole Lombard, both specialists in underplaying. Brooks and Bancroft go in the opposite direction, cheerfully allowing farce, slapstick, pratfalls, and puns into the story, until the whole movie seems strung together like one of the revues in Bronski's theater.

The supporting players, given license to overact, have fun. Charles Durning plays a rigid but peculiarly confused Nazi colonel, and Tim Matheson is the young aviator who excuses himself loudly and sneaks backstage to meet Bancroft. The veteran actor Jose Ferrer plays Professor Siletski, a two-faced collaborator.

It will probably always be impossible for Brooks to remain entirely within the dramatic logic of any story, and here he gives himself a lot of freedom with lines like "Sondheim! Send in the clowns!" But *To Be or Not To Be* works as well as a story as any Brooks film since *Young Frankenstein*, and darned if there isn't a little sentiment involved as the impresario and his wife, after years of marriage, surprise each other by actually falling in love.

Tootsie ★ ★ ★ ★
PG, 116 m., 1982

Dustin Hoffman (Michael), Jessica Lange (Julie), Charles Durning (Les Nichols), Teri Garr (Sandy), Bill Murray (Roommate), Dabney Coleman (Ron), Doris Belack (Rita), Sydney Pollack (Agent). Directed by Sydney Pollack and produced by Dick Richards. Screenplay by Larry Gelbart.

One of the most endearing things about *Tootsie*, a movie in which Dustin Hoffman plays a middle-aged actress, is that the actress is able to carry most of her own scenes as herself—even if she weren't being played by Hoffman. *Tootsie* works as a story, not as a gimmick. It also works as a lot of other things. *Tootsie* is the kind of Movie with a capital M that they used to make in the 1940s, when they weren't afraid to mix up absurdity with seriousness, social comment with farce, and a little heartfelt tenderness right in there with the laughs. This movie gets you coming and going.

Hoffman stars as Michael Dorsey, a character maybe not unlike Hoffman himself in his younger days. Michael is a New York actor: bright, aggressive, talented—and un-employable. "You mean *nobody in New York* wants to hire me?" he asks his agent, incredulously. "I'd go farther than that, Michael," his agent says. "Nobody in Hollywood wants to hire you, either." Michael has a bad reputation for taking stands, throwing tantrums, and interpreting roles differently than the director. How to get work? He goes with a friend (Teri Garr) to an audition for a soap opera. The character is a middle-age woman hospital administrator. When his friend doesn't get the job, Michael goes home, thinks, decides to dare, and dresses himself as a woman. And, improvising brilliantly, he gets the role.

That leads to *Tootsie's* central question: Can a fortyish New York actor find health, happiness, and romance as a fortyish New York actress? Dustin Hoffman is actually fairly plausible as "Dorothy," the actress. If his voice isn't quite right, a Southern accent allows it to squeak by. The wig and the glasses are a little too much, true, but in an uncanny way the woman played by Hoffman looks like certain actual women who look like drag queens. Dorothy might have trouble passing in Evanston, but in Manhattan, nobody gives her a second look.

Tootsie might have been content to limit itself to the complications of New York life in drag; it could have been *Victor/Victoria Visits Elaine's*. But the movie's a little more ambitious than that. Michael Dorsey finds to his interest and amusement that Dorothy begins to take on a life of her own. She's a liberated eccentric, a woman who seems sort of odd and funny at first, but grows on you and wins your admiration by standing up for what's right. One of the things that bothers Dorothy is the way the soap opera's chauvinist director (Dabney Coleman) mistreats and insults the attractive young actress (Jessica Lange) who plays Julie, a nurse on the show. Dorothy and Julie become friends and finally close confidantes. Dorothy's problem, however, is that the man inside her is gradually growing uncontrollably in love with Julie. There are other complications. Julie's father (Charles Durning), a gruff, friendly, no-nonsense sort, lonely but sweet, falls in love with Dorothy. Michael hardly knows how to deal with all of this, and his roommate (Bill Murray) isn't much help.

Surveying Dorothy in one of her new outfits, he observes dryly, "Don't play hard to get."

Tootsie has a lot of fun with its plot complications; we get almost every possible variation on the theme of mistaken sexual identities. The movie also manages to make some lighthearted but well-aimed observations about sexism. It *also* pokes satirical fun at soap operas, New York show business agents, and the Manhattan social pecking-order. *And* it turns out to be a touching love story, after all—so touching that you may be surprised how moved you are at the conclusion of this comedy.

Top Secret! ★ ★ ★ ½
R, 90 m., 1984

Val Kilmer (Nick Rivers), Lucy Gutteridge (Hillary), Omar Sharif (Cedric), Peter Cushing (Bookseller). Directed by Jim Abrahams, David Zucker, and Jerry Zucker and produced by Jon Davison and Hunt Lowry. Written by Abrahams, Zucker and Zucker, with Martyn Burke.

I have a friend who claims he only laughed real loud on five occasions during *Top Secret!* I laughed that much in the first ten minutes. It all depends on your sense of humor. My friend claims that I have a cornpone sense of humor, because of my origins deep in central Illinois. I admit that is true. As a Gemini, however, I contain multitudes, and I also have a highly sophisticated, sharply intellectual sense of humor. Get me in the right mood, and I can laugh all over the map. That's why I liked *Top Secret!* This movie will cheerfully go for a laugh wherever one is even remotely likely to be found. It has political jokes and boob jokes, dog poop jokes, and ballet jokes. It makes fun of two completely different Hollywood genres: the spy movie and the Elvis Presley musical. It contains a political refugee who fled America by balloon during the Carter administration, a member of the French underground named Escargot, and Omar Sharif inside a compacted automobile.

To describe the plot would be an exercise in futility. This movie has no plot. It does not need a plot. One does not attend movies like *Top Secret!* in order to follow the story line. I think you can figure that out right away, in the opening sequence, which is devoted to the sport of "skeet surfin'" and has beach boys on surfboards firing at clay targets. Instead of a plot, it has a funny young actor named Val Kilmer as the hero, a 1950s-style American rock 'n' roller who is sent on a concert tour behind the Iron Curtain, and manages to reduce East Germany to a shambles while never missing a word of "Tutti Frutti" (he never even stumbles during *a-wop-bop-a-doo bop, a bop-bam-boom*).

The movie is physical humor, sight gags, puns, double meanings, satire, weird choreography, scatalogical outrages, and inanity. One particular sequence, however, is such an original example of specifically cinematic humor that I'd like to discuss it at length. (Do not read further if you don't like to understand jokes before laughing at them.) The sequence involves a visit by the hero to a Swedish bookshop. Never mind why he goes there. The scene depends for its inspiration on this observation: People who run tape recorders backward often say that English, played backward, sounds like Swedish (especially, of course, to people who do not speak Swedish). What *Top Secret!* does is to film an entire scene and play it backward, so that the dialogue sounds Swedish, and then translate it into English subtitles. This is funny enough at the beginning, but it becomes inspired at the end, when the scene finally gives itself away.

There are other wonderful moments. The dance sequence in the East Berlin nightclub develops into something Groucho Marx would have been proud of. The malt shop musical number demolishes a whole tradition of Elvis Presley numbers. And how the ballerina makes her exit in *Swan Lake* will, I feel confident, be discussed for years wherever codpieces are sold.

Tough Enough ★ ★ ★
PG, 197 m., 1983

Dennis Quaid (Art Long), Stan Shaw (Coolidge), Warren Oates (Neese), Carlene Watkins (Caroline Long), Pam Grier (Myra), Wilford Brimley (Art's father). Directed by Richard O. Fleischer and produced by William S. Gilmore. Screenplay by John Leone.

There were articles in all the papers a few years ago about Tough Man Contests, a brilliant method of exploiting saloon fighters and street-corner brawlers. A promoter comes to town, rents a hall, and says he wants to find the toughest man in town. Every macho drunk for miles around signs up. On the appointed night, the tough guys climb into the ring and hammer each other, and the winner gets a cash prize and a chance to move on to the semifinals. The genius of Tough Man contests is that they combine the violence of prizefighting, the buffoonery of pro wrestling, the show business of Roller Derby, and the chance to see local boys making idiots out of themselves. Given all the energy expended annually in saloon brawls, it was probably only a matter of time until someone found a way to package it.

Tough Enough is a nice little movie about Tough Guy contests, a goofy entertainment that has some good moments and a couple of interesting characters. The movie stars Dennis Quaid as a would-be country singer who signs up for a contest to get money to pay the rent. Stan Shaw is a local kid who gets eliminated in an early round and stays on as Quaid's trainer. And the late Warren Oates turns up as the originator and promoter of the Tough Man empire.

The movie's really two stories in one. The most obvious story involves the fights themselves, and the movie's major flaw is that it has too many fight scenes—so many that it repeats itself and we lose interest (the *Rocky* pictures always saved the best fight for the last). It's the secondary story that's more interesting—the story about Quaid and his discontented wife, Shaw and his ringside quarterbacking, and Oates and his con man's dream. The screenplay, by John Leone, tries to slip as much quirky characterization as possible in between the prizefight scenes, and there are nice little dialogue touches in the movie, and quiet, funny little moments that show somebody was thinking.

One of my favorite scenes is a locker room confrontation between Quaid and Oates. The promoter tells him he's going to lose the big $100,000 fight. It's not so much a fix as a sure thing: There's no way Quaid can beat the bruiser he's up against. This scene could have been played as a showdown with an oily con man. Instead, the Oates character takes the situation in a direction we don't anticipate.

I also liked the scenes between Quaid and Shaw and especially Shaw's quick, comic advice from ringside. These scenes made me want to know more about the characters and less about the endless parade of Tough Man contestants. The movie also introduces a couple of female characters; Carlene Watkins plays Quaid's wife as a boringly one-dimensional scold, and the magnetic Pam Grier is thrown away in yet another disappointing role, as Shaw's wife. *Tough Enough* never quite breaks out of its prize-fight clichés, but it's fun anyway, and there are moments when it really works.

Trading Places ★ ★ ★ ½
R, 106 m., 1983

Dan Aykroyd (Louis Winthorpe III), Eddie Murphy (Billy Ray Valentine), Ralph Bellamy (Randolph Duke), Don Ameche (Mortimer Duke), Denholm Elliott (Coleman), Jamie Lee Curtis (Ophelia), Jim Belushi (King Kong). Directed by John Landis and produced by Aaron Russo. Screenplay by Timothy Harris and Herschel Weingrod.

Trading Places resembles *Tootsie* and, for that matter, some of the classic Frank Capra and Preston Sturges comedies: It wants to be funny, but it also wants to tell us something about human nature and there are whole stretches when we forget it's a comedy and get involved in the story. And it's a great idea for a story: A white preppy snot and a black street hustler trade places, and learn new skills they never dreamed existed.

This isn't exactly a new idea for a story (Mark Twain's *The Prince and the Pauper* comes to mind). But like a lot of stories, it depends less on plot than on character, and the characters in *Trading Places* are wonderful comic inventions. Eddie Murphy plays Billy Ray Valentine, the con man who makes his first appearance as a blind, legless veteran. Dan Aykroyd is Louis Winthorpe III, the stuck-up commodities broker. And, in a masterstroke of casting, those aging veterans Ralph Bellamy and Don Ameche are cast as the Duke brothers, incalculably rich men who compete by making little wagers involving human lives.

One day a particularly tempting wager occurs to them. Aykroyd has had Murphy arrested for stealing his briefcase. It's an unfair charge and Murphy is innocent, but Murphy is black and had the misfortune to bump into Aykroyd in front of a snobby club. To Mortimer Duke (Ameche), a believer that enviroment counts for more than heredity, this is a golden opportunity to test his theory. He bets his brother that if Aykroyd and Murphy were to change places, the black street kid would soon be just as good at calling the shots in the commodity markets as the white Ivy Leaguer ever was. Because the Dukes are rich, they can make almost anything happen. They strip Aykroyd of everything—his job, his home, his butler, his fiancée, his limousine, his self-respect. They give Murphy what they've taken from Aykroyd. And the rest of the movie follows the fortunes of the two changelings as they painfully adjust to their new lives, and get involved in a commodities scam the Duke brothers are trying to pull off.

This is good comedy. It's especially good because it doesn't stop with sitcom manipulations of its idea, and it doesn't go only for the obvious points about racial prejudice in America. Instead, it develops the quirks and peculiarities of its characters, so that they're funny because of who they are. This takes a whole additional level of writing on top of the plot-manipulation we usually get in popular comedies, and it takes good direction, too.

But what's most visible in the movie is the engaging acting. Murphy and Aykroyd are perfect foils for each other in *Trading Places*, because they're both capable of being so specifically eccentric that we're never just looking at a "black" and a "white" (that would make the comedy unworkable). They both play characters with a lot of native intelligence to go along with their prejudices, peculiarities, and personal styles. It's fun to watch them thinking. The supporting cast has also been given detailed attention, instead of being assigned to stand around as stereotypes. Jamie Lee Curtis plays a hooker with a heart of gold and a lot of T-bills; Ameche and Bellamy have a lot of fun with the Duke brothers; and Denholm Elliott successfully plays butler to both Aykroyd and Murphy, which is a stretch. The movie's invention extends all the way to the climactic scenes, which involve, not the usual manic chase, but a commodities scam, a New Year's Eve party on a train, and a gay gorilla.

Tribute ★ ★ ★
PG, 123 m., 1981

Jack Lemmon (Scottie Templeton), Robby Benson (Jud Templeton), Lee Remick (Maggie Stratton), Colleen Dewhurst (Gladys Petrelli), John Marley (Lou Daniels), Kim Cattrall (Sally Haines). Directed by Bob Clark and produced by Joel B. Michaels and Garth H. Drabinski. Screenplay by Bernard Slade.

I am aware that *Tribute* hauls out some of the oldest Broadway clichés in the book, that it shamelessly exploits its melodramatic elements, and that it is not a movie so much as a filmed stage play. And yet if I were to review it just on those grounds, I would be less than honest. In the abstract, *Tribute* may not be a very good film at all. But in its particulars, and in the way they affected me, it is a touching experience.

It's supposed to be cheating to make an admission like that. I myself believe that it is a film's form, more than its message, that makes it great. And yet *Tribute* is not a visually distinguished film. It has been directed, by Bob Clark, as a straightforward job of work. There are long sequences that are obviously just filmed scenes from Bernard Slade's original stage play. Yet the characters transcend these limitations and become people that we care about.

The film is mostly Jack Lemmon's, and he deserved his seventh Academy Award nomination for his performance as Scottie Templeton, the movie's hero. We all know somebody like Scottie—if we are not, God forbid, a little like Scottie ourselves. He's a wisecracking, popular guy with hundreds of deeply intimate passing acquaintances. He also has a few friends. One of them is his business partner (John Marley) and another is his ex-wife (Lee Remick). They love him and stand by him, but he can't allow himself to reveal how much that means to him. He is also hurt by his relationship with his son (Robby Benson), who has the usual collection of post-adolescent grudges against his father. All of these relationships suddenly become much more important when Scottie discovers he is dying. The movie begins at about that point in Scottie's life, and exam-

ines how the fact of approaching death changes all of Scottie's ways of dealing with the living.

His son comes home to visit for a few weeks. His wife returns to New York for a college reunion and stays to become involved in the crisis. The friend, Marley, acts as counsel and adjudicator. Other characters pass through, including a young woman (Kim Cattrall) who Scottie thinks would be ideal for his son (after all, she'd previously been ideal for Scottie himself). Veteran playgoers can already predict the obligatory scenes growing out of this situation. Scottie will be brave at first, then angry, then depressed, then willing to reach out to his son, and finally reconciled to his fate. Scottie's friends will rally around. His son will learn to love the old man. Everybody will become more human and sensitive, and the possibility of death will provide an occasion for a celebration of life. Et cetera.

What's amazing is that when these predictable situations appear, the movie makes them work. A great deal of the credit for that belongs to Lemmon and Benson. They are both actors with a familiar schtick by now: Benson trembling with emotions, Lemmon fast-talking his way into sincerity. In *Tribute*, though, the movie's characters are so close to the basic strengths of Lemmon and Benson that everything seems to work.

Take Lemmon, for example. Another actor, playing Scottie Templeton, might simply seem to be saying funny lines, alternating with bittersweet insights. Lemmon makes us believe that they're not lines; they're the way this guy talks. The big emotional changes take place underneath the surface wisecracks, making them all the more poignant. Robby Benson sometimes comes across as too vulnerable, almost affected in his sensitivity. Here, he's good, too: Examine the early scene where his father asks what the hell's going on, and Benson begins, "Let me try to explain about that . . . ." with touching formality.

Maybe your reaction to *Tribute* will depend on your state of mind. I know people who say they "saw through it," dismissing it as merely a well-made play. I know others, myself included, who were really touched by it. Perhaps the film works better because it's *willing* to be a bittersweet soap opera. Life itself, after all, is rarely a great directorial achievement, but almost always seems to work on the melodramatic level.

Tron ★ ★ ★ ★
PG, 96 m., 1982

Jeff Bridges (Flynn/Clu), Bruce Boxleitner (Alan/Tron), David Warner (Dillinger/Sark), Cindy Morgan (Lora/Yori), Barnard Hughes (Gibbs/Dumont), Dan Shor (Ram). Directed by Steven Lisberger and produced by Donald Kushner. Screenplay by Lisberger.

The interior of a computer is a fine and private place, but none, I fear, do there embrace, except in *Tron*, a dazzling movie from Walt Disney in which computers have been used to make themselves romantic and glamorous. Here's a technological sound-and-light show that is sensational and brainy, stylish and fun.

The movie addresses itself without apology to the computer generation, embracing the imagery of those arcade video games that parents fear are rotting the minds of their children. If you've never played Pac-Man or Space Invaders or the Tron game itself, you probably are not quite ready to see this movie, which begins with an evil bureaucrat stealing computer programs to make himself look good, and then enters the very mind of a computer itself to engage the villain, the hero, and several highly programmable bystanders in a war of the wills that is governed by the rules of both video games and computer programs.

The villain is a man named Dillinger (David Warner). The hero is a bright kid named Flynn (Jeff Bridges) who created the original programs for five great new video games, including the wonderfully named "Space Paranoia." Dillinger stole Flynn's plans and covered his tracks in the computer. Flynn believes that if he can track down the original program, he can prove Dillinger is a thief. To prevent that, Dillinger uses the very latest computer technology to break Flynn down into a matrix of logical points and insert him *into* the computer, and at that point *Tron* leaves any narrative or visual universe we have ever seen before in a movie and charts its own rather wonderful path.

In an age of amazing special effects, *Tron* is a state-of-the-art movie. It generates not just one imaginary computer universe, but a multitude of them. Using computers as their tools, the Disney filmmakers literally have been able to imagine any fictional landscape, and then have it, through an animated computer program. And they integrate their human actors and the wholly imaginary worlds of Tron so cleverly that I never, ever, got the sensation that I was watching some actor standing in front of, or in the middle of, special effects. The characters *inhabit* this world. And what a world it is! Video gamesmen race each other at blinding speed, hurtling up and down computer grids while the movie shakes with the overkill of Dolby stereo (justified, for once). The characters sneak around the computer's logic guardian terminals, clamber up the sides of memory displays, talk their way past the guardians of forbidden programs, hitch a ride on a power beam, and succeed in entering the mind of the very Master Control Program itself, disabling it with an electronic Frisbee. This is all a whole lot of fun. *Tron* has been conceived and written with a knowledge of computers that it mercifully assumes the audience shares. That doesn't mean we *do* share it, but that we're bright enough to pick it up, and don't have to sit through long, boring explanations of it.

There is one additional observation I have to make about *Tron*, and I don't really want it to sound like a criticism: This is an almost wholly technological movie. Although it's populated by actors who are engaging (Bridges, Cindy Morgan) or sinister (Warner), it is not really a movie about human nature. Like *Star Wars* or *The Empire Strikes Back*, but much more so, this movie is a machine to dazzle and delight us. It is not a human-interest adventure in any generally accepted way. That's all right, of course. It's brilliant at what it does, and in a technical way maybe it's breaking ground for a generation of movies in which computer-generated universes will be the background for mind-generated stories about emotion-generated personalities. All things are possible.

True Confessions ★ ★ ★
R, 110 m., 1981

Robert De Niro (Des Spellacy), Robert Duvall (Tom Spellacy), Charles Durning (Jack Amsterdam), Ed Flanders (Dan T. Campion), Burgess Meredith (Seamus Fargo). Directed by Ulu Grosbard and produced by Irwin Winkler and Robert Chartoff. Screenplay by John Gregory Dunne and Joan Didion.

True Confessions contains scenes that are just about as good as scenes can be. Then why does the movie leave us disoriented and disappointed, and why does the ending fail dismally? Perhaps because the attentions of the filmmakers were concentrated so fiercely on individual moments that nobody ever stood back to ask what the story was about. It's frustrating to sit through a movie filled with clues and leads and motivations, only to discover at the end that the filmmakers can't be bothered with finishing the story.

The film is about two brothers, one a priest, the other a cop. In a nice insight in casting, Robert De Niro plays the priest and Robert Duvall plays the cop; offhand, we'd expect it to be the other way around, but Duvall is just right, seedy and wall-faced, as the cop, and after a scene or two we begin to accept De Niro as a priest (although he seems too young for a monsignor).

The brothers live in Los Angeles in 1948. It is a Los Angeles more or less familiar from dozens of other movies, especially *Chinatown* and the Robert Mitchum *Farewell, My Lovely*—a small town, really, where the grafters and the power brokers know each other (and in some cases are each other). The movie's plot is complicated on the surface but simple underneath. It centers around a creep named Amsterdam (Charles Durning), a construction tycoon who got his start as a pimp. Both brothers have had dealings with the man. When Duvall was a vice cop, he helped handle the protection for Amsterdam's whorehouses. Now De Niro, the cardinal's right-hand man, oversees the building projects of the Los Angeles archdiocese. And Amsterdam gets most of the contracts for new schools and hospitals, even though his operation is tainted with scandal.

It's tainted with more than that after the dead body of a young woman is found in a field, cut in two. Duvall's investigation leads to a madam who once took a rap for him, long ago, and to a sleazy L.A. porno filmmaker. Eventually, certain clues point all the way back to Amsterdam. Try to follow this closely: Amsterdam met the girl through a business associate, who met her as a hitchhiker. When he first gave her a lift in his car, De Niro was another passenger. The movie makes a great deal of the fact that the monsignor once shared a car with the "virgin tramp," as the newspapers label the victim. But so what? One of the maddening things about *True Confessions* is that it's shot through with such paranoia that innocent coincidences take on the same weight as evil conspiracies.

The movie's emotional center is in the cop character. He's painted as a man who's not above taking a bribe. But at the same time he has a moral code that's stiffer than his brother's. (The monsignor, for example, isn't above rigging a church raffle so that a city councilman's daughter will win the new car.) What begins to eat away at Duvall is that this Amsterdam, honored as the Catholic Layman of the Year, is a grafter and former pimp. Did he also murder the girl? Duvall frankly doesn't care: The guy is such slime he should be arrested for the crime just on general principles.

True Confessions spends a lot of effort in laying the groundwork for its complex plot, but then it refuses to ever settle things. Instead, there are inane prologues and epilogues showing the two brothers years later, their hair gray, as they sigh philosophically over impending death and shake their heads at the irony and tragedy of it all—whatever it all was.

Since this isn't a thriller, we are invited, I guess, to take it as a cynical meditation on the corruptibility of man. Joan Didion and John Gregory Dunne, who based the screenplay on his novel, see the social institutions in their story as just hiding places for hypocrites and weary, defeated men. But they never follow through on their insights. The movie has, for example, a major subplot involving an old priest (Burgess Meredith) who is being put out to pasture. The priest is evidently a symbol of something, especially since the young De Niro gets the dirty job of firing him. But the movie never comes to terms with this story; it just leaves it sitting there.

At the end of *True Confessions*, we're just sitting there, too. We have been introduced to clearly drawn and well-acted characters, we've entered a period in time that is carefully reconstructed, we've seen moments between men and women that are wonderfully well-observed. But we haven't seen a film that cares to be about anything in particular, to state its case or draw its lines, or be much more than a skilled exercise in style.

Turk 182! ★

PG-13 97 m., 1985

Timothy Hutton (Jimmy Lynch), Robert Urich (Terry Lynch), Kim Cattrall (Danny Boudreau), Robert Culp (Mayor Tyler), Darren McGavin (Detective Kowalski), Peter Boyle (Detective Ryan). Directed by Bob Clark and produced by Ted Field and Rene Dupont. Screenplay by James Gregory Kinston, Denis Hamill, and John Hamill.

Turk 182! tells the story of an angry young man who plays humiliating practical jokes on the mayor of the world's dumbest city—which, for the purposes of this movie, is New York. The city is dumb because not a single one of its citizens can figure out who the mysterious man signing himself *Turk 182!* really is. No, not even the character whose nickname is Turk and whose fire deparment badge is number 182. The inspiration for *Turk 182*'s exploits possibly comes from the Fox, the anti-pollution activist whose exploits were recorded in the early 1970s by Mike Royko. Like the Fox, the Turk is morally indignant, and embarrasses public officials by staging harmless but dramatic stunts. Unlike the Fox, the Turk is trapped in a screenplay that takes this idea and turns it into an insult to the intelligence of the audience.

The movie stars Timothy Hutton in the title role. He is a talented young actor, and you can see that for yourself by watching *The Falcon and the Snowman*. In *Turk 182!* Hutton plays the kid brother of a New York fireman (Robert Urich), who is injured while rescuing a baby girl from a fire. Because Urich was off-duty at the time, he was

in violation of department policy and is refused city health benefits. Hutton thinks that stinks. So do I. So would the mayor of New York. That's why the movie rings false from the very first; no mayor of New York would commit political hari-kari by attacking a heroic fireman at a press conference. But this one does. And so Hutton goes underground, displaying the words "Turk 182!" on subway trains, public monuments, and even the Queensboro Bridge. Every time the mayor makes a public appearance, the Turk is there—despite the best efforts of detectives Darren McGavin and Peter Boyle to stop him.

For a change of pace, the movie also throws in scenes involving the brother, who tries to kill himself and spends much of the movie in an unintentionally hilarious head-to-toe cast. And there are lots of authentic, macho New York saloon scenes, in which everybody stands around doing the Miller Time commercials as amateur hour. If the movie wants to reek of New York authenticity, why don't any of its characters have any street-smarts? Example: Although the Queensboro Bridge is placed under police surveillance, Turk 182 not only manages to sabotage a giant electric sign, but also to grease the girders of the bridge so the cops can't climb up and stop him. How much grease would that take? How many people? How much time? In this movie, you don't ask.

The sad thing about *Turk 182!* is that the whole project sounds like a High Concept movie, in which the *idea* of the Turk was allowed to substitute for a story about him. Sure, it would be neat to see a movie about a guy like this. But not this movie.

Twilight Zone—the Movie

Prologue and Segment 1. Written and directed by John Landis. Starring Dan Aykroyd, Albert Brooks, Vic Morrow, and Doug McGrath. ★ ★

Segment 2. Directed by Steven Spielberg. Written by George Johnson. Starring Scatman Crothers. ★ ½

Segment 3. Directed by Joe Dante. Written by Richard Matheson. Starring Kathleen Quinlan, Jeremy Light, and Kevin McCarthy. ★ ★ ★ ½

Segment 4. Directed by George Miller. Written by Richard Marheson. Starring John Lithgow and Abbe Lane. ★ ★ ★ ½

PG, 101 m., 1983

Produced by Steven Spielberg and inspired by the television series created by Rod Serling.

Every year at Oscar time, somebody comes up with the bright idea of making the Academy Awards into a fair fight. Instead of making the voters choose among five widely different performances, they say, they ought to have five actors playing the same scene. That way you'd really be able to see who was best. It's an impractical idea, but *Twilight Zone—the Movie* does almost the same thing. It takes four stories that are typical of the basic approach of the great "Twilight Zone" TV series, and has four different directors try their hand at recapturing Rod Serling's "wondrous land whose boundaries are that of imagination." And the surprising thing is, the two superstar directors are thoroughly routed by two less-known directors whose previous credits have been horror and action pictures.

The superstars are John *(Blues Brothers)* Landis and Steven *(E.T.)* Spielberg. The relative newcomers are Joe Dante, whose *The Howling* was not my favorite werewolf movie, and George Miller, whose *The Road Warrior* is some kind of a manic classic. Spielberg, who produced the whole project, perhaps sensed that he and Landis had the weakest results, since he assembled the stories in an ascending order of excitement. *Twilight Zone* starts slow, almost grinds to a halt, and then has a fast comeback.

Landis directed the first episode, which stars Vic Morrow in the story of a bigot who

is transported back in time to Nazi Germany and Vietnam and forced to swallow his own racist medicine. This segment is predictable, once we know the premise, and Landis does nothing to surprise us. Because we know that Morrow was killed in a helicopter accident during the filming of the segment, an additional pall hangs over the whole story.

Spielberg's segment is next. It stars Scatman Crothers as a mysterious old man who turns up at an old folks' home one day and literally gives the residents what they think they want; to be young again. The easily anticipated lesson is that one lifetime is enough. Spielberg's visual style in this segment is so convoluted and shadowy that the action is hard to follow; the master of clearcut, sharp-edged visuals is trying something that doesn't work.

But then comes Joe Dante's weird, offbeat segment about a traveler (Kathleen Quinlan) who strays off the beaten path and accepts an offer of hospitality from a fresh-faced young kid who looks healthy and harmless. Once Quinlan is inside the roadside farmhouse where the kid lives, however, she's in another dimension—a bizarre world telepathically projected by the boy's imagination. The kid loves video games and TV cartoons, and he's trapped a whole group of adults in his private fantasies. The art direction in this segment is especially good at giving the house interior a wonderland quality.

George Miller's fourth segment stars John Lithgow in a remake of a famous "Twilight Zone" TV story in which a nervous air traveler sees (or imagines that he sees) a little green man hacking away at the engine of his airplane. But there *couldn't* be a little green man out there—could there? The beauty of *Twilight Zone—the Movie* is the same as the secret of the TV series: It takes ordinary people in ordinary situations and then zaps them with "next stop—the Twilight Zone!"

Two of a Kind ½ ★
PG, 87 m., 1983

John Travolta (Zack), Olivia Newton-John (Debbie). Directed by John Herzfeld and produced by Roger M. Rothstein and Joe Wizan. Screenplay by Herzfeld.

Give me a break. Don't send me any more

movies where four angels in heaven ask God to give mankind a second chance, and God agrees—on the condition that John Travolta reforms. This movie should have been struck by a lightning bolt.

Two of a Kind begins with a heavenly golf game involving a WASP (Charles Durning), a black (Scatman Crothers), a Latino (Castulo Guerra), and a woman (Beatrice Straight). James Watt should have been the caddy. They've been in charge of heaven for the last twenty-five years, while God took a little vacation, but now God (a glowing light with a voice by Gene Hackman) is back. And God is not happy. Mankind has screwed up again. The only thing to do is send another flood, and start all over. The angels persuade God to reconsider: Maybe a typical man can reform, and thus prove that mankind is not irredeemable. The typical man is Travolta, who is an inventor of useless gizmos. And Travolta, threatened by a juice-loan collector from the mob, has just stuck up a bank. Are you following this? It sounds like the results of an all-night script conference at the funny farm. Anyway, Olivia Newton-John is the bank teller who Travolta points a gun at. But she substitutes worthless deposit slips for his money, and keeps the money herself. Travolta tracks her down to get his money, and they fall in love.

The romance, alas, never gets airborne, if only because Travolta, Newton-John, and the plot are followed everywhere by countless unnecessary supporting characters. There are the angels, for example, who spy on Travolta but never contact him directly (so he never knows the fate of the world rests on his shoulders). There are the two guys from the mob. Also a weird landlord, and the devil. The funny thing is, for all of this heavy traffic, the script is amazingly lightweight. Hardly anything happens. Let's take inventory. The movie contains a food fight (always a sign of desperation at the concept level), several chase scenes, one of your basic Lovers-Walking-Down-the-Sidewalk-Talking-Angrily-to-Each-Other-While-New-Yorkers-Look-On scenes, and no less than two examples of our old friend, the Semi-Obligatory Lyrical Interlude. In both of them, Newton-John sings on the sound track while the lovers make goo-goo eyes at each other.

The movie never explains certain key elements. For example: (1) What are the rules? What, exactly, *does* Travolta have to do to redeem mankind? (2) To what extent can he be said to exercise free will when the angels can shout "Freeze!" and "Rewind!" and change history? (3) Does the devil have real power, or is he just a walk-on? (4) Why, after one handful of dollars is thrown into the air, does it rain bills for minutes on end? (5) Where does God go on vacation?

2010 ★ ★ ★
PG, 157 m., 1984

Roy Scheider (Heywood Floyd), John Lithgow (Curnow), Helen Mirren (Kirbuk), Bob Balaban (Chandra), Keir Dullea (Bowman), Douglas Rain (HAL 9000). Directed and produced by Peter Hyams. Screenplay by Hyams.

All those years ago, when *2001: A Space Odyssey* was first released, I began my review with a few lines from a poem by e.e. cummings:

I'd rather learn from one bird how to sing than teach ten thousand stars how not to dance.

That was my response to the people who said they couldn't understand *2001*, that it made no sense and that it was one long exercise in self-indulgence by Stanley Kubrick, who had sent a man to the stars, only to abandon him inside some sort of extraterrestrial hotel room. I felt that the poetry of *2001* was precisely in its mystery, and that to explain everything was to ruin everything—like the little boy who cut open his drum to see what made it bang.

2001 came out in the late 1960s, that legendary time when yuppies were still hippies, and they went to see the movie a dozen times and slipped up to the front of the theater and lay flat on their backs on the floor, so that the sound-and-light trip in the second half of the movie could wash over them and they could stagger to the exits and whisper "far out" to one another in quiet ecstasy. Now comes *2010*, a continuation of the Kubrick film, directed by Peter Hyams, whose background is in more pragmatic projects such as *Outland*, the Sean Connery space station thriller. The screenplay is by Arthur C. Clarke (who, truth to tell, I always have suspected was a little bewildered by what Kubrick did to his original ideas). *2010* is very much a 1980s movie. It doesn't match the poetry and the mystery of the original film, but it does continue the story, and it offers sound, pragmatic explanations for many of the strange and visionary things in *2001* that had us arguing endlessly through the nights of 1968.

This is, in short, a movie that tries to teach 10,000 stars how not to dance. There were times when I almost wanted to cover my ears. Did I really want to know (a) why HAL 9000 disobeyed Dave's orders? or (b) the real reason for the Discovery's original mission? or (c) what the monoliths were trying to tell us? Not exactly. And yet we live in a most practical time, and they say every decade gets the movies it deserves. What we get in *2010* is not an artistic triumph, but it is a triumph of hardware, of special effects, of slick, exciting filmmaking. This is a movie that owes more to George Lucas than to Stanley Kubrick, more to *Star Wars* than to *Also Sprach Zarathustra*. It has an ending that is infuriating, not only in its simplicity, but in its inadequacy to fulfill the sense of anticipation, the sense of wonder we felt at the end of *2001*.

And yet the truth must be told: This is a good movie. Once we've drawn our lines, once we've made it absolutely clear that *2001* continues to stand absolutely alone as one of the greatest movies ever made, once we have freed *2010* of the comparisons with Kubrick's masterpiece, what we are left with is a good-looking, sharp-edged, entertaining, exciting space opera—a superior film of the *Star Trek* genre.

Because *2010* depends so much upon its story, it would be unfair to describe more than the essentials: A joint Soviet-American expedition sets out for the moons of Jupiter to investigate the fate of the Discovery, its crew, and its on-board computer HAL 9000. There is tension on board between the American leader (Roy Scheider) and the Soviet captain (Helen Mirren), and it's made worse because back on Earth, the superpowers are on the brink of nuclear war over Central America. If Kubrick sometimes seemed to be making a bloodless movie with faceless characters, Hyams pays a great deal of attention to story and personality. But

only one of the best moments in his movie grows out of character (the touching scene where a Soviet and an American hold onto each other for dear life during a terrifying crisis). The other great moments are special effects achievements: a space walk threatened by vertigo, the awesome presence of Jupiter, and a spectacular flight through the planet's upper atmosphere.

It is possible that *no* conclusion to *2010* could be altogether satisfying, especially to anyone who still remembers the puzzling, awesome simplicity of the Star Child turning to regard us at the end of *2001*. This sequel has its work cut out for it. And the screenplay compounds the difficulty by repeatedly informing us that "something wonderful" is about to happen. After we've been told several times about that wonderful prospect, we're ready for something *really* wonderful, and we don't get it. We get a disappointly mundane conclusion worthy of a 1950s sci-fi movie, not a sequel to *2001*. I, for one, was disappointed that the monoliths would deign to communicate with men at all—let alone that they would use English, or send their messages via a video screen, like the latest generation of cable news.

So. You have to make some distinctions in your mind. In one category, *2001: A Space Odyssey* remains inviolate, one of the handful of true film masterpieces. In a more temporal sphere, *2010* qualifies as superior entertainment, a movie more at home with technique than poetry, with character than with mystery, a movie that explains too much and leaves too little to our sense of wonderment, but a good movie all the same. If I nevertheless sound less than ecstatic, maybe it's because the grave eyes of the *2001* Star Child still haunt me, with their promise that perhaps someday man would learn to teach 10,000 stars how to sing.

Under Fire ★ ★ ★ ½
R, 128 m., 1983

Nick Nolte (Russell Price), Gene Hackman (Alex Grazier), Joanne Cassidy (Claire), Ed Harris (Oates). Directed by Roger Spottiswoode and produced by Jonathan Taplin. Screenplay by Ron Shelton and Clayton Frohman.

This is the kind of movie that almost always

feels phony, but *Under Fire* feels real. It's about American journalists covering guerrilla warfare in Central America, and so right away we expect to see Hollywood stars transplanted to the phony jungles of one of those movie nations with madeup names. Instead, we see Hollywood stars who create characters so convincing we forget they're stars. And the movie names names: It's set in Nicaragua, in 1979, during the fall of the Somoza regime, period.

We meet three journalists who are there to get the story. This is not the first small war they've covered, and indeed we've already seen them packing up and leaving Africa. Now they've got a new story. Nick Nolte is Price, a photographer. Gene Hackman is Grazier, a TV reporter who dreams of becoming an anchorman. Joanna Cassidy is a radio reporter. During the course of the story, Cassidy will fall out of love with Hackman and into love with Nolte. These things happen under deadline pressure. Hackman cares, but not enough to affect his friendship with both of them.

The story is simply told, since *Under Fire* depends more upon moments and atmosphere than on a manufactured plot. During a lull in the action, Hackman heads back for New York and Nolte determines to get an interview with the elusive leader of the guerrillas. He doesn't get an interview, but he begins to develop a sympathy for the rebel cause. He commits the journalistic sin of taking sides, and it leads him, eventually, to a much greater sin: faking a photograph to help the guerrilla forces. That is, of course, wrong. But *Under Fire* shows us a war in which morality is hard to define and harder to practice. One of the key supporting characters in the movie is a mysterious American named Oates (played by Ed Harris). Is he CIA? Apparently. He's always in the thick of the dirty work, however, and if his conscience doesn't bother him, Nolte excuses himself for not taking an ethical stand. There are, in fact, a lot of ethical stands not taken in this movie. It could almost have been written by Graham Greene; it exists in that half-world between exhaustion and exhilaration, between love and cynicism, between covering the war and getting yourself killed. This is tricky ground, and the wrong performances could have made it ridiculous (cf. Richard Gere's sleek sexual athlete in *Beyond the Limit*). The actors in *Under Fire* never step wrong.

Nolte is great to watch as the seedy photographer with the beer gut. Hackman never really convinced me that he could be an anchorman, but he did a better thing. He convinced me that he thought he could be one. Joanna Cassidy takes a role that could have been dismissed as "the girl" and fills it out as a fascinating, textured adult. *Under Fire* surrounds these performances with a vivid sense of place and becomes, somewhat surprisingly, a serious and moving film.

Under the Volcano ★ ★ ★ ★
R, 109 m., 1984

Albert Finney (Geoffrey Firmin), Jacqueline Bisset (Yvonne Firmin), Anthony Andrews (Hugh Firmin), Ignacio Lopez Tarso (Dr. Vigil), Kathy Jurado (Senora Gregoria). Directed by John Huston and produced by Michael Fitzgerald. Screenplay by Guy Gallo.

The consul drinks. He has been drinking for so many years that he has arrived at that peculiar stage in alcoholism where he no longer drinks to get high or to get drunk. He drinks simply to hold himself together and continue to function. He has a muddled theory that he can even "drink himself sober," by which he means that he can sometimes find a lucid window through the fog of his life. *Under the Volcano* is the story of the last day in his drinking.

He lives in Cuernavaca, Mexico, in the years just before World War II. He is not really the British consul anymore: he was only a vice consul, anyway, and now that has been stripped from him, and he simply drinks. He has a few friends and a few acquaintances, and his long days are spent in a drunk's neverending occupation, monitoring his own condition. On this morning, for example, he had a bit too much and passed out in the road. One of those things. Earlier, or later, sometime in there, he had stumbled into a church and prayed for the return of his wife, who had left him. Now he sits on his veranda talking with his half-brother. He turns his head. His wife is standing in the doorway. He turns back. It cannot be her. He looks again. She is still there. Turns away. It cannot be. Looks again. A hallucination. But it persists, and eventually he is forced to admit that his wife has indeed returned, in answer to his prayers.

He drinks. He passes out. He wakes. The three of them set off on a bus journey. A peasant is found dead on a roadside. Later, in a bar, there is an unpleasantness with a whore. Still later, the day ends in a ditch. The consul's day is seen largely through his point of view, and the remarkable thing about *Under the Volcano* is that it doesn't resort to any of the usual tricks that movies use when they portray drunks. There are no trick shots to show hallucinations. No spinning cameras. No games with focus. Instead, the drunkenness in this film is supplied by the remarkably controlled performance of Albert Finney as the consul. He gives the best drunk performance I've ever seen in a film. He doesn't overact, or go for pathos, or pretend to be a character. His focus is on communication. He wants, he desperately desires, to penetrate the alcoholic fog and speak clearly from his heart to those around him. His words come out with a peculiar intensity of focus, as if every one had to be pulled out of the small hidden core of sobriety deep inside his confusion.

The movie is based on the great novel by Malcolm Lowry, who used this day in the life of a drunk as a clothesline on which to hang several themes, including the political disintegration of Mexico in the face of the rising tide of Nazism. John Huston, the surefooted old veteran who directed the film, wisely leaves out the symbols and implications and subtexts and just gives us the man. Lowry's novel was really about alcoholism, anyway; the other materials were not so much subjects as they were attempts by the hero to focus on something between his ears.

The movie belongs to Finney, but mention must be made of Jacqueline Bisset as his wife and Anthony Andrews as his halfbrother. Their treatment of the consul is interesting. They understand him well. They love him (and, we gather, each other). They realize nothing can be done for him. Why do they stay with him? For love, maybe, or loyalty, but also perhaps because they respect the great effort he makes to continue to function, to "carry on," in the face of his disabling illness. Huston, I think, is interested in the same aspect of the story, that within every drunk is a man with self-respect trying to get free.

Until September ½★
R, 95 m., 1984

Karen Allen (Mo), Thierry Lhermitte (Xavier). Directed by Richard Marquand. Produced by Michael Gruskoff. Screenplay by Janice L. Graham.

I knew we were in trouble when Karen Allen told Thierry Lhermitte he had the most beautiful eyes she'd ever seen. His eyes looked more to me like the kind of eyes where, when you turned up looking like that, the nuns sent you to see the school nurse. But then perhaps I am being unfair. Perhaps I do not like Thierry Lhermitte. Perhaps I think he is the biggest drip I've seen in a love story in years. He is the kind of romantic leading man who has the audience wondering when the *real* leading man is going to turn up and wipe this guy out of the picture. But *Until September* denies us that relief. This is a dumb, pointless, boring romance from beginning to end. Some measure of its desperation comes during the French toast scene, where the two lovers discuss the proper way to hold a fork. This is a scene that cries out for a Groucho Marx to pop up at the first mention of a fork, and cackle, "Your place or mine?"

A word about the plot. Karen Allen plays an American tour guide who misses her group's flight to Warsaw. That means she is stuck in Paris for three weeks. She goes to stay in a friend's apartment. Another apartment on the same landing is occupied by Lhermitte, who is an international banker. That means he makes phone calls about "the half-billion line of credit," and then takes the rest of the day off to debate about French toast. A movie like this depends entirely on chemistry, and unfortunately, there's never a moment when I could believe that Allen and Lhermitte were really attracted to each other. They discuss nothing of substance. They share no real confidences. The Allen character occasionally makes a show of being a liberated woman, and yet Lhermitte's big scenes are when he plays the worldly tutor for the wide-eyed female, explaining why different wines come in different kinds of bottles.

There is another fundamental problem with the film: Lhermitte is married and has kids. He believes in "honesty," by which he means he tells Allen about his wife but doesn't tell his wife about Allen because it would hurt her. Mistresses are hurt-proof, apparently. The movie is so manipulative that at the end, after the obligatory running-into-each-other's-arms-at-the-airport scene, we are supposed to be happy that this man has abandoned his family to be with a woman he has nothing of interest to discuss with. Meanwhile, do we see the glories of Paris, at least? Not really. The movie doesn't even manage to make the city into an interesting character. And a visit to the country—a weekend on the Riviera—is so strangely constructed that we have the impression all sorts of things happened in the screenplay that were cut from the film.

Because there are so few adult love stories made, it's a shame that *Until September* didn't try harder and have more intelligence. It feels like a movie that was conceived right from the beginning as a compilation of clichés. Love itself, of course, often is made up of clichés, but if the chemistry is right, they don't feel like clichés.

Up the Creek ★ ★ ★
R, 95 m., 1984

Tim Matheson (Bob McGraw), Jennifer Runyon (Heather Merriweather), Stephen Furst (Gonzer), Dan Monahan (Max), Sandy Helberg (Irwin), John Hillerman (Dean Burch). Directed by Robert Butler and produced by Michael L. Meltzer. Screenplay by Jim Kouf.

Up the Creek is in the great tradition of the Undergraduate Slob Movie, a genre that was created by *Animal House*, perfected by Bill Murray, and defiled by the 1984 *Where the Boys Are*. We know where we stand right in the first few minutes, when a fat kid throws his sandwich out the car window, it hits a motorcyclist in the face, and the motorcyclist hurtles over a cliff. This is not what you call subtle, but Undergraduate Slob Movies do not quibble.

The movie is about an intercollegiate white-water raft race. The defending champions are from a hard-ass military academy. The favorites are from the Ivy League. Our team is from Lepetoname University, described by its dean as the worst university in the world. (In French, by the way, le pe-

toname is the kind of guy who was sitting around the campfire in *Blazing Saddles*.) This university has never won anything. Its students have transferred to it from dozens of other universities—each. The dean makes them a deal. If they win the race, he will give them the diplomas of their choice.

The Lepetoname team is made up of an all-star Undergraduate Slob Movie cast: Tim Matheson and Stephen Furst are from *Animal House*, Dan Monahan is from *Porky's*, and Sandy Helberg was in *History of the World—Part One*, which was a Historical Slob Movie. They pile into a car and head for the race, accompanied by Chuck the Wonder Dog, a dog who is so instrumental to the success of this movie that I will even give you its real name, which is Jake.

One of the joys of this kind of movie comes during the scenes where we meet the competitors. The guys from the military school are led by an uptight, future general. The guys from the Ivy League are all blond, rich, good-looking, and unscrupulous: They plan to use bombs, torpedoes, and even radio-controlled model airplanes to shoot their enemies out of the water. There is, of course, a big beer blast before the race gets underway. The party scene has been an obligatory element of Undergraduate Slob Movies ever since the toga party in *Animal House*. But there are good parties and bad ones. In *Where the Boys Are*, the party is a shapeless confusion. In *Up the Creek*, it's a funny, sustained sequence that establishes all the important characters and sets up the tension.

There's one other scene in the movie that has to be singled out. That's when one of the Lepetoname team members is kidnapped, and Chuck the Wonder Dog uses charades to explain where he is. That's a great scene—and so, by the way, are the scenes of the actual race itself, where some skillful and difficult photography makes the river and its rapids seem convincingly dangerous. *Up the Creek* belongs to an honorable movie tradition, the slapstick comedy. It is superficial, obvious, vulgar, idiotic, goofy, sexy, and predictable. Those are all, by the way, positive qualities—at least, in an Undergraduate Slob Movie.

Used Cars ★ ★
R, 113 m., 1980

Kurt Russell (Rudy Russo), Jack Warden (The Fuchs Brothers), Gerrit Graham (Jeff), Frank McRae (Jim), Deborah Harmon (Barbara Fuchs). Directed by Robert Zemekis and produced by Bob Gale. Screenplay by Zemekis and Gale.

I wonder where the idea got started that it's intrinsically funny to see cars crashing into each other. It's not. It is also not *more* funny when there are dozens or hundreds of cars; the delicate timing you need for comedy is lost when a scene becomes a logistical demonstration. When it comes to cars in movies, more is less—a lesson *Used Cars* does not demonstrate.

When the movie isn't manipulating cars, it does have its good moments. It involves an ancient family feud between two brothers who own competing used car lots across the street from each other. The brothers, both played by Jack Warden, have been treated differently by fate: One is rich and successful; the other is on his last legs, like the cars on his lot. Warden does a good enough job in the dual role, but I always wonder why dual roles seem like a good idea in the first place. If you want two brothers, why not cast two brothers, and accentuate their differences? Why cast one actor and settle for one tour de force instead of two undistracting performances?

Anyway, the movie's plot thickens when it appears that the rich brother will run the poor brother out of business. The plot, in fact, does more than thicken, it congeals. There are so many different characters and story lines in the movie that it's hard to keep everything straight, and harder still to care.

The great comedies almost always have very simple story structures, upon which complex gags can be elaborated. Remember, for example, Buster Keaton's *The General*, in which magnificent complexities were developed out of a story that essentially amounted to Keaton driving a locomotive from point A to point B and back again. *Used Cars* makes the fatal error of achieving the reverse effect: Simple gags are generated out of bafflingly complex situations.

Meanwhile, back at the used car lot . . . Kurt Russell plays a used car salesman who

hopes to save the failing business in order to raise money for his political campaign. Gerrit Graham has some funny moments as a superstitious, sex-mad salesman. Deborah Harmon is the long-lost daughter of the less successful brother; her surprise reappearance gives him an heir just when he needs one the most.

Used Cars was written, directed, and produced by the team of Bob Zemekis and Bob Gale, two young filmmakers who seem to be higher on kinetic energy than on structure and comedic instinct. Their first collaboration, which I really enjoyed, was *I Wanna Hold Your Hand*, a fantasy about the Beatles' first concert in New York. Their next collaboration was the screenplay for Steven Spielberg's unsuccessful *1941*. Next came *Used Cars*. The second and third projects, in particular, are filled with too many ideas, relationships and situations—with plot overkill. And they seem to share the notion that if something is big enough and expensive enough, it will also be funny enough.

Valley Girl ★ ★ ★
R, 95 m., 1983

Nicholas Cage (Randy), Deborah Foreman (Julie), Elizabeth Dailey (Loryn), Michael Bowen (Tommy), Colleen Camp (Mom), Frederic Forrest (Dad). Directed by Martha Coolidge and produced by Wayne Crawford and Andrew Lane. Screenplay by Crawford and Lane.

Disgruntled and weary after slogging through Sex-Mad Teen-ager Movies, I came upon *Valley Girl* with low expectations. What can you expect from a genre inspired by *Porky's?* But this movie is a little treasure, a funny, sexy, appealing story of a Valley Girl's heartbreaking decision: Should she stick with her boring jock boyfriend, or take a chance on a punk from Hollywood? Having seen many Sex-Mad Teen-ager Movies in which a typical slice of teen-ager life consisted of seducing your teacher, being seduced by your best friend's mom, or driving off to Tijuana in search of hookers, I found *Valley Girl* to be surprisingly convincing in its portrait of kids in love. These *are* kids. They're uncertain about sex, their hearts send out confusing signals, and they're slaves to peer pressure.

The movie stars Deborah Foreman as Julie, a bright, cute high school girl who is in the process of breaking up with her blond jock boyfriend (Michael Gowen). He's gorgeous to look at, but he's boring and conceited and he does the one thing that drives all teen-age girls mad: He sits down next to them in a burger joint and casually helps himself to their lunch. One night at a party, Julie meets Randy (Nicholas Cage). He's a lanky, kind of goofy-looking kid with an appealing, crooked smile. He's also a punk from across the hills in Hollywood. Julie likes him. He makes her laugh. He's tender. It's awesome. She falls in love. And then her friends start working her over with all sorts of dire predictions, such as that she'll be "totally dropped" if she goes out with this grotty punk. Caving in to peer pressure, Julie agrees to go to the prom with the jock. And then there's the big climax where the punk gets his girl.

One of the nicest things about this movie is that it allows its kids to be intelligent, thoughtful, and self-analytical. Another thing is that it allows the *parents* to be modern parents. Have you ever stopped to think how *dated* all the parents in teen-ager movies are? They seem to have been caught in a time warp with Dagwood and Blondie. In *Valley Girl*, the parents (Frederic Forrest and Colleen Camp) are former hippies from the Woodstock generation, now running a health food restaurant and a little puzzled by their daughter's preppy friends. It's a perfect touch.

And here's one more nice thing about *Valley Girl*. Maybe because it was directed by a woman, Martha Coolidge, this is one of the rare teen-ager movies that doesn't try to get laughs by insulting and embarrassing teen-age girls. Everybody's in the same boat in this movie—boys and girls—and they're all trying to do the right thing and still have a good time. It may be the last thing you'd expect from a movie named *Valley Girl*, but the kids in this movie are human.

The Verdict ★ ★ ★ ★
R, 122 m., 1982

Paul Newman (Frank Galvin), Charlotte Rampling (Laura Fischer), Jack Warden (Mickey Morrissey), James Mason (Ed Concannon), Milo O'Shea (Judge Hoyle), Edward Binns (Bishop Brophy), Julie Bovasso (Maureen Rooney), Lindsay Crouse (Kaitlin Costello). Directed by Sidney Lumet and produced by Richard Zanuck and David Brown. Screenplay by David Mamet.

There is a moment in *The Verdict* when Paul Newman walks into a room and shuts the door and trembles with anxiety and with the inner scream that people should *get off his back*. No one who has ever been seriously hung over or needed a drink will fail to recognize the moment. It is the key to his character in *The Verdict*, a movie about a drinking alcoholic who tries to pull himself together for one last step at salvaging his self-esteem.

Newman plays Frank Galvin, a Boston lawyer who has had his problems over the years—a lost job, a messy divorce, a disbarment hearing, all of them traceable in one way or another to his alcoholism. He has a "drinking problem," as an attorney for the archdiocese delicately phrases it. That means that he makes an occasional guest appearance at his office and spends the rest of his day playing pinball and drinking beer, and his evening drinking Irish whiskey and looking to see if there isn't at least one last lonely woman in the world who will buy his version of himself in preference to the facts. Galvin's pal, a lawyer named Mickey Morrissey (Jack Warden) has drummed up a little work for him: An open-and-shut malpractice suit against a Catholic hospital in Boston where a young woman was carelessly turned into a vegetable because of a medical oversight. The deal is pretty simple. Galvin can expect to settle out-of-court and pocket a third of the settlement—enough to drink on for what little future he is likely to enjoy.

But Galvin makes the mistake of going to see the young victim in a hospital, where she is alive but in a coma. And something snaps inside of him. He determines to try this case, by God, and to prove that the doctors who took her mind away from her were guilty of incompetence and dishonesty. In Galvin's mind, bringing this case to court is one and the same thing with regaining his self-respect—with emerging from his own alcoholic coma. Galvin's redemption takes place within the framework of a courtroom thriller. The screenplay by David Mamet is a wonder of good dialogue, strongly seen characters, and a structure that pays off in the big courtroom scene—as the genre requires. As a courtroom drama, *The Verdict* is superior work. But the director and the star of this film, Sidney Lumet and Paul Newman, seem to be going for something more; *The Verdict* is more a character study than a thriller, and the buried suspense in this movie is more about Galvin's own life than about his latest case.

Frank Galvin provides Newman with the occasion for one of his great performances. This is the first movie in which Newman has looked a little old, a little tired. There are moments when his face sags and his eyes seem terribly weary, and we can look ahead clearly to the old men he will be playing in ten years' time. Newman always has been an interesting actor, but sometimes his resiliency, his youthful vitality, have obscured his performances; he has a tendency to always look great, and that is not always what the role calls for. This time, he gives us old, bone-tired, hung over, trembling (and heroic) Frank Galvin, and we buy it lock, stock, and shot glass.

The movie is populated with finely tuned supporting performances (many of them by British or Irish actors, playing Bostonians not at all badly). Jack Warden is the old law partner; Charlotte Rampling is the woman, also an alcoholic, with whom Galvin unwisely falls in love; James Mason is the ace lawyer for the archdiocese; Milo O'Shea is the politically connected judge; Wesley Addy provides just the right presence as one of the accused doctors. The performances, the dialogue, and the plot all work together like a rare machine.

But it's that Newman performance that stays in the mind. Some reviewers have found *The Verdict* a little slow-moving, maybe because it doesn't always hum along on the thriller level. But if you bring empathy to the movie, if you allow yourself to think about what Frank Galvin is going through, there's not a moment of this movie that's not absorbing. *The Verdict* has a lot of truth in it, right down to a great final scene in which Newman, still drinking, finds that if you wash it down with booze, victory tastes just like defeat.

Victor/Victoria ★ ★ ★
R, 133 m., 1982

Julie Andrews (Victor/Victoria), James Garner (King), Robert Preston (Toddy), Lesley Ann Warren (Norma), Alex Karras (Squash), John Rhys-Davis (Cassell). Directed by Blake Edwards and produced by Edwards and Tony Adams.

I've always felt this way about female impersonators: They may not be as pretty as women, or sing as well, or wear a dress as well, but you've got to hand it to them; they sure look great and sing pretty—for men. There are no doubt, of course, female impersonators who practice their art so skillfully that they cannot be told apart from real women—but that, of course, misses the point. A drag queen should be maybe 90 percent convincing as a woman, tops, so you can applaud while still knowing it's an act.

Insights like these are crucial to Blake Edwards's *Victor/Victoria*, in which Julie Andrews plays a woman playing a man playing a woman. It's a complicated challenge. If she just comes out as Julie Andrews, then of course she looks just like a woman, because she is one. So when she comes onstage as "Victoria," said to be "Victor" but really (we know) actually Victoria, she has to be an ever-so-slightly imperfect woman, to sell the premise that she's a man. Whether she succeeds is the source of a lot of comedy in this movie, which is a lighthearted meditation on how ridiculous we can sometimes become when we take sex too seriously.

The movie is made in the spirit of classic movie sex farces, and is in fact based on one (a 1933 German film named *Viktor und Viktoria*, which I haven't seen). Its more recent inspiration is probably *La Cage Aux Folles*, an enormous success that gave Hollywood courage to try this offbeat material. In the movie, Andrews is a starving singer, out of work, down to her last franc, when she meets a charming old fraud named Toddy, who is gay, and who is played by Robert Preston in the spirit of Ethel Mertz on "I Love Lucy." Preston is kind, friendly, plucky, and comes up with the most outrageous schemes to solve problems that wouldn't be half so complicated if he weren't on the case. In this case, he has a brainstorm: Since there's no market for girl singers, but a constant demand for female impersonators, why shouldn't Andrews assume a false identity and pretend to be a drag queen? "But they'll *know* I'm not a man!" she wails. "Of course!" Preston says triumphantly.

The plot thickens when James Garner, as a Chicago nightclub operator, wanders into Victor/Victoria's nightclub act and falls in love with him/her. Garner refuses to believe that lovely creature is a man. He's right, but if Andrews admits it, she's out of work. Meanwhile, Garner's blonde girlfriend (Lesley Ann Warren) is consumed by jealousy, and intrigue grows between Preston and Alex Karras, who plays Garner's bodyguard. Edwards develops this situation as farce, with lots of gags depending on split-second timing and characters being in the wrong hotel rooms at the right time. He also throws in several nightclub brawls, which aren't very funny, but which don't much matter. What makes the material work is not only the fact that it is funny (which it is), but that it's about likable people.

The three most difficult roles belong to Preston, Garner, and Karras, who must walk a tightrope of uncertain sexual identity without even appearing to condescend to their material. They never do. Because they all seem to be people first and genders second, they see the humor in their bewildering situation as quickly as anyone, and their cheerful ability to rise to a series of implausible occasions makes *Victor/Victoria* not only a funny movie, but, unexpectedly, a warm and friendly one.

Videodrome ★ ½
R, 87 m., 1983

James Woods (Max Renn), Sonja Smith (Bianca O'Blivion), Deborah Harry (Nicki Brand), Peter Dvorsky (Harlan), Jack Creley (Brian O'Blivion). Directed by David Cronenberg and produced by Claude Heroux. Screenplay by Cronenberg.

The colors in *Videodrome* are mostly shades of dried blood. The characters are bitter and hateful, the images are nauseating, and the ending is bleak enough that when the screen fades to black it's a relief. This is the kind of movie that makes you want to see a different movie. Yet the film has its interesting qualities. If the director, David Cronenberg, had been prepared to allow just a little humanity and humor into what is basically a good idea for a screenplay, *Videodrome* might have worked. But it's relentlessly grim. The movie stars James Woods as a fly-by-night cable TV operator who starts fooling around with a saucer antenna and picks up a cable show that isn't listed in any of the guides. It's pretty rough stuff: Women being tortured and killed. Where does it come from? He tracks it down to Pittsburgh. Meanwhile, some of the scenarios from the weird cable network start getting instant replays in his own bedroom. His girlfriend, Deborah Harry (formerly of the rock group Blondie), makes kinky suggestions and eventually burns herself with a cigarette, in a scene I could easily have lived without.

Woods is a video freak. Come to think of it, he's almost always a freak of one sort or another in the movies; he gets the roles that are too weird for Bruce Dern, and he usually does a great job with them (I especially liked his work as the psychopathic cop-killer in *The Onion Field*). This time, he's one of those video junkies who talks like the letters column of *BYTE* magazine. He becomes fascinated by the Pittsburgh operation and eventually goes there, tracking down a strange skid-row establishment named the Cathode Ray Mission, where bums get a TV set instead of a soup line. What's going on here? What's the master plan of the mysterious Brian O'Blivion, who runs the mission and the underground cable show? (And why, while we're at it, don't directors ever learn that few things make a character less interesting than a funny name?) Without giving away too many of O'Blivion's secrets, I can say that his sexy daughter (Sonja Smith) is the true force behind the Videodrome conspiracy.

I suppose there's a serious subtext lurking in *Videodrome*. The movie symbolizes television as a consuming, engulfing, devouring monster—most memorably in scenes where Woods's TV set turns into a sort of living, pulsing version of Deborah Harry. Television has been seen as a sinister force before, but never this sinister. As I was watching this parade of horrors, I began to wonder why Cronenberg is so unremittingly negative in his filmmaking. His movies are soaked with gloom and defeatism, with ugly images and worthless characters. It's a world view, I guess, but even the most pessimistic director in the history of movies, Luis Bunuel, sometimes found a way to express his bitterness as a joke. *Videodrome*, whatever its qualities, has got to be one of the least entertaining movies ever made.

Vision Quest ★ ★ ★ ½
R, 108 m., 1985

Matthew Modine (Louden Swain), Linda Fiorentino (Carla), Michael Schoeffling (Kuch), Ronny Cox (Louden's Dad), Harold Sylvester (Tanneran), Charles Hallahan (Coach), R.H. Thomson (Kevin), J.C. Quinn (Elmo), Frank Jasper (Shute). Directed by Harold Becker and produced by Jon Peters and Peter Guber. Screenplay by Darryl Poniscan.

We think we know the story pretty well already: Young wrestler has two dreams: (a) to win the state championship, and (b) to win the love of a girl. The defending state champion is a man-mountain who carries telephone poles to the top of stadiums. The girl is an independent drifter who is twenty years old and doesn't take the hero seriously. By the end of the movie, the only suspense is whether it will end with a victory in bed or in the ring. Although *Vision Quest* sticks pretty close to that outline, it is nevertheless a movie with some nice surprises, mostly because it takes the time to create some interesting characters. The movie's hero, Louden Swain, is probably the closest thing to a standard movie character, but Matthew Modine plays him with such an ingratiating freshness that he makes the character quirky and interesting, almost in spite of the script.

The other people in the movie are all real originals. They include Louden's father (Ronny Cox), who has lost the family farm and his wife, but still retains the respect of his son; Louden's best pal (Michael Schoeffling), who bills himself as a "half-Indian spiritual adviser"; a black history teacher (Harold Sylvester) who cares about Louden and listens to him; an alcoholic short-order cook (J.C. Quinn) who works in the kitchen

of the hotel where Louden's a bellboy, and a wrestling coach (Charles Hallahan) who has mixed feelings about Louden's drive to get down to the 168-pound class so he can wrestle the toughest wrestler in the state. All of those characters are written, directed, and acted just a little differently than we might expect; they have small roles, but they don't think small thoughts.

And then there is the movie's most original creation, the twenty-year-old drifter, Carla (Linda Fiorentino). Without having met the actress, it's impossible for me to speculate on how much of Carla is original work and how much is Fiorentino's personality. What comes across, though, is a woman who is enigmatic without being egotistical, detached without being cold, self-reliant without being suspicious. She has a way of talking—kind of deliberately objective—that makes you listen to everything she says.

All of these people live in Spokane, which looks sort of wet and dark in many scenes, and feels like a place that prizes individuality. Instead of silhouetting the Modine character against the city and a lot of humble supporting roles, and turning him into a Rocky of wrestlers, the movie takes time to place the character in the city and in the lives of the other people. We begin to value his relationships, and it really means something when the short-order cook puts on a clean shirt and goes to the big wrestling meet.

The movie's plot doesn't really equal its characters. After the Rocky movies and *Breaking Away* and *The Karate Kid* and a dozen other movies with essentially the same last scene, it's hard to care about the outcome of the big fight, or race, or match, because, let's face it, we know the hero's going to win. Just once, why couldn't they give us characters as interesting as the ones in *Vision Quest*, in a movie where they'd be set free from the same tired old plot and allowed to live?

WarGames ★ ★ ★ ★
PG, 110 m., 1983

Matthew Broderick (David), Dabney Coleman (McKittrick), John Wood (Falken), Ally Sheedy (Jennifer), Barry Corbin (General Beringer). Directed by John Badham and produced by Harold Schneider. Screenplay by Lawrence Lasker and Walter F. Parkes.

Sooner or later, a self-satisfied, sublimely confident computer is going to blow us all off the face of the planet. That is the message of *WarGames*, a scary and intelligent thriller that is one of the best films of 1983. The movie stars Matthew Broderick as a bright high school senior who spends a lot of time locked in his bedroom with his home computer. He speaks computerese well enough to dial by telephone into the computer at his school and change grades. But he's ready for bigger game. He reads about a toy company that's introducing a new computer game. He programs his computer for a random search of telephone numbers in the company's area code, looking for a number that answers with a computer tone. Eventually, he connects with a computer. Unfortunately, the computer he connects with does not belong to a toy company. It belongs to the Defense Department, and its mission is to coordinate early warning systems and nuclear deterrents in the case of World War III. The kid challenges the computer to play a game called "Global Thermonuclear Warfare," and it cheerfully agrees.

As a premise for a thriller, this is a masterstroke. The movie, however, could easily go wrong by bogging us down in impenetrable computerese, or by ignoring the technical details altogether and giving us a *Fail Safe* retread. *WarGames* makes neither mistake. It convinces us that it knows computers, and it makes its knowledge into an amazingly entertaining thriller. (Note: I do not claim the movie is *accurate* about computers—only convincing.) I've described only the opening gambits of the plot, and I will reveal no more. It's too much fun watching the story unwind. Another one of the pleasures of the movie is the way it takes cardboard characters and fleshes them out. Two in particular: the civilian chief of the U.S. computer operation, played by Dabney Coleman as a man who has his own little weakness for simple logic, and the Air Force general in charge of the war room, played by Barry Corbin as a military man who argues that men, not computers, should make the final nuclear decisions.

WarGames was directed by John Badham,

best known for *Saturday Night Fever* and *Blue Thunder*, a thriller that I found considerably less convincing on the technical level. There's not a scene here where Badham doesn't seem to know what he's doing, weaving a complex web of computerese, personalities, and puzzles; the movie absorbs us on emotional and intellectual levels at the same time. And the ending, a moment of blinding and yet utterly elementary insight, is wonderful.

The Watcher in the Woods ★ ★
PG, 83 m., 1981

Bette Davis (Mrs. Aylwood), Lynn-Holly Johnson (Jan Curtis), Carroll Baker (Helen Curtis), David McCallum (Paul Curtis), Ian Bannon (John Keller). Directed by John Hough and produced by Ron Miller. Screenplay by Brian Clemons, Harry Spalding, and Rosemary Anne Sisson.

I walked into *The Watcher in the Woods* suspecting that there was going to be something watching in the woods, and I walked out knowing that there *was* something watching in the woods, but somewhere in between I never quite figured out *what* was watching in the woods. If Walt Disney Productions' movie was that obscure for me, what is a nine-year-old watcher going to make out of it?

The movie begins with your basic teen-age gothic plot. An adolescent girl (Lynn-Holly Johnson) and the rest of her family move into a vast old mansion in the middle of the woods. The mean old lady who owns the mansion (Bette Davis) lives in the guest cottage. The family is always the same in stories like this. In addition to the teen-age heroine, who is the brains of the outfit, it also consists of a father who immediately has to leave for the city on business, a mother who keeps talking bravely about how this old house is going to be great once they get some air in these rooms, and a little sister who hears voices. Meanwhile, as these obligatory characters are being established, *something* is watching in the woods. We know that because the movie contains incessant POV shots within the woods. "POV" means "point of view" in the language of Hollywood—and when the camera slinks through the underbrush and sneaks up on people and swoops through the leaves, you know *something* is out there watching everything. And sometimes a mysterious blue ray beam zaps out of the woods and blinds people or starts fires.

Who, or what, is it? For a while, it doesn't matter. It turns out that Bette Davis's teenage daughter Karen, a dead ringer for Lynn-Holly Johnson, was killed thirty years ago during a children's game in the old chapel, which burned down in the process. They say her body was never found. Meanwhile, Lynn-Holly's little sister begins drawing "Karen" backwards on dirty windows and names her little dog "Nerak," which is "Karen" backward. And Lynn-Holly herself begins to see a blindfolded girl in every mirror she looks in.

What does it all mean? That Karen is trapped behind the looking glass? That Karen is the watcher in the woods? That Karen's body is still buried in the chapel? That Lynn-Holly is the reincarnation of Karen? That the pet dog is trying to tell us something? No, it doesn't mean any of these things. What it all *does* mean is . . . well, sort of hard to say. The ending of *The Watcher in the Woods* was reshot by the Disney folks, after an unsuccessful test run for the original version of the film. And the current ending left me completely baffled.

Without giving away too much, I can say that the explanation involves other planets, the fourth dimension, a strange ritual, and imprisonment in time. It involves all those things, I should add, in ways that are completely obscure. The movie doesn't exactly arrive at a conclusion; it almost defiantly announces that it is over. This sort of narrative must be terribly frustrating for young kids. They love to be told stories, and here's a story that refuses to explain itself. I'm frustrated, too. I still don't know what was causing that blue light to zap out of the woods. You know how it is. You spend a couple of hours with a movie like this, you want to find out what was with the blue light ray.

The Weavers: Wasn't That a Time!
★ ★ ★ ★
PG, 78 m., 1982

Featuring Lee Hays, Ronnie Gilbert, Fred Hellerman, and Pete Seeger. Directed by Jim Brown and produced by Brown, George Stoney, and Harold Leventhal.

Here is one of the most joyous musical documentaries in a long time, a celebration of the music and the singers that made up the Weavers. There are, I suppose, a lot of people who don't know who the Weavers were, but for a time in the fifties they were the top pop quartet in America, and for twenty years their recordings were a key influence on modern American folk music.

The owners of old Weavers record albums treasure them. I have four or five, and when things get depressing and the sky turns overcast and grim, I like to play one of them. There's just something magical about the joy with which the Weavers sing "Goodnight, Irene" or "Kisses Sweeter than Wine" or "The Sloop John B." or "This Land is Your Land."

The Weavers reached their popular peak in the fifties, with a string of Top Ten hits, which also included "On Top of Old Smokey," "Tzena, Tzena," and "If I Had a Hammer" (which was written by the Weavers, and not, as many people believe, by Bob Dylan). The height of their popularity unfortunately coincided with the height of McCarthyism, and the Weavers, all of them longtime left-wing activists, were blacklisted. They couldn't get jobs on television or in nightclubs, and their records were banned.

For several years in the late fifties, the group existed primarily on records. And the artists went their separate ways: Ronnie Gilbert into theater, Fred Hellerman into San Franciso-area media projects, Pete Seeger into a successful solo concert career, and Lee Hays into semi-retirement on his New England farm.

There were many calls for a Weavers reunion (in some circles, an event more fervently desired than the Beatles reunion). And in May of 1980, Lee Hays himself convened such a reunion, inviting the other Weavers and their families and friends to a picnic on his farm. As they sat around and sang and played, the idea of a public reunion began to take shape, and on November 28 and 29 of 1980, they held one last historic concert at Carnegie Hall.

The Weavers: Wasn't That a Time! is not

simply a concert film, however, but a documentary about the Weavers. The director, Jim Brown, was a neighbor of Hays, and grew to admire the old man who kept on singing after his legs were amputated for diabetes and his heart needed a pacemaker.

Brown's film begins with the picnic at Hays's farm, flashes back to newsreel and archive footage of the Weavers in their prime, and then concludes with the concert in Carnegie Hall. It is impossible not to feel a lump in your throat as the Weavers gather once again on stage, and it's hard not to tap your feet when they start to sing.

Seeing this film is a wonderful experience. I'd recommend it wholeheartedly to those who don't know about the Weavers. I imagine that Weavers fans won't need any encouragement.

A Week's Vacation ★ ★ ★ ½
NO MPAA RATING, 102 m., 1980

Nathalie Baye (Laurence Cuers), Gerard Lanvin (Pierre). Directed by Bertrand Tavernier. Screenplay by Tavernier, Colo Tavernier, and Marie-Francoise Hans.

It's nothing special, just an overcast day in Lyons when everybody's going to work just as usual. A car pulls out of the stream of traffic, and a young woman gets out. Her name is Laurence, she is a schoolteacher, and this day she does not feel like teaching school. It is more than that: She cannot. There is no particular crisis. A great tragedy has not descended on her life. In fact, things are going fairly well. She is thirty-one years old, she lives with her boyfriend, she has been teaching at the same school for ten years. It is simply that large and inarticulate emotions are welling up inside her, and she is desperately unhappy. She goes to see her doctor, and he prescribes a week's vacation.

A Week's Vacation is as simple, and as complicated, as that. It was directed by Bertrand Tavernier, the gifted French filmmaker who has made his hometown of Lyons the locale for some of his best work, including The Clockmaker (1974). That movie was based on a novel by Georges Simenon, and A Week's Vacation could well have been; it has the same matter-of-fact fascination with the great depths and unexpected secrets in the lives of people who outwardly seem ordi-

nary. A Week's Vacation follows the schoolteacher, played by Nathalie Baye, as she spends her week of freedom wandering without a plan through her city, her past, and her sexuality. She meets a friendly café owner and talks to him. She goes out to the country to visit her father, who is so old he has surely discovered the answer to the puzzle of life, but it has made him speechless. Returning to the city, she has an embarrassing encounter. The café owner, mistaking her friendliness for sexual interest, tries to kiss her. She was not thinking along those lines. As they both try to free themselves from the awkward situation, as he damns himself for being such a fool, there comes a turning point in her week's vacation: It seems to me that this foolish encounter, this mundane sexual pass based on mistaken assumptions, is the catalyst she needs to get back into life again.

What is best about Tavernier is his feeling for the ordinary currents of everyday life. He creates such empathy between his audiences and his characters that when they fall into a reverie, we have no difficulty imagining their thoughts. In A Week's Vacation, he has taken the occasional feeling we all have that we just can't go on any longer, not because of sadness or illness or tragedy, but simply because we have forgotten why we set out in the first place on this journey of life. And he has shown us the answer. The key is in that funny, embarrassing, fumbling little attempt at a kiss: We keep on plugging away because we never know when someone might decide to kiss us, and, better still, because it's so interesting to see how we'll react.

Where the Boys Are ½ ★
R, 93 m., 1984

Lisa Hartman (Jennie), Russell Todd (Scott), Lorna Luft (Carole), Wendy Schaal (Sandra), Howard McGillin (Chip) Lynn-Holly Johnson (Laurie). Directed by Hy Averback and produced by Allan Carr. Screenplay by Jeff Burkhart, Stu Krieger, and Carr.

Close your eyes and you can hear her even now. It's 1960 and you're parked in the Steak n' Shake in your red and white Chevy convertible and on the radio, Connie Francis is singing "Where the Boys Are." It's a love song to a time and a place. And as you tip the curb girl a dime, you close your eyes, and dream about pointing that Chevy right down Route 45 to Fort Lauderdale.

There is a certain innocence in that vision. A certain wistful optimism that maybe in Fort Lauderdale, or somewhere, somehow, sometime, you'll meet that special girl who will look into your eyes and whisper "I know" when you say you love her. It's a kind of innocent, romantic vision that has nothing to do with the 1984 movie also named *Where the Boys Are*, which is an exercise in exhausted cynicism. This movie has nothing to do with the song and the 1960 movie whose name it appropriates. It isn't a sequel and isn't a remake and isn't, in fact, much of anything. The press release contains this priceless line: "Allan Carr is producing *'Where the Boys Are'* from a screenplay based on an original story idea by himself, Jeff Burkhart, and Stu Krieger." What could the original story idea have been? "Hey, Jeff and Stu, let's write a new movie called 'Where the Boys Are'!" Don't laugh. People have made millions in Hollywood with even less-inspired story ideas. Also with even more-inspired ideas, of course, like this one I've just had: Hey, Allan, Jeff, and Stu—let's not rip-off that old title!

The movie stars a cast of aging would-be college kids who do, indeed, head south for Fort Lauderdale for the annual college week in the sun. But their sexual appetites are considerably more decadent than those of the 1960 cast. Before this movie is over, we will witness:

• Four college girls practicing foreplay with an inflatable male doll, which explodes during an experiment in nipple-biting.

• A girl who dreams of making it with a Conan-type body builder, only to find, when she arrives at Conan's apartment, that he is a male prostitute. What does she do then? Walk out in horror and disgust? No, she orders him to disrobe and then tells him he doesn't measure up.

There's also an idiotic subplot out of left field, about a wimpy concert pianist and his domineering mother, and how the whole gang crashes a lawn party at his mother's waterfront mansion. And the usual "Hot Bod" contests and drunken orgies, all written, acted, and directed at such a plodding pace that Valium seems to be the week's drug of choice.

Where the Buffalo Roam ★ ★
R, 98 m., 1980

Peter Boyle (Lazlo), Bill Murray (Hunter S. Thompson), Bruno Kirby (Marty Lewis), Rene Auberjonois (Harris of the Post), R.G. Armstrong (Judge Simpson), Danny Goldman (Porter). Directed and produced by Art Linson. Screenplay by John Kaye.

Dr. Hunter S. Thompson is the high priest of Gonzo journalism, a reporting style in which the reporter throws himself wildly into the event he is reporting, so that in a way he becomes the event. Karl Lazlo (not his real name) was a Mexican-American attorney Thompson met in the late 1960s and immortalized in *Fear and Loathing in Las Vegas*, a book in which, "speaking as your attorney," Lazlo regularly advised his client to ingest large quantities of booze, drugs, and pills. The purpose: to ward off paranoia and insanity as the two engaged on a drunken odyssey through the craziness of the Vegas Strip.

The Vegas book was followed by *Fear and Loathing on the Campaign Trail*, in which Thompson terrorized the 1972 presidential campaign as a correspondent for *Rolling Stone*. His mere presence was enough to cause terror in the hearts of advance men. The last appearance—or rather disappearance—of Lazlo in Thompson's writing is in "The Banshee Screams for Buffalo Meat," a 1976 *Rolling Stone* article in which the doctor speculates that his attorney has disappeared for good and been murdered.

Where the Buffalo Roam is a comedy inspired by the relationship between Thompson (Bill Murray) and Lazlo (Peter Boyle). The credits say it's "based on the twisted legend of Dr. Hunter S. Thompson." The doctor has become an American folk legend not only through his increasingly infrequent and incoherent *Rolling Stone* articles, but also through his frequent walk-ons (as Duke) in the comic strip Doonesbury. We know his uniform: eyeshade, cigarette holder, garish Hawaiian shirt, Bermuda shorts, bottle of Wild Turkey or similar beverage.

In Doonesbury, the character fights crisis with paranoia. In real life, Thompson has proven no more immune to the effects of alcohol and drug addiction than anybody else, and lives in isolation in his cabin in Woody Creek, Colorado, where he has written almost nothing worth reading since his original brilliant books. He seems to be spending these latter days of his fame having almost as much fun as Brendan Behan did.

But *Where the Buffalo Roam* is a celebration of the self-created public legend of Hunter Thompson, with no insights or hints into the dark night of his soul. That's a legitimate approach, and there are times during the movie when it works: There are really funny moments here, as when we learn that Thompson's dog has been trained to go berserk at the mention of the name Nixon, or when Thompson covers the Super Bowl by staging a football game in his hotel suite, or when he pulls a gun on a telephone, or turns a hospital room into an orgy, or attempts to impersonate a correspondent from the *Washington Post*. An amazing number of these scenes are inspired by real life—although it was Senator George McGovern, not Richard Nixon, who found himself being interviewed by Thompson while standing at a urinal.

We laugh at a lot of these moments; this is the kind of bad movie that's almost worth seeing. But there are large things wrong with *Where the Buffalo Roam*. One of them is its depiction of the relationship between Thompson and Lazlo. That's what the movie is supposed to be about, and yet we never discover why these two characters like one another. What *is* their relationship, aside from the coincidence that they happen to get stoned or drunk together under bizarre circumstances? Are they even really friends? Because the movie's central relationship just isn't there, the events don't matter so much: We get bizarre episodes but no insights.

The other problem is that the Dr. Thompson character never seems to really feel the effects of the chemicals he hurls so recklessly at his system. Murray plays Thompson well, but in a mostly one-level performance: He walks through the most insane situations with a quizzical monotone, a gift for understatement, a drug-induced trance. Any real person drinking and drugging like Thompson would have an occasional high,

and a more than occasional disastrous low. Here he has neither.

And so the movie fails to deal convincingly with either Thompson's addictions or with his friendship with Lazlo. It becomes just a series of set-pieces, oft-told tales about the wild and crazy things he's done while he was zonked. We wish him well, but we end up wondering, a little cynically, if Thompson has had as much fun destroying himself as we've had watching him.

Where the Green Ants Dream ★ ★ ★
NO MPAA RATING, 100 m., 1985 ✔

Bruce Spence (Geologist), Wandjuk Marika (Tribal Elder), Roy Marika (Dayipu), Ray Barrett (Cole, Foreman), Norman Kaye (Mining, Vice President), Colleen Clifford (Widow). Directed by Werner Herzog and produced by Lucki Stipetic. Screenplay by Herzog.

Werner Herzog believes in the voodoo of locations, in the possibility that if he shoots a movie in the right place and at the right time, the reality of the location itself will seep into the film and make it more real. He has filmed on the slopes of active volcanoes and a thousand miles up the Amazon, and in his new movie, *Where the Green Ants Dream,* he goes to a godforsaken, heat-baked stretch of Australian Outback. This is grim territory, but it is sacred land to the Aborigines, who believe that this is the place where the green ants go to dream, and that if their dreams are disturbed, unspeakable calamities will rain down on future generations. The Aborigines' belief is not shared by a giant mining company, which wants to tear open the soil and search for uranium.

As the movie opens, the company is in the process of setting off explosions, so geologists can listen to the echoes and choose likely mining sites. The Aborigines sit passively in the way of the explosions, refusing to move, insisting that the ants must not be awakened. We meet the characters on both sides: the tall, gangly mining engineer, the implacable tribal leaders, the supercilious president of the mining company, and the assorted eccentrics who have washed up on this desert shore.

Herzog has said that he thinks in images,

not ideas, and that if he can find the correct pictures for a film, he's not concerned about its message. In *Where the Green Ants Dream,* his images include an old woman sitting patiently in the Outback, an opened can of dog food on the ground in front of her, waiting for a pet dog that has been lost in a mine shaft. Then we see a group of Aborigines sitting in the aisle of a supermarket, on the exact spot where the last tree in the district once stood; it was the tree under which the men of the tribe once stood to "dream" their children before conceiving them. We also see an extraordinary landscape, almost lunar in its barren loneliness.

We do not see any ants, but then perhaps that is part of Herzog's plan. One of the strangest things about this film (strange if you are not familiar with Herzog, who is the strangest of all living directors) is that nothing in this movie is based on anthropological fact. The beliefs, customs, and behavior of the Aborigines, for example, are not inspired by research into their actual lives—but are a fiction, made up by Herzog for his screenplay. The confrontation between the mining company and the Aborigines is likewise not based on yesterday's headlines, but is symbolic, representing for Herzog similar "real" stories, but in a more dramatic form. Even the details about the life cycles of the ants are made up; Herzog has no idea if there are really ants in the Outback.

But there is a reality, nevertheless, in this odd film, and it comes out of the two conflicting sets of beliefs. The Aborigines sit and wait, inspired by deep currents of faith and tradition, and the engineers are always in motion, convinced that success lies in industry and activity. The conflict is everywhere in the world today, and Herzog didn't need to make it up, only to find the pictures for it.

Willie and Phil ★ ★ ★
R, 116 m., 1980

Michael Ontkean (Willie), Margot Kidder (Jeannette), Ray Sharkey (Phil), Jan Miner (Mrs. Kaufman), Tom Brennan (Mr. Kaufman), Julie Bovasso (Mrs. D'Amico), Louis Guss (Mr. D'Amico), Kathleen Maguire (Mrs. Sutherland). Directed and written by

Paul Mazursky and produced by Mazursky and Tony Ray.

Willie and Phil meet after a screening of Truffaut's *Jules and Jim,* which is a movie about two good friends and how they both fall in love with the same woman, who becomes the third good friend. Shortly after they see the movie, in Greenwich Village in 1970, Willie and Phil meet Jeannette, and then the three of them spend the 1970s working out their own version of a triangle.

If Paul Mazursky's *Willie and Phil* is supposed to be a psychologically plausible telling of this story, then it doesn't work. The movie gives away its own game right at the beginning, with the reference to *Jules and Jim.* These aren't real people in this movie; they're characters. They don't inhabit life, they inhabit Mazursky's screenplay—which takes them on a guided tour of the cults, fads, human potential movements, and alternative life-styles of the decade during which zucchini replaced Faulkner as the most popular subject on campus.

But I don't think *Willie and Phil* was intended to work on a realistic level, or that we're intended to believe that Willie, Phil, and Jeannette are making free choices throughout the movie. In a subtle, understated sort of way, Mazursky is giving us a movie that hovers between a satirical revue and a series of life-style vignettes. The characters in his movie are almost exhausted by the end of the decade (weren't we all?). Not only have they experimented with various combinations of commitments to one another, but they've also tried out most of the popular 1970s belief systems.

Willie (Michael Ontkean) is a high school teacher as the movie opens, but he wants to be more, to feel deeply, to think on more exalted levels, and his journey through the decade takes him into radicalism, back to the earth, and all the way to India for lessons in meditation. Phil (Ray Sharkey) says he wants love and security, but he holds himself at arm's length from Jeannette and other possible sources of love. Unable to communicate, he channels all of his energy into making it in the communications industries. Jeannette (Margot Kidder) . . . well, what does she want? To love, to be loved, to be possessed, to be free, to commit, but not to be trapped, to . . . have kids? A career? Willie? Phil?

I think Mazursky's suggesting something interesting about the 1970s. It was a decade without a consuming passion, without an overall subject or tone. Every decade from the 1920s to the 1960s had an overriding theme, at least in our collective national imagination, but in the 1970s we went on life-style shopping trips, searching for an impossible combination of life choices that would be morally good, politically correct, personally entertaining, and outperform the market—all at once.

And what were we left with in the 1980s? Confusion, vague apprehension, lack of faith in belief systems, EPA mileage estimates, megavitamins as the last blameless conspicuous consumption, and, echoing somewhere in the back of our minds, Peggy Lee singing "Is That All There Is?" How'd we get stuck? Why'd we wind up with a sense of impending doom when we tried every possible superficial substitute for profound change? Mazursky finds this note and strikes it in *Willie and Phil*, and that's what's best about his movie.

But like the decade itself, *Willie and Phil* is not completely substantial or satisfying. What redeems it, curiously, are the scenes involving Willie's Jewish parents, Phil's Italian parents, and Jeannette's Southern mother. Their scenes are reactions to what's happening to their kids in the 1970s, and they work like field trips from other decades. The parents observe, try to understand, are baffled, react with resentment, anger, love, confusion. I loved it when the Italian mother, trying to figure out how Jeannette was going to sleep with her boyfriend in the house of her ex-husband while the ex-husband bunked downstairs and the parents took the guest room, got up, said it was all just too complicated for her, and left for the airport. That's sort of the motif for this movie.

Winter of Our Dreams ★ ★ ★
R, 89 m., 1983

Judy Davis (Lou), Bryan Brown (Rob), Cathy Downes (Gretel), Baz Luhrmann (Pete). Directed by John Duigan and produced by Richard Mason. Screenplay by Duigan.

Rob runs a bookstore and lives in one of those houses where the bedrooms hang under the eaves; one false move and you dash your brains out onto the living room floor below. Lou is a prostitute who lives on the streets. They both once had a friend named Lisa, back in the late 1960s when they were all part of the Australian protest movement. Now Lisa has been murdered, and Lou, searching for a meaning in her life or death, runs into Rob again. She thinks he's a trick. He thinks she's an interesting, complicated person who deserves his attention. I think she's closer to the mark.

This is the setup for *Winter of Our Dreams*, an Australian film starring two popular Australian new wave actors, Judy Davis (of *My Brilliant Career*) and Bryan Brown (of *Breaker Morant* and TV's "A Town Like Alice"). Davis brought a kind of wiry, feisty intelligence to *My Brilliant Career*, playing an Australian farm woman who rather felt she would do things her own way. She's wonderful this time, in a completely different role as an insecure, distrustful, skinny street waif. It's Brown who is the trouble. Maybe it's the performance, maybe it's the character, or maybe it's Brown, but I've rarely seen a more closed-off person on the screen. When the story calls for him to reach out to Davis, we feel he's holding his nose. Sometimes there are movies where the leading actors cannot stand one another (Ken Wahl said he was only able to kiss Bette Midler in *Jinxed!* by thinking of his dog), and maybe Brown just couldn't express the feelings that were in the script. But I was never really convinced that he cared for Davis.

That's less of a handicap later in the movie, however, when the Brown character is *required* to draw back from any involvement with this pathetic street kid. The relationships in *Winter of Our Dreams* are very tangled—maybe too tangled. Brown's character has been married for six years to Gretel (Kathy Downes), a handsome, smart woman who has a lover. They have an open marriage, and there's no objection when Brown brings Davis home for the night. Davis, taking this all in, can't understand it. Trying to learn how to feel again, she can't understand why anyone would deliberately trivialize his feelings. The key passages in the film involve Brown's discovery that Davis is a heroin junkie, and then her tortured period of drug withdrawal. They are both pretending to care for one another, and after Davis gets straight maybe Brown will become her lover, while his wife disappears into the woodwork. That is not, however, even remotely in the cards, and there's a painful scene during a party at Brown's house, where Davis realizes that Brown is *very* married, open marriage or not.

There seem to be two movements in *Winter of Our Dreams*. One is Davis's movement away from the cynicism and despair of prostitution, and back toward an ability to care for another person. The other is Brown's initial concern for this girl, and then his retreat back into his shell. Davis performs her movement magnificently. Brown didn't win my sympathy for a moment. What just barely saves this film is the fact that we're not *supposed* to like the Brown character. As for Davis, she's a wonder.

Without a Trace ★ ★ ★ ½
PG, 119 m., 1983

Kate Nelligan (Susan Selky), Judd Hirsch (Menetti), David Dukes (Graham Selky), Stockard Channing (Jocelyn). Directed and produced by Stanley Jaffe. Screenplay by Beth Gutcheon.

"A woman's bravery and a police detective's relentless search for her missing son provide the elements of suspenseful human drama in *Without a Trace*."
—Press release

They have it exactly wrong. The press release describes what might have happened to this story if it had been turned into one of those TV docudramas where every emotion is predictably computed. What makes *Without a Trace* interesting is that it's *not* predictable, because it goes with the ebbs and flows of imperfect human beings. It's not about a woman's bravery but about her intelligence and vulnerability. It's not about a detective's relentless search, but about routine police work, made up of realism and hunches.

Without a Trace opens with a sequence that is very painful, since we know from the movie's title what's about to happen. A young mother (Kate Nelligan), who lives alone with her first-grader, gets him up, gets

him his breakfast, scolds him for feeding his breakfast to the dog, tells him he's a good boy, and sends him off to school. He's almost seven—sort of young to walk alone to school, but it's only two blocks and there's a crossing guard. Nelligan goes off to school herself. She's an English professor at Columbia University. She comes home and waits for her child. He's late. She makes a call. He never arrived at the school. She calls the police and a search begins at once, but her son has apparently disappeared into thin air. There are door-to-door canvasses, helicopter searches, anonymous phone calls, predictions by psychics, and a neighborhood campaign to put "missing" posters in store windows. But there is no little boy.

One of the unexpected things about *Without a Trace* is that it's not really about the police search for the child. Instead, it's about what happens to people when tragedy turns into open-ended frustration. The mother waits and waits. The detective in charge of the case (Judd Hirsch) follows up leads and does all the things a competent cop is supposed to do. The city lends its resources and pays for an expensive investigation. But everything leads to nothing.

The central passages of the film are the best, as Nelligan plays an intelligent, civilized woman fighting to keep control. She feels rage, yes, but she is a rational person and she tries to behave reasonably. Underneath, she is deeply grieving. It takes her best friend (Stockard Channing) to suggest, after several months, that perhaps it is time to give up and admit that the little boy must be dead. It's time to let go of the past and rebuild her own life. Nelligan rejects that reasoning. And the movie remains neutral. What *is* the right answer: Should she accept what looks like the inevitable, or should she continue to hope? Nelligan's performance grows immensely subtle at this point. We can almost read her mind, and what we are reading is a battle between instinct and intelligence, between common sense and a mother's love.

Then a "suspect" is arrested—a gay sadomasochist. The circumstantial evidence against him is overwhelming. But Nelligan refuses to be bullied into agreement by a police department eager to close its books on the case. She becomes convinced that the man is innocent. And *Without a Trace*, which could so easily have been just another police drama, grows into a thought-provoking movie about how we behave, and why. It asks hard questions. It also has its moments of joy, but it earns every one of them.

Witness ★ ★ ★ ★
R, 120 m., 1985 ✔

Harrison Ford (John Book), Kelly McGillis (Rachel), Josef Sommer (Schaeffer), Lukas Haas (Samuel), Alexander Godunov (Daniel Hochleitner). Directed by Peter Weir and produced by Edward S. Feldman. Screenplay by Earl Wallace.

Witness comes billed as a thriller, but it's so much more than a thriller that I wish they hadn't even used the word "murder" in the ads. This is, first of all, an electrifying and poignant love story. Then it is a movie about the choices we make in life and the choices that other people make for us. Only then is it a thriller—one that Alfred Hitchcock would have been proud to make.

The movie's first act sets up the plot, leaving it a lot of time to deal with the characters and learn about them. The film begins on an Amish settlement in Pennsylvania, where for two hundred years a self-sufficient religious community has proudly held onto the ways of their ancestors. The Amish are deeply suspicious of outsiders and stubbornly dedicated to their rural life-style, with its horses and carriages, its communal barn-raisings, its gas lanterns instead of electricity, hooks instead of buttons.

An Amish man dies. His widow and young son leave on a train journey. In the train station in Philadelphia, the little boy witnesses a murder. Harrison Ford plays the tough big-city detective who gets assigned to the case. He stages lineups, hoping the kid can spot the murderer. He shows the kid mug shots. Then it turns out that the police department itself is implicated in the killing. Ford is nearly murdered in an ambush. His life, and the lives of the widow and her son, are in immediate danger. He manages to drive them all back to the Amish lands of Pennsylvania before collapsing from loss of blood.

And it's at this point, really, that the movie begins. Up until the return to Pennsylvania, *Witness* has been a slick, superior thriller. Now it turns into an intelligent and perceptive love story. It's not one of those romances where the man and woman fall into each other's arms because their hormones are programmed that way. It's about two independent, complicated people who begin to love each other because they have shared danger, they work well together, they respect each other—*and* because their physical attraction for each other is so strong it almost becomes another character in the movie.

Witness was directed by Peter Weir, the gifted Australian director of *The Year of Living Dangerously.* He has a strong and sure feeling for places, for the land, for the way that people build their self-regard by the way they do their work.

In the whole middle section of this movie, he shows the man from the city and the simple Amish woman within the context of the Amish community. It is masterful filmmaking. The thriller elements alone would command our attention. The love story by itself would be exciting. The ways of life in the Amish community are so well-observed that they have a documentary feel. But all three elements work together so well that something organic is happening here; we're *inside* this story.

Harrison Ford has never given a better performance in a movie. Kelly McGillis, the young actress who plays the Amish widow, has a kind of luminous simplicity about her; it is refreshing and even subtly erotic to see a woman who doesn't subscribe to all the standard man-woman programmed responses of modern society.

The love that begins to grow between them is not made out of clichés; the cultural gulf that separates them is at least as important to both of them as the feelings they have. When they finally kiss, it is a glorious, sensuous moment, because this kiss is a sharing of trust and passion, not just another plug-in element from your standard kit of movie images.

We have been getting so many pallid, bloodless little movies—mostly recycled teen-age exploitation films made by ambitious young stylists without a thought in their heads—that *Witness* is like a fresh new day. It is a movie about adults, whose lives have dignity and whose choices matter to them. And it is also one hell of a thriller.

The World According to Garp ★ ★ ★
R, 126 m., 1982

Robin Williams (Garp), Mary Beth Hurt (Helen Holm), Glenn Close (Jenny Fields), John Lithgow (Roberta), Hume Cronyn (Mr. Fields), Jessica Tandy (Mrs. Fields), Swoozie Kurtz (Hooker), Amanda Plummer (Ellen James). Directed by George Roy Hill and produced by Hill and Robert L. Crawford. Screenplay by Steve Tesich.

John Irving's best-selling novel, *The World According to Garp,* was cruel, annoying, and smug. I kept wanting to give it to my cats. But it was wonderfully well-written and was probably intended to inspire some of those negative reactions in the reader. The movie version of *Garp,* however, left me entertained but unmoved, and perhaps the movie's basic failing is that it did not inspire me to walk out on it. Something has to be wrong with a film that can take material as intractable as *Garp* and make it palatable.

Like a lot of movie versions of novels, the film of *Garp* has not reinterpreted the material in its own terms. Indeed, it doesn't interpret it at all. It simply reproduces many of the characters and events in the novel, as if the point in bringing *Garp* to the screen was to provide a visual aid for the novel's readers. With the book we at least know how we feel during the saga of Garp's unlikely life; the movie lives entirely within its moments, keeping us entirely inside a series of self-contained scenes.

The story of Garp is by now part of best-selling folklore. We know that Garp's mother was an eccentric nurse, a cross between a saint and a nuisance, and that Garp was fathered in a military hospital atop the unconscious body of a brain-damaged technical sergeant. That's how much use Garp's mother, Jenny Fields, had for men. The movie, like the book, follows Garp from this anticlimactic beginning through a lifetime during which he is constantly overshadowed by his mother, surrounded by other strange women and women-surrogates, and asks for himself, his wife and children only uneventful peace and a small measure of happiness.

A great deal happens, however, to disturb the peace and prevent the happiness. Garp is accident-prone, and sadness and disaster surround him. Assassinations, bizarre airplane crashes, and auto mishaps are part of his daily routine. His universe seems to have been wound backward.

The movie's method in regarding the nihilism of his life is a simple one. It alternates two kinds of scenes: those in which very strange people do very strange things while pretending to be sane, and those in which all of the dreams of those people, and Garp, are shattered in instants of violence and tragedy.

What are we to think of these people and the events in their lives? The novel *The World According to Garp* was (I *think*) a tragicomic counterpoint between the collapse of middle-class family values and the rise of random violence in our society. A protest against that violence provides the most memorable image in the book, the creation of the Ellen James Society, a group of women who cut out their tongues in protest against what happened to Ellen James, who had her tongue cut out by a man. The bizarre behavior of the people in the novel, particularly Garp's mother and the members of the Ellen Jamesians, is a cross between activism and insanity, and there is the clear suggestion that without such behavior to hold them together, all of these people would be unable to cope at all and would sign themselves into the nearest institution. As a vision of modern American life, *Garp* is bleak, but it has something to say.

The movie, however, seems to believe that the book's characters and events are somehow real, or, to put it another way, that the *point* of the book is to describe these colorful characters and their unlikely behavior, just as Melville described the cannibals in *Typee.* Although Robin Williams plays Garp as a relatively plausible, sometimes ordinary person, the movie never seems bothered by the jarring contrast between his cheerful pluckiness and the anarchy around him.

That created the following dilemma for me. While I watched *Garp,* I enjoyed it. I thought the acting was unconventional and absorbing (especially by Williams, by Glenn Close as his mother, and by John Lithgow as a transsexual). I thought the visualization of the events, by director George Roy Hill, was fresh and consistently interesting. But when the movie was over, my immediate response was not at all what it should have been. All I could find to ask myself was: What the hell was *that* all about?

Xanadu ★ ★
PG, 93 m., 1980

Olivia Newton-John (Kira), Gene Kelly (Danny McGuire), Michael Beck (Sonny Malone). Directed by Robert Greenwald and produced by Lawrence Gordon. Screenplay by Richard Christian Danus and Marc Reid Rubel.

Xanadu is a mushy and limp musical fantasy, so insubstantial it evaporates before our eyes. It's one of those rare movies in which every scene seems to be the final scene; it's all ends and no beginnings, right up to its actual end, which is a cheat. There are, however, a few—a very few—reasons to see *Xanadu*, which I list herewith: (1) Olivia Newton-John is a great-looking woman, brimming with high spirits, (2) Gene Kelly has a few good moments, (3) the sound track includes "Magic," and (4) it's not as bad as *Can't Stop the Music.*

It is pretty bad, though. And yet it begins with an inspiration that I found appealing. It gives us a young man (Michael Beck) who falls in love with the dazzling fantasy figure (Newton-John) who keeps popping up in his life. Beck works as a commercial artist, designing record album covers, and when he tries to include Olivia in one of his paintings he gets into trouble at work.

That's okay, because he's met this nice older guy (Gene Kelly) who's very rich and wants to open a nightclub like the one he had back in New York in the 1940s. Kelly used to be a sideman in the Glenn Miller Orchestra, and in a quietly charming fantasy scene, he sings a duet with his old flame, the girl singer in the old Miller band—who, lo and behold, is Olivia Newton-John.

That means both men are in love with the same dream girl, who, we discover, is not of this earth. They team up to convert a run-down old wrestling amphitheater into Xanadu, a nightclub that will combine the music of the 1940s and 1980s. And that is the whole weight of the movie's ideas, except for a scene where Michael Beck visits Olivia in heaven, which looks like a computer-generated disco light show.

Musicals have been made with thinner plot lines than this one, but rarely with less style. The movie is muddy, it's underlit, characters are constantly disappearing into shadows, there's no zest to the movie's look. Even worse, I'm afraid, is the choreography by Kenny Ortega and Jerry Trent, especially as it's viewed by Victor Kemper's camera. The dance numbers in this movie do not seem to have been conceived for film.

For example: When Beck and Kelly visit the empty amphitheater, Kelly envisions a forties band in one corner and an eighties rock group in another. The movie gives us one of each: Andrews Sisters clones in close harmony, and the Electric Light Orchestra in full explosion. Then the two bandstands are moved together so that they blend and everyone is on one bandstand, singing one song. It's a great idea, but the way this movie handles it, it's an incomprehensible traffic jam with dozens of superfluous performers milling about.

The Ortega-Trent choreography of some of the other numbers is just as bad. They keep giving us five lines of dancers and then shooting at eye level, so that instead of seeing patterns we see confusing cattle calls. The dancers in the background muddy the movements of the foreground. It's a free-for-all.

The movie approaches desperation at times in its attempt to be all things to all audiences. Not only do we get the 1940s swing era, but a contemporary sequence starts with disco, goes to hard rock, provides an especially ludicrous country and western sequence, and moves on into prefabricated New Wave. There are times when *Xanadu* doesn't even feel like a movie fantasy, but like a shopping list of marketable pop images. Samuel Taylor Coleridge dreamed the poem Xanadu but woke up before it was over, a possibility overlooked by the makers of this film.

The Year of Living Dangerously
★ ★ ★ ★
PG, 114 m., 1983

Mel Gibson (Guy Hamilton), Linda Hunt (Billy Kwan), Sigourney Weaver (Jill Bryant), Michael Murphy (Pete Curtis), Noel Ferrier

(Wally O'Sullivan), Bill Kerr (Colonel
Henderson). Directed by Peter Weir and
produced by Jim McElroy. Screenplay by
David Williamson, Weir, and C.J. Koch.

The Year of Living Dangerously achieves one
of the best re-creations of an exotic locale
I've ever seen in a movie. It takes us to
Indonesia in the middle 1960s, a time when
the Sukarno regime was shaky and the war in
Vietnam was just heating up. It moves us
into the life of a foreign correspondent, a
radio reporter from Australia who has just
arrived in Jakarta, and who thrives in an
atmosphere heady with danger. How is this
atmosphere created by Peter Weir, the director? He plunges into it headfirst. He doesn't
pause for travelogue shots. He thrusts us
immediately into the middle of the action—
into a community of expatriates, journalists,
and embassy people who hang out in the
same bars, restaurants, and clubs, and speculate hungrily on the possibility that Sukarno might be deposed. That would be a really
big story, a corrective for their vague feelings
of being stuck in a backwater.

Guy Hamilton, the journalist (Mel Gibson), is a lanky, Kennedyesque, chain-smoking young man who has a fix on excitement.
He doesn't know the ropes in Indonesia, but
he learns them quickly enough, from a
dwarfish character named Billy Kwan. Billy
is half-Oriental and half-European, and
knows everybody and can tell you where all
the bodies are buried. He has a warm smile
and a way of encouraging you to do your
best, and if you sometimes suspect he has
unorthodox political connections—well, he
hasn't crossed you yet. In all the diplomatic
receptions he's a familiar sight in his gaudy
tropical shirts. *The Year of Living Dangerously* follows Guy and Billy as they become
friends, and something more than friends;
they begin to share a common humanity and
respect. Billy gets Guy a good interview with
the local Communist Party chief. He even
introduces Guy to Jill Bryant (Sigourney
Weaver), a British attaché with two weeks
left on her tour. As the revolution creeps
closer, as the stories get bigger, Guy and Jill
become lovers and Billy, who once proposed
to Jill, begins to feel pushed aside.

This sounds, no doubt, like a foreign
correspondent plot from the 1940s. It is not.

The Year of Living Dangerously is a wonderfully complex film about personalities more
than events, and we really share the feeling
of living in that place, at that time. It does for
Indonesia what Bogdanovich's *Saint Jack*
did for Singapore. The direction is masterful; Weir (whose credits include *Picnic at
Hanging Rock*) is as good with quiet little
scenes (like Billy's visit to a dying child) as
big, violent ones (like a thrilling attempt by
Guy and Billy to film a riot).

The performances of the movie are a good
fit with Weir's direction, and his casting of
the Billy Kwan character is a key to how the
film works. Billy, so small and mercurial,
likable and complicated and exotic, makes
Indonesia seem more foreign and intriguing
than any number of standard travelogue
shots possibly could. That means that when
the travelogue shots *do* come (and they do,
breathtakingly, when Gibson makes a trip
into the countryside), they're not just scenery; they do their work for the film because
Weir has so convincingly placed us in Indonesia. Billy Kwan is played, astonishingly,
by a woman—Linda Hunt, a New York stage
actress who enters the role so fully that it
never occurs to us that she is not a man. This
is what great acting is, a magical transformation of one person into another. Mel Gibson
(of *The Road Warrior*) is just right as a basically conventional guy with an obsessive
streak of risk-taking. Sigourney Weaver has
a less interesting role but is always an interesting actress. This is a wonderfully absorbing film.

Yentl ★ ★ ★ ½
PG, 134 m., 1983

Yentl (Barbra Streisand), Mandy Patinkin
(Avigdor), Amy Irving (Hadass), Nehemiah
Persoff (Papa). Directed and produced by
Barbra Streisand. Screenplay by Jack
Rosenthal and Streisand.

To give you a notion of the special magic of
Yentl, I'd like to start with the following
complicated situation:

Yentl, a young Jewish girl, wants to be a
scholar. But girls are not permitted to study
books. So she disguises herself as a boy, and
is accepted by a community of scholars. She
falls in love with one of them. He thinks she
is a boy. He is in love with a local girl. The

girl's father will not let him marry her. So he convinces Yentl to marry his girlfriend, so that at least he can visit the two people he cares for most deeply. (The girlfriend, remember this, thinks Yentl is a boy.) Yentl and the girl are wed. At first Yentl manages to disguise her true sex. But eventually she realizes that she must reveal the truth. That is the central situation in *Yentl*. And when the critical moment came when Yentl had to decide what to do, I was quietly astonished to realize that I did not have the slightest idea how this situation was going to turn out, and that I really cared about it.

I was astonished because, quite frankly, I expected *Yentl* to be some kind of schmaltzy formula romance in which Yentl's "secret identity" was sort of a running gag. You know, like one of those plot points they use for Broadway musicals where the audience is really there to hear the songs and see the costumes. But *Yentl* takes its masquerade seriously, it treats its romances with the respect due to genuine emotion, and its performances are so good that, yes, I really did care.

Yentl is Barbra Streisand's dream movie. She had been trying to make it for ten years, ever since she bought the rights to the Isaac Bashevis Singer story it's based on. Hollywood told her she was crazy. Hollywood was right—on the irrefutable logical ground that a woman in her forties can hardly be expected to be convincing as a seventeen-year-old boy. Streisand persisted. She worked on this movie four years, as producer, director, cowriter, and star. And she has pulled it off with great style and heart. She doesn't really look like a seventeen-year-old boy in this movie, that's true. We have to sort of suspend our disbelief a little. But she *does* look seventeen, and that's without a lot of trick lighting and funny filters on the lens, too. And she sings like an angel.

Yentl is a movie with a great middle. The beginning is too heavy-handed in establishing the customs against women scholars (an itinerant book salesman actually shouts, "Serious books for men . . . picture books for women"). And the ending, with Yentl sailing off for America, seemed like a cheat; I missed the final scene between Yentl and her "bride." But the middle 100 minutes of the movie are charming and moving and

surprisingly interesting. A lot of the charm comes from the cheerful high energy of the actors, not only Streisand (who gives her best performance) but also Mandy Patinkin, as her long-suffering roommate, and Amy Irving, as the girl Patinkin loves and Streisand marries.

There are, obviously, a lot of tricky scenes involving this triangle, but the movie handles them all with taste, tact, and humor. It's pretty obvious what strategy Streisand and her collaborators used in approaching the scenes where Yentl pretends to be a boy. They began by asking what the scene would mean if she *were* a male, and then they simply played it that way, allowing the ironic emotional commentaries to make themselves.

There was speculation from Hollywood that *Yentl* would be "too Jewish" for middle-American audiences. I don't think so. Like all great fables, it grows out of a particular time and place, but it takes its strength from universal sorts of feelings. At one time or another, almost everyone has wanted to do something and been told they couldn't, and almost everyone has loved the wrong person for the right reason. That's the emotional ground that *Yentl* covers, and it always has its heart in the right place.

Young Doctors in Love ★ ★
R, 96 m., 1982

Michael McKean (Dr. August), Sean Young (Dr. Brody), Harry Dean Stanton (Dr. Ludwig), Patrick MacNee (Dr. Jacobs), Hector Elizondo (Angelo), Dabney Coleman (Dr. Prang). Directed by Garry Marshall and produced by Jerry Bruckheimer. Screenplay by Michael Elias and Rich Eustis.

The basic joke in *Young Doctors in Love* was anticipated five years ago, in Mel Brooks's *Silent Movie*. Remember the scene where Brooks and his cohorts stand by Sid Caesar's bedside, watching his heartbeat reflected on a television monitor, when suddenly the heart beep turns into a Pong game? That combination of gallows humor and contemporary cross-references is repeated again and again in *Young Doctors in Love*, and it's finally not very funny. Yet the movie sounds like a good idea. Maybe it was a good idea, lost in the execution. *Young Doctors in Love* has as its modest ambition to be to "General Hospital" what *Airplane!* was to the *Airport* movies and ABC's "Police Squad" was to TV cop shows. Maybe there are two problems here: (1) It is rather hard to outflank "General Hospital," a parody of itself, and (2) If you do, you wind up skirting the edges of very unpleasant comic material about blood and death. Hospitals are just not very funny.

The movie takes place in a loony Los Angeles city hospital, where we meet all the standard types: the monomaniac surgeon, the befuddled chief of staff, and sex-and-dope crazed interns and nurses, and the ambitious young medical students in their first year of residence. There also are several long-running gags, the unfunniest being about a hit man who is turned into the hapless victim of accidents and near-fatal emergency treatments. The movie looks at times like a real-life version of one of those drawings by *Mad* magazine's Jack Davis, in which lunatics chase each other in circles.

Are there funny moments in the middle of the chaos? Yes, there are. There is, in fact, one wonderfully funny moment, starring that superb character actor Harry Dean Stanton, he of the long face, the quivering eyelids, and the perpetual hangover. He attempts to explain the secretion of bodily fluids to the amazed young medical students, and by the time he is finished with his amazing catalog, there is not an orifice left untapped.

That's a great scene, and Dabney Coleman has some nice moments as the egotistical surgeon, obviously modeled on the sorts of Texas super doctors who do most of their operations on the cover of *Life* magazine. Coleman reminds us again here of his versatility; his roles also have included the boss in *9 to 5* and Jane Fonda's fiancé in *On Golden Pond*. But for the rest, *Young Doctors in Love* is not very funny and not very inventive. God knows it tries. Like *Airplane!*, it spends its energy trying to wedge laughs into every crevice of the plot. There are some nice moments, especially a gag about *E.T.* But most of the time I wasn't laughing, and toward the end I wasn't even smiling. When a comedy goes wrong, it goes very wrong. *Young Doctors in Love* goes very wrong.

Zelig ★ ★ ★
PG, 79 m., 1983

Woody Allen (Leonard Zelig), Mia Farrow (Dr. Fletcher). Interviews: Susan Sontag, Irving Howe, Saul Bellow, Bricktop, Bruno Bettelheim, Professor John Morton Blum. Directed by Woody Allen. Produced by Robert Greenhut. Screenplay by Allen.

Woody Allen's *Zelig* represents an intriguing idea for a movie, and it has been made with great ingenuity and technical brilliance. That's almost enough. In fact, if *Zelig* were only about an hour long, it would be enough, but the unwritten code of feature films requires that it be longer, and finally there is just so much Zelig that we say enough, already.

The movie is a fake documentary, a film that claims to tell the story of Leonard Zelig, a once-famous American who suffered from a most curious disease: He was a human chameleon. He was so eager to please, so loath to give offense, so willing to blend right in, that perhaps some change took place at a cellular level, and Zelig began to take on the social, intellectual, and even physical characteristics of people that he spent time with. Put him with a psychiatrist, and he began to discuss complexes. Put him next to a Chinese man, and he began to look Oriental. This ability to fit right in propelled Zelig, we are told, to the heights of fame in the earlier decades of this century. He hobnobbed with presidents, was honored by ticker-tape parades, and his case was debated by learned societies. *Zelig* at first seems to be simply the documentary record of Zelig's case, but then another level begins to sneak in.

We are introduced (always through the documentary means of newsreel film, still photos, old radio broadcasts, and narration) to one Dr. Eudora Fletcher, who is a psychiatrist. She takes Zelig as a patient, and eventually they fall in love (we can see it happening, by implication, in documentary footage that apparently concerns other matters). The best thing about *Zelig*, apart from its technical accomplishment, is the way Woody Allen develops the human story of his hero; we get a portrait of a life and a poignant dilemma, peeking out from behind the documentary façade. The technical approach of *Zelig* has been experimented with before, most memorably in the fictional *March of Time* newsreel that introduced *Citizen Kane*. In that movie, we saw Charles Foster Kane apparently standing on balconies with Hitler and talking with Mussolini. In *Zelig*, the actors (Woody Allen, Mia Farrow, and dozens more) are so successfully integrated into old footage that we give up trying to tell the real from the fictional.

Zelig is a technical success, and it is also a success as a statement: Allen has a lot to say here about the nature of celebrity, science, and the American melting pot. He has also made an essay about film itself; the way that *Zelig*'s documentary material goes at right angles to its human story makes us think about the line between documentary and poetic "truth."

But the problem is, all of those achievements are easily accomplished at less length than the movie takes. The basic visual approach is clear from the first frames, and although it continues to impress us, it ceases after a while to amaze us. The emerging of Zelig's personality is intriguing, but the documentary framework allows it to emerge only so far, and no farther. We're left wanting more of Zelig and less of the movie's method; the movie is a technical masterpiece, but in artistic and comic terms, only pretty good.

Zorro, the Gay Blade ★ ★
PG, 96 m., 1981

George Hamilton (Don Diego/Bunny), Lauren Hutton (Charlotte), Brenda Vaccaro (Florinda), Ron Liebman (Esteban), Donovan Scott (Paco), James Booth (Velasquez). Directed by Peter Medak and produced by George Hamilton and E.O. Erickson. Screenplay by Hal Dresner.

It is hard to reconstruct these fragments from the memories of childhood but as nearly as I can remember, the Zorro craze came after the Davy Crockett craze and before Elvis. Kids made Z-marks everywhere—on walls, fences, blackboards, and with ballpoints on the shirts of the kids sitting in front of them—and my personal notion is that Datsun sells half of their Z-cars to guys harboring sublimated Zorro fantasies.

Here's the curious thing. I remember a lot about Zorro. I even remember that he was once played by Clayton Moore, who got to keep wearing his Lone Ranger mask. But I cannot remember if the Zorro movies were ever supposed to be funny. I assume that the Zorros played by Douglas Fairbanks, Tyrone Power, and John Carroll were more or less serious, within the broad outlines of the adventure genre. But what about all the Zorro movies and TV shows that Guy Williams made for Disney? Were we laughing at him, or with him?

I ask because I am just as confused after seeing *Zorro, the Gay Blade*, which stars George Hamilton in a dual role as Don Diego Vega and his twin brother, Bunny. (The brother was originally a Vega, too, but after enlisting in the British Navy he changed his name to Bunny Wigglesworth.) This movie is, of course, intended as a comedy, and it has some funny moments. But it's just not successful, and I think the reason is that Hamilton never for a second plays Zorro as if he were really playing Zorro. We could laugh at the previous movie Zorros because they were so serious about their ridiculous codes and vows and pledges of loyalty and chivalric passions. They were funny as long as they played it straight. But when a movie sets out a create a funny Zorro, that's bringing coals to Newcastle. By playing every scene for laughs, Hamilton has nothing to play against.

Zorro, the Gay Blade was no doubt inspired by the enormous success of Hamilton's spoof of a durable Hollywood character, when he played Dracula in *Love at First Bite* (1979). Hamilton demonstrated in that movie, and demonstrates again in this one, that he is a gifted comic actor. He can have fun with his improbably handsome appearance, he can poke fun at his character's vanity, and he can look convincing enough as Zorro (or Dracula) to remind us of the quintessential Hollywood leading men whose footsteps he is stalking.

But . . . should Zorro be funny because of his puffed-up self-importance, or because his role in life is inescapably ridiculous any way you look at it? Should he be funny because of what he is (my theory), or what he does (this movie's theory)? A funnier comedy might have been made out of a more genuinely satirical examination of the Zorro character. Instead, this one provides Zorro with a gay brother who's a screamingly limp-wristed stereotype, and then goes for jokes that are disappointingly predictable. It also gives him a leading lady (Lauren Hutton) who has all she can do to play her role at all, much less play it satirically. And it never provides a comprehensive story to hold the jokes together. Too bad. I think I remember now: We laughed more at the old Zorros, because they didn't know they were funny.

Afterword

Judging the Classics

Are these the sixteen greatest films of all time, or do 122 of the world's film critics only think they are?

1. *Citizen Kane* (Orson Welles, U.S.)
2. *The Rules of the Game* (Jean Renoir, France)
3. (tie) *The Seven Samurai* (Akira Kurosawa, Japan)
   Singin' in the Rain (Stanley Donen and Gene Kelly, U.S.)
5. *8½* (Federico Fellini, Italy)
6. *Battleship Potemkin* (Sergei Eisenstein, USSR)
7. (tie) *L'Avventura* (Michelangelo Antonioni, Italy)
   The Magnificent Ambersons (Orson Welles, U.S.)
9. (tie) *Vertigo* (Alfred Hitchcock, U.S.)
   The General (Buster Keaton, U.S.)
   The Searchers (John Ford, U.S.)
12. (tie) *2001: A Space Odyssey* (Stanley Kubrick, Great Britain)
    Andrei Roublev (Andrei Tarkovsky, USSR)
14. (tie) *Greed* (Erich von Stroheim, U.S.)
    Jules and Jim (Francois Truffaut, France)
    The Third Man (Carol Reed, Great Britain)

Those sixteen films were the 1982 winners of the fourth International Critics' Poll, conducted every ten years by *Sight & Sound*, the authoritative film quarterly published by the British Film Institute. The magazine's instructions to critics voting from all over the world were simple: "Personal choices of the films which have seemed most significant or relevant to you, which you have enjoyed or admired most. Ten titles only, please, in alphabetical order or in order of preference, of films made anywhere, at any time."

The *Sight & Sound* poll is to movies what the wire service polls are to college sports and the Dow Jones average is to the stock market. It represents an imperfect, subjective, unscientific, and highly influential sampling of the critical stock of the great films and filmmakers of the world. And when the 1982 results were announced, they created shock waves, at least in that little corner of the world where such things matter.

The big news in the 1982 poll was the surprising critical devaluation of the work of Ingmar Bergman, the great Swedish filmmaker whose name seems almost synonymous with cinematic art. In the 1972 poll, Bergman and Orson Welles were the only directors to place two films on the list.[1] This year, Welles's *Citizen Kane* and *Magnificent Ambersons* remain, but Bergman is missing; his *Persona* (tied for fifth in 1972) and *Wild Strawberries* (tied for tenth) dropped off the list altogether, and his more recent contenders, especially *Cries and Whispers* and *Autumn Sonata*, failed to place.

Maybe that was just a statistical aberration? Perhaps Bergman's support was so widely distributed among his more than forty films that no single Bergman movie had the votes to make the list? Not so. In a separate compilation, *Sight & Sound* totaled all of the times any film by a director was voted for. In 1972, Bergman placed a strong third on that list; his thirty-seven votes were close behind Welles's forty-six and Jean Renoir's forty-one. By 1982, Bergman's total vote didn't even qualify him for the top ten![2]

Why did Bergman drop so suddenly from the pantheon? My guess is that the jury changed. In 1972, a majority of the voters would still have belonged to what science-fiction fans call the "sercon" party; they would have been serious, constructive critics looking for meaning, significance, and Art. By 1982, the film generation of the 1960s would have joined in the balloting, probably with a preference for "movies" over "cinema." Perhaps Bergman seemed too heavily laden with symbolism and angst for them, and they wanted to make room for a Western or a musical. Bergman is gone, but not forgotten; look for him on the 1992 list.

Other conclusions from the 1982 balloting:

—Orson Welles continues to stand astride the world of film as an undisputed colossus—at least, as far as the film critics are concerned. Despite the fact that his most important work was done more than forty years ago (*Kane* and *Ambersons* are his first two films), he has strengthened his position since 1972; both times, Welles and *Kane* placed ahead of Renoir and *Rules*, but in 1982, it was a landslide.

Citizen Kane is, of course, widely described as the greatest film ever made— so frequently, and by so many different people, that it has moved into the same quasi-official stratosphere as *King Lear* or Beethoven's Fifth Symphony. What is remarkable is that in 1952, when *Sight & Sound* first conducted its poll, *Citizen Kane* didn't even make the list![3] In 1952, *Citizen Kane* was a masterpiece much talked about but rarely seen, after its original 1941 release was botched. (Because the Hollywood establishment feared to offend publishing

[1] The top ten, 1972: *Citizen Kane, Rules of the Game, Battleship Potemkin, 8½, L'Avventura* tied with Dreyer's *The Passion of Joan of Arc, The General* tied with *The Magnificent Ambersons, Ugetsu Monogatari* tied with *Wild Strawberries*.

[2] Voting by directors, 1982: Orson Welles, 71; Jean Renoir, 51; Charles Chaplin, 37; John Ford, 34; Luis Bunuel and Akira Kurosawa, both 33; Federico Fellini and Alfred Hitchcock, both 32; Jean-Luc Godard and Buster Keaton, both 30.

[3] The top four films in 1952, according to both the magazine poll and a vote of filmmakers at the Brussels World Fair, were De Sica's *Bicycle Thief,* Chaplin's *City Lights* and *Gold Rush,* and Eisenstein's *Battleship Potemkin.*

tycoon William Randolph Hearst, whose life inspired Kane's, the major
theater chains wouldn't touch the film, and it got scattered release; not until
1957, when a new print was widely distributed, did the film win really wide
audiences.)

Why is the film so widely admired? "Citizen Kane is perhaps the one
American talking picture that seems as fresh now as the day it opened. It may
even seem fresher," Pauline Kael wrote in the opening words of her landmark
The Citizen Kane Book. If you do not believe her, see it for yourself. The film is
endlessly inventive as it circles closer and closer to the mystery of a man's life, a
mystery that seems to be summed up by his dying word, "Rosebud."[4] One
reason the film always seems fresh is that we never know what's coming next;
the film has such an unpredictable structure, leaping about in Kane's life and
from flashback to flashback, that it is all but impossible to remember what will
follow. I have seen *Citizen Kane* at least thirty times, and yet when I walk in on
the middle of a screening, or start my tape at random, I am unable to remember
for sure what will come next.

—*The Seven Samurai* and *Singin' in the Rain,* were not even also-rans in
1972; this time, they tied for third. *Seven Samurai,* a saga about medieval
warlords that introduced Toshiro Mifune to world movie audiences and inspired the Hollywood remake *The Magnificent Seven,* became the only film on
the list from Japan, one of the great centers of cinema; last time, Japan was
represented by Mizoguchi's *Ugetsu Monogatari,* the story of a poor man's
infatuation with a dreamlike geisha. *Singin' in the Rain* is routinely called the
best of the Hollywood musicals, and its high place is a tribute to the whole
genre.

—Two veteran Hollywood filmmakers who died in the decade between the
polls made it into the top ten. Alfred Hitchcock's *Vertigo* and John Ford's *The
Searchers,* were runners-up in 1972, possibly because both directors had been
so prolific and made so many great films that no single title could gather a
following. By 1982, the consensus was in.

Many movie buffs would name *Rear Window, Psycho,* or *Notorious* as
Hitchcock's best picture, but *Vertigo,* starring James Stewart and Kim Novak
in the story of a man obsessed with a woman he thinks is dead, has been named
by Hitchcock's biographers as perhaps his most personal work. Because the
copyrights to *Vertigo* and four other Hitchcock titles (*Rope, The Man Who
Knew Too Much, Rear Window,* and *The Trouble with Harry*) were owned by
Hitchcock's estate, they had not been publicly screened for years when the
1982 poll was held. In 1984, however, they were bought from the estate by
Universal, and are all now available in video.

The Searchers is not everybody's favorite film by the man who once said "My
name is Ford. I make Westerns." Some viewers would name *Stagecoach, My*

[4]But who heard him say "rosebud"? Although Kane's butler claims late in the film that he
heard it, the death chamber seems empty except for the lonely tycoon. A nurse enters after he
drops the paperweight.

Darling Clementine, or *Three Godfathers.* Many critics have questions about the plot of *The Searchers,* which has John Wayne so appalled when his niece is kidnapped by Indians that he spends seventeen years in the wilderness on a relentless, obsessive search for her. They see the film as a racist portrait of Indians and a male chauvinist story, in which the real importance of the girl (played by Natalie Wood) is as a pawn for the men in the film. Still, *The Searchers* has inspired the stories of many other films, notably Martin Scorsese's *Taxi Driver* and Paul Schrader's *Hardcore.*

—The battle of the two greatest silent clowns continues in the 1982 results. Buster Keaton's *The General,* an amazingly ambitious epic in which he played the engineer of a lengendary Civil War train, slipped from eighth to ninth. Chaplin failed to place any titles on the list, but in the closely bunched vote by directors, he placed somewhat higher than Keaton—third, with thirty-seven votes, to ninth, with thirty. Perhaps the totals reflect the consensus that *The General* is Keaton's greatest film, and an inability to choose among such Chaplin masterpieces as *The Gold Rush, City Lights,* and *Modern Times.* Since most silent films are out of copyright, they can be purchased fairly cheaply in video, often under $20.

Is the *Sight & Sound* poll all that important? It's like the football coaches' poll: Everybody cares when it comes out, nobody can remember it by next year. The real importance is that if you set out to see every film on it, you will see sixteen great films, and each one will suggest avenues for further investigation, a few of which I cheerfully outline below, only occasionally venturing from the sublime to the ridiculous:

AFTER SEEING	THEN VIEW	BECAUSE
Citizen Kane	*Providence*	Similar opening shots, narrative ideas
Rules of the Game	*The Grand Illusion*	After and before
The Seven Samurai	*The Magnificent Seven*	The remake
Singin' in the Rain	*An American in Paris*	Gene Kelly
8½	*Day for Night*	Lives of a director
Battleship Potemkin	*Das Boot*	Under pressure
L'Avventura	*Blow Up*	Missing persons
The Magnificent Ambersons	*Breaking Away*	Family life in Indiana
Vertigo	*Body Double*	De Palma's homage
The General	*Modern Times*	Man over machines
The Searchers	*Taxi Driver*	Same underlying story
2001	*My Dinner with André*	"If we could really understand the cigar store next door—wouldn't that be as amazing as climbing Everest?"
Andrei Roublev	*The Seventh Seal*	Medieval legends
Greed	*Sunset Boulevard*	von Stroheim

Jules and Jim	*Two English Girls*	Same author, same director, two approaches
The Third Man	*Night and the City*	Postwar locations, similar feel

I'm not sure this chart has the slightest significance, but drawing it up was amusing, and it duplicated one of the pleasures that the VCR has brought into my life—the random walk through movie history, with one film leading to another, one vision suggesting another. It is probably true that some of the films on the list are not available in most video stores; this might be the occasion for a call to Home Film Festival (1-800-258-3456), which rents hard-to-find classics by mail. Or it might be an occasion for a random walk in another direction altogether. Have fun.

My Ten Great Films, and Why

What are my own nominations for the ten best films of all time? Making such a list is, of course, a form of gamesmanship, and the list is sure to change from day to day. On the day in 1982 when I drew up my list for *Sight & Sound,* these were the titles I decided upon, listed alphabetically:

Aguirre, the Wrath of God. Werner Herzog believes we are starving for images in these modern times, and that without them, we will die. His *Aguirre,* one of the great, mad, passionate, foolhardy masterpieces—as reckless and as brilliant as *Greed* or *Apocalypse Now*—stars Klaus Kinski in the story of a member of Pizarro's expedition to find the lost El Dorado. After the main body turns back, Aguirre presses on with a small band of followers, all of them weighted down by the armor which is suicidal in the rain forest. Among the film's great images, are the first, of a string of desperate men winding their way down an unimaginably long mountain path, and one of the last, of Aguirre on a raft overrun by chattering monkeys. Herzog believes in the voodoo of locations, and shot this film deep in the Amazon jungle. There is a legend that Kinski threatened to walk off the film, and Herzog held a gun to him and said he would shoot him if he left. It is probably only an apocraphal story, but neither Herzog nor Kinski denies it.

Bonnie and Clyde. Arthur Penn's film still seems to have the same freshness, after eighteen years, that Kael talks about with *Kane.* It works as comedy, as tragedy, as entertainment, as a meditation on the place of guns and violence in American society. And it was perfectly cast; Warren Beatty and Faye Dunaway have become icons as Clyde and Bonnie, but remember, too, Michael J. Pollard as C.W. Moss, Gene Hackman as Buck Barrow (his first major role), Estelle Parsons as Buck's wife Blanche, Gene Wilder as the hapless undertaker taken along for the ride, and Dub Taylor as C.W.'s greedy father. Scene after scene plays with perfect, almost dreamlike, emotional control: Clyde and the tenant farmer shooting out windows, the cloud passing in front of the sun and shadowing Bonnie and Clyde in the wheat field, Bonnie's farewell to her mother, C.W. parking the getaway car, Blanche screaming and running across the lawn with a spatula in her hand, Buck's dying delirium, and of course the final scene, which has been copied in so many other movies it has become a cliché, except here, where it retains all of its power.

Casablanca. I saw it again just a few weeks ago, at the University of Colorado, where I go every year to take a week and study a film shot-by-shot with a stop-action film analyzer. I was struck once again by what a perfect love story there is here, requiring the lovers to be true to their ideas of each other by choosing a greater good than love. The supporting characters (Claude Rains, Sidney Greenstreet, Peter Lorre, and, always, Dooley Wilson) transform what was, after all, only a set on the back lot at the Burbank Studios and turn it into a teeming, conspiring, colorful Casablanca.

The key to the movie's drama is Bogart's gradual transition, from a man who "sticks his neck out for no one" to a man who embraces once again the ideals of his youth. In remembering *Casablanca*, we think of it as a love story between Bogart and Bergman. (The pale Paul Henreid, as the freedom fighter Victor Laslo, is permitted a chaste peck on Bergman's cheek, and scarcely has the presence in the film to qualify as the third point of a love triangle.) But see the film again and you may be surprised at how bitter Bogart is when he sees Bergman again. His cruelty to her in the late-night drunk scene in Rick's Place is painful—because we see how much it hurts both of them. Only gradually does Bogart come around to the right feelings, and the right decisions. *Casablanca* is not the story of lost love, but of rediscovered idealism.

Citizen Kane. Of course. But for the little touches as well as for the big ones. For Kane's shadow-play with his hands the first time he meets Susan Alexander. For Kane applauding alone, defiantly, maniacally, after Susan's opera debut. For the remarkable visual illusion in Thatcher's office, when Kane, brought in to sign away his empire, is first seen in the foreground in front of what look like normal windows—and then, as Kane walks into the background of the shot, they are revealed as giant cathedral-scale windows, and Kane is diminished into a miniature. And for Mr. Bernstein's sad and wonderful line, "One day, back in 1896, I was crossing over to Jersey on a ferry, and as we pulled out, there was another ferry pulling in, and on it there was a girl waiting to get off. A white dress she had on. She was carrying a white parasol. I only saw her for one second. She didn't see me at all, but I'll bet a month hasn't gone by since, that I haven't thought of that girl." The power of that line is such that, in the years since I first heard it, I'll bet a month hasn't gone by that I haven't thought of it.

La Dolce Vita. Federico Fellini's 1959 film is a page-marker in my own life. It tells the story of a gossip columnist named Marcello, who roams the night world of Rome's Via Veneto, pursuing dreams of fame and sex and money, promising himself and his friend Steiner that someday he will write a great novel. Marcello seems almost afraid to stop moving, for fear that the silence of the emptiness of his life will overwhelm him. Fellini's great images come in profusion: The bearded dancer in the nightclub, lit from beneath as if from hell; the bas reliefs on the walls of the villa, each ancient Roman face the exact duplicate of a guest at the party; the Christ statue carried by helicopter over

Rome; the cat and the fountain at dawn; the children running here and there in the rain, taunting the sick and dying with their sudden sightings of the Virgin Mary. Marcello is thirty in the film. When I first saw it, I was twenty, and it represented a great and wonderful world I wanted to enter. When I was thirty and saw it again, it represented the trap I was in. I saw it again at forty, and saw it as what I had survived and perhaps even learned from. This is, I believe, Fellini's best film, too often overlooked on the short lists of unquestionably great films.

Notorious. This is my favorite Hitchcock film, and the best love story he ever told. In some ways, its triangle resembles *Casablanca's*; Cary Grant, like Humphrey Bogart, loves Ingrid Bergman but is cruel to her because she feels she has been unfaithful to him—and all the time Bergman has chosen the greater good. Although Claude Rains, the other man who loves Bergman, plays a Nazi in this film, he is in many ways more sympathetic than the cool Paul Henreid in *Casablanca.* He does, after all, really love her—and he will be denied her love, along with so many other things in his life, because of his monstrous mother and his fatal politics. The film is filled with great shots: The introduction of Cary Grant, seen from behind but nevertheless the focus of attention; an overview of an entrance hall, with the camera moving in one unbroken take to a close-up of a key in a hand; the inexorable procession down the stairs and past the Nazis waiting at the bottom. (For fun, and to reveal one of Hitchcock's secrets, watch for the one scene where Cary Grant completely ascends the staircase in Rains's home, and count the number of steps he takes. Then, in the scene where Grant, Bergman, Rains, and Madame Constantine descend the stairs, count how many steps they descend. Hitchcock prolongs the suspense by editing to add extra steps.)

Persona. Ingmar Bergman's 1967 film has been described as almost impossible to understand, but perhaps it can be approached, instead, as a very simple story. An actress, horrified by the suffering in the world, simply stops speaking one day. She is sent by her therapist to spend some time in the country with a nurse. During their months together, a strange personalities transference takes place, until the impressionable young nurse forgets exactly who she is—and then remembers again, when the spell is broken. The film itself "breaks" in the middle, as if the pain from the shard of glass has broken the power of fiction to contain it. The scene of the merging faces is famous (Liv Ullmann and Bibi Andersson told me they had no idea Bergman was going to do it), but even more mysterious is the dream sequence in which both women seem to share the actress's husband. The long monologue about the encounter with the boys on the beach has a strange after-effect; although it is only described, never seen, we visualize it so strongly that, months later, we may swear it was in the film.

Taxi Driver. I think Martin Scorsese's work is the best American film made since I've been reviewing movies, and Robert DeNiro's performance as Travis

Bickle, the lonely, violent taxi driver, has entered into folklore ("Are you looking at *me?*"). The film is visually fascinating, especially the repeated motif of overhead shots (a hack license, junk food, guns on a bed, push-ups, the final killing scene) that Scorsese says has a sacramental significance for him. American history has been rewritten by the loners like Travis who have come out of the woodwork: Oswald, Ruby, Ray, Sirhan, and, a colossal irony, John Hinckley, who shot at President Reagan because of his obsession with Jodie Foster in this film. Some said the film inspired his actions. I would say it predicted them, because the real-life Hinckley bore such an unsettlingly similarity to Bickle. If any film can explain to us how and why our society has created creatures like Travis Bickle, and can help us to enter their savagely narrow, driven visions, *Taxi Driver* can; it is a film to place beside the novel *Crime and Punishment* for its knowledge of a deviant personality.

The Third Man. I would have thought this was a great film anyway, but seeing it for the first time in a little cinema on the Left Bank, on a rainy Paris day, on my first trip to Europe, made it, on that day, a perfect film, and ever since it has occupied a special place in my memory. Once again, a story of doomed love; Joseph Cotten, as Holly Martin, the author of trash Westerns, journeys to postwar Vienna to find his best friend, Orson Welles as Harry Lime ("lie-me"). He discovers that Lime is dead, but meets his girl (Alida Valli), and falls in love with her, and finds that she still loves Lime—no matter that his black market penicillin killed innocent children. It's as if Bergman stayed with Rains in *Notorious,* or moved in with Greenstreet in *Casablanca.* Carol Reed's images are remarkable: The balloon man's shadow on the wall, Orson Welles's first entrance (which is the greatest entrance in the history of the movies), Welles approaching almost sideways across the amusement park, the chase in the sewers, and, of course, the great final shot and the perfect emotional parabola described as Cotten throws away his cigarette. The line about the cuckoo clocks is justly famous; I also like "Is that what you say when someone dies? How inconvenient?"

2001. One of the greatest stores of powerful, mysterious images in all of film history. What the film means, what it says, no longer matters to me so much (although like all critics I have a detailed explanation, if you have an evening to spare sometime). What is important here is the sense of wonder. The bone transforms itself into a spaceship, the Strauss waltzes are incongruously appropriate for the sexually charged moment when the ship penetrates the space station, and the appearances of the monolith are so disturbing that you realize the utter strangeness of man's right angles and straight lines amid the careless jumble of nature.

Eliot said he would show us fear in a handful of dust, and Stanley Kubrick shows us infinity in a bedroom, a glass of red wine, and a few green peas. The ending sequence of his film is so great because it does not dare to imagine what other intelligences would look or think like; he shows us a man placed by them, whatever they are, in a room of man's own tradition—and that is so much more frightening than any fantastical alternative. The sequel, *2010*, is a superior space action picture, and I praised it for that. But in explaining the mysteries of *2001*, it diminishes them. e.e. Cummings, who said he'd rather learn from one bird how to sing than teach ten thousand stars how not to dance, wrote in those words the definitive review of both pictures.

In fact, he wrote in those words the definitive review of a lot of pictures.

Glossary of Movie Terms

The basic movie reference books are filled with definitions of terms like *close-up* and *auteur theory*. Nobody needs to know those words. What you need is the *Movie Home Companion* Glossary of Terms for the Cinema of the 1980s. What follows is an attempt to compile such a list—a practical, everyday guide to enhance your moviegoing pleasure and help you categorize what you find on the screen.

A.C.N.E. Acronym for Adolescent Character's Neurotic Envy Syndrome, which usually afflicts shrill teen-age blondes in movies about how the good girl wins the hero away from the syndrome sufferer. See *Secret Admirer.*

Ali MacGraw's Disease. Movie illness in which only symptom is that the sufferer grows more beautiful as death approaches.

Beginning, The. Word used in the titles of sequels to movies in which everyone was killed at the end of the original movie, making an ordinary sequel impossible. Explains to knowledgeable filmgoers that the movie will concern, for example, what happened in the Amityville house *before* the Lutzes moved in. See also: *The First Chapter, The Early Days,* etc.

Balloon Rule. No good movie has ever contained a hot-air balloon.

Box Rule. Useful rule-of-thumb about movie advertisements which have a row of little boxes across the bottom, each one showing the face of a different international star and the name of a character (i.e., "Curt Jurgens as the Commandant"). The rule states: Automatically avoid such films. Example: *The Cassandra Crossing, Force 10 from Navarone,* most films made from Agatha Christie novels.

Brotman's Law. "If nothing has happened by the end of the first reel, nothing is going to happen." (Named for Chicago movie exhibitor Oscar Brotman.)

Crash Scene. Alternative to dialogue; substitute for Burt Reynolds's continuing growth as an actor.

Chop-Socky Movie. Any film involving a karate fight and including the dialogue, "Ha! Ha! Now you die!"

Dead Teen-ager Movie. Generic term for any movie primarily concerned with killing teen-agers, without regard for logic, plot, performance, humor, etc. Often imitated, never worse than in the *Friday the 13th* sequels.

Docudrama. TV term for extended-length program which stars a disease or social problem and co-stars performers willing to give interviews on how they experienced personal growth through their dramatic contact with same.

First Law of Funny Names. No names are funny unless used by W.C. Fields or Groucho Marx. Funny names, in general, are a sign of desperation at the screenplay level. See "Dr. Hfuhruhurr" in *The Man With Two Brains*.

"Food fight!" Dialogue which replaced "Westward ho!" as American movies ended the long frontier trek and began to look inward for sources of inspiration.

"Fruit cart!" An expletive used by knowledgeable film buffs during any chase scene involving a foreign or ethnic locale, reflecting their certainty that a fruit cart will be overturned during the chase, and an angry peddler will run into the middle of the street to shake his fist at the departing Porsche.

Hollywood Car. Looks like a normal automobile, but backfires after being purchased from used car lot by movie heroine who is starting out again in life and is on her own this time.

Horny Teen-ager Movie. Any film primarily concerned with teen-age sexual hungers, usually male. Replaced, to a degree, by Dead Teen-ager Movies (q.v.), but always popular with middle-aged movie executives, who like to explain to their seventeen-year-old starlets why the logic of the dramatic situation and the teachings of Strasberg and Stanislavsky require them to remove their brassieres.

Idiot Plot. Any plot containing problems which would be solved instantly if all of the characters were not idiots.

Impregnable Fortress Impregnated. Indispensable scene in all James Bond movies and many other action pictures, especially war films. The IFI sequence begins early in the picture, with long shots of a faraway fortress and Wagnerian music on the sound track. Eventually the hero gains entry to the fortress, which is inevitably manned by technological clones in designer uniforms. Sequence ends with destruction of fortress, as clones futilely attempt to save their marvelous machines. See *The Guns of Navarone*, etc.

Intelligence. In most movies, "all that separates us from the apes." In *Sheena, Queen of the Jungle*, what we have in common with them.

Kookalouris. Name for a large sheet of cardboard or plywood with holes in it, which is moved back and forth in front of a light to illuminate a character's face with moving light patterns. Popular in the 1930s; back in style again with the movies of Steven Spielberg, who uses a kookalouris with underlighting to show faces that seem to be illuminated by reflections from pots of gold, buckets of diamonds, pools of fire, pirate maps, and radioactive kidneys.

Mad Slasher Movies. Movies starring a mad-dog killer who runs amok, slashing all of the other characters. The killer is frequently masked (as in *Halloween* and *Friday the 13th*), not because a serious actor would be ashamed to be seen in the role, but because then no actor at all is required; the only skills necessary are the ability to wear a mask and wield a machete. For additional reading, see *Splatter Movies*, by John ("multilation is the message") McCarty.

Make My Day. First line of movie dialogue quoted at a presidential press conference since Jimmy Carter said, "I'll never lie to you."

Me-Push-Pull-You. Literal translation of the body language in many Hollywood action pictures, in which, as the hero and heroine flee from danger, the man takes the woman's hand and pulls her along meekly behind him. This convention is so strong that it is seen even in films where it makes no sense, such as *Sheena*, in which a jungle-woman who has ruled the savage beasts since infancy is pulled along by a TV anchorman fresh off the plane.

Seeing-Eye Man. Function performed by most men in Hollywood feature films. Involves a series of shots in which (1) the man sees something, (2) he points it out to the woman, (3) she then sees it too, often nodding in agreement, gratitude, amusement, or relief.

Semi-Obligatory Lyrical Interlude (Semi-OLI). Scene in which soft focus and slow motion are used while a would-be hit song is performed on the sound track and the lovers run through a pastoral setting. Common from the mid-1960s to the mid-1970s; replaced in 1980s with the Semi-Obligatory Music Video (q.v.).

Semi-Obligatory Music Video. Three-minute sequence within otherwise ordinary narrative structure, in which a song is played at top volume while movie characters experience spasms of hyperkinetic behavior and stick their faces into the camera lens. If a band is seen, the Semi-OMV is inevitably distinguished by the director's inability to find a fresh cinematic approach to the challenge of filming a slack-jawed drummer.

Sequel. A filmed deal.

Still Out There Somewhere. Obligatory phrase in Dead Teen-ager and Mad Slasher Movies, where it is triggered by the words, "The body was never found. They say he/she is . . ."

Tijuana. In modern Horny Teen-ager Movies, performs the same symbolic function as California did for the Beats and Paris did for the Lost Generation.

Wet. In Hollywood story conferences, suggested alternative to nude, as in: "If she won't take off her clothes, can we wet her down?" Suggested by Harry Cohn's remark about swimming star Esther Williams: "Dry, she ain't much. Wet, she's a star."

The We're Alive! Let's Kiss! Scene. Inevitable conclusion to any scene in which hero and heroine take cover from gunfire by diving side-by-side into a ditch, and find themselves in each other's arms, usually for the first time. See *High Road to China*.

Ukulele picks. What will happen to you if you are a bad movie.

Index

Titles in bold-face type are on Roger Ebert's ten-best list for the year in which they opened.